ANTHROPOLOGY
Sixth Edition

ANTHROPOLOGY

Sixth Edition

WILLIAM A. HAVILAND

University of Vermont

HOLT, RINEHART AND WINSTON, INC.
Fort Worth   Chicago   San Francisco   Philadelphia
Montreal   Toronto   London   Sydney   Tokyo

Acquisitions Editor: Christopher P. Klein
Developmental Editor: Meera Dash
Project Editor: Mark Hobbs
Production Manager: Tad Gaither

Design Supervisor: John Ritland
Cover Designer: Pat Sloan
Photo Researchers: Don Haddock, Barbara Stephenson
Compositor: York Graphic Services, Inc.

Library of Congress Cataloging-In-Publication Data
Haviland, William A.
  Anthropology/William A. Haviland — 6th ed.

  p. cm.
  Includes bibliographical references and index.
  1. Anthropology   I. Title.
GN25.H38   1990   301 — dc20   90-5302
                                                                      CIP

ISBN 0-03-043537-4

Printed in the United States of America

1234-069-98765432

Address for orders: Holt, Rinehart and Winston, Inc., 6277 Sea Harbor Drive, Orlando, FL 32887.

Address for editorial correspondence: Holt, Rinehart and Winston, Inc., Suite 3700, 301 Commerce Street, Fort Worth, TX 76102.

Holt, Rinehart and Winston
The Dryden Press
Saunders College Publishing

CREDITS

The author is indebted to the following for photographs and permission to reproduce them. Copyright for each photograph belongs to the photographer or agency credited, unless specified otherwise.

Part I: Part Opener, *1*, Dallas Museum of Art. **Chapter 1:** Chapter Opener, *4*, Gilcrease Museum. *7 (left and right)*, The Granger Collection. *8*, Dr. W. Montague Cobb. *10 (upper)*, Southern Illinois University/Biomedical Communications/Photo Researchers; *(lower)*, Lawrence Migdale/Photo Researchers. *12*, Mark Godfrey. *13*, Mel Konner/Anthro-Photo. *17*, Al Danegger/Courtesy of the University of Mary-

land. *19*, UPI/Bettmann Newsphotos. *21 (left)*, The Bettmann Archives; *(middle)*, The Granger Collection; *(right)*, Culver Pictures. *22*, Richard B. Lee, Department of Anthropology, University of Toronto. *24*, Arthur B. Palmer. **Chapter 2:** Chapter Opener, *28*, Bob Daemmrich. *32 (upper left)*, Windover Project/James P. Blair; *(upper right and center)*, Windover Project. *34*,

(Credits continue on page 689.)

PREFACE

PURPOSE OF THE BOOK

This text is designed for college-level introductory anthropology courses. It treats the basic divisions of anthropology—physical and cultural anthropology, including ethnology, linguistics, and prehistoric archeology—and presents the key concepts and terminology germane to each.

The aim of the text is to give the student a thorough introduction to the principles and processes of anthropology. Because it draws from the research and ideas of a number of schools of anthropological thought, the text will expose students to a mix of such approaches as evolutions, historical particularism, diffusionism, functionalism, French structuralism, structural functionalism, and others. This inclusiveness reflects my conviction that, while each of these approaches has important things to say about human behavior, to restrict oneself to one approach, at the expense of the others, is to cut oneself off from important insights. Thorough and scholarly in its coverage, the book is nonetheless simply written and attractively designed to appeal to students. Thus, they will find that it pleases as it teaches.

UNIFYING THEME OF THE BOOK

Although each chapter has been developed as a self-contained unit of study and may be used in any sequence the instructor wishes, a common theme runs through all the chapters. This, along with part introductions which support that theme, serves to convey to students how material in one chapter relates to that in others.

In earlier editions of this book, for want of a better designation, I referred to this common theme as one of environmental adaptation, although I was never very happy with that phrase. Its principal defect is that it implies a fairly straightforward behavioral response to environmental stimuli. But, of course, people don't just react to an environment as given; rather, they react to it as they perceive it, and different groups of people may perceive the same environment in radically different ways. People also react to things other than the environment: their own biological natures, for one, and their beliefs, attitudes, and the consequences of their own behavior, for others. All of these things present them with problems, and people maintain cultures to deal with problems, or matters that concern them. To be sure, their cultures must produce behavior that is generally adaptive, or at least not maladaptive, but this is not the same as saying that cultural practices necessarily arise because they are adaptive in a particular environment.

OUTSTANDING FEATURES OF THE BOOK

1. READABILITY

The purpose of a textbook is to transmit and register ideas and information, to induce the readers to see old things in new ways, and to think about what they see. A book may be the most elegantly written, most handsomely designed, most lavishly illustrated text available on the subject, but if it is not interesting, clear, and comprehensible to the student, it is valueless as a teaching tool. The trick is not just to present facts and concepts, it is to make them *memorable*.

The readability of the text is enhanced by the writing style. The book is designed to present even the most difficult concepts in prose that is clear, straightforward, and easy for today's first and second year students to understand, without feeling that they are being "spoken down to." Where technical terms are necessary, they appear in bold-faced type, are carefully defined in the text, and defined again in the glossary in simple, clear language.

Because much learning is based on analogy, numerous and colorful examples have been used to illustrate, emphasize, and clarify anthropological concepts. Wherever appropriate, there is a cross-cultural perspective—comparing cultural practices in several different societies, often including the student's own. But while the student should be made aware of the fact that anthropology has important things to say about the student's own society and culture, the emphasis in introductory anthropology should be on non-Western societies and cultures for illustrative purposes. It is a fact of modern life that North Americans share the same planet with great numbers of people who are not only not North Americans but are non-Western as well. Moreover, North Americans constitute a minority, for they account for far less than half the world's population. Yet traditional school curricula emphasize our own surroundings and backgrounds, saying little about the rest of the world. In its March 8, 1976, issue (p. 32), the *Chronicle of Higher Education* documented an increasing tendency toward cultural insularity and ethnocentrism in North American higher education. That the problem persists is clear from a report made public in 1989 by the National Governor's Association, which warned that the economic well-being of the United States was in jeopardy because so many of its citizens are ignorant of the languages and cultures of other nations. More than ever, college students need knowledge about the rest of the world and its peoples. Such a background gives them the global perspective they need to better

understand their own culture and society and their place in today's world. Anthropology, of all disciplines, with its long-standing commitment to combating ethnocentrism, has a unique obligation to provide this perspective.

2. ORIGINAL STUDIES

A special feature of this text consists of the "Original Studies" that are included with each chapter. These studies are selections from case studies and other original works of men and women who have done, or are doing, important anthropological work. Each study, integrally related to the material in the text, sheds additional light on some important anthropological concept or subject area found in the chapter.

The idea behind this feature is to coordinate the two halves of the human brain, which have different functions. While the left (dominant) hemisphere is "logical" and processes verbal input in a linear manner, the right hemisphere is "creative" and less impressed with linear logic. Psychologist James V. McConnell has described it as "an analogue computer of sorts—a kind of intellectual monitor that not only handles abstractions, but also organizes and stores material in terms of Gestalts [that] include the emotional relevance of the experience." Logical thinking, as well as creative problem solving, occurs when the two sides of the brain cooperate. The implication for textbook writers is obvious: To be truly effective, they must reach both sides of the brain. The Original Studies help to do this by conveying some "feel" for humans and their behavior and how anthropologists actually go about studying them. For example, included in Chapter 14 is an Original Study extracted from *The Mbuti Pygmies: Change and Adaptation* by Colin M. Turnbull, who presents an absorbing picture of a way of growing up that stands in marked contrast to the experience of most students who will use this textbook.

Because women have always been an important part of the anthropological enterprise, and students need to realize this, women are well represented as authors of Original Studies in the sixth edition. Thirteen are by women alone, and another two are authored jointly by women and men.

3. ILLUSTRATIONS

Another means of appealing to the nondominant hemisphere of the brain is through the use of illustrations and other graphic materials. In this text, numerous four-color photos have been used to make important anthropological points by catching the student's eye and mind. Many are unusual in that they are not the "standard" anthropological textbook photographs; each has been chosen because it complements the text in some distinctive way. For example, the pictures on pages 667 and 670 lend an immediacy to the theoretical concept of structural violence by relating it to things students are likely to have heard about on the news: exposure to toxic substances and starvation in the Third World. The line drawings, maps, charts, and tables were selected especially for their usefulness in illustrating, emphasizing, or clarifying certain anthropological concepts and should prove valuable teaching aids.

4. PREVIEWS AND SUMMARIES

An old and effective pedagogical technique is repetition: "Tell'em what you're going to tell'em, do it, and then tell'em what you've told'em." In order to do just this, each chapter begins with a set of "preview" questions, setting up a framework for studying the contents of the chapter. Following each chapter is a summary containing the kernels of the most important ideas presented in the chapter. The summaries provide handy reviews for the student, without being so long and detailed as to seduce the student into thinking that he or she can get by without reading the chapter itself.

5. SUGGESTED READINGS AND BIBLIOGRAPHY

Also following each chapter is a list of suggested readings that will supply the inquisitive student with further information about specific anthropological points of interests. Each reading is fully annotated and provides information as to content, value, and readability. The books suggested are oriented toward either the general reader or the interested student who wishes to explore further the more technical aspects of some subject. In addition, the bibliography at the end of the book contains a listing of over 500 books, monographs, and articles from scholarly journals and popular magazines on virtually every topic covered in the text that a student might wish to investigate further.

6. GLOSSARY

In addition to the traditional "end-of-the-book" glossary, this text has a running glossary — marginal definitions of terms from the accompanying text. This catches the student's eye as he or she reads and, so, reinforces the meaning of each newly introduced term. It is also useful for chapter review, as the student may readily isolate those terms introduced in one chapter from those terms introduced in others.

At the same time, the "end-of-the-book" glossary makes it easy to look up terms when the student is not sure which chapter it first appeared in. This glossary is thus an anthropological dictionary in miniature, with each term defined in clear, understandable language. As a result, less class time is required going over terms, leaving instructors free to pursue matters of greater moment.

7. LENGTH

Careful consideration has been given to the length of this book. On the one hand, it had to be of sufficient length to avoid superficiality and/or misrepresentation of the discipline by ignoring or otherwise slighting some important aspects of anthropology. On the other hand, it could not be so long as to present more material than can reasonably be dealt with in a single semester or to be prohibitively expensive. The resultant text is comparable in length to introductory texts in the sister disciplines of economics, psychology, and sociology, even though there is more ground to be covered in an introduction to general anthropology.

ADVANTAGES OF THE SIXTH EDITION

The planning of the sixth edition of *Anthropology* was based on extensive review and criticism by instructors, some of whom were users of the fifth edition of the sister text, *Cultural Anthropology*, and some of whom were users of other texts. In addition, it was my privilege to be chosen as a Participating Author in the American Anthropological Association's Project on Gender and the Anthropological Curriculum, and as such, I was assigned a project member, Lila Abu-Lughod, with whom I worked closely on this revision. Her constructive critical review of chapters from the fifth edition, as well as revisions for the sixth, and her helpful suggestions all along the way were enormously helpful; I am grateful to her as well as to the project's co-directors, Sandra L. Morgen and Mary H. Moran. As all this suggests, one of the major thrusts in the sixth edition was to substantially expand coverage of sex and gender material. In doing so, the decision was made to integrate this with other material, rather than to "ghetto-ize" it in a separate chapter by itself (although the old Chapter 17 on Marriage and the Family has been divided into two new chapters, 17 and 18, largely to accommodate expanded material on sex- and gender-related issues). My position is that gender considerations are so intertwined with the other things that people do that the subject should not be presented as a thing apart. Thus, the reader will find something on gender in almost *every* chapter of the book, while overall coverage in terms of quantity and quality is equivalent to a good solid chapter on the subject.

The other major thrust in this revision was to increase the coverage given Applied Anthropology. Again I have chosen an integrated approach and have added seven new "Applications" boxes to the eleven that were in the fifth edition. Each box relates in some way to the subject matter of the chapter in which it is included. The advantage of this is that the student is constantly reminded that anthropology has many practical applications and that there is a wide range of job opportunities available outside of academia for people with anthropological training.

The above changes, coupled with the necessary fine tuning and up dating, have improved every feature of the book: topic coverage, readability, continuity, illustrations, Original Studies, Chapter Summaries, Suggested Readings, Glossary, and Bibliography. Many of the illustrations are new to this edition, and captions have been altered or rewritten to ensure that the illustrations supplement the text and clarify concepts that are not always easily rendered into words.

In addition to the substantial rewriting and updating of the text's contents, ten of the twenty-five Original Studies are new. Their topics include "Participant Study on a Motorcycle" by Andrew Cornish (Chapter 1), "*Homo erectus* and the Use of Bamboo" by Geoffrey G. Pope (Chapter 7), "Subsistence Practices of Mousterian Peoples" by Paul Mellars (Chapter 8), "The Importance of Trobriand Women" by Annette B. Weiner (Chapter 12), "Sexism in the English Language" by Robin Lakoff (Chapter 13), "Men and Women in Egalitarian Societies" by Eleanor Leacock (Chapter 15), "Marriage and Affinal Relationships Among the Kiowa" by Jane F. Collier (Chapter 18), "Coping as a Woman in a Man's World" by Margery Wolf (Chapter 19), "Limits on Power in Bedouin Society" by Lila Abu-Lughod (Chapter 21), and "The 'Little Songs' of the Awlad 'Ali" by Lila Abu-Lughod (Chapter 23).

SUPPLEMENTS TO THE TEXT

Ancillaries to be used with *Anthropology*, Sixth Edition, have been skillfully prepared and coordinated by Susan Parman of California State University, Fullerton. They are a student's *Study Guide*, an *Instructor's Manual and Test Bank*, and a *Computerized Test Bank*.

A separate *Study Guide* is now provided to aid student comprehension of the text material. Each chapter of the *Study Guide* presents concise learning objectives and then offers review materials, exercises, and self-tests to help students achieve these objectives. This supplement to the textbook also includes hints on reading anthropology texts, thinking critically, and relating anthropology to one's life.

The *Instructor's Manual and Test Bank* offers lecture and class activity suggestions corresponding to every chapter of the text, teaching objectives corresponding to the learning objectives in the student's *Study Guide*, and a large selection of multiple-choice test questions coordinated with the teaching/learning objectives and page-referenced to the text.

Introduced with this edition is the publisher's new *ExaMaster*™ software program, which offers the test bank in a computerized version in the following formats: IBM, Apple, and Macintosh.

Through common learning and teaching objectives, these supplements are intended to work together as a fully integrated instructional package that is adaptable to different teaching situations. It is my hope that they will encourage interaction between teacher and student, as well.

Instructors also are offered video cassettes from the acclaimed television course, *Faces of Culture*. Each cassette features footage from leading anthropological film makers.

ACKNOWLEDGMENTS

Many people assisted in the preparation of this book, some of them directly, some of them indirectly. In the latter category are all of the anthropologists under whom I was privileged to study at the University of Pennsylvania: Robbins Burling, William R. Coe, Carleton S. Coon, Robert Ehrich, Loren Eisley, J. Louis Giddings, Ward H. Goodenough, A. Irving Hallowell, Alfred V. Kidder II, Wilton M. Grogman, Froelich Rainey, Ruben Reina, and Linton Satterthwaite. They may not always recognize the final product, but they all contributed to it in important ways.

A similar debt is owed to all those anthropologists with whom I have worked or discussed research interests and the field in general. There are too many of them to list here, but surely they have had an important impact on my own thinking and, so, on this book. Finally, the influence of all those who assisted in the preparation of the first five editions must linger on in this new one. They are all listed in the prefaces to the earlier editions, and the sixth edition benefits from their influence.

This revision must also benefit from my continued association with valued colleagues at the University of Vermont: Robert Gordon, William E. Mitchell, Carroll McC. P. Lewin, Stephen L. Pastner, Marjory Power, Peter A. Thomas, and A. Peter Woolfson. All have responded graciously at one time or another to my requests for sources and advice in their various fields of expertise. We all share freely our successes and failures in trying to teach anthropology to introductory students.

Just over five years ago, I was given the opportunity to participate in a free and open discussion between textbook authors and users at the American Anthropological Association's 1984 Annual Meeting (a session organized and chaired by Walter Packard and the Council on Anthropology and Education). From this I got a good sense of what instructors at institutions ranging from community colleges to major universities were looking for in anthropology texts; subsequent insights have come from a special symposium on the teaching of anthropology at the University of Vermont in 1986 (organized by A. Peter Woolfson), and a meeting of textbook authors with members of the Gender and the Anthropology Curriculum Project at the American Anthropological Association's Annual Meeting in 1988. To the organizers and sponsors of all these events, my sincere thanks.

Thanks are also due the anthropologists who made suggestions for this edition, foremost of whom was Lila Abu-Lughod of the Gender Project. Others include Anita Alvarado, University of New Mexico; David Glassman, Southwest Texas State University; Robert Hoover, California Polytech State University; Barry Mitchie, Kansas State University; Richard Seaghon, University of Pittsburgh; Edwin Segal, University of Louisville; Allyn Stearman, University of Central Florida; and John Swetnam, University of Nevada, Las

Vegas. All of their comments were carefully considered; how I have responded of them has been determined by my own perspective of anthropology, as well as my twenty-seven years of experience with undergraduate students. Therefore, neither they nor any of the other anthropologists mentioned here should be held responsible for any defects in this book.

I also wish to acknowledge my debt to a number of nonanthropologists who helped me with this book. The influence of David Boynton, winner of the 1985 Distinguished Service Award of the American Anthropological Association and my editor at Holt, Rinehart and Winston until his retirement in 1983, I am sure lingers on. So, too, does the influence of Kirsten Olson who has moved on to new challenges. My present editors, Chris Klein and Meera Dash, have been immensely helpful in seeing this edition through to production and have been a pleasure to work with.

I also wish to thank the skilled new editing, design, and production team at Holt, Rinehart and Winston in Forth Worth, including Tad Gaither, Production Manager; Mark Hobbs, Senior Project Editor; and John Ritland, Art and Design Supervisor.

The greatest debt of all is owed my wife, Anita de Laguna Haviland, who has had to put up with my preoccupation with this revision, reminding me when it's time to feed the livestock or play midwife to the sheep in the barn. In addition, she took on the task of feeding revised text into the word processor, bringing me at last into the world of "high tech" and delivering my editors from the frustration of dealing with cut-and-paste copy full of pencilled-in changes. As if this were not enough, she has been a source of endless good ideas on things to include and ways to express things. The book has benefitted enormously from her involvement.

ABOUT THE AUTHOR

 Dr. William A. Haviland is professor of anthropology at the University of Vermont, where he has taught since 1965. He holds bachelor's, master's, and doctoral degrees in anthropology from the University of Pennsylvania and has published widely on archaeological, ethnological, and physical anthropological research carried out in Guatemala, Maine, and Vermont. In 1989, he served as an expert witness for the Abenaki Indians in a court case concerned with aboriginal fishing rights. Dr. Haviland is a member of many professional societies, including the American Anthropological Association and the American Association for the Advancement of Science. In 1988, he participated in *Gender and the Anthropology Curriculum*, a project sponsored by the American Anthropological Association.

One of Dr. Haviland's greatest loves is teaching, which originally prompted him to write textbooks in anthropology. He says that he learns something new every year from his students about what they need to get out of their first college course in anthropology. In addition to *Anthropology*, Dr. Haviland has written two other popular textbooks published by Holt, Rinehart and Winston for students of anthropology.

BRIEF CONTENTS

CONTENTS

PART IV
CULTURE AND SURVIVAL: COMMUNICATING, RAISING CHILDREN, AND STAYING ALIVE   275

INTRODUCTION   276

CHAPTER 12
The Nature of Culture   278

**PART VI
THE SEARCH FOR ORDER: SOLVING THE PROBLEM
OF DISORDER   525**

INTRODUCTION 526

CHAPTER 21
Political Organization and Social Control   528

FEATURES

North America: Native Americans

Dozier, Hano: A Tewa Indian Community in Arizona (1966) •
Grobsmith, Lakota of the Rosebud: A Contemporary Ethnography
(1981) • *Hoebel*, The Cheyennes, *Second Edition* (1978) • *Kehoe*, The
Ghost Dance Religion: Ethnohistory and Revitalization (1989) •
Laughlin, Aleuts: Survivors of the Bering Land Bridge (1981) •
Trigger, The Huron: Farmers of the North, *Second Edition* (1990)

Pacific Oceania

Hart/Pilling/Goodale, The Tiwi of North Australia, *Third Edition*
(1988) • *Heider*, Grand Valley Dani: Peaceful Warriors (1979) •
Herdt, The Sambia: Ritual and Gender in New Guinea (1987) •
Keesing, 'Elota's Story: The Life and Times of a Solomon Islands Big
Man (1983) • *O'Meara*, Samoan Planters: Tradition and Economic
Development in Polynesia (1990) • *Pospisil*, The Kapauku Papuans of
West New Guinea (1978) • *Tonkinson*, The Mardudjara Aborigines:
Society and Spirit in a Desert Culture (1978) • *Weiner*, The
Trobrianders of Papua New Guinea (1988)

Other Titles

Hickerson, Linguistic Anthropology (1980) • *Lancaster*, Primate
Behavior and the Emergence of Human Culture (1975) • *Schusky*,
Variation in Kinship (1974).

Locations of the cultures mentioned in the textbook

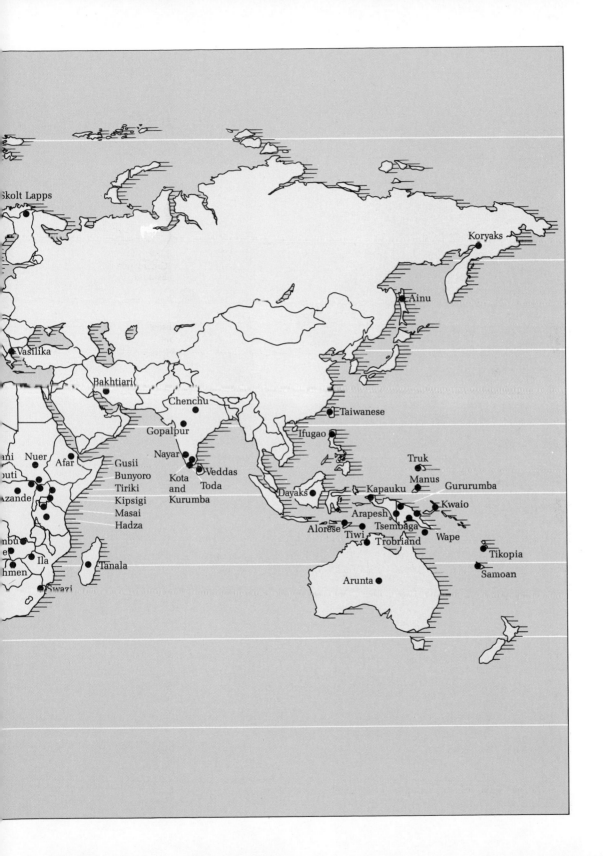

Skolt Lapps

Koryaks

Ainu

Vasilika

Bakhtiari

Chenchu

Taiwanese

Gopalpur

Ifugao

Nayar

Truk

Gusii
Bunyoro
Tiriki
Kipsigi
Masai
Hadza

Nuer   Afar

Veddas

Manus
Kapauku   Gururumba

Kota
and
Kurumba

Toda

Dayaks

Kwaio

Arapesh

Azande

Alorese   Tsembaga
Tiwi   Wape

Trobriand

nbu
e
hmen   Ila

Tanala

Tikopia

Swazi

Arunta

Samoan

In their attempt to understand human behavior, anthropologists study all peoples, past and present, Western and non-Western. This pottery vessel, from the North Coast of Peru, was made between A.D. 200 and 500 and depicts hunting scenes.

THE STUDY OF HUMANKIND

INTRODUCTION

Anthropology is the most liberating of all the sciences. Not only has it exposed the fallacies of racial and cultural superiority, but its devotion to the study of all peoples, regardless of where and when they lived, has cast more light on human nature than all the reflections of sages or the studies of laboratory scientists. If this sounds like the assertion of an overly enthusiastic anthropologist, it is not; it was all said by the philosopher Grace de Laguna in her 1941 presidential address to the Eastern Division of the American Philosophical Association.

The subject matter of anthropology is vast, as we shall see in this book: It includes everything that has to do with human beings, past and present. Of course, many other disciplines are concerned in one way or another with human beings. Some, such as anatomy and physiology, study humans as biological organisms. The social sciences are concerned with the distinctive forms of human relationships, while the humanities examine the great achievements of human culture. Anthropologists are interested in all of these things, too, but they try to deal with them all together, in all places and times. It is this unique, broad perspective that equips anthropologists so well to deal with that elusive thing called human nature.

Needless to say, no single anthropologist is able to investigate personally everything that has to do with people. For practical purposes, the discipline is divided into various subfields, and individual anthropologists specialize in one or more of these. Whatever their specialization, though, they retain a commitment to a broader, overall perspective on humankind. For example, cultural anthropologists specialize in the study of human behavior, while physical anthropologists specialize in the study of humans as biological organisms. Yet neither can afford to ignore the work of the other, for human behavior and biology are inextricably intertwined, with each affecting the other in important ways. We can see, for example, how biology affects a cultural practice: color-naming behavior. Human populations differ in the density of pigmentation within the eye itself, which in turn affects people's ability to distinguish the color blue from green, black, or both. For this reason, a number of cultures identify blue with green, black, or both. We can see also how a cultural practice may affect human biology, as exemplified by the sickle-cell trait and related conditions. In certain parts of the Old World, when humans took up the practice of farming, they altered the ecology in a way that, by chance, created ideal conditions for the breeding of mosquitoes. As a result, malaria became a serious problem, and a biological response to this was the spread of certain genes that, in substantial numbers of people living in malarial areas, produced a built-in resistance to the disease.

To begin our introduction to the study of anthropology, we will look closely at the nature of the discipline. In Chapter 1 we will see how the field of anthropology is subdivided, how the subdivisions relate to one another, and how they relate to the other sciences and humanities. Chapter 1 introduces us as well to the methods anthropologists use to study human cultures, especially those of today or the very recent past. However, since the next two parts of the book take us far back into the human past, to see where we came from and how we got to be the way we are today, furhter discussion of methods used to study contemporary cultures is deferred to Parts IV and VII (especially Chapter 12). The very different methods used to find out about the ancient past are the subject of Chapter 2, which discusses the nature of fossils and archaeological materials, where they are found, how they are (quite literally) unearthed, and how they must be treated once unearthed. From this, one can begin to appreciate what the evidence can tell us if handled properly, as well as its limitations.

In order to understand what fossils have to tell us about our past, some knowledge of how biological evolution works is necessary. But fossils, unlike flesh and blood people, do not speak for themselves, and so they must be interpreted. If we are to have confidence in an interpretation of a particular fossil, we must be sure that the interpretation is consistent with what we know about the workings of evolution; therefore, Chapter 3 is devoted to a discussion of evolution.

The zoological order that gave rise to human beings includes lemurs, lorises, indriids, tarsiers, monkeys, and apes: the Primate order. In Chapter 4 we shall examine the modern primates in order to understand how we humans are like the other primates; in particular we can begin to appreciate that many of the physical characteristics we think of as distinctively human are simply exaggerated versions of characteristics common to other primates. For example, primate brains tend to be large and heavy relative to body size and weight; in humans, this trait is realized to a greater degree than it is in other primates. We can begin to appreciate as well the kind of behavioral versatility of which present-day members of this order are capable. In the range of modern primate behavior patterns, we find clues to patterns that were characteristic of primates that lived in the past, from which humans are descended. With these things done, we will have set the stage for our detailed look at human biological and cultural evolution in Parts II and III.

1

THE NATURE OF ANTHROPOLOGY

In this sixteenth-century depiction of a meeting between Frenchmen and Indians, the latter look more like scantily clad Europeans than Native Americans. The tendency to see other people as we are conditioned to see them, rather than as they really are, is still a major problem in the world today.

PREVIEW

What Is Anthropology?

Anthropology, the study of humankind, seeks to produce useful generalizations about people and their behavior and to arrive at the fullest possible understanding of human diversity.

What Do Anthropologists Do?

Physical anthropologists study humans as biological organisms, tracing the evolutionary development of the human animal and looking at the biological variations within the species. Cultural anthropologists are concerned with human cultures, or the ways of life in societies. Within the field of cultural anthropology are archaeologists, who seek to explain human behavior by studying material objects, usually from past cultures; linguists, who study languages, by which cultures are maintained and passed on to succeeding generations; and ethnologists, who study cultures as they can be experienced and discussed with persons whose culture is to be understood.

How Do Anthropologists Do What They Do?

Anthropologists, in common with other scientists, are concerned with the formulation and testing of hypotheses, or tentative explanations of observed phenomena. In so doing, they hope to arrive at a system of validated hypotheses, or a theory, although they recognize that no theory is ever completely beyond challenge. In order to frame hypotheses that are as objective and free of cultural bias as possible, anthropologists typically develop them through a kind of total immersion in the field, becoming so familiar with the minute details of the situation that they can begin to recognize patterns inherent in the data. It is also through fieldwork that anthropologists test existing hypotheses.

A common component of the mythology of all peoples is a legend that explains the appearance of humans on earth. For example, the Nez Perce of the American Northwest believe that humanity is the creation of Coyote, one of the animal people that inhabited the earth before humans. Coyote chased the giant beavermonster, Wishpoosh, in an epic chase whose trail formed the Columbia River. When Coyote caught Wishpoosh, he killed him and dragged his body to the river bank. Ella Clark retells the legend:

> With his sharp knife Coyote cut up the big body of the monster.
>
> "From your body, mighty Wishpoosh," he said, "I will make a new race of people. They will live near the shores of Big River and along the streams which flow into it."
>
> From the lower part of the animal's body, Coyote made people who were to live along the coast. "You shall live near the mouth of Big River and shall be traders."
>
> "You shall live along the coast," he said to others. "You shall live in villages facing the ocean and shall get your food by spearing salmon and digging clams. You shall always be short and fat and have weak legs."
>
> From the legs of the beaver monster he made the Klickitat Indians. "You shall live along the rivers that flow down from the big white mountain north of Big River. You shall be swift of foot and keen of wit. You shall be famous runners and great horsemen."
>
> From the arms of the monster he made the Cayuse Indians. "You shall be powerful with bow and arrows and with war clubs."
>
> From the ribs he made the Yakima Indians. "You shall live near the new Yakima River, east of the mountains. You shall be the helpers and the protectors of all the poor people."
>
> From the head he created the Nez Perce Indians. "You shall live in the valleys of the Kookooskia and Wallowa rivers. You shall be men of brains, great in council and in speechmaking. You shall also be skillful horsemen and brave warriors."
>
> Then Coyote gathered up the hair and blood and waste. He hurled them far eastward, over the big mountains. "You shall be the Snake River Indians,"

said Coyote. "You shall be people of blood and violence. You shall be buffalo hunters and shall wander far and wide."[1]

For as long as they have been on earth, people have needed answers to questions about who they are, where they came from, and why they act the way they do. Throughout most of their history, though, people had no extensive and reliable body of data about their own behavior and background, and so they relied on myth and folklore for their answers to these questions. Anthropology, over the last 200 years, has emerged as a more scientific approach to answering these questions. Simply stated, anthropology is the study of humankind. The anthropologist is concerned primarily with a single species — *Homo sapiens* — the human species, its ancestors, and near relatives. Because anthropologists are members of the species being studied, it is difficult to be completely objective. They have found, however, that the use of the scientific approach produces useful generalizations about humans and their behavior. With the scientific approach, anthropologists are able to arrive at a reasonably reliable understanding of human diversity, as well as those things that all humans have in common.

THE DEVELOPMENT OF ANTHROPOLOGY

Anthropology, as we know it, is a relatively recent product of Western civilization. In the United States, for example, the first course in general anthropology to carry credit in a college or university was offered at the University of Rochester, but not until 1879. If people have always been concerned about themselves and their origins, why then did it take such a long time for a systematic discipline of anthropology to appear?

The answer to this is as complex as human history. In part, the question of anthropology's slow

---

[1]Ella E. Clark, *Indian Legends of the Pacific Northwest* (Berkley: University of California Press, 1966), p. 174.

growth may be answered by reference to the limits of human technology. Throughout most of history, people have been restricted in their geographical horizons. Without the means of traveling to distant parts of the world, observation of cultures and peoples far from one's own was a difficult — if not impossible — venture. Extensive travel was usually the exclusive prerogative of a few; the study of foreign peoples and cultures was not likely to flourish until adequate modes of transportation and communication could be developed.

This is not to say that people have always been unaware of the existence of others in the world who look and act differently from themselves. The Jewish and Christian Bibles, for example, are full of references to diverse peoples, among them Jews, Egyptians, Hittites, Babylonians, Ethiopians, Romans, and so forth. Different though they may have been, however, these peoples were at least familiar to one another, and familiar differences are one thing, while unfamiliar differences are another. It was the massive encounter with hitherto unknown peoples, which came as Europeans sought to extend their trade and political domination to all parts of the world, that focused attention on human differences in all their glory.

Another significant element that contributed to the slow growth of anthropology was the failure of Europeans to recognize the common humanity

In the United States, anthropology began in the nineteenth century, when a number of dedicated amateurs, many of them women, went into the field to find out for themselves whether prevailing ideas about so-called savage and barbarian peoples had any validity. Shown here are Alice Fletcher, who spent the better part of 30 years documenting the ways of the Omaha Indians, and Frank Hamilton Cushing, who lived for four and a half years with the Zuni in New Mexico.

that they share with people everywhere. Societies that did not subscribe to the fundamental cultural values of the European were regarded as "savage" or "barbarian." It was not until the late eighteenth century that a significant number of Europeans considered the behavior of foreigners to be at all relevant to an understanding of themselves. This awareness of human diversity, coming at a time when there were increasing efforts to explain things in terms of natural laws, cast doubts on the traditional biblical mythology, which no longer adequately "explained" human diversity. From the reexamination that followed came the awareness that the study of "savages" is a study of all humankind.

ANTHROPOLOGY AND THE OTHER SCIENCES

It would be incorrect to infer from the foregoing that serious attempts were not made to analyze human diversity before the eighteenth century. Anthropology is not the only discipline that studies people. In this respect it shares its objectives with the other social and natural sciences. Anthropologists do not think of their findings as something quite apart from those of psychologists, economists, sociologists, or biologists; rather, they welcome the contributions these other disciplines have to make to the common goal of understanding humanity, and they gladly offer their own findings for the benefit of these other disciplines. Anthropologists do not expect, for example, to know as much about the structure of the human eye as anatomists, or as much about the perception of color as psychologists. As synthesizers, however, they are better prepared to understand these things in analyzing color-naming behavior in different human societies than any of their fellow scientists. Because they look for the broad basis of human behavior without limiting themselves to any single social or biological aspect of that behavior, anthropologists can acquire an especially extensive overview of the complex biological and cultural organism that is the human being.

> **Physical anthropology:** The systematic study of humans as biological organisms.

> **Cultural anthropology:** The branch of anthropology that focuses on the patterns of life of a society.

THE DISCIPLINE OF ANTHROPOLOGY

Anthropology is traditionally divided into four fields: physical anthropology and the three branches of cultural anthropology, which are archaeology, linguistic anthropology, and ethnology. **Physical anthropology** is concerned primarily with humans as biological organisms, while **cultural anthropology** deals with humans as cultural animals. Both, of course, are closely related; we cannot understand what people do unless we know what people are. And we want to know how biology does and does not influence culture, as well as how culture affects biology.

Physical anthropologists do not just study fossil skulls. Head of the Anatomy Department for many years in Howard University's Medical School, W. Montague Cobb's special research interest in aging in the adult human skeleton has made him a sought-after consultant as a forensic expert by the FBI and other agencies.

APPLICATION
Forensic Anthropology

In the public mind, anthropology is often identified with the recovery of the bones of remote human ancestors, the uncovering of ancient campsites and "lost cities", or the study of present-day tribal peoples whose way of life is all too often seen as being something "out of the past". What people are often unaware of are the many practical applications of anthropological skills and knowledge. One field of applied anthropology — known as **forensic anthropology** — specializes in the identification of human skeletal remains. Forensic anthropologists are routinely called upon by law enforcement officials to identify the remains of murder victims, missing persons, or people who have died in disasters such as plane crashes. From their skeletons, the forensic anthropologist can establish the age, sex, race, and stature of the deceased and, often, whether they were right or left handed, exhibited any abnormalities or evidence of trauma (broken bones and the like). In addition, some details of an individual's health and nutritional history can be read from the bones.

One well-known forensic anthropologist is Clyde C. Snow, who has been practicing in this field for 30 years. In addition to the usual police work, Snow has studied the remains of General George Custer and his men from the battlefield at Little Big Horn, and in 1985, he went to Brazil, where he identified the remains of convicted Nazi war criminal Josef Mengele.

He also has been instrumental in establishing the first forensic team devoted to documenting cases of human rights abuses around the world. This began in 1984, when he went to Argentina at the request of the newly elected civilian government as part of a team to help with the identification of remains of the *desaparecidos*, or "disappeared ones", the 9,000 or more people who were eliminated by government death squads during seven years of military rule. A year later, he returned to give expert testimony at the trial of nine junta members and to teach Argentineans how to recover, clean, repair, preserve, photograph, x-ray, and analyze bones.

Besides providing factual accounts of the fate of victims to their surviving kin, the work of Snow and his Argentinean associates has helped to send several military officers to prison. Moreover, evidence provided by them is critical to the prosecution of many of the men who still await trial for kidnapping, torture, and execution. Meanwhile, Snow and two of his Argentine associates have been invited to the Philippines to look into the disappearance of 600 or more suspected victims of the Marcos regime. Similar requests have come from other South American countries, and when he has time, Snow plans to look into the case of a prison in Arkansas where, prior to the 1950's, dozens of inmates seem to have disappeared.

PHYSICAL ANTHROPOLOGY

Physical anthropology (sometimes called biological anthropology) is the branch of anthropology that focuses on humans as biological organisms, and one of its many interests is human evolution. Whatever distinctions people may claim for themselves, they are mammals — specifically, primates — and, as such, they share a common ancestry with other primates, most specifically apes and monkeys. Through the analysis of fossils and the observation of living primates, the physical anthropologist tries to trace the ancestry of the human species in order to understand how, when, and why we became the kind of animal we are today.

Another concern of physical anthropology is the study of present-day human variation. Although we are all members of a single species, we differ from each other in many obvious and not so obvious ways. We differ not only in such visible traits as the color of our skins or the shape of our noses, but also in such biochemical factors as our blood types and our susceptibility to certain diseases. The modern physical anthropologist applies genetics and biochemistry to achieve fuller understanding of human variation and the ways in which it relates to the various environments in which people have lived.

CULTURAL ANTHROPOLOGY

Because the capacity for culture is rooted in our biological natures, the work of the physical anthropologist provides a necessary framework for the cultural anthropologist. In order to understand the work of the cultural anthropologist, we must clarify what we mean when we refer to culture. The subject will be taken up in more detail in Chapter 12, but for our purposes here, we may think of culture as the often unconscious standards by which societies — groups of people — operate. These standards are learned rather than acquired through biological inheritance. Since they determine, or at least guide, the day-to-day behavior of the members of a society, human behavior is above all cultural behavior. The manifestations of culture may vary considerably from place to place, but no person is "more cultured" in the anthropological sense than any other.

Just as physical anthropology is closely related to the other biological sciences, cultural anthropology is closely related to the other social sciences. The one to which it has most often been compared is sociology, since the business of both is the description and explanation of behavior of people within a social context. Sociologists, however, have concentrated heavily on studies of people living in modern — or at least recent — North American and European societies, thereby increasing the probability that their theories of human behavior will be **culture-bound** — that is, based on assumptions about the world and reality that are part of their Western culture, usually the middle-class version most typical of professional people. Cultural anthropologists, while not immune to culture-bound theorizing, constantly seek to minimize the problem by studying the whole of humanity in all times and places and do not limit themselves to the study of recent Western peoples;

anthropologists have found that to fully understand human behavior, all humans must be studied. More than any other feature, this unique cross-cultural and evolutionary perspective distinguishes cultural anthropology from the other social sciences. It provides anthropology with a far richer body of data than that of any other social science, and it can also be applied to any current issue. As a case in point, two different anthropologists have tested independently the validity of the argument that a high degree of military sophistication acts as a deterrent to war. By comparing the frequency of war in a number of different types of cultures, both found that the more sophisticated a

Sociologists have respondents who are interviewed and to whom questionnaires are administered, and psychologists have subjects with whom they experiment. Anthropologists, by contrast, have informants from whom they learn.

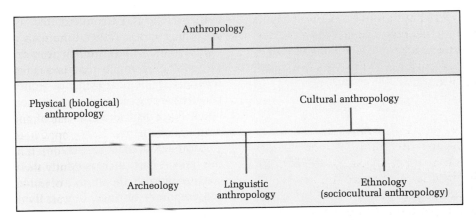

FIGURE 1.1 The subfields of anthropology.

community is militarily, the more frequently it engages in aggressive war and is attacked in turn. This at least suggests that as we ourselves expand our arsenal and develop new weapons systems, we will increase, rather than decrease, the likelihood of war.[2]

The emphasis cultural anthropology places on studies of prehistoric or more recent non-Western cultures has often led to findings that dispute existing beliefs arrived at on the basis of Western studies. Thus, cultural anthropologists were the first to point out "that the world does not divide into the pious and the superstitious; that there are sculptures in jungles and paintings in deserts; that political order is possible without centralized power and principled justice without codified rules; that the norms of reason were not fixed in Greece, the evolution of morality not consummated in England. . . . We have, with no little success, sought to keep the world off balance; pulling out rugs, upsetting tea tables, setting off firecrackers. It has been the office of others to reassure; ours to unsettle."[3] Although the findings of cultural anthropologists have often challenged the conclusions of sociologists, psychologists, and economists, anthropology is absolutely indispensable to them as the testing ground for their theories.

[2]John H. Bodley, *Anthropology and Contemporary Human Problems* (Palo Alto, Calif.: Mayfield, 1985), p. 207.

[3]Clifford Geertz, "Distinguished Lecture: Anti Anti-Relativism," *American Anthropologist* 86 (June 1984): 275.

Culture-bound: Based on assumptions about the world and reality that are part of one's own culture.

Cultural anthropology may be divided into the areas of archaeology, linguistic anthropology, and ethnology (often called sociocultural anthropology). (See Figure 1.1.) Although each has its own special interests and methods, all deal with cultural data. The archaeologist, the linguist, and the ethnologist take different approaches to the subject, but each gathers and analyzes data that are useful in explaining similarities and differences between human cultures, as well as the ways that cultures everywhere develop, adapt, and continue to change.

Archaeology

Archaeology is the branch of cultural anthropology that studies material remains in order to describe and explain human behavior. For the most part, it has focused on the human past, for things rather than ideas are all that survive of that past. The archaeologist studies the tools, pottery, and other enduring relics that remain as the legacy of extinct cultures, some of them as much as 2.5 million years old. Such objects, and the way they were left in the ground, reflect certain aspects of human behavior. For example, shallow, restricted concentrations of charcoal, in which occur oxidized earth, bone fragments, and charred plant remains, and around which are pieces of fire-cracked rock, pot-

Archaeologists study material remains in order to learn about human behavior. Shown here are archaeologists at work at the Great Temple of the Aztecs in Mexico City.

Archaeology: The study of material remains, usually from the past, to describe and explain human behavior.

tery, and tools suitable for food preparation, indicate cooking and associated food processing. From such remains much can be learned about a people's diet and subsistence activities. Thus the archaeologist is able to find out about human behavior in the past, far beyond the mere 5000 years to which historians are limited, owing to their dependence on written records. By contrast, archaeologists are not limited to the study of prehistoric societies, but may also study those for which historic documents are available to supplement the material remains that people left behind them. In most lit-

erate societies, written records are associated with governing elites, rather than with people at the "grass roots." Thus, while written records can tell archaeologists much that they might not know from archaeological evidence alone, it is equally true that archaeological remains can tell historians much about a society that is not apparent from its written documents.

Although archaeologists have concentrated on the human past, increasing numbers of them are concerned with the study of material objects in contemporary settings. One example is the University of Arizona's "Garbage Project," which, by a carefully controlled study of household waste, is producing information about contemporary social issues. One aim of this project is to test the validity of interview-survey techniques, on which sociologists, economists, and other social scientists rely heavily for their data. The tests clearly show a significant difference between what people say they do and what garbage analysis shows they actually do. For example, in 1973, conventional techniques were used to construct and administer a questionnaire to find out about the rate of alcohol consumption in Tucson. In one part of town, 15 percent of respondent households admitted consuming beer, and no household reported consumption of more than eight cans a week. Analysis of garbage from the same area, however, demonstrated that some beer was consumed in over 80 percent of households, and 50 percent discarded more than eight empty cans a week. Another interesting finding of the Garbage Project is that when beef prices reached an all-time high in 1973, so did the amount of beef wasted by households. Although common sense would lead us to suppose just the opposite, high prices and scarcity correlate with more, rather than less, waste. Obviously, such findings are important, for they suggest that ideas about human behavior based on conventional interview-survey techniques alone may be seriously in error.

Linguistic Anthropology
Perhaps the most distinctive human feature is the ability to speak. Humans are not alone in the use of

symbolic communication. Studies have shown that the sounds and gestures made by some other animals — especially by apes — may serve functions comparable to those of human speech; yet no other animal has developed so complex a system of symbolic communication as have humans. Ultimately, it is languages that allow people to preserve and transmit their culture from generation to generation.

The branch of cultural anthropology that studies human languages is called **linguistic anthropology.** Linguistics may deal with the description of a language (the way it forms a sentence or conjugates a verb) or with the history of languages (the way languages develop and influence each other with the passage of time). Both approaches yield valuable information, not only about the ways in which people communicate but also about the ways in which they understand the external world. The "everyday" language of North Americans, for example, includes a number of slang words, such as "dough," "greenback," "dust," "loot," and "bread," to identify what a Papuan would recognize only as "money." Such phenomena help identify things that are considered of special importance to a culture. Through the study of linguistics, the anthropologist is better able to understand how people perceive themselves and the world around them.

Anthropological linguists may also make a significant contribution to our understanding of the human past. By working out the genealogical relationships among languages and studying the distributions of those languages, they may estimate how long the speakers of those languages have lived where they do. By identifying those words in related languages that go back to an ancient ancestral tongue, they can also suggest where the speakers of the ancestral language lived, as well as how they lived.

Ethnology

As the archaeologist has traditionally concentrated on cultures of the past, so the **ethnologist,** or sociocultural anthropologist, concentrates on cultures of the present. While the archaeologist focuses on

Linguistic anthropology: The branch of cultural anthropology that studies human language.

Ethnologist: An anthropologist who studies cultures from a comparative or historical point of view.

Ethnography: The systematic description of a culture based on firsthand observation.

the study of material objects to learn about human behavior, the ethnologist concentrates on the study of human behavior as it can be seen, experienced, and discussed with those whose culture is to be understood.

Fundamental to the ethnologist's approach is descriptive **ethnography.** Whenever possible, the ethnologist becomes ethnographer by going to live among the people under study. By eating their food, speaking their language, and personally experiencing their habits and customs, the ethnographer is able to understand a society's way of life to a far greater extent than any nonparticipant anthropologist ever could; one learns a culture best by learning how to behave acceptably oneself in the society in which one is doing fieldwork. The ethnographer tries to become a participant observer in the culture under study. This does not mean that one must join in a people's battles in

Ethnographers learn about other people's cultures by actually living with them, as Marjory Shostak is here with the !Kung of Africa's Kalahari Desert.

order to study a culture in which warfare is prominent; but by living among a warlike people, the ethnographer should be able to understand the role of warfare in the overall cultural scheme. He or she must be a meticulous observer in order to be able to get a broad overview of a culture without emphasizing one of its parts to the detriment of another. Only by discovering how all cultural institutions — social, political, economic, religious — fit together can the ethnographer begin to understand the cultural system. Anthropologists refer to this as the **holistic perspective,** and it is one of the fundamental principles of anthropology. Robert Gordon, an anthropologist from Namibia, speaks of it in this way: "Whereas the sociologist or the political scientist might examine the beauty of a flower petal by petal, the anthropologist is the person that stands on the top of the mountain and

| **Holistic perspective:** A fundamental principle of anthropology, that things must be viewed in the broadest possible context in order to understand their interconnections and interdependence.

looks at the beauty of the field. In other words, we try and go for the wider perspective."[4]

So basic is ethnographic fieldwork to ethnology that the British anthropologist C. G. Seligman once asserted, "Field research in anthropology is what the blood of the martyrs is to the church."[5] Something of its flavor is conveyed by the experience of one young anthropologist working in Thailand.

[4]Robert Gordon, Interview for Coast Telecourses, Inc., Los Angeles, December 4, 1981.
[5]I. M. Lewis, *Social Anthropology in Perspective* (Harmondsworth, Eng.: Penguin, 1976), p. 27.

ORIGINAL STUDY
Participant Observation on a Motorcycle[6]

A short while after arriving in the field in southern Thailand, I managed to acquire a motorcycle. While I did not actually possess a licence to ride it, some kind words to those in high places by patrons who had taken me under their wing had cleared the way for me to be turned loose on the roads of Thailand without hindrance unless, it was sharply stressed, I was foolish enough to get involved in an accident. At an early stage I had wondered whether I should mention that my licence at home had been repossessed by a couple of incredulous policemen who took a very dim view of creative driving, but I felt that to try and explain this in Thai would probably lead to misunderstandings, and might well have caused my hosts unnecessary anxiety.

Come St David's Day, the inevitable accident occurred. I had been on an afternoon jaunt on my freshly cleaned motorcycle, merrily weaving through the traffic, and thinking how interesting it was that Thai motorists actually lived out the theory of loose structure in their driving. During this course of musing I decided to make a right-hand turn, and still being rather set in my Western ways, slowed down to do so. This was an ethnocentric mistake. As I began to turn, another motorcyclist, complete with an ice chest full of fish and a large basket of oranges on the pillion seat, decided that this was the ideal moment to overtake. I was much too slow, he was far too fast, and our subjective constructions of existence spectacularly collided with the limits of the material world.

What followed was actually quite pleasurable for the brief but slow-motion moments it lasted. A massive surge of metal, flesh, fish, and disintegrating oranges swept me from behind, then passed overhead in a surrealistic collage as my body easily performed a series of gymnastic stunts that I had been totally unable to master at school. As always in life, the brief pleasure had to be repaid with an extended flood of unwelcome pain, relieved only by the happy realization that I, and the other motorist who had flown so gracefully above me, had narrowly but successfully avoided truncating our skulls on a Burmese ebony tree.

Anxious to reassure myself that nothing was broken, I got quickly to my feet, dusted myself off, and walked over to switch off my motorcycle engine, which by now was making a maniacal noise without its exhaust pipe. Then I walked back to the other rider, who was still lying rigidly on his back and wondering whether he should believe what was happening. I politely asked him if he was all right, but the hypothesis that in a crisis everyone reverts to speaking English clearly required some revision. Months of Thai lessons began to trickle back, but far too slowly, and in the meantime he had also stood up. It was only then that I realized the pair of us had been surrounded by a rather large crowd of onlookers.

Television in Thailand does not commence broadcasting until 4:30 p.m. so our little accident had a good audience, with local residents coming out of their houses and shops, and cars, motorcycles, and trucks stopping to take in the scene. The other rider began talking to some people near him, and a shopkeeper who knew me came and asked if I was all right. From that moment, I never had a chance to speak to the other rider again. We were slowly but surely separated, each of us in the centre of a group, the two groups gathering slightly apart from one another. I had a sudden and horrible realization that I was in the middle of one of those dispute settlement cases that I had intermittently dozed through as an undergraduate. With an abrupt and sickening shock, participant observation had become rather too much participation and too little cosy observation.

Some of the other rider's newly acquired entourage came over to ask the fringes of my group what exactly had happened. I pleaded my version to those standing close to me, and it was then relayed—and, I should add, suitably amended—back through the throng to be taken away and compared with the other rider's tale of woe. While this little contest was going on, a number of people from both groups were inspecting the rather forlorn wreckages of our motorcycles and debating over which one appeared to be more badly damaged. "Look at this!" someone cried, lifting a torn section of the seat and helpfully making the tear more ostentatious in the process. "But look at this!" came the reply, as someone else wrenched a limply hanging indicator light completely off its mounting. After a series of such exchanges, the two groups finally agreed that both motorcycles were in an equally derelict state, though I could not help feeling, peering from the little prison within my group of supporters, that those judging the damage to the machines had played a more than passive role in ensuring a parity of demolition.

Physical injuries were the next to be subjected to this adjudication process. I found my shirt being lifted up, and a chorus of oohs and aahs issuing from the crowd, as someone with jolly animation prodded and pinched the large areas of my back which were now bravely attempting to stay in place without the aid of skin. My startled eyes began looking in opposite directions at the same time, while somewhat less than human groans gargled out of my mouth. From similar sounds in the distance I deduced that the other poor rider was being subjected to similar treatment. He frankly looked rather the worse for wear than I did, but whenever his group claimed this, my supporters would proceed to show just what excruciating pain I was suffering by prodding me in the back and indicating my randomly circumambulating eyes as if to say "see, we told you so."

On issues of damage, both mechanical and physical, we were adjudged by the two groups to be fairly evenly scored. Fault in relation to road rules had never been an issue. Then came a bit of a lull, as if something serious was about to happen. A senior person from the other group came over and spoke to me directly, asking if I wanted to call the police. A hush fell over everyone. I, of course, was totally terrified at the prospect—no licence, visions of deportation, and so far only one meagre book of field notes to my name. I put on my best weak pathetic smile and mumbled that I thought it was not really necessary unless the other chap insisted. A culturally appropriate move: Everyone looked happily relieved, and the other rider's spokesman said generously that it would only be a waste of time and cause unnecessary bother to bring the police out on an errand like this. It was to be a few months before I realized that, like many other motorcyclists, the other rider was also probably roaming the roads without a licence, and that in this part of the country calling the police was generally regarded as a last, and unsporting, resort.

The final agreement was that we should settle our own repairs—to both body and vehicle—and let the matter rest. A visible sigh of relief passed through the two groups that had gathered, and they slowly began to disperse. For the first time since the collision, I saw the other rider face to face, so I walked towards him to offer my apologies. I never managed to reach him. The dispersing groups froze in horror, then quickly regathered around me. "What is wrong now?" I was interrogated on all sides. Was I not happy with the result? I had clearly made a serious blunder, and it took a while to settle things down once more. A perceptive shopkeeper from nearby grabbed my arm and dragged me off to his shop for coffee, explaining to me that the matter had been settled and that further contact for any reason with the other rider or his group would only prolong an unpleasant situation that could now be forgotten by all involved.

So it was that later that evening I was able to start my second book of field notes with an entry on dispute settlement, though painful twinges up

my back and throbbing between the ears made me wish I had relied on some other informant to provide the ethnographic details. I made a silent vow to myself to discontinue this idiosyncratic method of participant observation, and managed to some extent to keep the vow for the rest of my stay. Thereafter I successfully steered clear of motorcycle accidents, and instead got shot at, electrocuted, and innocently involved in scandal and otherwise abused. But all that, as they say, is another story.

[6]Andrew Cornish, "Participant Observation on a Motorcycle," *Anthropology Today*, 3(6) (December 1987), pp. 15–16. By permission of the Royal Anthropological Institute of Great Britain and Ireland.

The popular image of ethnographic fieldwork is that it takes place among far-off, exotic peoples. To be sure, a lot of ethnographic work has been done in places like Africa, the islands of the Pacific Ocean, the deserts of Australia, and so on. One very good reason for this is that non-Western peoples were largely ignored by other social scientists. Still, anthropologists have recognized from the start that an understanding of human behavior depends on knowledge of all cultures and peoples, including their own. During the years of the Great Depression and World War II, for example, many anthropologists in the United States worked in settings ranging from factories to whole communities. One of the landmark studies of this period was W. Lloyd Warner's study of "Yankee City" (Newburyport, Massachusetts). Less well known, it was an anthropologist, Philleo Nash, working in the White House under Presidents Roosevelt and Truman, who was instrumental in moving the federal government into the field of civil rights.

In the 1950's, the availability of large amounts of money for research in foreign lands diverted attention from work at home. More recently, as fieldwork abroad has become increasingly difficult to carry out, there has been renewed awareness of important anthropological problems that need to be dealt with in North American society. Many of these problems involve people that anthropologists have studied in other settings. Thus, as Hispanic Americans have moved into the cities of the United States, or as refugees have arrived from southeast Asia, anthropologists have been there

not just to study them, but to help them adjust to their new circumstances. At the same time, anthropologists are applying the same research techniques that served them so well in the study of non-Western peoples to the study of such diverse things as street gangs, corporate bureaucracies, religious cults, health care delivery systems, schools, and how people deal with consumer complaints.

An important finding from such research is that the knowledge gained usually does not emerge from the kinds of research done by other social scientists. For example, the theory of cultural deprivation arose during the 1960s as a way of explaining the educational failure of many children of minorities. In order to account for their lack of achievement, some social scientists proposed that such children were "culturally deprived." They then proceeded to "confirm" this idea by studying children, mostly from Indian, black, and chicano populations, interpreting the results through the protective screen of their theory. Ethnographic research on the cultures of "culturally deprived" children, however, reveals a different story. Far from being culturally deprived, they have elaborate, sophisticated, and adaptive cultures that are simply different from the ones espoused by the educational system. Although some still cling to it, the cultural-deprivation theory is culture-bound and is merely a way of saying that people are "deprived" of "my culture." One cannot argue that such children do not speak adequate Spanish, black English, or whatever — that they do not do

Anthropologists carry out fieldwork at home, as well as abroad. Known on the road as "Dr. Truck," Michael Agar spends much of his time in the cabs of 18-wheelers, studying the culture of independent truckers.

well the things that are considered rewarding in *their* cultures.

Much though it has to offer, the anthropological study of one's own culture is not without its own special problems. Sir Edmund Leach, a noted British anthropologist, puts it in the following way:

> Surprising though it may seem, fieldwork in a cultural context of which you already have intimate first-hand experience seems to be much more difficult than fieldwork which is approached from the naive viewpoint of a total stranger. When anthropologists study facets of their own society their vision seems to become distorted by prejudices which derive from private rather than public experience.[7]

Probably the most successful anthropological studies of their own culture by North Americans have been done by those who first worked in some other culture. Lloyd Warner, for example, had studied the Murngin of Australia before he tackled Newburyport. In addition to getting ourselves

outside of our own culture before trying to study it ourselves, much is to be gained by encouraging anthropologists from Africa, Asia, and South America to do fieldwork in North America. From their outsiders' perspective come insights all too easily overlooked by an insider. Nonetheless, the special difficulties of studying one's own culture can be overcome; what it requires is an acute awareness of those difficulties.

Although ethnographic fieldwork is basic to ethnology, it is not the sole occupation of the ethnologist. What it does is provide the basic data the ethnologist may then use to study one particular aspect of a culture by comparing it with that same aspect in others. Anthropologists constantly make such cross-cultural comparisons, and this is another hallmark of the discipline. Interesting insights into our own practices may come from cross-cultural comparisons, as when one compares the time that people devote to what we consider to be "housework." In our own society, people generally believe that the ever-increasing output of household appliance consumer goods has resulted in a steady reduction in housework, with a consequent increase in leisure time. Thus, consumer appliances have become principal indicators of a high standard of living. Anthropological research among food foragers (people who rely on wild plant and animal resources for subsistence), however, has shown that they work far less at household tasks, and indeed less at all subsistence pursuits, than do people in industrialized societies. Aboriginal Australian women, for example, devote an average of approximately 20 hours per week to collecting and preparing food, whereas women in the rural United States in the 1920s, without the benefit of laborsaving appliances, devoted approximately 52 hours a week to their housework. Some 50 years later, contrary to all expectations, urban women who were not working for wages outside their homes were putting 55 hours a week at their housework, in spite of all their "laborsaving" dishwashers, washing machines, clothes dryers, vac-

[7]Edmund Leach, *Social Anthropology* (Glasgow: Fontana Paperbacks, 1982), p. 124.

uum cleaners, food processors, and microwave ovens.[8]

Cross-cultural comparisons highlight alternative ways of doing things and, so, have much to offer North Americans, significant numbers of whom, opinion polls show, continue to doubt the effectiveness of their own ways of doing things. In this sense, one may think of ethnology as the study of alternative ways of doing things. At the same time, by making systematic cross-cultural comparisons of cultures, ethnologists seek to arrive at valid conclusions concerning the nature of culture in all times and places.

ANTHROPOLOGY AND SCIENCE

The chief concern of all anthropologists is the careful and systematic study of humankind. Anthropology has been called a social or a behavioral science by some, a natural science by others, and one of the humanities by still others. Can the work of the anthropologist properly be labeled scientific? What exactly do we mean by the term "science"?

Science is a powerful and elegant way people have hit upon to understand the workings of the visible world and universe. Science seeks testable explanations for observed phenomena in terms of the workings of hidden but universal and immutable principles, or laws. Two basic ingredients are essential for this: imagination and skepticism. Imagination, though capable of leading us astray, is required in order that we may imagine the ways in which phenomena might be ordered, and think of old things in new ways. Without it, there can be no science. Skepticism is what allows us to distinguish fact from fancy, to test our speculations, and to prevent our imaginations from running away with us.

In their search for explanations, scientists do not assume that things are always as they appear on the surface. After all, what could be more obvious

[8]Bodley, *Anthropology*, p. 69.

Hypothesis: A tentative explanation of the relation between certain phenomena.

Theory: A system of validated hypotheses that explains phenomena systematically.

than that the earth is a stable entity, around which the sun travels every day? And yet, it isn't so. Supernatural explanations are rejected, as are all explanations that are not supported by strong observational evidence. Because explanations are constantly challenged by new observations and novel ideas, science is self-correcting; that is, inadequate explanations are sooner or later shown up as such and are replaced by more adequate explanations.

The scientist begins with a **hypothesis,** or tentative explanation of the relationship between certain phenomena. By gathering various kinds of data that seem to support such generalizations and, equally important, showing why alternative hypotheses may be falsified, or eliminated from consideration, the scientist arrives at a system of validated hypotheses, or a **theory.** Although a theory is actually a well supported body of knowledge, no theory is acknowledged to be beyond challenge. Truth, in science, is not considered to be absolute, but rather a matter of varying degrees of probability; what is considered to be true is what is most probable. This is true of anthropology, just as it is true of biology or physics. As our knowledge expands, the odds in favor of some theories over others are generally increased, but sometimes old "truths" must be discarded as alternative theories are shown to be more probable.

DIFFICULTIES OF THE SCIENTIFIC APPROACH

Straightforward though the scientific approach may appear to be, there are serious difficulties in its application in anthropology. One of them is that once one has stated a hypothesis, one is strongly motivated to verify it, and this can cause one unwittingly to overlook negative evidence, not to mention all sorts of other unexpected things. In the fields of cultural anthropology there is a fur-

Destruction in Nagasaki after the atomic bomb blast of August 13, 1945. Late in World War II, anthropologists and other social scientists working for the U.S. government predicted a Japanese surrender without the need to drop atomic bombs. Because this conflicted with preconceived notions, these scientists' prediction was not heeded, but evidence found after the war confirmed its correctness.

ther difficulty: In order to arrive at useful theories concerning human behavior, one must begin with hypotheses that are as objective and as little culture-bound as possible. And here lies a major — some people would say insurmountable — problem: It is difficult for someone who has grown up in one culture to frame objective hypotheses about another that are not culture-bound.

As our example of this sort of problem, we may look at attempts by archaeologists to understand the nature of settlement in the Classic period of Maya civilization. This civilization flourished between A.D. 250 and 900 in what is now northern Guatemala, Belize, and adjacent portions of Mexico and Honduras. Today much of this region is covered by a dense tropical forest of the sort that people of European background find difficult to deal with. In recent times this forest has been inhabited by few people, who sustain themselves through slash-and-burn farming. Yet numerous archaeological sites, featuring temples sometimes as tall as a modern 20-story building, other sorts of monumental architecture, and carved monuments are to be found there. Because of their cultural bias against tropical forests as places to live, and against slash-and-burn farming as a means of raising food, North American and European archaeologists asked the question: How could the Maya have maintained large, permanent settlements on the basis of slash-and-burn farming? The answer seemed self-evident — they couldn't; therefore, the great archaeological sites must have been ceremonial centers inhabited by few, if any, people. Periodically a rural peasantry, living scattered in small hamlets over the countryside, must have gathered in these centers for rituals, or to provide labor for their construction and maintenance.

This view was the dominant one for several decades, and it was not until 1960 that archaeologists working at Tikal, one of the largest of all

Maya sites, decided to ask the simplest and least biased questions they could think of: Did anyone live at this particular site on a permanent basis? If so, how many? And how were they supported? Working intensively over the next several years, with as few preconceived notions as possible, the archaeologists were able to establish that Tikal was a huge settlement inhabited by tens of thousands of people who were supported by intensive forms of agriculture. It was this work at Tikal that paved the way for a new understanding of Classic Maya civilization totally at odds with the older, culture-bound ideas.

Recognizing the problem of framing hypotheses that are not culture-bound, anthropologists have relied heavily on a technique that has proved successful in other fields of the natural sciences. As did the archaeologists working at Tikal, they immerse themselves in the data to the fullest extent possible. By doing so, they become so thoroughly familiar with the minute details that they can begin to see patterns inherent in the data, many of which might otherwise have been overlooked. It is these patterns that allow the anthropologist to frame hypotheses, which then may be subjected to further testing.

This approach is most easily seen in ethnographic fieldwork, but it is just as important in archaeology. Unlike many social scientists, the ethnographer usually does not go into the field armed with prefigured questionnaires; rather, the ethnographer recognizes that there are probably all sorts of unguessed things, to be found out only by maintaining as open a mind as one can. This is not to say that anthropologists never use questionnaires, for sometimes they do. Generally, though, they use them as a means of supplementing or clarifying information gained through some other means. As the field-work proceeds, ethnographers sort their complex observations into a meaningful whole, sometimes by formulating and testing limited or low-level hypotheses, but as often as not by making use of intuition and by playing hunches. What is important is that the results are constantly scrutinized for consistency, for if the parts fail to fit together in a manner that is internally consistent,

then the ethnographer knows that a mistake has been made and that further work is necessary.

The contrast between the anthropological and other social-science approaches is dramatically illustrated by the following example — one of several — presented by Robert Chambers in his book, *Rural Development*. Since Chambers is a highly respected professional in the field of international development, and not an anthropologist, he can scarcely be accused of trying to promote his own discipline at the expense of others.

> Sean Conlin lived as a social anthropologist in a village in Peru. While he was there a sociologist came and carried out a survey. According to the sociologist's results, people in the village invariably worked together on each others' individually owned plots of land. That was what they told him. But in the period of over a year during which Conlin lived in the village, he observed the practice only once. The belief in exchange relations was, he concludes, important for the people's understanding of themselves, but it was not an economic fact.[9]

This does not mean that all sociological research is bad and all anthropological research is good; merely that reliance on questionnaire surveys is a risky business, no matter who does it. Robert Chambers sums up the difficulties:

> Unless careful appraisal precedes drawing up a questionnaire, the survey will embody the concepts and categories of outsiders rather than those of rural people, and thus impose meanings on the social reality. The misfit between the concepts of urban professionals and those of poor rural people is likely to be substantial, and the questions asked may construct artificial chunks of "knowledge" which distort or mutilate the reality which poor people experience. Nor are questionnaire surveys on their own good ways of identifying causal relationships — a correlation alone tells us nothing definite about cause — or of exploring social relationships such as reciprocity, dependence, exploitation and so on. Their penetration is usually shallow, concentrating on what is measurable, answerable, and acceptable as a question, rather than probing less tangible and more

[9]Robert Chambers, *Rural Development: Putting the Last First* (New York: Longman, 1983), p. 51.

The unique character of anthropology among the social sciences in North America owes a great deal to the three men pictured here, all of whom were educated in the natural sciences: Boas in physics, Putnam in zoology, and Powell in geology. Although not the first to teach anthropology, Boas and his students made such courses a common part of college and university curricula. Similarly, Putnam established anthropology in the museum world, as did Powell within government.

qualitative aspects of society. For many reasons— fear, prudence, ignorance, exhaustion, hostility, hope of benefit—poor people give information which is slanted or false.

For these and many other reasons, conventional questionnaire surveys have many drawbacks if the aim is to gain insight into the lives and conditions of the poorer rural people. Other methods are required, either alone, or together with surveys. But extensive questionnaire surveys pre-empt resources, capturing staff and finance, and preventing other approaches.[10]

The end result of archaeological or ethnographic fieldwork is a coherent account of a culture, which provides an explanatory framework for understanding the behavior of the people who have been studied. And this, in turn, is what permits the anthropologist to frame broader hypotheses about human behavior. Plausible though such hypotheses may be, however, the consideration of a single society is generally insufficient for their testing. Without some basis for comparison, the hypothesis grounded on a single case may be no more than a historical coincidence. A single case may be adequate, however, to cast doubt on, if not

[10]Ibid., p. 51.

refute, a theory that had previously been held to be valid. The discovery in 1948 that aborigines living in Australia's Arnhem Land put in an average work day of less than 6 hours, while living well above a level of bare sufficiency, was enough to call into question the widely accepted notion that food foraging peoples are so preoccupied with finding food that they lack time for any of life's more pleasurable activities. Even today, economists are prone to label such peoples as "backward" (some examples will be given in Chapter 15 and the "Introduction" to Part Seven), even though the observations made in the Arnhem Land study have since been confirmed many times over in various parts of the world.

Hypothetical explanations of cultural phenomena may be tested by the comparison of archaeological and/or ethnographic data for several societies found in a particular region. Nonhistorical, controlled comparison provides a broader context for understanding cultural phenomena than does the study of a single culture. The anthropologist who undertakes such a comparison may be more confident that the conditions believed to be related really are related, at least within the region that is under investigation; however, an explana-

A Ju/wasi family relaxes in their Kalahari Desert home. Like most hunter-gatherers, these people spend a small percentage of their time working, in this case, no more than about 20 hours a week.

tion that is valid in one region is not necessarily so in another.

Ideally, theories in cultural anthropology are generated from worldwide comparisons. The cross-cultural researcher examines a worldwide sample of societies in order to discover whether or not hypotheses proposed to explain cultural phenomena seem to be universally applicable. Because the sample is selected at random, it is probable that the conclusions of the cross-cultural researcher will be valid; however, the greater the number of societies being examined, the less likely it is that the investigator will have a detailed understanding of all the societies encompassed by the study. The cross-cultural researcher depends on other ethnographers for data. It is difficult for any single individual personally to perform in-depth analyses of a broad sample of human cultures throughout the world.

In anthropology, cultural comparisons need not be restricted to ethnographic data. Anthropologists can, for example, turn to archaeological data for the testing of hypotheses about culture change. Cultural characteristics thought to be caused by

Ethnohistory: The study of cultures of the recent past through accounts left by explorers, missionaries, and traders and through the analysis of such records as land titles, birth and death records, and other archival materials.

certain specified conditions can be tested archaeologically by investigating situations where such conditions actually occurred. Also useful are data provided by the ethnohistorian. **Ethnohistory** is a kind of historic ethnography that studies cultures of the recent past through the accounts of explorers, missionaries, and traders and through the analysis of such records as land titles, birth and death records, and other archival materials. The ethnohistorical analysis of cultures, like archaeology, is a valuable approach to understanding change. By examining the conditions believed to have caused certain phenomena, we can discover whether or not those conditions truly predate those phenomena.

Ethnohistorical research, like the field studies of archaeologists, is valuable for testing and confirming hypotheses about culture. And like much of anthropology, it has practical utility as well. In the United States, ethnohistorical research has flourished, for it often provides the key evidence necessary for deciding legal cases involving American Indian land claims.

ANTHROPOLOGY AND THE HUMANITIES

Although the sciences and humanities are often thought of as mutually exclusive approaches to learning, they both come together in anthropology. That is why, for example, anthropological research is funded not only by such "hard science" agencies as the National Science Foundation, but also by such organizations as the National Endowment for the Humanities. The humanistic side of anthropology is perhaps most immediately evident in its concern with other cultures' languages, values, and achievements in the arts and literature (oral literature, among peoples who lack writing). Beyond this, anthropologists remain committed to the proposition that one cannot fully understand another culture by observing it; one must *experience* it as well. Thus, ethnographers spend prolonged periods of time living with the people whom they study, sharing their joys and suffering their deprivations, including sickness and, sometimes, premature death. They are not so naive as to believe that they can be, or even should be, dispassionate about the people whose trials and tribulations they share. As Robin Fox puts it, "our hearts, as well as our brains, should be with our men and women."[11] Nor are anthropologists so self-deceived as to believe that they can avoid dealing with the moral and political consequences of their findings.

Given their intense encounters with other peoples, it should come as no surprise that anthropologists have amassed as much information about human frailty and nobility—the stuff of the humanities—as any other discipline. Small wonder, too, that above all they intend to avoid allowing a "coldly" scientific approach to blind them to the fact that the human species is made up of individuals with rich assortments of emotions and aspirations that demand respect. Anthropology has

sometimes been called the most human of the sciences, a designation in which anthropologists take considerable pride.

QUESTIONS OF ETHICS

The kinds of research carried out by anthropologists, and the settings within which they work, raise a number of important questions concerning ethics. Who will make use of the findings of anthropologists? And for what purposes? In the case of a militant minority, for example, will others use anthropological data to suppress that minority? And what of traditional communities around the world? Who is to decide what changes should, or should not, be introduced for community "betterment"? By whose definition is it betterment—the community's or that of a remote national government? Then there is the problem of privacy. Anthropologists deal with people's private and sensitive matters, including things that people would not care to have generally known about them. How does one write about such matters and at the same time protect the privacy of informants? Not surprisingly, because of these and other questions, there has been a hot debate among anthropologists over the past two decades on the subject of ethics.

The present consensus among anthropologists about the ethics of their profession was summed up by Laura Nader in an interview:

> Anthropologists have obligations to three different sets of people. First, to the people that we study; secondly, to the profession which expects us to report back our findings; and thirdly, to the organizations that fund the research. Some people would order them differently—one, two, three, three, two, one, or whatever—but those three are in the minds of most anthropologists. Now, sometimes the obligations conflict. If I do fieldwork among a group of people and I learn certain things that, if revealed, might come back to hurt them, then reporting my findings back to the profession is going to be secondary because first and foremost I have to protect my informants because they trusted me. In the case of

[11]Robin Fox, *Encounter with Anthropology* (New York: Dell, 1968), p. 290.

the Zapotec, I was dealing with very sensitive materials about law and disputes and conflicts and so forth. And I was very sensitive about how much of that to report while people were still alive and while things might still be warm, so I waited on that. I'm just finishing my Zapotec monograph now. I've written certain things, but I waited for the most part, and I feel comfortable now releasing that information. With regard to a funder in that case, it was the Mexican government, and I feel that I have written enough to have paid off the $1200 which they gave me to support that work for a year. So, I've not felt particularly strained for my Zapotec work in those three areas. On energy research that I've done, it's been another story. Much of what people wanted me to do energy research for was ... to tell people in decision-making positions about American consumers in such a way that they could be manipulated better, and I didn't want to do that. So what I said was I would be willing to study a vertical slice. That is, I would never study the consumer without studying the producer. And once you take a vertical slice like that, then it's fair because you're telling the consumer about the producer and the producer about the consumer. But just to do a study of consumers for producers, I think I would feel uncomfortable.[12]

ANTHROPOLOGY AND CONTEMPORARY LIFE

Anthropology, with its long-standing commitment to the understanding of peoples in all parts of the world, coupled with its holistic perspective, makes it better equipped than any other discipline to grapple with a problem of overriding importance for all of humanity in this last quarter of the twentieth century. It is an inescapable fact of life that we North Americans live in a global community in which all the world's people are interdependent upon one another. Although there is widespread awareness of this in the business community, which relies on foreign sources for raw materials, sees the non-Western world as its major area for market expansion, and is more and more making its products abroad, citizens of the United States are on the whole as ignorant about

[12] Laura Nader, Interview for Coast Telecourses, Inc., Los Angeles, December 3, 1981.

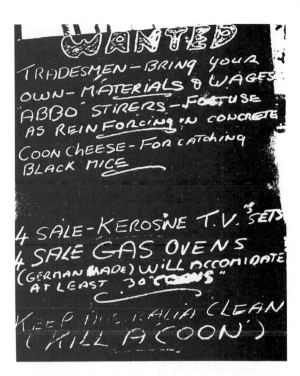

Ignorance about other peoples helps perpetuate stereotypes, such as those expressed on this sign, photographed in Australia in 1978 (the sign's message is that aborigines should be exterminated). Such attitudes have been responsible for much human misery. The interdependence of the world's peoples today, with their capability to do one another incalculable harm, has made an understanding of "other people" a matter of basic survival.

the cultures of the rest of the world as they have ever been. As a result, they are poorly equipped to handle the demands of living in the modern world.

Anthropologist Dennis Shaw sums up the implications of this state of affairs as follows:

Such provinciality raises questions about the welfare of our nation and the global context in which it is a major force. We have, as a nation, continued to interpret the political actions of other nations in terms of the cultural and political norms of our own culture and have thus made major misinterpretations of global political affairs. Our economic interests have been pursued from the perspective of our own cultural norms, and thus, we have failed to keep up with other nations that have shown a sensitivity to cultural differences. Domestically, a serious question can be raised about the viability of a democracy in which a major portion of the electorate is basically ignorant of the issues which our political leaders must confront. Internationally, one can speculate about the well-being of a world in which the citizens of one of the most powerful nations are seriously deficient in their ability to evaluate global issues.[13]

Former ambassador Edwin Reischauer puts it more tersely: "Education is not moving rapidly enough in the right directions to produce the knowledge about the outside world and attitudes toward other peoples that may be essential for human survival."[14] What anthropology has to contribute to contemporary life, then, are an understanding of, and a way of looking at, the world's peoples, which are nothing less than basic skills for survival in the modern world.

[13]Dennis G. Shaw, "A Light at the End of the Tunnel: Anthropological Contributions Towards Global Competence," *Anthropology Newsletter*, 25 (November 1984): 16.
[14]Quoted in Susan L. Allen, "Media Anthropology: Building a Public Perspective," *Anthropology Newsletter*, 25 (November 1984): 6.

CHAPTER SUMMARY

Throughout human history, people have needed to know who they are, where they came from, and why they behave as they do. Traditionally, myths and legends provided the answers to these questions. Anthropology, as it has emerged over the last 200 years, offers another approach to answering the questions people ask about themselves.

Anthropology is the study of humankind. In employing a scientific approach, anthropologists seek to produce useful generalizations about humans and their behavior and to arrive at a reasonably objective understanding of human diversity. The two major fields of anthropology are physical and cultural anthropology. Physical anthropology focuses on humans as biological organisms. Particular emphasis is given by physical anthropologists to tracing the evolutionary development of the human animal and studying biological variation within the species today. Cultural anthropologists study humans in terms of their cultures, the often unconscious standards by which societies operate.

Three areas of cultural anthropology are archaeology, anthropological linguistics, and ethnology. Archaeologists study material objects usually from past cultures in order to explain human behavior. Linguists, who study human languages, may deal with the description of a language or with the history of languages. Ethnologists concentrate on cultures of the present or of the recent past; in doing comparative studies of culture, they may also focus on a particular aspect of culture, such as religious or economic practices, or as ethnographers, they may go into the field to observe and describe human behavior as it can be seen, experienced, and discussed with persons whose culture is to be understood.

Anthropology is unique among the social and natural sciences in that it is concerned with formulating explanations of human diversity based on a study of all aspects of human biology and behavior in all known societies, rather than in European and North American societies alone. Thus, anthropologists have devoted much attention to the study of non-Western peoples.

Anthropologists are concerned with the objective and systematic study of humankind. The anthropologist employs the methods of other scientists by developing a hypothesis, or assumed explanation, using other data to test the hypothesis, and ultimately arriving at a theory—a system of validated hypotheses. The data used by the cultural anthropologist may be field data of one society or comparative studies of numerous societies.

In anthropology, the humanities and sciences come together into a genuinely human science. Anthropology's link with the humanities can be seen in its concern with people's values, languages, arts, and literature — oral as well as written — but above all in its attempt to convey the experience of living as other people do. As both science and humanity, anthropology has essential skills to offer the modern world, where understanding the other people with whom we share the globe has become a matter of survival.

SUGGESTED READINGS

Lett, James. *The Human Enterprise: A Critical Introduction to Anthropological Theory*. Boulder, Colo.: Westview, 1987. Part 1 examines the philosophical foundations of anthropological theory, paying special attention to the nature of scientific inquiry and the mechanisms of scientific progress. Part 2 deals with the nature of social science as well as the particular features of anthropology.

Peacock, James L. *The Anthropological Lens: Harsh Light, Soft Focus*. New York: Cambridge University Press, 1986. This lively and innovative book manages to give the reader a good understanding of the diversity of activities undertaken by anthropologists, while at the same time identifying the unifying themes that hold the discipline together.

Spradley, James P. *The Ethnographic Interview*. New York: Holt, Rinehart and Winston, 1979. This contains one of the best discussions of the nature and value of ethnographic research to be found. The bulk of the book is devoted to a step-by-step, easy-to-understand account of how one carries out ethnographic research with the assistance of native "informants." Numerous examples drawn from the author's own research in such diverse settings as Skid Row, courtrooms, and bars make for interesting reading. A companion volume, *Participant Observation*, is also highly recommended.

Van Willigen, John. *Applied Anthropology, An Introduction*. South Hadley, Mass.: Bergin and Garvey, 1986. In recent years, more and more anthropologists have been applying their knowledge and skills to activities other than teaching and research. This book is the first comprehensive survey of the field of applied anthropology by a master in the field.

Voget, Fred W. *A History of Ethnology*. New York. Holt, Rinehart and Winston, 1975. This history of cultural anthropology attempts to describe and interpret the major intellectual strands, in their cultural and historical contexts, that influenced the development of the field. The author tries for a balanced view of this subject rather than one that would support a particular theoretical position.

2

METHODS OF STUDYING THE HUMAN PAST

Excavation of a 10,000-year-old skeleton at Leander, Texas. Because excavation of ancient remains destroys the site in which they are found, meticulous records must be kept. Without such records, the finds tell us nothing about the human past.

CHAPTER
PREVIEW

What Are Archaeological Sites and Fossil Localities and How Are They Found?

Archaeological sites are places containing the remains of past human activity. They are revealed by the presence of artifacts — objects fashioned or altered by humans — as well as certain kinds of soil marks, changes in vegetation, irregularities of the surface, and the like. Fossil localities are places containing the actual remains of organisms that lived in the past. They are revealed by the presence of fossils — any trace or impression of an organism of past geological time that has been preserved in the earth. Although fossils are sometimes found in archaeological sites, not all archaeological sites contain fossils, and localities are often found apart from archaeological sites. Though often discovered by accident, sites and localities are usually located by systematically surveying a region.

How Are Sites and Localities Investigated?

Archaeologists and paleoanthropologists face something of a dilemma. The only way to thoroughly investigate a site or locality is by excavation, which results in its destruction. Thus, every attempt is made to excavate in such a way that the location of everything found, no matter how small, is precisely recorded. Without such records, little sense can be made of the data, and the potential of the site or locality to contribute to our knowledge of the past would be lost forever.

How Are Archaeological or Fossil Remains Dated?

Remains can be dated in relative terms by noting their stratigraphic position, by measuring the amount of fluorine contained in fossil bones, or by associating them with different floral or faunal remains. More precise dating is achieved by counting the growth rings in wood from archaeological contexts, by measuring the amount of Carbon 14 remaining in organic materials, or by measuring the percentage of potassium that has decayed to argon in volcanic materials. Some other techniques are less commonly used, but they are not always as widely available, or they have not been proved as reliable.

Archaeology and physical anthropology are the two branches of anthropology most involved in the study of the human past. Archaeologists, apart from those engaged in the analysis of modern garbage, study things left behind by people who lived in historic or prehistoric times — tools, trash, traces of shelters, and the like. Most of us are familiar with some kind of archaeological material: the coin dug out of the earth, the fragment of an ancient jar, the spear point used by some ancient hunter. The finding and cataloging of such objects is often thought by nonprofessionals to be the chief goal of archaeology. While this was true in the last century, the emphasis today is on using archaeological remains to reconstruct human societies that can no longer be observed firsthand, in order to understand and explain human behavior.

The actual remains of our ancestors, as opposed to the things they lost or discarded, are the concern of physical anthropologists. Those physical anthropologists engaged in the recovery and study of the fossil evidence for human evolution are generally known as **paleoanthropologists.** Just as the finding and cataloging of objects was once the chief concern of the archaeologist, so the finding and cataloging of fossils was once the chief concern of the paleoanthropologist. But, again, there has been a major change in the field; while recovery, description, and organization of fossil materials are still important, the emphasis now is on what those fossils can tell us about the processes at work in human biological evolution.

In Chapter 1, we surveyed at some length just what it is that anthropologists do, and why they do it. We also looked briefly at the ethnographic methods used by anthropologists to study living peoples (and we shall touch upon these again in Chapter 12). Other methods are required, however, when studying peoples of the past — especially those of the prehistoric past. In this chapter, we shall look at how archaeologists and paleoanthropologists go about their study of the human past.

Paleoanthropologist: An anthropologist who studies human evolution from fossil remains.

Artifact: Any object fashioned or altered by humans.

METHODS OF DATA RECOVERY

Archaeologists, one way or another, work with **artifacts,** that is, any object fashioned or altered by humans — a flint chip, a basket, an ax, a pipe, or such nonportable things as house ruins or walls. An artifact expresses a facet of human culture. Because it is something that someone made, archaeologists like to say that an artifact is a product of human behavior or, in more technical words, that it is a material representation of an abstract ideal.

Just as important as the artifacts themselves is the way they were left in the ground. What people do with the things they have made, how they dispose of them, and how they lose them also reflect important aspects of human behavior. Furthermore, it is the context in which the artifacts were found that tells us which objects were contemporary with which other objects, which are older, and which are younger. Without this information, the archaeologist is in no position at all to even identify, let alone understand, specific cultures of the past. Unfortunately, such information is easily lost if the materials have been disturbed, whether by bulldozers or by the activities of relic collectors.

While archaeologists work with artifacts, paleoanthropologists work with fossils — the remains of past forms of life. And just as the context of a find is as important to the archaeologist as is the find itself, so is the context of a fossil critical to the paleoanthropologist. Not only does it tell which fossils are earlier or later in time than other fossils, but by noting the association of human fossils with other nonhuman remains, the paleoanthropologist may also go a long way toward reconstructing the environmental setting in which the human lived.

THE NATURE OF FOSSILS

Broadly defined, a **fossil** is any trace or impression of an organism of past geological time that has been preserved in the earth's crust. Fossilization typically involves the hard parts of an organism; bones, teeth, shells, horns, and the woody tissues of plants are the most successfully fossilized materials. Although the soft parts of an organism are rarely fossilized, the casts of footprints, and even whole bodies, have sometimes been found.

An organism or part of an organism may be preserved in a number of ways. The whole animal may be frozen in ice, like the famous mammoths found in Siberia, safe from the actions of predators, weathering, and bacteria. Or it may be enclosed in a fossil resin such as amber. Specimens of spiders and insects dating back millions of years have been

Fossil: The preserved remains of plants and animals that lived in the past.

Unaltered fossil: Remains of plants and animals that lived in the past that have not been altered in any significant way.

preserved in resins found in the Baltic Sea area, which is rich in resin-producing conifers. It may be preserved in the bottoms of lakes and sea basins, where the accumulation of chemicals renders the environment antiseptic. The entire organism may also be mummified or preserved in tar pits, peat, oil, or asphalt bogs, in which the chemical environment prevents the growth of decay-producing bacteria. Such **unaltered fossils,** although not common, are often quite spectacular and may be particularly informative.

ORIGINAL STUDY
Peat Holds Clues to Early American Life[1]

Tenderly buried in a shallow pond in central Florida, the dead of an early American Indian society lay under an ever deepening shroud of peat for more than 7000 years. Recently resurrected, the bones and artifacts speak poignantly of a little-understood culture and reveal levels of craft previously undocumented in the New World during that era. The site is a genetic gold mine as well—brains preserved in this peat environment have yielded the oldest known human DNA.

Excavation directed by Florida State University began in 1984, two years after a construction crew turned up skulls in a Titusville housing development called Windover Farms. By late 1986 the Windover Archaeological Research Project had uncovered more than a hundred burials dating from 7000 to 8000 years ago. Few sites of this age in the Americas have held so large and diverse a group—nearly equally divided between male and female, adult and subadult.

In life they were hunter–gatherers, making seasonal rounds through this region today known for Walt Disney World and the Kennedy Space Center. At death they were placed in the foot-deep pond. Often laid on their side in a flexed position, they were wrapped in grass mats, then covered with peat and wood. A frame of branches secured the grave.

Fabric, perhaps from a blanket or poncho, clung to some skeletons. Analysis by Dr. James Adovasio at the University of Pittsburgh has unrav-

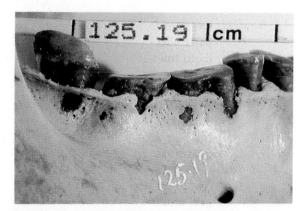

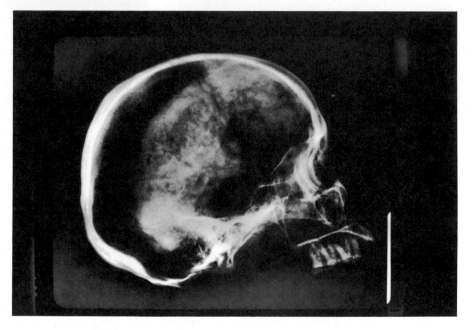

eled five distinct types of weaving more sophisticated than any known in the Americas from that time. Made without a loom, one weave is nearly as tight as a modern T-shirt. "There are lots of simpler ways to make durable cloth," says archaeologist Dr. Glen Doran, director of the excavation. "It challenges our traditional model of hunter–gatherer societies. These people had taken care of the basic necessities of life and had enough time to devote to a very complex nonessential activity." Further evidence comes from the skeleton of a teenager who suffered from a degenerative chronic spinal disorder. "It tells us they could support a nonproductive person for a long time," explains archaeologist and codirector Dr. David Dickel.

"They seem to have been oriented toward doing things for children," says Dickel, noting that the most bountiful grave offerings lie with children and teenagers. Artifacts found include a wooden pestle and a paddle, perhaps used to pound plant fibers for weaving. Antler from deer and bone from manatee, rabbit, and fish were shaped into awls and needles, a small hammer, devices to accelerate spear throwing, and tools of unknown function.

Under a tarpaulin shielding the drained pond, field archaeologist John Ricisak (*upper left*) slices peat from the skeleton of a child who died at about the age of the observing schoolchildren. Even at about 12 years, teeth (*upper right*) show wear from a diet of rough vegetation such as nuts and cabbage palm.

About ten feet of peat was cleared to reach the burials. Sealed from oxygen and saturated with minerals from Florida peatland waters, the preserved bones contain protein that may reveal diseases this population encountered. Unprotected soft tissue dissolved, but, locked in the skull, a shrunken brain often survived, as seen in this X ray of a middle-aged woman (*below*). The water's almost neutral pH balance also saved brain DNA. "One of this find's most significant aspects is that human DNA can be preserved," says Dr. William Hauswirth, a microbiologist at the University of Florida who, in collaboration with biochemist Dr. Philip Laipis, has extracted this genetic-coding molecule from the Windover-site brains. They are trying to clone it. "There are not many things we can do with it now, but it will be a resource for the future when we understand more about human genes."

In anticipation of such advances, the site was not totally excavated. Reflooded, it awaits archaeologists of another generation.

[1]Louise E. Levathes, "Mysteries of the Bog," *National Geographic* 171 (1987): 406–407.

Cases in which an entire organism is preserved in a relatively unaltered state are rare and comprise possibly less than 1 percent of all fossil finds. The majority of **fossils** have been **altered** in some way. They generally consist of such things as scattered teeth and fragments of bones and are found embedded in the earth's crust as part of rock deposits. Thousands, and even millions, of years ago, the organisms died and were deposited in the earth; they may then have been covered by sediments and silt, or sand. These materials gradually hardened, forming a protective shell around the skeleton of the organism. The internal cavities of bones or teeth and other parts of the skeleton are generally

Altered fossils: Remains of plants and animals that lived in the past that have been altered, as by the replacement of organic material by calcium carbonate or silica.

filled in with mineral deposits from the sediment immediately surrounding the specimen. Then the external walls of the bone decay and are replaced by calcium carbonate or silica.

Fossilization is most apt to occur among marine animals and other organisms that live near water, because their remains accumulate on shallow sea or river bottoms, away from waves and tidal action. These concentrations of shells and other parts of organisms are covered and completely enclosed by the soft marine sediments that eventually harden into shale and limestone.

Terrestrial animals, however, are not so successfully fossilized unless they happened to die in a cave, or their remains were dragged there by some other meat-eating animal. In caves, conditions are often excellent for fossilization, as minerals contained in water dripping from the ceiling may harden over bones left on the cave floor. In northern China, for example, many fossils of *Homo erectus* (discussed in Chapter 7) and other animals were found in a cave at a place called Zhoukoudian, in deposits consisting of consolidated clays and rock that had fallen from the cave's limestone ceiling. The cave had been frequented by both humans and predatory animals, who left remains of many a meal there.

Outside of caves, the bones of a land dweller, having been picked clean and often broken by predators and scavengers, are then scattered and exposed to the deteriorating influence of the elements. The fossil record for many primates, for example, is poor, because the acid soil of the tropical forests in which they lived decomposed the skeleton rather quickly. The record is much more complete for primates that lived on the grassy plains, or savannas, where conditions were much more favorable to the formation of fossils. This is particularly true in places where ash from volcanic eruptions, or waterborne sediments along lakes and streams, might quickly have covered the skeletons of primates that died there. At several localities in Ethiopia, Kenya, and Tanzania in East Africa, fossils important for our understanding of human evolution have been found near ancient lakes and streams, often "sandwiched" between layers of volcanic ash.

SITES AND FOSSIL LOCALITIES

Places containing archaeological remains of previous human occupation are known as **sites.** There are many kinds of sites, and sometimes it is diffi-

Site: In archaeology, a place containing remains of previous human occupants.

cult to define the boundaries of a site, for remains may be strewn over large areas. Some examples of sites are hunting campsites, in which hunters waited for game to pass; kill sites, in which game was killed and butchered; village sites, in which domestic activities took place; and cemeteries, in

Fossils are not always found in the ground. In this picture, paleoanthropologist Donald Johanson searches for fossils in a gully in Ethiopia. The fossils in the foreground were once buried beneath sediments on an ancient lake bottom, but rains in more recent times have eroded the sediments from around them so that they lie exposed on the surface.

which the dead, and sometimes their belongings, were buried.

Sometimes human fossil remains are present at archaeological sites. This is the case, for example, at certain early sites in East Africa. Sometimes, though, they are found at other localities. For example, in South Africa the fossil remains of early hominids have been found in rock fissures, where their remains seem to have been dropped by predators. Such places are usually referred to as **fossil localities.**

SITE AND LOCALITY IDENTIFICATION

Archaeological sites, particularly very old ones, frequently lie buried underground, and therefore, the first task for the archaeologist is actually finding sites to investigate. Most sites are revealed by the presence of artifacts. Chance may play a beneficial role in the discovery of artifacts and sites, but usually the archaeologist will have to survey a region in order to plot the sites available for excavation. A survey can be made from the ground, but nowadays, more and more use is being made of remote sensing techniques, many of them byproducts of space-age technology. Aerial photographs have been used off and on by archaeologists since the 1920s and are widely used today. Among other things, they were used for the discovery and interpretation of the huge geometric and zoomorphic markings on the coastal desert of Peru. More recently, use of high-resolution aerial photographs, including satellite imagery, resulted in the astonishing discovery of over 200 miles of prehistoric roadways connecting sites in the four-corners region (where Arizona, New Mexico, Colorado, and Utah meet) with other sites in ways that archaeologists had never suspected. This has led to a whole new understanding of prehistoric Pueblo Indian economic, social, and political organization. Evidently, large centers like Pueblo Bonito were able to exercise political control over a number of satellite communities, mobilize labor for large public works, and see to the regular redistribution of goods over substantial distances.

Fossil locality: In paleoanthropology, a place where fossils are found.

Soil marks: Stains that show up on the surface of recently plowed fields that reveal an archaeological site.

On the ground, sites can be spotted by **soil marks,** or stains, that often show up on the surface of recently plowed fields. From soil marks, many Bronze Age burial mounds were discovered in northern Hertfordshire and southwestern Cambridgeshire, England. The mounds hardly rose out of the ground, yet each was circled at its core by

An archaeological site best seen from the air: a network of roads built by American Indians at Chaco Canyon.

chalky soil marks. Sometimes the very presence of certain chalky rock is significant. A search for Stone Age cave sites in Europe would be simplified with the aid of a geological map showing where limestone — a mineral necessary in the formation of caves — is to be found.

Some sites may be spotted by the kind of vegetation they grow. For example, the topsoil of ancient storage and refuse pits is often richer in organic matter than that of the surrounding areas, and so it grows a distinct vegetation. At Tikal, an ancient Maya site in Guatemala (Chapter 10), breadnut trees usually grow near the remains of ancient houses, so that an archaeologist looking for the remains of houses at Tikal would do well to search where these trees grow. In England, a wooden monument of the Stonehenge type at Darrington, Wiltshire, was discovered from an aerial photograph showing a distinct pattern of vegetation growing where the ancient structure stood.

Documents, maps, folklore — ethnohistorical data — are also useful to the archaeologist. Heinrich Schliemann, the famous nineteenth-century German archaeologist, was led to the discovery of Troy after a reading of Homer's *Iliad*. He assumed that the city described by Homer as Ilium was really Troy. Place names and local lore often are an indication that an archaeological site is to be found in the area. Archaeological surveys in North America depend a great deal on amateur collectors who are usually familiar with local history.

Sometimes sites in eastern North America are exposed by natural agents, such as soil erosion or droughts. Many prehistoric Indian shell refuse mounds have been exposed by the erosion of river banks. A whole village of stone huts was exposed at Skara Brae in the Orkney Islands by the action of wind as it blew away sand. And during the long drought of 1853–1854, a well-preserved prehistoric village was exposed when the water level of Lake Zurich, Switzerland, fell dramatically.

Often, archaeological remains are accidentally discovered in the course of some other human activity. Ploughing sometimes turns up bones, fragments of pots, and other archaeological objects.

Stone quarrying revealed one of the most important sites of the Old Stone Age in England — at Swanscombe, Kent — in which human remains thought to be about 250,000 years old were found. In 1965, ground breaking for a new apartment complex in Nice, France, uncovered the remains of a campsite of *Homo erectus* (Chapter 7) 400,000 years old. So frequently do construction projects uncover archaeological remains that in many countries, including the United States, projects that require government approval will not be authorized unless measures are first taken to identify and protect archaeological remains on the construction sites. Increasingly, archaeological surveys in the United States are carried out as part of the environmental review process for federally funded or licensed construction projects.

Conspicuous sites such as the great mounds or *tells* of the Middle East are easy to spot, for the country is open. But where there is a dense forest cover, it is difficult to locate ruins, even those that are well above ground. Thus, the discovery of archaeological sites is strongly affected by local geography.

While archaeological sites may be found just about anywhere, the same is not true for fossil localities. One will find fossils only in geological contexts where conditions are known to have been right for fossilization. Once the paleoanthropologist has identified such regions, specific localities are identified in much the same ways as archaeological sites. Indeed, the discovery of ancient stone tools may lead to the discovery of human fossil remains. For example, it was the presence of very crude stone tools in Olduvai Gorge, East Africa, which prompted Mary and Louis Leakey to search there for the human fossils they eventually found.

SITE AND LOCALITY EXCAVATION

Before the archaeologist or paleoanthropologist plans an excavation, he or she must ask the question: "Why am I digging?" Then must be considered the amount of time, money, and labor that can be committed to the enterprise. The recovery of archaeological and fossil material has long since ceased to be the province of the enlightened amateur, as it once was when any enterprising collector went out to dig for the sake of digging. A modern excavation is carefully planned and rigorously conducted; not only should it shed light on the human past, but it should also help us to understand cultural and evolutionary processes in general.

Archaeological Excavation

After a site is chosen for excavation, on the basis of its potential contribution to the solution of some important research problem, the land is cleared and the places to be excavated are plotted. This is usually done by means of a **grid system.** The surface of the site is divided into squares, and then each square is numbered and marked with stakes. The starting point of a grid system may be a large

Grid system: A system for recording data from an archaeological excavation.

Datum point: Starting, or reference, point for a grid system.

rock, the edge of a stone wall, or an iron rod sunk into the ground. The starting point is also known as the reference or **datum point.** At a large site covering several square miles, this kind of grid system is not feasible because of the large size of the ruins. In such cases, the plotting may be done in terms of individual structures, numbered according to the square of a "giant grid" in which they are found (Figure 2.1).

In a gridded site, each square is dug separately with great care. Trowels are used to scrape the soil,

Sometimes archaeological sites are marked by dramatic ruins, as shown here. These are three of seven great temples standing in or near the ancient Mayan city of Tikal. Built by piling up rubble and facing it with limestone blocks held together with mortar, the temples served as funerary monuments for Tikal's rulers between ca. 700 and 810 A.D.

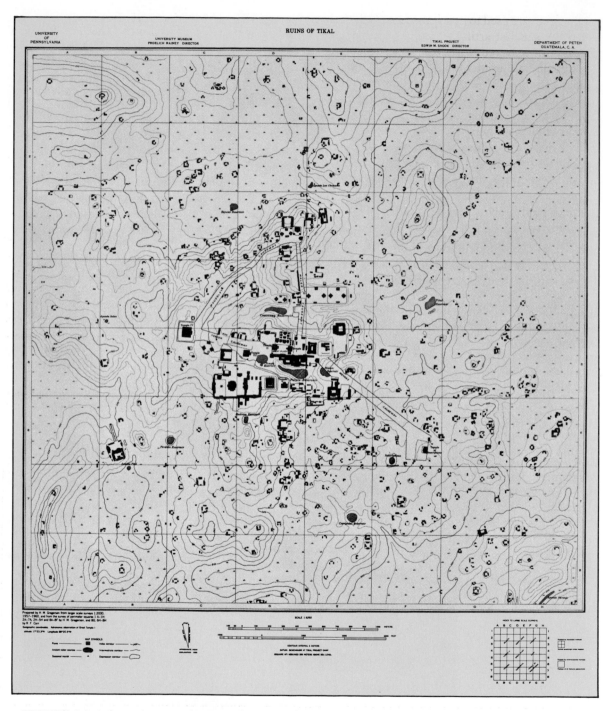

FIGURE 2.1 At large sites covering several square miles, a giant grid is constructed, as shown in this map of the center of the ancient Maya city of Tikal. Each square of the grid is one quarter of a square kilometer; individual structures are numbered according to the square in which they are found. The temple shown on page 37 can be located near the center of the map, on the east edge of the Great Plaza.

and screens are used to sift all the loose soils so that even the smallest artifacts, such as flint chips or beads, are recovered.

A technique used when looking for very fine objects, such as fish scales or very small bones, is called **flotation.** Flotation consists of immersing soil in water, causing the particles to separate. Some will float, others will sink to the bottom, and the remains can be easily retrieved. If the site is **stratified** — that is, if the remains lie in layers one upon the other — each layer, or stratum, will be dug separately (see Figure 2.2 for an example of stratigraphy). Each layer, having been laid down during a particular span of time, will contain artifacts deposited at the same time and belonging to the same culture. Culture change can be traced through the order in which artifacts were deposited. But, say archaeologists Frank Hole and Robert F. Heizer, "because of difficulties in analyzing stratigraphy, archaeologists must use the greatest caution in drawing conclusions. Almost all interpretations of time, space, and culture contexts depend on stratigraphy. The refinements of laboratory techniques for analysis are wasted if archaeologists cannot specify the stratigraphic position of their artifacts."[2] If no stratification is present,

> **Flotation:** An archaeological technique employed to recover very tiny objects by immersion of soil samples in water to separate heavy from light particles.
>
> **Stratified:** Layered; said of archaeological sites where the remains lie in layers, one upon another.

then the archaeologist digs by arbitrary levels. Each square must be dug so that its edges and profiles are straight; walls between squares are often left standing to serve as visual correlates of the grid system.

Excavation of Fossils
Excavating for fossils is in many ways like archaeological excavation, although there are some differences. The paleoanthropologist must be particularly skilled in the techniques of geology, or else have ready access to geological expertise, because a fossil is of limited use unless its temporal place in the sequence of rocks that contain it can be determined. In addition, the paleoanthropologist must be able to identify the fossil-laden rocks, their

[2] Frank Hole and Robert F. Heizer, *An Introduction to Prehistoric Archeology* (New York: Holt, Rinehart and Winston, 1969), p. 113.

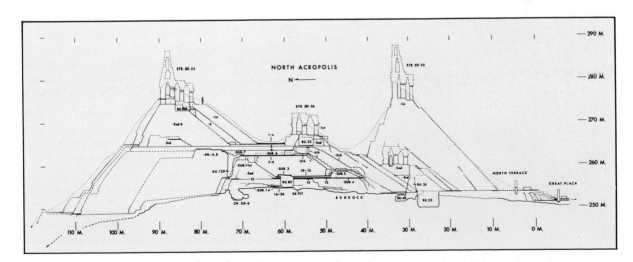

FIGURE 2.2 The drawing shows the strata (layers) uncovered on the North Acropolis of Tikal; the remains of at least 22 structures were found at this one location. The North Acropolis is shown near the center of the map in Figure 2.1, just north of the Great Plaza.

deposition, and other geological details. In order to provide all the necessary expertise, paleoanthropological expeditions these days generally are made up of teams of experts in various fields in addition to physical anthropology.

A great deal of skill and caution is required to remove a fossil from its burial place without damage. An unusual combination of tools and materials is usually contained in the kit of the paleoanthropologist — pickaxes, enamel coating, burlap for bandages, and plaster of paris.

To remove a newly discovered skeleton, the paleoanthropologist begins uncovering the specimen, using pick and shovel for initial excavation, then small camel hair brushes and dental picks to

The recovery of fossil material is often a delicate and tedious business.

remove loose and easily detachable debris surrounding the skeleton. Once the entire skeleton has been uncovered (a process that may take days of back-breaking, patient labor), the bones are covered with shellac and tissue paper to prevent cracking and damage during further excavation and handling.

Both the fossil skeleton and the earth immediately surrounding it, or the matrix, are prepared for removal as a single block. The skeleton and matrix are cut out of the earth (but not removed), and more shellac is applied to the entire block to harden it. The skeleton is covered with burlap bandages dipped in plaster of paris. Then the entire block is enclosed in plaster and burlap bandages, perhaps splinted with tree branches, and allowed to dry overnight. After it has hardened, the entire block is carefully removed from the earth, ready for packing and transport to a laboratory. Before leaving the discovery area, the investigator makes a thorough sketch map of the terrain and pinpoints the find on geological maps to aid future investigators.

STATE OF PRESERVATION OF ARCHAEOLOGICAL AND FOSSIL EVIDENCE

Just what is recovered in the course of excavation depends on the nature of the remains as much as on the excavator's digging skills. Inorganic materials such as stone and metal are more resistant to decay than organic ones such as wood and bone. Often an archaeologist comes upon an assemblage — a collection of artifacts made of durable inorganic materials, such as stone tools, and traces of organic ones long since decomposed, such as woodwork (Figure 2.3), textiles, or food.

The state of preservation is affected by climate; under favorable climatic conditions, even the most perishable objects may survive over vast periods of time. For example, predynastic Egyptian burials consisting of shallow pits in the sand often yield well-preserved corpses. Because these bodies were buried long before mummification was ever practiced, their preservation can only be the result of

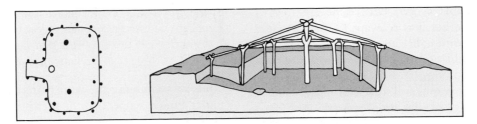

FIGURE 2.3 Although the wooden posts of a house may long since have decayed, their positions may still be marked by discoloration of the soil. The plan shown on the left, of an ancient posthole pattern and depression at Snaketown, Arizona, permits the hypothetical house reconstruction on the right.

rapid desiccation in the very warm, dry climate. The tombs of dynastic Egypt often contain wooden furniture, textiles, flowers, and papyri barely touched by time, seemingly as fresh looking as they were when deposited in the tomb 3000 years ago — as a result of the dryness of the atmosphere.

The dryness of certain caves is also a factor in the preservation of fossilized human or animal feces. Human feces are a source of information on prehistoric foods and can be analyzed for dietary remains. From such analysis can be determined not only what the inhabitants ate but also how the food was prepared. Because so many sources of food are available only in certain seasons, it is even possible to tell the time of year in which the food was eaten and the excrement deposited.

Certain climates can soon obliterate all evidence of organic remains. Maya ruins found in the very warm and moist tropical rain forests of Mesoamerica are often in a state of collapse — notwithstanding the fact that they are massive structures of stone — as a result of the pressure exerted on them by the heavy forest vegetation. The rain and humidity soon destroy almost all traces of woodwork, textiles, or basketry.

The cultural practices of ancient humans may also account for the preservation of archaeological remains. The ancient Egyptians believed that eternal life could be achieved only if the dead person were buried with his or her worldly possessions. Hence, their tombs are usually filled with a wealth of artifacts. Many skeletal remains of Neandertals

(Chapter 8) are known because they practiced burial, probably because they too believed in some sort of afterlife. By contrast, skeletal remains of pre-Neandertal peoples are rare and when found usually consist of mere fragments rather than complete skeletons.

SORTING OUT THE EVIDENCE

The value of archaeological materials is virtually destroyed if an accurate and detailed record of the excavations has not been kept.

> The excavator bears a very heavy burden of responsibility; as he excavates, he does in fact destroy the site he is investigating and, apart from the actual portable and removable objects he recovers, the essential circumstances of their findings will only survive in the form of his records.[3]

The records include a scale map of all the features, the stratification of each excavated square, a description of the exact location and depth of every artifact or fossil bone unearthed, and photographs and scale drawings of the objects. This is the only way archaeological evidence can later be pieced together in order to be able to arrive at a plausible reconstruction of a culture. Although the archaeologist may be interested only in certain

[3]Stuart Piggott, *Approach to Archeology* (New York: McGraw-Hill, 1965), p. 30.

kinds of remains, every aspect of the site must be recorded, whether it is relevant to the particular investigation or not, because such evidence may be useful to others and would otherwise be permanently lost.

After photographs and scale drawings are made, the materials recovered are processed in the laboratory. In the case of fossils, the block in which they have been removed from the field is cut open, and the fossil is separated from the matrix. Like the initial removal from the earth, this is a long, painstaking job involving a great deal of skill and special tools. This task may be done with hammer and chisel, dental drills, rotary grinders or pneumatic chisels, and, in the case of very small pieces, with awls and tiny needles under a microscope.

Chemical means, such as hydrochloric and hydrofluoric acid, are also used in the separation process. Some fossils require processing by other methods. For example, precise identification can be obtained by examining thin, almost transparent strips of some fossils under a microscope. Casts of the insides of skulls are made by filling the skull wall with an acid-resistant material, then removing the wall with acid. A skull may be cleaned out and the inside painted with latex. After the latex hardens, it is removed in a single piece, revealing indirect evidence of brain shape and nerve patterns. Such a cast of the internal skull is helpful in determining the size and complexity of the specimen's brain.

Archaeologists, as a rule of thumb, generally plan on at least three hours of laboratory work for each hour of fieldwork. In the lab, artifacts which have been recovered must first be cleaned and cataloged — often a tedious and time-consuming job — before they are ready for analysis. From the shapes of the artifacts and from the traces of manufacture and wear, archaeologists can usually determine their function. For example, the Russian archaeologist S. A. Semenov devoted many years to the study of prehistoric technology.[4] In the case of a flint tool used as a scraper, he was able to deter-

[4]A. Semenov, *Prehistoric Technology* (New York: Barnes & Noble, 1964).

Relative dating: In archaeology and paleoanthropology, designating an event, object, or fossil as being older or younger than another.

mine, by examining the wear patterns of the tool under a microscope, that the prehistoric individuals who used it began to scrape from right to left and then scraped from left to right, and in so doing avoided straining the muscles of the hand.

Analysis of vegetable and animal remains provides clues about the environment and the economic activities of the occupants of a site (see Figure 2.4). Such analysis may help clarify peoples' relationship to their environment and its influence upon the development of their technology — the knowledge they employ to make and use objects. For example, we know that the inhabitants of Serpent Mound, in Ontario, Canada, which is a mound consisting of burials and a shell midden, were there only in the spring and early summer, when they came to collect shellfish and perform their annual burial rites; apparently they moved elsewhere at the beginning of summer to pursue other seasonal subsistence activities. Archaeologists have inferred that the mound was unoccupied in winter, because this is the season when deer shed their antlers, yet no deer antlers were found on the site. Nor were duck bones found, and so archaeologists conclude that the mound was also unoccupied in the fall, when ducks stopped on their migratory route southward to feed on the wild rice which was growing in the region.

DATING THE PAST

Reliable methods of dating objects and events are necessary if archaeologists and paleoanthropologists are to know the sequence of events in the situation under study. But because archaeologists and paleoanthropologists deal mostly with peoples and events in times so far removed from our own, the calendar of historic times is of little use to them. So they must rely on two kinds of dating: relative and "absolute." **Relative dating** consists simply of finding out if an event or object is younger or older

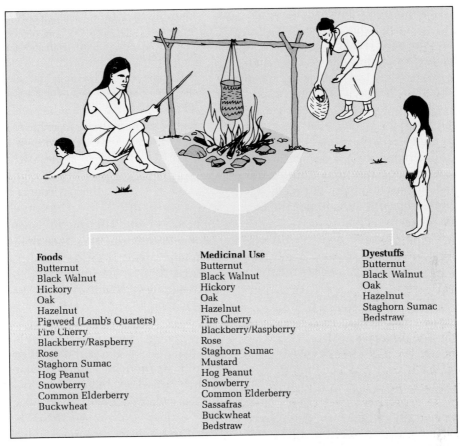

Foods	Medicinal Use	Dyestuffs
Butternut	Butternut	Butternut
Black Walnut	Black Walnut	Black Walnut
Hickory	Hickory	Oak
Oak	Oak	Hazelnut
Hazelnut	Hazelnut	Staghorn Sumac
Pigweed (Lamb's Quarters)	Fire Cherry	Bedstraw
Fire Cherry	Blackberry/Raspberry	
Blackberry/Raspberry	Rose	
Rose	Staghorn Sumac	
Staghorn Sumac	Mustard	
Hog Peanut	Hog Peanut	
Snowberry	Snowberry	
Common Elderberry	Common Elderberry	
Buckwheat	Sassafras	
	Buckwheat	
	Bedstraw	

FIGURE 2.4 Plant remains recovered from hearths used by people between one and two thousand years ago at an archaeological site in Vermont may have been utilized as shown here, based on our knowledge of how the same plants were used by Indians in the region when first encountered by Europeans. Occupation of the site must have been in the summer and fall, the seasons when these plants are available.

than another. **"Absolute"** or **chronometric dating** is based on solar years, and the resulting dates are reckoned in "years before the present" (B.P., with "present" defined as A.D. 1950) or years before and after the birth of Christ (B.C. and A.D.). Many relative and chronometric techniques are available; here, we will discuss only those most often relied on.

METHODS OF RELATIVE DATING
Of the many relative dating techniques available, **stratigraphy** is probably the most reliable. Stra-

Absolute, or chronometric, dating: In archaeology and paleoanthropology, dating archaeological materials in solar years, centuries, or other units of absolute time.

Stratigraphy: In archaeology and paleoanthropology, the most reliable method of relative dating by means of strata.

tigraphy is based on the principle that the oldest layer, or stratum, was deposited first (it is the deepest), while the newest layer was deposited last (it usually lies at the top). Thus, in an archaeological site, the evidence is usually deposited in chronological order. The lowest stratum contains the oldest artifacts and/or fossils, whereas the uppermost stratum contains the most recent ones.

Another method of relative dating is the **fluorine test.** It is based on the fact that the amount of fluorine deposited in bones is directly proportional to their age. The oldest bones contain the greatest amounts of fluorine, and vice versa. The fluorine test is useful in dating bones that cannot be ascribed with certainty to any particular stratum and cannot be dated according to the stratigraphic method. A shortcoming of this method is that the rate of fluorine formation is not constant, but varies from region to region.

Relative dating can also be done on the evidence of botanical and animal remains. A common method, known as **palynology,** involves the study

Fluorine test: In archaeology or paleoanthropology, a technique for relative dating based on the fact that the amount of fluorine in bones is proportional to their age.

Palynology: In archaeology and paleoanthropology, a method of relative dating based on changes in fossil pollen over time.

Radiocarbon analysis: In archaeology and paleoanthropology, a technique for chronometric dating based on measuring the amount of radioactive carbon (C-14) left in organic materials found in archaeological sites.

of pollen grains. The kind of pollen found in any geological stratum depends on the kind of vegetation that existed at the time that stratum was deposited. A site or locality can therefore be dated by determining what kind of pollen was found associated with it.

Another method relies on our knowledge of paleontology. Sites containing the bones of extinct animal species are usually older than sites in which the remains of these animals are absent. Very early North American Indian sites have yielded the remains of mastodons and mammoths — animals now extinct — and on this basis the sites can be dated to a time before these animals became extinct, roughly 10,000 years ago.

METHODS OF CHRONOMETRIC DATING

One of the most important methods of "absolute," or chronometric, dating is **radiocarbon analysis.** It is based on the fact that all living organisms absorb radioactive carbon (known as Carbon 14), which reaches equilibrium with that in the atmosphere, and that this absorption ceases at the time of death. It is possible to measure in the laboratory the amount of radioactive carbon left in a given organic substance, because radioactive substances break down or decay slowly over a fixed period of time. Carbon 14 begins to disintegrate, returning to Nitrogen 14, emitting radioactive (beta) particles in the process. At death, about 15 beta radiations per minute per gram of material are emitted.

Some ancient societies devised precise ways of recording dates that archaeologists have been able to correlate with our own calendar. Here is the tomb of the important ruler Stormy Sky, at the ancient Maya city of Tikal. The glyphs painted on the wall give the date of the burial in the Maya calendar, which is the same as March 18, A.D. 457 in our calendar. The tomb, Burial 48, is shown in Figure 2.2 above the 30 M. mark.

The rate of decay is known as "half-life," and the half-life of Carbon 14 is 5730 years. This means that it takes 5730 years for one-half of the original amount of Carbon 14 to decay into Nitrogen 14. Beta radiation will be about 7.5 counts per minute per gram. In another 5730 years, one-half of this amount of Carbon 14 will also have decayed. In 11,460 years, only one-fourth of the original amount of Carbon 14 will be present. Thus, the age of an organic substance such as charcoal, wood, shell, or bone can be measured by counting the beta rays emitted by the remaining Carbon 14. The radiocarbon method can adequately date organic materials up to 70,000 years old. Of course, one has to be sure that the association between organic remains and archaeological materials is valid. For example, charcoal found on a site may have gotten there from a recent forest fire, rather than more ancient activity, or wood used to make something by the people who lived at a site may have been retrieved from some older context.

Because there is always a certain amount of error involved, radiocarbon dates are not as "absolute" as is sometimes thought. This is why any stated date always has a plus-or-minus factor attached to it. For example, a date of 5200 ± 120 years ago means that there is a two out of three chance that the true date falls somewhere within the 240 years between 5080 and 5320 radiocarbon years ago. The qualification "radiocarbon" years

This picture shows some of the equipment used for radio-carbon dating.

Dendrochronology: In archaeology, a method of chronometric dating based on the pattern of growth rings found in wooden artifacts.

Potassium–argon analysis: In archaeology and paleoanthropology, a technique for chronometric dating which measures the ratio of radioactive potassium to argon in volcanic debris associated with human remains.

ago is necessary, because we have discovered that radiocarbon years are not precisely equivalent to calendar years.

The discovery that radiocarbon years are not precisely equivalent to calendar years was made possible by another method of "absolute" dating, **dendrochronology.** Originally devised for dating Pueblo Indian sites in the North American southwest, this method is based on the fact that in the right kind of climate, trees add a new growth ring to their trunks every year. The rings vary in thickness, depending on the amount of rainfall received in a year, so that climatic fluctuation is registered in the growth ring. By taking a sample of wood, such as a beam from a Pueblo Indian house, and by comparing its pattern of rings with those in the trunk of a tree known to be as old as the artifact, archaeologists can date the archaeological material. Dendrochronology is applicable only to wooden objects. Furthermore, it can be used only in regions in which trees of great age, such as the giant Sequoias and the bristlecone pine, are known to grow. On the other hand, radiocarbon dating of wood from bristlecone pines that have been dated by dendrochronology allows us to "correct" Carbon 14 dates so as to bring them into agreement with calendar dates.

Potassium–argon analysis, another method of absolute dating, is based on a technique similar to that of radiocarbon analysis. After intense heating, as from a volcanic eruption, radioactive potassium decays at a known rate to form argon, any previously existing argon having been released by the heating. The half-life of radioactive potassium is 1.3 billion years. Objects that are millions of years old can now be dated by measuring the ratio of potassium to argon in a given rock. Volcanic

Cultural Resource Management

In June 1979, on a knoll next to a river not far from Lake Champlain, a survey crew working for Peter A. Thomas of the University of Vermont discovered archaeological materials unlike any found before in the region. The following June, Thomas returned to the site with a crew of five, in order to excavate a portion of it. What they found were the remains of an 8000-year-old hunting and fishing camp that had been occupied for up to a few months in the spring or fall by perhaps one or two families. From the site they recovered a distinctive tool inventory never recognized before, as well as data related to hunting and fishing subsistence practices, butchery or hide processing, cooking, tool manufacture, and a possible shelter. Because many archaeologists had previously believed the region to be devoid of human occupation 8000 years ago, recovery of these data was especially important.

What sets this work apart from conventional archaeological research is that it was conducted as part of cultural resource management activities required by state and federal laws to preserve important aspects of the country's prehistoric and historic heritage. In this case, the Vermont Department of Highways planned to replace an inadequate bridge with a new one. Because the project was partially funded by the U.S. government, steps had to be taken to identify and protect any significant prehistoric or historic resources that might be adversely affected. To do so, the Vermont Agency of Transportation hired Thomas, first to see if such resources existed in the project area, and then to retrieve data from the endangered portions of the one site that was found. As a result, an important contribution was made to our knowledge of the prehistory of northeastern North America.

Since passage of the Historic Preservation Act of 1966, the National Environmental Policy Act of 1969, and the Archaeological and Historical Preservation Act of 1974, the field of cultural resource management has undergone something of a boom. Consequently, many archaeologists have been employed by such agencies as the National Park Service, The U.S. Forest Service, and the U.S. Soil and Conservation Service to assist in the preservation, restoration, and salvage of archaeological resources. Archaeologists are also employed by state historic preservation agencies. Finally, they do a considerable amount of consulting work for engineering firms, to help them prepare environmental impact statements. Some of these archaeologists, like Thomas, operate out of universities and colleges, whereas others are on the staffs of independent consulting firms.

debris, such as at Olduvai Gorge and other localities in East Africa, can be dated by potassium–argon analysis; thus, we know when the volcanic eruption occurred. If fossils or artifacts are found sandwiched between layers of volcanic ash, as they are at Olduvai, they can therefore be dated with some precision. But as with radiocarbon dates, there are limits to that precision, and potassium–argon dates are always stated with a plus-or-minus margin of error attached.

Radiocarbon and potassium–argon dating are only two of the several "high tech" dating methods that have been developed in relatively recent years. They are, however, the chronometric methods most heavily relied on by archaeologists and paleoanthropologists; other methods are not always as widely applicable, some are more difficult to carry out, whereas others have not yet been proven as reliable. Nonetheless, as we saw with dendrochronology, they may serve as valuable checks on the accuracy of other methods.

CHANCE AND THE STUDY OF THE PAST

It is important to understand the imperfect nature of the archaeological record. It is imperfect, first of all, because the chance circumstances of preservation have determined what has and what has not survived the ravages of time. Thus, cultures must be reconstructed on the basis of incomplete and, possibly, unrepresentative samples of artifacts. The problems are further compounded by the large role chance continues to play in the discovery of prehistoric remains. Thus, one must always be cautious when trying to interpret the human past. No matter how elegant a particular theory may be about what happened in the past, new evidence may at any time force its reexamination and modification, or even rejection in favor of some better theory.

CHAPTER SUMMARY

Archaeology and physical anthropology are the two branches of anthropology most involved in the study of the human past. Archaeologists study material remains to describe and explain human behavior; physical anthropologists study fossil remains to understand and explain the processes at work in human biological evolution.

Artifacts are objects fashioned or altered by humans, such as a flint chip, a pottery vessel, or even a house. A fossil is any trace of an organism of past geological time that has been preserved in the earth's crust. Fossilization typically involves the hard parts of an organism and may take place through freezing in ice, preservation in bogs or tar pits, immersion in water, or inclusion in rock deposits. Fossilization is most apt to occur among marine animals and other organisms that live near water because of the favorable chances that their corpses will be buried and preserved on sea and river bottoms. On the land, conditions in caves are often conducive to fossilization.

Places containing archaeological remains of previous human occupation are known as sites. Sometimes human fossils are present at archaeological sites, but they may occur by themselves at fossil localities. Sites and localities are generally located by means of a survey of a region. While fossil localities are revealed by the presence of fossils, archaeological sites are revealed by the presence of artifacts. Irregularities of the ground surface, unusual soil discoloration, and unexpected variations in vegetation type and coloring may also indicate the location of a site. Ethnohistorical data — maps, documents, and folklore — may pro-vide further clues to the location of archaeological sites. Sometimes both fossils and archaeological remains are discovered accidentally, for example, in plowing, quarrying, or in building construction.

Once a site or locality has been selected for excavation, the area is divided and carefully marked with a grid system; the starting point of the dig is the datum point. Each square within the grid is carefully excavated, and any archaeological or fossil remains are recovered through employment of various tools and screens; for very fine objects, the method of flotation is employed. The location of each artifact when found must be carefully noted. Once excavated, artifacts and fossils undergo further cleaning and preservation in the laboratory with the use of specialized tools and chemicals.

The durability of archaeological evidence depends on climate and the nature of the artifacts. Inorganic materials are more resistant to decay than organic ones. However, given a very dry climate, even organic materials may be well preserved. Warm, moist climates as well as thick vegetation act to decompose organic material quickly, and even inorganic material may suffer from the effects of humidity and vegetation growth. The durability of archaeological evidence is also dependent on the social customs of ancient people.

Because excavation in fact destroys a site, the archaeologist must maintain a thorough record in the form of maps, descriptions, scale drawings, and photographs of every aspect of the excavation. All artifacts must be cleaned and classified before being sent to the laboratory for analysis. Often the shape and markings of artifacts can determine their function, and the analysis of vegetable and animal remains may provide information.

There are two types of methods for dating archaeological and fossil remains. Relative dating is a method of determining the age of objects relative to each other. Methods of relative dating include stratigraphy, based on the position of the artifact or fossil in relation to different layers of soil deposits; the fluorine test, based on the determination of the amount of fluorine deposited in the bones; and the analysis of floral remains (including palynol-ogy) and faunal deposits. Methods of "absolute," or chronometric, dating include radiocarbon analysis, which measures the amount of Carbon 14 that remains in organic objects; potassium–argon analysis, which measures the percentage of radioactive potassium which has decayed to argon in volcanic material; and dendrochronology, which is based on tree rings. Other chronometric methods exist, but are not as widely used, owing to limited applicability, difficulty of application, or unproven reliability.

SUGGESTED READINGS

Cole, Sonia. *Leakey's Luck: The Life of Louis Seymour Bazett Leakey, 1903–1972*. New York: Harcourt Brace Jovanovich, 1975. No one accomplished and promoted more work dealing with human origins than Leakey. This is an honest and thorough account of the man and his work by an early protégée and friend of more than a quarter century.

Fagan, Brian M. *People of the Earth: An Introduction to World Prehistory*, 5th ed. Boston: Little, Brown, 1986. There are a number of good texts that, like this one, try to summarize the findings of archaeologists on a worldwide scale. This book, being one of the more recent ones, is reasonably up to date.

Joukowsky, Martha. *A Complete Field Manual of Archaeology: Tools and Techniques of Field Work for Archaeologists*. Englewood Cliffs, N.J.: Prentice-Hall, 1980. This book, encyclopedic in its coverage, explains for the novice and professional alike all of the methods and techniques used by archaeologists in the field. Two concluding chapters discuss fieldwork opportunities and financial aid for archaeological research.

Sharer, Robert J., and Wendy Ashmore. *Archaeology: Discovering Our Past*. Palo Alto, Calif.: Mayfield, 1987. One of the best presentations of the body of method, technique, and theory that most archaeologists accept as a foundation for their discipline. The authors confine themselves to the operational modes, guiding strategies, and theoretical orientations of anthropological archaeology in a manner well designed to lead the beginner into the discipline.

Thomas, David H. *Archaeology*. 2d ed. New York: Holt, Rinehart and Winston, 1988. Some books tell us how to do archaeology, some tell us what archaeologists have found out, but this one tells us why we do archaeology. It does so in a coherent and thorough way, and Thomas' blend of ideas, quotes, biographies, and case studies makes for really interesting reading.

White, Peter. *The Past Is Human*, 2d ed. New York: Maplinger, 1976. This book, written for a nonprofessional audience, is a response to those advocating extraterrestrial interference and other mystical "explanations" of the human past.

3

BIOLOGY AND EVOLUTION

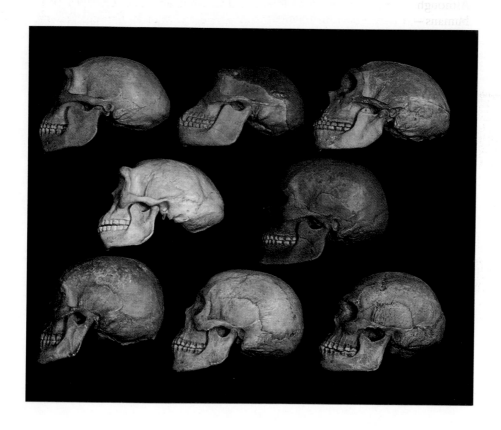

Skulls of human evolution. Such variation is not the result of progressive change, but rather the adaptation of organisms to conditions as they are. Once those conditions change, new adaptations are required.

PREVIEW

What Forces Are Responsible for the Diversity of Primates in the World Today?
Although all primates — lemurs, lorises, indriids, tarsiers, monkeys, apes, and humans — share a common ancestry, they have come to differ through the operation of evolutionary forces which have permitted them to adapt to a variety of environments in a variety of ways. Although biologists agree on the fact of evolution, they are still unraveling the details of how it has proceeded.

What Are the Processes of Evolution?
Evolution works through mutation, which produces genetic variation, which is then acted upon by drift (accidental changes in gene frequencies in a population), gene flow (the introduction of new genes from other populations), and natural selection. Natural selection is the adaptive mechanism of evolution, and works through differential reproduction as individuals with genes for adaptive traits produce more offspring than those without.

How Do These Processes Produce New Forms of Organisms?
Populations may evolve in a linear manner, as small changes from one generation to another improve that population's adaptation. Through the accumulation of such changes over many generations, an older species may evolve into a new one. Or evolution may proceed in a branching manner, in response to isolating mechanisms. These serve to separate populations, preventing gene flow between them so that drift and selection may proceed in different ways. This may lead to the appearance first of divergent races and then of divergent species.

Humans have long had close contact with other animals. Some, such as dogs, horses, and cows, have lived close to people for so long that little attention is paid to their behavior. We are interested only in how well they do what they were bred for — companionship, racing, milk-giving, or whatever. Domestic animals are so dependent on humans that they have lost many of the behavioral traits of their wild ancestors. Except to a small child, perhaps, and a dairy farmer, a cow is not a very interesting animal to watch.

By contrast, wild animals, especially exotic ones, have always fascinated people; circuses and zoos attest to this fascination. In cultures very different from ours, like those of some American Indians, people can have a special relationship with animals, believing themselves to be descended from them; such animals represent their "totems."

A curious feature of this interest is the desire of humans to see animals as mirror images of themselves, a phenomenon known as **anthropomorphism.** Stories in which animals talk, wear clothes, and exhibit human virtues and vices go back to antiquity. Many children learn of Mickey Mouse, Garfield the Cat, or Kermit the Frog and Miss Piggy; the animals created by Walt Disney, Jim Hensen, and others have become an integral part of contemporary North American culture. Occasionally one sees on television trained apes dressed like humans eating at a table, pushing a stroller, or riding a tricycle. They are amusing because they look so "human."

Over the ages, people have trained animals to perform tricks, making them mimic human behavior. But never did people suspect the full extent of the relationship they have with animals. The close biological tie between humans and the other **primates** — the group of animals which, in addition to humans, includes lemurs, lorises, indriids, tarsiers, monkeys, and apes — is now better understood. The diversity of primates seen today is the result of the operation of evolutionary forces which have permitted them to adapt to environments in a variety of ways. These evolutionary processes are the subject of this chapter.

Anthropomorphism: The ascription of human attributes to nonhuman beings.

Primate order: The group of mammals which includes lemurs, lorises, indriids, tarsiers, monkeys, apes, and humans.

Genes: Portions of DNA molecules that direct the development of observable or identifiable traits.

DNA: The genetic material — deoxyribonucleic acid; a complex molecule with information to direct the synthesis of proteins. DNA molecules have the unique property of being able to produce exact copies of themselves.

HEREDITY

In order to understand how evolution works, one must first have some understanding of the mechanisms of heredity, because heritable variation constitutes the raw material for evolution. Our knowledge of the mechanisms of heredity is fairly recent; most of the fruitful research into the molecular level of inheritance has taken place in the past three decades. Although certain aspects remain puzzling, the outlines by now are reasonably clear.

THE TRANSMISSION OF GENES

Biologists call the actual units of heredity **genes,** a term that comes from the Greek word for "birth." The presence and activity of genes were originally deduced rather than observed by an Austrian monk, Gregor Mendel, in the nineteenth century. Working shortly after publication of Darwin's theory of evolution, Mendel sought to answer some of the riddles posed by that theory by experimenting with garden peas to determine how various traits are inherited. Interestingly, his work was generally ignored until it was rediscovered at the turn of the century. Since then, the function of genes has been pretty well known, even though no one really knew what genes were until quite recently.

DNA
It is now known that genes are actually portions of molecules of deoxyribonucleic acid, or **DNA.**

DNA is a complex molecule with an unusual shape, rather like two strands of a rope twisted around one another (Figure 3.1). The way that smaller molecules are arranged in this giant molecule is actually a code that contains information to direct the synthesis of proteins. It is at this level that the development of certain traits occurs. The code directs the formation of such things as the protein that colors the iris of the eye (thereby determining eye color) or the hemoglobin molecule

Chromosome: In the cell nucleus, long strands of DNA combined with a protein, which can be seen under the microscope.

in red blood cells. Recently, there has been great progress in cracking the genetic code, in a series of events as fascinating as any spy story.

DNA molecules have the unique property of being able to produce exact copies of themselves. Thus, a copy can be made and passed to another organism; as long as there are no errors made in the replication process, new organisms will contain genetic material exactly like that in ancestral organisms.

Genes

A gene is a segment of the DNA molecule that directs the development of particular observable or identifiable traits. Thus, when we speak of the gene for a human blood type in the A-B-O system, we are referring to the portion of a DNA molecule that contains the genetic code for the proteins that result in the attachment of different sugar molecules to certain other molecules carried on the surface of red blood cells, and which determine one's blood type. A gene, then, is not really a separate structure, as had once been imagined, but a location, like a dot on a map. It is estimated that human DNA contains at least 100,000 different genes.

Chromosomes

DNA molecules do not float freely about in our bodies; they are located on structures called **chromosomes** found in the nucleus of each cell. Chromosomes are probably nothing more than long strands of DNA combined with protein to produce structures that can actually be seen under a conventional light microscope. Each kind of organism has a characteristic number of chromosomes, which are usually found in pairs. For example, the body cells of the fruit fly each contain four pairs of chromosomes; those of humans contain 23 pairs; those of some brine shrimp have as many as 160 pairs. The two chromosomes in each pair contain genes for the same traits. The gene for eye color,

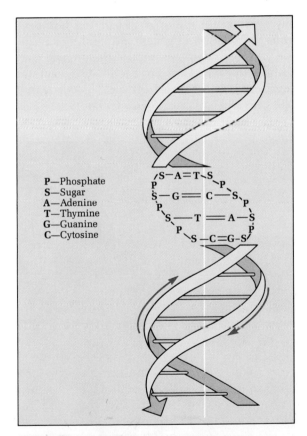

P—Phosphate
S—Sugar
A—Adenine
T—Thymine
G—Guanine
C—Cytosine

FIGURE 3.1 A diagrammatic representation of a portion of a deoxyribonucleic acid (DNA) molecule to indicate the double helix strands and the connecting nitrogenous base pairs. The helix strands are formed by alternating sugar and phosphate groups; the connection is produced by complementary bases — adenine, cytosine, guanine, and thymine — as shown for a section of the molecule.

for instance, will be found on each chromosome of a particular pair, but there may be variant forms of these genes. One might be for brown and the other for blue eyes. Genes that are located on paired chromosomes and are coded for different versions of the same trait are called **alleles.**

Cell Division

In order to grow and maintain good health, the body cells of an organism must divide and produce new cells. Cell division is initiated when the chromosomes and, hence, the genes replicate, forming a second pair that duplicates the original pair of chromosomes in the nucleus. This new pair then separates from the original pair, is surrounded by a membrane, and becomes the nucleus that directs the activities of a new cell. This kind of cell division is called **mitosis,** and it produces new cells that have exactly the same number of chromosome pairs and, hence, genes as did the parent cell.

When new individuals are produced through sexual reproduction, the process involves the merging of two cells, one from each parent. If two regular body cells, each containing 23 pairs of chromosomes, were to merge, the result would be a new individual with 46 pairs of chromosomes; such an individual, if it lived at all, would surely be a monster. But this increase in chromosome number never occurs, because the sex cells that join to form a new individual are the product of a different kind of cell division, called **meiosis.**

Although meiosis begins like mitosis, with the replication and doubling of the original genes and chromosomes, it goes on to divide that number into four new cells rather than two (Figure 3.2). Thus, each new cell has only half the number of chromosomes with their genes found in the parent cell. Human eggs and sperm, for example, have only 23 single chromosomes (half of a pair), whereas body cells have 23 pairs, or 46 chromosomes.

The process of meiotic division has important implications for genetics. Since paired chromosomes are separated, two different types of new cells will be formed; two of the four new cells will have one half of a pair of chromosomes, and the

Alleles: Alternate forms of a single gene.

Mitosis: A kind of cell division that produces new cells having exactly the same number of chromosome pairs and, hence, genes as the parent cell.

Meiosis: A kind of cell division that produces the sex cells, each of which has half the number of chromosomes and, hence, genes as the parent cell.

Homozygous: Description of a chromosome pair that bears identical alleles for a single gene.

other two will have the second half of the original chromosome pair. Of course, this will not make any difference if the original pair was **homozygous,** or identical in genetic material. For example, if in both chromosomes of the original pair, the gene for blood type in the A-B-O system was represented by the allele for Type A blood, then all new cells will have the "A" allele. But if the origi-

Gregor Mendel performed carefully controlled breeding experiments with garden peas that led to the discovery, in 1865, of the basic laws of heredity.

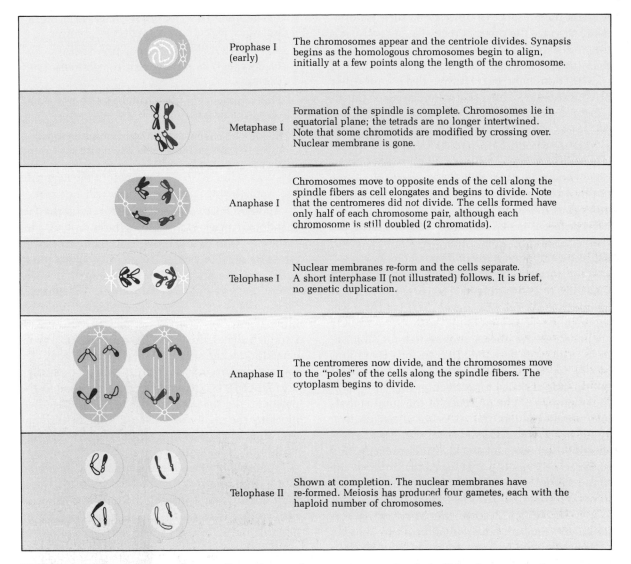

	Prophase I (early)	The chromosomes appear and the centriole divides. Synapsis begins as the homologous chromosomes begin to align, initially at a few points along the length of the chromosome.
	Metaphase I	Formation of the spindle is complete. Chromosomes lie in equatorial plane; the tetrads are no longer intertwined. Note that some chromotids are modified by crossing over. Nuclear membrane is gone.
	Anaphase I	Chromosomes move to opposite ends of the cell along the spindle fibers as cell elongates and begins to divide. Note that the centromeres did *not* divide. The cells formed have only half of each chromosome pair, although each chromosome is still doubled (2 chromatids).
	Telophase I	Nuclear membranes re-form and the cells separate. A short interphase II (not illustrated) follows. It is brief, no genetic duplication.
	Anaphase II	The centromeres now divide, and the chromosomes move to the "poles" of the cells along the spindle fibers. The cytoplasm begins to divide.
	Telophase II	Shown at completion. The nuclear membranes have re-formed. Meiosis has produced four gametes, each with the haploid number of chromosomes.

FIGURE 3.2 The separation of a pair of homologous chromosomes carrying their alleles during meiosis.

nal pair was **heterozygous,** with the "A" allele on one chromosome and the allele for Type O blood on the other, then half of the new cells will contain only the "O" allele; the offspring have a 50-50 chance of getting either one. It is impossible to predict any single individual's genotype, or genetic composition, but statistical probabilities can be established.

What happens when a child inherits the allele

Heterozygous: Description of a chromosome pair that bears different alleles for a single gene.

for Type O blood from one parent and that for Type A from the other? Will the child have blood of Type A, O, or some mixture of the two? Many of these questions were answered by Mendel's original experiments.

Mendel discovered that certain alleles are able

to mask the presence of others; one allele is dominant, whereas the other is recessive. Actually, it is the traits that are dominant or recessive rather than the alleles themselves; geneticists merely speak of dominant and recessive alleles for the sake of convenience. Thus, one might speak of the allele for Type A blood as being dominant to the one for Type O. An individual whose blood type genes are heterozygous, with one "A" and one "O" allele, will have Type A blood. Thus, the heterozygous condition (AO) will show exactly the same physical characteristic, or **phenotype,** as the homozygous AA, even though the two have a somewhat different genetic composition, or **genotype.** Only the homozygous recessive genotype (OO) will show the phenotype of Type O blood.

The dominance of one allele does not mean that the recessive one is lost or in some way blended. A Type A heterozygous parent (AO) will produce sex cells containing both "A" and "O" alleles. Recessive alleles, such as that for albinism in humans, can be handed down for generations before they are matched with another recessive in the process of sexual reproduction and show up in the phenotype. The presence of the dominant allele simply renders the recessive allele inactive.

All of the traits Mendel studied in garden peas showed this dominant–recessive relationship, and so for some years it was believed that this was the only relationship possible. Later studies, however, have indicated that patterns of inheritance are not always so simple. In some cases, neither allele is dominant; they are both codominant. An example of codominance in human heredity can be seen also in the inheritance of blood types. Type A is produced by one allele, Type B by another. A heterozygous individual will have a phenotype of AB, since neither allele can dominate the other.

The inheritance of blood types points out another complexity of heredity. The number of alleles is by no means limited to two; certain traits seem to have three or more allelic genes. Of course, only one allele can appear on each of the pairs of chromosomes, so each individual is limited to two alleles.

Phenotype: The physical appearance of an organism which may or may not reflect its genotype because the latter may include recessive alleles.

Genotype: The actual genetic composition of an organism.

Hemoglobin: The protein that carries oxygen in the red blood cells.

Sickle-cell anemia: An inherited form of anemia caused by the red blood cells assuming a sickled shape.

Another relatively recent discovery is the fact that dominance need not always be complete. This is the case with the alleles for normal **hemoglobin** (the protein that carries oxygen in the red blood cells) and the abnormal hemoglobin that is responsible for **sickle-cell anemia** in humans. Sickle-cell anemia occurs in individuals who are homozygous for a particular allele. In those with two such alleles, the red blood cells take on a characteristic sickle shape which, because they are more rapidly removed from the circulation than normal cells, leads to anemia. To compound the problem, the sickle cells tend to clump together, blocking the capillaries and so causing tissue damage. Such individuals normally die before reaching adulthood. The homozygous dominant condition (AA; normal hemoglobin is known as hemoglobin A, not to be confused with blood Type A) produces only normal molecules of hemoglobin, whereas the heterozygous condition (AS) produces some normal and abnormal molecules; except under low-oxygen conditions, such individuals suffer no ill effects. The normal seems dominant to the abnormal, but the dominance is incomplete, and therefore, the other allele is not completely inactive. It is now believed that many instances in which phenotypes appear to indicate complete dominance may show incomplete dominance on the molecular level. We shall return to the sickle-cell condition later, for we now know that under certain conditions the heterozygous condition is actually more advantageous than is the "normal" homozygous condition.

Polygenes

So far, we have spoken as if the traits of organisms are single-gene traits; that is, the alleles of one particular gene determine one particular trait. Certainly, this is the case with the A-B-O blood groups and some other things, but in humans, the most obvious traits are usually not single-gene traits. Skin color, for example, is programmed by the action of many genes, each of which produces a small effect. Such genes are called **polygenes,** two or more genes (as opposed to just two or more alleles) that work together to affect some phenotypic character. Because so many genes are involved, it is difficult to unravel the genetic underpinnings of a trait like skin color. Theoretically, the observed range of variation in human skin color seems to require the presence of at least three, if not as many as six, separate genes, each of which produces a small additive effect.

POPULATION GENETICS

At the level of the individual organism, the study of genetics indicates the way that traits are transmitted from one generation to the next and enables a prediction about the chances that any given individual will display some phenotypic characteristic. At the level of the group, the study of genetics takes on additional significance, revealing mechanisms that support evolutionary interpretations of the diversity of life.

A key concept in genetics is that of the **population,** or a group of individuals that can and does interbreed. It is on the population level that natural selection takes place: Some members of the population produce more than their share of the next generation, while others produce less than their share. Thus, over a period of generations, the population shows a measure of adaptation to its environment because of this evolutionary mechanism.

Polygenes: Two or more genes that work together to affect some phenotypic character.

Population: In biology, a group of similar individuals that can and do interbreed.

Sickle-cell anemia is caused by an abnormal hemoglobin, called "hemoglobin S." Those afflicted by the disease are homozygous for the allele S; heterozygotes are not afflicted. Shown are a normal red blood cell (*left*) and the sickle-shaped cells of the abnormal hemoglobin (*right*).

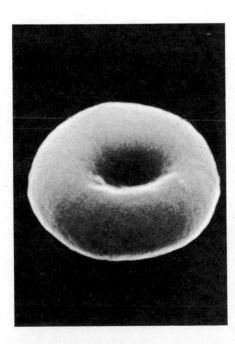

THE STABILITY OF THE POPULATION

In theory, the characteristics of any given population should remain remarkably stable. And indeed, generation after generation, the bullfrogs in my farm pond, for example, look much alike, have the same calls, and exhibit the same behavior when breeding. Another way to look at this remarkable consistency is to say that the **gene pool** of the population — the total number of different genes and alleles — seems to remain the same.

The theoretical stability of the gene pool of a population is not only easy to observe; it is also easy to understand. Mendel's experiments with garden peas, and all subsequent genetic experiments as well, have shown that, although some alleles may be dominant to others, the recessive alleles are not just lost or destroyed. Statistically, a heterozygous individual has a 50 percent chance of passing on to the next generation the dominant allele; he or she also has a 50 percent chance of passing on the recessive allele. The recessive allele may again be masked by the presence of a dominant allele in the next generation, but it is there nonetheless, and will be passed on again.

Since alleles are not just "lost" in the process of reproduction, the frequency with which certain ones occur in the population should remain exactly the same from one generation to the next. The **Hardy-Weinberg Principle,** named for the English mathematician and German physician who worked it out in 1908, demonstrates algebraically that the percentage of individuals that are homozygous for the dominant allele, homozygous for the recessive allele, and heterozygous will remain the same from one generation to the next provided that certain specified conditions are met. These are that mating is entirely random, that the population is sufficiently large for statistical averages to express themselves, that no new variants will be introduced into the population's gene pool, and that all individuals are equally successful at surviving and reproducing. In real life, however, these conditions are rarely met, because geographical, physiological, or behavioral factors may favor mat-

Gene pool: The total genes of a population.

Hardy–Weinberg Principle: Demonstrates algebraically that the percentage of individuals that are homozygous for the dominant allele, homozygous for the recessive allele, and heterozygous should remain constant from one generation to the next, provided that certain specified conditions are met.

Evolution: A heritable change in genotype which becomes effective in the gene pool of a population.

Mutation: Chemical alteration of a gene that produces a new allele.

ings between certain individuals over others; because populations — on islands, for example — may be quite small; because new genetic variants may be introduced through mutation or gene flow; and because natural selection may favor the carriers of some alleles over others. Thus, changes in the gene pools of populations, without which there could be no evolution, can and do take place. Formally defined, **evolution** is a heritable change in genotype which becomes effective in the gene pool of a population.

FACTORS FOR CHANGE

MUTATION

The ultimate source of change is **mutation** of genes. Although mutation rarely occurs, the large number of genes in each individual sex cell, the large number of sex cells produced (the human male ejaculates hundreds of millions of sperm cells at a single time), and the large number of individuals in a population mean that there will always be new mutant genes.

Geneticists have calculated the rate at which various types of mutant genes appear. In the human population, they run from a low of about five mutations per million sex cells formed, in the case of a gene abnormality that leads to the absence of an iris in the eye, to a high of about 100 per million, in the case of a gene that causes a form of muscular dystrophy. The average is about 30 mutants per million. Although mutations sometimes produce marked abnormalities, the great majority of them produce more subtle effects.

Research with viruses and bacteria indicates that certain factors increase the rate at at which mutations occur. These include certain chemicals, such as some dyes and also some antibiotics; some chemicals used in the preservation of food also have this property. Another important cause of increased mutation rates is irradiation. The ultraviolet rays of sunshine are capable of producing mutations, as are X rays. Radioactive rays have the same mutation-causing effect, as was so sadly demonstrated by the high rates of mutation found in the children of survivors of the bombings of Hiroshima and Nagasaki.

Genetic research studies with corn have shown that certain genes appear to have the function of causing mutations in seed color and plant size. It is speculated that such mutator genes may also occur in human DNA, which might explain why some mutations appear so frequently. The presence of these mutator genes has been likened to a fail-safe mechanism for preserving the variability of the gene pool; even if offspring with the mutant gene are selected against, the mutation will not disappear from the gene pool but will simply recur, as a result of the mutator gene's action.

Advantageous though mutator genes may be for a population, one must not assume that they evolved for that reason. Rather, they must have appeared by chance, and become common in a population's gene pool because for some reason they benefited the individuals who carried them.

GENETIC DRIFT

Each individual is subject to a number of chance events that determine life or death. For example, an individual squirrel in good health and possessed of a number of advantageous traits may be killed in a forest fire; a genetically superior baby cougar may not live longer than a day if its mother gets caught in an avalanche, whereas the weaker offspring of a mother that does not may survive. In a large population, such accidents of nature are unimportant; the accidents that preserve individuals

Genetic drift: Chance fluctuations of allele frequencies in the gene pool of a population.

Gene flow: The introduction of alleles from the gene pool of one population into that of another.

with certain genes will be balanced out by the accidents that destroy them. However, in small populations, such averaging out may not be possible. Since human populations are so large, we might suppose that human beings are unaffected by chance events. While it is true that a rock slide which kills five campers whose home community has a total population of 100,000 is not statistically significant, a rock slide which killed five hunters from a small group of food foragers could significantly alter frequencies of alleles in the local gene pool. The average size of local groups of modern food foragers (people who hunt, fish, and gather other wild foods for subsistence) varies between about 25 and 50.

Another sort of chance event may occur when an existing population splits up into two or more new ones, especially if one of these new populations is founded by a particularly small number of individuals. In such cases, it is unlikely that the gene frequencies of the smaller population will duplicate those of the larger population.

The effect of chance events on the gene pool of small populations is called **genetic drift.** Genetic drift plays an important role in causing the sometimes bizarre characteristics found in animals in isolated island populations. It is also thought to have been an important factor in human evolution, because until 10,000 years ago all humans were food foragers, who probably lived in relatively small, self-contained populations.

GENE FLOW

Another factor that brings change to the gene pool of a population is **gene flow,** or the introduction of new genes from nearby populations. Gene flow occurs when previously separated groups are once again able to interbreed, as, for example, when a river that once separated two populations of small mammals changes course. Migration of individuals or groups into the territory occupied by others may also lead to gene flow. This has been observed in several North American rodents that have been forced to leave their territory because of changes in environmental conditions. Gene flow has been an important factor in human evolution, both in terms of early hominid groups and in terms of current racial variation. For example, the last 400 years have seen the establishment of a new phenotype throughout much of Central and South America as a result of the introduction into the gene pool of Indians native to the area of genes from both the Spanish colonists and the Africans whom Europeans imported as slaves.

NATURAL SELECTION

Although the factors listed above may produce change in a population, that change would not necessarily make the population better adapted to

Adaptation: A process by which organisms achieve a beneficial adjustment to an available environment; the results of that process; and the characteristics of organisms that fit them to the particular set of conditions of the environment in which they are generally found.

its biological and social environment. By **adaptation** we mean both a process — by which organisms achieve a beneficial adjustment to an available environment — and its results, that is, the characteristics of organisms that fit them to the particular set of environmental conditions in which they are generally found. Genetic drift, for example, often produces strange characteristics that have no survival value; and mutation of genes may be either helpful or harmful to survival. It is the action of natural selection that makes evolutionary change adaptive.

In Central America, gene flow between Native Americans (*upper left*), Spaniards (*upper right*), and Africans (*lower left*) has led to the emergence of a new phenotype (*lower right*).

Charles R. Darwin (1809–1882)

Grandson of Erasmus Darwin (a physician, scientist, poet, and originator of a theory of evolution himself), Charles Darwin began the study of medicine at the University of Edinburgh. Finding himself unfitted for this profession, he then went to Christ's College, Cambridge, to study theology. On completion of his studies there, he took the position of naturalist and companion to Captain Fitzroy on the HMS Beagle, which was about to embark on an expedition to various poorly mapped parts of the world. The voyage lasted almost 5 years, taking Darwin along the coasts of South America, over to the Galapagos Islands, across the Pacific to Australia, and then across the Indian and Atlantic Oceans back to South America before returning to England. The observations he made on this voyage, and the arguments he had with the orthodox and dogmatic Fitzroy, had a powerful influence on the development of the ideas which culminated in Darwin's most famous book, *On the Origin of Species*, which was published in 1859.

Contrary to what a lot of people seem to think, Darwin did not "discover" or "invent" evolution. The general idea of evolution had been put forward by a number of writers, including his grandfather, long before Darwin's time. Nor is evolution a single theory, as some people seem to think, any more than gravity is a single theory. To be sure, there are competing theories of gravity — the Newtonian and Einsteinian — that seek to explain its workings; nevertheless, the evidence in favor of gravity is overwhelming. Similarly, the evidence in favor of evolution is overwhelming, even though there are competing theories that seek to explain how it works.

Darwin's contribution was one such theory, that of evolution through natural selection. His was the theory that was best able to account both for change within species and for the emergence of new species in purely naturalistic terms. As is usually the case with pioneering ventures, there were flaws in Darwin's original theory. Today, we can say that Darwin's basic idea has stood the test of scientific scrutiny remarkably well, and that the evidence in its favor is about as good as we had for the theory that the earth is spherical, until we were able to put up an astronaut who could see with his own eyes that this indeed is the case.

Natural selection refers to the evolutionary process through which the environment exerts pressure that selects some individuals and not others to reproduce the next generation of the group. In other words, instead of a completely random selection of individuals whose traits will be passed on to the next generation, there is a selection by the forces of nature. In the process, the frequency of genes for harmful or maladaptive traits within the population is reduced while the frequency of genes for adaptive traits is increased.

In popular writing, natural selection is often equated with the "survival of the fittest," in which the weak and the unfit are eliminated from the population by disease, predation, or starvation. Obviously, the survival of the fittest has some

> **Natural selection:** The evolutionary process through which factors in the environment exert pressure that favors some individuals over others to produce the next generation.

bearing on natural selection; one need hardly point out that the dead do not reproduce. But there may be many cases in which individuals survive but do not reproduce. They may be incapable of attracting mates, they may be sterile, or they may produce offspring that do not survive after birth. For example, among the Uganda Kob, a kind of antelope native to East Africa, males that are unable to attract females form all-male herds in which they live out their lives. As members of a herd, they are reasonably well protected against predators, and so they may survive to relatively ripe old ages. They do not, however, pass their genes on to succeeding generations. This is an instance of natural selection at work, leading to different rates of reproduction for different types of individuals within a population. Change brought about by natural selection in the frequency with which certain genes appear in a population is actually a very slow process. For example, the present frequency of the sickle-cell allele is .05 in the entire U.S. population. A 5 percent reduction per generation (about 25 years) would take about 2000 years to reach a frequency of .01, assuming complete selection against those homozygous for the allele. Yet given the great time span involved — life on earth has existed for three to four billion years — even such small and slow changes will have a significant cumulative impact on both the genotypes and phenotypes of any population.

Natural selection, as it acts to promote change in gene frequencies, is referred to as **directional selection.** Another form it may take is **stabilizing selection,** in which it acts to promote stability rather than change. This occurs in populations which are already well adapted, or at least where change would be disadvantageous. In humans, for instance, there has been no significant increase in brain size for the last 100,000 years or so. Stabilizing selection seems to be operating here, because

> **Directional selection:** Natural selection as it acts to promote change in a population's gene pool.
>
> **Stabilizing selection:** Natural selection as it acts to promote stability (rather than to promote change) in a population's gene pool.

the human birth canal is not adequate for the birth of larger-brained offspring. In cases where change is disadvantageous, natural selection will favor the retention of gene frequencies as they are. For this reason, the evolutionary history of most forms of life is not one of constant change, proceeding as a steady, stately progression over vast periods of time; rather, it is one of prolonged periods of stability punctuated by shorter periods of change (or extinction) when altered conditions require new adaptations.

Discussions of the action of natural selection typically focus on anatomical or structural changes, such as the evolutionary change in the types of teeth found in primates; ample evidence (fossilized teeth, for example) exists to interpret such changes. By extrapolation, biologists assume that the same mechanisms work on behavioral traits as well. It seems reasonable that a hive of bees capable of communicating the location of nectar-bearing flowers would have a significant survival advantage over those that must search for food by trial and error. Natural selection of behav-

Despite their different appearances, the brain housed in the modern human skull on the left is no bigger than the one housed in the 100,000-year-old skull on the right.

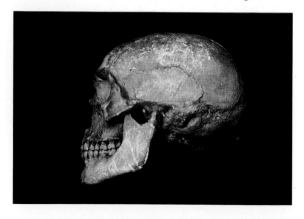 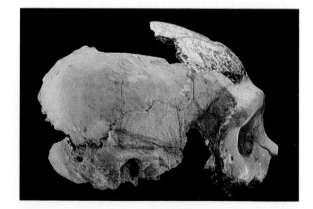

ioral and social traits was probably a particularly important influence on hominid evolution, since in the primates, social mechanisms began to replace physical structures for getting food, for defense, and for mate attraction.

Many anthropologists point out the close parallel between biological and cultural evolution, and therefore, they postulate that a process of natural selection continues to work on cultural traits within a society. By inventing better tools, more efficient means of organization, and the like, humans may make life significantly easier for themselves. As a result, selective pressures are reduced, reproduction becomes easier, more offspring survive than before, and so, populations grow. Because culture is learned rather than biologically inherited, cultural evolution can take place much more rapidly than biological evolution.

ADAPTATION

As a consequence of the process of natural selection, those populations that do not become extinct generally become well adapted to their environments. Anyone who has ever looked carefully at the plants and animals that survive in the deserts of the western United States can cite many instances of adaptation. For example, members of the cactus family have extensive root networks close to the surface of the soil, enabling them to soak up the slightest bit of moisture; they are able to store large quantities of water whenever it is available; they are shaped so as to expose the smallest possible surface to the dry air and are generally leafless as adults, thereby preventing water loss through evaporation; and a covering of spines discourages animals from chewing into the juicy flesh of the plant.

Desert animals are also adapted to their environment. The kangaroo rat can survive without drinking water; many reptiles live in burrows where the temperature is lower; most animals are nocturnal, or active only in the cool of the night. Many of the stories traditionally offered to explain observable cases of adaptation rely heavily on the purposeful acts of a world creator. The legend of

Coyote and Wishpoosh (Chapter 1) is one such example; the belief popular among Europeans early in the nineteenth century that God created each animal separately to occupy a specific place in a hierarchical ladder of being is another.

The adaptability of organic structures and functions, no matter how much a source of wonder and fascination, nevertheless falls short of perfection. That exquisite design is often not the rule is illustrated by the pains of aching backs and the annoyances of hernias that we humans must put up with because the body of a four-footed vertebrate, designed for horizontal posture, has been "jury rigged" to be held vertically above the two hind limbs. Furthermore, the structural alterations that enable us to walk erect have made it more difficult than it is for any other species of mammal to bear offspring. Yet, these defects have been favored by natural selection, because they are outweighed by other aspects of human adaptation that enhance the reproductive success of the species as a whole.

THE CASE OF SICKLE-CELL ANEMIA

Among human beings, a particularly well-studied case of an adaptation paid for by the misery of many individuals brings us back to the case of sickle-cell anemia. Sickle-cell anemia first came to the attention of geneticists when it was observed that most North Americans who suffer from it are black. Investigation traced the abnormality to populations that live in a clearly defined belt throughout central Africa.

Geneticists were curious to know why such a deleterious hereditary disability persisted in these populations. According to the theory of natural selection, any alleles that are harmful will tend to disappear from the group, since the individuals who are homozygous for the abnormality generally die — are "selected out" — before they are able to reproduce. Why, then, had this seemingly harmful condition remained in populations from central Africa?

The answer to this mystery began to emerge when it was noticed that the areas in which sickle-cell anemia is prevalent are also areas in which falciparum malaria is common (Figure 3.3). This severe form of malaria causes high fevers which significantly interfere with the reproductive abilities of those who do not actually die from the disease. Moreover, it was discovered that the same hemoglobin abnormalities are found in residents of parts of the Arabian Peninsula, Greece, Algeria, Syria, and East India, all of whom also live in regions where falciparum malaria is common. Further research established that the abnormal hemoglobin was associated with an increased ability to survive the effects of the malarial parasite; it seems that the effects of the abnormal hemoglobin in limited amounts were less injurious than the effects of the malarial parasite.

Thus, selection favored heterozygous individuals (AS). The loss of alleles for abnormal hemoglobin caused by the death of those homozygous for it (from sickle-cell anemia) was balanced out by the loss of alleles for normal hemoglobin, because those homozygous for it experienced reproductive failure.

This example also points out how specific adaptations tend to be; the abnormal hemoglobin was an adaptation to the particular parts of the world in which the malarial parasite flourished. When Africans who were adapted to that region moved to North America, where falciparum malaria is unknown, what had been an adaptive characteristic became an injurious one. Where there is no malaria to attack those with normal hemoglobin, the abnormal hemoglobin becomes comparatively disadvantageous. Although the rates of sickle-cell trait are still relatively high among North American blacks — about 9 percent show the sickling trait — this represents a significant decline from the approximately 22 percent who are estimated to have shown the trait when the first slaves were brought from Africa. A further decline over the next several generations is to be expected, because selection pressure continues to work against it.

This example also points out the important role culture may play even with respect to biological adaptation. In West Africa, falciparum malaria was not a significant problem until humans abandoned food foraging for farming a few thousand years ago. In order to farm, they had to clear areas of the natural forest cover. In the forest, decaying vegetation on the forest floor had imparted an absorbent quality to the ground so that the heavy rainfall of the region rapidly soaked into the soil. But once stripped of its natural vegetation, the soil lost this quality. Furthermore, the forest canopy was no longer there to break the force of the rainfall, and so the impact of the heavy rains tended to compact the soil further. The result was that stagnant puddles commonly formed after rains, and these were perfect for breeding mosquitoes. Mosquitoes then began to flourish, and it is mosquitoes that carry the malarial parasite and transmit it to humans. Thus, humans unwittingly created the kind of environment that made a hitherto disadvantageous

A Snowshoe Hare in its winter coat, and changing to its summer coat. The animal's coloration serves as camouflage, illustrating the principle of adaptation.

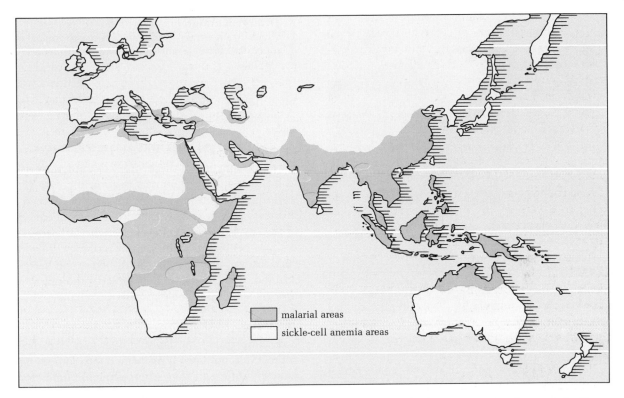

FIGURE 3.3 The allele which, in homozygotes, causes sickle-cell anemia makes heterozygotes resistant to the ill effects of falciparum malaria. Thus, the allele is most common in populations native to regions where this form of malaria is common.

trait, the abnormal hemoglobin associated with sickle-cell anemia, advantageous.

Although it is true that all living organisms have many adaptive characteristics, it is not true that all characteristics are adaptive. All male mammals, for example, possess nipples, even though they serve no useful purpose. To female mammals, however, nipples are essential to reproductive success, which is why males have them. The two sexes are not separate entities, shaped independently by natural selection, but are variants of a single ground plan, elaborated in later embryology. Precursors of mammary glands are built in all mammalian fetuses, enlarging later in the development of females, but remaining small and without function in males.

Nor is it true that current utility is a reliable guide to historical origin. For one thing, nonadaptive characteristics may be coopted for later utility

after their origin because of developmental consequences of changing patterns in embryonic and postnatal growth. The unusually large size of the kiwi egg, for example, enhances the survivability of kiwi chicks, in that they are particularly large and capable when hatched. Nevertheless, kiwi eggs probably did not evolve because they are adaptive. Kiwis evolved from large, moa-sized ancestors, and in birds, egg size reduces at a slower rate than does body size. Therefore, the out-sized eggs of kiwi birds seem to be no more than a developmental by-product of a reduction in body size.[1] Similarly, an existing adaptation may come under strong selective pressure for some new purpose, as did insect wings. These did not arise that insects might fly, but rather as devices useful in regulating

[1]Stephen Jay Gould, "Of Kiwi Eggs and the Liberty Bell," *Natural History* 95 (1986): 20–29.

This X ray illustrates the unusually large size of a kiwi's egg.

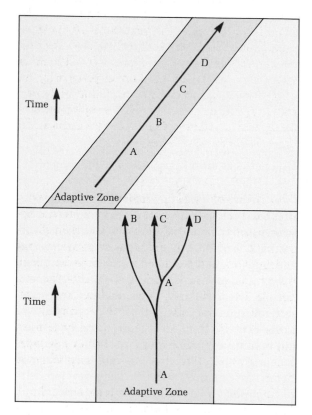

FIGURE 3.4 Linear evolution (*top*): As relatively small-scale changes accumulate over time, an old species may be gradually transformed into a new one. Divergent evolution (*bottom*): An increase in the number of species is achieved when the different populations become reproductively isolated.

> **Divergent evolution:** An evolutionary process in which an ancestral population gives rise to two or more descendant populations that differ from one another.

body temperature. Later, the larger ones by chance proved useful for purposes of flight.

EVOLUTION OF POPULATIONS

One consequence of the process of natural selection is that a population may become increasingly well adapted to its environment. This kind of evolutionary change can be thought of as a refinement of the organism. As it moves from the rather generalized prototype to more and more specialized versions, the organism becomes better and better adapted; each new "model" replaces the old in a process somewhat analogous to the changes that have been made to automobiles since their first appearance. Still, a car remains a car, no matter how "improved" the latest model may have become; it has not been transformed into something radically different. The same principle holds for linear evolution (Figure 3.4, top). Ultimately, stabilizing selection is likely to take over, as available alleles reach their most adaptive frequencies in a species' gene pool.

Alternatively, a species may become extinct if it becomes too well adapted. If the environment changes for some reason, those organisms most highly adapted to the old environment will have the greatest difficulty surviving in a new one. It appears that such changes took place a number of times during the course of vertebrate evolution; one of the most dramatic examples was the sudden extinction of the dinosaurs. In such cases, it is usually the more generalized organisms that survive; later, they may give rise to new lines of specialists.

But not all evolution is a linear progression from one form to more specialized forms of the same type. Evolution is also **divergent,** or branching (Figure 3.4, bottom). This happens when a single ancestral species gives rise to two or more descendant species. Divergent evolution is probably responsible for much of the diversity of life to be observed today. Evolution may also be **conver-**

gent, when two dissimilar forms develop greater similarities — birds and bats, for example. Convergent evolution takes place in circumstances where an environment exerts similar pressures on different organisms so that unrelated species become more like one another. Because evolution can take so many different courses, it is often difficult to reconstruct the sequence of events that led to the emergence of any given group or species, especially when that evidence, such as fossil remains, is often fragmentary and incomplete. We are fortunate, though, in that the fossil record for human evolution is particularly rich.

SPECIATION

Both linear and divergent evolution can result in the establishment of a new **species.** The term "species" is usually defined as a population or group of populations that is mechanically capable of interbreeding and reproductively isolated from other such populations. Thus, the bullfrogs in my farm pond are the same species as those in my neighbor's pond, even though the two populations may never actually interbreed; in theory, they are capable of it if they are brought together. This definition is not altogether satisfactory, because isolated populations are often in the process of evolving into different species, and it is hard to tell exactly when they become separate. For example, all dogs belong to the same species, but a male Saint Bernard and a female Chihuahua are not capable of producing offspring; even if they could somehow manage the feat of copulation, the Chihuahua would die trying to give birth to such large pups. On the other hand, Alaskan sled dogs are able to breed with wolves, even though they are of different species. In nature, however, wolves most often mate with their own kind. Although all species definitions are relative rather than absolute, the modern concept of species puts more stress on the question of whether breeding actually takes place in the wild than on the more academic question of whether breeding is technically feasible.

Populations within species that are quite capable of interbreeding but may not regularly do so

Convergent evolution: A process in which two phylogenetically unrelated organisms develop greater similarities.

Species: In biology, a population or group of populations that is capable of interbreeding, but that is reproductively isolated from other such populations.

Race: A population of a species that differs in the frequency of some allele or alleles from other populations of the same species.

Isolating mechanisms: Factors that separate breeding populations, creating divergent races and then divergent species.

are called **races.** Evolutionary theory suggests that species evolve from races through the accumulation of differences in the gene pools of the separated groups. In the case of humans, as we shall see in Chapter 11, the race concept is difficult to apply. For one thing, the human propensity for gene flow makes it difficult to define biological races; for another, there has been a deplorable tendency to mix cultural with biological phenomena under the heading of "race."

ISOLATING MECHANISMS

Certain factors, known as **isolating mechanisms,** separate breeding populations, leading to the appearance first of divergent races and then divergent species. This happens because mutations may appear in one of the isolated populations but not in the other, because genetic drift affects the two populations in different ways, and because selective pressures may come to differ slightly in the two places. Because isolation prevents gene flow, changes that affect the gene pool of one population cannot be introduced into the gene pool of the other.

Some isolating mechanisms are geographical, preventing gene flow between members of separated populations as a result of traveling individuals or bands. Anatomical structure can also serve as an isolating mechanism, as we saw in the case of the Saint Bernard and the Chihuahua. Other physical isolating factors include early miscarriage of the offspring; weakness or presence of maladaptive traits that cause early death in the offspring; or as in the case of horses and asses, sterility of the hybrid offspring (mules).

Although physical barriers to reproduction may develop in geographical isolation, because genetic differences accumulate in the gene pools of separate populations, they may also result from accidents in the course of meiosis. In the course of such accidents, genetic material may be broken off, transposed, or transferred from one chromosome to another. Even a relatively minor mutation, if it involves a gene that regulates the growth and development of an organism, may have a major effect on its adult form.

Isolating mechanisms may also be social rather than physical. Speciation due to this mechanism is particularly common among birds. For example, cuckoos (birds that do not build nests of their own but lay their eggs in other birds' nests) attract mates by mimicking the song of the bird species whose nests they borrow; thus, cuckoos that are physically capable of mating may have different courtship behavior, which effectively isolates them from others of their kind.

Social isolating mechanisms are thought to have been important factors in human evolution.

They continue to play a part in the maintenance of so-called racial barriers. Although mating is physically possible between any two mature humans of the opposite sex, the awareness of social and cultural differences often makes the idea distasteful, perhaps even unthinkable; in India, for example, someone of an upper caste would not think of marrying an "untouchable." This isolation results from the culturally implanted concept of a significant difference between "us" and "them." Yet, as evidenced by the blending of human populations that has so often taken place in the world, people are also capable of reasoning away social isolating mechanisms that would, in the case of other animals, lead separate races to evolve into separate species. Such speciation is very unlikely in *Homo sapiens*.

THE NONDIRECTEDNESS OF EVOLUTION

In the popular mind, evolution is often seen as leading in a predictable and determined way from one-celled organisms, through various multicelled forms, to humans, who occupy the top rung of a "ladder of progress." The fallacy of this notion is neatly made clear by paleontologist Stephen Jay Gould:

Although zebras and ponies can produce live offspring like the one shown here, sterility of the offspring maintains the reproductive isolation of the parental species.

O R I G I N A L   S T U D Y
Evolution and the Improbabilities of History[2]

Classical determination and complete predictability may prevail for simple macroscopic objects subject to a few basic laws of motion (balls rolling down inclined planes in high school physics experiments), but complex historical objects do not lend themselves to such easy treatment. In the history of life, all results are products of long series of events, each so intricately dependent upon particular environments and previous histories that we cannot predict their future course with any certainty. The historical sciences try to explain unique situations — immensely complex historical accidents. Evolutionary biologists, as historical scientists, do not expect detailed repetition and cannot use the actual results of history to establish probabilities for recurrence (would a Caesar again die brutally in Rome if we could go back to *Australopithecus* in Africa and start anew?). Evolutionists view the origin of humans (or any particular butterfly, roach, or starfish) as a historical event of such complexity and improbability that we would never expect to see anything exactly like it again (or elsewhere) — hence our strong opposition to the *specific* argument about humanoids on other worlds. Consider just two of the many reasons for uniqueness of complex events in the history of life.

1. Mass extinction as a key influence upon the history of life on earth. Dinosaurs died some 65 million years ago in the great worldwide Cretaceous extinction that also snuffed out about half the species of shallow water marine invertebrates. They had ruled terrestrial environments for 100 million years and would probably reign today if they had survived the debacle. Mammals arose at about the same time and spent their first 100 million years as small creatures inhabiting the nooks and crannies of a dinosaur's world. If the death of dinosaurs had not provided their great opportunity, mammals would still be small and insignificant creatures. We would not be here, and no consciously intelligent life would grace our earth. Evidence gathered since 1980 indicates that the impact of an extraterrestrial body triggered this extinction. What could be more unpredictable and unexpected than comets or asteroids striking the earth literally out of the blue. Yet without such impact, our earth would lack consciously intelligent life. Many great extinctions (several larger than the Cretaceous event) have set basic patterns in the history of life, imparting an essential randomness to our evolutionary pageant.

2. Each species as a concatenation of improbabilities. Any animal species — human, squid, or coral — is the latest link of an evolutionary chain stretching through thousands of species back to the inception of life. If any of these species had become extinct or evolved in another direction, final results would be markedly different. Each chain of improbable events includes adaptations developed for a local environment and only fortuitously

suited to support later changes. Our ancestors among fishes evolved a peculiar fin with a sturdy, central bony axis. Without a structure of this kind,
landbound descendants could not have supported themselves in a
nonbuoyant terrestrial environment. (Most lineages of fishes did not and
could not evolve terrestrial descendants because they lacked fins of this
form.) Yet these fins did not evolve in anticipation of future terrestrial
needs. They developed as adaptations to a local environment in water, and
were luckily suited to permit a new terrestrial direction later on. All evolutionary sequences include such a large set of *sine quibus non*, a fortuitous
series of accidents with respect to future evolutionary success. Human
brains and bodies did not evolve along a direct and inevitable ladder, but by
a circuitous and tortuous route carved by adaptations evolved for different
reasons, and fortunately suited to later needs.

[2]Stephen Jay Gould, *The Flamingo's Smile: Reflections in Natural History* (New York: W.W. Norton, 1985), pp. 408–410.

The history of life is not one of progressive advancement in complexity; if anything, it is one of
proliferation of enormously varied designs which
subsequently have been restricted to a few highly
successful forms. Even at that, imperfections remain. As Gould so aptly puts it:

Our world is not an optimal place, fine tuned by

omnipotent forces of selection. It is a quirky mass of
imperfections, working well enough (often admirably); a jury-rigged set of adaptations built of curious
parts made available by past histories in different
contexts.[3]

[3]Ibid, p. 54.

CHAPTER SUMMARY

Evolution may be defined as a heritable change in
genotype which becomes effective in the gene pool
of a population. Genes, the actual units of heredity, are portions of molecules of DNA (deoxyribonucleic acid), a complex molecule resembling two
strands of rope twisted around one another. The
way that smaller molecules are arranged in this
giant molecule is actually a code that contains information to direct the synthesis of proteins. DNA
molecules have the unique property of being able
to produce exact copies of themselves. As long as

no errors are made in the process of replication,
new organisms will contain genetic material exactly like that in ancestral organisms.

A gene is a unit of the DNA molecule that directs the development of observable traits, for example, blood type. Human DNA is believed to
contain at least 100,000 different genes.

DNA molecules are located on chromosomes,
structures found in the nucleus of each cell. Each
kind of organism has a characteristic number of
chromosomes, which are usually found in pairs.

Humans have 23 pairs. Genes that are located on paired chromosomes and coded for different versions of the same trait are called alleles.

Mitosis, one kind of cell division, begins when the chromosomes (hence, the genes) replicate, forming a second pair that duplicates the original pair of chromosomes in the nucleus. It results in new cells with exactly the same number of chromosome pairs as the parent cell. Meiosis, a different kind of cell division, results from sexual reproduction. It begins with the replication of original chromosomes, but these are divided into four cells, each containing 23 single chromosomes.

The Austrian monk Gregor Mendel studied the mechanism of inheritance with garden peas. He discovered that some alleles are able to mask the presence of others. They are dominant. The allele which is not expressed is recessive. The allele for Type A blood in humans, for example, is dominant to the allele for Type O blood.

Phenotype refers to the physical characteristics of an organism, whereas genotype refers to its genetic composition. Two organisms may have the same phenotype, but different genotypes.

An important concept is that of population, or a group of similar individuals within which most breeding takes place. It is populations, rather than individuals, that evolve. The total number of different genes and alleles available to a population is its gene pool. The frequency with which certain genes occur in the same gene pool theoretically remains the same from one generation to another; this is known as the Hardy-Weinberg principle. Nonetheless, change does take place in gene pools as a result of several factors.

The ultimate source of genetic change is mutation. Normally mutation is a rare occurrence, but some factors, such as certain chemicals or radioactive substances, can increase the mutation rate.

The effects of chance events on the gene pool of a small population is genetic drift. Genetic drift may have been an important factor in human evolution, because until 10,000 years ago, all humans probably lived in relatively small populations. Another factor that brings change to the gene pool of a population is gene flow, or the introduction of new genes from nearby populations. Gene flow occurs when previously separated groups are once able to breed again.

Natural selection is the force that makes evolutionary change adaptive. It reduces the frequency of alleles for harmful or maladaptive traits within a population and increases the frequency of alleles for adaptive traits. Adaptation is the process by which organisms achieve a beneficial adjustment to an available environment, and the results of the process, the characteristics of organisms that fit them to the particular set of conditions of the environment in which they are generally found. A well-studied example of adaptation through natural selection in humans is inheritance of the trait for sickling red blood cells. The sickle-cell trait, caused by the inheritance of an abnormal form of hemoglobin, is an adaptation to life in regions in which falciparum malaria is common. In these regions, the sickle-cell trait plays a beneficial role, but in parts of the world where malaria is uncommon, the sickling trait is no longer advantageous and the associated sickle-cell anemia becomes injurious. Geneticists predict that as malaria is brought under control, within several generations, there will be a decline in the number of individuals who carry the allele responsible for the sickle-cell anemia.

Evolution is the process whereby organisms change into a new form from a previous form. Evolution is not necessarily a linear progression. It may be divergent, or branching; or convergent, where two dissimilar forms develop similarities.

A species is a population or a group of populations that is mechanically capable of interbreeding. The concept of species is relative rather than absolute; whether or not breeding takes place in the wild is more important than the academic question of whether or not it is technically feasible. Populations within species that are capable of interbreeding but do so only to a limited extent are called races.

Isolating mechanisms serve to separate breeding populations, creating first divergent races and then divergent species. Isolating mechanisms can be geographical; physical, as in the differing anatomical structures of the Saint Bernard and Chihuahua; or social, such as in the caste system of India.

Evolution is not a "ladder of progress" leading in a predictable and determined way to ever more complex forms. Rather, it has produced, through a series of accidents, a diversity of enormously varied designs which subsequently have been restricted to a lesser number of still less-than-perfect forms.

SUGGESTED READINGS

Cavalli-Sforza, L. L. *Elements of Human Genetics*. Menlo Park, Calif.: Benjamin, 1977. A short book for those who want to know something about genetics, and who would like basic genetic principles discussed from a "human" angle.

Edey, Maitland A., and Donald Johanson. *Blueprints: Solving the Mystery of Evolution*. Boston: Little, Brown, 1989. This book is about the evolution of the idea of evolution, told as a scientific detective story. As much about the discoverors of evolution as it is about their discoveries, the book provides insights into the workings of science, and it gives readers the information they need to ponder the significance of our newfound ability, through genetic engineering, to actually direct the evolution of living things, including ourselves.

Gould, Stephen Jay. *The Flamingo's Smile: Reflections in Natural History*. New York: Norton, 1985. A collection of Gould's essays from *Natural History* magazine, in which he ranges over various issues in evolutionary biology. No one is better at explaining how evolution works, or exposing common fallacies, than Gould. Collections of his earlier essays, also highly recommended, are *Ever Since Darwin*, *The Panda's Thumb*, and *Hens' Teeth and Horses' Toes*.

Miller, Johnathan, and Brian Van Loon. *Darwin for Beginners*. New York: Pantheon, 1982. Witty, clever, yet informative and sophisticated, this is a "fun" introduction to Darwin's life and thought.

Stanley, Stephen M. *Macroevolution*. San Francisco: Freeman, 1979. Evolution, according to what is called the "Modern Synthesis," proceeds as relatively small-scale changes accumulate over many generations. Not all biologists agree that this is the whole story, however, and Stanley feels that the fossil record tells us things about evolution that the Modern Synthesis does not.

Suzuki, David T., Anthony J. F. Griffiths, Jeffrey H. Miller, and Richard C. Lewontin. *An Introduction to Genetic Analysis*, 3d ed. New York: W. H. Freeman, 1986. A recent text, in which there is a good mix of the classical and molecular approaches to genetics.

4

MONKEYS, APES, AND HUMANS: THE MODERN PRIMATES

From studying those primates closely related to us, as is the lowland gorilla shown here, we can discover which characteristics we share and which we do not. The former we presumably owe to a common ancestor; the latter are what make us distinctively human.

PREVIEW

What Is the Place of Humanity Among the Other Animals?
Humans are classified by biologists as belonging to the primate order, a group
that also includes lemurs, indriids, lorises, tarsiers, monkeys, and apes. They are
so classified on the basis of shared characteristics of anatomy, physiology,
protein structure, and even the genetic material itself. Among the primates,
humans resemble monkeys, but most closely resemble apes.

*What Are the Implications of the Shared Characteristics Between Humans
and the Other Primates?*
The similarities on which the modern classification of animals is based are
indicative of evolutionary relationships. Therefore, by studying the anatomy,
physiology, and molecular structure of the other primates, we can gain a better
understanding of what human characteristics we owe to our general primate
ancestry, and what traits are uniquely ours, as humans. Such studies indicate
that many of the differences between apes and humans are differences of degree
rather than kind.

Why Do Anthropologists Study the Social Behavior of Monkeys and Apes?
By studying the behavior of apes and monkeys living today — especially those
most closely related to us and those which have adapted to life on savannas to
which our earliest ancestors adapted — we may find essential clues that will
enable the reconstruction of adaptations and behavior patterns involved in the
emergence of our earliest ancestors.

All living creatures, be they great or small, fierce or timid, active or inactive, face a fundamental problem in common, that of survival. Simply put, unless they are able to adapt themselves to some available environment, they cannot survive. Adaptation requires the development of behavior patterns that will help an organism to utilize the environment to its advantage — to find food and sustenance, avoid hazards, and, if the species is to survive, reproduce its own kind. In turn, organisms need to have the biological equipment that makes possible the development of appropriate patterns of behavior. For the hundreds of millions of years that life has existed on earth, biological adaptation has been the primary means by which the problem of survival has been solved. This is accomplished because those organisms of a particular kind, whose biological equipment is best suited to a particular way of life, produce more offspring than those whose equipment is not. In this way, advantageous characteristics become more common in succeeding generations, while less advantageous ones become less common.

In this chapter, we will look at the biological equipment possessed by the primates, the group of animals to which humans belong. We shall also sample the behavior made possible by that biological equipment. The study of that behavior may then help us understand something of the origins of human culture and the origin of humanity itself.

THE CLASSIFICATION SYSTEM

In order to understand the exact place of humanity among the animals, it is helpful to describe briefly the system used by biologists to classify living things. The basic system was devised by the eighteenth-century Swedish naturalist Karl von Linné. The purpose of the Linnaean system was simply to classify the great mass of confusing biological data that had accumulated by that time. Von Linné — or Linnaeus, as he is generally called — classified living things on the basis of overall similarities into small groups, or species. Modern classification has

Analogies: In biology, structures that are superficially similar; the result of convergent evolution.

Homologies: In biology, structures possessed by two different organisms which arise in similar fashion and pass through similar stages during embryonic development. May or may not be similar in adults, but have evolved from a common ancestral stock.

Genus: In the system of plant and animal classification, a group of like species.

gone a step further by distinguishing superficial similarities between organisms — called **analogies** — from basic ones — called **homologies.** The latter are possessed by organisms that share a common ancestry; even though homologous structures may serve different functions (the arm of a human and the forefoot of a dog, for instance), they arise in similar fashion and pass through similar stages in embryonic development before their ultimate differentiation. On the basis of homologies, groups of like species were organized into larger, more inclusive groups, called **genera** (the singular term is "genus"). The characteristics on which Linnaeus based his system were as follows:

1. *Body structure:* A Guernsey cow and a Holstein cow are of the same species because they have identical body structure. A cow and a horse do not.
2. *Body function:* Cows and horses bear their young in the same way. Although they are of different species, they are closer than either cows or horses are to chickens, which lay eggs and have no mammary glands.
3. *Sequence of bodily growth:* Both cows and chickens give birth to — or hatch out of the egg — fully formed young. They are therefore more closely related to each other than either one is to the frog, whose tadpoles undergo a series of changes before attaining adult form.

Modern taxonomy (scientific classification) is based on more than body structure, function, and growth. Now, one must also compare chemical reactions of blood, protein structure, and even the genetic material itself. Even comparison of parasites is useful, for they tend to show the same degree of relationship as the forms they infest.

Through careful comparison and analysis, Linnaeus and those who have come after him have been able to classify specific animals into a series of larger and more inclusive groups up to the largest and most inclusive of all, the animal kingdom. In Table 4.1 are the main categories of the Linnaean system applied to the classification of the human species, with some of the more important distinguishing features noted for each category. (Other categories of primates will be dealt with later in this chapter.)

THE PRIMATE ORDER

The primate order is only one of several mammalian orders, such as rodents, carnivores, ungulates (hoofed mammals), and so on. As such, primates share a number of features with other mammals. Generally speaking, mammals are intelligent animals, having more in the way of brains than reptiles or other kinds of vertebrates. In most species,

> **Notochord:** A rodlike structure of cartilage which, in vertebrates, is replaced by the vertebral column.

the young are born live, the egg being retained within the womb of the female until it achieves an advanced state of growth. Once born, the young are nourished by their mothers with milk provided from the mammary glands, from which the class Mammalia gets its name. During this period of infant dependency, young mammals are able to learn some of the things that they will need for survival as adults.

Mammals are also active animals. This is made possible by their maintenance of a relatively constant body temperature, an efficient respiratory system featuring a separation between the nasal and mouth cavities, a diaphragm to assist in drawing in and letting out breath, and an efficient four-chambered heart that prevents mixing of oxygenated and deoxygenated blood. It is facilitated as well by a skeleton in which the limbs are positioned beneath the body, rather than out at the sides, for ease and economy of movement. The

TABLE 4.1

Classification of Humans	
Kingdom: Animals	Do not make their own food, but depend on intake of living food.
Phylum: Chordata	Have at some stage gill slits as well as a **notochord** (a rodlike structure of cartilage) and a nerve cord running along the back of the body.
Subphylum*: Vertebrata	Notochord replaced by vertebral column ("backbone") to form internal skeleton along with skull, ribs, and limb bones.
Class: Mammalia	Maintain constant body temperature; young nourished after birth by milk from mother's mammary glands.
Order: Primates	Hands and feet capable of grasping; tendency to erect posture with head balanced on spinal column; acute development of vision rather than sense of smell; tendency to larger brains.
Family: Hominidae	Ground-dwelling with bipedal locomotion; more reliance on learned, as opposed to biologically determined, behavior
Genus: *Homo*	Larger brains; reliance on cultural, as opposed to biological, adaptation.
Species: *sapiens*	Brains of modern size; relatively small faces.

*Most categories can be expanded or narrowed by adding the prefix "sub" or "super." A family could thus be part of a superfamily, and in turn contain two or more subfamilies.

bones of the limbs have joints that are constructed in such a way as to permit growth in the young, while at the same time they provide strong, hard joint surfaces that will stand up to the stresses of sustained activity.

The skeleton of most mammals is simplified, compared to that of most reptiles, in that it has fewer bones. For example, the lower jaw consists of a single bone rather than several. The teeth, however, are another matter. Instead of the relatively simple, pointed, peglike teeth of reptiles, mammals have special teeth for special purposes: incisors for nipping, gnawing, and cutting; canines for ripping, tearing, killing, and fighting; premolars that may either slice and tear or crush and grind (depending on the kind of animal); and molars for crushing and grinding. This enables mammals to make use of a wide variety of food—an advantage to them, since they require more food than do reptiles to sustain their high activity. But they pay a price: reptiles have unlimited tooth replacement, whereas mammals are limited to two sets. The first set serves the immature animal, and is replaced by the "permanent" or adult dentition.

The primate order is divided into two suborders (Table 4.2), of which one is the **Strepsirhini,** which includes lemurs, lorises, and indriids (all members of the infraorder **Lemuriformes**). On the whole, strepsirhines are cat sized or smaller,

Strepsirhini: A primate suborder that includes the single infraorder, Lemuriformes.

Lemuriformes: A strepsirhine infraorder that includes lemurs, indriids, and lorises.

Haplorhini: A primate suborder that includes tarsiers, monkeys, apes, and humans.

Tarsiiformes: A haplorhine infraorder that includes tarsiers.

Platyrrhinii: A haplorhine infraorder that includes the New World monkeys.

Catarrhinii: A haplorhine infraorder that includes Old World monkeys, apes, and humans.

although there have been some larger forms in the past. Generally, they do not exhibit the characteristics of their order to as great a degree as do the members of the other suborder, the **Haplorhini.** The Strepsirhines also retain certain mammalian features, such as claws and moist, naked skin on their noses, that have not been retained by the haplorhines.

The haplorhine suborder is divided into three infraorders: the **Tarsiiformes,** or tarsiers; the **Platyrrhinii,** or New World monkeys; and the **Catarrhinii,** consisting of the superfamilies Cercopithecoidea (Old World monkeys) and Hominoidea. Within the latter are the families Hominidae (modern and extinct forms of hu-

TABLE 4.2

The Primate Order

ORDER	SUBORDER	INFRAORDER	SUPERFAMILY	FAMILY
Primates	Strepsirhini	Lemuriformes	(lemurs, lorises, and indiriids)	
	Haplorhini	Tarsiiformes		
		Platyrrhinii	(New World monkeys)	
		Catarrhinii	Cercopithecoidea (Old World monkeys)	
			Hominoidea	Hylobatidae (small apes)
				Pongidae (great apes) Hominidae (humans and near humans)

mans), Hylobatidae (small apes, like the gibbon), and Pongidae (great apes, like today's chimpanzee, gorilla, and orangutan).[1]

PRIMATE CHARACTERISTICS

Although the living primates are a varied group of animals, they do share a number of features. These features are, however, displayed in varying degree by the different kinds of primate; in some, they are barely detectable, while in others they are greatly elaborated. All are useful in one way or another to **arboreal,** or tree-dwelling animals, although (as any squirrel knows) they are not essential to life in the trees. For animals preying on the many insects living on the fruit and flowers of trees and shrubs, however, such primate characteristics as manipulative hands and keen vision would have been enormously adaptive. Probably, it was as arboreal animals relying on visual predation of insects that primates got their start in life.

PRIMATE SENSE ORGANS

The primates' adaptation to their way of life in the trees coincided with changes in the form and function of their sensory apparatus: The senses of sight and touch became highly developed, and the sense of smell declined. When primates took to the trees in search of insects, they no longer needed to live a "nose-to-the-ground" existence, sniffing close to the ground in search of food. The haplorhines have the least-developed sense of smell of all land animals.

Catching insects in the trees, as the early primates did and many still do, demands quickness of movement and the ability to land in the right place without falling. Thus, they had to be adept at judging depth, direction, distance, and the relationships of objects in space, abilities that remain useful to animals that travel through the trees (as most

Arboreal: Tree dwelling.

Stereoscopic vision: Three-dimensional vision.

Fovea centralis: A shallow pit in the retina of the eye that enables an animal to focus on an object while maintaining visual contact with its surroundings.

primates still do today), even though they may have given up most insect eating in favor of fruits and leaves. In the haplorhines, these abilities are provided by their **stereoscopic vision,** the ability to see the world in three dimensions—height, width, and depth. It requires two eyes set apart from one another on the same plane. Each eye thus views an object from a slightly different angle, and the object assumes a three-dimensional appearance, indicating spatial relationships. Stereoscopic vision is one of the most important factors in primate evolution, for it is believed to have led to increased brain size in the visual area and a great complexity at nerve connections.

Visual acuity, however, varies throughout the primate order. Lemuriformes, for example, are the most visually primitive of the primates. Lacking stereoscopic vision, their eyes look out from either side of their muzzle or snout, much like a cow or a rabbit. Nor do they possess color vision. All other primates possess both color and stereoscopic vision, as well as a unique structure called the **fovea centralis,** or central pit in the retina of each eye. Like a camera lens, this remarkable feature enables the animal to focus on a particular object for very clear perception, without sacrificing visual contact with the object's surroundings.

Primate sense of touch also became highly developed as a result of arboreal living. Primates found useful an effective feeling and grasping mechanism to grab their insect prey, and to prevent them from falling and tumbling while moving through the trees. The primitive mammals from which primates descended possessed tiny tactile hairs that gave them extremely sensitive tactile capacities. In primates, these hairs were replaced by informative pads on the tips of the animals' fingers and toes.

[1]The classification used here, which differs from the traditional ones dividing primates into prosimians and anthropoids, is the one favored by most primatologists today.

THE PRIMATE BRAIN

By far, the most outstanding characteristic of primate evolution has been the enlargement of the brain among members of the order. Primate brains tend to be large, heavy in proportion to body weight, and very complex. The cerebral hemispheres, the areas of conscious thought, have enlarged dramatically and, in catarrhines, completely cover the cerebellum, which is the part of the brain that coordinates the muscles and maintains body equilibrium.

The reasons for this important change in brain size are many, but it may have begun when the earliest primates, along with many other mammals, began to carry out their activities in the daylight hours. Before 65 million years ago, mammals seem to have been nocturnal in their habits, but with the extinction of the dinosaurs, inconspicuous, nighttime activity was no longer the key to survival. With the change to diurnal, or daytime, activity, the sense of vision took on greater importance, and so visual acuity was favored by natural selection. Unlike reptile vision, where the information-processing neurons are in the retina, mammalian vision is processed in the brain, permitting integration with information received by hearing and smelling.

If the evolution of visual acuity began the trend to larger brains, it is likely that the primates' arboreal existence played a major role in furthering that trend. Paleontologist Alfred S. Romer states:

> Locomotion in the trees requires great agility and muscular coordination, which in itself demands development of the brain centers; and it is of interest that much of the higher mental faculties are apparently developed in an area alongside the motor centers of the brain.[2]

An interesting hypothesis that may help account for primate brain development involves the use of the hand as a tactile organ to replace the teeth and jaws or snout. The hands assumed some of the grasping, tearing, and dividing functions of the snout, again requiring development of the

brain centers for more complete coordination. Thus, while the skull and brain expanded, the teeth and jaws grew smaller. Certain areas of the brain became more elaborate and intricate. One of these areas is the cortex, generally considered to be the center of an animal's intelligence; it receives impressions from the animal's various sensory receptors, analyzes them, and sends responses back down the motor nerves to the proper receptor.

An animal living in the trees is constantly acting on and reacting to the environment. Messages from the hands, feet, eyes, and ears, as well as from the sensors of balance, movement, heat, touch, and pain, are relayed to the cortex, individually and simultaneously. The cortex, then, must be developed to a considerable degree of complexity to receive and coordinate these impressions and to transmit the appropriate responses back. It is assumed that such development must have occurred early in the history of the primates.

The enlarged cortex not only provided the primates with a greater degree of efficiency in the daily struggle for survival, but it also gave them the basis for more sophisticated cerebration, or thought. The ability to think probably played a decisive role in the evolution of the primates from which human beings emerged.

PRIMATE DENTITION

Although primates have added other things than insects to their diets, they have retained less-specialized teeth than other mammals. According to primatologist W. E. LeGros Clark:

> An arboreal life obviates the necessity for developing highly specialized grinding teeth, since the diet available to most tree-living mammals in the tropics, consisting of leaves, shoots, soft fruits and insects, can be adequately masticated by molar teeth of relatively simple structure.[3]

In most primates, on each side of each jaw, in front, are two straight-edged, chisel-like broad teeth called "incisors" (Figure 4.1). Behind the

[2]Alfred S. Romer, *Vertebrate Paleontology* (Chicago: University of Chicago Press, 1945), p. 103.

[3]W. E. LeGros Clark, *History of the Primates*, 5th ed. (Chicago: University of Chicago Press, 1966), p. 271.

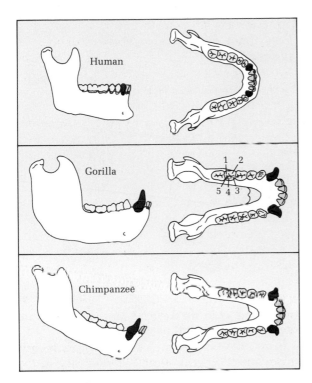

FIGURE 4.1 Lower jaws of a human, a gorilla, and a chimpanzee; incisors are shown in green, canines in red, premolars and molars in yellow. On one of the gorilla molars, the cusps are numbered to enhance their identification.

incisors is a canine, which in many mammals is large, flaring, and fanglike and is used for defense as well as for tearing and shredding food. Among some catarrhines the canine is reduced in size somewhat, especially in females, though it is still large in males. In humans, though, incisors and canines are practically indistinguishable. Behind the canines are the premolars. Last are the molars, usually with four or five cusps, used mostly for crushing or grinding food. This basic pattern of dentition contrasts sharply with that of nonprimate mammals.

On the evidence of comparative anatomy and the fossil record, LeGros Clark postulated the existence of an early primate ancestor that possessed three incisors, one canine, four premolars, and three molars on each side of the jaw, top and bottom, for a total of 44 teeth. In the early stages of

■ **Cranium:** The brain case of the skull.

primate evolution, four incisors (one on each side of each jaw) were lost. This change differentiated the primates, with their two incisors on each side of each jaw, from other mammals. The canines of most primates develop into long, daggerlike teeth that enable them to rip open tough husks of fruit and other foods. In combat, male baboons, apes, and other primates flash these formidable teeth at their enemy, hoping to scare it off. Only on rare occasions, when this bluffing action fails, are teeth used to inflict bodily harm.

Other evolutionary changes in primate dentition involve the premolar and molar teeth. Over the millennia, the first and second premolars became smaller and eventually disappeared altogether, while the third and fourth premolars grew larger with the addition of a second pointed projection, or cusp, thus becoming "bicuspid." The molars, meanwhile, evolved from a three-cusp pattern to one with four and even five cusps. This kind of molar economically combined the functions of grasping, cutting, and grinding in one tooth.

The evolutionary trend for primate dentition has generally been toward economy, with fewer, smaller, and more efficient teeth doing more work. Thus, our own 32 teeth are fewer in number than those of some, and more generalized than those of most, primates. Indeed, the absence of third molars in many individuals indicates that the human dentition is undergoing further reduction.

THE PRIMATE SKELETON

The skeleton gives an animal its basic shape or silhouette, supports the soft tissues, and helps protect the vital internal organs. In primates (Figure 4.2), for example, the skull protects the brain and the eyes. A number of factors are responsible for the shape of the primate skull as compared with those of most other mammals: changes in dentition, changes in the sensory organs of sight and smell, and increased brain size. The primate brain case, or **cranium,** tends to be high and vaulted. A

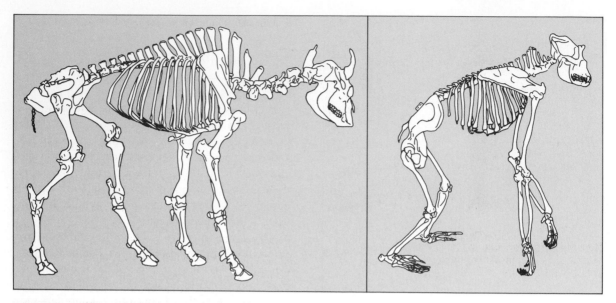

FIGURE 4.2 Skeleton of a bison (*left*) and gorilla (*right*), compared. Note where the skulls and vertebral columns are joined; in the bison (as in most mammals) the skull projects forward from the vertebral column, but in the semierect gorilla, the vertebral column is well down beneath the skull.

solid partition exists in most primate species between the eye and the temple, affording maximum protection to the eyes in their vulnerable forward position.

The **foramen magnum** (the large opening in the skull through which the spinal cord passes and connects to the brain) is an important clue to evolutionary relationships. In primates, the evolutionary trend has been for this to shift forward, toward the center of the skull's base so that it faces downward, as in humans, rather than directly backward, as in dogs, horses, and other mammals. Thus, the skull does not project forward from the vertebral column. Instead, the vertebral column joins the skull toward the center of its base, thereby placing the skull in a balanced position in animals which frequently assume upright posture.

In most primates, the snout or muzzle portion of the skull has grown smaller as the acuity of the sense of smell declined. The smaller snout offers less interference with stereoscopic vision; it also enables the eyes to be placed in the frontal position. As a result, primates have more of a human-like face than other mammals. Below the primate

> **Foramen magnum:** A large opening in the skull through which the spinal cord passes and connects to the brain.
>
> **Clavicle:** The collar bone.
>
> **Scapula:** The shoulder blade.
>
> **Brachiate:** To use the arms to move from branch to branch, with the body hanging suspended from them.

skull and the neck is the **clavicle,** or collarbone, a holdover from primitive mammal ancestors. This serves as a strut that prevents the arm from collapsing inward when brought across the front of the body. It allows greater maneuverability of the arms, permitting them to swing sideways and outward from the trunk of the body. The clavicle also supports the **scapula,** or shoulder blade, and allows for the muscle development that is required for flexible, yet powerful, arm movement. This shoulder and limb structure is associated with considerable acrobatic agility and, in the case of all apes and some New World monkeys, the ability to **brachiate**—use their arms to swing and hang among the branches of trees.

A young spider monkey clings to its mother. Since her hands and arms are used in locomotion, she cannot herself carry her infant; consequently, it must be able to hold on for itself.

Primates have also retained the characteristic, found in early mammals, of **pentadactyly.** Pentadactyly, which means possessing five digits, is found in many nonarboreal animals, but it proved to be of special advantage to tree-dwelling primates. Their grasping feet and hands (Figure 4.3)

Pentadactyly: Possessing five digits (fingers and toes).

Prehensile: Having the ability to grasp.

have sensitive pads at the tips of their digits, protected except in some strepsirhines by flattened nails. This unique combination of pad and nail provides the animal with an excellent **prehensile,** or grasping, device for use when moving from tree to tree. The structural characteristics of the primate foot and hand make grasping possible; the digits are extremely flexible, the big toe is fully opposable to the other digits in most species, and the thumb is opposable to the other digits to varying degrees.

Hindsight indicates that the flexible, unspecialized primate hand was to prove a valuable asset for future evolution of this group. Had they not had generalized grasping hands, early hominids would not have been able to manufacture and use tools and thus embark on the new and unique evolutionary pathway that led to the revolutionary ability to adapt through culture.

FIGURE 4.3 The hands of primates are similar. Human hands are distinguished by well-developed thumbs that can be used in opposition to the fingers; the hands of brachiators (gibbons and chimpanzees) are characterized by long fingers and weakly developed thumbs.

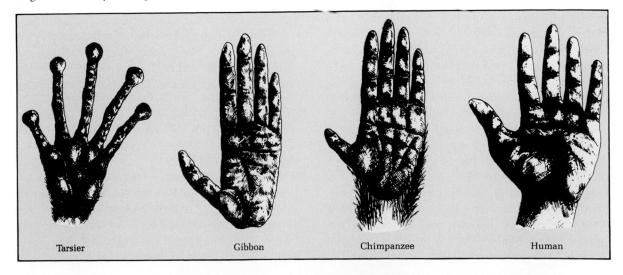

Tarsier   Gibbon   Chimpanzee   Human

REPRODUCTION AND CARE OF YOUNG

The breeding of most mammals occurs once or twice a year, but most primate species seem able to breed at any time during the course of the year. Generally, the male is ready to engage in sexual activity whenever females are receptive; whereas the female's receptivity is cyclical, corresponding to her period of **estrus.**

This is not to say that females are receptive regularly each month. Rather, the average adult female monkey or ape spends most of her time either pregnant or nursing, at which times she is not sexually receptive. But after her infant is weaned, she will come into estrus for a few days each month, until she becomes pregnant again. Since this can happen at any time, it is advantageous to have males present throughout the year. Thus, sex plays a role in keeping both sexes constantly together, although it is by no means the only, or even the most important, cause of males and females remaining together.

One of the most noticeable adaptations to arboreal life among primates is a trend toward reduction in the number of offspring born at one time to a female. The most primitive primates, lemurs and marmosets, produce two or three young at each birth. Catarrhines, however, usually produce only a single offspring at a time. Natural selection may have favored single births among primate tree dwellers because the primate infant, which has a highly developed grasping ability (the grasping reflex can also be seen in human infants), must be transported about by its mother and more than one clinging infant would seriously encumber her as she moved about the trees. Moreover, a female pregnant with a large litter would be unable to lead a very active life as a tree dweller.

Primates bear fewer young at a time, and they must devote more time and effort to their care if the species is to survive. This usually means a longer period during which the infant is dependent on its mother. As a general rule, the more closely related to humans the species is, the smaller, more helpless, and more immature the newborn offspring tend to be. For example, a

Estrus: In primate females, the time of sexual receptivity during which ovulation takes place.

lemur is dependent on the mother for only a few months after birth, an ape for 4 or 5 years, and a human for over a decade. Longer infancy is typically associated with an increase in longevity (see Figure 4.4). If the breeding life of primates had not extended, the lengthened infancy could have led to a decrease in numbers of individuals. Something approaching this can be seen in the great apes: A female chimpanzee, for example, does not reach sexual maturity until about the age of 10 years, and once she produces her first live offspring, there is a period of about 5.6 years before she will bear another. Furthermore, a chimpanzee infant cannot survive if its mother dies before it reaches the age of four at the very least. Thus, assuming that none of her offspring die before adulthood, a female chimpanzee must survive for at least 20 or 21 years just to maintain the size of chimpanzee populations at their current levels. In fact, chimpanzee infants and juveniles do die from time to time, and all females do not live full reproductive lives. This is one reason why apes are not as abundant in the world today as are monkeys.

The young of catarrhine, and especially hominoid, species are born with relatively underdeveloped nervous systems; moreover, they are lacking in the social knowledge that guides behavior. Thus, they depend on adults not only for protection but also for instruction, for they must learn how to survive. The longer period of dependence in these primates makes possible a longer period of learning, which appears to be a distinct evolutionary advantage.

ESTABLISHING EVOLUTIONARY RELATIONSHIPS

Most of the primate characteristics so far discussed are present at least in a rudimentary sort of way in the strepsirhines, but all are seen to a much greater degree in the haplorhines. The differences between humans and the other haplorhines, especially catarrhines, are rather like those between strepsirhines and haplorhines. Humans have developed most of the characteristic primate traits to a degree not realized by any other species. Among some strepsirhines, some of the distinctive primate traits are missing, while others are clearly present, so that the borderline between primate and non-primate becomes blurred, and the difference is one of degree rather than kind. All of this is fully expectable, given an evolutionary history in which primitive primates, having a rough resemblance to today's strepsirhines, developed out of some other mammalian order, and eventually gave rise to primitive haplorhines; from these, emerged the catarrhines and, ultimately, hominids.

Just how close our evolutionary relationship is to other primates is indicated by molecular evidence. There is a striking similarity in blood and protein chemistry among the anthropoids, indicating close evolutionary relationships. On the basis of tests with blood proteins, the chimpanzee and gorilla are closest to humans, next is the orangutan, then the smaller apes (gibbons and

siamangs), Old World monkeys, New World monkeys, and finally the strepsirhines. Measurements of genetic affinity confirm these findings, providing further evidence of humanity's close kinship to the great apes, especially those of Africa (Figure 4.5). For example, humans and chimpanzees are at least 98 percent identical at the genetic level; the only difference is that chimpanzees have an extra pair of chromosomes, and of the others, the 22nd pair shows some difference. With respect to the extra pair, in humans, these have fused with another pair to form the single 22nd pair, so even this is not a major difference.

MODERN PRIMATES

The modern primates are mostly restricted to warm areas of the world. As already noted, they are divided into two suborders, Strepsirhini and Haplorhini. Strepsirhines are small, mostly quadrupedal Old World animals; haplorhines include tarsiers, monkeys, apes, and humans.

FIGURE 4.4 Primates are born at earlier stages of development than other animals. Humans are born at a particularly early stage because of their larger brain size; later, the baby's head would be too large for the mother's pelvis.

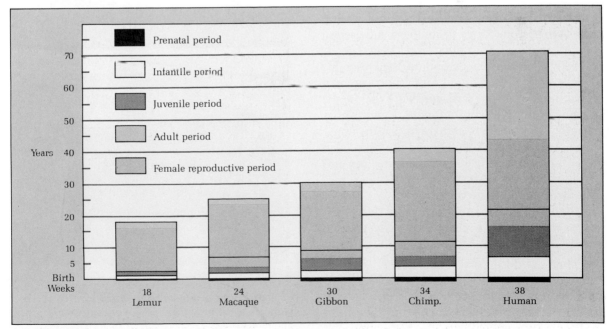

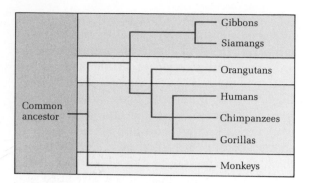

FIGURE 4.5 The relationships among the various catarrhine primates, as revealed by molecular similarities and differences, are shown in this diagram. Its authors, V. M. Sarich and A. C. Wilson, have stated that it is difficult to consider seriously any date in excess of 10 million years for the origin of the separate lineages for chimpanzees, gorillas, and humans.

STREPSIRHINES

Members of the suborder Strepsirhini (from the Greek for "turned nose") are considered to be the most primitive primates. The suborder is represented by the single infraorder Lemuriformes, within which are the lemurs, indriids, and lorises. Although lemurs and indriids are restricted to the island of Madagascar, off the east coast of Africa, lorises range from Africa to southern and eastern Asia. All are small, with none larger than a good-sized dog. In general body outline, they resemble rodents and insectivores, with short pointed snouts, large pointed ears, and big eyes. In the anatomy of the upper lip and snout, lemuriformes resemble nonprimate mammals, in that the upper lip is bound down to the gum and the naked skin on the nose around the nostrils is moist. They also have long tails, with that of a ring-tail lemur somewhat like the tail of a raccoon.

In brain structure, lemuriformes are clearly primates, and they have characteristically primate "hands," which they use in pairs rather than one at a time. They move on all fours, with the forelimbs in a "palms down" position, and also cling in near vertical positions to branches. Although they retain a claw on their second toe, which they use for scratching and grooming, all other digits are

Modern strepsirhines represent highly evolved variants of an early primate model. In them, primate characteristics are not as prominent as they are in monkeys, apes, and humans.

equipped with flattened nails. With their distinctive mix of characteristics, strepsirhine primates appear to occupy a place between the haplorhines and insectivores.

HAPLORHINES

The suborder Haplorhini (from the Greek for "simple nose") is divided into three infraorders: the Tarsiiformes (tarsiers), the Platyrrhinii (New World monkeys), and Catarrhinii (Old World monkeys, apes, and humans). Most haplorhines are bigger than the strepsirhines and are strikingly humanlike in appearance. Actually, it is more accurate to say that humans are remarkably like monkeys, but even more like apes, in appearance. The defining traits of the strepsirhines — large cranium, well-developed brain, acute vision, chisel-like incisors, prehensile digits — are even more apparent in the haplorhines. Most haplorhines generally move on all four limbs, but many stand erect to reach fruit hanging in trees; some apes occasionally walk on two feet. Monkeys are often highly arboreal, and New World species have prehensile tails that wrap around a tree branch, freeing the forelimbs to grasp food. Some New World monkeys brachiate; Old World monkeys almost never do.

All apes may once have been fully arboreal brachiators, but among modern apes, only the gibbon and siamang still are. The chimpanzee and the gorilla spend most of their time on the ground, but they sleep in the trees and may also find food there. Orangutans, too, spend time on the ground, but they are somewhat more arboreal than the African apes. When on the ground, they move mostly on all fours.

Tarsiers

Tarsiers are the haplorhine primates most like the lemuriformes, and in the past, they were usually classified in the same suborder with them. The head, eyes, and ears of these kitten-sized arboreal creatures are huge in proportion to the body. They have the remarkable ability to turn their heads 180 degrees, so they can see where they have been as

In tarsiers, primate characteristics are somewhat more prominent than among strepsirhines.

well as where they are going. The digits end in platelike, adhesive discs. Tarsiers are named for the elongated tarsal, or foot bone, that provides leverage for jumps of six feet or more. Tarsiers are mainly nocturnal insect eaters. In the structure of the nose and lips, and the part of the brain governing vision, tarsiers resemble monkeys.

New World Monkeys

New World monkeys live in forests and swamps of South and Central America. They are characterized by flat noses with widely separated, outward flaring nostrils, from which comes their name of platyrrhine monkeys. Many are entirely arboreal, and some have long, prehensile tails by which they hang from trees. These and the presence of three, rather than two, premolars on each side of each jaw distinguish them from the Old World monkeys, apes, and humans. Platyrrhines walk on all fours with their palms down and scamper along tree branches in search of fruit, which they eat sitting upright. Spider monkeys are accomplished brachiators as well. Although other New World monkeys spend much of their time in the trees, they do not often hang or swing from limb to limb by their arms and have not developed the extremely long forelimbs characteristic of brachiators.

Old World Monkeys

Old World, or catarrhine, monkeys are characterized by noses with closely spaced, downward-pointing nostrils, the presence of two, rather than three, premolars on each side of each jaw, and their lack of prehensile tails. They may be either arboreal or terrestrial. The arboreal species include the guereza monkey, the Asiatic langur, and the strange-looking proboscis monkey. Some are equally at home on the ground and in the trees, such as the macaques, of which there are some 19 species ranging from Gibraltar (The Barbary ape) to Japan.

Several species of baboons are largely terrestrial, living in the savannas, deserts, and highlands of Africa. They have long, fierce faces and move quadrupedally, with all fours in the palms-down position. Their diet consists of leaves, seeds, insects, and lizards, and they live in large, well-organized troops. Because baboons have abandoned trees (except for sleeping) and live in environments like that in which humans may have originated, they are of great interest to primatologists.

Small and Great Apes

The apes are the closest living relatives we humans have in the animal world. Their general appearance and way of life are related to their semierect posture. In their body chemistry, the position of their internal organs, and even their diseases, they are remarkably close to humans. They are arboreal to varying degrees, but their generally greater size and weight are obstacles to their swinging and jumping as freely as monkeys. The small, lithe gibbon can both climb and swing freely through the trees and so spends virtually all of its time in them.

At the opposite extreme are gorillas, who climb trees, using their prehensile hands and feet to grip the trunk and branches. Their swinging is limited to leaning outward as they reach for fruit, clasping a limb for support. Most of their time is spent on the ground.

The apes, like humans, have no external tail. But, unlike humans, their arms are longer than their legs, indicating that their ancestors remained arboreal brachiators long after our own had become terrestrial. In moving on the ground, the African apes "knuckle-walk" on the backs of their hands, resting their weight on the middle joints of the fingers. They stand erect when reaching for fruit, looking over tall grass, or in any activity where they find the erect position advantageous. The semierect position is natural in apes when on the ground because the curvature of their vertebral column places their center of gravity, which is high in their bodies, in front of their hip joint. Thus, they are both "top heavy" and "front heavy." Furthermore, the structure of the ape pelvis is not well suited to support the weight of the torso and limbs easily. Nor do apes have the arrangement of leg muscles that enables humans to stand erect and swing their legs freely before and behind.

Gibbons and siamangs, which are found in Southeast Asia and Malaya, have compact, slim bodies and disproportionately long arms and short legs, and stand about three feet high. Although their usual form of locomotion is brachiation, they can run erect, holding their arms out for balance. Gibbons and siamangs resemble monkeys in size and general appearance more than the other apes.

Orangutans are found in Borneo and Sumatra. They are somewhat taller than gibbons and siamangs and are much heavier, with the bulk characteristic of apes. In the closeness of the eyes and facial prominence, an orangutan looks a little like a chimpanzee, except that its hair is reddish. It has very small ears, and its sparse hair, wrinkled face, and sad expression give it the look of an old man. Orangutans walk with their forelimbs in a fists-sideways, or a palms-down, position. Shy and rather solitary animals, they are somewhat more arboreal than the African apes.

Gorillas, found in equatorial Africa, are the largest of the apes; an adult male can weigh over 400 pounds. The body is covered with a thick coat of glossy black hair, and mature males have a silvery gray upper back. There is a strikingly human look about the face, and like humans, gorillas focus on things in their field of vision by directing the eyes rather than moving the head. Gorillas are mostly ground dwellers, but may sleep in trees in carefully constructed nests. Because of their weight, brachiation is limited to raising and lowering themselves among the tree branches when searching for fruit. They "knuckle-walk," standing erect to reach for fruit or to see something more easily. Although gorillas are gentle and tolerant, bluffing is an important part of their behavioral repertoire.

Chimpanzees are widely distributed throughout Africa. They are probably the best known of the apes, and because they are fast learners and good mimics, have long been favorites in zoos and circuses. Studies in genetics, biochemistry, and anatomy suggest that they are humanity's closest relative. Chimpanzees forage on the ground much of the day and build tree nests at sunset.

Gibbons and orangutans are Southeast Asian apes. Gibbons are brachiators who use their long arms and hands to swing through the trees. Although orangutans are sometimes brachiate, their legs move like arms and their feet are like hands; thus, much of their movement is by "four-handed" climbing.

Chimpanzees and goril-
las are African apes. The
photo at far right shows
a mature female gorilla
with her infant.

THE SOCIAL BEHAVIOR
OF PRIMATES

The physical resemblance of human beings to the other catarrhines is striking, but the most startling resemblance of all is in their social behavior. Because of their highly developed brains, monkeys and apes behave in a manner far more complex than most other animals except humans. Only over the past three decades have primatologists made prolonged close-range observations of catarrhines in their natural habitats, and we are discovering much about social organization, learning ability, and communication among our closest relatives in the animal kingdom. In particular, we are finding that a number of behavioral traits that we used to think of as distinctively human are found to one degree or another among other primates.

The range of behavior shown by living primates is great — too great to be adequately surveyed in this book. Instead, we shall look primarily at the behavior of those species most closely related to humans — chimpanzees and gorillas — or those that have adapted to an environment somewhat like the one to which our own ancestors adapted millions of years ago — savanna baboons.

THE GROUP

Primates are social animals, living and traveling in groups that vary in size from species to species. In most species, females and their offspring constitute the core of the social system. Among baboons, these females are all related in that they remain for life in the group into which they were born, whereas males generally move to other groups as adolescents. Among chimpanzees, females sometimes leave their natal group to join another, but their sons, and often their daughters, remain in their mother's group for life. Among gorillas, either sex may or may not leave its natal group for another.

Savanna baboons live in large troops which may number more than 100 animals. They have male and female status hierarchies, and males dominate

At present, no less than 76 species of primates are recognized as being in danger of extinction. Included among them are all of the great apes as well as such formerly widespread and adaptable species as rhesus macaques. In the wild, they are threatened by destruction of their habitat in the name of "development," by hunting for food and trophies, and by trapping for pets and research. Because monkeys and apes are so closely related to humans, they are regarded as essential for biomedical research in which humans cannot be used. It is ironic that trade in live primates to supply laboratories can be a major factor in their local extinction.

Because of their vulnerability, the conservation of primates has become a matter of urgency. Two approaches to the problem may be taken, both of which require application of knowledge gained from studies of free-ranging animals. One is to maintain some populations in the wild, either by establishing preserves where animals are already living, or by moving populations to localities where suitable habitat exists. In either case, constant monitoring and management are necessary to assure that sufficient space and resources remain available. The other approach is to maintain breeding colonies in captivity, in which case care must be taken to provide the kind of physical and social environment that will encourage reproductive success. Without such amenities as things to climb, materials to use for nest building, others to socialize with, and places to withdraw not only from humans but from each other, primates in zoos and laboratories do not successfully reproduce.

The value of field studies for effective wild animal management is illustrated by Shirley Strum's relocation in 1984 of three troops of free-ranging baboons in Kenya. The troop she had been studying for 15 years had become a problem, raiding peoples' crops and garbage. Accordingly, it was decided to move this and two other local troops—130 animals in all—to more sparsely inhabited country 150 miles away. Knowing their habits, Strum was able to trap, tranquilize, and transport the animals to their new home in such a way as not to disrupt their social relationships, cause them to abandon their new home, or block the transfer into their troops of new males, with their all-important knowledge of local resources. The success of her effort, which had never been tried with baboons before, proves that relocation is a realistic technique for saving endangered primate populations.

females, unless a female is supported by another male (males are twice as big as females). Each animal knows its place, and the hierarchies are maintained by the self-assertiveness of dominant animals and their success in securing the support of other animals, as well as by the deference of subordinates. High dominance brings with it priority of access to choice food, water, and (sometimes) mates; moreover, high-ranking females are more often groomed by others of their sex as well as by juveniles, and are less vulnerable to harassment by others when caring for young infants. Although adult females tend to avoid one another when foraging, closely related females sit together and groom each other when at rest. They will also support one another during aggressive encounters with other troop members. Males, by contrast, rarely associate with members of their own sex. Instead, they strike up friendships with one or more females.

Among chimps, the largest organizational unit is the community, composed of 50 or more individuals. Rarely, however, do all these animals come together at a single time. Instead, they are usually found ranging singly or in small subgroups consisting of adult males together, females with their young, or males and females together with the young. In the course of their travels, subgroups may join forces and forage together, but sooner or later, these will break up again into smaller units.

When they do, members are often exchanged so that new subunits are different in their composition from the ones that initially came together.

Although relationships between individuals within the community are relatively harmonious, dominance hierarchies do exist. Generally, males outrank females, although high-ranking females may dominate low-ranking males. Physical strength and size are important determinants of an animal's rank, as are the rank of its mother, its effectiveness at enlisting the aid of other individuals, and, in the case of the male, its motivation to achieve high status. Highly motivated males may bring considerable intelligence and ingenuity to bear in their quest for high rank. For example, one chimpanzee in the community studied by Jane Goodall, a pioneer in the study of primate behavior, was able to figure out how to incorporate noisy kerosene cans into his charging displays, thereby intimidating all the other males.[4] As a result, he rose from relatively low status to the number one (alpha) position.

The gorilla group is a "family" of 5 to 20 individuals led by a mature, silver-backed male and includes younger, black-backed males, females, the young, and sometimes other silver backs. Subordinate males, however, are usually prevented by the dominant male from mating with the group's females, although he may occasionally allow access to lower-ranking ones. Thus, young silver backs often leave their natal family to start their own families by winning outside females. If the dominant male is weakening with age, however, one of his sons may remain with the group to succeed to his father's position. Unlike chimpanzees, gorillas rarely fight over food, territory, or sex, but will fight fiercely to maintain the cohesiveness of the group.

INDIVIDUAL INTERACTION

One of the most notable primate activities is grooming, the ritual cleaning of another animal's coat to remove parasites, shreds of grass, or other

[4]Jane Goodall, *The Chimpanzees of Gombe: Patterns of Behavior.* (Cambridge, Mass.: Belknap Press, 1986), p. 424.

Catarrhine primates, like these baboons, spend a lot of time grooming one another. Such behavior is important in maintaining group cohesion.

matter. The grooming animal deftly parts the hair of the one being groomed with two fingers, and with the thumb and forefinger of the other hand removes any foreign object, often eating it. Among gorillas, grooming is mainly hygienic; but among chimpanzees and baboons, it is a gesture of friendliness, submission, appeasement, or closeness. Embracing, touching, and jumping up and down are forms of greeting behavior among chimpanzees. Touching is also a form of reassurance.

Gorillas, though gentle and tolerant, are also aloof and independent, and individual interaction among adults tends to be quite restrained. Friendship or closeness between adults and infants is more evident. Among baboons, chimpanzees, gorillas, and most other primates, the mother–infant bond is the strongest and most long lasting in the group. A new infant baboon is an object of tremendous interest to the group, and shortly after birth, mother and infant are surrounded by attention. The adults lipsmack and touch the infant with their fingers or mouths, and young females may even try to take it to practice "mothering" on their own. The new mother aligns herself with a male friend, who protects her from animals that may threaten her or her infant. Two incidents reported by primatologist Barbara Smuts are indicative of the care males may invest in their friends' offspring. Two infants of the group she was studying lost their mothers while they were still quite young. In each case, their bond with the mother's male friend intensified, and was probably critical in the youngsters' survival.[5] Although such friends are not always the fathers, this grouping of adult males, adult females, and juveniles suggests the kind of situation that may have been a forerunner of human family organization.

Among gorillas and chimpanzees, the mother–infant bond is especially strong and may last for many years; commonly for the lifetime of the mother. Gorilla infants and young juveniles share their mothers' nests and have been seen sharing nests with mature, childless females. Both chimpanzee and gorilla males are attentive to juveniles, and may share in parental responsibilities. Male chimpanzees, however (as among human food foragers), may wander apart from the females and juveniles. Thus, it is the females who provide stability in the chimpanzee group, whereas it is the dominant silver back who provides this in the gorilla family.

SEXUAL BEHAVIOR

Among the three foregoing species, as with humans, there is no fixed breeding season. Sexual activity, however — initiated by either the male or the female — occurs only during the period each month when the female is receptive to impregnation. Once impregnated, females are not sexually receptive until their offspring are weaned (at about age four among chimpanzees and gorillas; sooner among baboons). Baboon females typically mate with several different males, but they clearly prefer to mate with those with whom they have a prior friendship. Thus, friendship often precedes, rather than follows, a sexual relationship. When they are at the height of estrus, females commonly spend most of their time in proximity to males with whom they maintain exclusive mating relationships.

To a degree, chimps are promiscuous in their sexual behavior, and 12 to 14 males have been ob-

[5]Barbara Smuts, "What Are Friends For?" *Natural History* 96 (1987): 41.

Sexual dimorphism: Within a single species, the presence of marked anatomical differences between males and females.

served to have as many as 50 copulations in one day with a single female. Nevertheless, dominant males try to monopolize females in full estrus, although cooperation from the female is usually required for this to succeed. An alpha male, however, is able to monopolize the females to some extent, and some alphas have been seen to monopolize several estrus females at the same time.

In gorilla families, the dominant silver back has exclusive breeding rights with the females, although he may allow a young silver back occasional access to a low-ranking female. Otherwise, the young silver back must leave "home" in order to find sex partners, usually by luring them away from other established groups.

Although the vast majority of primate species are not "monogamous" in their mating habits, many smaller species of New World monkeys, a few island-dwelling populations of leaf-eating Old World monkeys, and all of the smaller apes (gibbons and siamangs) do mate for life with a single individual of the opposite sex. None of these species is closely related to human beings, nor do "monogamous" species ever display the degree of **sexual dimorphism** — anatomical differences be-

Among chimpanzees, as among most primates, the mother–infant bond is strong. This mother is playfully tickling her offspring.

tween males and females — that is characteristic of our closest primate relatives, or that seems to have been characteristic of our own ancient ancestors.

PLAY

Frequent play activity among primate infants and juveniles is a means of learning about the environment, testing strength (rank in dominance hierarchies is based to some degree on strength), and generally learning how to behave as adults. Chimpanzee infants mimic the food-getting activities of their mothers, "attack" dozing adults, and "harass" adolescents.

Observers have watched young gorillas do somersaults, wrestle, and play tug o' war, follow the leader, and king of the mountain. One juvenile, becoming annoyed at repeated harassment by an infant, picked it up, climbed a tree, and deposited it on a branch from which it was unable to get down on its own and its mother had to retrieve it.

COMMUNICATION

Primates, like many animals, vocalize. They have a great range of calls that are often used together with movements of the face or body to convey a message. Observers have not yet established the meaning of all the sounds, but a good number have been distinguished, such as warning calls, threat calls, defense calls, and gathering calls; the behavioral reactions of other animals hearing the call have also been studied. Among chimpanzees and gorillas, vocalizations are mainly emotional rather than propositional. Much of their communication takes place by the use of specific gestures and postures. Indeed, some of these, such as kissing and embracing, are in practically universal use today among humans as well.

Primatologists have classified numerous kinds of chimpanzee vocalization and visual communication (see Figure 4.6). Together, these facilitate group protection, coordination of group efforts, and social interaction in general. Experiments with captive apes, discussed in Chapters 12 and 13, reveal that their communicative abilities exceed what they make use of in the wild. From such ex-

Home range: The area within which a group of primates usually move.

periments, we may learn something about the origin of human language.

HOME RANGES

Primates usually move about within circumscribed areas, or **home ranges,** which are of varying sizes, depending on the size of the group and on ecological factors such as availability of food. Ranges are often moved seasonally. The distance traveled by a group in a day varies; baboons may travel as many as 12 miles in a day. Some areas of a range, known as "core areas," are used more often than others; they may contain water, food sources, resting places, and sleeping trees. The ranges of different groups may overlap, and often a tree-dwelling species will share a range with ground dwellers. In such cases, the two species are not necessarily competing for the same resources; they may be using the range at different times and eating somewhat different foods.

Neither baboons nor gorillas defend their home ranges against incursions of others of their kind, although they certainly will defend their group if it is in any way threatened. Thus, they may be said to be nonterritorial. Chimpanzees, by contrast, have been observed patrolling their territories to ward off potential trespassers. Moreover, Goodall has recorded the destruction of one chimpanzee community by another which invaded the first one's turf. Although Goodall has interpreted this as territorial behavior [6] another interpretation is possible. In Africa today, human encroachment is squeezing chimpanzees into ever smaller pockets of forest. This places considerable stress on animals whose levels of violence tend to increase in the absence of sufficient space. Perhaps the violence that Goodall witnessed was a response to crowding as a consequence of human encroachment. Among primates in general, the clearest territoriality appears in forest species rather than in those that are more terrestrial in their habits.

[6]Goodall, p. 525.

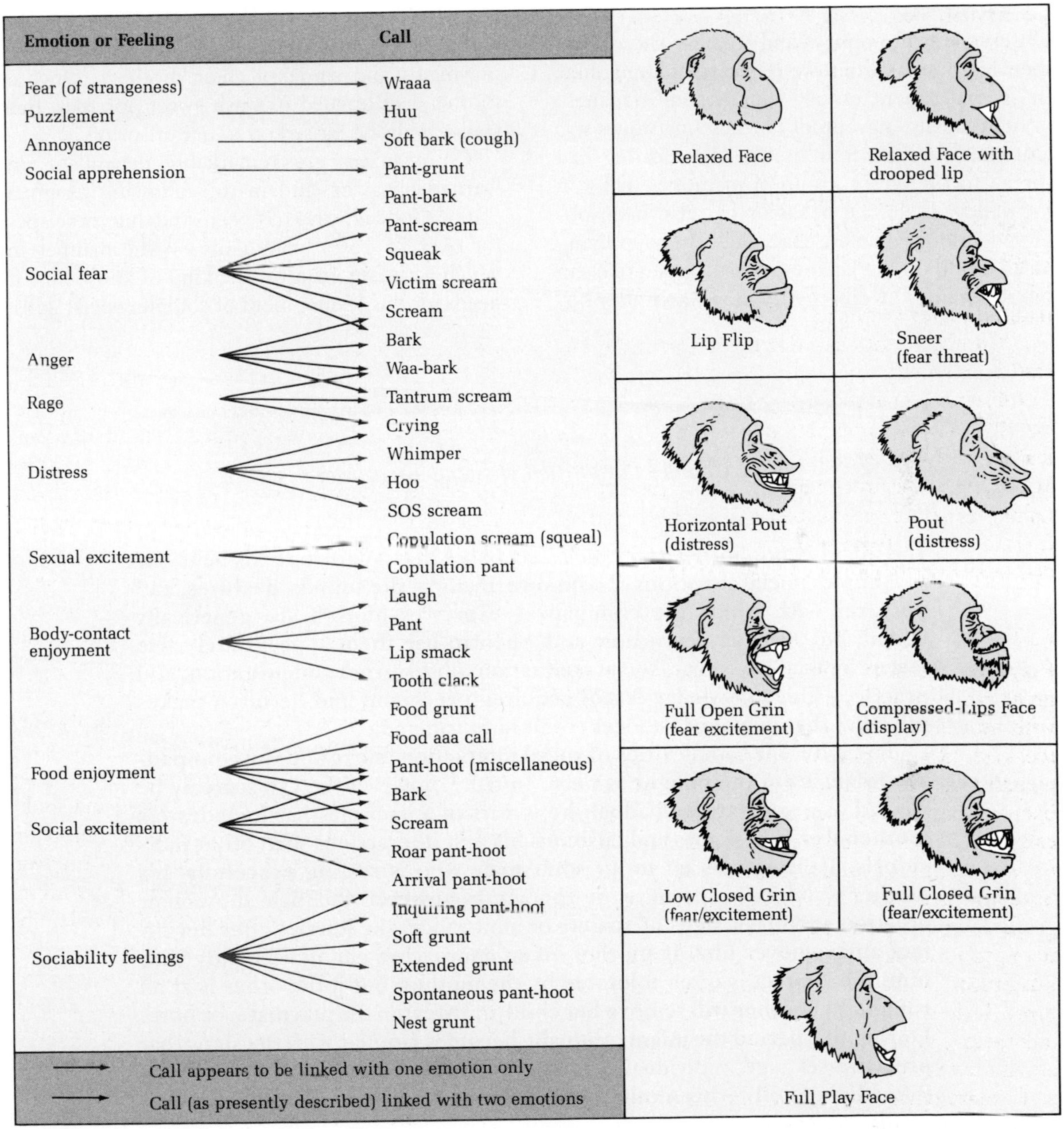

Emotion or Feeling	Call
Fear (of strangeness) ⟶	Wraaa
Puzzlement ⟶	Huu
Annoyance ⟶	Soft bark (cough)
Social apprehension ⟶	Pant-grunt
	Pant-bark
	Pant-scream
	Squeak
Social fear	Victim scream
	Scream
	Bark
Anger	Waa-bark
Rage	Tantrum scream
	Crying
	Whimper
Distress	Hoo
	SOS scream
	Copulation scream (squeal)
Sexual excitement	Copulation pant
	Laugh
Body-contact	Pant
enjoyment	Lip smack
	Tooth clack
	Food grunt
	Food aaa call
Food enjoyment	Pant-hoot (miscellaneous)
	Bark
Social excitement	Scream
	Roar pant-hoot
	Arrival pant-hoot
	Inquiring pant-hoot
	Soft grunt
Sociability feelings	Extended grunt
	Spontaneous pant-hoot
	Nest grunt

⟶ Call appears to be linked with one emotion only

⟶ Call (as presently described) linked with two emotions

Relaxed Face

Relaxed Face with drooped lip

Lip Flip

Sneer (fear threat)

Horizontal Pout (distress)

Pout (distress)

Full Open Grin (fear excitement)

Compressed-Lips Face (display)

Low Closed Grin (fear/excitement)

Full Closed Grin (fear/excitement)

Full Play Face

FIGURE 4.6 Chimpanzee communication.

LEARNING

Observation of monkeys and apes has shown that their learning abilities are remarkably humanlike. In an experiment carried out by some Japanese primatologists, a group of Japanese macaques was fed wheat; within four hours, wheat eating had spread to the entire group of macaques living in the valley. Inventive behavior has also been observed among Japanese macaques. A group living on an island off the Japanese coast learned to clean sweet potatoes by dipping them in water after ob-

serving the young macaque who had first done it. From this youngster, the behavior spread to its playmates and some of their mothers. Once a mother had learned to wash sweet potatoes, this skill was always passed on to her offspring.

Chimpanzees are remarkably dependent on learned behavior, and in the following Original Study, Goodall, who has been studying these apes for over 25 years, comments on the manner in which an infant acquires the kind of knowledge it needs for the development of complex social skills.

ORIGINAL STUDY
A Chimp's Acquisition of Social Knowledge[7]

The infant is not born with built-in responses that will dictate his behavior in complex social situations. To be sure, many of the sounds, gestures, and postures with which the chimpanzee expresses himself are genetically coded, but he must learn how and when to use them appropriately. He learns by trial and error, social facilitation, observation and imitation, and practice. This knowledge is not acquired overnight, and he often makes mistakes that in many instances result in reprimand.

The inherent complexities of social interactions surround the chimpanzee infant from the time he is born. Initially, however, he can scarcely be viewed as a separate individual: he is part of a package that includes his mother also. She shapes and cushions his first interactions with other individuals. If he totters up to an adult male who is resting peacefully, his mother watches but permits the contact. If, however, the male shows hair erection and other signs of anxiety or annoyance, she hurries after her infant and removes him. If another infant approaches and plays gently with him, the contact is often tolerated by the mother; but if the other is at all rough, the mother will remove her child, or threaten the playmate, or both. During this period the infant gradually becomes familiar with the signs that proclaim sex, age, individuality, and mood in those around him. His own immediate family — his mother and siblings — he will of course know best of all.

As he gets older, his mother increasingly permits contact with other individuals and he has more opportunity to experiment with behaviors that previously he has only watched. He may sometimes be mildly rebuffed, but his vigilant mother usually removes him from situations where punishment might be too severe. Moreover, other adults are for the most part highly

tolerant of small infants. His first serious rejections are often administered by his mother herself, and she is seldom overpunitive. Thus his confidence — and knowledge — grow.

As a result of gradually accumulating experience, along with increasing motor skills and independence, he finds out that a given individual, B, is liable to behave differently toward him when he, A, is close to his mother than when he is farther away from her. He discovers that there are things he cannot do — such as taking food from B — unless his mother is nearby, in which case she will protect him from retaliation by B. And so he learns to keep close to her in potentially unsafe social situations. He next finds out that if B's ally, C, is present, he may have to be more cautious even if his own mother is there, unless she is higher ranking than B and C combined. Having mastered this fact, he may discover that when his mother is with her close ally, D (perhaps an adult son or daughter), this coalition may be able to intimidate B + C. He sees that other individuals (such as siblings) may stand in for his mother. He learns their relationships with others, and how this too varies relative to the distance from his (and their) mother; her rank, of course, is still crucial. And so, stage by stage, radiating out from the focal relationships with his mother, he learns more and more about his society.

As a result of these *direct* learning experiences, our youngster should eventually be in a position to respond appropriately in a variety of social situations and to predict the probable effect of his own behavior (and that of his allies) on various individuals. But he must also learn from his role as an observer, from watching interactions between others which, even though neither he nor his all-important mother is involved, may at any moment affect him. If, for example, C attacks D, D may turn and attack A, our chimpanzee pupil, in redirected aggression. If A is able to predict an outcome of this sort, he may be able to avoid such an attack. Moreover, if A can learn, from watching an interaction between C and D, that C is dominant over D, he has obtained some helpful information: he will then know that C will be more useful to him as an ally against D than will D against C (although it may be that A and D, acting together, can intimidate C). Some social events, such as a dominance reversal, can have significant ramifications, and the more A can learn from careful observation of the behavior of others, the greater will be his ability to manipulate his fellows to his own advantage.

In order to acquire and make reasoned use of the kind of information outlined above, the young chimpanzee must have an attention span sufficient to follow long-drawn-out social maneuvers, and he must be able to remember all that he has learned from one occasion to the next. He also needs to know how to integrate information received through different sensory modalities, and how to form concepts. For example, when he hears a pant-hoot in the distance, he needs to relate the sound in some way to the individual who made it and, moreover, have some kind of symbolic representation of the message conveyed. If he has an understanding of the wants, purposes, and emotional attitudes of his companions — a "theory of mind" —

he will be able to anticipate their future behavior and better plan his own. Finally, he must be able to combine his isolated pieces of knowledge, drawing on past experience and surveying the present scene, if he is to respond appropriately to each new encounter.

[7]Jane Goodall, *The Chimpanzees of Gombe: Patterns of Behavior.* (Cambridge, Mass.: Belknap Press, 1986), pp. 568–569. Copyright © 1986 by the President and Fellows of Harvard College.

THE USE OF OBJECTS AS TOOLS

Although neither baboons nor gorillas make or use tools in any significant way, chimpanzees do. Not only do they modify objects to make them suitable for particular purposes, but chimps can to some extent modify them to regular and set patterns. They can also pick up, and even prepare, objects for future use at some other location, and they can use objects as tools to solve new and novel problems. For example, chimps have been observed using stalks of grass, twigs that they have stripped of leaves, and even sticks up to three feet long, to "fish" for termites. They insert the stick into a termite nest, wait a few minutes, pull the stick out, and eat the insects clinging to it, all of which requires considerable dexterity. Chimpanzees are equally deliberate in their nest building. They test the vines and branches to make sure they are us-

able. If they are not, the animal moves to another site.

Other examples of chimpanzee use of objects as tools involve leaves, used as wipes, or as sponges to get water out of a hollow to drink. Large sticks may serve as clubs or as missiles (as may stones) in aggressive or defensive displays. Stones or rocks are also used as hammers and anvils to open palm nuts and hard fruits. Interestingly, the use of tools to fish for termites or to crack open nuts is most often exhibited by females, whereas aimed throwing of rocks and sticks is most often exhibited by males. Such tool-using behavior, which young animals learn from their mothers and other adults in their group, may reflect one of the preliminary adaptations that, in the past, led to human cultural behavior.

HUNTING

The hunting, killing, and eating of small to medium-sized mammals, which is unusual among primates, has been observed among baboons and chimps, but not among gorillas. Such behavior is exhibited less often by baboons than by chimps, who are less opportunistic in their meat eating. Although chimpanzee females sometimes hunt, males do so far more frequently. When on the hunt, they may spend up to two hours watching, following, and chasing intended prey. Moreover, in contrast to the usual primate practice of each animal finding its own food for itself, hunting frequently involves teamwork to trap and kill prey. The most sophisticated examples of this occur

This chimpanzee is using a tool to "fish" for termites.

when hunting baboons; once a potential victim has been partially isolated from its troop, three or more adults will carefully position themselves so as to block off escape routes while another climbs toward the prey for the kill. Once a kill has been made, it is common for most of those present to get a share of the meat, either by grabbing a piece as the chance affords, or by sitting and begging for a piece.

Perhaps limited predation is a very old pattern among chimpanzees. Equally possible, it may be a recent development on the part of chimpanzees living at the edge of the savanna; they may just be starting to exploit a food source that our own ancestors tapped in similar circumstances millions of years earlier. Consistent with this behavior, when out on the savanna chimpanzees are known to increase their predation on eggs and vertebrate animals, probably because they cannot so easily satisfy their amino acid requirements (necessary for growth and tissue replacement) from the plants there as they can from those in the forest.[8] In any case, it is interesting to note that, in primates,

[8]Ann Brower Stahl, "Hominid Dietary Selection Before Fire," *Current Anthropology* 25 (1984): 155.

more cooperation seems to go hand in hand with predation and meat eating.

PRIMATE BEHAVIOR AND HUMAN EVOLUTION

Studies of monkeys and apes living today—especially the gorilla and chimpanzee, which are so closely related to us, and baboons, which have adapted to life on savannas like those to which our earliest ancestors adapted—afford essential clues in the reconstruction of adaptations and behavior patterns involved in the emergence of our earliest ancestors. At the same time, we must be careful about how we reconstruct this development. Primates have changed in various ways from earlier times, and undoubtedly certain forms of behavior that they now exhibit were not found among their ancestors. Furthermore, it is important to remember that present-day primate behavior shows considerable variation, not just from one species to another but also from one population to another of a single species. To ignore such variation is to run the risk of faulty generalization—something often seen in the popular literature.

CHAPTER SUMMARY

The Linnaean system classifies living things on the basis of overall similarities into small groups, or species. The characteristics on which Karl von Linné based his system were body structure, body function, and sequence of bodily growth. Modern taxonomy also utilizes such characteristics as chemical reactions of blood, protein structure, and even the makeup of the genetic material itself.

The modern primates, like most mammals, are intelligent animals that bear their young live and then nourish them with milk from their mothers. Like other mammals, they maintain constant body temperature and have respiratory and circulatory systems that will sustain high activity. Their skeleton and teeth also resemble those of other mammals, although there are differences of detail.

Modern primates are divided into two suborders. The strepsirhines include lemurs, indriids, and lorises, which resemble small rodents in body outline. The haplorhines include tarsiers, New and Old World monkeys, apes, and humans. To a greater degree among the haplorhines, and a lesser degree among the strepsirhines, primates show a number of characteristics that developed as adaptations to insect predation in the trees. These adaptive characteristics include a generalized set of teeth, suited to eating insects and also a variety of fruits and leaves. These teeth are fewer in number and set in a smaller jaw than in most mammals. Other evolutionary adaptations in the primate line include stereoscopic vision, or depth perception, and an intensified sense of touch. Each of these developments had an effect on the primate brain, resulting in a general trend toward larger size and greater complexity. There were also changes in the primate skeleton, in particular, a reduction of the snout, a larger brain case, and numerous adaptations for upright posture and flexibility of limb movement. In addition, changes in the reproductive pattern took place so that fewer offspring were born to each female and a longer period of infant dependency developed.

The apes are the closest relatives humans have. These include gibbons, siamangs, orangutans, gorillas, and chimpanzees. In genetic structure, biochemistry, and anatomy, chimpanzees and gorillas are closest to humans.

The social life of primates is very complex. Primates are social animals, and most species live and travel in groups. Among savanna baboons, females remain for life in the group of their birth, whereas males transfer at adolescence to another. Among chimpanzees, it is females that may transfer, though not all do so; their sons and often their daughters remain with their mothers for life. Among gorillas, either males or females may transfer. In all three species, both males and females are organized into dominance hierarchies. In the case of females, the better food and reduced harassment that are a consequence of high rank enhance reproductive success.

A characteristic primate activity is grooming, which is a sign of closeness between individuals. Among baboons, gorillas, and chimpanzees, sexual interaction generally takes place only when a female is in estrus. Although dominant males try to monopolize females while they are in estrus, the cooperation of the females is usually required for this to succeed. Among baboons, females clearly prefer males with whom they already have a friendship as sex partners. Primates have elaborate systems of communication based on vocalizations and gestures. Usually primates move about within home ranges rather than defended territories.

The diet of most primates is made up of a variety of fruits, leaves, and insects, but baboons and chimpanzees sometimes hunt, kill and eat animals as well. Among chimpanzees, most hunting is done by males, and may require considerable teamwork. Once a kill is made, most animals present get a share of the meat.

SUGGESTED READINGS

Fossey, Dian. *Gorillas in the Mist.* Burlington, Mass.: Houghton Mifflin, 1983. Dian Fossey is to gorillas what Jane Goodall is to chimpanzees. Up until the time of her death, Fossey had devoted years to study gorilla behavior in the field. This book is about the first 13 years of her study; as well as being readable and informative, it is well illustrated.

Goodall, Jane. *The Chimpanzees of Gombe: Patterns of Behavior.* Cambridge, Mass.: Belknap Press, 1986. This magnificent book presents the results of Goodall's 25 years of study of wild chimpanzees living in Tanzania. Because she relates her work to all previous and ongoing research into the behavior of these apes, this can be called the definitive work on chimpanzees. Beautifully written and documented, the book is profusely illustrated.

Jolly, Allison. *The Evolution of Primate Behavior*, 2d ed. New York: Macmillan, 1985. The first edition of this book was the standard text on primate behavior for 13 years. In this as in the original edition, the author surveys current knowledge about primate behavior and its relevance for human behavior. Comprehensive and up to date, the book is also exciting, amusing, and well illustrated.

LeGros Clark, W. E. *History of the Primates*, 5th ed. Chicago: University of Chicago Press, 1966. An old classic, this remains a fine introduction to the comparative anatomy of the primates.

Patterson, Francine, and Eugene Linden. *The Education of Koko.* New York: Holt, Rinehart and Winston, 1981. Several experiments with captive apes have sought to investigate the full potential of their communicative abilities, and one of the most interesting is that involving Koko the gorilla. This is a particularly readable account of those experiments and their results.

An Upper Paleolithic "Laurel leaf" blade from Europe. Beginning about 2.5 million years ago, our ancient ancestors began to make crude but serviceable tools of stone. By 30,000 years ago, by which time anatomically modern humans had appeared, tool making capabilities had improved to the point where some could be considered works of art. For an understanding of what our ancient ancestors were like, we must rely not only on their bones, but also on the things they made.

PART II

HUMAN BIOLOGICAL AND CULTURAL EVOLUTION THROUGH THE OLD STONE AGE

INTRODUCTION

In Chapter 1, we saw how the Nez Perce Indians of North America explained their existence in the world. Indeed, all human cultures of which we have record have grappled with such age-old questions as where do we come from and what is our place in the overall scheme of things? Each culture has answered these questions in its own way, through bodies of myth and folklore, as did the Nez Perce. It was not really until the twentieth century that hard scientific evidence could be brought to bear on these questions. In particular, as physical anthropologists and archaeologists have unearthed the bones and tools of our earliest ancestors, we have begun to glimpse the outline of a fantastic saga in which a tropical-dwelling apelike creature is transformed into a creative being capable of inventing solutions to problems of existence rather than passively accepting what the environment and its own biology dictate.

We begin our discussion of this transformation, in Chapter 5, with a review of the fossil evidence for primate evolution, interpreting the important fossils in light of evolutionary theory, our understanding of the biological variation of modern primates, and the behavioral correlates of that variation. This brings us to the apelike creatures of 8 to 14 million years ago, from some of which human ancestors evolved. These early apelike ancestors seem to have spent more and more time on the ground, and probably possessed mental abilities more or less equivalent to those of a modern chimpanzee. Because they were rather small and vulnerable, we think that the greatest measure of reproductive success came to those who were able to rear up on their hind limbs and scan the savanna, threaten predators with their forelimbs, transport food to a tree or other place where it could be eaten in relative safety, and transport offspring instead of relying on them to hang on by themselves.

Chapter 6 continues the saga of the human transformation by showing how improved mental abilities came to play an important role in human survival. The stage was set for this with the appearance some 4 to 6 million years ago of *Australopithecus*, the first undoubted hominid. *Australopithecus* may best be thought of as an apelike human; it walked bipedally in a fully human manner, but its mental abilities do not seem to have differed greatly from those of its ancestors of a few million years earlier. By 2.3 million years ago, however, some hominids were beginning to manipulate the physical world, inventing solutions to the problems of existence. These earliest members of the genus *Homo* had far smaller brains than ours, but they were significantly larger than those of *Australopithecus*. Their appearance is associated with a new way of surviving. Instead of foraging, as do most primates, on a more or less individualistic basis for vegetables and fruits, supplemented by eggs, grubs, lizards, and similar sources of animal protein, our earliest ancestors invented stone tools with which they could butcher the carcasses of larger animals. This made possible a degree of economic specialization; males scavenged for meat, and females gathered a wide variety of other wild foods. It also made possible new patterns of social interaction; females and males began sharing the results of their food-getting activities on a regular basis.

Over the next nearly 2 million years, a period known as the Paleolithic, or Old Stone Age, the evolving genus *Homo* relied increasingly on improved mental abilities for survival, as we shall see in Chapters 7 and 8. In the process, hunting replaced scavenging as the main means by which meat was procured, and other improvements of this food-foraging way of life took place. As a consequence, the human species, essentially a tropical one, was able to free itself from its tropical habitat and, through invention, adapt itself to colder climates. By 100,000 years ago, humans had acquired essentially modern brains. Shortly thereafter, they achieved the ability to survive under true arctic conditions. To invent ways of surviving under such forbidding and difficult conditions ranks as no less an achievement than sending the first man to the moon.

5

FOSSIL PRIMATES

Our knowledge of the earliest catarrhine primates is based primarily on fossils from Egypt's Fayum Depression, in the desert west of Cairo. Here, winds and flash floods have uncovered sediments over 22 million years old, exposing the remains of a tropical rainforest that was home to a variety of monkeylike animals.

CHAPTER
PREVIEW

When Did the First Primates Appear, and What Were They Like?
The earliest primates had developed by 65 million years ago and were small, arboreal insect eaters. In some ways, they resembled the tree shrews of today. Their initial adaptation to life in the trees set the stage for the subsequent appearance of other primate models.

When Did the First Monkeys and Apes Appear, and What Were They Like?
By the Oligocene Epoch, which began about 38 million years ago, monkeys and apes about the size of modern house cats were living in Africa. By about 20 million years ago, they had proliferated and soon spread over many parts of the Old World. Some forms remained relatively small, while others became quite large, comparable to present-day chimpanzees and gorillas.

What Group of Primates Gave Rise to the Human Line of Evolution?
Present evidence suggests that our own ancestors are to be found among the "ramapithecines," which lived between approximately 17 and 8 million years ago. Small versions of these apelike primates seem to have had the right kind of anatomy, and at least some of them lived in situations in which the right kind of selective pressures existed to transform them into primitive hominids.

A little more than a century ago, Charles Darwin shattered the surface calm of the Victorian world with his startling theory that humans are cousins of the living apes and monkeys and are descended from their prehistoric ancestors. What would have been the public reaction, one wonders, if they had known, as we do, that an even earlier ancestor is thought to have resembled a small squirrel-like tree shrew that possessed a long nose and claws and subsisted chiefly on insects?

Such primitive tree shrews date back about 65 million years. These ancient forebears of ours evolved over time into different species as mutations produced variation, which was acted on by natural selection and genetic drift.

Although many of the primates discussed in this chapter no longer exist, their descendants, which were reviewed in Chapter 4, are to be found living throughout the world. The successful adaptation of the primate line is believed to be due largely to their intelligence, a characteristic that reaches its culmination in human beings and which provides for adaptive flexibility. Other physical traits, such as stereoscopic vision and a grasping hand, have also been instrumental in the success of the primate line.

What is the justification for studying a form of life whose history is, at best, fragmentary, and which existed millions of years ago? The study of these prehistoric primates tells us something we can use to interpret the evolution of the entire primate line, including ourselves. It gives us a better understanding of the physical forces that caused these primitive creatures to evolve into today's primates. Ultimately, the study of these ancient ancestors gives us a fuller knowledge of the processes through which an insect-eating, small-brained animal evolved into a toolmaker and thinker that is recognizably human.

PRIMATE FOSSILS

Considering that primates have shown a tendency through the ages to live in environments where the conditions for fossilization are generally not good, we have a surprising number of fossils to work

Adaptive radiation: Rapid diversification of an evolving population as it adapts to a variety of available niches.

with. While some nearly complete skeletons of ancient primates do exist, more often what we have are specimens of teeth and jawbones, because these structures are durable and are often the only remains of an animal to be found. Thus, a whole branch of fossil study based on tooth structures, or dentition, has arisen. Dentition is most important in helping to identify and classify different fossil forms; often, investigators are able to infer a good deal about the total animal on the basis of only a few teeth found lying in the earth. For example, knowledge of the way the teeth fit together indicates much about the operation of the jaws, suggesting the types of muscles needed. This in turn indicates how the skull must have been shaped to provide accommodation for the musculature. The shape of the jaws and the efficiency of the teeth also define the type of food that they were suited to deal with, indicating the probable diet of the specimen. Thus, a mere jawbone can tell physical anthropologists a great deal about the animal from which it came.

MAMMALIAN EVOLUTION AND PRIMATE ORIGINS

An interesting fact about the evolution of the mammals is that the diverse forms with which we are familiar today, including the primates, are the products of an **adaptive radiation** that did not begin until after mammals had been present on the earth for over 100 million years. Actually, the story of mammalian evolution starts as long ago as 230 to 280 million years ago (Figure 5.1). From deposits of this period, which geologists call the Permian, we have the remains of reptiles with features pointing in a distinctly mammalian direction. These mammal-like reptiles were slimmer than most other reptiles, and were flesh eaters. In a series of graded fossils, we can see in them a reduction of bones to a more mammalian number, the shifting of limbs underneath the body, develop-

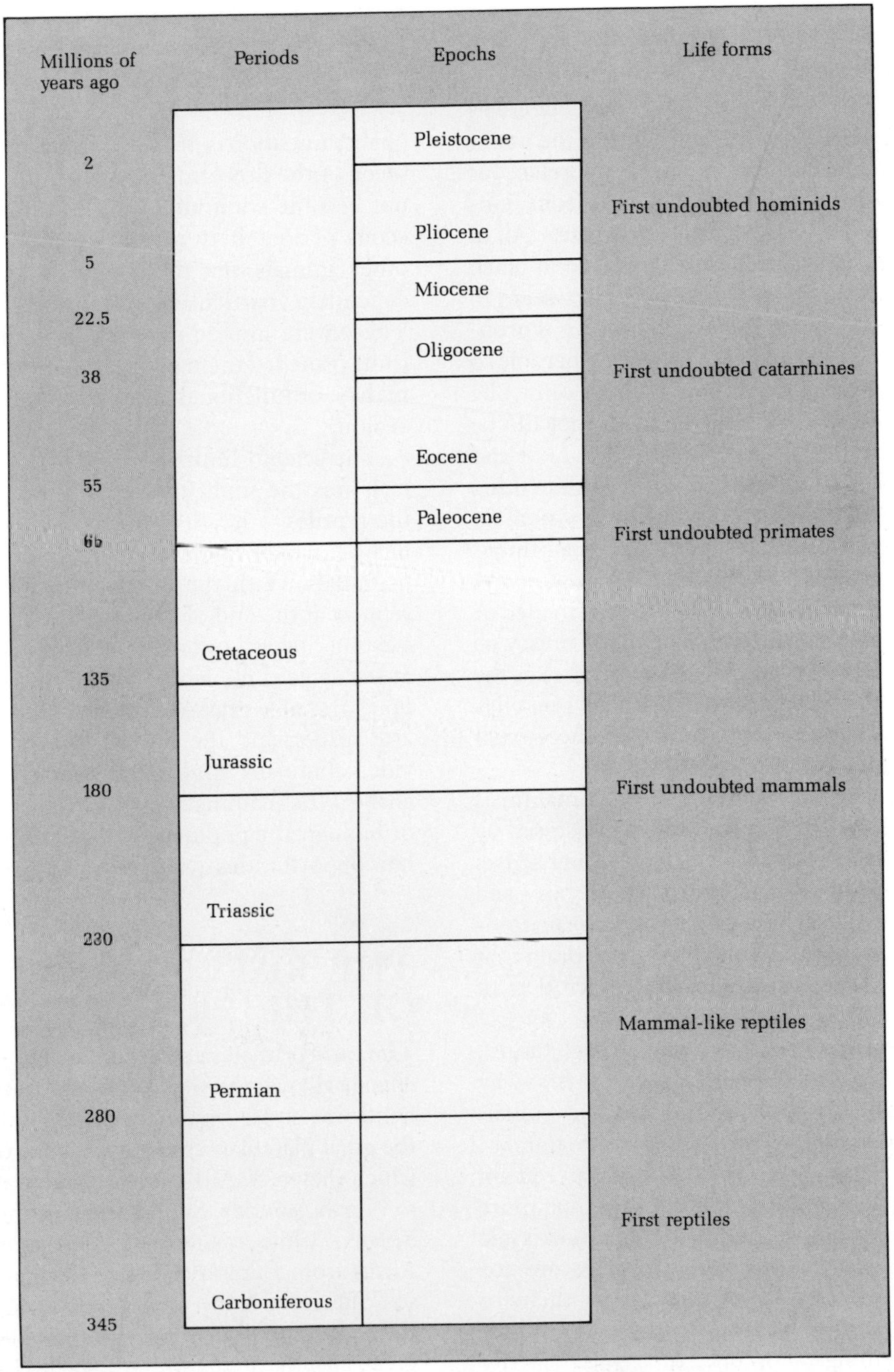

Millions of years ago	Periods	Epochs	Life forms
2		Pleistocene	
		Pliocene	First undoubted hominids
5		Miocene	
22.5		Oligocene	
38			First undoubted catarrhines
55		Eocene	
66		Paleocene	First undoubted primates
135	Cretaceous		
180	Jurassic		First undoubted mammals
230	Triassic		
280	Permian		Mammal-like reptiles
345	Carboniferous		First reptiles

FIGURE 5.1 Major "milestones" in the evolution of the mammals.

ment of a separation between the mouth and nasal cavity, differentiation of the teeth, and so forth.

By 180 million years ago — the end of what geologists call the Triassic period — true mammals were on the scene. We know these and the mammals from the succeeding Jurassic and Cretaceous periods (180 to 65 million years ago) from hundreds of finds of mostly teeth and jaw parts. All of these creatures were small and flesh eaters — such things as insects, worms, and eggs. They seem to have been nocturnal in their habits, which is probably why the senses of smell and hearing became so developed in mammals. Although things cannot be seen as well in the dark as in the light, they can be heard and smelled just as well. Both sound and smell are more complex than sight. If something can be seen it is right there in the line of vision. By contrast, it is possible to smell and hear things around corners and in other hidden places, and in addition to figuring out what it is that is smelled or heard and how far away it is, the animal must also figure out where it is. A further complication is the fact that smells linger, and so the animal must figure out if the cause of an odor is still there or, if not, how old the odor is.

As the hearing and sense of smell of mammals became keener, they lost the ability (possessed by reptiles) to see in color. But the new keener senses and the importance of outwitting both prey and predators served to improve their information-processing capacities and the part of the brain that handles this — the cerebral cortex — over that of reptiles.

Since mammals were developing as such bright, active creatures, it may seem puzzling at first why reptiles continued to be the dominant land animals for over 100 million years. After all, mammals, with their constant body temperature, can remain active at any time, whereas reptiles become more sluggish unless the surrounding temperature is just right. Furthermore, mammals provide care for their young, whereas most reptiles leave theirs to fend for themselves. But the mammals were limited by two things. For one, their high activity demanded more in the way of nutrition than did the less constant activity of reptiles. Such high-

Ecological niche: A species' way of life considered in the context of its environment, including other species found in that environment.

quality nutrition is provided by the fruits, nuts, and seeds of the flowering plants, but these plants did not become common until the end of the Cretaceous period. It is also provided by the flesh of other animals, but the mammals were small and dependent particularly on insects and worms. These were limited in numbers until flowers and fruits provided them with a host of new **ecological niches,** or functional positions in their habitats, to exploit.

The second limitation that affected the mammals was the slight temporal priority enjoyed by the reptiles — they had preempted most available niches, which therefore were not available to mammals. With the mass extinction of so many reptiles at the end of the Cretaceous, a number of existing niches became available to the mammals; at the same time, whole new niches were opened up as the new grasses provided abundant food in arid places, and the other flowering plants provided abundant, high-quality food elsewhere. By chance, the mammals had what it took in the way of biological equipment to take advantage of the new opportunities available to them.

THE RISE OF THE PRIMATES

The early primates emerged during a time of great change all over the world. The separation of continents was under way as the result of movement of the great platelike segments of the earth's crust on which they rest. Although Europe was still joined to North America, South America and India were isolated, while a narrow body of water separated Africa from Eurasia (Figure 5.2). On the land itself, the great dinosaurs had but recently become extinct, and the mammals were undergoing the great adaptive radiation which ultimately led to the development of the diverse forms with which we are familiar today. At the same time, the newly

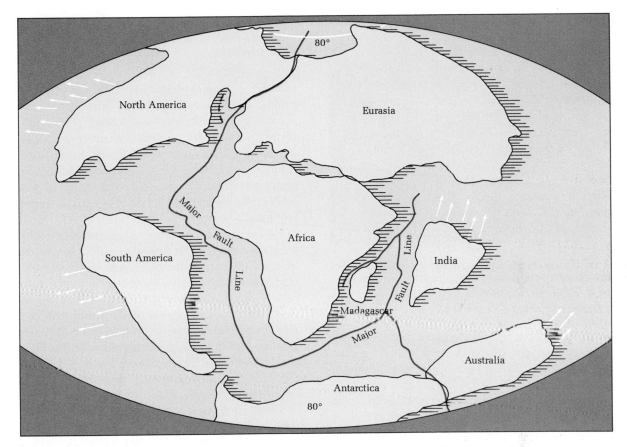

FIGURE 5.2 Position of the continents at end of the Cretaceous period (ca. 65 million years ago).

evolved grasses, ivies, shrubs, and other flowering plants were undergoing an enormous proliferation. This, along with a new, mild climate, favored the spread of dense, lush tropical and subtropical forests over much of the earth, including North and South America, much of Eurasia, and Africa.

With the spread of these huge belts of forest, the stage was set for the evolution of some mammals from a rodentlike ground existence to the arboreal primate condition. Forests would provide our early ancestors with the ecological niches in which they would flourish.

The move to an arboreal existence brought a combination of the problems of earth-bound existence with those of flight. In their move into the air, birds developed highly stereotyped behavior;

tree-dwelling primates, on the other hand, exhibit flexible behavior in response to decision making. The initial forays into the trees must have produced many misjudgments and errors of coordination, leading to falls that injured or killed the individuals badly adapted to arboreal life. Natural selection favored those that judged depth correctly and gripped the branches strongly. It is quite likely that the early primates that took to the trees were in some measure preadapted, with better vision and more dexterous fingers than their contemporaries.

The relatively small size of the early primates allowed them to make use of the smaller branches of trees; larger, heavier competitors, and most predators, could not follow. The move to the

The ability to judge depth correctly and grasp branches strongly are of obvious use to animals as active in the trees as this South American squirrel monkey.

Plesiadapiformes: A primate suborder, now extinct, that includes earliest members of the primate order.

the latter characteristic was reflected in their brains, which were larger than those of the tree shrews they otherwise resembled. Plesiadapiformes, of which there were a number of species, are known from a series of fossils from North America and Europe. Clearly, they were successful animals in their day, for in North America they account for over a third of late Paleocene mammalian fossils.

These creatures were so primitive that biologists were reluctant at first to classify them as primates. One bit of evidence came from an examination of fossilized molars, which are more like those of primates than those of moles and shrews. Moreover, the olfactory region of the brain (the part concerned with the sense of smell) is noticeably smaller than the analogous area of the brain in tree shrews. A final piece of evidence was that the middle ear of plesiadapiformes resembled that of strepsirhine primates.

Plesiadapiformes are thought to resemble the tree shrews of today that, although they look very much like other shrews, differ in that they have seeds in their diet, possess keener vision, and have a larger visual cortex and smaller olfactory area.

smaller branches also opened up a more abundant food supply; the primates were able to gather leaves, flowers, fruits, and insects directly rather than waiting for them to fall to the ground.

The utilization of a new environment led to an acceleration in the rate of change of primate characteristics. Paradoxically, these changes eventually made possible a return to the ground on the part of some primates, including the ancestors of the genus *Homo*.

PALEOCENE PRIMATES

Far back in the reaches of geological time, small, squirrel-like animals resembling today's tree shrews scampered along the branches of trees in tropical forests. Members of the now extinct suborder **Plesiadapiformes,** these creatures appeared during the Paleocene Epoch, about 65 million years ago. They lived mostly on seeds and insects; their muzzles were long and pointed; their ears were small; their wrists and ankles were capable of turning toward each other, enabling them to climb trees; and their digits were flexible and suitable for grasping despite the presence of claws.

Since their survival depended on catching live food, these animals had to be quick and intelligent;

EOCENE PRIMATES

The Eocene Epoch, about 55 to 38 million years ago, was characterized by a warm, wet climate. Numerous new forms of lemurlike and tarsierlike

FIGURE 5.3 Trends in the evolution of the primates. Faces became flatter; crania became larger to accommodate bigger brains; and teeth became more generalized. *Plesiadapis*, a plesiadapiform primate, in some ways resembles today's tree shrew; *Smiledectes* was a strepsirhine with a shorter snout, a larger front portion of the brain, and more forwardly positioned eyes than *plesiadapis*. *Aegyptopithecus* was an Oligocene catarrhine, probably ancestral to later hominoids. *Pliopithecus* was a small ape of the Miocene, while *Proconsul* was a larger Miocene ape ancestral to *Dryopithecus*.

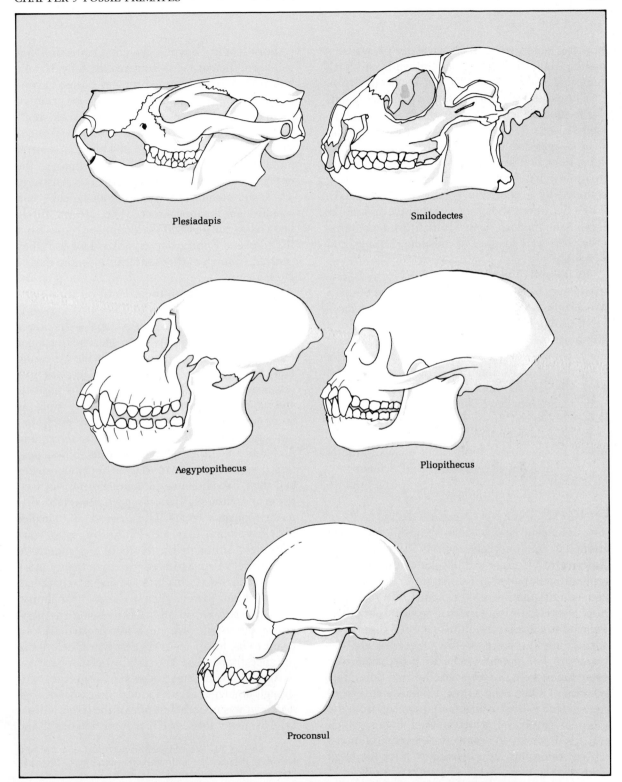

Plesiadapis

Smilodectes

Aegyptopithecus

Pliopithecus

Proconsul

primates emerged to fill a diversity of available niches. Major fossil forms are known from North America, Europe, and Asia, but few from Africa.

The earliest strepsirhines were remarkably similar to modern lemurs, especially in some specialized features of the skull; for example, the brain case is larger than that of plesiadapiformes, there is some reduction of the snout, and the eye orbits are in a somewhat more forward position and are surrounded by a complete bony ring (Figure 5.3). Their dentition, though, was primitive and unlike that of the modern forms. In their limb skeleton, they were well adapted to grasping, leaping, and perching.

By the end of the Eocene, all the North American lemurs became extinct, and the range of those in Europe, Africa, and Asia was reduced considerably. This was probably brought about by a combination of factors. In the late Eocene, many climates became cooler and drier, causing a reduction of environments to which early primates were adapted. At the same time, some early primate niches may have been more effectively used by newly evolved rodent forms. Finally, new types of primates, the precursors of monkeys and apes, may have taken over some other niches formerly occupied by lemurlike and tarsierlike primates.

OLIGOCENE MONKEYS AND APES

The Oligocene Epoch began about 37, and ended about 26, million years ago. At its start, North America and Europe had not yet completed their separation, but northern climates were sufficiently cool and dry that New World and Old World primates were effectively isolated from one another. Primate fossils that have thus far been discovered and definitely placed in the Oligocene are not common, but enough exist to prove that true catarrhines were on the scene by this time. The scarcity of Oligocene primate fossils stems from the reduced habitat available to them and from the arboreal nature of primates then living, which restricted them to damp forest environments where conditions are exceedingly poor for fossil formation.

Fortunately, Egypt's Fayum Depression has yielded sufficient fossils to reveal that, by 31 million years ago, catarrhine primates existed in considerable diversity.[1] Included among one group of them may be the ancestors of the Old World monkeys. These belong to the genus *Parapithecus*, a small primate about the size of a modern squirrel monkey. While the dentition is primitive, the upper molars are monkeylike in their cusp pattern. The lower molars, however, are more apelike than monkeylike in appearance. The earliest surely known fossil of an Old World monkey comes from the Miocene Epoch, but its molars look as if they evolved from an earlier pattern much like that of *Parapithecus*.

Far more apelike in their dentition are a number of other genera, of which the best known is *Aegyptopithecus* (the "Egyptian ape"). Its lower molars have the five cusps of an ape, and the upper canine and lower first premolar provide a shearing mechanism such as is found in apes. Its skull possesses eye sockets that are in a forward position and completely protected by a bony wall, as is typical of modern monkeys and apes, but not lemuriformes. Evidently, *Aegyptopithecus*, and probably the other Oligocene catarrhines, possessed vision superior to that of Eocene primates and their descendants, the lemuriformes. In fact, the inside of the skull of *Aegyptopithecus* reveals that its brain had a larger visual cortex and smaller olfactory lobes than do lemuriformes or tarsiiformes. Although the brain of *Aegyptopithecus* was smaller relative to body size than that of more recent catarrhines, this primate seems to have had a larger brain than any lemuriform or tarsiiform.

Aegyptopithecus, in addition to being the best-known Oligocene primate, is also of particular interest to us, for its teeth suggest that it belongs in the ancestry of those Miocene forms that gave rise to both humans and today's African apes. Although no bigger than a modern house cat, *Aegyptopithecus* was nonetheless one of the larger Oligocene primates. Possessed of a monkeylike skull and

[1] E. L. Simons, D. T. Rasmussen, and D. L. Gebo, "A New Species of Propliopithecus from the Fayum, Egypt," *American Journal of Physical Anthropology* 73 (1987): 139–147.

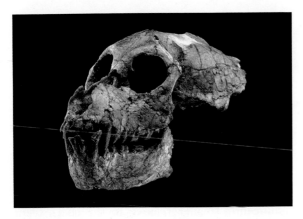

Skull of *Aegyptopithecus*, whose enclosed eye sockets and dentition mark it as a catarrhine primate, probably ancestral to *Proconsul*.

body, it evidently moved about in a quadrupedal monkeylike manner. Differences between males and females include more formidable canine teeth and deeper mandibles (lower jaws) in the males. In modern catarrhines, species with these traits generally live in groups that include several adult females with one or more adult males.

MIOCENE APES

The Miocene Epoch, which succeeded the Oligocene about 26 million years ago, saw the proliferation and spread of apes over many parts of the Old World. These apes probably developed in the forest belt that extended from Africa eastward into Asia.

East Africa is an area particularly rich in the fossils of apes from the early through the middle part of the Miocene. The earliest of these apes, *Proconsul*, is one of the best known, owing to the preservation of much of its skeleton. Species of *Proconsul* varied considerably in size, the smallest being no larger than a small-sized monkey, while the largest was the size of a chimpanzee. That they were apes is clearly shown by their dentition, particularly the five-cusped lower molars. Moreover their skull, compared with that of the Oligocene proto-apes, shows a reduced snout and a fuller, more rounded brain case. Still, some features are reminiscent of

Hominoid: A catarrhine primate superfamily that includes apes and humans.

monkeys, particularly the forward thrust and narrowness of the face.

Although its overall configuration is not quite like any living monkey or ape, the elbow, shoulder, and foot anatomy of *Proconsul* is similar to what one sees in a chimpanzee, while the wrist is monkeylike and the lumbar vertebrae are like those of a gibbon. The consensus is that *Proconsul* represents an unspecialized tree-dwelling, fruit-eating **hominoid** (the catarrhine superfamily to which modern apes and humans belong). Easily derivable from an animal like *Aegyptopithecus*, it was almost certainly ancestral to the hominoids of the middle Miocene. Like its probable ancestor, as well as its descendants, all species of *Proconsul* were sexually dimorphic, the males being larger with more formidable canine teeth.

Hominoids of the middle and late Miocene (from, roughly, 16 million to 5 million years ago) can be divided into two broad groups, informally labeled "dryopithecines" and "ramaphithecines." In the former group are several species of primates having teeth and jaws very much like those of the earlier *Proconsul*. They seem to have become somewhat more apelike rather than monkeylike in their overall appearance, however. Dryopithecines ranged over a remarkably wide geographical area:

Skeletal remains of *Proconsul*, an unspecialized tree-dwelling, fruit-eating hominoid of the early Miocene.

Their fossils have been found in Europe, Asia, and Africa. Such abundance and wide distribution indicates that these primates were very successful animals.

RAMAPITHECINES

Also living in parts of Africa, Asia, and Europe were the various hominoids lumped together as **ramapithecines** (sometimes called "ramamorphs" and sometimes "sivapithecines") (Figure 5.4). Closely related to the dryopithecines, they too may be descendants of the earlier *Proconsul*. According to David Pilbeam, who has made the study of Miocene hominoids his life work: "Any of [the ramapithecines] would make excellent ancestors for the living hominoids: human bipeds, chimpanzee and gorilla knucklewalkers, Orangutan contortionists."[2] For many years, ramapith-

[2]David Pilbeam, *Human Origins.* David Skamp Distinguished Lecture in Anthropology, Indiana University, 1986: 6.

Ramapithecines: A group of hominoids ancestral to orangutans, and probably to chimpanzees, gorillas, and humans as well.

ecines were known exclusively from the remains of teeth and jaws. Relative to the size of the cheek teeth (premolars and molars), their incisor teeth are comparable in size to those of the dryopithecines, although they are placed a bit more vertically in the mouth. The canines are far larger in males, than in females, but even in males, they are significantly smaller relative to the cheek teeth than the canines of any dryopithecine. Still, they do project beyond adjacent teeth so that, when closed, the jaws of ramapithecines interlock. Furthermore, the shearing function of the upper canine with the first lower premolar is retained. The molars, which show the same five-cusp pattern as the dryopithecines, have noticeably thicker enamel. The shape of the tooth row tends to be

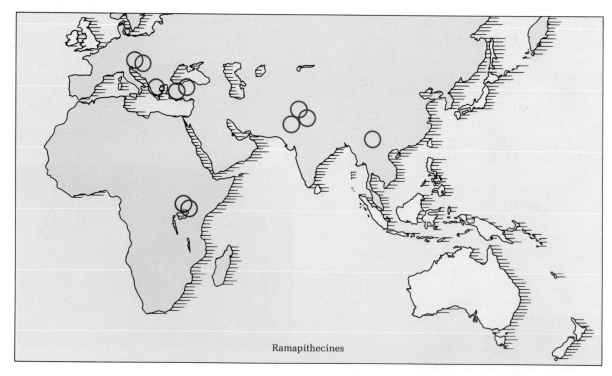

Ramapithecines

FIGURE 5.4 Localities where ramapithecine fossils have been found.

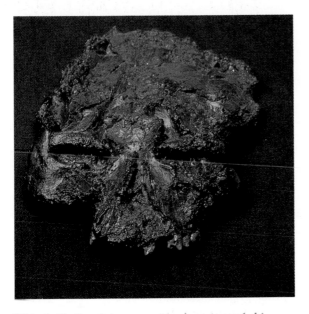

This skull of an Asian ramapithecine is remarkably similar to skulls of modern orangutans, so much so that an ancestor descendant relationship is probable. The last common ancestor of chimpanzees, gorillas, and humans may lie among African ramapithecines.

slightly V shaped, while that of the dryopithecines is more U shaped, with the rows of cheek teeth parallel to one another (Figure 5.5). The palate, or roof of the mouth, is high and arched. Finally, the lower facial region of the ramapithecines is narrow, short, and deep. Overall, the dental apparatus was built for powerful chewing, especially on the back teeth.

In the past few years, our dependence on teeth and jaws for our knowledge of the ramapithecines has lessened as a number of their skull and limb bone fragments have been found in China, Hungary, and Pakistan. In many respects, these are remarkably orangutanlike, even down to small details of the palate.

RAMAPITHECINES AND HUMAN ORIGINS

As long as ramapithecines were known only from fossils of teeth and jaws, it was easy to postulate some sort of relationship between ramapithecines and ourselves. This was because a number of fea-

FIGURE 5.5 The lower jaws of *Dryopithecus* (*A*), an early ape; a ramapithecine (*B*); and *Australopithecus* (*C*) from Laetoli, East Africa. The latter is a hominid who lived nearly 4 million years ago. Relative to the cheek teeth, all have comparably small teeth at the very front of the jaw. There is a general similarity between (*A*) and (*B*), as well as between (*B*) and (*C*). The major difference between the ramapithecine and *Australopithecus* is that the rows of cheek teeth are farther apart in the hominid.

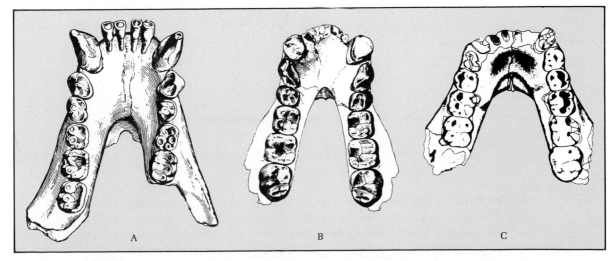

Although not identical, the modern ape most like the ramapithecines is the orangutan. Chimpanzees and gorillas, like humans, have come to differ more from the ancestral condition than have these Asian apes.

Hominid: Hominoid family to which humans belong.

somewhat human direction. Some fossils even show a shallow concavity above the position of the canine tooth, a feature not found in any ape, but often found in humans. indeed, some even went so far as to label ramapithecines as definitely **hominid** (belonging to the human family). With the discovery of orangutanlike skulls and limb bones, however, it became clear that this could not be so, and many anthropologists concluded that ramapithecines could have nothing to do with human origins. Rather, orangutans were seen as the sole modern survivors of an ancient group that had branched off of the evolutionary line that led to the African apes and humans.

Recently, opinion has begun to shift back to a middle position. While the link between Miocene ramapithecines and modern orangutans seems undeniable, this does not rule out the possibility of a link with African apes and humans as well.[3] How anthropologists are reassessing the "ramapithecine problem" is illustrated in the following Original Study by Roger Lewin, who reports on developments in paleoanthropology for *Science*, a journal of the American Association for the Advancement of Science.

tures — the position of the incisors, the reduced canines, the thick enamel of the molars, and the shape of the tooth row — seemed to point in a

[3]Russell L. Ciochon and John G. Fleagle, "Ramapithecus and Human Origins," in *Primate Evolution and Human Origins*, ed. Russell L. Ciochon and John G. Fleagle (Hawthorne, N.Y.: Aldine de Gruyter, 1987), p. 208.

ORIGINAL STUDY
Tooth Enamel Tells a Complex Story[4]

The thickness of the enamel layer on teeth once assumed an especially pertinent diagnostic significance in paleoanthropology: thick enamel permitted entry to the human family (the hominids), thin enamel betokened an ape. This simple equation has crumbled in recent years, and a current pub-

lication by Lawrence Martin, of University College, London, reveals something of the true complexity of enamel morphology.

Tooth enamel in modern humans is thick, which contrasts with the thin coating on chimpanzee and gorilla teeth. The anthropocentric interpretation was that thick enamel represented the specialized, or derived, condition, whereas thin enamel was primitive. The discovery of thick enamel in the australopithecines, fossil hominids that lived in south and east Africa between 4 and 1 million years ago, fitted this preconception. And thick enamel was one of the supposed human attributes of *Ramapithecus*, an ape-like creature that lived in Africa and Asia between 15 and 8 million years ago. *Ramapithecus* is no longer considered by most to be a hominid. Just recently enamel thickness was adduced in support of a proposed ancestral relationship between humans and orangutans, which, unlike their African cousins, have a relatively thick tooth cap.

Martin's work shows, however, that thickness is only one property of enamel that must be examined in taxonomic comparisons: details of enamel formation are also diagnostic. But, most important, thick enamel turns out to be a primitive, not derived, character for the great ape and human group and therefore cannot be used to define hominids, according to Martin's interpretation.

Enamel is deposited in two basic patterns in the teeth of hominoids, the group to which apes and humans belong. The first is a fast mode, which produces a characteristic appearance known as pattern 3 and is primitive for hominoids. The second is a slow mode, whose product is pattern 1 and is derived within the hominoid group.

In gibbons, for instance, a relatively short-lived burst of pattern 3, fast enamel deposition leaves a thin tooth cap. A longer period of maturation in humans builds up thick enamel by the same, pattern 3, growth. Now, chimpanzees and gorillas, like gibbons, have thin enamel, but deposition proceeds in two stages. The bulk (60 percent) of the initial phase is fast growth, but there is an abrupt switch to slow deposition for the remainder. Martin terms this pattern thin, slowed growth, which is developmentally and phylogenetically distinct from the thin, fast pattern in gibbons.

Orangutans, which have intermediate thick enamel, also go through a two-stage deposition, but again it is not homologous with that in the African apes. After the initial fast phase (80 percent of the total), deposition slows to 2.5 μm per day for about 200 μm, and then slows again to the African apes' lower rate for the final 50 μm.

A phylogenetic picture begins to emerge, into which the data for the fossil ape *Sivapithecus* fit very neatly. This creature, which existed in Eurasia and Africa 15 to 8 million years ago and represents the group to which *Ramapithecus* belongs, turns out to have thick, fast-forming enamel, like humans. On the basis of facial morphology, this fossil is considered to be related to the orangutan. Overall, then, the hominoids' primitive dental structure is with thin fast-forming enamel, which is represented today by gibbons. An increase in deposition time produced a derived state of thick, fast-forming enamel, as displayed by the extinct *Sivapithecus*, possibly via intermediate stages. The orangutan evolved a secondary slowing.

The scheme, as interpreted by Martin, now shows that the common ancestor of the African great apes and humans had thick, fast-forming enamel. He considers that the African apes shared a common ancestor, in which the characteristic slowing process developed: both then derived from this ancestor, which had thin, slow-forming enamel. Once again, there may have been transitional forms with intermediate thick and intermediate thin, slow-forming enamel. If true, the identification of putative African great ape ancestors in the fossil record will be facilitated.

Martin's version of the hominoid family tree runs counter to a newly emerging notion, based, among other things, on DNA-DNA hybridization studies: to wit, that gorillas diverged first, leaving humans and chimpanzees briefly to share a common ancestor. This interpretation would require that chimpanzees and gorillas developed their identical slow enamel deposition process independently. Martin considers this to be possible but unlikely. In a recent study of 125 morphological characters in humans and the African apes he concluded that chimpanzees and gorillas form an ancestral group, with humans having split off separately, which is in accord with the enamel data.

[4]Roger Lewin, "Tooth Enamel Tells a Complex Story," *Science* 228 (1983): 707. Copyright 1985 by the AAAS.

That the ancestry of humans may ultimately be among the apelike ramapithecines, then, is consistent with dental evidence. It is consistent as well with resemblances between the shoulder girdle of the earliest undoubted hominid, *Australopithecus* (discussed in the next chapter), and that of orangutans. This suggests that hominids evolved from a primate capable of arm movements like those of orangutans, and the ramapithecines were capable of just such arm movements. Finally, the opinion that ramapithecines are ancestral to hominids as well as today's great apes (Figure 5.6) is in accord with estimates based on molecular similarities and differences between humans, chimpanzees, and gorillas that they could not have separated from a common ancestral stock more than 8 million years ago.[5] We know from the fossils that the

ramapithecines survived until 8 million years ago and also that hominids were going their own separate evolutionary way by at least 4 million, if not 6 million, years ago.

RAMAPITHECINE ADAPTATIONS

Molar teeth like those of the ramapithecines, having low crown relief, thick enamel, and surfaces poorly developed for cutting, are found in a number of modern primates.[6] Some of these species are terrestrial and some are arboreal, but all have one thing in common: They eat very hard nuts, fruits with very tough rinds, and some seeds. This provides them with a rich source of easily digested nutrients that are not accessible to species with thin molar enamel incapable of standing up to the

[5]Roger Lewin, "Is the Orangutan a Living Fossil?" *Science* 222 (1983): 1223.

[6]Richard F. Kay, "The Nut-Crackers — A New Theory, of the Adaptations of the Ramapithecinae," *American Journal of Physical Anthropology* 55 (1981): 141–151.

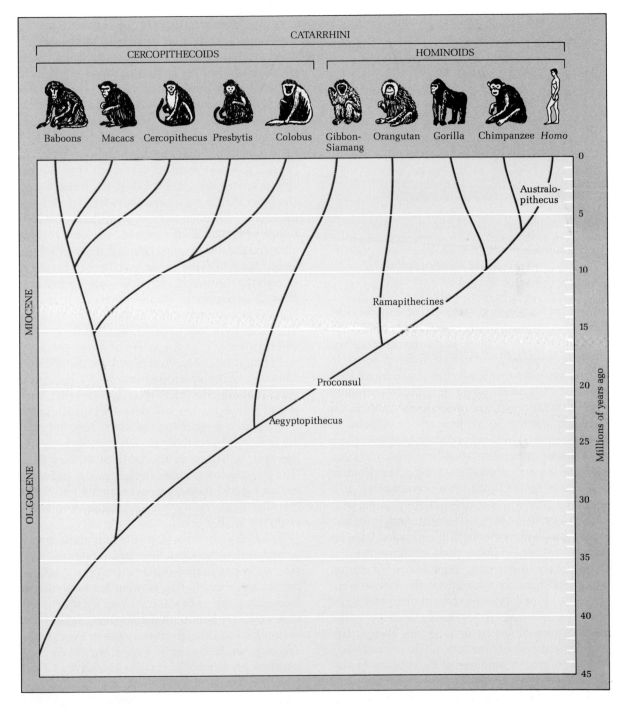

FIGURE 5.6 Although debate continues over details, this chart presents a reasonable reconstruction of evolutionary relationships among the catarrhine primates.

Ground-dwelling primates, like this male baboon, depend heavily on their massive canine teeth for protection from other animals. Ramapithecines, by contrast, lacked such massive weapons of defense.

stresses of tough rind removal or nutcracking. Thus, the ramapithecines probably ate food similar to that eaten by these latter-day nutcrackers.

Analysis of other materials from deposits in which ramapithecine fossils have been found suggests use of a broad range of habitats, including tropical rain forests and drier bush country. Of particular interest to us, from the standpoint of human origins, are those populations that lived on the edge of open country, where food could be obtained through foraging on the ground out in the open as well as in the trees of the forests. As it happened, there was a climatic shift under way, causing a gradual but persistent breaking up of forested areas, with a consequent expansion of open savanna country. Under such circumstances, it seems likely that those populations of ramapithecines living at the edge of the forests were obliged to supplement food from the forest more and more with other foods readily available on the open savannas. Consistent with this theory, late ramapithecine fossils are typically found in association with greater numbers of the remains of animals adapted to grasslands than are earlier ones.

Because ramapithecines already had large, thickly enameled molars, those that had to were capable of dealing with the tough and abrasive foods available on the savanna. What they lacked,

however, were canine teeth of sufficient size to have served as effective "weapons" of defense. By contrast, most modern monkeys and apes that spend much time down on the ground rely heavily for defense on the massive, fanglike canines possessed by the males. Since catlike predators were even more numerous on the savanna then than now, ramapithecines, especially the smaller ones (which probably weighed no more than about 40 pounds[7]), would seem to have been very vulnerable primates indeed. Probably, the forest fringe was more than just a source of foods different from those of the savanna; its trees would have provided refuge when danger threatened. Yet, with continued expansion of savanna country, trees for refuge would have become fewer and farther between.

Slowly, however, physical and behavioral changes must have improved these primates' chances for survival on the savanna. For one thing, those that were able to gather food on the ground and then carry it to the safety of a tree probably had a better rate of survival than those that did not. Although many species of monkeys have cheek pouches in which to carry food, apes do not. Occasionally, modern apes will assume a bipedal stance in order to transport food in their arms, but they are quite awkward about it. The center of gravity, however, is higher in the body of modern apes than it seems to have been in their earlier ancestors so that bipedal food transport may not have been quite so awkward for the ramapithecines, especially the smaller ones.

Food may not have been the only thing transported. Among modern primates, infants must be able to cling to their mothers in order to be transported; since the mother is using her forelimbs in locomotion, either to walk or swing by, she cannot very well carry her infant. Chimpanzee infants, for example, must cling for themselves to their mothers, and even at the age of 4 years, they make long journeys on her back. Injuries caused by falling from the mother are a significant cause of infant

[7]D. R. Pilbeam, "Rethinking Human Origins," ed. Ciochon and Fleagle, p. 217.

A gorilla mother and her offspring. The ability of these apes to carry their infants is limited by their need to use their arms in locomotion.

mortality.[8] Thus, females able to carry their infants would have made a significant contribution to the survivorship of their offspring.

Other advantages of at least the occasional assumption of a bipedal stance would have been the ability to scan the savanna so that predators could be spotted before they got too close. Such scanning can be seen from time to time among baboons and chimps today when out on the savanna, even though their anatomy is less suited for this than the ramapithecines' was. Another advantage of bipedalism would have been the ability to use the hands to wield and throw things at predators. Among primates, "threat gestures" typically involve shaking branches and large sticks, while on the ground, chimpanzees have been observed throwing rocks at leopards. Lacking the large body size and formidable canines of chimpanzees, there is every reason to suppose that the ramapithecines,

when away from the trees and faced by a predator, indulged in the same kind of behavior.

One final incentive to stand bipedally would be to make use of one of the more abundant food sources on the savanna[9] — the thorn bushes that provide edible seeds, leaves, and pods that would have been too high to pick while standing on four (or three) feet; yet, they are too spiny and are not sturdy enough to be climbed.

EARLY APES AND HUMAN EVOLUTION

Although the ramapithecines display a number of features from which hominid characteristics may be derived, and may occasionally have walked bipedally, they were much too apelike to be considered hominids. No matter how much some of them may have resorted to bipedalism, they had not yet developed the anatomical specializations for this mode of locomotion that are seen in the earliest known hominids. Nevertheless, existing evidence allows the hypothesis that apes and humans separated from a common evolutionary line sometime during the later Miocene, and some fossils, particularly the smaller ramapithecines, do possess traits associated with humans. Moreover, the Miocene apes possessed a limb structure less specialized for brachiation than modern apes; this structure could well have provided the basis for the development of human as well as ape limb types.

Clearly, not all ramapithecines evolved into hominids. Those that remained in the forests and woodlands continued to develop as arboreal apes, although, ultimately, some of them took up a more terrestrial life. These are the chimpanzees and gorillas, who have changed far more from the ancestral condition than have the still arboreal orangutans.

[8]C. Owen Lovejoy, "The Origin of Man," *Science* 211 (1981): 344, 349.

[9]Clifford J. Jolly and Fred Plog, *Physical Anthropology and Archaeology*, 4th ed. (New York: Knopf, 1986), p. 216.

CHAPTER SUMMARY

Although the study of comparative anatomy and biochemistry of living animals indicates much about their evolution, the most direct evidence comes from fossils. For animals that have often lived where conditions for fossilization are generally poor, we do have a substantial number of primate fossils. Some are relatively complete skeletons, while most are teeth and jaw fragments.

The primates arose as part of a great adaptive radiation that began more than 100 million years after the appearance of the first mammals. The reason for this late diversification of mammals was that most ecological niches that they have since occupied were not available until the flowering plants became widespread, beginning about 75 million years ago, and the reptiles had already preempted most other niches.

The first primates were arboreal insect eaters, and the characteristics of all primates developed as an adaptation to the initial tree-dwelling environment. While some primates no longer inhabit the trees, it is certain that those adaptations which evolved to a life in the trees were preadaptive to the adaptive zone now occupied by the hominids.

The earliest primates, as represented by plesiadapiformes, had developed by about 65 million years ago in the Paleocene Epoch and were small arboreal creatures. Lemuriformes developed in the Eocene, as did numerous species of tarsiiformes. By the Oligocene Epoch, beginning about 37 million years ago, small catarrhine primates were on the scene. Oligocene fossil finds seem to indicate that monkeys and apes began to head in different evolutionary directions at a very early date. In the Miocene Epoch apes proliferated and spread over many parts of the Old World. Among them were the ramapithecines, which appeared by 16 million years ago and remained until perhaps as recently as 8 million years ago. Although remarkably similar to orangutans in overall appearance, details of dentition suggest that hominids, as well as the modern apes, arose from the ramapithecines. At least some populations of ramapithecines lived where the right kind of selective pressures existed to transform a creature just like it into a primitive hominid. Other populations remained in the forests, developing into today's chimpanzee, gorilla, and orangutan. Of these, the orangutan has changed less from the ancestral condition than have the chimp and the gorilla.

SUGGESTED READINGS

Ciochon, Russell L., and John Fleagle, eds. *Primate Evolution and Human Origins.* Hawthorne, New York: Aldine de Gruyter, 1987. Articles in Part IV of this book summarize current knowledge of early catarrhine evolution, while those in Part V examine the ramapithecines and their possible significance with respect to human origins. Editors' introductions to each section provide the necessary overall perspective on the issues discussed in the articles.

Lasker, Gabriel W., and Robert Tyzzer. *Physical Anthropology.* New York: Holt Rinehart and Winston, 1982. This is a very readable textbook in physical anthropology. The chapter on fossil primates is particularly good, with one of the best descriptions of the Fayum deposits from which so many fossils have come.

Simons, Elwyn L. *Primate Evolution.* New York: Macmillan, 1972. Although beginning to show its age, this volume is still a good survey of humanity's place in nature. An extensive analysis of other primates is presented, followed by a consideration of what differentiates humans.

6

THE EARLIEST HOMINIDS AND CULTURAL ORIGINS

Mary Leakey at work in the field. Through her work, as well as that of Louis and Richard Leakey and other paleoanthropologists working in Africa, hundreds of fossils of hominids that lived over 1.5 million years ago have been recovered.

When Did the First Hominids Appear, and What Were They Like?

By at least 4 million years ago, the first undoubted hominids, known as *Austra-lopithecus*, had appeared. *Australopithecus* was remarkably human from the waist down and had become fully adapted for moving about on the open savanna on its hind legs in the distinctive human manner. But from the waist up, *Australo-pithecus* was still remarkably apelike, with a brain suggesting intellectual abilities roughly comparable to those of a modern-day chimpanzee or gorilla.

Why Had **Australopithecus** *Become a Bipedal Walker?*

Present evidence suggests that the ancestors of *Australopithecus* were small and vulnerable creatures on an open savanna teeming with predators. Bipedal loco-motion would have enabled them to scan the savanna for danger, carry their food to places where it could be consumed in safety, transport their offspring, and grab hold of objects with which to threaten predators.

When and How Did Human Culture Develop?

Human culture appears to have developed as some populations of early homi-nids began making stone tools with which they could butcher animals for their meat. Actually, the earliest stone tools and evidence of significant meat eating date to about 2.5 million years ago, just before the appearance of the genus *Homo*.

When Did Reorganization and Expansion of the Human Brain Begin?

Reorganization and expansion of the human brain did not begin until at least 2 million years after the development of bipedal locomotion. It began in conjunc-tion with scavenging and the making of stone tools. This marks the appearance of the genus *Homo*, an evolutionary offshoot of *Australopithecus*. The two forms appear to have coexisted for a million years or so, during the course of which *Australopithecus* emphasized a vegetarian diet while becoming more robust. In contrast, *Homo* ate more meat and became brainier.

The period between about 7.5 and 4.5 million years ago was one of change; climates became dramatically drier than before, and in Africa, as many species of forest or bush-loving mammals became extinct, several new groups made their appearance. Among the latter was the first undoubted hominid, known as ***Australopithecus.*** Several of its fossils have been found in Tanzania that are almost 4 million years old, and fragments of mandibles from two localities in Kenya suggest that *Australopithecus* may be as much as 6 million years old. What is certain is that *Australopithecus* habitually walked about on two (rather than four) feet and possessed manipulative and dexterous hands capable of using objects as tools. In most other respects, though, it was a most apelike hominid. Despite its ability to walk in a human manner, its behavior patterns otherwise were probably more apelike than human. Nonetheless, by 2.3 million years ago, it had given rise to a new kind of hominid that could not only use tools, but make them as well. The beginnings of brain expansion and stone toolmaking both date from about this time, probably along with some kind of social organization featuring a greater degree of group cooperation and division of labor.

THE EFFECTS OF ENVIRONMENT AND DIET

In order to understand the evolutionary forces at work to produce *Australopithecus*, we must take into account the effects of climatic changes profound enough to cause the temporary drying up of the Mediterranean Sea. On the land, tropical forests underwent reduction or, more commonly, broke up into mosaics where patches of forest were interspersed with savanna or other types of open country. The forebears of the hominid line, probably to be found among the African ramapithecines, lived in places where there was access to both trees and open country. With the breaking up of forests, these early ancestors of ours found themselves spending more and more time on the ground and had to adapt to this new open environment.

Australopithecus: The first undoubted hominid; lived between 1 and 4 or 6 million years ago, and included one (or two) robust species and one (or two) smaller, lightly built species.

The most obvious problem facing these hominid ancestors in their new situation was acquiring food. As the forest shrank, the traditional ape-type foods found in trees became less available to them. Therefore, more emphasis was placed on foraging on the ground for foods such as seeds, grasses, and roots. Associated with this change in diet is a change in their dentition; male canines (used by other primates as defensive weapons) became as small as those of females (Figure 6.1), leaving both sexes relatively defenseless on the open plain and easy targets for numerous carnivorous predators. Many investigators have concluded that the hands of early hominids took over the weapon functions of the reduced canines, enabling them to threaten predators by using wooden objects as clubs and by throwing stones at them. This set the stage for the later manufacture of more efficient weapons from bone, wood, and stone. There is no evidence that the australopithecines ever made stone tools. The earliest known stone tools are at least 1.5 million years younger than the oldest undoubted fossils of *Australopithecus*, nor has anyone been able to establish a link between stone tools and later *Australopithecus* fossils. Considering the number of sites and fossils known (several hundred), this appears to be significant. However, *Australopithecus* certainly had no less intelligence and dexterity than do modern great apes, all of whom are capable of using tools when it is to their advantage to do so.[1] The most adept and inventive tool user in captivity is the orangutan, although chimpanzees are the only apes that have been seen to use tools in the wild — throwing rocks and wielding clubs for defense as just described, but also for such purposes as procuring and processing food (termite probes and "nutting stones," for example).

[1]Roger Lewin, "Why Is Ape Tool Use So Confusing?" *Science* 236 (1987): 776–777.

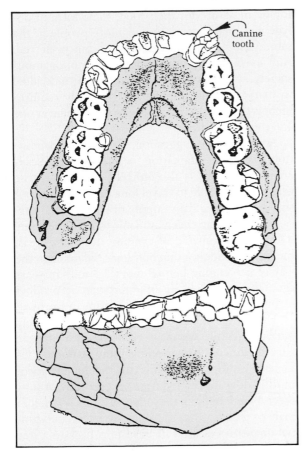

FIGURE 6.1 This lower jaw from Laetoli, Tanzania, is between 3.6 and 3.8 million years old, and belonged to a hominid known as *Australopithecus*. Although its canine tooth projects a bit beyond the other teeth, it is a far cry from what one sees in most other primates.

It is reasonable to suppose, then, that australopithecines were tool users, though not tool makers. Unfortunately, few tools that they used are likely to have survived for a million and more years, and any that did would be unrecognizable as such. Although we cannot be certain about this, in addition to clubs and missiles for defense, stout sticks may have been used to dig up edible roots, and convenient stones may have been used to crack open nuts. We may also allow the possibility that, like chimpanzees, females may more often have used tools to get and process food than males, but the latter may more often have made use of tools as "weapons."[2]

HUMANS STAND ON THEIR OWN TWO FEET

From an apelike carriage, the early hominids developed a fully erect posture; they became bipedal. Ramapithecines seem to have been primates who combined quadrupedal climbing with at least some brachiation and who, on the ground, were capable of assuming an upright stance, at least on occasion. Since no hominid fossils have been found dating from the period of 2 or more million years between the last known ramapithecines and the first known *Australopithecus*, we may assume that those hominid ancestors who did exist during the period were evolving into fully erect bipeds. *Australopithecus* is the first fully bipedal hominid of which we have a record.

Bipedalism, as a means of locomotion, has its drawbacks. For example, it makes an animal more visible to predators, exposes its "soft underbelly," or gut, and interferes with the ability to change direction instantly while running. Nor does it make for particularly fast running; quadrupedal chimpanzees and baboons, for example, are 30 to 34 percent faster than we bipeds. For 100 meter distances, our best athletes today may attain speeds of 34 to 37 kilometers per hour, but the larger African carnivores can attain speeds up to 60 to 70 kilometers per hour. Since all of these would have placed our early hominid ancestors at risk from predators, what, we may ask, made bipedal locomotion worthwhile?

One suggestion that has received a great deal of attention is that it allowed males to gather food on the savanna and transport it back to females, who were restricted from doing so by the dependence of their offspring.[3] This is unlikely, however, in

[2]Jane Goodall, *The Chimpanzees of Gombe: Patterns of Behavior* (Cambridge, Mass.: Belknap Press, 1986), pp. 552, 564.
[3]C. Owen Lovejoy, "The Origin of Man," *Science* 211 (1981): 341–350.

Sufficient parts of the skeleton of "Lucy," a hominid that lived between 2.6 and 3.3 million years ago, survived to permit this reconstruction. Her hip and leg bones reveal that she walked about in a distinctively human manner.

view of the fact that female apes, as well as women among food-foraging peoples, routinely combine infant care with foraging for food. Indeed, among food foragers, it is the women who normally supply the bulk of the food eaten by both sexes. Moreover, the pair bonding (one male attached to one female) required by this model is not characteristic of territorial primates, nor of those displaying the degree of sexual dimorphism that was characteristic of *Australopithecus.* Nor is it really characteristic of *Homo sapiens;* in a substantial majority of recent human societies, including those in which people forage in nature for their food, some form of polygamy—marriage to two or more people at the same time—is not just permitted, but preferred. And even in our own supposedly monogamous society, it is relatively common for one individual to marry two or more others (the only requirement is that one may not be married to them at one and the same time).

A more recent suggestion, that bipedal locomotion arose as an adaptation for nonterritorial scavenging of meat,[4] is also unlikely. While it is true that a biped is able to travel long distances without tiring and that a daily supply of dead animal carcasses would have been available to hominids only if they were capable of ranging over vast areas, there is no evidence that hominids did much in the way of scavenging before about 2.5 million years ago. Thus, it was likely an unforeseen by-product of bipedal locomotion rather than a cause of it.

The causes of bipedal locomotion are probably multiple. While we may reject the idea of male "breadwinners" provisioning "stay-at-home" females as culture bound, it is true that bipedal locomotion does make food transport possible. A fully erect biped out on the open savanna—whether male or female—has the ability to gather substantial quantities of food for transport back to a tree or other place of safety for consumption; the animal does not have to remain out in the open, exposed and vulnerable, to do all of its eating. But food may not have been the only thing transported. As we saw in Chapter 4, primate infants must be able to cling to their mother in order to be transported; since the mother is using her forelimbs in locomotion, to either walk or swing by, she cannot very well carry her infant. Chimpanzee infants, for example, must cling for themselves to their mother, and even at the age of 4 years, they make long journeys on their mothers' backs. Injuries caused by falling from the mother are a significant cause of infant mortality. Thus, mothers able to carry their infants would have made a significant contribution to the survivorship of their offspring,

[4]Roger Lewin, "Four Legs Good, Two Legs Bad," *Science* 235 (1987): 969–971.

and the ancestors of *Australopithecus* would have been capable of doing just this.

In addition to making food transport possible, bipedalism could have facilitated the food quest in other ways. With their hands free and body upright, the animals can reach otherwise unobtainable food on savanna thorn trees too flimsy to climb. Furthermore, with both hands free, they can gather food twice as fast. And in times of scarcity, their ability to travel far without tiring would help get them between widely distributed sources of food. Since the head is positioned higher than in a quadrupedal stance, sources of food and water may be spotted from afar, thereby facilitating their location.

Still other advantages of bipedalism would have enhanced survivability. With their heads well up above the ground, bipeds are able to spot predators before they get too close for safety. Finally, if they did get caught away from a safe place of refuge by a predator, manipulative and dexterous hands freed from locomotion provided hominids with a means of protecting themselves by brandishing and throwing objects at their attackers.

BRAIN REORGANIZATION AND EXPANSION

By 2 million years or so after early hominids became fully bipedal, the size and structure of the brain were beginning to change. Up until about 2.5 million years ago, early hominids lived on foods that were around to be picked or gathered: plants, fruits, invertebrate animals such as ants and termites, and perhaps even an occasional piece of meat scavenged from kills made by other animals. After 2.5 million years ago, meat became more important in their diet, and they began to scavenge for it on a more regular basis.

Since early hominids lacked size and strength to drive off predators or to compete directly with other scavengers attracted to kills, they must have had to rely on their wit and cunning for success. One may imagine them lurking in the vicinity of a kill, sizing up the situation as the predator ate its fill while hyenas and other scavengers gathered,

and devising strategies to outwit them all so as to seize a piece of the carcass. A hominid depending on stereotyped instinctual behavior in such a situation would have been at a competitive disadvantage. One that could anticipate problems, devise distractions, bluff competitors into temporary retreat, and recognize, the instant it came, its opportunity to rush in and grab what it could of the carcass stood a much better chance of surviving, reproducing, and proliferating.

For reasons that will be discussed in Chapter 15, it was probably the early hominid males, rather than females, who did most of the scavenging. What set them up for this may have been the foraging habits of the earlier australopithecines. Dental and skeletal differences between males and females suggest that males may have fed on the ground and lower levels of trees more heavily than females, who had a higher proportion of fruit in their diet.[5] Something like this pattern is seen today among orangutans, where it is a response to highly dispersed resources. As a consequence, males consume larger amounts of low-quality food such as bark than do females. A major difference, of course, is that orangutan males still forage in the forest, whereas male *Australopithecus* did not. In such a situation, the latter may have been tempted to try out supplementary sources of food on the ground, especially if existing sources became scarcer, as they may have; a cold, dry episode has been identified in the crucial period between 2.6 and 2.3 million years ago.[6] Already bipedal, australopithecines were capable of covering, in an energetically efficient way, the vast distances necessary to ensure a steady supply of meat.

As early hominid males increased their scavenging, the females, for their part, continued to gather the same kinds of foods that their ancestors had been eating all along. But instead of consuming all this food themselves as they gathered it, they pro-

[5]William R. Leonard and Michelle Hegmon, "Evolution of P3 Morphology in *Australopithecus afarensis,*" *American Journal of Physical Anthropology* 73 (1987): 61.

[6]Randall R. Skelton, Henry M. McHenry, and Gerrell M. Drawhorn, "Phylogenetic Analysis of Early Hominids," *Current Anthropology* 27 (1986): 31.

vided some to the males who, in turn, provided the females with meat. In order for this sharing to work, the females, like the males, had to "sharpen their wits." They had to plan ahead so as to know where food would be found in sufficient quantities, devise means by which it could be transported to some agreed upon location for division, while at the same time preventing its loss through spoilage, or to such animals as rats and mice. Thus, female gathering played no less important a role in the development of better brains than did male scavenging.

The new interest in meat on the part of evolving hominids is a point of major importance. Out on the savanna, it is hard for a primate with a digestive system like that of humans to satisfy its amino-acid requirements from available plant resources. Moreover, failure to do so has serious consequences: growth depression, malnutrition, and ultimately death. The most readily accessible plant sources would have been the proteins available in leaves and legumes (nitrogen-fixing plants, familiar modern examples being beans and peas), but these are hard for primates like us to handle digestively, unless they are cooked. The problem is that leaves and legumes contain substances that cause the proteins to pass right through the gut without being absorbed.[7]

Chimpanzees have a similar problem when out on the savanna. In such a setting, they spend about 37 percent of their time searching for insects like ants and termites on a year-round basis, while at the same time increasing their predation on eggs and vertebrate animals. Such animal foods not only are easily digestible, but they provide high-quality proteins that contain all the essential amino acids in just the right percentages. No one plant food does this by itself; only if the right combination is consumed can plants provide what meat does by itself in the way of amino acids. Moreover, there is abundant meat to be had on the savanna. All things considered, then, we should not be surprised if our own ancestors solved their

Homo habilis: Earliest representative of the genus *Homo*; lived between 2.3 and 1.8 million years ago. Compared with *Australopithecus*, characterized by expansion and reorganization of the brain.

Homo erectus: Members of the genus *Homo*, which immediately precede *Homo sapiens*.

"protein problem" in somewhat the same way that chimpanzeess on the savanna do today.

Increased meat consumption on the part of early hominids did more than merely ensure an adequate intake of essential amino acids, important though this was. Animals that live on plant foods must eat large quantities of vegetation, and obtaining such foods consumes much of their time. Meat eaters, by contrast, have no need to eat so much, or so often. Consequently, meat-eating hominids may have had more leisure time available to explore and manipulate their environment; like lions and leopards, they would have time to spend lying around and playing. Such activity, coupled with the other factors already mentioned, probably was a stimulus to hominid brain development.

The importance of meat eating for early hominid brain development is suggested by the size of hominid brains: The size of the inside of the braincase (cranial capacity) of the largely plant-eating *Australopithecus* ranged from 380 to 530 cubic centimeters; that of the most primitive known meat eater, **Homo habilis** from East Africa, ranged from 580 to 775 cubic centimeters; whereas **Homo erectus**, who hunted as well as scavenged for meat, possessed a cranial capacity of 775 to 1225 cubic centimeters.

THE EARLIEST SIGNS OF CULTURE: TOOLS

The use of specially made tools of stone appears to have arisen as a result of the need for implements to butcher and prepare meat, because hominid teeth were inadequate for the task. Even chimpanzees, whose canine teeth are far larger and sharper, frequently have trouble tearing through the skin of other animals.[8] In addition to overcoming this

---

[7]Ann Brower Stahl, "Hominid Dietary Selection before Fire," *Current Anthropology* 25 (1984): 151–168.

[8]Goodall, p. 372.

problem, the manufacturing of stone tools must have played a role in the evolution of the human brain, first by putting a premium on manual dexterity and fine manipulation, as opposed to hand use emphasizing power rather than precision. This in turn put a premium on improved organization of the nervous system. Second, the transformation of a lump of stone into a "chopper," "knife," or "scraper" is a far cry from what a chimpanzee does when it transforms a stick into a termite probe. While the probe is not unlike the stick, the stone tool is unlike the lump of stone. Thus, the toolmaker must have in mind an abstract idea of the tool to be made as well as a specific set of steps that will accomplish the transformation. Furthermore, only certain kinds of stone have the flaking properties that will allow the transformation to take place, and the toolmaker must know about these.

COOPERATION AND SHARING

With an apelike brain and a diet like that of monkeys and apes when out on the savanna, *Australopithecus* probably behaved much like other hominoids. Like apes, adults probably foraged for their own food, which was rarely shared with other adults. Among modern apes, however, there is one notable exception to this behavior: Although adult chimpanzees rarely share plant food with one another, males almost always share meat, frequently with females.[9] Thus, increased consumption of meat on the part of *H. habilis* may have promoted even more sharing among adults. Moreover, a regular supply of meat would have required that substantial amounts of time and energy be devoted to the search for carcasses, and food gathered by females and shared with males could have provided the latter with both.

Sharing and cooperation between the sexes need not necessarily have been between mated males and females, but may just as well have been between brothers and sisters and mothers and sons. On the other hand, the ability to engage in sexual activity at any time on the part of females may have promoted sharing and cooperation be-

[9]Ibid.

Fossil bone fragments are assembled in a laboratory where they are inspected for cut and gnaw marks. These marks may indicate how the animal was killed, butchered, and eaten.

tween a male and one or more sex partners, for among most catarrhine primates, males attempt to monopolize females when the latter are at the height of sexual receptivity. As discussed in Chapter 17, the ability to engage in sex at any time that is characteristic of the human female alone among the primates probably was an incidental by-product of bipedal locomotion; hence, it should have been characteristic of the earliest hominids.

Although chimpanzees can and do hunt alone, they frequently cooperate in the task. In the case of *H. habilis*, cooperation would seem to have been even more crucial to success in scavenging. It is hard to imagine a creature lacking the formidable canines of a chimpanzee competing on an individual basis with carnivores far more powerful than itself.

In summary, then, it seems reasonable to assume that *H. habilis* engaged in more sharing and cooperative behavior than one sees among present-day chimpanzees. How much more is certainly not known, and probably fell far short of what has been observed among any historically known food-foraging peoples. After all, *H. habilis* was not just a different sort of hominid from *Australopithecus*; it was different from *H. sapiens* as well.

FOSSIL EVIDENCE

Until recently, the fossil evidence of the early stages of human evolution under discussion here has been both sparse and tenuous. In the 1960s, however, there began a rush of paleoanthropologists into the field. Numerous international expeditions, including over 100 researchers from Belgium, Great Britain, Canada, France, Israel, Kenya, the Netherlands, and the United States, have swarmed over parts of East Africa, where they have unearthed more fossil remains in 25 years than had been unearthed previously. So much material, coming all at once, has been difficult to digest, and our ideas of hominid evolution are constantly being revised. Nonetheless, there is widespread agreement over the broad outline, even though debate continues over details. What is clear is that the course of hominid evolution has not been a simple, steady "advance" in the direction of modern humanity. Rather, it appears that at least three divergent lines evolved in the past.

AUSTRALOPITHECUS

In 1924, an unusual fossil was brought to the attention of Professor Raymond Dart of the University of Witwatersrand in Johannesburg; it was the cranium of an animal unlike any he had ever seen before in South Africa. Recognizing in this unusual fossil a fascinating mixture of simian and hominid characteristics, anatomist Dart named his discovery *Australopithecus africanus*, or southern ape of Africa. Based on the position of the foramen magnum, the large hole in the skull where the spinal cord enters, Dart claimed that *Australopithecus* was probably a biped.

Since Dart's original find, hundreds of other fossils of *Australopithecus* have been found, first in South Africa and then in Tanzania, Kenya, and Ethiopia (Figure 6.2). As they were discovered, many were given a number of different specific and generic names, but all are now considered to belong to the single genus *Australopithecus*. On the other hand, most anthropologists recognize at least two species of the genus: *A. africanus* and

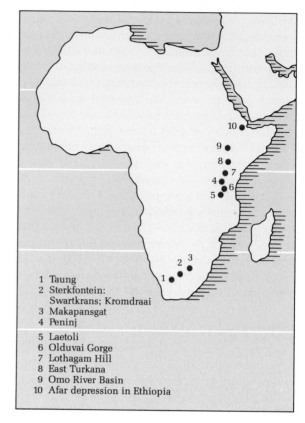

1 Taung
2 Sterkfontein: Swartkrans; Kromdraai
3 Makapansgat
4 Peninj

5 Laetoli
6 Olduvai Gorge
7 Lothagam Hill
8 East Turkana
9 Omo River Basin
10 Afar depression in Ethiopia

FIGURE 6.2 Australopithecine localities in Africa.

■ **Gracile:** Small and lightly built.

A. robustus. Some refer to this latter as *A. boisei*, while others would reserve this name for a third, super-robust species. Finally, a fourth species, *A. afarensis*, has been proposed for the earliest *Australopithecus* fossils from the Afar Depression of Ethiopia and Laetoli, in Tanzania.

Despite differences of opinion over the exact number of species, it is generally agreed that there were basically two kinds of *Australopithecus*. One, represented by *A. robustus* and *A. boisei*, was heavy with a robust frame and jaws that are massive, relative to the size of the brain case. The other, represented by *A. africanus* and *A. afarensis*, was smaller and more lightly built, or **gracile.**

Gracile Australopithecines

The gracile form of *Australopithecus* is well known from numerous fossils found in the 1930s and 1940s at Sterkfontein and Makapansgat in South Africa. These are included today in the species *A. africanus*. In the 1970s, parts of between 35 and 64 gracile australopithecines that date between 2.9 and 3.2 million years ago were found in northern Ethiopia's Afar region. These include the famous "Lucy," represented by bones from almost all parts of a single skeleton, and "the First Family," a collection of bones from at least 13 individuals of both sexes, ranging in age from infancy to adulthood, that died together as a result of some single calamity.

Similar material, close to 4 million years old, has been found by a team led by Mary Leakey at Laetoli, in Tanzania. The name *A. afarensis* has been proposed to refer to both, although there has been debate about this. Some have interpreted the wide variation exhibited by the *afarensis* specimens as indicative of the presence of two separate species. Two recent studies, however, support the single-species hypothesis,[10] and indicate that *afarensis* was sexually dimorphic, with the males about twice the size of females. In this respect, they were like the Miocene apes and all recent great apes except chimpanzees, whose males are only one third bigger than females. Predictably, these early australopithecines are a bit more primitive than the South African fossils, which, although not securely dated, appear to be not quite so old. Whether this is sufficient to justify a different species name is questionable; clearly, both are variants of the gracile form.

Other pieces of gracile australopithecines have been found at other East African sites that generally are 2 million or more years old. The oldest of all may be fragments of jaws from two sites in Kenya which are 5.5 and 6 million years old. Unfortunately, they are too fragmentary to be absolutely sure that they are *Australopithecus*.

The gracile australopithecines were erect, bipedal hominids about the size of modern pygmies, though far more powerfully built. Their stature ranged between 3.5 and 5 feet, and they are estimated to have weighed between 60 and 150 pounds. Their physical appearance was unusual by our standards: They have been described as looking like an ape from the waist up and like a human from the waist down. Their cranium was relatively low, the forehead sloped backward, and the brow ridge that helps give apes such massive-looking foreheads was also present. The lower half of the face was chinless and accented by jaws that were quite large, relative to the size of the skull.

Much has been written about *Australopithecus* teeth. Speaking generally, gracile *Australopithecus* possessed small incisors, short canines in line with adjacent teeth, and a rounded dental arch. The molars and premolars are larger in size but similar in form to modern human teeth (Figure 6.3). The molars are unevenly worn; the upper cheek teeth are worn from the inside, and the lower cheek teeth are worn from the outside. This indicates that gracile *Australopithecus* chewed food in a hominid fashion, even though it was probably capable of two to four times the crushing force of modern human beings. There is no gap between the canines and the teeth next to them on the upper jaw, a trait common in apes. Further, the large mandible is very similar to that of the later hominid, *H. erectus*.

As one might expect, these features are most evident in the later fossils of gracile *Australopithecus*; the earlier ones, from Ethiopia and especially from Laetoli, show numerous features reminiscent of the late Miocene ramapithecines which the later ones do not (see Figure 5.5). Generally, the incisors and canines are a bit larger in the earlier ones, the canines tend to project noticeably, the first lower premolars are less like molars and show more shearing wear, and the dental arch is less rounded. One jaw from Laetoli even shows a partial interlock of upper canines with lower canines and premolars. All of this strongly suggests a ramapithecinelike ancestor for gracile *Australopithecus* back in Miocene times.

[10]Leonard and Hegmon, p. 60.

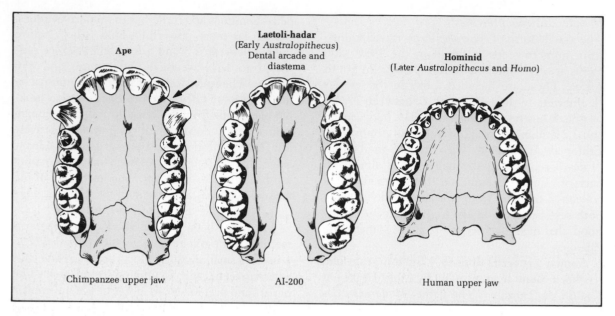

FIGURE 6.3 Upper jaws of an ape, *Australopithecus*, and modern human. Only in the earliest australopithecines can a diastema be seen.

In addition to differences in the teeth between earlier and later forms, there were also differences between the sexes. In gracile *Australopithecus*, for example, there is a clear evolutionary trend for the first lower premolar of males to become more molarlike, through development of a second cusp. Those of females, by contrast, do not. Such differences are to be expected if male and female foraging patterns were not quite the same; for example, if females got more of their food from the trees, while males consumed large amounts of lower-quality food found on or near the ground. Consistent with this, some features of the skeleton are somewhat more apelike and better suited to climbing in females than in males.[11]

Although the brain is small and apelike and the general conformation of the skull seems non-human, the foramen magnum of *Australopithecus* is placed forward and is downward looking, as it is in later bipedal hominids of the **genus *Homo***. Cranial capacity, frequently used as an index of brain

> **Genus *Homo*:** Hominid genus characterized by expansion of brain and reduction of jaws; includes three species: *habilis*, *erectus*, and *sapiens*.

volume, varied from 350 to 485 cubic centimeters, which is roughly the size of a large chimpanzee brain and about a third the size of a modern human brain. Intelligence, however, is not indicated by absolute brain size alone, but is roughly indicated by the ratio of brain to body size. Unfortunately, with such a wide range of adult weights it is not clear whether brain size was larger than an ape's relative to body size. Although some researchers think they see evidence for some expansion of the brain, others vigorously disagree. Moreover, the outside appearance of the brain, as revealed by natural casts of the inside of the skull, is more apelike than human, suggesting that cerebral reorganization toward a human condition had not yet occurred.[12] At the moment, the weight of the evidence favors mental capabilities on the part of

[11]Elwyn L. Simons, "Human Origins," *Science* 245 (1989): 1346.

[12]Dean Falk, "Ape-like Endocast of 'Ape-man' Taung," *American Journal of Physical Anthropology* 80 (1989): 339.

This comparison of two skulls illustrates the degree of sexual dimorphism exhibited by australopithecines about 2 million years ago. Earlier australopithecines were equally dimorphic.

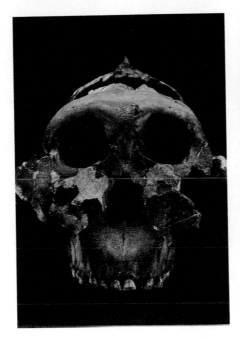
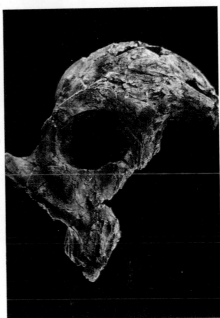

gracile *Australopithecus* as being comparable to those of modern great apes.

The fossil remains of gracile *Australopithecus* have provided anthropology with two striking facts. First, as early as 4 million years ago, this hominid was bipedal, walking erect. This is indicated, first of all, by the curvature of the spine, which is like that of humans and unlike that of apes. This served to place the center of gravity over, rather than in front of, the hip joint. In addition, an upper arm bone from "Lucy," which is shorter than that of an ape, suggests that the upper limb was lighter and the center of gravity lower in the body than in apes. Still, gracile australopithecines had longer forearms than *Homo*, the shoulder girdle was more adapted to arboreal performance, and fingers and toes show more curvature. Such traits suggest that *Australopithecus* still engaged in a significant amount of tree climbing.

Bipedal locomotion is also indicated by a number of leg and hip remains (Figure 6.4). There is general agreement that these are much more human than apelike. In fact, a trait-by-trait comparison of individual bones shows that *Australo-*pithecus frequently falls within the range of modern *Homo*, even though the overall configuration is not exactly the same. But the most dramatic confirmation of *Australopithecus'* walking ability comes from Laetoli, where, nearly 4 million years ago, two individuals walked across newly fallen volcanic ash. Because it was damp, the ash took the impressions of their feet and these were sealed beneath subsequent ash falls until discovered by Dr. Paul Abell in 1978. The shape of the footprints, the linear distance between the heels where they struck, and the amount of "toe out" are all fully human.

The second striking fact provided by the gracile *Australopithecus* is that hominids acquired their erect bipedal position long before they acquired their highly developed and enlarged brain. Not only is the latter more apelike than human in its size and structure, but it is now evident that *Australopithecus* did not have prolonged maturation as do modern humans; instead, they grew up rapidly like apes.[13] Thus, no matter how important bipedal locomotion may have been in setting the

[13]Simons, p. 1344.

FIGURE 6.4 Upper hip bones and lower limbs of *Homo sapiens*, *Australopithecus*, and an ape (the reconstruction of the australopithecine limb is based on the knee joint shown in the photograph above). The similarities of the human and australopithecine bones are striking and are indicative of bipedal locomotion.

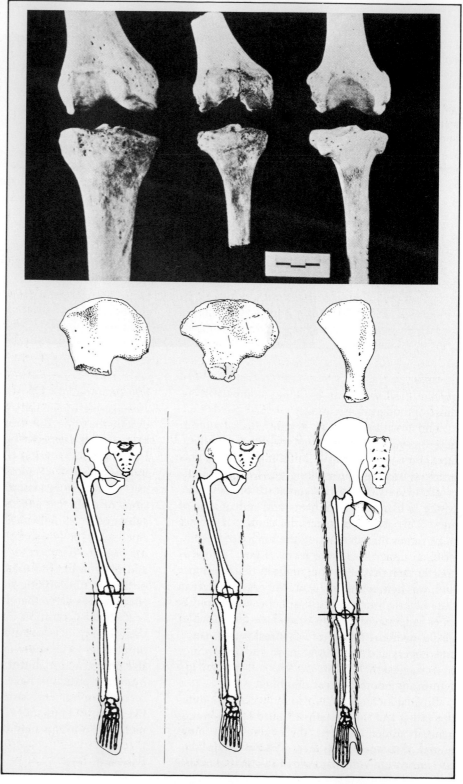

stage for the later expansion and elaboration of the human brain, it cannot by itself account for those developments.

Robust Australopithecus

The remains of what is now known as *A. robustus* were first found at Kromdraai and Swartkrans in South Africa by Robert Broom and John Robinson in 1948 in deposits that, unfortunately, cannot be securely dated. Current thinking puts them anywhere from 1.5 to 2 million years ago.

A. robustus shared practically all of the traits listed for gracile *Australopithecus*, especially *A. africanus* from South Africa. *A. robustus* was much larger than *africanus*, regularly weighing over 80 pounds. The bones of its body were thick for their size, with prominent markings where their muscles attached. The skull of *A. robustus* was thicker and larger than that of *africanus*, with a slightly larger cranial capacity (500 cubic centimeters).

The *robustus* form possessed a skull with a simianlike sagittal crest running from front to back along the top of the skull. This feature provides sufficient area on a relatively small braincase for attachment of the huge temporal muscles required to operate powerful jaws, such as both gorillas and *A. robustus* possessed, and is an example of convergent evolution in gorillas and hominids.

The first robust *Australopithecus* found in East Africa was discovered by Mary Leakey in the summer of 1959, the centennial year of the publication of Darwin's *On the Origin of Species* She found it in Olduvai Gorge, a fossil-rich area near Ngorongoro Crater, on the Serengeti Plain of East Africa. Olduvai, sometimes called the "Grand Canyon" of East Africa, is a huge gash in the earth, about 25 miles long and 300 feet deep, which cuts through Pleistocene and recent geological strata revealing close to 2 million years of the earth's history.

Mary Leakey's discovery was reconstructed and studied by her husband, Louis, who gave it the name *"Zinjanthropus boisei."* At first, he thought this hominid seemed more advanced than *Australopithecus* and extremely close to modern humans in evolutionary development. Further study, however, revealed that *"Zinjanthropus,"* the remains of

which consisted of a skull and a few limb bones, was an East African variety of *Australopithecus*. Consequently, the designation often given this species is *A. boisei*; it has also been classified as a variant of *A. robustus*. Potassium–argon dating places this early hominid at about 1.75 million years old.

Since the time of Mary Leakey's original find, numerous other fossils of robust *Australopithecus* have been found at Olduvai, as well as north and east of Lake Turkana in Ethiopia and Kenya. While one is known to be as much as 2.5 million years old, some date to as recently as 1 million years ago.

The size of the teeth and certain cranial features indicate that *A. boisei* is probably related to *A. robustus*; they could even be regional variants of a single species. Molars and premolars are enormous, as is the palate. The heavy skull, more massive even than its robust South African relative's, has a sagittal crest and prominent brow ridges; cranial capacity ranges from about 506 to 530 cubic centimeters. In short, *A. boisei* is a super-robust australopithecine, but whether one should refer to it as an extreme version of *A. robustus* or as a separate robust species of *Australopithecus* is not settled.

Although debate continues over details, anthropologists generally agree that robust *Australopithecus* evolved from earlier gracile ancestors. In many respects, the two forms are scaled versions of the same animal, differing in size rather than design. Among mammals, including primates, larger size brings with it larger brains, but brain size increases at a slower rate than body size. In fact, brain size in robust *Australopithecus* is just what it should be in an enlarged version of *A. africanus*. Another consequence of larger size is that relatively larger cheek teeth (molars and premolars) are required to process the extra food needed to sustain the animal. Because body size (volume) increases by the cube power, while tooth surface (area) increases by the square power, tooth size has to increase at a faster rate than body size, or the teeth will not be sufficient for the larger animal. In robust australopithecines, the cheek teeth are both absolutely and relatively larger than in *A. africanus*, as expected,

Louis S. B. Leakey (1903–1972)
Mary Leakey (1913–19)

Few figures in the history of paleoanthropology have discovered so many key fossils, received so much public acclaim, or stirred up as much controversy as Louis Leakey and his second wife, Mary. Born in Kenya of missionary parents, Louis received his early education from an English governess, and subsequently was sent to England for a university education. He returned to Kenya in the 1920s to begin his career there.

It was in 1931 that Louis and Mary began working in their spare time at Olduvai Gorge in Tanzania, searching patiently and persistently for remains of early hominids. It seemed a good place to look, for there were numerous animal fossils, as well as crude stone tools lying scattered about on the ground and eroding out of the walls of the gorge. Their patience and persistence were not rewarded until 1959, when Mary found the first hominid fossil. A year later, another skull was found, and Olduvai was on its way to being recognized as one of the most important sources of hominid fossils in all of Africa. While Louis reconstructed, described,

and interpreted the fossil material, Mary made the definitive study of the Oldowan tools.

The Leakeys' important discoveries were not limited to those at Olduvai. In the early 1930s, they found the first *Dryopithecus* fossils in Africa at Rusinga Island in Lake Victoria. Also in the 1930s, Louis found a number of skulls at Kanjera, Kenya, which show a mixture of modern and more primitive features. In 1961, at Fort Ternan, Kenya, the Leakeys found the first ramapithecine remains in Africa. Most recently, a member of an expedition led by Mary Leakey found the first footprints of *Australopithecus*, at Laetoli, Tanzania. In addition to all of this, Louis Leakey promoted a good deal of important work on the part of others. He made it possible for Jane Goodall to begin her landmark field studies of chimpanzees; and later on, he was instrumental in getting similar studies started among gorillas and orangutans.

Louis Leakey had a flamboyant personality and a way of making interpretations of fossil materials that frequently did not stand up very well to careful scrutiny, but this did not stop him from publicly presenting his views as if they were the gospel. It was this aspect of the Leakeys' work that generated controversy. Nonetheless, the Leakeys accomplished and promoted more work that resulted in the accumulation of knowledge about human origins than anyone before them. Anthropology clearly owes them a great deal.

---

and by the same degree as can be seen in smaller and larger forms of living great apes. Larger teeth require more bone to support them, hence the prominent jaws of the robust form. Finally, the larger jaws and the chewing of more food require more in the way of jaw musculature which attaches to the skull. The marked crests seen on the skulls of robust australopithecines provide for the attachment of such a musculature on a skull that has increased very little in size. In sum, most of the distinctive features of the robust form can be accounted for as necessities to preserve the function

of the smaller prototype, given an increase in size.

Anthropologist David Pilbeam and paleontologist Stephen Jay Gould, who have observed that *A. boisei* is precisely the creature predicted if one were to build *A. africanus* at 1.5 times its average body weight, liken the difference between the two forms to those between chimpanzees and gorillas. If so, robust australopithecines, like gorillas, may have had a more specialized vegetarian diet than their smaller, more omnivorous relatives. Clearly, the immense cheek teeth and powerful chewing muscles of the robust form bespeak the kind of

Law of competitive exclusion: States that when two closely related species compete for the same niche one will out compete the other, bringing about its extinction.

heavy chewing a diet restricted to uncooked plant foods requires. Many anthropologists believe that, by becoming a specialized consumer of plant foods, robust australopithecines avoided competing for the same niche with early *Homo*, with which they were contemporaries. In the course of evolution, the **law of competitive exclusion** dictates that, when two closely related species compete for the same niche, one will out compete the other, bringing about the "loser's" extinction.

EARLY REPRESENTATIVES OF THE GENUS *HOMO*

When the Leakeys began work at Olduvai Gorge, they did so on account of the presence of crude stone tools in deposits dating back to very early in the Pleistocene Epoch, which began about 2 million years ago. When they found the bones of *A. boisei* in 1959, in association with some of these tools, they thought they had found the remains of one of the toolmakers. They later changed their minds, however, and suggested that these tools were not produced by *A. boisei*, nor were the bones of the birds, reptiles, antelopes, and an extinct kind of pig found with the remains of *A. boisei* the remains of the latter's dinner. Instead, *A. boisei* may have been a victim of a rather different contemporary who created the tools, ate the animals, and possibly had the unfortunate *A. boisei* for dessert. That contemporary was called by the Leakeys *H. habilis* ("handy man").

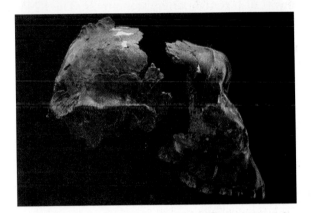

The Leakeys discovered the remains of this second hominid in 1960, only a few months after their earlier discovery, just a few feet below it. The remains, which were those of more than one individual, consisted of a few cranial bones, a lower jaw, a clavicle, some finger bones, and the nearly complete left foot of an adult. These fossils date from about 1.8 million years ago and indicate a lightly built hominid with a cranial capacity in the range

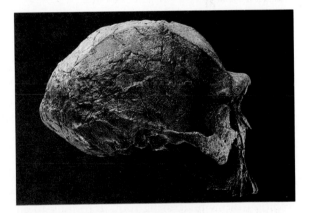

Skulls of gracile *Australopithecus* (reconstructed from fragments 3 to 3.6 million years old), a robust *Australopithecus* 1.75 million years old, and *Homo erectus* (the 1470 skull from East Turkana). All represent males of their respective species.

of 650 to 690 cubic centimeters, a skull that lacks noticeable bony crests, and almost modern-looking hands and feet.

Since the late 1960s, a number of other fossils have been discovered east and north of Lake Turkana as well as in South Africa, which have been attributed to the same species. One of the best, known as KNM ER 1470, was discovered by the Leakeys' son, Richard. (The letters KNM stand for Kenya National Museum, the ER for East Rudolf, the former name for Lake Turkana.) The deposits in which it was found are about 1.9 million years old; these deposits, like those at Olduvai, also contain crude stone tools. The KNM ER 1470 skull is more modern in appearance than any *Australopithecus* skull and has a cranial capacity of 775 cubic centimeters.

Despite their more modern-looking heads, the skeleton of *H. habilis* from the neck down does not differ in any significant way from that of gracile *Australopithecus*; overall size was about the same, males were twice the size of females, and they still climbed trees.[14] Moreover, dental evidence suggests that, as with gracile *Australopithecus*, the period of infancy and childhood in *H. habilis* was not significantly prolonged, as it is in modern humans, but was more in line with apes.[15]

LOWER PALEOLITHIC TOOLS

The earliest tools known to have been made by hominids have been found in the vicinity of Lake Turkana in Kenya and southern Ethiopia, Olduvai Gorge, Tanzania, and Hadar, Ethiopia. Their appearance marks the beginning of the **Lower Paleolithic,** the first part of the Old Stone Age.

These early tools show striking similarities, indicating that they were the results of a cultural tradition of manufacturing tools according to an

[14]Roger Lewin, "The Earliest 'Humans' Were More Like Apes," *Science* 236 (1987): 106–163.
[15]Roger Lewin, "Debate Over Emergence of Human Tooth Pattern," *Science* 235 (1987): 749.

Lower Paleolithic: The first part of the "Old Stone Age"; its beginning is marked by the appearance of Oldowan tools.

ideal model or pattern. At Olduvai and Lake Turkana, these tools are close to 2 million years old. The Hadar tools have been found below a deposit dated by potassium–argon analysis to about 1.8 million years ago, but above another dated to about 2.8 million years; thus, they are estimated to be about 2.5 million years old.

OLDUVAI GORGE

What is now Olduvai Gorge was once a lake. Almost 2 million years ago, its shores were inhabited not only by numerous wild animals but also by groups of hominids, including robust australopithecines and *H. habilis* — the earliest members of the genus *Homo* — as well as the later *H. erectus* (Chapter 7). The gorge, therefore, is a rich source of Paleolithic remains as well as an important site providing evidence of human evolutionary development. Among the finds are assemblages of stone tools that are about 2 million years old. These lay undisturbed, exactly as they were left, together with the bones of now extinct animals which were eaten. At one spot, in the lowest level of the gorge, the bones of an elephant lay in close association with more than 200 stone tools. Apparently, the animal was butchered here; there are no indications of any other activity. At another spot, on a "living floor" 1.8 million years old, basalt stones were found grouped in small heaps so as to form a circle. The interior of the circle was practically empty, while numerous tools and food debris littered the ground outside, right up to the edge of the circle. Some interpret this as evidence for some sort of shelter, seeing the stone piles as supports for the framework of a protective fence of thorn branches, or perhaps a hut with a covering of animal skins or grass. Another possibility is that the stones were "stock piled" ahead of time to be made into tools as needed or to be hurled as missiles to hold off other scavengers while the hominids extracted meat, marrow, hide, and sinew from bones.

Oldowan tool tradition: The earliest identifiable stone tools.

Percussion method: A technique of stone tool manufacture by striking the raw material with a hammerstone or by striking raw material against a stone anvil to remove flakes.

OLDOWAN TOOLS

The oldest tools found at Olduvai Gorge belong to the **Oldowan tool tradition,** which is characterized by an all-purpose generalized chopping tool, produced by removing a few flakes from a stone (often a large water-worn pebble) either by using another stone as a hammer (hammerstone) or by striking the pebble against a large rock (anvil) to remove the flakes. This system of manufacture is called the **percussion method** (Figure 6.5). The finished product had a jagged sharp edge, effective for cutting and chopping. The generalized form of the chopping tool suggests that it served many purposes, such as butchering meat, splitting bones for marrow, and perhaps also defending the owner. Also used were the flakes, which had sharp, useful edges (in fact, many so-called choppers may be no more than by-products of flake manufacture). Some flakes were used "as is," for cutting tools, while others were retouched for use as scrapers.

Crude as they were, Oldowan choppers and flakes mark an important technological advance for early hominids; previously, they depended on found objects requiring little or no modification, such as bones, sticks, or conveniently shaped stones. Oldowan tools made possible new additions to the diet, because, without such tools, hominids could eat only animals that could be skinned by tooth or nail; therefore, their diet was limited in terms of animal proteins. The advent of Oldowan choppers and flakes meant more than just saving labor and time — they made possible the addition of meat to the diet on a regular, rather than occasional, basis. Much of a popular nature has been written about this, often with numerous colorful references to "killer apes." Such references are quite misleading, not only because hominids are not apes but also because killing has been greatly

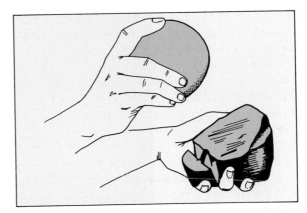

FIGURE 6.5 By 2.5 million years ago, hominids had invented the percussion method of stone tool manufacture. This technological breakthrough, which is associated with a significant increase in brain size, made possible the butchering of meat from scavenged carcasses.

overemphasized. Meat can be obtained, after all, by scavenging or by stealing it from other predators. What is significant is that a dentition such as that possessed by *Australopithecus* and *H. habilis* is poorly suited for meat eating. What is needed if substantial amounts of meat are to be used, in the absence of teeth like those possessed by carnivorous animals, are sharp tools for butchering.

The initial use of tools was probably the result of adaptation to an environment that was changing from forests to grasslands. The physical changes that adapted hominids to living in the new grassy terrain encouraged toolmaking. It has been observed that monkeys and apes, for example, often use objects, such as sticks and stones, in conjunction with threat gestures. The change to a nearly upright bipedal posture, coupled with existing flexibility at the shoulder, arms, and hands, helped hominids to compete with, and survive despite, the large predatory carnivores that shared their environment.

What else do these assemblages of Oldowan tools and broken animal bones have to tell us about the life ways of early *Homo?* Opinions have differed, for reasons given in the following Original Study.

The stone tools used by *Homo habilis* included lava cobbles, choppers, and flakes like these shown here. Most choppers were probably the result of flakes being struck from one cobble by another. These flakes were used to remove meat from bones, leaving cut marks (*lower left*); cobbles and choppers were used to break open bones (*middle left*) to get at the marrow.

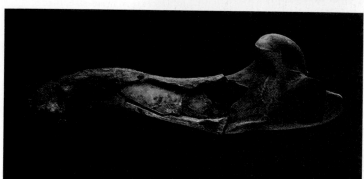

ORIGINAL STUDY
ORIGINAL STUDY
Archaeological Evidence for Early Human Social Life[16]

The assumption that the earliest hominids practiced a way of living that was somewhere along a direct line between the generalized lifeway of the chimpanzee and that of the contemporary hunter–gatherer is best exemplified by the earlier work of Glynn Isaac. Several of Isaac's papers began by listing the traits that distinguish modern humans, *Homo sapiens*, from the common chimpanzee, *Pan troglodytes*, and attempting to identify the time periods in the archaeological and paleontological record when these distinctively human traits first appeared. As Isaac himself acknowledged in his recent papers, there was a strong tendency to extrapolate the modern traits as far back into the record as possible. The earliest hominids were credited with complex social, intellectual, and technological abilities, not quite at the level of modern hunter–gatherers, but recognizably "human" nonetheless.

More recently, there has been a reassessment of the archaeological evidence for, and interpretations of, early hominid behavior. Although the study of human evolution often has been characterized by heated debate, not all of it enlightening, these recent attempts to test fundamental archaeological assumptions and to develop alternative ways of explaining the material evidence have been, in Isaac's own words, "liberating" and an "exciting exercise of alternating leaps of imagination with rigorous testing." Most of these new problem-oriented studies and experimental investigations of the processes that produce archaeological remains are beyond the range of this review, but the recognition that early hominids may have been very different in lifeway from modern humans has also been liberating from the perspective of sex role reconstruction. And the most important aspect of this minor paradigmatic revolution for women's roles concerns the new interpretations of bone-and-artifact associations, or what were traditionally known as "home bases."

Isaac had developed a "sharing" model which was founded on the fact that in the early East African sites of around 2 million years ago, tools are found in dense patches in association with the bony remains of many animal species. Both stones and bones appear to have been transported to "central locations." Beginning with this one piece of material evidence, Isaac suggested that humans carried food and possessions to consistent locations as part of a social system involving home bases, division of labor, hunting and gathering, substantial meat eating, food sharing, and food preparation. As Potts has noted, Isaac's model could as appropriately have been entitled a "home base" model as a "sharing" model, since all the other social charac-

[16]Linda Marie Fedigan, "The Changing Role of Women in Models of Human Evolution," *Annual Review of Anthropology* 15 (1986): 55–57. Reproduced with permission. Copyright © 1986 by annual reviews inc.

teristics are constructed upon the initial interpretation that stone–bone associations are evidence of "social and industrial foci in the lives of the early hominid toolmakers to which food was brought for collective consumption."

Several researchers have now challenged the home base interpretation. Binford analyzed some of the published evidence from Olduvai Gorge to argue that the "so-called" living sites or home bases were in fact the remains of carnivore activities. Isaac countered that the published data sets on which Binford worked were declared by their author (M. D. Leakey) to be incomplete and preliminary, and that Binford had not accounted for the fact that the bone assemblages come from patches in which thousands of human artifacts (tools) also occur. Thus Potts's detailed, firsthand analysis of the Olduvai Gorge and Koobi Fora stone–bone concentrations was to be very influential.

Potts came to a different, but nonetheless startling, conclusion from both Binford and Isaac about the processes which formed the bone–stone tool assemblages. He argued that the animal bones at these sites were marked *both* by carnivore teeth and by stone tools, including tooth marks from gnawing and cutmarks made by slicing, scraping, and chopping with stone. Somehow, both early hominids and large carnivores were active at these locations, in some cases upon the same parts of the carcass, even the same bones. However, it is not whole carcasses of animals that are represented and the bones were not completely processed for meat and marrow, suggesting that hominids were abandoning considerable portions of the available food. Finally, the incredible density of bones at some of the sites and the patterns of weathering indicate bone accumulation spanning 5–10 years. All four factors, according to Potts, argue against a home base interpretation of the sites. The presence of large carnivores would certainly have restricted the activities of early hominids at such locations, and surely campsites would never have been established in such unsafe places. Modern hunter–gatherers carry whole or nearly whole carcasses back to camp, not restricted portions, and they intensively modify the bones of animal food. Finally, hunter–gatherers rarely occupy a campsite for a long period of time, and seldom reoccupy an old site. Thus Potts concluded that it is not possible to assume that the behaviors associated with home bases (sharing, division of labor) occurred at the early sites in Olduvai.

How then can one explain the presence of hominids at these sites? Potts argued that the sites represent stone tool caches and meat-processing locations. Because animal carcasses attract many meat-eaters, the hominids were forced to transport parts of the animal away from the original location where it was obtained either by scavenging or hunting. These portions of meat were taken to the nearest stone tool cache in the foraging area, where raw stone, manufactured tools, and bones remained from previous visits. Even chimpanzees are known to take food, in this case vegetable food, to consistent locations where tools have been left for processing. It is hypothesized that the hominids processed the meat quickly with the stone tools in the cache and abandoned the site before direct confrontation occurred with the carnivores who were attracted to the remains. Thus, over the years, many remains of partially processed, gnawed bones and large numbers of stone tools were accumulated in one location. Such sites could represent the antecedents of home bases, but Potts believes that until hominids gained the controlled use of fire to make home bases safe from carnivores, and the first evidence of controlled use of fire is much more recent in the record, they may well have continued to sleep in trees and to range widely during the day as do the other primate species.

RELATIONS BETWEEN EARLY *HOMO* AND *AUSTRALOPITHECUS*

A consideration of brain size relative to body size clearly indicates that *H. habilis* had undergone enlargement of the brain far in excess of values predicted on the basis of body size alone. This means that there was a marked advance in information-processing capacity over that of the australopithecines. Furthermore, although these hominids had teeth that are large by modern standards — or even those of a half million years ago — they are smaller in relation to the size of the skull than those of australopithecines. Since major brain-size increase and tooth-size reduction are important trends in the evolution of the genus *Homo*, but not of *Australopithecus*, it looks as if ER 1470 and similar

hominids were evolving in a more human direction. Consistent with this, the brain of KNM ER 1470 appears less apelike and more human in structure.[17] It is probably significant that the earliest fossils to exhibit these features appear by 2.3 million years ago, soon after the earliest evidence for stone toolmaking and increased consumption of meat.

As noted earlier, the Australopithecine diet seems to have consisted for the most part of plant foods, although the gracile form may have consumed some animal protein as well. Later australopithecines evolved into more specialized "grinding machines" as their jaws became markedly larger (Figure 6.6), while their brain size did not. Nor is there evidence that they made stone tools.

[17]Simons, p. 1348.

FIGURE 6.6 Premolars (*left*) and molars (*right*) of *Australopithecus* and *Homo habilis*. The teeth of *Australopithecus* show a clear tendency to enlarge with time over those of *A. afarensis*, while the teeth of *H. habilis* differ little from those of *A. afarensis*.

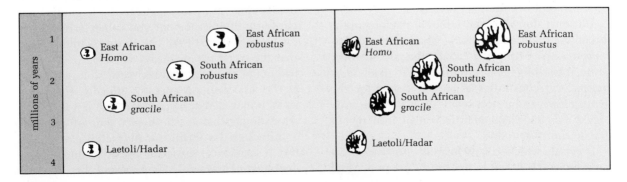

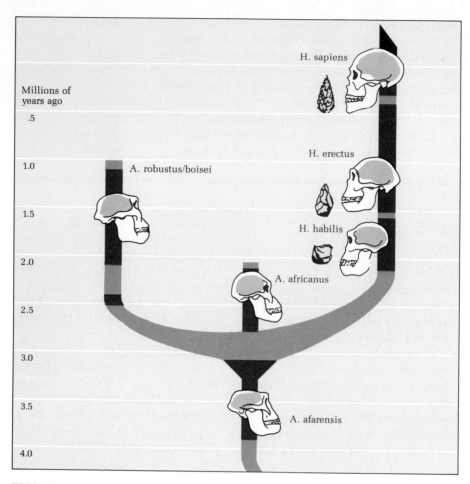

FIGURE 6.7 A plausible view of early human evolution. Equally plausible, South African *Australopithecus robustus* may represent a separate continuation of the *africanus* line until about 1.5 million years ago.

Thus, in the period between 2.5 and 1 million years ago, two kinds of hominid were headed in very different evolutionary directions.

If robust *Australopithecus* does not belong in the direct line of human ancestry, what of gracile *Australopithecus*? From the standpoint of anatomy alone, it has long been recognized that gracile *Australopithecus* constitutes a good ancestor for the genus *Homo*, and it now seems clear that the body of *H. habilis* had changed little, if at all, from that of gracile *Australopithecus*.

Precisely which gracile form of *Australopithecus* gave rise to *H. habilis* is vigorously debated. Most

see *A. afarensis* as sufficiently generalized to have given rise to both the *Homo* and robust patterns, noting that *A. africanus* shows the beginnings of cheek tooth enlargement and other features that are characteristic of the robust line. Others argue that the trend toward heavy chewing in *africanus* had not gone so far as to be irreversible, and see it as the last common ancestor. Finally, there is a small minority that would place the last common ancestor just before the appearance of *afarensis*.

Although the gracile line ultimately gave rise to two descendant lines, it did not itself immediately disappear (Figure 6.7). It persisted, briefly, as a

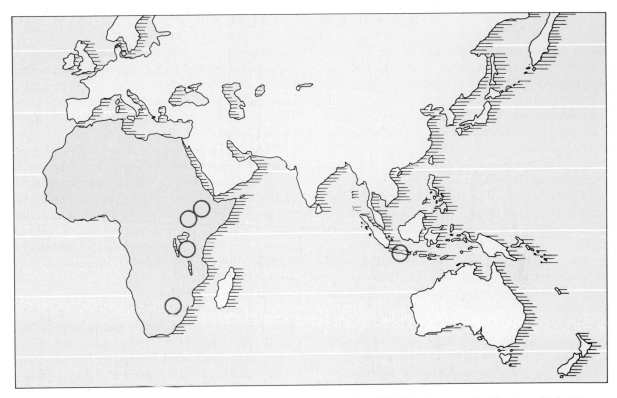

FIGURE 6.8 Localities at which fossils of *Homo habilis* have been found. Unlike the australopithecines, *H. habilis* was not restricted to Africa alone.

third line, which became extinct by 2 million years ago, by which time the descendant lineages had become widespread in nonforested parts of Africa and, in the case of *Homo*, even beyond (Figure 6.8). The latter is signified by pieces of jawbone from Java which were originally given the name *"Meganthropus."* Not only do these predate *H. erectus* fossils in Java, but they are practically identical to corresponding pieces of jaw from *H. habilis* at Olduvai Gorge. Evidently, such was the success of its adaptation that hominids, for the first time, were able to spread to tropical regions outside of Africa.

Homo habilis from Olduvai Gorge compared with *"Meganthropus"* from Java. The two are so similar as to suggest that they represent the same hominid.

CHAPTER SUMMARY

By at least 4 million years ago, in the Pliocene Epoch, the first undoubted hominids had appeared. Although they had by then developed the anatomical structure that enabled them to walk erect on two feet, it was not until about 2.5 million years ago that some of them began to scavenge for meat and make stone tools. The beginnings of brain expansion date from this time.

During the late Miocene and Pliocene, the climate became cooler and drier; many areas that had once been heavily forested became woodland and open savanna. The ancestors of hominids found themselves spending more and more time on the ground; they had to adapt to this altered, open environment, and acquiring food became a problem. As their diet changed, so did their dentition. On the whole, teeth became smaller, and many of the defensive functions once performed by the teeth seem to have been taken over by the hands.

Ramapithecines are believed to have been part-time brachiators who may at times have walked erect. *Australopithecus* is the first full biped hominid with erect posture whom we know about. Some disadvantages of bipedalism as a means of locomotion are that it makes an animal more visible to predators, exposes its soft underbelly, is relatively slow, and interferes with the ability to change direction instantly while running. Its advantages are that it provides hominids with a means of protecting themselves and of holding objects while running, the ability to travel long distances without tiring, and the ability to see further.

Some changes in the brain structure of early hominids seem to have been the result of a changed diet. Increased consumption of meat, beginning about 2.5 million years ago, made new demands on their coordination and behavior. Successful procurement of meat through scavenging depended on the hominid's ability to out-think far more powerful predators and scavengers. Obtaining animal food presented problems that very often had to be solved on the spot; a small scavenger depending on stereotyped instinctual behavior alone would have been at a competitive disadvantage in such a situation. Moreover, eaters of high-protein foods, such as meats, do not have to eat as often as vegetarians do. Consequently, meat-eating hominids may have had more leisure time available to explore and experiment with their environment.

Toolmaking and use also favored the development of a more efficient brain. To make stone tools, one must have in mind at the beginning a clear vision of the tool to be made, one must know the precise set of steps necessary to transform the raw material into the tool, and one must be able to recognize the kind of stone that can be successfully worked. Advanced eye-hand coordination is also required.

A prime factor in the success of early hominids was the development of some cooperation in the procurement of foods. While the males probably supplied much of the meat, the females continued to gather the sorts of food eaten by other primates; however, instead of consuming what they gathered as they gathered it, they shared a portion with the males in exchange for meat. This required foresight and planning on the part of females, which was just as important as male scavenging in favoring the development of better brains. Food sharing with a sexual division of labor is characteristic of modern food foragers, and some hint of it can be seen among chimpanzees, among whom meat is frequently shared.

The course of hominid evolution, we know from fossil finds, has not been a simple, steady "advance" in the direction of modern humans. One early hominid was *Australopithecus*, a genus that anthropologists divide into gracile and robust species. Gracile *Australopithecus* walked erect; it was about the size of a modern human pygmy; it chewed food like a human; and its general appearance was that of an apelike human. The size and outward appearance of its brain suggest a degree of intelligence probably not greatly different from that of a modern chimpanzee or gorilla. Like chimpanzees, it may have made some use of objects as tools.

Robust *Australopithecus* shared practically all of the traits listed for the gracile form, but it was larger and more heavily muscled. Although the two differ primarily in size, but not design, the robust form seems to have been more highly specialized for the consumption of plant foods than the gracile form.

In the summer of 1959, Mary Leakey discovered the remains of a hominid in Olduvai Gorge, East Africa, which Louis Leakey called *"Zinjanthropus,"* but it is now generally accepted as an East African variant of robust *Australopithecus.* Stone tools found with the *"Zinjanthropus"* remains at Olduvai were probably not made by *"Zinjanthropus,"* but by an early member of the genus *Homo.*

Since 1960, a number of fossils have been found in East Africa at Olduvai Gorge and east of Lake Turkana and in South Africa at Sterkfontein, which have been attributed to *H. habilis,* the earliest representative of this genus. Among them is the well-known KNM ER 1470 skull, which is more modern in appearance than any *Australopithecus* skull. From the neck on down, however, the skeleton of *H. habilis* is practically indistinguishable from that of *Australopithecus.* Because they do show a significant increase in brain size, and some reorganization of its structure, their mental abilities must have exceeded those of *Australopithecus.* By

2.3 million years ago, the evolution of *Homo* was proceeding in a direction different from that of *Australopithecus.*

The same geological strata that have produced *Homo habilis* have also produced the earliest known stone tools. These Lower Paleolithic artifacts from Olduvai Gorge, Lake Turkana, and Hadar, Ethiopia, are remarkably similar, suggesting that they were the products of a cultural tradition in which tools were manufactured according to a model.

Finds made at Olduvai Gorge have provided important evidence of human evolutionary development. The oldest Lower Paleolithic tools found at Olduvai are in the Oldowan tool tradition, which is characterized by all-purpose generalized chopping tools and flakes. Lower Paleolithic people used the percussion method to manufacture tools. The crude Oldowan choppers and flakes made possible the addition of meat to the diet on a regular basis, because people could now butcher meat, skin any animal, and split bones for marrow. Many Oldowan archaeological sites appear to be where meat was scavenged or processed rather than campsites.

Although fossils of *Australopithecus* have never been found outside of Africa, the new adaptation of *H. habilis* allowed it to spread as far afield as southeast Asia.

SUGGESTED READINGS

Brace, C. Loring, Harry Nelson, and Noel Korn. *An Atlas of Human Evolution,* 2d ed. New York: Holt, Rinehart and Winston, 1979. The core of this atlas consists of a series of drawings that provide a pictorial survey of the most important fossils which form the basis of our knowledge of human evolution. To facilitate comparison, each drawing highlights the diagnostic character of the fossil find and is accompanied by notes on date, geological age, place of discovery, and interpretations. Maps showing the distribution of important sites and stone tool distributions are included for each stage.

Campbell, Bernard G. *Humankind Emerging,* 5th ed. Boston: Little, Brown, 1988. Several physical anthropology texts have good coverage of the earliest hominids; this one is distinguished by its accessible writing style and lavish illustrations from the Time-Life *Emergence of Man* and *Life Nature Library* series.

Ciochon, Russell L., and John G. Fleagle, eds. *Primate Evolution and Human Origins.* Hawthorne, N.Y.: Aldine de Gruyter, 1987. In Part VI of this book, the editors have assembled articles to survey different theories on the evolution and diversification of the earliest hominids. A short editors' introduction to the section places these various articles in context.

Johanson, Donald, and Maitland Edey. *Lucy: The Beginnings of Humankind.* New York: Simon and Schuster, 1981. This book tells the story of the discovery of "Lucy" and the other fossils of *Australopithecus afarensis,* and why they have enhanced our understanding of the early stages of human evolution. It reads like a first-rate detective story, at the same time giving one of the best descriptions of australopithecines and one of the best accounts of how paleoanthropologists analyze their fossils, to be found in literature.

7

HOMO ERECTUS AND THE EMERGENCE OF HUNTING AND GATHERING

Understanding how our earliest ancestors lived requires more than the unearthing of fossils and artifacts. Experiments such as using stone tools on an elephant's carcass, shown in this photograph, help us to understand how our ancestors dealt with the resources at their disposal.

PREVIEW

Who Was Homo erectus?

Homo erectus was the direct descendant of the earliest members of the genus *Homo*, as have been found in East Africa and Java. Populations of *H. erectus* were widespread between about 1.6 million and 300,000 years ago, living in Africa, China, Europe, and Southeast Asia.

What Were the Cultural Capabilities of Homo erectus?

Having larger brains than its ancestors, *Homo erectus* became better able to adapt to different situations through the medium of culture. This is reflected by better-made tools, a greater variety of tool types, regional diversification of tool kits, use of fire, and improved organizational skills.

What Were the Consequences of Homo erectus' Improved Abilities to Adapt through Culture?

As culture became more important as the vehicle through which this species secured its survival, life became somewhat easier than it had been. As a result, selective pressures, other than those favoring increased capacity for culture, were reduced, reproduction became easier, and more offspring survived than before. This allowed populations to grow, causing "spillover" into previously uninhabited regions. This in turn contributed to the further evolution of culture, as populations of *Homo erectus* had to find solutions to new problems of existence in newly inhabited regions.

In 1891, the Dutch army surgeon Eugene Dubois, intent on finding the fossils of a "missing link" between humans and apes, set out for Java, which he considered to have provided a suitable environment for such a creature. At Trinil, Java, Dubois found what he was searching for: the fossil remains of a primitive kind of hominid, consisting of a skull cap, a few teeth, and a thigh bone. Its features seemed to Dubois part ape, part human. Indeed, Dubois at first thought the remains did not even belong to the same individual. The flat skull, for example, with its enormous brow ridges and small size, appeared to be like that of an ape; but it possessed a cranial capacity much larger than an ape's. The femur, or thigh bone, was clearly human in shape and proportions and indicated the creature was a biped. Although Dubois called his find *Pithecanthropus erectus*, or "erect ape man," it has since been assigned to the species *Homo erectus*.

HOMO ERECTUS FOSSILS

No previous hominids were as widespread as *Homo erectus*, whose fossils are now known from a number of localities in Africa, China, and Europe, as well as Java (Figure 7.1). Despite the fact that remains of this species have been found in so many different places in three continents, the remains show very little significant physical variation. Evidence suggests, however, that populations of

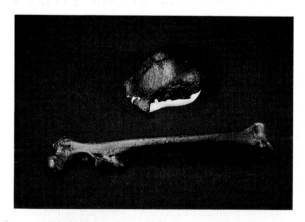

The original skull cap and thigh bone of *Homo erectus* found by E. Dubois at Trinil, Java.

H. erectus in different parts of the world do show some differences from one another on a subspecific level.

HOMO ERECTUS FROM JAVA

For a long time, the scientific community was reluctant to accept Dubois' claim that his Javanese fossils were of human lineage. It was not until the 1930s, particularly when other fossils of *H. erectus* were discovered by G.H.R. von Koenigswald at Sangiran, Java, in the Early Pleistocene Djetis beds that scientists almost without exception agreed both discoveries were the remains of an entirely new kind of early hominid. Von Koenigswald found a small skull that fluorine analysis and (later) potassium–argon dating indicated to be older than Dubois' approximately 500,000-to-700,000-year-old Trinil specimen. Since 1960, additional fossils have been found in Java. A long continuity of *H. erectus* populations in Southeast Asia is indicated, from perhaps as much as 1.3 million years to about 500,000 years ago at least.

HOMO ERECTUS FROM CHINA

A second population of *H. erectus* was found in the mid-1920s by Davidson Black, a Canadian anatomist then teaching at Peking Union Medical College. After purchasing in a Peking drugstore a few teeth sold to local inhabitants for their supposed medicinal properties, Black set out for the nearby countryside to discover the owner of the teeth and perhaps the species of early hominid. At a place called "Dragon Bone Hill" in Zhoukoudian, 30 miles from Beijing, he found one molar tooth on the day before closing camp at the end of his first year of excavation. Subsequently, a skull encased in limestone was found by W. C. Pei, and from 1929 until 1934, the year of his death, Black labored along with Pei in the fossil-rich deposits of Zhoukoudian, uncovering fragment after fragment of the hominid Black had named, on the basis of that first molar tooth, *Sinanthropus pekinesis*, or "Chinese man of Peking" — now recognized as an East Asian representative of *H. erectus*.

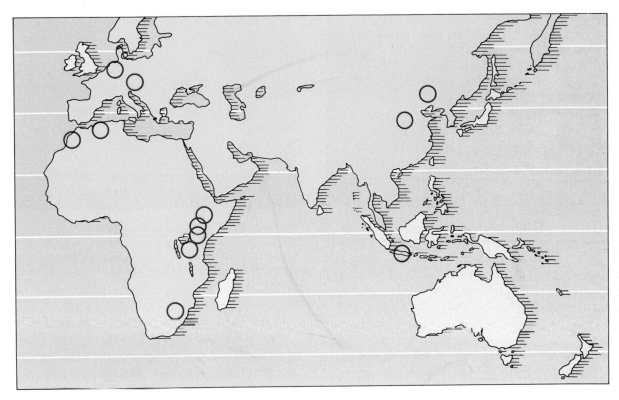

FIGURE 7.1 Localities at which the remains of *Homo erectus* have been found.

After his death, Black's work was continued by Franz Weidenreich, a Jewish refugee from Nazi Germany. By 1938, the remains of over 40 individuals, consisting of teeth, jawbones, and incomplete skulls, had been dug out of the limestone. World War II brought a halt to the digging, and the original Zhoukoudian specimens were lost during the Japanese invasion of China. Fortunately, Weidenreich had made superb casts of most of the fossils and sent them to the United States. After the war, other specimens of *H. erectus* were discovered in China, at Zhoukoudian and at Lantian in Shensi Province. The latter include a skull about 700,000 years old, while the Zhoukoudian remains appear to be about 500,000 years old.

Although the two populations overlap in time, the Chinese fossils are, on the whole, not quite so old as those from Java. Not surprisingly, Chinese *H. erectus* is a bit less "primitive" looking. Its average cranial capacity is about 1000 cubic centimeters, compared with 900 cc for Javanese *H. erectus*. The smaller teeth, short jaw, and lack of diastema in the lower dentition—a gap in the teeth to accommodate a large upper canine when the jaws are closed—of the Chinese are further evidence of their more modern status.

HOMO ERECTUS FROM AFRICA

Although fossils now assigned to *H. erectus* were discovered in Africa as long ago as 1933, the better-known finds have been made since 1960, at Olduvai and at Lake Turkana. Among them is the oldest—at 1.6 million years—and most complete *H. erectus* skeleton ever found, that of a boy who died at about the age of 12 years. Another partial skeleton, that of an adult, had diseased bones, possibly the result of a massive overdose of Vitamin A. This could have come from eating the livers of carnivorous animals, for they accumulate this vitamin

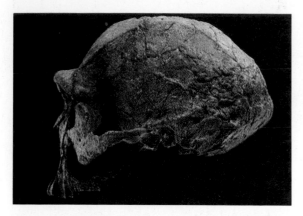

This 1.5 million-year-old skull from Lake Turkana, Kenya, is one of the most complete skulls of *Homo erectus* ever found.

This late *Homo erectus* skull from Petralona in Greece, in common with its contemporaries from other parts of Africa and Asia, retains much of the shape of earlier *H. erectus* skulls, but its brain is a bit larger.

in their livers at levels that are poisonous to human beings.

Generally speaking, African *H. erectus* skulls are quite similar to those from Asia; one difference is that their bones are not quite as thick. It may be, too, that individuals living in China were shorter and stockier, on the whole, than those living in Africa. Overall, however, the Africans reveal no more significant physical variations from their Asian counterparts than are seen if modern human populations from East and West are compared. As in Asia, the most recent fossils are less "primitive" in appearance, and the oldest fossils display features reminiscent of the earlier *Homo habilis.*

HOMO ERECTUS FROM EUROPE

Although Europe seems to have been inhabited by 700,000 years ago, few fossils attributable to *H. erectus* have so far been found there. A large lower jaw from Mauer, Germany, that may be almost a half million years old certainly came from a skull wide at the base, as is that of *H. erectus.* A skull from Petralona, in Greece, probably belongs to this species as well. Until other equally old fossils are found, knowledge of *H. erectus* in Europe must remain limited.

PHYSICAL CHARACTERISTICS OF *HOMO ERECTUS*

Apart from its skull, the skeleton of *H. erectus* differs only subtly from that of modern humans. Although its bodily proportions are like ours, it was more heavily muscled, its rib cage was conical rather than barrel shaped, and its hips were narrower. With a small birth canal, gestation must have been short, with infants born in a relatively immature state. Stature seems to have been in the modern range, as the youth from Lake Turkana was about 5 feet 4 inches tall. Compared to *H. habilis,* *H. erectus* was significantly larger but displayed considerably less sexual dimorphism.

Cranial capacity in *H. erectus* ranged from 775 to 1225 cubic centimeters (average, 1000 cubic centimeters), which compares with 775 cubic centimeters for the nearly 2 million-year-old ER 1470 skull from East Africa, and 1000 to 2000 cubic centimeters (average, 1300 cubic centimeters) for modern human skulls (Figure 7.2). The cranium itself had a low vault, and the head was long and narrow. When viewed from behind, its width was greater than its height, with its greatest width at the base. The skulls of modern humans, when similarly viewed, are higher than they are wide, with the widest dimension in the region above the ears.

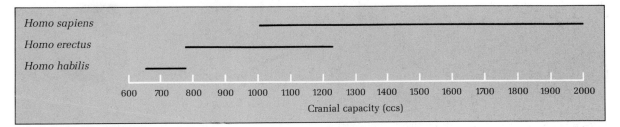

FIGURE 7.2 Cranial capacity for the genus *Homo*. Note the continuous range of variation, from the smallest skull of *H. habilis* to the largest skull of *H. sapiens*.

Moreover, the shape of the inside of *H. erectus'* brain case showed near-modern development of the brain, especially in the speech area. Although some anthropologists argue that the vocal apparatus was not adequate for speech, others argue that asymmetries of the brain suggest the same pattern of righthandedness with left cerebral dominance that, in modern peoples, is correlated with the capacity for language.[1]

Massive ridges over the eyes gave this early hominid a somewhat simian, "beetle-browed" appearance. *H. erectus* also possessed a sloping forehead and a receding "chin." Powerful jaws with large teeth, protruding mouth, and huge neck muscles added to the generally rugged appearance. Nevertheless, the face, teeth, and jaws of this hominid are smaller than those of *H. habilis*.

RELATIONSHIP BETWEEN *HOMO ERECTUS* AND *HOMO HABILIS*

The smaller teeth and larger brains of *H. erectus* seem to mark continuation of a trend first seen in *H. habilis*. What is new is the increased body size, reduced sexual dimorphism, and more "human" body form of *erectus*. Nonetheless, there is some resemblance to *habilis*, for example, in the conical shape of the rib cage, the long neck and low neck angle of the thigh bone, and smaller brain size in the earliest *erectus* fossils. Presumably, the one

Acheulean tradition: The toolmaking tradition of *Homo erectus* in Africa, Europe, and Southwest Asia in which hand axes were developed from the earlier Oldowan chopper.

form evolved from the other, evidently fairly abruptly, in the period between 1.8 and 1.6 million years ago.[2]

THE CULTURE OF *HOMO ERECTUS*

As one might expect given its larger brain, *H. erectus* outstripped its predecessors in cultural development. In Africa, Europe, and Southwest Asia, there was refinement of the stone toolmaking technology begun by the makers of earlier flake and chopper tools. At some point, fire began to be used for protection, warmth, and cooking, though precisely when is still a matter for debate. Finally, there is indirect evidence that the organizational abilities of *H. erectus*, or at least the later ones, were improved over those of their predecessors.

THE ACHEULEAN TOOL TRADITION

Associated with the remains of *Homo erectus* in Africa, Europe, and Southwest Asia are tools of the **Acheulean tradition.** Characteristic of this tradi-

[1]Ralph L. Holloway, "The Indonesian *Homo erectus* Brain Endocasts Revisited," *American Journal of Physical Anthropology* 55 (1981): 521.

[2]Roger Lewin, "The Earliest 'Humans' Were More Like Apes," *Science* 236 (1987): 1061.

Improvements in tool-
making abilities are illustrated by comparison of
two hand axes. The one
at the *right* is not as old
as the one at the *left*.

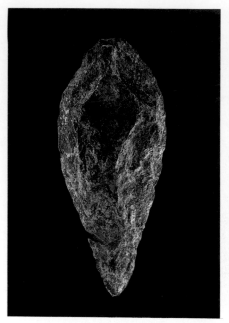 

tion are hand axes, pear-shaped tools pointed at
one end with a sharp cutting edge all around. In
East Africa, the earliest hand axes are about 1.4
million years old; those found in Europe and
Southwest Asia are no older than about 750,000
years. In East Asia, chopping tool traditions reminiscent of the Oldowan, rather than Acheulean
and derived traditions, continued through much of
the **Paleolithic.**

That the Acheulean grew out of the Oldowan
tradition is indicated by an examination of the evidence discovered at Olduvai. In Bed 1, the lowest
level, chopper tools were found along with remains of *H. habilis.* In lower Bed 2, the first crude
hand axes were found intermingled with chopper
tools. Acheulean hand axes having a more "finished" look about them appear in middle Bed 2,
together with *H. erectus* remains.

Early Acheulean tools represent a definite improvement over the generalized cutting, chopping, and scraping tools of the Oldowan tradition.
Like chopper tools, the hand axes were probably
general-purpose implements for food procurement, processing, and defense. However, they

Paleolithic: The Old Stone Age, characterized by
manufactured use of chipped stone tools.

were more standardized in form, having been
shaped by regular blows rather than by random
strikes. In this way, sharper points and more regular cutting edges were produced, and more cutting
edge was available from the same amount of stone.

During this period, tool cultures began to diversify (Figure 7.3). In addition to hand axes,
H. erectus used tools that functioned as cleavers
(these were hand axes with a straight edge where
the point would otherwise be) and flake tools (generally smaller tools made by hitting a flint core
with a hammerstone, thus knocking off flakes with
sharp edges). Many flake tools were by-products of
hand ax and cleaver manufacture. Their sharp
edges made them useful as is, but many were retouched to make points, scrapers, borers, and
other sorts of tools. Diversification of tool kits is
also indicated by the smaller numbers of hand axes
in northern and eastern Europe, where people relied more on simply flaked choppers, a wide vari-

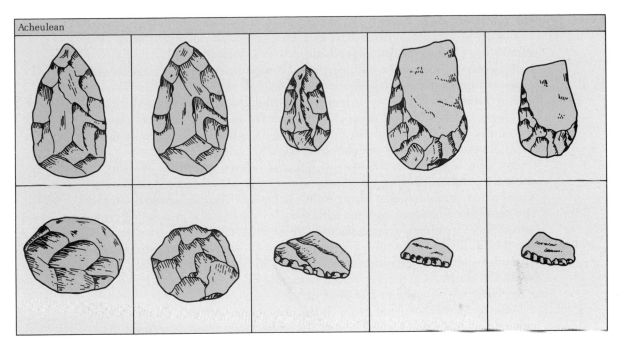

FIGURE 7.3 Each tool drawn here represents 10 percent of the shaped tools in a typical Acheulean assemblage.

ety of unstandardized flakes, and supplementary tools of bone, antler, and wood. Evidently, these people expended less effort in their toolmaking than did their contemporaries living to the south and west. In East Asia, by contrast, many tools may have been made of bamboo and other local woods, from which excellent knives, scrapers, and the like comparable to those of stone can be made.

O R I G I N A L S T U D Y

Homo erectus and the Use of Bamboo[3]

Bamboo provides, I believe, the solution to a puzzle first raised in 1943, when the late archeologist Hallam Movius of Harvard began to publish his observations on paleolithic (Old Stone Age) cultures of the Far East. In 1937 and 1938 Movius had investigated a number of archeological localities in India, Southeast Asia, and China. Although most of the archeological "cultures" that he recognized are no longer accepted by modern workers, he made another, more lasting contribution. This was the identification of the "Movius line" (which his colleague Carleton Coon named in his honor): a geographical boundary, extending through northern India, that separates two long-lasting paleolithic cultures. West of the line are found collections of tools with a high percentage of symmetrical and consistently proportioned hand axes (these are called Acheulean tools, after the French site of Saint Acheul). More or less similar tool kits also occur in Mongolia and Siberia, but with few exceptions (which are generally relatively late in time), not in eastern China or Southeast Asia, where more crudely made tools known as choppers and chopping tools prevail (Figure 7.4).

My own research on the Movius line and related questions evolved almost by accident. During the course of my work in Southeast Asia, I excavated many sites, studied a variety of fossil faunal collections, and reviewed the scientific literature dealing with Asia. As part of this research I compared fossil mammals from Asia with those recovered from other parts of the world. In the beginning, my purpose was biostratigraphic—to use the animals to estimate the most likely dates of various sites used by early hominids. On the basis of the associated fauna, for example, I estimate that Kao Pah Nam may be as old as 700,000 years.

After years of looking at fossil collections and faunal lists, I realized that something was very strange about the collections from Southeast Asia: there were no fossil horses of Pleistocene age or for a considerable time before that. The only exceptions were a few horse fossils from one place in southern China, the Yuanmou Basin which was and is a special small grassland habitat in a low, dry valley within the Shan-Yunnan Massif.

To mammalian biostratigraphers this is unusual, since members of the horse family are so common in both the Old and New World that they are a primary means of dating various fossil localities. Fossil horses have been reported from western Burma, but the last one probably lived there some twenty million years ago. Not a single fossil horse turns up later than that in Southeast Asia, although they are known from India to the west and China to the north and every other part of Europe and Asia.

I then began to wonder what other normally common animals might be missing. The answer soon became apparent: camels—even though they too were once widespread throughout the world—and members and relatives of the giraffe family. Pleistocene Southeast Asia was shaping up as a kind of "black hole" for certain fossil mammals! These animals—horses, camels, and giraffids—all dwell in open country. Their absence on the Southeast Asian mainland and islands (all once connected, along with the now inundated Sunda Shelf) is indicative of a forested environment. The mammals that are present—orangutans, tapirs, and gibbons—confirm this conclusion.

The significance of this is that most reconstructions of our evolutionary past have emphasized the influence of savanna grassland habitats, so important in Africa, the cradle of hominid evolution. Many anthropologists theorize that shrinking forests and spreading grasslands encouraged our primarily tree-dwelling ancestors to adapt to ground-dwelling conditions,

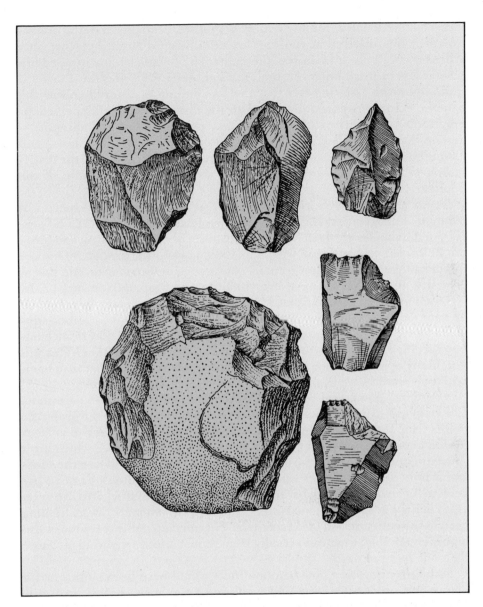

FIGURE 7.4 Choppers and flakes used by *Homo erectus* at Zhoukoudian, China.

giving rise to the unique bipedal gait that is the hallmark of hominids. Bipedalism, in turn, freed the hands for tool use and ultimately led to the evolution of a large-brained, cultural animal. Tropical Asia, instead, apparently was where early hominids had to readapt to tropical forest.

In studying the record, I noticed that the forested zone — the zone that lacked open-dwelling mammals — coincided generally with the distribution of the chopper-chopping tools. The latter appeared to be the products of a forest adaptation that, for one reason or another, deemphasized the utilization of standardized stone tools. At least this held for Southeast Asia; what at first I could not explain was the existence of similar tools in northern China, where fossil horses, camels, and giraffids were present. Finally, I came upon the arresting fact that the distribution of naturally occurring bamboo coincided almost directly with the distribution of chopper-chopping tools. The only exceptions that may possibly be of real antiquity — certain hand ax collections from Kehe and Dingcun, in China, and Chonggok-Ni, in Korea — fall on the northernmost periphery of the distribution of bamboo and probably can be attributed to fluctuation of the boundary.

Today there are, by various estimates, some 1,000 to 1,200 species of bamboo. This giant grass is distributed worldwide, but more than 60 percent of the species are from Asia. Only 16 percent occur in Africa, and those on the Indian subcontinent — to an unknown extent the product of human importation and cultivation — are discontinuous in distribution and low in diversity. By far, the greatest diversity occurs in East and Southeast Asia.

Based on these observations, I hypothesized that the early Asians relied on bamboo for much of their technology. At first I envisioned bamboo simply as a kind of icon representing all nonlithic technology. I now think bamboo specifically must have been an extremely important resource. This was not, in my opinion, because appropriate rock was scarce but because bamboo tools would have been efficient, durable, and highly portable.

There are few useful tools that cannot be constructed from bamboo. Cooking and storage containers, knives, spears, heavy and light projectile points, elaborate traps, rope, fasteners, clothing, and even entire villages can be manufactured from bamboo. In addition to the stalks, which are a source of raw material for the manufacture of a variety of artifacts, the seeds and shoots of many species can be eaten. In historical times, bamboo has been to Asian civilization what the olive tree was to the Greeks. In the great cities of the Far East, bamboo is still the preferred choice for the scaffolding used in the construction of skyscrapers. This incomparable resource is also highly renewable. One can actually hear some varieties growing, at more than one foot per day.

Some may question how bamboo tools would have been sufficient for killing and processing large and medium-size animals. Lethal projectile and stabbing implements can in fact be fashioned from bamboo, but their importance may be exaggerated. Large game accounts for a relatively small proportion of the diet of many modern hunters and gatherers. Furthermore, animals are frequently trapped, collected, killed, and then thrown on a fire and cooked whole prior to using bare hands to dismember the roasted carcass. There are many ethnographic examples among forest peoples of this practice.

The only implements that cannot be manufactured from bamboo are axes or choppers suitable for the working of hard woods. More than a few archeologists have suggested that the stone choppers and resultant

"waste" flakes of Asia were created with the objective of using them to manufacture and maintain nonlithic tools. Bamboo can be easily worked with stone flakes resulting from the manufacture of choppers (many choppers may have been a throwaway component in the manufacture of flakes).

[3]Adapted from "Bamboo and Human Evolution," Geoffrey G. Pope. Excerpted with permission from *Natural History*, October 1989; copyright © The American Museum of Natural History, 1989.

The greater number of tool types found in the Acheulean and contemporary traditions is indicative of *H. erectus'* increased efficiency in dealing with the environment. The greater the range of tool types used, the greater the range of natural resources capable of being exploited in less time, with less effort, and with a higher degree of efficiency. For example, hand axes may have been used to kill game and dig up roots; cleavers to butcher; scrapers to process hides for bedding and clothes; and flake tools to cut meat and shape wooden objects. As argued in the Original Study, the differences between tool kits for the Far East and West are likely indicative of adaptation to specific regions. The same may be indicated by the differences between the tool kits of northern and eastern Europe on the one hand, and southern and western Europe on the other. One suggested explanation for this is that resources were scarcer in the latter region, which was more heavily forested than the former, and that this scarcity was a spur to increasing the efficiency of technology.[4]

The improved technological efficiency of *H. erectus* is also evident in the selection of raw materials. While Oldowan toolmakers frequently used coarse-grained stone such as basalt, their Acheulean counterparts generally used such stone only for their heavier implements, preferring flint or other stones with a high silica content for the smaller ones. During later Acheulean times, two techniques were developed which produced thinner, more sophisticated axes with straighter, sharper cutting edges. The **baton method** of percussion manufacture involved using a bone or antler punch to hit the edge of the flint core. This

Baton method: The technique of stone tool manufacture by striking the raw material with a bone or antler "baton" to remove flakes.

method produced shallow flake scars rather than the crushed edge that the hammerstone method produced on the earlier Acheulean hand axes. In later Acheulean times, the striking platform method was also used to create sharper, thinner axes; the toolmakers would often strike off flakes to create a flat surface near the edge. These flat surfaces, or striking platforms, were set up along the edge of the tool perpendicular to its sides so that the toolmaker could remove long thin flakes stretching from the edge across each side of the tool.

THE USE OF FIRE

Another sign of *H. erectus'* developing technology is the evidence of fires and cooking. Although use of fire may be indicated by burned layers in the cave at Zhoukoudian, this is problematical. Most of the bones and tools in the cave were probably carried there by carnivorous animals and/or water, and the burned layers appear to have resulted from combustion of extensive guano deposits.[5] This could have occurred naturally; yet, *H. erectus* did enter the cave, at least occasionally, and could have been responsible for the fires that ignited the guano. Better evidence comes from the 700,000 year old Kao Poh Nam rock shelter in Thailand, where a roughly circular arrangement of fire-cracked basalt cobbles has been found in associa-

[4]Clive Gamble, *The Paleolithic Settlement of Europe* (Cambridge: Cambridge University Press, 1986), p. 310.

[5]Lewis R. Binford and Chuan Kun Ho, "Taphonomy at a Distance: Zhonkoudian, The Cave Home of Beijing Man?" *Current Anthropology* 26 (1985): 428–429.

tion with artifacts and animal bones. Since such rocks are not native to the rock shelter, and are quite heavy, they probably had to have been carried in by hominids. The reason more readily available limestone rocks were not used for hearths is that when burned, they produce a quicklime, which causes itchy and burning skin rashes.[6] The bones associated with the hearth (which was located near the rock shelter entrance, away from the deeper recesses favored by denning animals) show clear evidence of cut marks from butchering as well as burning.

Although we do not know precisely when *H. erectus* learned to use fire, once they did so, it enabled them to do more than just keep warm. In places like Europe and China, food would have been hard to come by in the long, cold winters, because edible plants were unavailable and the large herds of animals, whose mobility exceeded the potential of humans to maintain contact, dispersed and migrated. One solution would have been to search out the frozen carcasses of animals that had died naturally in the late fall and winter, using long wooden probes to locate them beneath the snow, wooden scoops to dig them out, and fire to thaw them so that they could be butchered and eaten.[7] Furthermore, such fire-assisted scavenging would have made available meat and hides of wooly mammoths, wooly rhinoceroses, and bison, which were probably beyond the ability of *H. erectus* to kill, at least until late in the species' career.

Perhaps it was the use of fire to thaw carcasses that led to the idea of cooking food, thereby altering the forces of natural selection, which previously favored individuals with heavy jaws and large, sharp teeth (food is tougher and needs more chewing when it is uncooked), thus promoting further reduction in tooth size as well as supportive facial architecture. Cooking did more than this, though; because it detoxifies a number of other-

At Olorgesailie in Kenya, 400,000-year-old sites are littered with hundreds of stone tools including hand axes and cleavers.

wise poisonous plants, alters digestion-inhibiting substances so that important vitamins, minerals, and proteins can be absorbed while in the gut, rather than just passing through it unused, and makes complex carbohydrates like starch — high-energy foods — digestible, the basic resources available to humans were substantially increased and made more secure.

Like tools, then, fire gave people more control over their environment. Possibly, *H. erectus* in Southeast Asia used fire, as have more recent populations living there, to keep areas in the forest clear for foot traffic. Certainly, the resistance to burning characteristic of many hardwood trees in this forest today indicates that fire has for a long time been important in their evolution. Fire may also have been used at least occasionally by *H. erectus*, as it was by subsequent hominids, to frighten away cave-dwelling predators so that they might live in the caves themselves; and it could then be used to provide warmth and light in these cold and dark habitations. Even more, it modified the natural succession of day and night, perhaps encouraging *H. erectus* to stay up after dark to review the day's events, and plan the next day's activities.

Although the interpretation is controversial, evidence from a site in Spain has been used to argue that late *H. erectus* used fire to drive ele-

[6]Geoffrey G. Pope, "Bamboo and Human Evolution," *Natural History* Oct 1989, p. 56
[7]Gamble, p. 387.

phants into a bog, where the trapped creatures could easily be slaughtered. If so, such drives must have required cooperation between different groups, which suggests improved organizational techniques and advanced planning.

OTHER ASPECTS OF *HOMO ERECTUS'* CULTURE

There is no evidence that populations of *H. erectus* lived anywhere outside the Old World tropics before a million years ago. Presumably, control of fire was a key element in permitting them to move into cooler regions like Europe and China. In cold winters, however, a fire is of little use without adequate shelter, and *H. erectus'* increased sophistication in the construction of shelters is indicated by the remains of what may be several huts at Terra Amata (Figure 7.5). Here, several huts appear to have been built, probably of saplings. They seem to have been seasonally reoccupied over a number of years, and each apparently had a hearth in the center of its floor.

Keeping warm by the hearth is one thing, but keeping warm away from the hearth when procuring food or other necessities is another. Studies of modern humans indicate that they can remain rea-

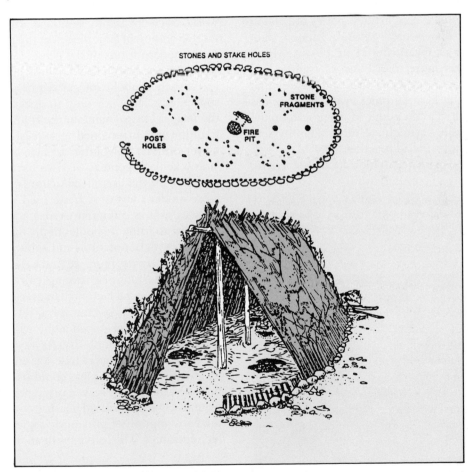

FIGURE 7.5 Terra Amata: plan of hut and artist's reconstruction.

sonably comfortable down to 50° F with a minimum of clothing so long as they are active; below that temperature, the extremities cool to the point of pain;[8] thus, the dispersal of humans into regions where winter temperatures regularly went below 50° F, as they must have in China and Europe, was probably not possible without more in the way of clothing than hominids had hitherto worn. Unfortunately, we have no direct evidence as to the kind of clothing worn by *H. erectus;* we only know that it must have been more sophisticated than before.

That *H. erectus* was able to organize in order to hunt live animals is suggested by remains such as those from Olorgesailie, a site in southwestern Kenya. Here, the bones of at least 13 juvenile and 50 adult members of an extinct species of baboon much larger than today's savanna baboon were found in an area measuring 21 by 14 feet. Mixed with them was more than a ton of cobbles and stone tools including hand axes and cleavers, all from sources at least 20 miles away. The site has been interpreted as the result of an ambush on the baboons, possibly at night to catch them by surprise when they were all together.

There is no evidence to indicate that *H. erectus*

became an accomplished hunter all at once. Presumably, the most ancient members of this species, like *H. habilis* before them, got the bulk of their meat through scavenging. As their cultural capabilities increased, however, they could have devised ways of doing their own killing rather than waiting for animals to die or be killed by other predators. As they became more proficient predators over time, they would have been able to count on a more reliable supply of meat.

Evidence for a developing symbolic life comes from a site in France, where an engraved ox rib was found in an Acheulean context. This could be the earliest of a number of Paleolithic artifacts which have no obvious utility or model in the natural world. Such apparently symbolic artifacts became more common in later phases of the Paleolithic, as more modern forms of the genus *Homo* appeared on the scene. Alexander Marshack argues that the use of such symbolic images requires some sort of spoken language, not only to assign meaning to the images but to maintain the tradition.[9] That a tradition was maintained is suggested by similar motifs on later Paleolithic artifacts. It is also in a late Acheulean context that we have our earliest evidence for the use of red ochre, a pigment that more modern forms of *Homo* used to color symbolic as well as utilitarian artifacts, the bodies of the dead, to paint the bodies of the living and (ultimately) to make notations and paint pictures.

With *H. erectus,* then, we find a clearer manifestation of the interplay among cultural, physical, and environmental factors than ever before. However slowly, social organization, technology, and communication developed along with an increase in brain size and complexity. As a consequence of these, *H. erectus'* resource base was enlarged significantly; the supply of meat could be increased by hunting as well as by scavenging, and the supply of plant foods was increased because cooking allowed the consumption of previously toxic or indigestible vegetables. This, along with an increased abil-

[8]John W. M. Whiting, John A. Sodergem, and Stephen M. Stigler, "Winter Temperature as a Constraint to the Migration of Preindustrial Peoples," *American Anthropologist* 84 (1982): 289.

At Terra Amata in France, a hearth was found that consists of a depression surrounded by stones.

[9]Alexander Marshack, "Some Implications of the Paleolithic Symbolic Evidence for the Origin of Language," *Current Anthropology* 17 (1976): 280.

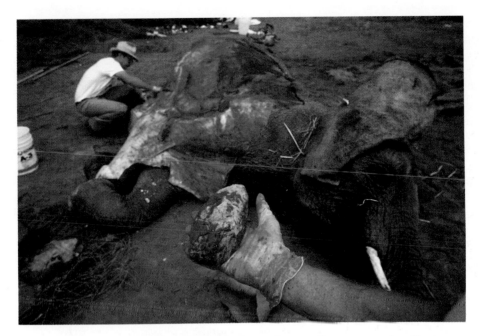

Experimentation on an elephant that died of natural causes demonstrates the effectiveness of Acheulean tools. Simple flint flakes easily slice through the thick hide, while hand axes sever large muscles. With such tools, two men can butcher 100 pounds of meat each in an hour.

ity to modify the environment in advantageous ways — for example, by using fire to provide warmth — undoubtedly contributed to a population increase and territorial expansion. In humans, as in other mammals, any kind of adaptation that makes life significantly easier than it had been reduces selective pressures, reproduction becomes easier, more offspring survive than before, and so

populations grow. This causes fringe populations to "spill over" into neighboring regions previously uninhabited by the species.

Thus, just as *H. habilis* was able to move into areas outside of Africa for the first time, *H. erectus* was able to move into areas outside the tropics — Europe and China that had never been inhabited by hominids before (Figure 7.6).

CHAPTER SUMMARY

The remains of *Homo erectus* have been found at several sites in Africa, Europe, China, and Java. The earliest is 1.6 million years old, and the species endured until about 300,000 years ago. It appears to have evolved, rather abruptly, from *Homo habilis*. From the neck on down, the body of *H. erectus* was essentially modern in appearance. The brain, although small by modern standards, was larger than that of *H. habilis*. The skull was

generally low, with maximum breadth near its base, and massive brow ridges. Powerful teeth and jaws added to a generally rugged appearance.

With *H. erectus*, we find a greater interaction among cultural, physical, and environmental factors than ever before. Social organization and advanced technology developed along with an increase in brain size. The Oldowan chopper evolved into the Acheulean hand ax. These tools,

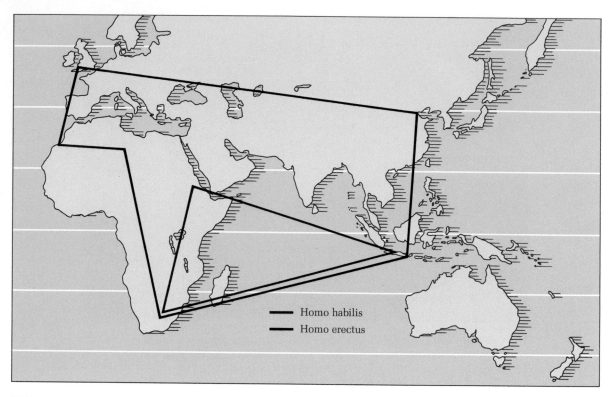

FIGURE 7.6 Areas in which fossils of *Homo habilis* and *Homo erectus* have been found. Evidently, there was a steady expansion of hominid populations into new areas. As the efficiency of cultural adaptation increased, the genus *Homo* expanded into areas previously uninhabited by hominids.

the earliest of which are about 1.4 million years old, are pear shaped, with pointed ends and sharp cutting edges. Like the chopper, they served a general purpose. During Acheulean times, tool cultures began to diversify. Along with hand axes, tool kits included cleavers, scrapers, and flakes. Further signs of *H. erectus'* developing technology was the selection of different stone for different tools and the use of fires for protection, warmth, light, thawing frozen carcasses, and cooking. Cooking is a significant cultural adaptation; it resulted in the decline of certain physical adaptations such as large heavy jaws and teeth because cooked food is easier to chew. During later Acheulean times,

H. erectus used the baton and striking platform methods to make thinner axes with straighter, sharper cutting edges. From France comes evidence of the building of huts and the making of nonutilitarian artifacts; from Africa comes evidence of cooperative efforts to kill large amounts of game.

H. erectus' improved organizational, technological, and communicative abilities led to more effective hunting and a greater ability to modify the environment in advantageous ways. As a result, the populations of these early hominids increased and they expanded into new geographic areas.

SUGGESTED READINGS

Brace, C. Loring, Harry Nelson, and Noel Korn. *An Atlas of Human Evolution*, 2d ed. New York: Holt, Rinehart and Winston, 1979. This useful atlas includes a map of important *Homo erectus* sites and distribution of Lower Paleolithic tools, an illustration of Acheulean tools, and drawings of *H. erectus* fossils from Java, China, Africa, and Europe. These are accompanied by notes on dating, place of discovery, and interpretation.

Campbell, Bernard G. *Humankind Emerging*, 5th ed. Boston: Little, Brown, 1988. This book, incorporating material from the Time-Life *Emergence of Man* series, has good, up-to-date coverage of *Homo erectus* and their way of life.

Gamble, Clive. *The Paleolithic Settlement of Europe*. Cambridge: Cambridge University Press, 1986. Although it does not deal exclusively with *Homo erectus*, it does discuss material from Europe associated with this species. In doing so, it takes a critical stance to conventional interpretations and offers new explanations of *H. erectus'* behavior based on a better understanding of the process of archeological site formation.

White, Edmond, Dale Brown, and the editors of Time-Life. *The First Men*. New York: Time-Life, 1973. This magnificently illustrated volume in the Time-Life *Emergence of Man* series deals with *Homo erectus*. Its one drawback is that it portrays early *H. erectus* as too much of a "big game hunter"; nonetheless, it remains a good introduction to the fossils, sites, and tools associated with this hominid.

8

HOMO SAPIENS AND THE LATER PALEOLITHIC

The intellectual capabilities of Upper Paleolithic peoples, whose skeletons differ in no significant ways from our own, are reflected in the efficiency with which some of them hunted game far larger and more powerful than themselves, as well as the sophistication of their art. Shown here is a painting of a bull—one of the animals hunted—by an artist who was not only a master of the medium, but also knew intimately the anatomy of the animal depicted.

CHAPTER

PREVIEW

Who Was "Archaic" Homo sapiens?

"Archaic" *Homo sapiens* is the name used for members of this species who lived before about 35,000 years ago. Included are the Neandertals, descendants of *H. erectus*, who lived in Europe and western Asia between about 100,000 and 35,000 years ago, and other populations somewhat like them who lived in Africa, China, and Southeast Asia. All had essentially modern-sized brains in skulls which still retained a number of primitive features.

When Did More Modern Forms of Homo sapiens *Appear?*

By about 90,000 years ago, populations of *Homo sapiens* were living in Africa, and at least parts of Asia, that did not differ greatly in appearance from modern humans. In Europe, however, anatomically modern forms of *H. sapiens* were present no earlier than about 40,000 years ago.

What Happened to Culture after Humans Achieved Modern-Sized Brains?

By 100,000 years ago, human culture had become rich and varied. People not only made a wide variety of stone tools for special purposes, but they also made objects for purely symbolic purposes, engaged in ceremonial activities, and cared for the old and disabled. Although the human brain has not become larger since then, culture has continued to evolve and change to the present time. In the latter part of the Paleolithic, cultural diversity increased as people adapted ever more specifically to the diverse regions in which they already lived, and into which expanding human populations were moving. In the Meso-lithic, or Middle Stone Age, the process of regional adaptation continued as environments throughout the world changed in the immediate postglacial era.

The anthropologist attempting to piece together the innumerable parts of the puzzle of human evolution must be as good a detective as a scholar, for the available evidence is often scant, enigmatic, or full of misleading clues. The quest for the origin of modern humans from more ancient representatives of the genus *Homo* has some of the elements of a detective story, for it contains a number of mysteries concerning the emergence of humanity, none of which has been completely solved to this day. The mysteries involve the appearance of the first fully sapient humans, the identity of the Neandertals, and the relationship of both to more modern forms.

This skull, from Ethiopia, is one of several from Africa indicative of a transition from *Homo erectus* to *Homo sapiens*.

THE APPEARANCE OF *HOMO SAPIENS*

At various sites in Europe and Africa, a number of hominid fossils have been found which seem to date, roughly, between 300,000 and 200,000 years ago. These include skulls and skull fragments from Casablanca and Salé in Morocco, Arago in France, Steinheim and Bilzingsleben in Germany, Swanscombe in England, Vertessöllös in Hungary, and Bodo in Ethiopia (although this one could be older); and jaws and jaw fragments from Casablanca (two sites), Rabat, and Temara in Morocco, and Arago and Montmaurin in France. Some of these—most commonly the African fossils, but also the Arago skull—have been called *Homo erectus;* others—most commonly those from Steinheim and Swanscombe—have been called *H. sapiens.* In fact, most of them show a mixture of characteristics of both forms, which is what one would expect of remains transitional between the two. For example, the skulls from Bodo, Steinheim, and Swanscombe had rather large brains for *H. erectus.* The overall appearance of the skulls, however, is different from ours. They are large and robust with their maximum breadth lower on the skull, and they had more prominent brow ridges, larger faces, and bigger teeth. Even the Salé skull,

which had a rather small brain for *H. sapiens* (about 930–960 cubic centimeters), looks surprisingly modern from the back. Finally, the various jaws from Morocco and France seem to combine features of *H. erectus* with those of the European Neandertals.

Whether one chooses to call these early humans "primitive" *H. sapiens* or "advanced" *H. erectus* seems to be a matter of taste; whichever one calls them does not alter their apparently transitional status.

LEVALLOISIAN TECHNIQUE

The culture of the hominids transitional between *H. erectus* and *H. sapiens* seems little changed from that of their predecessors. Primitive *sapiens* (or advanced *H. erectus*, if that is what one wishes to call them), for example, used the kinds of heavy-duty tools such as hand axes and smaller flake tools used by *H. erectus* for thousands of years; however, by 200,000 years ago, the **Levalloisian technique** of tool manufacture had come into use. Levalloisian flake tools have been found widely in Africa, Europe, the Middle East, and even China, where practically no hand axes have been uncovered. It is likely that this is a case of independent invention, since eastern Asia is quite distinct culturally from the west. In the Levalloisian technique, the core was shaped by removal of flakes over its surface, following which a striking platform was made by a crosswise blow at one end of the core of stone (Figure 8.1). Then the platform was struck, removing three or four long flakes, leaving a nodule that looked like a tortoise shell. This method produced a longer edge for the same amount of flint than the previous ones. The edges were sharper and could be produced in less time.

ARCHAIC *HOMO SAPIENS*

The scarcity of *H. sapiens* fossils predating 100,000 years ago is in marked contrast to the situation after that date, by which time the Neandertals were becoming widespread in Europe and western Asia, while other representatives of archaic *H. sapiens* are known from East Asia and Africa.

In 1856, three years before publication of Darwin's *On the Origin of Species*, the skeletal remains of an early man were discovered in the Neander Valley — *Neandertal* in German — near Dusseldorf, Germany. Although the discovery was of considerable interest, the experts were generally at a loss as to what to make of it. Examination of the fossil skull, a few ribs, and some limb bones revealed that the individual was a human being, showing primitive and modern characteristics. The cranial capacity had reached modern proportions, but the skull was still primitive looking. Some people believed the bones were those of a sickly and deformed contemporary. Others thought the skeleton belonged to a soldier who had succumbed to "water on the brain" during the Napoleonic Wars. A prominent anatomist thought the remains were those of an idiot suffering from malnutrition,

Levalloisian technique: Toolmaking technique developed about 200,000 years ago by which three or four long triangular flakes were detached from a specially prepared core.

Neandertals: Representatives of "archaic" *Homo sapiens* in Europe and western Asia, living from about 100,000 years ago to about 35,000 years ago.

whose violent temper had gotten him into many scrapes, flattening his forehead and making his brow ridges bumpy.

The idea that **Neandertals** were somehow deformed or aberrant was given impetus by an analysis of a Neandertal skeleton found in 1908 near La Chapelle-Aux-Saints in France. The analysis mistakenly concluded that the specimen's brain was apelike and that it walked like an ape. Although a team of North American investigators subsequently proved that this French Neandertal specimen was that of an elderly *H. sapiens* who had suffered from malnutrition, arthritis of the spine, and other deformities, the apelike image has persisted. To many nonanthropologists, Neandertal has become the quintessential "caveman," portrayed by imaginative cartoonists as a slant-headed, stooped, dim-witted individual clad in animal skins and carrying a big club as he plods across the prehistoric landscape, perhaps dragging behind him an unwilling female or a dead leopard. In the best-selling novel, *Clan of the Cave Bear*, Neandertals are depicted as bow legged and barrel chested, with extra long arms — more like those of apes than humans — and incapable of the full range of human arm movements; also, muzzlelike jaws and a body covering of coarse brown hair — not quite a pelt but not far from it. This brutish image is completed by portraying them as incapable of spoken language, abstract thought, thinking in new ways, or even thinking ahead.

With the discovery that Neandertals were nowhere near as brutish and apelike as originally portrayed, some scholars began to see them as no more than "less finished" versions of the anatomically modern populations that held exclusive sway

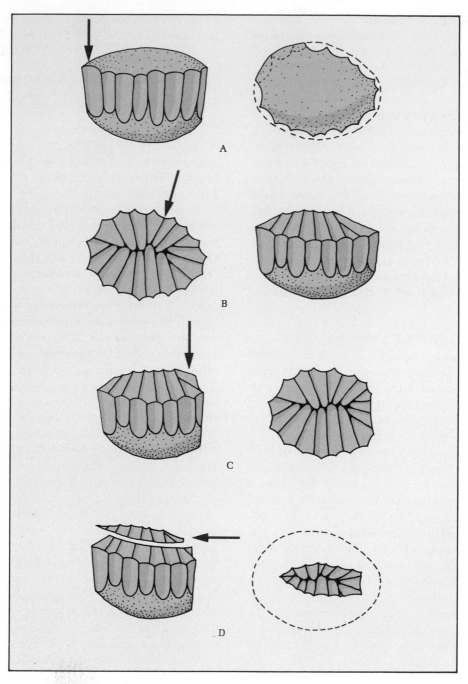

FIGURE 8.1 These drawings show top and side views of the steps in the Levalloisian technique. *A*, the trimming of the edge of the stone nucleus; *B*, the trimming of the top surface; *C*, the striking platform; *D*, the final step.

in Europe and the Middle East after 30,000 years ago. For example, Ashley Montagu argued that some faint ancestral Neandertal characteristics may still be seen even in today's Middle Eastern and European populations, with their relatively prominent brow ridges, deep eye sockets, and receding foreheads and chins.[1] Nevertheless, recent work has shown that significant differences do exist between Neandertals and anatomically modern populations. Although they had modern-sized brains (average cranial capacity, 1400 vs. 1300 cubic centimeters for modern *H. sapiens*), Neandertal skulls are distinctive in the midfacial projection of their noses and teeth, which form a kind of prow. This is due at least in part to the large size of their front teeth, which were heavily used for tasks other than chewing. In many individuals, they were worn down to the stubs of their roots by 35 to 40 years of age. The eye sockets were also positioned well forward, with prominent brow ridges above them. At the back of the skull, a bony mass provided for attachment of powerful neck muscles.

Both sexes were extraordinarily muscular, with extremely robust and dense limb bones. Details of the shoulder blades indicate the importance of overarm and downward thrusting movements; their arms were exceptionally powerful, and pronounced attachments on their hand bones attest to a remarkably strong grip. Their massive foot and leg bones (their shin bones, for example, were twice as strong as those of any recent human population) suggests a high level of endurance; evidently, Neandertals spent long hours walking and scrambling about. Since brain size is related to overall body mass as well as intelligence, the large average size of the Neandertal brain (compared to that of modern humans) is accounted for by their heavy robust bodies.

Although the shape of the Neandertal pelvis differs from that of anatomically modern humans, the size of the pelvic inlet was not significantly different, and the length of gestation was probably the same as it is in people today.[2] The differences in pelvic shape are easily accounted for by the larger size of Neandertal infants, locomotor differences, and deviation in anatomically modern humans from the shape characteristic of earlier hominids. On the other hand, Neandertal infants did mature more rapidly than do our own, as the characteristic Neandertal robustness can be dis-

[1]Ashley Montagu, *Man: His First Two Million Years* (New York: Columbia University Press, 1969).

[2]Connie M. Anderson, "Neandertal Pelves and Gestational Length," *American Anthropologist* 91 (1989): 336.

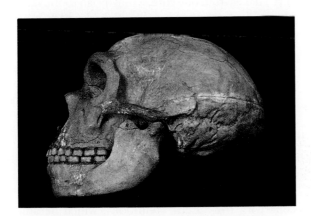
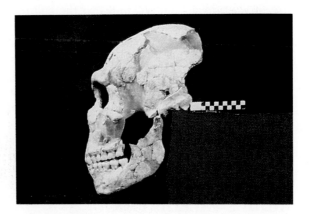

Two typical Neandertal skulls from Europe. The one on the *right* is from Saint-Césaire, France, and is one of the most recent Neandertal skulls known.

cerned in the bones of children who died even be-fore the age of five years. Furthermore, their teeth erupted earlier, and their brains grew more rapidly after birth than do our own.

AFRICAN, CHINESE, AND JAVANESE POPULATIONS

Because Neandertal fossils are so numerous, have been known for so long, and are relatively well dated, they have received much more attention than have other populations of archaic *H. sapiens*. Nevertheless, outside of Europe and western Asia, a number of skulls have been found in Africa, China, and Java, which, though poorly dated, are roughly contemporary with the Neandertals, or at least the earliest ones. They differ from the Nean-dertals primarily in their lack of midfacial projec-tion and the absence of such massive muscle at-tachments on the back of their skull. Basically, they look like robust versions of the early modern populations that lived in the same regions or, if one looks backward, somewhat less primitive ver-sions of the *H. erectus* populations that preceded them. All had fully modern-sized brains.

THE CULTURE OF ARCHAIC *HOMO SAPIENS*

As the first hominids to possess brains of modern size, it is not surprising to find that the cultural capabilities of archaic *H. sapiens* were significantly improved over those of earlier hominids. Such a brain made possible an advanced technology as well as conceptual thought of considerable sophis-tication, and communication was almost surely by speech. In short, Neandertals and others like them were a fully sapient species of human being, rela-tively successful in surviving and even thriving in environments that would seem to us impossibly cold and hostile.

MIDDLE PALEOLITHIC

The improved toolmaking capabilities of archaic *H. sapiens* are represented by various **Middle Pa-leolithic** traditions, of which the best known are

Middle Paleolithic: That part of the Paleolithic characterized by the emergence of archaic *Homo sapiens* and the development of the Mousterian tra-dition of toolmaking.

Mousterian tradition: Toolmaking tradition of the Neandertals and their contemporaries of Europe, western Asia, and northern Africa, featur-ing flake tools lighter and smaller than Levalloisian flake tools.

the Mousterian and Mousterianlike traditions of Europe, western Asia, and North Africa, which date from about 100,000 to 40,000 years ago; they represent a technological advance over Acheulean and Levalloisian tools. The 16 inches of working edge that an Acheulean flint worker could get from a 2-pound core compares with the 6 feet the Mousterian could get from the same core.

The Mousterian Tradition

The **Mousterian tradition** is named after the Neandertal site of Le Moustier, France. The pres-ence of Acheulean hand axes at Neandertal sites is one indication that Mousterian culture was ulti-mately rooted in the older Acheulean tradition. Neandertals improved upon Levalloisian tech-niques; Mousterian flake tools are lighter and smaller than those of the Levalloisian. Whereas Levalloisian toolmakers obtained only two or three flakes from one core, Mousterian toolmakers obtained many more smaller flakes, which were then skillfully retouched and sharpened.

The Mousterian tool kits contained a much greater variety of tool types than the previous tra-ditions: hand axes, flakes, scrapers, borers, gravers, notched flakes for sawing and shredding wood, and many types of points that could be attached to wooden shafts to form thrusting spears. This vari-ety of tool types indicates that the Mousterian tool kit intensified human utilization of food resources and increased the availability and quality of cloth-ing and shelter. For the first time, people could cope with truly arctic conditions, which became prevalent in Europe beginning about 70,000 years ago.

People may have come to live in cold climates as

Two characteristic
Mousterian tools; a side
scraper and a point.

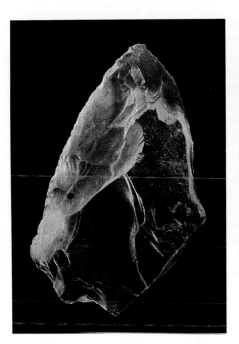 

a result of a slow but steady population increase during the Paleolithic era. As this caused populations to "spill over" into previously uninhabited colder regions, humans developed a series of cold-climate adaptations that increased their cultural variability. Under arctic conditions, vegetable foods are only rarely or seasonally available, and meat is the staff of life. In particular, animal fats, rather than carbohydrates, become the chief source of energy on account of their slower rate of metabolism. Abundant animal fat in the diets of cold-climate meat eaters provides them with the extra energy needed for full-time hunting as well as needed body heat. Insufficient fat in the diet produces lower resistance to disease, lassitude, and a loss of the will to work. That meat was important to the makers of Mousterian tools is indicated by the following Original Study.

ORIGINAL STUDY
Subsistence Practices of Mousterian Peoples[3]

Most of the recent discussions of changes in subsistence strategies across the archaic/modern human transition have focused on a series of generalizations formulated in the recent publications of Binford. In essence, these can be reduced to three basic propositions:

1. Prior to the emergence of anatomically modern populations, the exploitation of animal resources was focused primarily on the scavenging of meat

and bone marrow from carnivore kills and included only a relatively minor and secondary component of deliberate hunting of game.

2. Where some hunting was practiced by these archaic populations, it was focused almost entirely on the smaller species of game, especially various species of cervids [deer family] and some of the smaller species of bovids [cattle family].

3. Any deliberate hunting or killing of game by archaic populations was undertaken essentially on an opportunistic or encounter basis and involved little if any deliberate planning, forethought, or "logistical organization" on the part of the human groups.

Binford's interpretations are original and provocative and have undoubtedly served to stimulate more sharply focused research on the problems of Lower and Middle Paleolithic subsistence. Recently, however, they have been challenged from a number of perspectives. In particular, Chase and others have drawn attention to at least three aspects of the current data which would appear to run directly counter to Binford's hypotheses:

1. The faunal assemblages recovered from several Middle Paleolithic sites in Europe reveal a heavy bias in favor of one particular species, which would seem difficult if not impossible to account for by any hypothesis of essentially random or opportunistic exploitation. Examples of these heavily single-species-dominated faunas have been recorded at Staroselje in the Crimea, Ilskaya, Teshik-Tash, and Volgograd in southern Russia, and Ehringsdorf in Germany, as well as at several recently excavated sites in France. One of the most striking illustrations of this single-species orientation has been documented in the recent excavations at Mauran in the French Pyrenees, where (according to preliminary reports) well over 90% of the faunal assemblage (representing at least 108 animals) consists of the remains of large bovids (*Bos/Bison*). As Chase points out, it is difficult to visualize these heavily specialized faunas as the result of either opportunistic scavenging or unstructured encounter hunting on the part of Neanderthal groups. Both of the latter sample the whole range of animal species within the immediate catchment areas of the sites, roughly in proportion to their relative frequencies in the local faunal communities. The fact that the faunal assemblage from Mauran (as well as other) sites consisted almost entirely of very large game (large bovids, with individual carcass weights of up to 900 kg) runs counter to Binford's hypothesis that hunting was focused exclusively on the smaller species of game.

2. The detailed studies carried out by Chase, Levine, and others of the faunal assemblages from the long Mousterian succession at Combe Grenal (southwestern France) have produced results which conflict in several respects with those reported by Binford from his earlier studies at this site. Thus, Chase has demonstrated that the remains of both horses and large bovids at Combe Grenal (which Binford has maintained were exclusively *scavenged*) are represented more frequently by the major meat-bearing

bones from the *upper* parts of the limbs than by the meat-poor bones from the lower limbs and that these bones frequently bear clear cut marks (presumably through fresh flesh) as opposed to indications of heavy chopping through the remains of partially desiccated carcasses. Both these observations are much more consistent with the notion of deliberate hunting of large game than with that of scavenging of remains from natural-death carcasses or abandoned carnivore kills. Similarly, Levine has shown that the age profiles of the horse remains from three separate levels at Combe Grenal appear to indicate an essentially "catastrophic" pattern closely similar to that to be expected in a living herd. This pattern again bears little resemblance to what one would anticipate from the scavenging of carnivore kills, which would be likely to reflect a primary emphasis on the oldest and youngest age-classes, the most vulnerable elements in the animal herds. As Levine points out, these age profiles would conform best to some form of unselective, mass hunting strategies on the part of the Mousterian groups.

3. Finally, the specific character and location of several Middle Paleolithic sites in Europe may well provide some direct insight into the methods by which large game was hunted by Mousterian groups. At the site of La Quina in western France, for example, a dense accumulation of bones of bovids, horses, and reindeer (many with clear indications of butchery marks) occurs immediately at the base of a steep cliff, the only topographic feature of this kind within several kilometres of the site. As Jelinek, Debenath, and Dibble and Chase have pointed out, there would seem to be a strong implication in this case that the site represents a typical jump or cliff-fall hunting site, in which the animals were deliberately driven over the cliff as part of a systematic hunting strategy. A similar situation has been documented in the recent excavations at Mauran, where an accumulation of several thousands of bones of large bovids again occurs immediately at the foot of a steep riverside escarpment. And in a slightly different context, Scott has recently argued that the highly localized and dense accumulations of mammoth and woolly rhinoceros bones at the site of La Cotte de Saint-Brelade (Channel Islands) can only be plausibly explained in terms of some similar strategy of cliff-fall hunting — in this case into a deep coastal ravine. In none of these cases is there any convincing way of explaining the bone accumulations as accidental death assemblages. The strong implication, in other words, is that Middle Paleolithic populations in Europe were practicing some form of organized, systematic cliff-fall hunting in many ways reminiscent of that reflected in the Paleo-Indian bison-jump kill sites of North America [see p. 194]. As a further indication of the deliberate killing of game in Middle and Lower Paleolithic contexts, one could refer to the well-documented discoveries of wooden spears at the sites of Clacton (England) and Lehringen (Germany) and the recent confirmation from microwear studies that at least certain forms of Mousterian and Levallois points would seem to have functioned as the hafted tips of either thrusting or throwing spears.

The combination of the preceding data leaves little doubt that the Neandertal populations of Europe *were* practicing a good deal of deliberate hunting of very large game, and in a way that can hardly be described as totally unstructured or opportunistic.

[3]Paul Mellars, "Major Issues in the Emergence of Modern Humans," *Current Anthropology* 30 (1989): 356–357. Copyright © 1989 by the University of Chicago Press. Reprinted by permission.

The importance of hunting to Mousterian peoples may also be reflected in their hunting implements, which are more standardized with respect to size and shape than are their domestic and maintenance implements. The complexity of the tool kit needed for survival in a cold climate may have played a role in lessening the mobility of the "owners" of all of these possessions. That they were less mobile is suggested by the greater depth of deposits at Mousterian sites compared with those from the earlier Paleolithic. Similarly, evidence for long sequences of production, resharpening and discarding of tools, large-scale butchery and cooking of game, and evidence of efforts to improve accommodations in some caves and rock shelters through pebble paving, construction of simple walls, and the presence of postholes and artificial pits all suggest that Mousterian sites were more than mere stop overs in peoples' constant quest for food. The large number of Mousterian sites uncovered in Europe and western Asia, as well as clear differences between them are closely related to Neandertal's improved hunting techniques, based on superior technology in weapon and toolmaking and more efficient social organization than before. These, in turn, were closely related to Neandertal's increased brain size.

Neandertal society had developed even to the point of being able to care for the handicapped members of the group; it appears that the disabled were often cared for by their fellows. The remains of a blind amputee discovered in Shanidar Cave in Iraq and a man crippled by arthritis unearthed at La Chapelle attest to this fact. Whether or not this indicates true "compassion" on the part of these early people is not known; what is certain is that culture had become more than barely adequate to ensure survival.

Although earlier reports of evidence for some sort of "cave bear cult" have turned out to be far fetched, indications of some sort of symbolic life do exist. At some sites, there is clear evidence for deliberate burial of the dead. For example, at Shanidar Cave evidence was found of a burial accompanied by funeral ceremonies. In the back of the cave a Neandertal was buried in a pit. Pollen analysis of the soil around the skeleton indicated that flowers had been placed below the body and in a wreath about the head. Moreover, the flowers consist solely of varieties valued in historic times for their medicinal properties.

Other evidence for symbolic behavior in Mousterian culture comes from the use of two different pigments: manganese dioxide and red ochre. These show clear evidence of scraping to produce powder, as well as crayonlike facets. Thus, Mousterian peoples were clearly using these for applying color to things. One example is the carved and shaped section of a mammoth tooth illustrated on page 181 that was worked by Mousterian peoples about 50,000 years ago. One of a number of carved and engraved objects that may have been made for purely symbolic purposes, it is similar to a number of plaques of bone and ivory made by later Paleolithic peoples, and it is also similar to the "churingas" made of wood by Australian Aborigines for ritual purposes. The Mousterian object, which was once smeared with red ochre, has a highly polished face as if from long handling. Microscopic examination reveals that it was never provided with a working edge for any utilitarian purpose.

Carved symbolic plaque or "churinga" made from a section of a mammoth molar excavated at the Mousterian site of Tata, Hungary. The edge is rounded and polished from long handling. The plaque has been symbolically smeared with red ochre. *Right*, reverse face of the plaque, indicating the beveling and shaping of the tooth.

NEANDERTALS AND SPOKEN LANGUAGE

Among modern humans, the sharing of thoughts and ideas, as well as the transmission of culture from one generation to the next, is dependent on a spoken language. Since the Neandertals had modern-sized brains and a tool kit comparable to that being used in historic times by Australian Aborigines, it might be supposed that they had some form of spoken language. Despite this, the argument has been made that the Neandertals lacked the physical features necessary for spoken language. It has been shown, however, that the reconstruction of the Neandertal larynx, on which this argument is partially based, is faulty. Moreover, the brain (as reflected by endocranial casts) suggests that Neandertals had the neural development necessary for language. Finally, modern adults with as much flattening of the skull base and facial protrusion as some Neandertals have no

trouble talking. Talking Neandertals make a good deal of sense in view of the evidence, sparse though it may be, for the manufacture objects of apparently symbolic significance. Objects such as the mammoth tooth "churinga" already described would seem to have required some form of linguistic explanation. On the other hand, any language spoken by Neandertals need not have been as complex as those used by their later Paleolithic successors.

ARCHAIC *HOMO SAPIENS* AND MODERN HUMAN ORIGINS

One of the hot debates in paleoanthropology today is over the question: Did populations of archaic *H. sapiens* in most, if not all, parts of the Old World evolve simultaneously into anatomically modern humans, or was there a single, geographic place of origin from which anatomically modern *H. sapiens* spread to replace existing populations of the archaic species everywhere else? Based on the fossil evidence from Africa and some parts of Asia, a good case can be made for the former, as opposed to the latter hypothesis. As several anthropologists have noted, African, Chinese, and Southeast Asian fossils of archaic *H. sapiens* imply local population continuity across the *H. erectus* to modern transition,[4] lending strong support to the interpretation that there was genetic continuity in these regions. Instead of evolving extremely pointed faces and massive neck musculature, as did the Neandertals, these other populations experienced a reduction in total facial protrusion as facial robusticity decreased, while the backs of their skulls took on a more modern form.

One evident exception to this scenario consists of the Neandertals of Europe and western Asia. In the Middle East, there is now clear evidence for coexistence between Neandertals and more modern forms for at least 20,000 to 30,000 years. At Qafzeh, in Israel, for example, 90,000-year-old skeletons show none of the Neandertal hallmarks; although their faces and bodies are large and heavily built by today's standards, they are nonetheless within the range of present day peoples. For a time, both populations made and used Mousterian tools, but about 40,000 to 47,000 years ago, the more modern people began to make and use tools of the **Aurignacian tradition,** which mark the beginning of the **Upper Paleolithic** period in western Eurasia. This new technology spread into Europe by about 35,000 to 40,000 years ago, and when found in association with human skeletons, the latter are invariably modern in their features. Nevertheless, Neandertals are known to have survived in western Europe until 33,000 to 35,000 years ago, so again, coexistence between the two forms of *sapiens* is indicated. Given the striking anatomical differences between the two, some form of population replacement, rather than sim-

> **Aurignacian tradition:** Toolmaking tradition of anatomically modern *H. sapiens* in Europe and western Asia at the beginning of the Upper Paleolithic.
>
> **Upper Paleolithic:** The last part of the Paleolithic, characterized by the emergence of anatomically modern hominids and the development of the blade technique of toolmaking.

ple evolution from one to the other, must have occurred.

How or why this replacement took place remains a mystery. There seems to have been nothing in the physical or mental makeup of Neandertals to prevent them from leading a "typical" Upper Paleolithic way of life, as in fact the final Neandertals of western, central, and eastern Europe did.[5] Borrowing many ideas and techniques from the Aurignacians, they created their own Upper Paleolithic cultures (see Figure 8.2). As paleoanthropologist Elwyn Simons observes:

> For me it is difficult to see how two genetically isolated species of humans could have so recently arisen. Primates often produce hybrids in the wild when two species or subspecies come into contact. Humans in conflict typically capture and incorporate unrelated women and children into their bands. Hunting and eating a species that is vastly different, as far as intelligence is concerned, might explain the disappearance of *A. boisei* at the hands of *Homo*, but Neandertals and modern humans shared equal brain size, tool kits, and other advanced practices.[6]

THE EVE HYPOTHESIS

Recently, some anthropologists have argued that anatomically modern humans are descended from one specific population of *H. sapiens*, replacing not just the Neandertals, but other populations of archaic *H. sapiens* as our ancestors spread out of their original homeland. Evidence for this hypothesis comes not from fossils, but from a relatively new technique which uses mitochondrial DNA to re-

[4]Erik Trinkhaus, "The Neandertals and Modern Human Origins," *Annual Review of Anthropology* (1986): 196–197.

[5]Paul Mellars, "Major Issues in the Emergence of Modern Humans," *Current Anthropology*, 1989, 30: 356–357.
[6]Elwyn L. Simons, "Human Origins," *Science* 245 (1989): 1349.

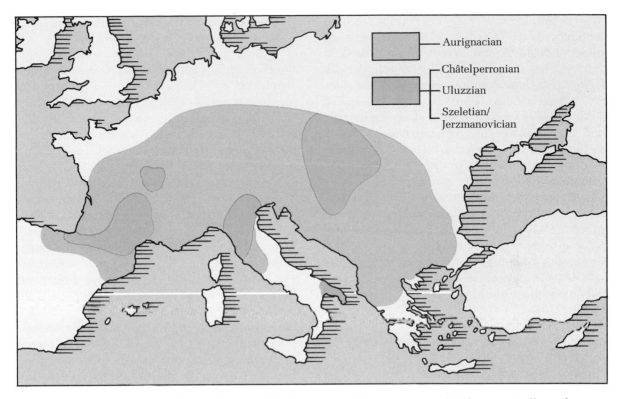

FIGURE 8.2 This map shows the distribution of the Aurignacian industry, associated with anatomically modern *Homo sapiens*, and the Mousterian-derived Upper Paleolithic industries of the last Neandertal populations in Europe, about 30,000 to 40,000 years ago.

construct family trees. Unlike the DNA that determines physical traits, mitochondrial DNA is located outside the cell nucleus in compartments that produce energy needed to keep cells alive. Since the male sperm is not large enough to carry mitochondrial DNA, it is inherited only from one's mother and is not "rescrambled" with each succeeding generation. Therefore, it should be altered only by mutation. By comparing the mitochondrial DNA of living individuals from diverse geographical populations, anthropologists and molecular biologists seek to determine when and where modern *H. sapiens* originated. As widely reported in the popular press, preliminary results suggest that the mitochondrial DNA of all living humans can be traced back to a "Mitochondrial Eve" who lived in Africa (though some say Asia)

some 200,000 years ago. If so, all other populations of archaic *H. sapiens*, as well as early *H. erectus*, would have to be ruled out of the ancestry of modern humans.

Although modern features do seem to appear earlier in African fossils than in those from other regions, this "Eve hypothesis" has been criticized on several grounds. For one thing, it conflicts with the fossil evidence for continuity between older and more recent populations in many, though not all, parts of the Old World. It seems to ask too much of coincidence that many features seen in premodern populations in places like China, the Middle East (excluding Neandertals), and Southeast Asia should reappear in recent populations in those same regions if these latter populations represent unrelated newcomers. There are methodological problems as well; for example, debate continues as to whether rates of change in mitochondrial DNA are as regular and as rapid as claimed. New calculations suggest movement out of Africa may have been some 1 million or so years ago,[7] which is more in line with when a pre-*sapiens* species of *Homo* spread beyond its ancient homeland. Furthermore, the technique is new, and all the problems may not yet be worked out. Even well-established techniques of molecular analysis sometimes yield conflicting results, and may be perturbed by such things as transfer of DNA between populations as a consequence of shared viral infections.[8] For the moment, it pays to be cautious; analysis of mitochondrial DNA, while undoubtedly promising, is still in its infancy and probably does not yet yield results that are as clear and precise as we would like.

UPPER PALEOLITHIC PEOPLES: THE FIRST MODERN HUMANS

Although populations of archaic and anatomically modern *H. sapiens* managed to coexist in some parts of the world for 50,000 years or so, by 30,000 years ago, anatomically modern peoples with Upper Paleolithic cultures had the world to themselves. The remains of these ancient peoples who looked so much like us were first discovered in 1868 at Les Eyzies in France in a rock shelter called Cro-Magnon, and so European remains from the Upper Paleolithic are often referred to as **Cro-Magnons.** Between 1872 and 1902, the fossils of 13 other specimens were unearthed in the caves of the Cote d'Azur near the Italian Riviera. Since then, various other Cro-Magnon skeletons have been unearthed in various parts of Europe.

The Cro-Magnons have suffered their share of idealization on the part of physical anthropologists; at one time, they were made to look like

---

[7]Simons, p. 1349.
[8]Roger Lewin, "Molecular Clocks Turn a Quarter Century," *Science* 239 (1988): 562; Timothy Rowe, "New Issues for Phylogenetics," *Science* 239 (1988): 1184.

| **Cro-Magnons:** The first fully modern Europeans, of Upper Paleolithic times.

Greek gods, in contrast to the Neandertals, who supposedly stood just a step ahead of the ape. The idea lives on in *The Clan of the Cave Bear*, in which the heroine is portrayed as a tall, slender, blonde-haired blue-eyed beauty. As more Upper Paleolithic remains have been found, in Africa, Asia, and Europe, more physical variability has been shown, as is to be expected from any human population. Therefore, it is hardly surprising to find specimens that exhibit distinct features. In some ways, such as in the size of the brain, in the narrow nasal openings, and in the high, broad forehead, the European Cro-Magnons resembled modern Europeans. But their faces, for example, were shorter and broader than those of modern Europeans, and their brow ridges were a bit more prominent. Nor were they usually as tall as modern Europeans.

Generally speaking, Upper Paleolithic people in all parts of the world evolved a modern-looking face; the full-sized brain had already been achieved by archaic *H. sapiens*, no doubt as a consequence of increased reliance on cultural adaptation. Ultimately, this emphasis on cultural adaptation led to the development of more complex tool kits. The modernization of the face of Upper Paleolithic peoples is the result of a reduction in the size of the teeth, and eventually the jaw, as specialized tools increasingly took over the cutting, softening, and clamping functions once performed by the front teeth. The cooking of food (which began with *H. erectus*) had already favored a reduction in size of the teeth and muscles involved in chewing; consequently, the jaws reduced in size, accompanied by loss of robust sites for muscle attachment and features like brow ridges that buttress the skull from the stresses and strains imposed by massive jaw muscles.

Technological improvements also reduced the intensity of selective pressures favoring especially massive, robust bodies. With more emphasis on elongate tools with greater mechanical advantages, more effective techniques of hafting, and a switch from thrusting to throwing spears, there

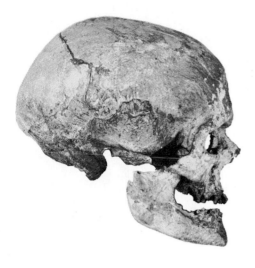
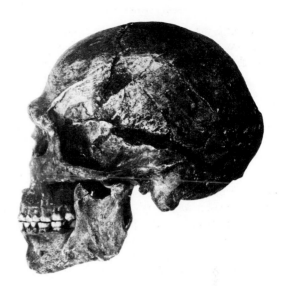

Left, the original Cro-Magnon skull, which differs very little from modern European skulls. *Right*, a much earlier anatomically modern skull from the 90,000-year-old site of Qafzeh, Israel.

was a marked reduction in overall muscularity. Moreover, the skeletons of Upper Paleolithic peoples show far less evidence of trauma than do those of archaic *H. sapiens*, whose bones almost always show evidence of injury.

Upper Paleolithic peoples also tended to live longer than their archaic predecessors. Furthermore, the prolonged period of development characteristic of the human species today, which allows people to learn so much before they are responsible for themselves as adults, was associated with the appearance of anatomically modern peoples. Perhaps both have something to do with the burst of creativity that was a part of Upper Paleolithic culture. Being too old for most day-to-day subsistence activities, but able to recall events beyond the experience of younger adults, elders could have spent more time, passing on a greater store of wisdom, to youngsters who were capable of absorbing it all.

UPPER PALEOLITHIC TOOLS

The typical Upper Paleolithic tool was the blade, a flint flake at least twice as long as it is wide. Although Middle Paleolithic toolmakers, especially

> **Blade technique:** A technique of stone tool manufacture by which long, parallel-sided flakes are struck off the edges of a specially prepared core.
>
> **Pressure flaking:** A technique of stone tool manufacture in which a bone, antler, or wooden tool is used to press, rather than strike off, small flakes from a piece of flint or similar stone.

in Africa, occasionally made blades, they did not do so to the extent that their Upper Paleolithic successors did. What made this possible were new techniques of core preparation which allowed more intensive production of highly standardized blades. To make these, the toolmaker formed a cylindrical core, struck the blade off near the edge of the core, and repeated this procedure, going around the core in one direction until finishing near its center (Figure 8.3). The procedure is analogous to peeling long leaves off an artichoke. With this **blade technique,** an Upper Paleolithic flint knapper could get 75 feet of working edge from a 2-pound core; his Mousterian counterpart could get only 6 feet from the same-sized core.

Other efficient techniques of tool manufacture also came into common use at this time. One such method was **pressure flaking,** in which a bone,

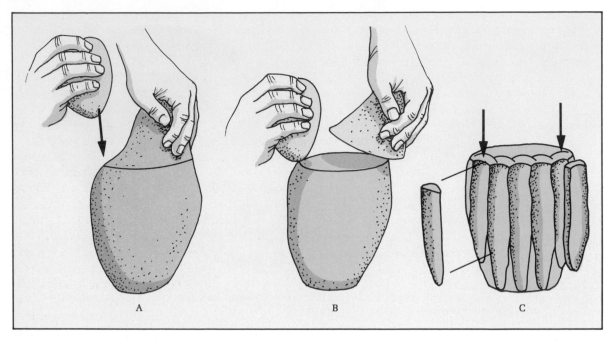

FIGURE 8.3 During the Upper Paleolithic, a new technique was used to manufacture blades. The stone is broken to create a striking platform, then vertical pieces are flaked off the side of the flint, forming sharp-edged tools.

antler, or wooden tool was used to press rather than strike off small flakes as the final step in stone tool manufacture (Figure 8.4). The advantage of this technique was that the toolmaker had greater control over the final shape of the tool than is possible with percussion flaking. The Solutrean laurel leaf blades found in Spain and France are examples of this technique. The longest of these blades is 13 inches long and only about a quarter of an inch thick. Pressure flaking also provided great precision in retouching cutting edges for extra sharpness.

FIGURE 8.4 Two examples of pressure flaking.

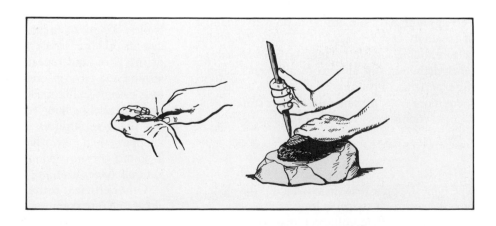

Another Upper Paleolithic development was the **burin,** a stone tool with chisel-like edges. Although invented in the Middle Paleolithic, burins became common only in the Upper Paleolithic. They facilitated the working of bone, horn, antler, and ivory into such useful things as fishhooks, harpoons, and eyed needles, all of which made life easier for *H. sapiens,* especially in northern regions. The spear-thrower also appeared at the time. Spear-throwers are wooden devices, one end of which is gripped in the hunter's hand, while the other end has a hole or hook, in or against which the end of the spear is placed (Figure 8.5, lower right). It is held so as to increase the length of the hunter's arm, thereby increasing the velocity of the spear when thrown. The spear and spear-thrower when used together make for more efficient hunting than does the use of the spear alone. With hand-held spears, hunters had to get close to their quarry to make the kill, and since many of the animals they hunted were quite large and fierce, this was a dangerous business. The need to approach closely, and the improbability of an instant kill, exposed the spear hunter to considerable risk. But with the spear-thrower, the effective killing distance was increased; experiments indicate that the effective killing distance of a spear when used with a spear-thrower is between 18 and 27 meters.[9]

A further improvement of hunting techniques came with the invention of the bow and arrow, which appeared first in North Africa but not until the end of the Upper Paleolithic in Europe. The greatest advantage of the bow is that it increases the distance between hunter and prey; beyond 18 to 27 meters, the accuracy and penetration of a spear thrown with a spear-thrower is quite poor, whereas even a poor bow will shoot an arrow farther, with greater accuracy and penetrating power. A good bow is effective even at 91 meters. Thus, hunters were able to maintain a safe distance be-

Burins: Stone tools of the Upper Paleolithic with a chisel-like edge used for working bone and antler.

tween themselves and dangerous prey, dramatically decreasing their chances of being seriously injured by an animal fighting for its life.

These changes in hunting weaponry had important consequences for human biology. Spear hunting, particularly where large, fierce animals are the prey as they were in Upper Paleolithic Europe, demands strength, power, and overall robusticity on the part of the hunter. Without them, the hunter is poorly equipped to withstand the rigors of close-quarter killing. A high nutritional price must be paid, however, for large, powerful, and robust bodies, but in severe cold climates such as that of Upper Paleolithic Europe, adequate nutritional resources cannot always be relied upon. Thus, it is not surprising that when Europeans at the end of the Upper Paleolithic began to use bows and arrows to hunt game that was at the same time somewhat smaller and less aggressive, the men underwent a further reduction in body size and robusticity. With the personal danger to the hunters reduced, natural selection favored reduced body size as a form of nutritional conservation.[10]

The invention of the bow did more than just improve hunting techniques. Long before anyone thought of beating swords into plowshares, some genius discovered that bows could be used not just for killing, but to make music as well. Just when and where this discovery was made we do not know, but we do know that there was music in the lives of Upper Paleolithic peoples, for bone flutes and whistles as much as 30,000 years old have been found. We also know that the musical bow is the oldest of all the stringed instruments, and its invention ultimately made possible the development of all of the stringed instruments with which we are familiar today.

Upper Paleolithic peoples not only had better tools but also a greater diversity of types than earlier peoples. The highly developed Upper Paleo-

[9]David W. Frayer, "Body Size, Weapon Use, and Natural Selection in the European Upper Paleolithic and Mesolithic," *American Anthropologist* 83 (1981): 58.

[10]Ibid., p. 58.

FIGURE 8.5 This figure, which continues on the following two pages, shows a variety of tools commonly found in Upper Paleolithic tool kits, along with an artist's reconstruction of the way they were used.

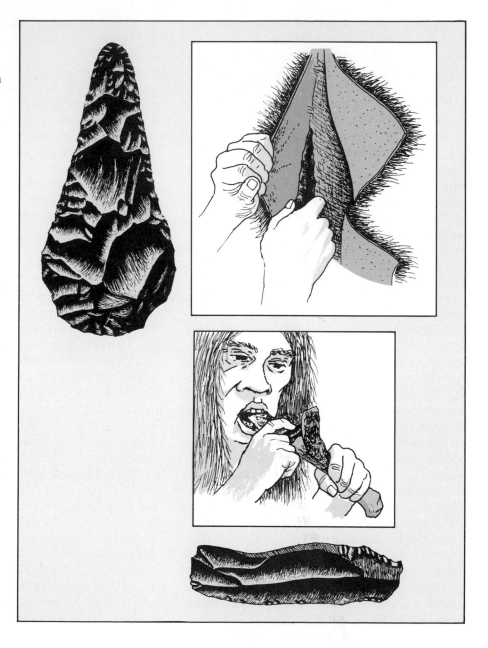

lithic kit included tools for use during different seasons, and regional variation in tool kits was greater than ever before. (See Figure 8.4 for some examples of Upper Paleolithic tools.) Thus, it is really impossible to speak of an Upper Paleolithic culture, even in a relatively small region like Europe; instead, one must make note of the many different traditions that made it possible for people to adapt ever more specifically to the various environments in which they were living. Just how pro-

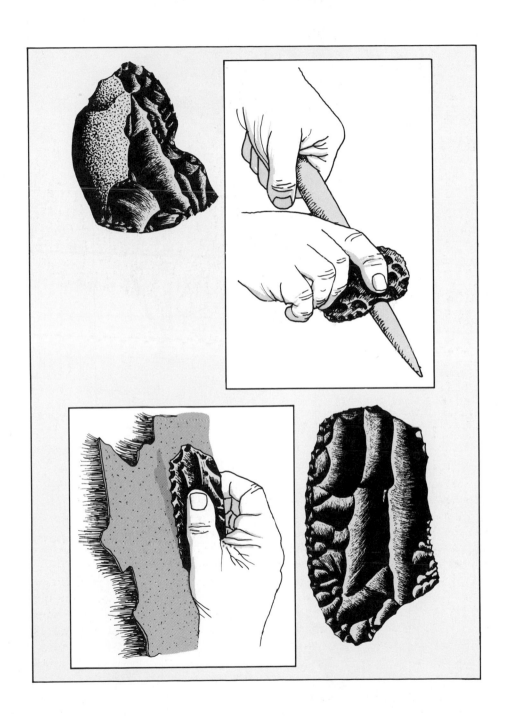

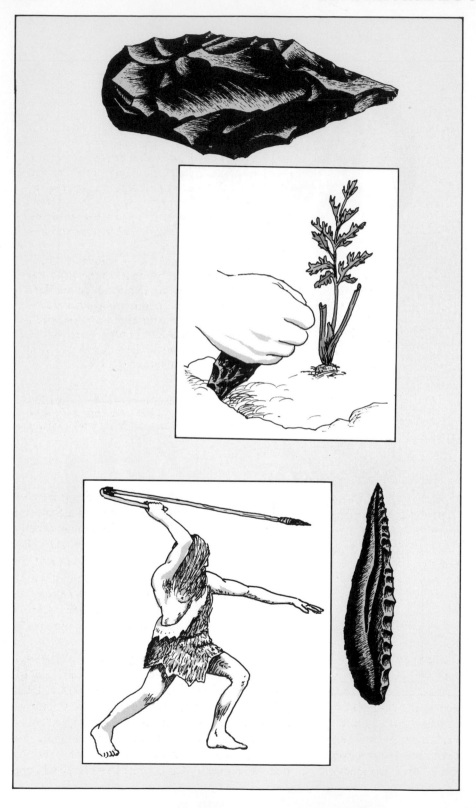

In 1975, Don Crabtree, then at the Idaho State University Museum, underwent heart surgery; in 1980, an unnamed patient in Boulder, Colorado, underwent eye surgery; and in 1986, David Pokotyle of the Museum of Anthropology at the University of British Columbia underwent reconstructive surgery on his hand. What these operations had in common was that the scalpels used were not of surgical steel. Instead, they were made of obsidian (a naturally occurring volcanic "glass") by the Upper Paleolithic blade technique. In all three cases, the scalpels were handmade by archaeologists who specialized in the study of ancient stone tool technology: Crabtree himself, Payson Sheets at the University of Colorado, and Pokotyle with his colleague Len McFarlane of the Museum of Anthropology.

The reason for the use of scalpels modeled on ancient stone tools, rather than modern steel, or even diamond scalpels, is that obsidian is superior in almost every way: Obsidian blades are 210 to 1050 times sharper than surgical steel, 100 to 500 times sharper than a razor blade, and three times sharper than a diamond blade (which costs many times more and has no more than 3 millimeters of cutting edge). They are easier to cut with, and they do less damage in the process. (Under a microscope, incisions made with the sharpest steel blades show torn ragged edges and are littered with bits of displaced flesh.)* As a consequence, the surgeon has better control over what she or he is doing and the incisions heal faster—with less scarring and less pain.

In order to develop and market obsidian scalpels, Sheets has formed a corporation in partnership with Boulder, Colorado, eye surgeon Dr. Firmon Hardenbergh. So far, they have developed a means of producing cores of uniform size from molten glass, as well as a machine to detach blades from the cores. Once this equipment is tested and refined, they hope to go into production for the surgical supply trade.

*Payson D. Sheets, "Dawn of a New Stone Age in Eye Surgery," in Robert J. Sharer and Wendy Ashmore, *Archaeology: Discovering Our Past* (Palo Alto, Calif.: Mayfield, 1987), p. 231.

ficient (and even wasteful) people had become at securing a livelihood is indicated by bone yards containing thousands of skeletons. At Solutré in France, for example, Upper Paleolithic hunters killed 10,000 horses; at Predmost in Czechoslovakia, they were responsible for the deaths of 1000 mammoths.

UPPER PALEOLITHIC ART

Although the creativity of Upper Paleolithic peoples is evident in the tools and weapons they made, it is nowhere more evident than in their outburst of artistic expression. In Europe, the earliest of this art took the form of sculpture and engravings often portraying such animals as reindeer, horses, bears, and ibexes, but there are also numerous portrayals of voluptuous women with exaggerated sexual and reproductive characteristics. These so-called "Venus" figures have been found at sites from southwestern France as far east as Siberia. Made of stone, ivory, antler, or baked clay, they differ little in style from place to place, testifying to the sharing of ideas over vast distances. Although some have interpreted the Venuses as objects associated with a fertility cult, others suggest that they may have been exchanged to cement alliances between groups.

Most spectacular are the paintings on the walls of 200 or so caves in southern France and northern Spain, the oldest of which date from about 15,000 years ago. Most common are visually accurate portrayals of ice-age mammals, including bison, bulls, horses, mammoths, and stags, often painted one on top of another. Rarely portrayed are humans, nor are scenes or depictions of events at all com-

Some examples of Upper Paleolithic art: A carved antler spear-thrower ornamented by two headless ibexes (from Enlene Cave, France); a female Venus figurine of yellow steatite (from a cave at Liguria, Italy); and one of the sandstone lamps by which artists worked in caves (from Lascaux Cave, France.)

mon. Instead, the animals are usually abstracted from nature and rendered two-dimensionally without regard to the confirmations of the surfaces they are on — no small achievement for these early "artists." Often, the paintings are in hard-to-get-at places, while suitable surfaces in more accessible places remain untouched. In some caves, the lamps by which the artists worked have been found; these are spoon-shaped objects of sandstone in which animal fat was burned. Experimentation has shown that such lamps would have provided adequate illumination over several hours.

Hypotheses to account for this early art are difficult because they must depend on conjectural and subjective interpretations. Some have argued that it is art for art's sake; if that is so, why were animals so often painted over one another, and why were they so often placed in inaccessible places? The latter might suggest that they were for ceremonial purposes and that the caves served as religious sanctuaries. One suggestion is that the animals were drawn to ensure success in the hunt, another that their depiction was seen as a way to promote fertility and increase the size of the herds on which humans depended. Some support for this comes from a major reassessment of the art of Altimira Cave in northern Spain. Here, the ceiling of the great hall does seem to be a true composition, representing a herd of bison in the rutting season. Elsewhere in the cave, too, the art shows a pervasive concern for the sexual reproduction of the bison.[11] In other caves, though, the species depicted are not always those most frequently hunted, there are few depictions of animals being hunted or killed, nor are there depictions of animals copulating or with exaggerated sexual parts as there are in the Venus figures. Another suggestion is that rites by which youngsters were initiated into adulthood took place in the painted galleries. In support of this idea, footprints, most of which are small, have been found in the clay floors of several caves, and in one, they even circle a modeled clay bison. The animals painted may have had to do with knowledge being transmitted from the elders to the youths. Whether or not that was so, the transmission of information is suggested by countless so-called signs, apparently abstract designs that accompany much Upper Paleolithic art. Some have interpreted these as tallies of animals killed or a reckoning of time according to a lunar calendar. Perhaps all Upper Paleolithic art reflects an increased need to communicate information, and if so, it may have paralleled an increase in the complexity of spoken language. But when all is said and done, according to Henri Delaporte of France's Musé des Antiquités Nationales, "There were probably many different reasons why people produced art of different kinds, and we shouldn't just think of single explanations."[12]

Artistic expression, whatever its purpose may have been, was not confined to cave walls and portable objects alone. Upper Paleolithic peoples also ornamented their bodies with necklaces of perforated animal teeth, shells, beads of bone, stone, and ivory; rings; bracelets; and anklets. Clothing, too, was adorned with beads. This should alert us to the probability that quite a lot of art was executed in perishable materials — wood carving, paintings on bark or animal skins, and the like. Thus, the rarity or absence of Upper Paleolithic art outside Europe and western Asia may be more

apparent than real, as people elsewhere worked with materials unlikely to survive so long in the archeological record.

OTHER ASPECTS OF UPPER PALEOLITHIC CULTURE

Upper Paleolithic peoples lived not only in caves and rock shelters, but also in structures built out in the open. In the Ukraine, for example, the remains have been found of sizeable settlements, in which huts were built on frameworks of intricately stacked mammoth bones. Where the ground was frozen, cobblestones were heated and placed in the earth to sink in, thereby providing sturdy, dry floors. Their hearths, no longer shallow depressions or flat surfaces that radiated back little heat, were instead stone-lined pits that conserved heat for extended periods and made for more efficient cooking. For the outdoors, they had the same sort of tailored clothing worn in historical times by the natives of Siberia, Alaska, and Canada. And they engaged in long-distance trade, as indicated, for example, by the presence of sea shells and Baltic amber at sites several hundred kilometers from the sources of these materials. Although Middle Paleolithic peoples made use of rare and distant materials, they did not do so with the regularity seen in the Upper Paleolithic.

THE SPREAD OF UPPER PALEOLITHIC PEOPLES

Such was the effectiveness of their cultures that Upper Paleolithic peoples were able to expand into regions previously uninhabited by their archaic forebears. Colonization of Siberia can be clearly documented by 30,000 to 35,000 years ago, but even before that — perhaps as early as 40,000 to 45,000 years ago — people had traveled to Australia and New Guinea. To get there, they used some kind of water craft to make the difficult crossing of at least 90 kilometers of water that separated Australia and New Guinea from the Asian continent throughout Paleolithic times. Once in Australia, these people created the world's first sophisticated rock art some 5,000 to 10,000 years

[11]John Halverson, "Review of *Altimira Revisited and Other Essays on Early Art,*" *American Antiquity* 54 (1989): 883.
[12]Roger Lewin, "Myths and Methods in Ice Age Art," *Science* 234 (1986): 938.

Remains of a hut, built on a framework of intricately stacked mammoth bones, from an Upper Paleolithic site in the Ukraine.

Paleoindian: Inhabitants of North America around 12,000 years ago who hunted big game, such as mammoths, with spears tipped with distinctive fluted points.

first Americans. Securely dated remains from Meadowcraft Rockshelter in southwestern Pennsylvania indicate that populations had spread as far as the eastern United States by 15,000 years ago, if not earlier, and people seem to have gotten as far south as central Chile, where remains of huts have been found at Monte Verde and dated at about 13,000 years ago.

Technologies roughly comparable to the old East Asian chopper tool industries gave rise in North America, about 12,000 years ago, to the distinctive fluted spear points of **Paleoindian** hunters of big game, such as mammoths, caribou, and now extinct forms of bison. Fluted points are finely

earlier than the more famous European cave paintings. Other evidence for sophisticated ritual activity in early Australia is provided by 26,000-year-old cremation burials associated with red ochre. What is especially interesting in view of such accomplishments is that the tools used by these people are remarkably similar to those of the Eurasian Middle Paleolithic. Clearly, simplicity of tool kits does not bespeak absence of sophisticated intellectual capabilities.

To get to the Americas, voyages of the sort undertaken by the first Australians were not necessary. With much of the world's water supply taken up by the great continental glaciers, there was a worldwide lowering of sea levels, causing an emergence of land joining Siberia to Alaska. With expanding populations in Asia, brought about by increasingly effective cultural adaptations, it was only a matter of time before human populations began to drift gradually eastward over this dry land. But because the cold of the last glaciation was more intense at some times than others, there were occasional minor recessions of ice. One of these took place about 33,000 years ago, releasing enough water to drown the land bridge between Siberia and Alaska. By then, there may have been people in North America who, being cut off from their fellow Asians, became, in effect, the

Paleoindians, like their Upper Paleolithic contemporaries in Eurasia, were such accomplished hunters that they, too, could kill more animals than could possibly be used at one time. These bones are the remains of some 200 bison that Paleoindian hunters stampeded over a cliff 8500 years ago.

Paleoindian fluted spear points.

made, with large channel flakes removed from one or both surfaces. They are found from the Atlantic seaboard to the Pacific coast, and from Alaska down into Panama. So efficient were the hunters who made these points that they may have hastened the extinction of the mammoth and other large Pleistocene mammals. By driving large numbers of animals over cliffs, they killed many more than they could possibly use, thus wasting huge amounts of meat.

WHERE DID UPPER PALEOLITHIC PEOPLE COME FROM?

As noted earlier in this chapter, we cannot be sure whether the transition from archaic to anatomically modern *H. sapiens* took place in one specific population or was the result of in situ evolution on the part of populations living in Africa and Asia between 100,000 and 40,000 years ago. Still, in all of these regions, since the time of *H. erectus*, more and more emphasis was placed on cultural, as opposed to biological, adaptation. To handle environmental stress, reliance was placed more and more on the development of appropriate tools, clothes, shelter, use of fire, and so forth, as opposed to alteration of the human organism itself.

Cognitive capacity: A broad concept including intelligence, educability, concept formation, self-awareness, self-evaluation, attention span, sensitivity in discrimination, and creativity.

This was true whether human populations lived in hot or cold, wet or dry, forest or grassland areas. Since culture is learned and not carried by genes, it is ultimately based on what might loosely be called "brain power" or, more formally, **cognitive capacity.** While this includes intelligence, in the IQ sense, it is broader than that, for it also includes such things as educability, concept formation, self-awareness, self-evaluation, reliability of performance under stress, attention span, sensitivity in discrimination, and creativity.

The major thrust in the evolution of the genus *Homo*, then, has been toward improved cognitive capacity through the evolution of the brain regardless of the environmental and climatic differences between the regions in which populations of the genus lived. Hence, there has been a certain similarity of selective pressures in all regions. In addition, this evolution of all populations of the genus *Homo* would have been helped along by a certain amount of gene flow between populations.

In an evolving species, genes having survival value anywhere tend to spread from one population to another. In the case of the human species, these would be whatever genes happen to relate to cognitive capacity. It is impossible to know just how much gene flow took place between ancient human populations. All we can really say is that historically known humans show a remarkable tendency to swap genes between populations, even in the face of cultural barriers to gene flow. Given this, some gene swapping on the part of our ancient ancestors seems likely.

THE MESOLITHIC ERA

By 12,000 years ago, glacial conditions in the world were moderating, causing changes in human habitats. Throughout the world, sea levels were on the rise, ultimately flooding many areas that had been above sea level during periods of glaciation, such as the Bering Straits, parts of the North Sea, and an extensive area that had joined Indonesia to Southeast Asia. In northern regions, milder climates brought about marked changes as tundras were ultimately replaced by hardwood forests. In the process, the herd animals on which northern Paleolithic peoples had depended for food, clothing, and shelter disappeared from many areas. Some, like the reindeer and musk ox, moved to colder climates; others, like the mammoths, died out completely. Thus, the northerners especially were forced to adapt to new conditions. In the new forests, animals were more solitary in their habits and so not as easy to hunt as they had been, and large, cooperative hunts were no longer very productive. However, plant food was more abundant than before, and there were new and abundant sources of fish and other food around lake shores, bays, and rivers. Hence, human populations developed new and ingenious ways to catch and kill animals, while at the same time, they devoted more energy to fishing and the collection of wild plant foods. This new way of life marks the end of the Paleolithic and the start of the **Mesolithic,** or **Middle Stone Age.** In a sense, it marks a return to more typical hominid subsistence patterns.

Mesolithic, or Middle Stone Age: Began about 10,000 B.C.

Microlith: A small flint blade characteristic of the Mesolithic, several of which were hafted together in wooden handles to make tools.

MESOLITHIC TOOLS AND WEAPONS

New technologies were developed for the changed postglacial environment (Figure 8.6). Ground stone tools, shaped and sharpened by grinding the tool against sandstone (often with sand as an additional abrasive), made effective axes and adzes. Such implements are less prone to breakage, given heavy-duty usage, than are those made of chipped stone. Thus, they were helpful in clearing forest areas and in the woodwork needed for the creation of dugout canoes and skin-covered boats. Although some kind of water craft had been developed early enough to get humans to Australia by about 40,000 years ago, boats become prominent only in Mesolithic sites, indicating that human hunting and gathering activities frequently took place on the water as well as the land. Thus, it was possible to make use of deep water resources as well as those of coastal areas.

The characteristic Mesolithic tool was the **microlith,** a small but hard, sharp blade. Microliths could be mass produced because they were small, easy to make, and could be of materials other than flint. Also, they could be attached to arrow shafts by using melted resin as a binder. Thus, the bow and arrow with the microlith arrowhead became the deadliest and most common weapon of the Mesolithic.

The development by Mesolithic peoples of microliths provided them with an important advantage not found in one-piece Upper Paleolithic tools: The small size of the microlith enabled people to devise composite tools made out of stone and wood or bone (Figure 8.5, top). Thus, they could make sickles, harpoons, arrows, and daggers by fitting microliths into grooves in wood or bone

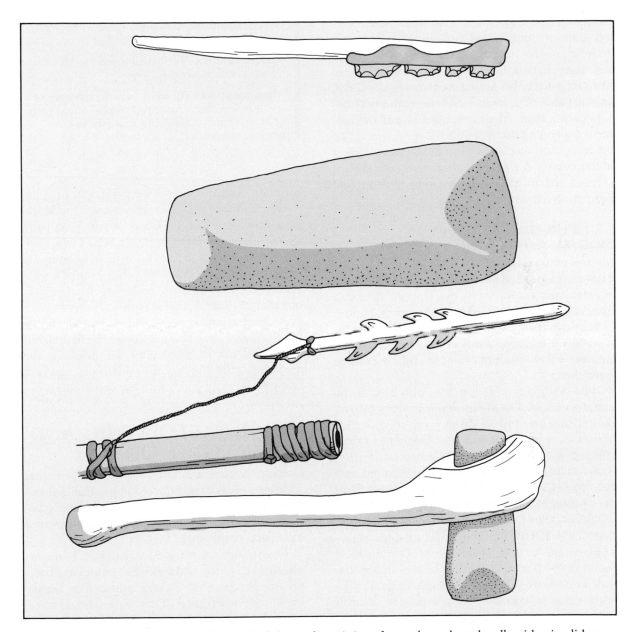

FIGURE 8.6 The drawing above shows a Mesolithic tool consisting of a wooden or bone handle with microliths set into it. Below is a bone tool of a somewhat earlier date, fitted out for service as a harpoon. The ground stone ax at the bottom has a smooth stone blade set in a wooden handle that gives increased leverage.

handles. Later experimentation with these forms led to more sophisticated tools and weapons.

It is possible that the Mesolithic was a more sedentary period for humans than earlier eras. Dwellings from this period seem more substantial, an indication of permanency. Indeed, this is a logical development: Most hunting cultures and cultures depending on herd animals are nomadic. To be successful, one must follow the game. This is not necessary for peoples subsisting on a diet of seafood and plants, as the location of shore and vegetation remains relatively constant.

CULTURAL DIVERSITY IN THE MESOLITHIC

In the warmer parts of the world, the collection of wild plant foods had been more of an equal partner in subsistence activities in the Upper Paleolithic than had been the case in the colder north. Hence, in areas like the Middle East, the Mesolithic represents less of a changed way of life than was true in Europe. Here, the important **Natufian culture** flourished.

The Natufians were a people who lived at the eastern end of the Mediterranean Sea in caves, rock shelters, and small villages with stone-walled houses. A small shrine is known from one of their villages, a 10,500-year-old settlement at Jericho. Basin-shaped depressions in the rocks found outside homes at Natufian sites are thought to have been storage pits. Plastered storage pits beneath the floors of the houses were also found, indicating that the Natufians were the earliest known Mesolithic people to have stored crops. Certain tools found in the Natufian remains bear evidence that they were used to cut grain. These Mesolithic sickles, for that is what they were, consisted of small stone blades set in straight handles of wood or bone.

In the Americas, cultures comparable to Mesolithic cultures of the Old World developed, but here they are referred to as **Archaic cultures.** Outside of the Arctic, microlithic tools are not prominent in them, as they are in parts of the Old World, but ground stone tools such as axes, adzes, gouges, plummets, and spear-thrower weights are

Natufian culture: A Mesolithic culture of Israel, Lebanon, and western Syria.

Archaic cultures: Term used to refer to Mesolithic cultures in the Americas.

Maritime archaic culture: An archaic culture of northeastern North America, centered on the Gulf of St. Lawrence, which emphasized the use of marine resources.

common. Archaic cultures were widespread in the Americas; one of the more dramatic was the **Maritime archaic,** which developed about 7000 years ago around the Gulf of St. Lawrence. These people developed an elaborate assortment of bone and ground slate tools with which they hunted a wide variety of sea mammals, including whales; fish, including swordfish; and sea birds. To get some of these, they regularly paddled their dugout canoes far off shore. They also developed the first elaborate burial cult in North America, involving the use of red ochre ("red paint") and the placement of finely made grave goods with the deceased.

MAJOR PALEOLITHIC AND MESOLITHIC TRENDS

Certain trends stand out from the information anthropologists have gathered about the Old and Middle Stone ages. These are general progressions that occurred from one culture to the next in most parts of the world.

One trend was toward increasingly more sophisticated, varied, and specialized tool kits. Tools became progressively lighter and smaller, resulting in the conservation of raw materials and a better ratio between length of cutting edge and weight of flint. Tools became specialized according to region and function. Instead of crude all-purpose tools, more effective particularized devices were made to better deal with the differing conditions of savanna, forest, and shore.

This more efficient tool technology enabled human populations to increase and spill over into more diverse environments; it also was responsible for the dropping of heavy physical features, favoring instead decreased size and weight of face and teeth, the development of larger and more complex brains, and ultimately a reduction in body size and robusticity. This dependence on intelligence rather than bulk provided the key for peoples' increased reliance on cultural rather than physical adaptation. As the brain became modernized, conceptual thought developed, as evidenced by symbolic artifacts and remains of magicoreligious ceremonies.

Through Paleolithic times, at least in the colder parts of the world, there appeared a trend toward the importance of and proficiency in hunting. People's intelligence enabled them to develop tools that exceeded other animals' physical equipment, as well as the improved social organization and cooperation so important for survival and population growth. This trend was reversed during the Mesolithic, when hunting lost its preeminence and the gathering of plants and seafood became increasingly important.

As human populations grew and spread, regionalism also grew. Tool assemblages developed at different times in different areas. General differences appeared between north and south, east and west. Although there are some indications of cultural contact and intercommunication, such as the development of long-distance trade in the Upper Paleolithic, regionalism was a dominant characteristic of the Paleolithic and Mesolithic eras. The persistence of regionalism is probably due in large part to the need to adapt to differing environments. Paleolithic peoples eventually spread over all the continents of the world, including Australia and America, and as they did so, changes in climate and environment called for new kinds of adaptations. Thus, Paleolithic and Mesolithic tool kits had to be altered to meet the requirements of many varying locations. In forest environments, people needed strong axes for working wood; on the open savanna and plains, they used the bow and arrow to hunt the game they could not stalk closely; the people in settlements that grew up around lakes and along rivers and coasts developed harpoons and hooks; in the subarctic regions, they needed tools to work the heavy skins of seals and caribou; in the grasslands, they needed tools for harvesting grain and separating the usable part from the chaff. The fact that culture is first and foremost an adaptive mechanism meant that it was of necessity a regional thing.

CHAPTER SUMMARY

At various sites in Europe and Africa, a number of fossils have been found which date between about 200,000 and 300,000 years ago and which show a mixture of traits characteristic of both *H. erectus* and *H. sapiens*. They are indicative of evolution from the older into the younger species. Their culture was much like that of *H. erectus*; however, about 200,000 years ago, they developed a new method of tool manufacture known as the Levalloisian technique.

By 100,000 years ago, populations of archaic *H. sapiens* lived in all parts of the inhabited world. Although some populations of this species, most notably the Neandertals of Europe and western Asia, survived until at least 35,000 years ago, oth-

ers evolved into anatomically modern humans. By 90,000 years ago, anatomically modern populations were coexisting with Neandertals in places like the Middle East.

The brains of archaic *H. sapiens* had reached modern size, although their skills retained some primitive characteristics. With a larger brain, they were able to use culture as a means of environmental adaptation to a far greater extent than any of their predecessors; they were capable of an advanced technology and sophisticated conceptual thought.

The cultures of archaic and early anatomically modern *H. sapiens* are known as Middle Paleolithic, and the best known is the Mousterian of Europe, northern Africa, and western Asia. Mousterian tools included hand axes, flakes, scrapers, borers, wood shavers, and spears. Flake tools were lighter and smaller than those of the Levalloisian technique. Mousterian tools increased the availability and quality of food, shelter, and clothing. Archaeological evidence indicates that Mousterian peoples cared for the disabled, and made a number of objects for purely symbolic purposes.

All populations of archaic *H. sapiens* are easily derivable from earlier populations of *H. erectus* from the same regions. With the exception of the Neandertals, all populations of archaic *H. sapiens* could be ancestral to more modern populations in the same regions. An alternative hypothesis is that the transition from archaic to anatomically modern *H. sapiens* took place in one specific population, probably in Africa. From here, people spread to other regions, replacing older populations as they did so.

The Cro-Magnons and the other anatomically modern peoples that held exclusive sway in the world after 30,000 years ago, in addition to a full-sized brain, possessed a physical appearance somewhat similar to our own. The modernization of the face of Upper Paleolithic peoples is a result of a reduction in the size of the teeth and the muscles involved in chewing as a consequence of the fact that teeth were no longer being used as tools. Similarly, bodies became somewhat less massive and robust as improved technology reduced the need for brute strength.

The emphasis in evolution of the genus *Homo* in all parts of the world has been toward increasing cognitive capacity through development of the brain. This progression took place regardless of environmental or climatic conditions under which the genus lived. In addition, evolution of the genus *Homo* may have been aided by gene flow between populations.

Upper Paleolithic cultures evolved from the Middle Paleolithic cultures of Africa and Asia. The typical Upper Paleolithic tool was the blade. The blade technique of toolmaking saved much more flint than Middle Paleolithic methods. Other efficient Upper Paleolithic toolmaking techniques were pressure flaking, and using chisel-like stones

called burins to fashion bone, antler horn, and ivory into tools. The cultural adaptation of Upper Paleolithic people became specific; they developed different tools for different seasons. There is no one Upper Paleolithic culture, as different environments produced different cultures. Northern Upper Paleolithic cultures supported themselves by the hunting of large herd animals. Upper Paleolithic cultures contain the earliest remains of pictorial art.

The ending of the glacial period caused great physical changes in human habitats. Sea levels were raised, vegetation changed, and herd animals disappeared from many areas. The European Mesolithic period marked a return to more typical hominid ways of subsistence, as big game hunters returned to more of a balance between hunting and gathering. Increased reliance on seafood and plants made the Mesolithic a more sedentary period for people. Ground stone tools, including axes and adzes, answered postglacial needs for new technologies. The characteristic Mesolithic tool in the Old World was made with microliths, small, hard, sharp flint blades which could be mass produced and hafted with others to produce implements like sickles. Reliance on the bow and arrow to hunt generally smaller, less aggressive animals resulted in a reduction of the size and robusticity of men, at least in Europe.

Three trends emerged from the Paleolithic and Mesolithic periods. First was a trend toward more sophisticated, varied, and specialized tool kits. This trend enabled people to increase their population and spread to new environments. It also was adaptive, leading to decreased size and weight of face and teeth, the development of larger, more complex brains, and ultimately a reduction in body size and mass. Second was a trend toward the importance of and proficiency in hunting. The importance of hunting was somewhat reversed during the Mesolithic period, as the hunting of large game became less important than smaller game and the gathering of plants and seafood. Third was a trend toward regionalism, as people's technology and life habits increasingly reflected their association with a particular environment.

SUGGESTED READINGS

Campbell, Bernard G. *Humankind Emerging*, 5th ed. Boston: Little, Brown, 1988. Adapted in part from Time-Life's *Emergence of Man* and *Life Nature Library*, this is a richly illustrated, up-to-date account of the Paleolithic. In it, Campbell integrates paleontological and archaeological data with ethnographic data on modern food foragers to present a rich picture of evolving Paleolithic ways of life.

Gamble, Clive. *The Paleolithic Settlement of Europe.* Cambridge: Cambridge University Press, 1986. Although not the easiest book to read, it is important for the way it looks at old data in new ways. Instead of presenting yet another descriptive synthesis of archaeologically recovered things, it tries to explain what happened in the past in light of a better understanding of how archeological sites are formed.

Pfeiffer, John E. *The Creative Explosion.* Ithaca, N.Y.: Cornell University Press, 1985. A fascinating and readable discussion of the origins of art and religion.

Prideaux, Tom, and the Editors of Time-Life. *Cro-Magnon Man.* New York: Time-Life, 1973. This beautifully illustrated volume in Time-Life's *Emergence of Man* series covers the period between 10,000 and 40,000 years ago. A whole chapter is devoted to "The Subtle Mind of Cro-Magnon."

Mosaic death mask of jade, pyrite, and shell worn by Jaguar Paw Skull, a king of the Maya city of Tikal who died ca. 527 A.D. Although the human species is the same today as 10,000 years ago, the evolution of human culture over the same period of time has seen the invention of farming, animal husbandry, and the rise of civilization.

PART III

HUMAN BIOLOGICAL AND CULTURAL EVOLUTION SINCE THE END OF THE OLD STONE AGE

INTRODUCTION

In the Upper Paleolithic, by 30,000 years ago, anatomically modern varieties of humans, with cultures comparable to those known for recent food foraging peoples, had sole possession of the inhabited parts of the world. The story of human evolution in the Paleolithic is one of a close interrelation between developing culture and developing humanity. The critical importance of culture as the human adaptive mechanism seems to have imposed selective pressures favoring a better brain, and a better brain, in turn, made possible improved cultural adaptation. Indeed, it seems fair to say that modern humans look the way they do today because cultural adaptation came to play such an important role in the survival of our ancient ancestors. Because cultural adaptation worked so well, human populations were able to grow, probably rather slowly, with a consequent expansion into previously uninhabited parts of the world. And this, too, affected cultural adaptation as adjustments were made to meet new conditions.

Although food foraging served humans well for hundreds of thousands of years in the Paleolithic, far-reaching changes began to take place in some parts of the world as much as 11,000 years ago. This second major cultural revolution consisted of the emergence of food production, the subject of Chapter 9. Eventually, most of the world's people became food producers, even though food foraging remained a satisfactory way of life for some. At the present time, no more than a quarter of a million people — less than .05

percent of a world population of 5 billion — remain food foragers. Just as the emergence of food foraging was followed by modifications and improvements leading to regional variants of this pattern, so the advent of food production opened the way for new cultural variants based upon it. Chapter 10 discusses the result: further cultural diversity, out of which developed civilization, the basis of modern life.

Despite the increasing effectiveness of culture as the primary mechanism by which humans adapt to diverse environments, our species has continued to evolve biologically. In the course of their movement into other parts of the world, humans had already developed considerable biological variation from one population to another. On top of this, populations of food producers were exposed to selective pressures of a different sort than those affecting food foragers, thereby inducing further changes in human gene pools. Such changes continue to affect the human species today, even though it remains the same species now as it was at the end of the Paleolithic. Chapter 11 discusses how the variation to be seen in *Homo sapiens* today came into existence as the result of forces acting to alter the frequencies of genes in human gene pools, and why such variation probably has nothing to do with intelligence. The chapter concludes with a look at forces apparently active today to produce further changes in those same gene pools.

9

CULTIVATION AND DOMESTICATION

Beginning about 11,000 years ago, some of the world's people embarked on a new way of life based on food production. This included new attitudes toward the earth and forces of nature, reflected in monumental construction. Shown here is Stonehenge, the famous ceremonial and astronomical center in England, which dates back to about 2500 B.C.

PREVIEW

When and Where Did the Change from Food Foraging to Food Production Begin?
Centers of early plant and animal domestication exist in Africa, China, Meso-america, South America, and Southwest and Southeast Asia. From these places, food production spread to most other parts of the world. It began at different times in these different places; for example, it began about 11,000 years ago in Southwest Asia, but began sometime between 8800 and 5000 years ago in Southeast Asia.

Why Did the Change Take Place?
Since food production by and large requires more work than hunting and gathering, is not necessarily a more secure means of subsistence, and requires people to eat more of the foods that food foragers eat only when they have no other choice, it can be assumed that people probably did not become food producers through choice. Of various theories that have been proposed, the most likely is that food production came about as a largely accidental by-product of existing food resource management practices. In some other places, people may have been forced into it through a failure of traditional wild food resources.

What Were the Consequences of the Change to Food Production?
Although food production generally provides less leisure time than food foraging, it does permit some reallocation of the work load. Some people can produce enough food to allow others to spend more time at other tasks, and so a number of technological developments, such as weaving and pottery making, generally accompany food production. In addition, it makes possible a more sedentary way of life in villages, with more substantial housing. Finally, the new modes of work and resource allocation require new ways of organizing people, generally into lineages, clans, and common-interest associations.

Throughout the Paleolithic, people depended exclusively on wild sources of food for their survival. In cold northern regions, they came to rely primarily on the hunting of herds of mammoth, bison, and reindeer. Elsewhere, they hunted, fished, or gathered whatever nature was kind enough to provide. There is no evidence in Paleolithic remains to indicate that livestock was kept or plants cultivated. Paleolithic people followed wild herds and gathered wild plant foods, relying on their wits and muscles to acquire what nature provided. Whenever favored sources of food became scarce, as sometimes happened, people adjusted by increasing the variety of food eaten, and incorporating less-favored food into their diet.

About 12,000 years ago, the subsistence practices of some people began to change in ways that were to transform radically their way of life, although no one involved had any way of knowing it at the time. Not until these changes were well advanced could people become aware that their mode of subsistence differed from that of other cultures — that they had become farmers rather than food foragers.[1] This change in the means of obtaining food had important implications for human development, for it meant that by taking matters into their own hands, people could become more sedentary. Moreover, by reorganizing the work load, some of them could be freed from the food quest to devote their energies to other sorts of tasks. With good reason, the **Neolithic period,** when this change took place, has been called a revolutionary one in human history. This period, and the changes that took place within it, are the subjects of this chapter.

THE MESOLITHIC ROOTS OF FARMING AND PASTORALISM

The Mesolithic may be viewed either as the final stage of the Paleolithic or as the beginning of the Neolithic. Fixed as having begun around 12,000

[1]David Rindos, *The Origins of Agriculture: An Evolutionary Perspective* (Orlando, Fla.: Academic Press, 1984), p. 99.

| **Neolithic period:** The New Stone Age, which began about 11,000 years ago in Southwest Asia.

years ago, people during this period turned increasingly toward abundant food supplies to be found in the rivers, lakes, and oceans. These waterways were teeming with aquatic life because of the rising seas brought about by warmer temperatures and melting glaciers. In addition, people gathered a broad spectrum of plant foods on land, and hunted a variety of birds and smaller mammals. Generally, this new way of life offered more secure supplies of food and therefore an increased margin of survival. In some parts of the world, people started living in larger and more sedentary groups, now cooperating with others outside the sphere of family or hunting band. They became settled village dwellers, and some of these settlements were shortly to expand into the first farming villages, towns, and ultimately cities.

THE NEOLITHIC REVOLUTION

The Neolithic, or New Stone Age, was characterized by the transition from foraging for food to dependence on domesticated plants and animals. It was by no means a smooth or rapid transition; in fact, it spread over many centuries and was a direct outgrowth of the preceding Mesolithic. Where to draw the line between the two is not always clear.

The term "New Stone Age" is derived from the polished stone tools that are characteristic of this period. But more important than the presence of these tools is the transition from a hunting, gathering, and fishing to a food-producing economy, representing a major change in the subsistence patterns of early peoples. One of the first regions to undergo this transition was Southwest Asia. The remains of domesticated plants and animals are known from parts of Israel, Jordan, Syria, Turkey, Iraq, and Iran, all before 7000 years ago.

DOMESTICATION: WHAT IS IT?

A **domesticated plant** or **animal** is one which has come to depend for its protection and reproductive success on some other species that feeds upon it. Although commonly thought of as the result of human manipulation, domestication need not involve conscious intent, or even humans. In the case of plants, there are numerous species that rely on some type of animal — in some instances birds, in others mammals, and in yet others, insects — for protection and dispersal of their seeds. The important thing is that both parties benefit from the arrangement; reliance on animals for seed dispersal ensures that the latter will be carried farther afield than would otherwise be possible, thereby cutting down on competition for sun and nutrients between young and old plants and reducing the likelihood that any diseases or parasites harbored by one will be transmitted to the others. Added vigor is apt to come to plants that are freed from the need to provide themselves with built-in defensive mechanisms such as thorns or chemical compounds that make them taste bad. This enhanced vigor may be translated into larger and more tasty edible parts to attract the animals that feed upon them, thereby cementing the relationship between domesticate and protector.

EVIDENCE OF EARLY PLANT DOMESTICATION

The characteristics of plants under human domestication that set them apart from their wild ancestors, and have made them attractive to those who eat them, include increased size, at least of edible parts; reduction or loss of natural means of seed dispersal; reduction or loss of protective devices such as husks or distasteful chemical compounds; and loss of delayed seed germination (important to wild plants for survival in times of drought or other adverse conditions of temporary duration), along with simultaneous ripening of the seed or fruit. Many of these characteristics can be seen in plant remains from archaeological sites; thus, paleobotanists can often tell the fossil of a wild plant

> **Domestic plant or animal:** One which has come to depend for its protection and reproductive success on some other species that feeds on it.
>
> **Unconscious selection:** The preservation of valued representatives of a plant or animal species and the destruction of less-valued ones, with no thought as to the long-range consequences.

species from a domesticated one, for example, by studying the seed of cereal grasses, such as barley, wheat, and maize (corn). Wild cereals have a very fragile stem, whereas domesticated ones have a tough stem. Under natural conditions, plants with fragile stems scatter their seed for themselves, while those with tough stems do not. The structural change from a soft to a tough stem in early domesticated plants involves a genetic change, undoubtedly the result of what Darwin referred to as **unconscious selection:** the preservation of valued individuals and the destruction of less valued ones, with no thought as to long-range consequences.[2] When the grain stalks were harvested, their soft stem would shatter at the touch of sickle or flail, and many of their seeds would be lost. Inevitably, most of the seeds that people harvested would have been taken from the tough plants. Early domesticators probably also tended to select seed from plants having few husks or none at all — eventually breeding them out — because husking before pounding the grains into meal or flour was much too time consuming. Size of plants is another good indicator of the presence of domestication. For example, the large ear of corn we know today is a far cry from the tiny ears (about an inch long) characteristic of early corn. In fact, the ear of corn may have arisen as a simple gene mutation transformed male tassel spikes of the wild grass, Teosinte, into small and primitive versions of the female corn ear.[3] Small and primitive though these were, however, they were radically different in structure from the ears of Teosinte.

[2]Ibid., p. 86.
[3]Stephen Jay Gould, *The Flamingo's Smile, Reflections in Natural History* (New York: Norton, 1985), p. 368.

Wild wheat kernels from a site in Syria (*top*), compared with those of a domestic variety grown in Greece 2000 or 3000 years later (*bottom*). Increased size of edible parts is a common feature of domestication.

EVIDENCE OF EARLY ANIMAL DOMESTICATION

Domestication also produced changes in the skeletal structure of some animals. For example, the horns of wild goats and sheep differ from those of their domesticated counterparts (domesticated female sheep have none). Another structural change that occurred in domestication involves the size of the animal or its parts. For example, certain teeth of domesticated pigs are smaller than those of wild ones.

A study of age and sex ratios of butchered animals at a site may indicate whether or not animal domestication was practiced. Investigators have assumed that if the age and/or sex ratios at the site differ from those in wild herds, the imbalances are due to conscious selection. For example, at the site of Zawi Chemi Shanidar, in northern Iraq, about 50 percent of the sheep killed were under 1 year of age. Evidently, the occupants of Zawi Chemi Shanidar were slaughtering the young males for food and saving the females for breeding. Although this does not prove that the sheep were fully domesticated, such herd management does suggest a first step in the domestication process.

In Peru, the prominence of bones of newborn llamas at archaeological sites (up to 72 percent at some), dating to about 6300 years ago, is probably indicative of at least incipient domestication. Such high mortality rates for newborn animals are uncommon in wild herds, but are common where animals are penned up. Under such conditions, a build up of mud and filth harbors bacteria that cause diarrhea and enterotoxemia, both of which are fatal to newborn animals.

THE BEGINNINGS OF DOMESTICATION

Over the past 30 years, a good deal of information has accumulated about the beginnings of domestication, primarily in Southwest Asia as well as Central and South America. We still do not have all the answers about how and why it took place. Nonetheless, some observations of general validity can be made which help us to understand how the switch to food production may have taken place.

The first of these observations is that the switch to food production was not the result of such discoveries that seeds, if planted, grow into plants. Food foragers are far from ignorant about the forces of nature and are perfectly aware of the role of seeds in plant growth, that plants grow better under certain conditions than others, and so forth. In fact, they frequently put their knowledge to work so as to manage actively the resources on which they depend. For example, Indians living in the northern part of Canada's Alberta province put to use a sophisticated knowledge of the effects of fire to create local environments of their own design. And in northern Australia, runoff channels of creeks were deliberately altered so as to flood extensive tracts of land, converting them into fields of wild grain. Food foragers do not remain as such through ignorance, but through choice.

A second observation is that a switch from food foraging to food production does not free people from hard work. The available ethnographic data indicate just the opposite — that farmers, by and large, work far longer hours than do most food foragers. Furthermore, it is clear that early farming required people not only to work longer hours but also to eat more "third choice" food. Typically, food foragers divide potentially edible food resources into first, second, and third choice categories; third choice foods are eaten only by necessity, when there is no other option. And in Southwest Asia and Mexico, at least, the plants that were brought under domestication were clearly third choice plants.

A final observation is that food production is not necessarily a more secure means of subsistence than food foraging. Seed crops in particular, of the sort domesticated in Southwest Asia, Mexico, and Peru, are highly productive but very unstable on account of low species diversity. Without constant human attention, their productivity suffers.

From all of this, it is little wonder that food foragers do not necessarily regard farming and animal husbandry as superior to hunting, gathering, and fishing. Thus, there are some people in the world who have remained food foragers down into the 1980s, although it has become increasingly difficult for them, because food-producing peoples have deprived them of more and more of the land base necessary for their way of life. But as long as existing practices worked well, there was no felt need to abandon them. After all, their traditional way of life gave them all the food they needed and an eminently satisfactory way of living in small, intimate groups. Free from tedious routine, their lives were often more exciting than those of farmers. Food could be hunted, gathered, or fished for as needed, but in most environments, food foragers could relax when they had enough to eat. Why

raise crops by backbreaking work, when the whole family could camp under a tree bearing tasty and nutritious nuts? Farming brings with it a whole new system of human relationships that offers no easily understood advantages, and disturbs an age-old balance between humans and nature as well as the people who live together (for more on the food-foraging way of life, see Chapter 15).

WHY HUMANS BECAME FOOD PRODUCERS

In view of what has been said so far, we may well ask: Why did any human group abandon food foraging in favor of food production?

Several theories have been proposed to account for this change in human subsistence practices. One older theory, stated by V. Gordon Childe, is the "desiccation," or "oasis," theory based on climatic determinism. Its proponents advanced the idea that the glacial cover over Europe and Asia caused a southern shift in rain patterns from Europe to northern Africa and Southwest Asia. When the glaciers retreated northward, so did the rain patterns. As a result, North Africa and Southwest Asia became drier, and people were forced to congregate at oases for water. Because of the scarcity of wild animals in such an environment, people were driven by necessity to collect the wild grasses and seeds growing around the oases. Eventually, they had to cultivate the grasses to provide enough food for the community. According to this theory, animal domestication began because the oases attracted hungry animals, such as wild goats, sheep, and also cattle, which came to graze on the stubble of the grain fields. People, finding these animals too thin to kill for food, began to fatten them up.

Although it was once quite popular, evidence has failed to sustain the oasis theory. For one thing, the earliest evidence for domestication does not occur where the theory would predict. For another, climatic conditions in Southwest Asia seem to have been better at the time that people there made the transition from food foraging to food production than they had been before or have been since.[4]

A theory that became popular in the 1960s is one in which population growth played a central role. In Southwest Asia, so this theory goes, people adapted to the cool dry conditions of the last glacial period by developing a mixed pattern of resource utilization: They hunted such animals as were available, harvested wild cereal grasses, collected nuts, and collected a wide variety of birds, turtles, snails, crabs, and mussels.

They did so well that their populations grew, requiring the development of new ways of providing sufficient food. The result, especially in marginal situations where wild foods were least abundant, was to improve productivity through the domestication of plants and animals.

Just as there are problems with the "oasis" theory, so are there problems with this one. The most serious is that it requires an intentional decision on the part of the people involved to become producers of domestic crops, whereas, as we have already seen, domestication does not require intentional design. Furthermore, prior to domestication, people could have had no way of knowing that plants and animals could be so radically transformed as to permit a food-producing way of life (even today, the long-term outcome of plant breeding cannot be predicted). Finally, even if people had wanted to become producers of their own food, there is no way such a decision could have had an immediate and perceptible effect; in fact, domestication took a few thousand years to accomplish. Although this may seem a relatively short period of time compared to the 200,000 or 300,000 years since the appearance of *H. sapiens*, it was still too long to have made any difference to people concerned with immediate food shortages. Under such conditions, the usual response is to make use of a wider variety of foods than before, which acts as a brake on domestication by diverting attention from potential domesticates, while alleviating the immediate problem.

[4]O. Bar-Yosef, "The Walls of Jericho: An Alternative Interpretation," *Current Anthropology* 27 (1986): 160.

Transhumance: Among pastoralists, the grazing of sheep and goats in the low steppelands in the winter, moving to high pastures on the plateaus in the summer.

Another theory, in accord with the evidence as we now know it, but also more in accord with the role played by chance both in evolution (Chapter 3) and in cultural innovation (Chapter 4), is that the change to food production took place originally in environmentally diverse regions where plants and animals with the potential for domestication, along with other sources of food, were being used by food-foraging peoples. One case was in Mesolithic times in the hill country of Southwest Asia, which stretches northward from the Judean Highlands of Israel through the mountains of Lebanon and Syria to Turkey and from there eastward through northern Iraq and Iran (Figure 9.1). Here were to be found large herds of wild sheep and goats as well as large stands of wild wheat and barley. Here, too, is found environmental diversity. From the low, alluvial plains of the valley of the Tigris and Euphrates rivers, for example, travel to the north or east takes one into high country through three other zones: first steppeland, then oak and pistachio woodlands, and, finally, high plateau country with grass, scrub, or desert vegetation. Valleys that run at right angles to the mountain ranges afford relatively easy access between these zones. Today, a number of pastoral peoples in the region practice a pattern of **transhumance,** in which they graze their herds of sheep and goats on the low steppelands in the winter and then move to high pastures on the plateaus in the summer.

Moving 12,000 years backward in time to the Mesolithic, we find that the region was inhabited by peoples whose subsistence pattern was one of food foraging. The wild plants they gathered included wheat and barley. Different plants were found in different ecological zones, and because of the difference in altitude, plant foods matured at different times in different zones. So it was that, as winter gave way to summer, the people moved up to higher altitudes, gathering the wild foods as

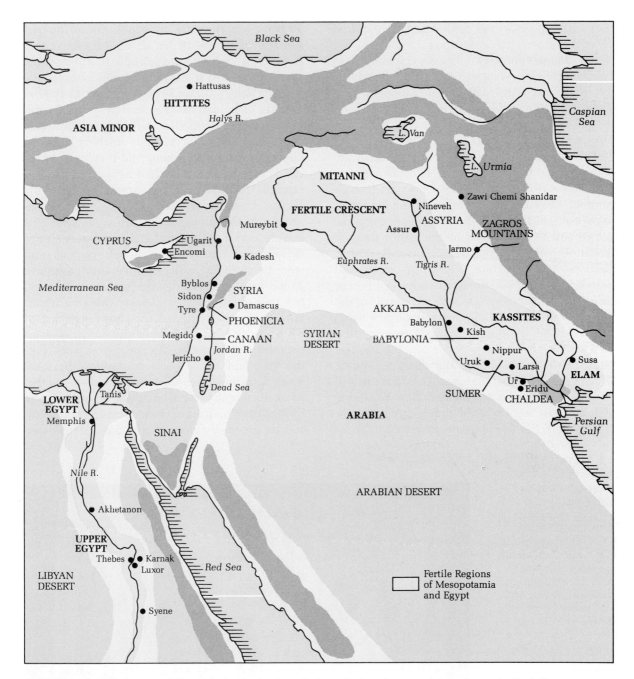

FIGURE 9.1 In Southwest Asia, early domestication of wheat, barley, sheep, and goats began in the hill country around the Fertile Crescent.

they matured. As winter approached, they moved down to warmer, lower elevations.

The animals hunted for meat and hides by these people included several species, among them bear, fox, boar, and wolf. Most notable, though, were the hoofed animals: deer, gazelles, wild goats, and wild sheep. Their bones are far more common in human refuse piles than those of other animals. This is significant, for most of these animals are naturally transhumant in the Middle East, moving back and forth from low winter pastures to high summer pastures. People followed these animals in their seasonal migrations, making use along the way of other wild foods in the zones through which they passed: dates in the lowlands; acorns, almonds, and pistachios higher up; apples and pears higher still; wild grains maturing at different times in different zones; woodland animals in the forested zone between summer and winter grazing land. All in all, it was a rich, varied fare.

There was in hunting, then, a concentration on hoofed animals, including wild sheep and goats, which provided meat and hides. At first, animals of all ages and sexes were hunted. But, beginning about 11,000 years ago, the percentage of immature sheep eaten, for example, increased to about

50 percent of the total. At the same time, the percentage frequency of female animals decreased. Apparently, people were learning that they could increase yields by sparing the females for breeding, while feasting on ram lambs. This marks the beginning of human management of sheep. As this management of flocks became more and more efficient, sheep were increasingly shielded from the effects of natural selection. And they were introduced into areas outside their natural habitat. For example, sheep were kept at ancient Jericho, in the Jordan River Valley, 9000 years ago. As a consequence of this human intervention, variants that usually were not successful in the wild were able to survive and reproduce. Although variants that were perceived as being of immediate advantage would have attracted peoples' attention, they did not arise out of need, but independent of it at random, as mutations do. In such a way did those features characteristic of domestic sheep, such as greater fat and meat production, excess wool (Figure 9.2), and so on, begin to develop. By 9000 years ago, the bones of domestic sheep had become distinguishable from those of wild sheep.

The development of plant domestication seems to have proceeded along similar lines. Many of the

Although sheep and goats were first valued for their meat, hides, and sinew, the changes wrought by domestication made them useful for other purposes as well. This impression, from a 4500-year-old seal, shows a goat being milked.

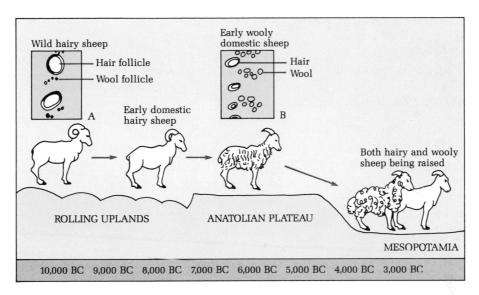

FIGURE 9.2 Steps in the evolution of domestic sheep. *A,* a section, as seen through a microscope, of skin of wild sheep, showing the arrangement of primary (hair) and secondary (wool) follicles. *B,* a section similarly enlarged of skin of domestic sheep, showing the changed relationship and the change in the size of follicles that accompanied the development of wool.

plants that became domesticated were colonizers, which do particularly well in disturbed habitats, including those created by humans. Such habitats include latrines, garbage dumps, areas cleared of trees around campsites, or burned-over areas. In nature, disturbed conditions usually are restricted and relatively short lived, but those created by humans are less so. Thus, as human populations grew, as they continued to do after the Paleolithic, disturbed ecologies became more extensive, providing more stable environments for colonizing plants. Under such circumstances, higher yielding plants were bound to out produce low yielders, making them more attractive to humans. At the same time, as people made use of wild plant foods to be found in different environmental zones, some of these were carried out of their native habitats. The inevitable result of all this would have been the creation of altered niches in which, by chance, mutants previously selected against were able to flourish. Again, by chance, some of these

would have been useful to humans. For example, barley, which in its wild state can be tremendously productive but difficult to harvest and process, had developed the tougher stems that make it easier to harvest by 9000 years ago; by 8000 years ago "naked" barley, which is easier to process, was common, and by 7500 years ago, six-row barley, which is more productive than the original two-row, was widespread.

Apparently, the domesticators of plants and animals sought only to increase to the maximum extent the food sources available to them. They were not aware of the revolutionary consequences their actions were to have. But as the process continued, the productivity of the domestic species increased, relative to wild species. Thus, they became increasingly more important to subsistence, resulting in further intensification of interest in, and management of, the domesticates. Inevitably, the result would be further increases in productivity.

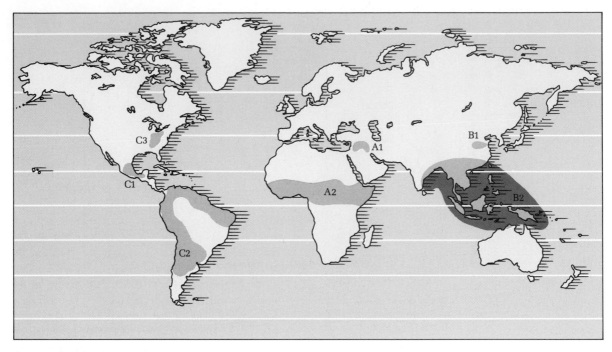

FIGURE 9.3 Areas of early plant and animal domestication: *A1*, Southwest Asia; *A2*, central Africa; *B1*, China; *B2*, Southeast Asia; *C1*, Mesoamerica; *C2*, South America; *C3*, North America.

OTHER CENTERS OF DOMESTICATION

In addition to Southwest Asia, the domestication of plants and, in some cases, animals took place independently in Southeast Asia, parts of the Americas (southern Mexico, Peru, and the Amazon Basin of South America) and possibly northern China and other regions (Figure 9.3). In Southeast Asia, domestication took place sometime between 8800 and 5000 years ago. Plant remains, none of them showing any detectable differences from wild strains, have been found in Spirit Cave in northern Thailand in levels dating back as far as 10,000 years. The oldest domestic plant so far identified is rice, in pottery dated to sometime before 5000 years ago. In addition to rice, Southeast Asians domesticated root crops, most notably yams and taro. Root crop farming, or **vegeculture,** typically involves the growing of many different species together in a single field.

Vegeculture: The cultivation of domesticated root crops, such as yams and taro.

Because this approximates the complexity of the natural vegetation, vegeculture tends to be more stable than seed crop cultivation.

In Mexico, the domestication of plants took place between 9000 to 3500 years ago. Archaeological evidence from the Tehuacan Valley in the Mexican state of Puebla shows that crops such as maize, beans, and squash very gradually came to make up a greater percentage of the food eaten (Figure 9.4). Like the hill country of Southwest Asia, the Tehuacan Valley is environmentally diverse, and the people living there had a cyclical pattern of hunting and gathering which made use of the resources of different environmental zones. It is not surprising then that the change to food production in Mexico took place in much the same

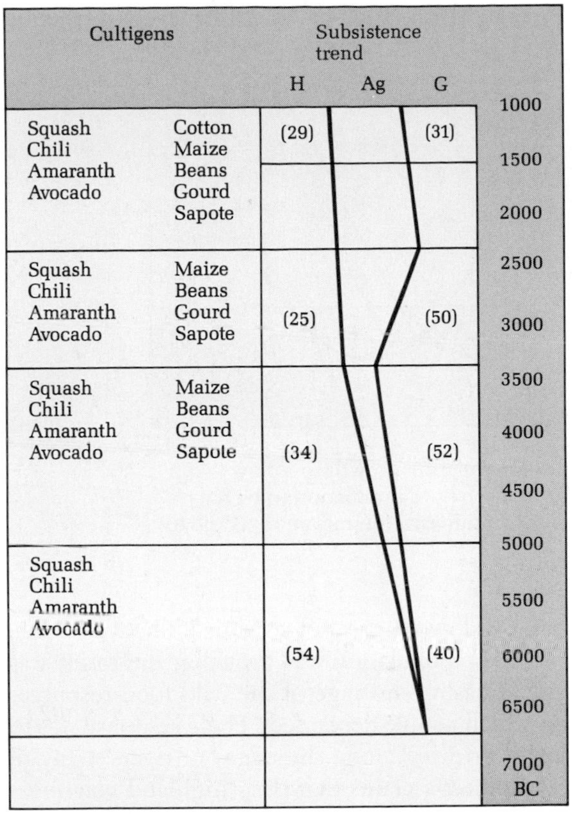

Cultigens		Subsistence trend			
		H	Ag	G	
Squash Chili Amaranth Avocado	Cotton Maize Beans Gourd Sapote	(29)		(31)	1000 1500 2000
Squash Chili Amaranth Avocado	Maize Beans Gourd Sapote	(25)		(50)	2500 3000
Squash Chili Amaranth Avocado	Maize Beans Gourd Sapote	(34)		(52)	3500 4000 4500 5000
Squash Chili Amaranth Avocado		(54)		(40)	5500 6000 6500
					7000 BC

FIGURE 9.4 Tehuacán Valley subsistence trends. H = % hunting; AG = % horticulture; G = % wild plant use.

way that it did in Southwest Asia. The one major difference is that the domestication of animals did not proceed hand in hand with the domestication of plants.

The change to food production also took place in South America, earliest in the highlands of Peru; again an environmentally diverse region. Although a number of crops first grown in Mexico eventually came to be grown here, there was more of an emphasis on root crops, such as potatoes, sweet potatoes, and manioc. South Americans domesticated guinea pigs, llamas, alpacas, and ducks, whereas the Mexicans were limited to dogs, turkeys, and bees.

THE SPREAD OF FOOD PRODUCTION

Although population growth and the need to feed more people cannot explain the origin of the food-producing way of life, it does seem to have a lot to do with its subsequent spread. As already noted, domestication inevitably leads to higher yields, and higher yields make it possible to feed more people. In addition, farmers have available a variety of foods that are soft enough to be fed to infants, which food foragers usually do not. Hence, farmers do not need to nurse their children so intensively, nor for so many years. In humans, prolonged nursing, so long as it involves frequent stimulation of the nipple by the infant, has a dampening effect on ovulation. As a result, women in food-foraging societies are less likely to become fertile as soon after childbirth as they are in food-producing societies. Coupled with this, too many children to care for at once interferes with the foraging activities of women in hunting, gathering, and fishing societies. Among farmers, however, numerous children are frequently seen as assets to help out with the many household chores. Small wonder, then, that a sharp upsurge in the birth rate commonly follows a switch from food foraging to farming.

Paradoxically, while domestication increases productivity, so does it increase instability. This is so because those varieties with the highest yields become the focus of human attention, while other varieties are less valued and ultimately ignored. As a result, farmers become dependent on a rather narrow range of resources compared to the wide range used by food foragers. Modern agriculturists, for example, rely on about 20 crops, whereas the !Kung of Africa's Kalahari Desert regard more than 100 species as edible. This dependence on fewer varieties means that when a crop fails, for whatever reason, farmers have less to fall back on than do food foragers. Furthermore, the likelihood of failure is increased by the common farming practice of planting crops together in one locality so that a disease contracted by one plant can easily spread to others. Moreover, by relying on seeds from the most productive plants of a species

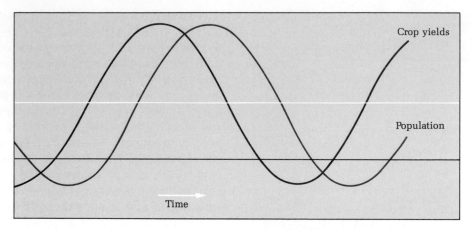

FIGURE 9.5 This graph illustrates the tendency of population growth to follow increases in farming yields. Inevitably, this results in too large a population to be fed when crops fail, as they periodically do. The result is an outward migration of people to other regions.

to establish next year's crop, farmers favor genetic uniformity over diversity. The result is that if some virus, bacterium, or fungus is able to destroy one plant, it will likely destroy them all. This is what happened in the famous Irish potato famine of 1845–1846, which sent waves of Irish immigrants to the United States.

The Irish potato famine illustrates how the combination of increased productivity and vulnerability may contribute to the geographical spread of farming. Time and time again in the past, population growth followed by crop failures has triggered movements of people from one place to another, where they have reestablished the subsistence practices with which they were familiar. Thus, once farming came into existence, it was more or less guaranteed to spread to neighboring regions (Figure 9.5). From Southwest Asia, for instance, it spread to southeastern Europe by 8000 years ago, reaching Central Europe and the Netherlands by 4000 years ago, and reaching England between 4000 and 3000 years ago.

In some instances, farming appears to have been adopted by food foragers from food-producing neighbors. By way of illustration, a crisis developed on the coast of Peru some 4500 years ago as continental uplift caused lowering of the water

table and destruction of marine habitats at a time when the population was growing; the result was an increasing shortage of the wild food resources on which people depended. Their response was to begin growing along the edges of rivers many of the domestic plants that their highland neighbors to the east had begun to cultivate a few thousand years earlier. Here, then, farming appears to have been a subsistence practice of last resort, which a food-foraging people took up only because they had no real choice.

CULTURE OF NEOLITHIC SETTLEMENTS

A number of Neolithic settlements have been excavated, particularly in Southwest Asia. The structures, artifacts, and food debris found at these sites have revealed much about the daily activities of their former inhabitants as they pursued the business of making a living.

EARLIEST FULL-FLEDGED FARMING SETTLEMENTS

Dated to about 9000 years ago, the earliest known sites containing domesticated plants and animals are found in Southwest Asia. These sites occur in a

In the Middle East, the first domestic animals (aside from dogs) were sheep and goats. Pigs, however, followed not long afterward. This pottery vessel in the shape of a pig, found at a site in Turkey, was made about 5600 B.C.

region extending from the Jordan Valley eastward across the flanks of the Taurus Mountains into northern Syria and northeastern Iran, and southward into Iraq and Iran along the hilly flanks of the Zagros Mountains. The sites contain evidence of domesticated barley, wheat, goats, sheep, dogs, and pigs.

These sites are generally the remains of small village farming communities — small clusters of houses built of mud, each with its own storage pit and clay oven. Their occupants continued to use stone tools of Mesolithic type, plus a few new types of use in farming. Probably the people born into these communities spent their lives in them in a common effort to make their crops grow and their animals prosper. At the same time, they participated in long-distance trade networks. Obsidian found at Jarmo, Iraq, for instance, was imported from 300 miles away.

JERICHO: AN EARLY FARMING COMMUNITY

At the biblical city of Jericho, excavation has revealed the remains of a sizable farming community occupied as early as 10,350 years ago. Located in the Jordan River Valley, what made the site attractive was the presence of a bounteous spring and the rich soils of an ice age lake that had dried up about 3000 years earlier. Here, crops could be grown almost continuously, since the fertility of the soil was regularly renewed by flood-borne deposits originating in the Judean Highlands, to the west. To protect their settlement against these floods and associated mudflows, the people of Jericho built massive walls of stone around it.[5] Within these walls, an estimated 400 to 900 people lived in houses of mud brick with plastered floors arranged around court yards. In addition to these houses, a stone tower that would have taken 100 men 104 days to build was located inside one corner of the wall, near the spring. A staircase inside it probably led to a mud brick building on top. Nearby were mud brick storage facilities as well as peculiar structures of possible ceremonial significance. A village cemetery also indicates the sedentary life of these early people; nomadic groups, with few exceptions, rarely buried their dead in a single central location.

Evidence of domestic plants and animals is scant at Jericho. However, indirect evidence in the form of harvesting tools and milling equipment has been uncovered at the site, and wheat, barley, and other domestic plants are known from sites of similar age in the region. We do know that the people of Jericho were keeping sheep and goats by 9000 years ago, although some hunting still went on. Some of the meat from wild animals may have been supplied by food-foraging peoples whose campsites have been found everywhere in the desert of the Arabian peninsula. Close contacts between these people and the farmers of Jericho and other villages are indicated by common features in art, ritual, use of prestige goods, and burial practices. Other evidence of trade consists of obsidian and turquoise from Sinai as well as marine shells from the coast, all discovered inside the walls of Jericho.

[5]My description of the prepottery Neolithic settlement of Jericho takes account of its recent reinterpretation; see Bar-Yosef, pp. 157–162.

These two photos show the stone tower and the remains of one of the houses of early Neolithic Jericho.

NEOLITHIC TECHNOLOGY

Early harvesting tools were made of wood or bone with serrated flints inserted. Later tools continued to be made by chipping and flaking stone, but during the Neolithic period, stone that was too hard to be chipped was ground and polished for tools (Figure 9.6). People developed scythes, forks, hoes, and plows to replace their simple digging sticks. Pestles and mortars were used for preparation of grain. Plows were later redesigned when domesticated cattle became available for use as draft animals, after 8000 years ago.

Pottery

In addition to the domestication of plants and animals, one of the characteristics of the Neolithic period is the extensive manufacture and use of pottery. In food-foraging societies, most people are involved in the food quest. In food-producing societies, even though people have to work as long — if not longer — at subsistence activities than food foragers, this need not be the case. Hard work on the part of those producing the food may free other members of the society to devote their energies to other craft specialties. One such craft is pottery making, and different forms of pottery were created for transporting and storing food, artifacts, and other material possessions. Because pottery vessels are impervious to damage by insects, rodents, and dampness, they could be used for storing small grain, seeds, and other materials. Moreover, food can be boiled in pottery vessels directly over the fire rather than by such ancient techniques as dropping stones heated directly in the fire into the food being cooked. Pottery is also

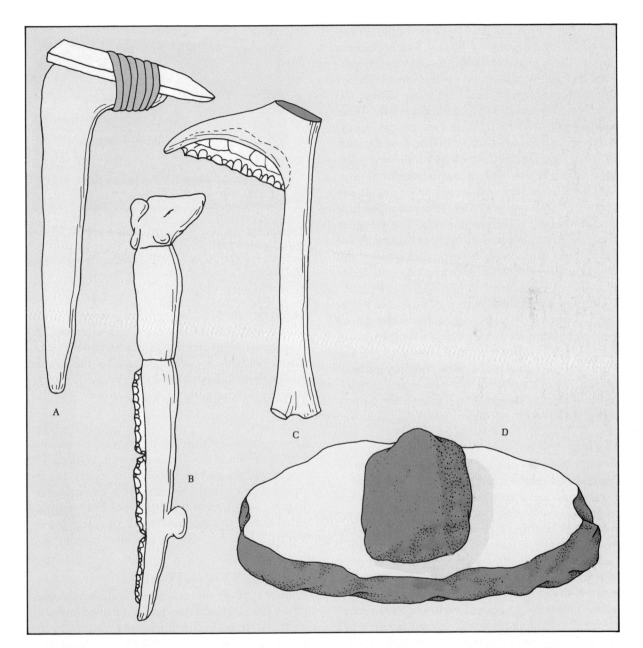

FIGURE 9.6 Some of the tools used by Neolithic peoples. In Southwest Asia, many tools made use of flint microliths in bone or wood handles, as had been done in the Mesolithic, but some used ground and polished stone.

used for pipes, ladles, lamps, and other objects, and some cultures used large vessels for burial of the dead. Significantly, pottery containers remain important for much of humanity today.

The invention of pottery, which is manufactured from clay and fired, is discussed in Chapter 24. Its widespread use is a good, though not foolproof, indication of a sedentary community, and it is found in abundance in all but a few of the earliest Neolithic settlements. At ancient Jericho, for example, the earliest Neolithic people lacked pottery. Its fragility and weight make it impractical for use by nomads and hunters, who use baskets and hide containers. Nevertheless, there are some modern nomads who make and use pottery, just as there are farmers who lack it. In fact, food foragers in Japan were making pottery by 13,000 years ago, long before it was being made in Southwest Asia.

The manufacture of pottery is a difficult art and requires a high degree of technological sophistication. To make a useful pot requires a knowledge of clay and the techniques of firing or baking. Neolithic pots, for example, are often coarse and poorly made because of improper clay mixture or faulty firing technique.

Pottery is decorated in various ways. For example, designs can be engraved on the vessel before firing, or special rims, legs, bases, and other details may be made separately and fastened to the finished pot. Painting is the most common form of pottery decoration, and there are literally thousands of painted designs found among the pottery remains of ancient cultures.

Housing

Food production and the new sedentary life-style engendered another technological development — house building. Permanent housing is of limited interest to food foragers who usually have to move from time to time. Cave shelters, pits dug in the earth, and simple lean-tos made of hides and tree limbs serve their purpose of keeping the weather out. In the Neolithic, however, dwellings became more complex in design and more diverse in type. Some, like Swiss Lake Dwellings, were constructed of wood;, housed several families per building; had doors; and contained beds, tables, and other furniture. More elaborate shelters were made of stone, sun-dried brick, or branches plastered together with mud or clay.

Although permanent housing frequently goes along with food production, there is archaeological evidence that one can have substantial houses without food production. For example, at

Textiles like this one, produced in ancient Peru, remain unsurpassed anywhere in the world, even though weaving began later in the Americas than in parts of the Old World.

Mureybit, in Southwest Asia, storage pits and year-round occupation of stone houses indicate that its occupants had definitely settled down between 10,200 and 9500 years ago. Yet the remains and artifacts indicate that the occupants were food foragers, not farmers.

Clothing

During the Neolithic, for the first time in human history, clothing was made of woven textiles. The raw materials and technology necessary for the production of clothing came from three sources: flax and cotton from farming, wool from domesticated sheep, and the spindle for spinning and the loom for weaving from the inventive human mind.

SOCIAL STRUCTURE

Evidence of all the economic and technological developments listed thus far has enabled archaeologists to draw certain inferences concerning the organization of Neolithic society. The general absence of elaborate buildings in all but a few settlements may suggest that neither religion nor government was yet a formally established institution able to wield real social power. Although there is evidence of ceremonial activity, no firm evidence of a centrally organized and directed religious life has been found. Since no early Neolithic graves have been found containing tomb ornaments or burial equipment, it is believed that no person had attained the superior social status that would have required an elaborate funeral. The smallness of most villages suggests that the inhabitants knew each other very well so that most of their relationships were probably highly personal ones, charged with emotional significance.

The general picture that emerges is one of an egalitarian society with little division of labor and probably little development of new and more specialized social roles. Villages seem to have been made up of several households, each providing for its own needs. The organizational needs of society beyond the household level were probably met by kinship groups and common-interest associations, such as are discussed in Chapters 19 and 20.

NEOLITHIC CULTURE IN THE NEW WORLD

Outside of Mesoamerica (southern Mexico and northern Central America) and Peru, hunting, fishing, and the gathering of wild foods remained important elements in the economy of Neolithic peoples in the New World. Apparently, most American Indians never experienced a complete change from a food-foraging to a food-producing mode of life, even though maize and other domestic crops were cultivated where climate permitted. Farming developed independently of Europe and Asia, and the crops differed because of different natural conditions and cultural traits.

The Neolithic developed later in the New World than in the Old. For example, Neolithic agricultural villages developed in Southwest Asia about 9000 to 8000 years ago, but similar villages did not appear in the New World until about 4500 years ago, in Mesoamerica and Peru. Moreover, pottery, which arose in the Old World shortly after plant and animal domestication, did not develop in the New World until about 4500 years ago. Neither the potter's wheel nor the loom and spindle were used by early Neolithic people in the New World. Both pottery and textiles were manufactured by manual means, and evidence of the loom and spindle does not appear in the New World until 3000 years ago. None of these indicate any "backwardness" on the part of New World peoples; rather, older practices continued to be satisfactory for relatively long periods of time.

THE NEOLITHIC AND HUMAN BIOLOGY

Although we tend to think of the invention of food production in terms of its cultural impact, it obviously had a biological impact as well. From studies of human skeletons from Neolithic burials, physical anthropologists have found evidence for a somewhat lessened mechanical stress on peoples' bodies and teeth. Although there are exceptions, the teeth of Neolithic peoples show less wear, their bones are less robust, and osteoarthritis (the result of stressed joint surfaces) is not as marked as in the skeletons of Paleolithic and Mesolithic peoples. On the other hand, there is clear evidence for a marked deterioration in health and mortality. Anthropologist Anna Roosevelt sums up our knowledge of this in the following Original Study.

O R I G I N A L   S T U D Y
History of Mortality and Physiological Stress[6]

Although there is a relative lack of evidence for the Paleolithic stage, enough skeletons have been studied that it seems clear that seasonal and periodic physiological stress regularly affected most prehistoric hunting–gathering populations, as evidenced by the presence of enamel hypoplasias

Harris lines near the ends of these youthful thigh bones, found in a prehistoric farming community in Arizona, are indicative of recovery after growth arrest, caused by famine or severe disease.

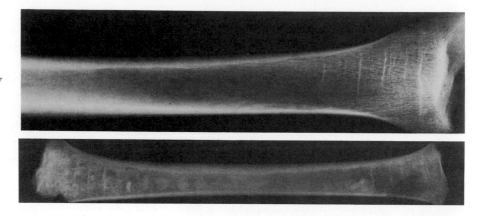

Enamel hypoplasias such as those shown on these teeth are indicative of arrested growth caused by severe disease or famine. The teeth are from an adult who lived in an ancient farming community in Arizona.

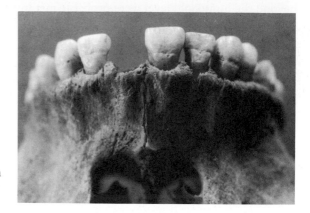

[horizontal linear defects in tooth enamel] and Harris lines [horizontal lines near the ends of long bones]. What also seems clear is that severe and chronic stress, with high frequency of hypoplasias, infectious disease lesions, pathologies related to iron-deficiency anemia, and high mortality rates, is not characteristic of these early populations. There is no evidence of frequent, severe malnutrition, and so the diet must have been adequate in calories and other nutrients most of the time. During the Mesolithic, the proportion of starch in the diet rose, to judge from the increased occurrence of certain dental diseases, but not enough to create an impoverished diet. At this time, diets seem to have been made up of a rather large number of foods, so that the failure of one food source would not be catastrophic. There is a possible slight tendency for Paleolithic people to be healthier and taller than Mesolithic people, but there is no apparent trend toward increasing physiological stress during the Mesolithic. Thus, it seems that both hunter–gatherers and incipient agriculturalists regularly underwent population pressure, but only to a moderate degree.

During the periods when effective agriculture first comes into use there seems to be a temporary upturn in health and survival rates in a few regions: Europe, North America, and the Eastern Mediterranean. At this stage, wild foods are still consumed periodically and a variety of plants are cultivated, suggesting the availability of adequate amounts of different nutrients. Based on the increasing frequency of tooth disease related to high carbohydrate consumption, it seems that cultivated plants probably increased the storable calorie supply, removing for a time any seasonal or periodic problems in food supply. In most regions, however, the development of agriculture seems not to have had this effect, and there seems to have been a slight increase in physiological stress.

Stress, however, does not seem to have become *common* and widespread until after the development of high degrees of sedentism, population density, and reliance on intensive agriculture. At this stage in all regions the incidence of physiological stress increases greatly, and average mortality rates increase appreciably. Most of these agricultural populations have high frequencies of porotic hyperostosis and cribra orbitalia [bone deformities indicative of chronic iron-deficiency anemia] and there is a substantial increase in the number and severity of enamel hypoplasias and pathologies associated with infectious disease. Stature in many populations appears to have been considerably lower than would be expected if genetically determined height maxima had been reached, which suggests that the growth arrests documented by pathologies were causing stunting. Accompanying these indicators of poor health and nourishment, there is a universal drop in the occurrence of Harris lines, suggesting a poor rate of full recovery from the stress. Incidence of carbohydrate-related tooth disease increases, apparently because subsistence by this time is characterized by a heavy emphasis on a few starchy food crops. Populations seem to have grown beyond the point at which wild food resources could be a meaningful dietary supplement, and even domestic animal resources were commonly reserved for farm labor and transport rather than for diet supplementation.

It seems that a large proportion of most sedentary prehistoric populations under intensive agriculture underwent chronic and life-threatening malnutrition and disease, especially during infancy and childhood. The causes of the nutritional stress are likely to have been the poverty of the staple crops in most nutrients except calories, periodic famines caused by the instability of the agricultural system, and chronic lack of food due to both population growth and economic expropriation by elites. The increases in infectious disease probably reflect both a poorer diet and increased interpersonal contact in crowded settlements, and it is, in turn, likely to have aggravated nutritional problems.

[6]Anna Curtenius Roosevelt, "Population, Health, and the Evolution of Subsistence: Conclusions from the Conference," in Mark N. Cohen and George J. Armelegos, eds., *Paleopathology and the Origins of Agriculture* (Orlando, Fla.: Academic Press, 1984), pp. 572–574.

For the most part, the crops on which Neolithic peoples came to depend were selected for their higher productivity and storability rather than their nutritional value. Moreover, their nutritional shortcomings would have been exacerbated by their susceptibility to periodic failure, as already noted, particularly as populations grew in size. Thus, the worsened health and mortality of Neolithic peoples is not surprising.

Another important contributor to the increased incidence of disease and mortality was probably the new mode of life in Neolithic communities. Sedentary life in fixed villages brings with it sanitation problems that do not exist for small groups of people who move about from one campsite to another. Moreover, airborne diseases are more easily transmitted in such villages. Another factor, too, may have been close association between humans and their domestic animals, a situation conducive to the transmission of some animal diseases to humans. Smallpox, chicken pox, and in fact all of the infectious diseases of childhood that were not overcome by medical science until the latter half of the present century seem to have been transmitted to humans through their close association with domestic animals.

Another example of the biological impact of food production on human biology is that of the abnormal hemoglobin responsible for sickle-cell anemia, discussed in Chapter 3. Other abnormal hemoglobins are associated with the spread of farming from Southwest Asia westward around the Mediterranean, and also with the spread of farming in Southeast Asia. In all these regions, changes in human gene pools took place as a biological response to malaria, which had become a problem as a result of farming practices.

Higher mortality rates in Neolithic villages seem to have been offset by increased fertility, for population growth accelerated dramatically at precisely the moment that health and mortality worsened. The factors responsible for this increased natality have already been discussed earlier in this chapter.

THE NEOLITHIC AND THE IDEA OF PROGRESS

One of the more deeply held biases of Western culture is that human history is basically a record of steady progress over time. The transition from food foraging to food production is generally viewed as a great step upward on a supposed "ladder of progress." To be sure, farming allowed people to increase the size of their population, to live together in substantial sedentary communities, and to reorganize the work load in ways that permitted craft specialization. If one chooses to regard this as "progress," that is fine — progress is, after all, whatever it is defined as and different cultures hold different views of this.

Whatever the benefits of food production, however, a substantial price was paid. As anthropologists Mark Cohen and George Armelegos put it:

> Taken as a whole, indicators fairly clearly suggest an overall decline in the quality — and probably in the length — of human life associated with the adoption of agriculture. This decline was offset in some regions, but not in others, by a decline in physical demands on the body. The studies support recent ethnographic statements and theoretical arguments about the relatively good health and nutrition of hunter–gatherers. They also suggest that hunter–gatherers were relatively well buffered against episodic stress. These data call in question simplistic popular ideas about human progress. They also call in question models of human population growth that are based on assumed progressive increases in life expectancy. The data suggest that the well-documented expansion of early farming populations was accomplished in spite of general diminution of both child and adult life expectancy rather than being fueled by increased survivorship."[7]

Rather than imposing ethnocentric notions of progress on the archaeological record, it is best to view food production as contributing to the diver-

[7]Mark N. Cohen and George J. Armelegos, "Paleopathology and the Origins of Agriculture: Editors' Summation," in Cohen and Armelegos, p. 594.

sification of cultures that had begun in the Paleolithic. While some societies continued to practice hunting, gathering, and fishing, others became **horticultural** — small communities of gardeners working with simple hand tools and using neither irrigation nor the plow. Horticulturists typically cultivate different varieties of crops in small gardens they have cleared by hand. Some horticultural societies, however, became **agricultural.** Technologically more complex than the horticulturalists, agriculturalists often use irrigation, fertilizers, and the wooden or metal plow pulled by two harnessed draft animals, such as oxen or water buffalo, to produce food on larger plots of land. The distinction between horticulturalist and agriculturalist is not always an easy one to make. For example, the Hopi Indians of the North American Southwest traditionally employed irrigation in their farming, while at the same time using simple hand tools.

> **Horticulture:** Cultivation of crops with hand tools such as digging sticks or hoes.
>
> **Agricultural:** Intensive farming of large plots of land, using fertilizers, plows, and/or extensive irrigation.
>
> **Pastoralists:** People who rely on herds of domestic animals for their subsistence.

Some societies became specialized **pastoralists** in environments that were too dry or too grassy for effective horticulture or agriculture. For example, the Russian steppes, with their heavy grass cover, were not suitable to farming without a plow, but they were ideal for herding. Thus, a number of peoples living in the arid grasslands and deserts that stretch from North Africa into Central Asia kept large herds of domestic animals, relying on their neighbors for plant foods. Finally, some societies went on to develop civilizations — the subject of the next chapter.

CHAPTER SUMMARY

Throughout the Paleolithic, people were strictly food foragers moving from place to place as the food supply became exhausted. The change to food production, which began about 12,000 years ago, meant that people could become more sedentary and reorganize the work load, freeing some people from the food quest to pursue other tasks. From the end of the Mesolithic, human groups became larger and more permanent as people turned to animal breeding and crop growing.

A domesticated plant or animal is one which has become dependent for its protection and reproductive success on some other species that feeds upon it. Analysis of plant and animal remains at a site will usually indicate whether or not its occupants were food producers. Wild cereal grasses, for example, usually have fragile stems, whereas cultivated ones have tough stems. Domesticated plants can also be identified because they are usually larger than their wild counterparts. Domestication produces skeletal changes in some animals.

The horns of wild goats and sheep, for example, differ from those of domesticated ones. Age and sex imbalances in herd animals may also indicate selection practices by domesticators.

Several theories have been proposed to account for the changes in the subsistence patterns of early humans. One theory, the "oasis" or "desiccation" theory, is based on climatic determination. Domestication began because the oasis attracted hungry animals, which were domesticated instead of killed by early humans. Although once popular, no evidence exists to support such a theory. Another hypothesis, popular in the 1960s, saw domestication as a response to population growth, but this would require a deliberate decision on the part of people who could have had no knowledge of the long-range consequences of domestication. The most probable theory is that domestication came about as the largely accidental by-product of existing food resource management practices. This happened independently in Southwest and Southeast Asia, highland Mexico and Peru, and South America's Amazon forest.

Two major consequences of domestication are that crops become more productive but also more vulnerable. This combination periodically causes population to outstrip food supplies, whereupon people are apt to move into new regions. In this way, farming has often spread from one region to another, as into Europe from Southwest Asia. Sometimes, food foragers will adopt the cultivation of crops from neighboring peoples, in response to the shortage of wild foods, as happened in ancient Peru.

Among the earliest known sites containing domesticated plants and animals, about 11,000 to 9000 years old, are those of Southwest Asia. These sites were mostly small villages of mud huts with individual storage pits and clay ovens. There is evidence not only of cultivation and domestication but also of trade. At the biblical city of Jericho, remains of tools, houses, and clothing indicate the oasis was occupied by Neolithic people as early as 10,350 years ago. At its height, Jericho had a population of 400 to 900 people. Similar villages developed independently in Mexico and Peru by about 4500 years ago.

During the Neolithic, stone that was too hard to be chipped was ground and polished for tools. People developed scythes, forks, hoes, and plows to replace simple digging sticks. The Neolithic was also characterized by the extensive manufacture and use of pottery. The widespread use of pottery is a good indicator of a sedentary community; it is found in all but a few of the earliest Neolithic settlements. The manufacture of pottery requires a knowledge of clay and the techniques of firing or baking. Neolithic pottery is often coarse. Other technological developments that accompanied food production and the sedentary life were the building of permanent houses and the weaving of textiles.

Archaeologists have been able to draw some inferences concerning the social structure of Neolithic society. No evidence has been found indicating that religion or government was yet a centrally organized institution. Society was probably egalitarian, with little division of labor and little development of specialized social roles.

The development of food production had biological, as well as cultural, consequences. New diets, living arrangements, and farming practices led to increased incidence of disease and higher mortality rates. Increased fertility of women seems to have more than offset mortality.

SUGGESTED READINGS

Childe, V. Gordon. *Man Makes Himself.* New York: New American Library, 1951. In this old classic, originally published in 1936, Childe presented his concept of the "Neolithic Revolution." He places special emphasis on the technological inventions that helped transform humans from food gatherers to food producers.

Rindos, David. *The Origins of Agriculture: An Evolutionary Perspective.* Orlando, Fla.: Academic Press, 1984. This is the most important book on agricultural origins to appear in recent times. After identifying the weaknesses of existing theories, Rindos presents his own evolutionary theory of agricultural origins.

Smith, Philip F. L. *Food Production and Its Consequences,* 2d ed. Menlo Park, Calif.: Cummings, 1976. This book is the author's personal interpretation of the ways in which food production influenced and transformed the more important aspects of humans and society, through its effects on demography, settlements, technology, social and political organization, religion, and so on.

Struever, Stuart, ed. *Prehistoric Agriculture.* Garden City, N.Y.: Natural History Press, 1970. This book presents a worldwide survey of the when, where, and how of the rise of agriculture and the development of agrarian societies. The emphasis is upon the adaptation of a society to a particular environment. There are studies of agrarian societies of Europe, the Near East, and North and South America.

Wernick, Robert, and the Editors of Time-Life Books. *The Monument Builders.* New York: Time-Life, 1973. This volume of the Time-Life *Emergence of Man* series deals with the spread of the Neolithic to Europe and the emergence of distinctive patterns there of this way of life. Like all volumes in this series, it is richly illustrated and contains a useful bibliography.

10

THE RISE OF CITIES AND CIVILIZATION

One of the largest cities of the ancient world was Teotihuacán, in central Mexico. At its height, just before its violent end in the eighth century A.D., a population of 125,000 people may have lived there. This photo shows some of the buildings at the city's center.

CHAPTER

PREVIEW

When and Where Did the World's Cities First Develop?
Cities—urban settlements with well-defined nuclei, populations that are large, dense, and diversified both economically and socially — are characteristic of civilizations which developed initially in China, the Indus and Nile Valleys, Mesopotamia, Mesoamerica, and Peru. The world's oldest cities were those of Mesopotamia, but one of the world's largest was located in Mesoamerica.

What Changes in Culture Accompanied the Rise of Cities?
Four basic culture changes mark the transition from Neolithic village life to that in civilized urban centers. These are agricultural innovation as new farming methods were developed; diversification of labor as more people were freed from food production to pursue a variety of full-time craft specialties; the emergence of centralized governments to deal with the new problems of urban life; and the emergence of social classes as people were ranked according to the work they did, or the position of the families into which they were born.

Why Did Civilizations Develop in the First Place?
A number of theories have been proposed to explain why civilizations develop. Most of them emphasize the interrelation of people and what they do on the one hand, and their environment on the other. For example, some civilizations may have developed as populations grew, causing competition for space and scarce resources, which necessitated the development of centralized authority to control resources and organize warfare. Some civilizations, though, appear to have developed as a result of certain beliefs and values which brought people together into large, heavily populated centers, again necessitating centralized authority to manage the problems — of which there are many — of living in such a way. Thus, it may be that civilizations arose in different places for somewhat different reasons.

A walk down a street of a busy North American city brings us in contact with numerous activities that are essential to the well being of North American society. The sidewalks are crowded with people going to and from offices and stores. The traffic of cars, taxis, and trucks is heavy, sometimes almost at a standstill. In a brief two-block stretch, there may be a department store; shops selling clothing, appliances, or books; a restaurant; a newsstand; a gasoline station; and a movie theater. Perhaps there will also be a museum, a police station, a school, a hospital, or a church. That is quite a number of services and specialized skills to find in such a small area.

Each of these services or places of business is dependent on others. A butcher shop, for instance, depends on slaughterhouses and beef ranches. A clothing store depends on designers, farmers who produce cotton and wool, and workers who manufacture synthetic fibers. Restaurants depend on refrigerated trucking and vegetable and dairy farmers. Hospitals depend on a great variety of other institutions to meet their more complex needs. All institutions, finally, depend on the public utilities — the telephone, gas, and electric companies. Although interdependence is not immediately apparent to the passerby, it is an important aspect of modern cities.

The interdependence of goods and services in a big city is what makes so many products readily available to people. For example, refrigerated air transport makes it possible to buy fresh California artichokes on the East Coast. This same interdependence, however, has undesirable effects if one service stops functioning, for example, because of strikes or bad weather. In recent years, a number of major North American cities have had to do without services as vital as newspapers, subways, schools, and trash removal. The question is not so much "Why does this happen?" but rather "Why doesn't it happen more often, and why does the city continue to function as well as it does when one of its services stops?" The answer is that services are not only interdependent, but they are also adaptable. When one breaks down, others take over its functions. During a long newspaper strike in New York City in the 1960s, for example, several new magazines were launched, and television expanded its coverage of news and events.

On the surface, city life seems so orderly that we take it for granted; but a moment's pause reminds us that the intricate fabric of city life did not always exist, and the goods which are so accessible to us were once simply not available.

WHAT CIVILIZATION MEANS

This complicated system of goods and services available in such a small space is a mark of civilization itself. The history of civilization is intimately bound up with the history of cities. This does not mean that civilization is to be equated with modern industrial cities or with present-day North American society. As an example, consider the following description of the great market at Tlaltelolco, sister city of the Aztec capital. It was written over 500 years ago by one of the Spaniards who was with Cortés when he first visited the Aztecs of Mexico.

O R I G I N A L   S T U D Y
The Great Aztec Market at Tlaltelolco[1]

Our Captain and all of those who had horses went to Tlaltelolco on horseback, and nearly all of us soldiers were fully equipped, and many Caciques whom Montezuma had sent for that purpose went in our company. When we arrived at the great market place, called Tlaltelolco, we were astounded at the number of people and the quantity of merchandise that it contained, and at the good order and control that was maintained, for we had never seen such a thing before. The chieftains who accompanied us acted as guides. Each kind of merchandise was kept by itself and had its fixed place marked out. Let us begin with the dealers in gold, silver, and precious stones, feathers, mantles, and embroidered goods. Then there were other wares consisting of Indian slaves both men and women; and I say that they bring as many of them to that great market for sale as the Portuguese bring negroes from Guinea; and they brought them along tied to long poles, with collars round their necks so that they could not escape, and others they left free. Next there were other traders who sold great pieces of cloth and cotton, and articles of twisted thread, and there were *cacahuateros* who sold cacao. In this way one could see every sort of merchandise that is to be found in the whole of New Spain. There were those who sold cloths of henequen and ropes and the sandals with which they are shod, which are made from the same plant, and sweet cooked roots, and other tubers which they get from this plant, all were kept in one part of the market in the place assigned to them. In another part there were skins of tigers and lions, of otters and jackals, deer and other animals and badgers and mountain cats, some tanned and others untanned, and other classes of merchandise.

Let us go on and speak of those who sold beans and sage and other vegetables and herbs in another part, and to those who sold fowls, cocks with wattles, rabbits, hares, deer, mallards, young dogs and other things of that sort in their part of the market, and let us also mention the fruiterers, and the women who sold cooked food, dough and tripe in their own part of the market; then every sort of pottery made in a thousand different forms from great water jars to little jugs, these also had a place to themselves; then those who sold honey and honey paste and other dainties like nut paste, and those who sold lumber, boards, cradles, beams, blocks and benches, each article by itself, and the vendors of *ocote* [pitch-pine for torches] firewood, and other things of a similar nature. But why do I waste so many words in recounting what they sell in that great market? — for I shall never finish if I tell it all in detail. Paper, which in this country is called *amal*, and reeds scented with *liquidambar*, and full of tobacco, and yellow ointments and things of that sort are sold by themselves, and much cochineal is sold under the arcades which are in that great market place, and there are many vendors of herbs and other sorts of trades. There are also buildings where three magistrates sit in judgment, and there are executive officers like *Alguacils* who inspect the merchandise. I am forgetting those who sell salt, and those who make the stone knives, and how they split them off the stone itself; and the fisherwomen and others who sell some small cakes made from a sort of ooze which they get out of the great lake, which curdles, and from this they make a bread having a flavour something like cheese. There are for sale axes of brass and copper and tin, and gourds and gaily painted jars made of wood. I could wish that I had finished telling of all the things which are sold there, but they are so numerous and of such different quality and the great market place with its surrounding arcades was so crowded with people, that one would not have been able to see and inquire about it all in two days.

Then we went to the great Cue, and when we were already approaching its great courts, before leaving the market place itself, there were many more merchants, who, as I was told, brought gold for sale in grains, just as it is taken from the mines. The gold is placed in thin quills of the geese of the country, white quills, so that the gold can be seen through, and according to the length and thickness of the quills they arrange their accounts with one another, how much so many mantles or so many gourds full of cacao were worth, or how many slaves, or whatever other thing they were exchanging.

[1]Excerpted from *The Discovery and Conquest of Mexico: 1517–1521* by Bernal Diaz del Castillo. Copyright © 1956 by Farrar, Straus and Cudahy. Renewal copyright © 1984 by Farrar, Straus and Giroux, Inc. Reprinted by permission of Farrar, Straus and Giroux, Inc.

Both the ancient preindustrial Aztecs and the industrial North Americans of today are included in the term "civilization," but each represents a very different kind. It was with the development of the earliest preindustrial cities, however, that civilization first developed (Figure 10.1). In fact, the word comes from the Latin civis, which refers to one who is an inhabitant of a city, and civitas, which refers to the community in which one dwells. The word "civilization" contains the idea of "citification," or "the coming-to-be of cities."

THE EMERGENCE OF CIVILIZATION

The world's first cities sprang up in some parts of the world as Neolithic villages of the sort discussed in Chapter 9 grew into towns, some of which in turn grew into cities. This happened first in Mesopotamia (in modern-day Iraq), then in Egypt and the Indus Valley, between 6000 and 4500 years ago. The inhabitants of Sumer, in Mesopotamia, developed the world's first civilization about 5000 years ago. In China, civilization was under way by 4100 years ago. Independent of these developments in the Old World, the first cities appeared in Mesoamerica and Peru 2000 and 3000 years ago.

What characterized these first cities? Why are they called the birthplaces of civilization? The first characteristic of cities — and of civilization — is their large size and population. But the first cities were far more than expanded Neolithic villages. The changes that took place in the transition from village to city were so great that the emergence of urban living is considered by some to be one of the greatest "revolutions" in human culture. The following case study gives us a glimpse of one of the world's ancient cities, how it was studied by archaeologists, and how it may have grown from a smaller farming community.

TIKAL: A CASE STUDY

The ancient city of Tikal, one of the largest lowland Maya centers in existence, is situated about 200 miles by air from Guatemala City. Tikal was built on a broad limestone terrace in a rain-forest setting. Here the Maya settled in the last millennium B.C., and their civilization flourished until about A.D. 869.

At its height, Tikal covered about 120.5 square kilometers, and its center was the Great Plaza, a large, paved area surrounded by about 300 major structures and thousands of houses. Starting from

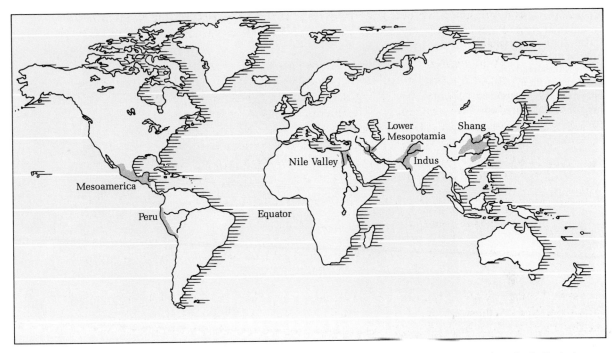

FIGURE 10.1 Locations of major early civilizations. Those of North and South America developed wholly independently of those in Africa and Asia; Chinese civilization may well have developed independently of Southwest Asian (including the Nile and Indus) civilizations.

a small, dispersed population, the population of Tikal swelled to large proportions. By A.D. 600, the density of Tikal was on the order of 600 to 700 persons per square kilometer, six times that of the surrounding regions.

From 1956 through the 1960s, Tikal and the surrounding region were intensively explored under the joint auspices of the University Museum of the University of Pennsylvania and the Guatemalan government. Until 1959, the Tikal Project had investigated only the major temple and palace structures found in the vicinity of the Great Plaza. It became evident, however, that in order to gain a balanced view of Tikal's development and composition, considerable attention would have to be devoted to hundreds of small mounds, thought to be the remains of dwellings, which surround the larger buildings. just as one cannot get a realistic view of Washington, D.C., by looking at its monu-

mental public buildings alone, so one cannot obtain a realistic view of Tikal without examining the full range of ruins in the area.

It became evident that a long-range program of excavation of small structures, most of which were probably houses, was necessary at Tikal. Such a program would provide some basis for an estimate of population size and density at Tikal; this information is critical to test the traditional assumption that the Maya could not have sustained large concentrations of population, because their subsistence patterns were not adequate. Extensive excavation would also provide a sound basis for a reconstruction of the everyday life of the Maya, previously known almost entirely through a study of ceremonial remains. Moreover, the excavation might shed light on the social organization of the Maya. For example, differences in house construction and in the quality and quantity of associated

View of the civic and ceremonial heart of Tikal. In the foreground are the palaces where the city's rulers lived and carried out their administrative tasks; beyond are the temples erected over the tombs of past kings.

remains might suggest social class differences; or features of house distribution might indicate the existence of extended families or other types of kin groups. The excavation of both large and small structures could reveal the variations in architecture and associated artifacts and burials; such variations might reflect the social structure of the total population of Tikal.

SURVEYING THE SITE

Six square miles surrounding the Great Plaza had already been extensively surveyed by mapping crews by the time the first excavations of small structures were undertaken. For this mapping, aerial photography was worthless because the tree canopy in this area is often 100 feet above the ground and obscures all but the tallest temples; many of the small ruins are practically invisible even to the observer on the ground. The only way to explore the region is on foot. Once a ruin is found, it is not easy to mark its exact location. After 4 years of careful mapping, the limits of the site still had not been revealed. Ancient Tikal was

far larger than the 6 square miles so far surveyed. More time and money were required to continue surveying the area in order to define the boundaries of Tikal. To simplify this problem, straight survey trails oriented toward the four cardinal directions, with the Great Plaza as the center point, were cut through the forest, measured, and staked by government surveyors. The distribution of ruins was plotted, using the trails as reference points, and the overall size of Tikal was estimated.

The area selected for the first small structure excavation was surveyed in 1957 while it was still covered by forest. A map was drawn, and 2 years later, the first excavations were undertaken. Six structures, two plazas, and a platform were investigated. The original plan was to strip each of the structures to bedrock to obtain every bit of information possible. But three obstacles prevented this. First was the discovery of new structures not visible before excavation; second, the structures turned out to be much more complex architecturally than anyone had expected; and, finally, the enormous quantity of artifacts found then had to be washed and cataloged; a time-consuming process. Consequently, not every structure was completely excavated, and some remained uninvestigated.

EVIDENCE FROM THE EXCAVATION

After this initial work, over 100 additional small structures were excavated in different parts of the site to ensure that a representative sample was investigated. Numerous test pits were sunk in various other small structure groups to supplement the information gained from more extensive excavations.

Excavation at Tikal revealed evidence of trade in nonperishable items. Granite, quartzite, hematite, pyrite, jade, slate, and obsidian were all imported, either as raw materials or finished products. Marine materials came from Atlantic and Pacific coastal areas. Tikal itself is located on a source of abundant flint, which may have been exported in the form of raw material and finished objects. The site is also located between two river systems to the east and west, and so may have been on a major overland trade route between the two. There is indirect evidence that trade went on in perishable goods such as textiles, feathers, salt, and cacao. We can safely conclude that there were full-time traders among the Tikal Maya.

In the realm of technology, specialized woodworking, pottery, obsidian, and shell workshops have been found. The skillful stone carving displayed on carved monuments suggests that this was done by occupational specialists. The complex Maya calendar required astronomers, and in order to control the large population, estimated to have been at least 50,000 people, there must have been some form of bureaucratic organization. We do know that the government was headed by a hereditary ruling dynasty. Although we do not have direct evidence, there are clues to the existence of textile workers, dental workers, makers of bark cloth "paper," and other occupational specialists.

The religion of the Tikal Maya probably developed as a means to cope with the uncertainties of

Carved monuments like this were commissioned by Tikal's rulers to commemorate important events in their reigns. Portrayed on this one is a king who ruled between A.D. 768 and 790 or a bit later. Such skilled stone carving could only have been carried out by a specialist. (For a translation of the inscription, see Figure 10.2.)

agriculture. When people are faced with problems unsolvable by technological or organizational means, they resort to manipulation of magic and the supernatural. Soils at Tikal are thin, and there is no water except that which can be collected in ponds. Rain is abundant in season, but its onset tends to be unreliable. Once the wet season arrives, there may be dry spells of varying duration which can seriously affect crop productivity. Or there may be too much rain so that crops rot in the fields. Other risks include storm damage, locust plagues, and incursions of wild animals. To this day, the native inhabitants of the region display great concern about these very real risks involved in agriculture over which they have no direct control.

The Maya priesthood devoted much of its time to calendrical matters; the priests tried not only to placate the deities in times of drought but also to propitiate them in times of plenty. They determined the most auspicious time to plant crops and were concerned with other agricultural matters. The dependence of the population in and around Tikal on their priesthood to manipulate supernatural beings and forces in their behalf, in order that their crops would not fail, tended to keep them in or near the city, despite the fact that a slash-and-burn method of agriculture, which was probably the prevailing method early in Tikal's history, required the constant shifting of plots and consequently tended to disperse the population over large areas.

As the population increased, land for agriculture became scarcer, and the Maya were forced to find new methods of food production that could sustain the dense population concentrated at Tikal. From slash-and-burn agriculture as their main form of subsistence, they turned to collecting the very nutritious fruit of the breadnut tree for food. It may be that breadnut trees were abundant and the fruit could be easily picked. Along with increased reliance on breadnuts for subsistence went the construction of artificially raised fields in areas that were flooded each rainy season. In these fields, crops could be intensively cultivated year after year, so long as they were carefully maintained. As these changes were taking place, a class of artisans, craftspeople, and other occupational specialists emerged to serve the needs first of religion, then of an elite consisting of the priesthood and a ruling dynasty. The arts flourished, and numerous temples, public buildings, and houses were built.

For several hundred years, Tikal was able to sustain its ever-growing population. Then the pressure for food and land reached a critical point, and population growth was halted. This event is marked archaeologically by a pull back from prime land, by the advent of nutritional problems as evidenced by the bones from burials, and by the construction of a system of ditches and embankments that probably served in the defense of the city and as a means of regulating commerce by limiting its accessibility. In other words, a period of readjustment set in, which must have been directed by an already strong central authority. Activities then continued as before, but without further population growth for another 250 years or so.

CITIES AND CULTURAL CHANGE

If someone who grew up in a small village of Maine, Wyoming, or Mississippi were to move to Chicago, Detroit, or Los Angeles, that person would experience a number of marked changes in his or her way of life. Some of the same changes in daily life would have been felt 5000 years ago by a Neolithic village dweller on moving into one of the world's first cities in Mesopotamia. Of course, the differences would be less extreme today. In the twentieth century, every North American village, however small, is part of civilization; back when cities first developed, they were civilization, and the villages for the most part represented a continuation of Neolithic life.

Four basic culture changes mark the transition from Neolithic village life to life in the first urban centers.

AGRICULTURAL INNOVATION

The first culture change characteristic of life in cities — hence, of civilization itself — was change in farming methods. The ancient Sumerians, for example, built an extensive system of dikes, canals, and reservoirs to irrigate their farmlands. With such a system, they could control water resources at will; water could be held and then run off into the fields as necessary. Irrigation was an important factor affecting an increase of crop yields. Because farming could now be carried on independently of the seasons, more crops could be harvested in

APPLICATION
Economic Development and Tropical Forests

Prime targets for development in the world today, in the eyes of governments and private corporations alike, are vast tracts of tropical forests. On a global basis, forests are being rapidly cleared for lumber and fuel, as well as to make way for farms, ranches, mines, and other forms of economic development. The world's largest uninterrupted tracts are the forests of the Amazon and Orinoco watersheds of South America, which are being destroyed at about the rate of 4 percent a year. Just what the rate is for the world as a whole no one is quite sure, but it is clearly accelerating. And already there are signs of trouble, as extensive tracts of once-lush growth have been converted to semidesert. What happens is that essential nutrients are lost, either through erosion (which increases by several orders of magnitude under deforestation), or by leaching too deeply, as soils are exposed to the direct force of the heavy tropical rains.

The problem is that developers, until recently, have lacked reliable models by which the long-term impact of their actions might be assessed. Such a model now exists, thanks to the efforts of archaeologists unraveling the mystery of how the ancient Maya, in a tropical rain-forest setting, carried out large-scale urban construction and sustained huge numbers of people successfully for two millennia. The key to the Maya success was their implementation of sophisticated practices to reduce region-wide processes of nutrient loss, deterioration of soil structure, destabilization of water flows, soil erosion, and loss of productive components of their environment.* These included construction of terraces, canals, and raised fields, the fertility of which was maintained through mulching with water plants and the addition of organic wastes. Coupled with all this, crops were planted in such a way as to produce complex patterns of foliage distribution, canopy heights, and nutrient demands. Far different from "modern" monocrop agriculture, this reduced the impact on the soils of intensive farming, while making maximum use of nutrients and enhancing their cycling in the system.

In Mexico, where population growth has threatened the country's ability to provide sufficient food for its people, archaeologists and agriculturalists are already cooperating to apply our knowledge of ancient Maya techniques to the problems of modern food production in the tropics. Application of these techniques in other tropical forested countries, like Brazil, could do much to alleviate food shortages.

*Don S. Rice and Prudence M. Rice, "Lessons from the Maya" *Latin American Research Review* 19 (1984): 24–28.

---

1 year. On the other hand, this intensification of agriculture did not necessarily mean that people ate better than before. Under centralized governments, intensification was generally carried out with less regard for human health than when such governments did not exist.[2]

The ancient Maya who lived at Tikal developed systems of tree cultivation and constructed raised fields in seasonally flooded swamplands to supplement their earlier slash-and-burn farming. The resultant increase in crop yields provided for a higher population density. Increased crop yields, resulting from agricultural innovations such as those of the ancient Maya and Sumerians, were probably a factor contributing to the high population densities of all civilized societies.

[2]Anna C. Roosevelt, "Population, Health, and the Evolution of Subsistence: Conclusions from the Conference," in Mark N. Cohen and George J. Armelagos, eds., *Paleopathology and the Origins of Agriculture* (Orlando, Fla.: Academic Press, 1984), p. 568

DIVERSIFICATION OF LABOR

The second culture change characteristic of civilization is diversification of labor. In a Neolithic village that possessed neither irrigation nor plow

This clay tablet map of farmland outside of the Mesopotamian city of Nippur dates to 1300 B.C. Shown are irrigation canals separating the various fields, each of which is identified with the name of the owner.

Bronze Age: In the Old World, the period marked by the production of tools and ornaments of bronze; began about 3000 B.C. in Southwest Asia.

ners, engravers, butchers, carpenters, spinners, barbers, cabinetmakers, bakers, clerks, and brewers. At the ancient Maya city of Tikal we have evidence of traders, potters, woodworkers, obsidian workers, sculptors, and perhaps, textile workers, dental workers, shell workers, and paper makers.

With specialization came the expertise that led to the invention of new and novel ways of making and doing things. In the Old World, civilization ushered in what archaeologists often refer to as the **Bronze Age,** a period marked by the production of tools and ornaments of this metal. Metals were in great demand for the manufacture of farmers' and artisans' tools, as well as for weapons. Copper, tin (the raw materials from which bronze is made), and eventually iron were separated from their ores, then smelted, purified, and cast to make plows, swords, axes, and shields. In wars over border disputes or to extend a state's territory, stone knives, spears, and slings could not stand up against bronze spears, arrowheads, swords, and armor.

The native civilizations of the Americas also made use of metals — in South America, for tools as well as ceremonial and ornamental objects, but in Mesoamerica, for ceremonial and ornamental objects alone. Why people like the Aztecs and Maya continued to rely on stone for their everyday tools has puzzled those who assume that metal is inherently superior. The answer, however, is simple: The availability of obsidian (a glass formed by volcanic activity), its extreme sharpness (many times sharper than the finest steel) and the ease with which it could be worked made it perfectly suited to their needs.

In order to procure the raw materials needed for their technologies, extensive trade systems were developed by the early civilizations. Extensive trade agreements were maintained with distant peoples, not only to secure basic raw materials but to provide luxury items as well.

Boats gave greater access to trade centers; they

farming, the members of every family were primarily concerned with the raising of crops. The high crop yields made possible by new farming methods and the increased population freed more and more people from farming. For the first time, a sizable number of people were available to pursue nonagricultural activities on a full-time basis. In the early cities, some people still farmed, but a large number of the inhabitants were skilled workers or craftspeople.

Ancient public records indicate there was a considerable variety of such skilled workers. For example, an early Mesopotamian document from the city of Lagash lists the artisans, craftspeople, and others paid from crop surpluses stored in the temple granaries. Among them were coppersmiths, silversmiths, sculptors, merchants, potters, tan-

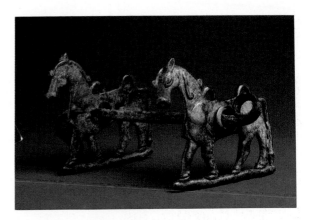

Bronze tools and weapons were more effective and durable than their stone counterparts. *Left*, a bronze axe from Mesopotamia. *Right*, the cheek piece from an Iranian horse's harness — a fine example of the artistry that became possible with the introduction of bronze into craftsmanship.

Aztec spears tipped and edged with obsidian blades are shown in this sixteenth-century drawing of battles with their Spanish conquerors. Though superior to steel for piercing, cutting, and slashing, the brittleness of obsidian placed the Aztecs at a disadvantage when faced with Spanish swords.

could easily carry back to cities large loads of imports at less cost than if they had been brought back overland. A one-way trip from Egypt to the northern city of Byblos in Phoenicia took only 4 to 8 days by rowboat. With a sailboat, it took even less.

Egyptian pharaohs sent expeditions to the Sinai Peninsula for copper; to Nubia for gold; to Arabia for spices and perfumes; to Asia for lapis lazuli (a blue semiprecious stone) and other jewels; to Lebanon for cedar, wine, and funerary oils; and to central Africa for ivory, ebony, ostrich feathers, leopard skins, cattle, and slaves.

With technological innovation, along with increased contact with foreign peoples through trade, came new knowledge. It was within the early civilizations that sciences such as geometry and astronomy were first developed. Geometry was used by the Egyptians for such purposes as measuring the area of a field or staking off an accurate right angle at the corner of a building.

Astronomy grew out of the need to know when to plant and harvest crops or to hold religious observances and to find exact bearings on voyages. Astronomy and mathematics were used to devise calendars. The Maya calculated that the solar year was 365 days (actually, it is 365¼ days), accurately predicted the appearances of the Planet Venus as

Among occupational specialists in ancient civilizations were astronomers. This structure, at the ancient Maya city of Chichen Itza in Mexico, was built as an observatory.

morning and evening "star," and were able to predict eclipses. The Babylonians were able to calculate the exact date of the new moon.

CENTRAL GOVERNMENT

The third culture change characteristic of civilization is the emergence of a governing elite, a strong central authority required to deal with the many problems arising within the new cities, owing to their size and complexity. The new governing elite saw to it that different interest groups, such as farmers, craftsmen, or money lenders, provided the services that were expected of them and did not infringe on each other's rights. It ensured that the city was safe from its enemies by constructing walls and raising an army. It levied taxes and appointed tax collectors so that construction workers, the army, and other public expenses could be paid. It saw to it that merchants, carpenters, or farmers who made legal claims received justice. It guaranteed safety for the lives and property of ordinary people and assured that any harm done one person by another would be justly dealt with. In addition, surplus food had to be stored for times of scarcity, and public works such as extensive irrigation systems had to be supervised by competent, disinter-

ested individuals. The mechanisms of government served all these functions.

Evidence of Centralized Authority

Evidence of a centralized authority in ancient civilizations comes from such sources as law codes, temple records, and royal chronicles. Excavation of the city structures themselves provides further evidence. For example, archaeologists believe that the cities of Mohenjodaro and Harappa in the Indus Valley were governed by a centralized authority because they show definite signs of city planning. They are both over 3 miles long; their main streets are laid out in a rectangular grid pattern; and both contain city-wide drainage systems.

Monumental buildings and temples, palaces, and large sculptures are usually found in civilizations. The Maya city of Tikal contained over 300 major structures, including temples, ball courts, and "palaces" (residences of the aristocracy). The Pyramid of the Sun in the pre-Aztec city of Teotihuacán is 700 feet long and over 200 feet high. Its interior is filled by more than one million cubic yards of sun-dried bricks. The tomb of the Egyptian pharaoh Cheops, known as the Great Pyramid, is 755 feet long and 481 feet high. It contains about 2,300,000 stone blocks, each with an

This Tikal palace may be compared with the lower-class houses shown in Figure 10.3.

average weight of 2.5 tons. The Greek historian Herodotus reports that it took 100,000 men 20 years to build this tomb. Such gigantic structures could be built only because the considerable manpower, engineering skills, and raw materials necessary for their construction could be harnessed by a powerful central authority.

Another indicator of the existence of centralized authority is writing. In the Old World, early governments found it useful to keep records of state affairs, such as accounts of their food surplus, tribute records, and other business receipts. The earliest documents appear to be just such records — lists of vegetables and animals bought and sold, tax lists, and storehouse inventories. Writing was an extremely important invention, because governments could keep records of their assets instead of simply relying on the memory of administrators.

Before 5000 years ago, "writing" consisted of pictures drawn or carved on stone, bone, or shell to commemorate a notable event, such as a hunt, a military victory, or the deed of some king. The earliest picture writing — pictographs — functioned much like historical paintings or newspaper photos.

The figures in such pictures gradually became simplified and generalized and stood for ideas of things rather than for the things themselves. Thus, a royal palace could be represented by a simple stick drawing of a house with a crown placed above it. This representation of the idea of a palace is an ideogram. In the older pictographic writing, it would have been necessary to draw a likeness of an actual palace in order to convey the message effectively. Ideographic writing was faster, simpler, and more flexible than pictographic writing. Over the centuries, the ideograms became more simplified, and although their meaning was clear to their users, they looked less and less like the natural objects they had originally depicted.

In Mesopotamia, about 6000 years ago, a new writing technique emerged, which used a stylus to make wedge-shaped markings on a tablet of damp clay. Originally, each marking stood for a word. Since most words in this language were monosyllabic, the markings came, in time, to stand for syllables. There were about 600 signs, half of them ideograms, the others functioning either as ideograms or as syllables.

In the New World, systems of writing came into use among various Mesoamerican peoples, but the most sophisticated system was that of the Maya. Their hieroglyphic system had less to do with keeping track of state belongings than with "dynastic bombast." Maya lords glorified themselves by recording their dynastic genealogies, important conquests, and royal marriages, by using grandiose titles to refer to themselves, and by associating their actions with important astrological events (Figure 10.2). Often, the latter involved complicated mathematical calculations.

The Earliest Governments

The government organization of the earliest cities was typically headed by a king and his special advisers. In addition, there were sometimes councils of lesser advisers. Formal laws were enacted and courts sat in judgment over the claims of rival litigants or the criminal charges brought by the government against an individual.

Of the many ancient kings known, one stands out as truly remarkable for the efficient government organization and highly developed legal system that characterized his reign. This is Hammurabi, the Babylonian king who lived sometime

	The day 13 Ahau Eighteenth day of the month, Cumku,
	End of the seventeenth katun. The completion of its period.
	[Part of the ruler's name?] Chitam
	In the dynastic line, lord of Tikal, [A title]
	The ninth plus twenty, In the count of the rulers
	[Successor to?] His lord father,
	Yax Kin Caan Chac [A probable title,]
	In the dynastic line, lord of Tikal, In his fourth katun [period of 20 tuns, or 360 day years]
	The leader [batab] Sixteen days plus one period of twenty days,
	Plus two tuns [back to], The day 11 Kan,
	Twelfth day of the month of the parrot, Kayab, He took the throne,
	At the place of leadership, He who scatters blessings.

FIGURE 10.2
Translation of the text on the monument shown on p. 237. The "scattering" mentioned may refer to bloodletting as part of the ceremonies associated with the end of one 20-year period, or *Katun*, and the beginning of the next.

between 1950 and 1700 B.C. He promulgated a set of laws for his kingdom, known as the Code of Hammurabi, which is important because of its thorough detail and standardization. It prescribes the correct form for legal procedures and determines penalties for perjury, false accusation, and injustice done by judges. It contains laws applying to property rights, loans and debts, family rights, and damages paid for malpractice by a physician. There are fixed rates to be charged in various trades and branches of commerce. The poor, women, children, and slaves are protected against injustice. The Code was publicly displayed on huge stone slabs so that no one accused could plead ignorance. Even the poorest citizen was supposed to know his or her rights.

Some civilizations flourished under a ruler with extraordinary governing abilities, such as Hammurabi. Other civilizations possessed a widespread governing bureaucracy that was very efficient at every level. The government of the Inca civilization is a case in point.

The Inca empire of Peru reached its zenith in the sixteenth century A.D., just before the arrival of the Spanish. In the mid-1400s, the Inca kingdom probably did not extend more than 20 miles beyond the modern-day city of Cuzco, which was then its center. Within a 30-year period, in the late 1400s, the Inca kingdom enlarged a thousand times its original size. By A.D. 1525, it stretched 2500 miles from north to south and 500 miles from east to west, making it at the time the greatest empire on the face of the earth. Its population numbered in the millions, composed of people of various ethnic groups. In the achievements of its governmental and political system, Inca civilization surpassed every other civilization of the New World and most of those of the Old World. At the head of the government was the emperor, regarded as semidivine, followed by the royal family, the aristocracy, imperial administrators, the lower nobility, and the masses of artisans, craftsmen, and farmers.

The empire was divided into four administrative regions, further subdivided into provinces, and so on down to villages and families. Planting, irrigation, and harvesting were closely supervised by government agricultural experts and tax officials. Teams of professional relay runners could carry messages up to 250 miles in a single day over a network of roads and bridges that remains impressive even today. The Inca are unusual in that they had no writing that we know about; public records and historical chronicles were kept in the form of an ingenious system of colored beads, knots, and ropes.

SOCIAL STRATIFICATION

The rise of large, economically diversified populations presided over by centralized governing authorities brought with it the fourth culture change characteristic of civilization: social stratification, or the emergence of social classes. The nature of social stratification is discussed in Chapter 20. Here, we may note that symbols of special status and privilege appeared for the first time in the ancient cities of Mesopotamia, and people were ranked according to the kind of work they did or the family into which they were born.

People who stood at or near the head of government were the earliest holders of high status. Although economic specialists of one sort or another — metal workers, tanners, traders, or the like — generally outranked farmers, such specialization did not necessarily bring with it high status. Rather, people engaged in economic activity were either of the lower class or outcasts.[3] The exception was those merchants who were in a position to buy their way into some kind of higher class status. With time, the possession of wealth, and the influence it could buy, became in itself a requisite for status.

Evidence of Social Stratification

How do archaeologists know that there were different social classes in ancient civilizations? There are four main ways:

1. Burial customs. Graves excavated at early Neolithic sites are mostly simple pits dug in the

[3]Gideon Sjoberg, *The Preindustrial City* (New York: Free Press, 1960), p. 325.

ground, containing few grave goods. Grave goods consist of things such as utensils, figurines, and personal possessions, which are placed in the grave in order that the dead person might use them in the afterlife. The lack of much variation between burials in terms of the wealth implied by grave goods in Neolithic sites indicates an essentially classless society. Graves excavated in civilizations, by contrast, vary widely in size, mode of burial, and the number and variety of grave goods. This indicates a stratified society — one divided into social classes. The graves of important persons contain not only a great variety of artifacts made from precious materials, but sometimes, as in some early Egyptian burials, even the remains of servants evidently killed to serve their master in his afterlife. The skeletons from the burials may also give evidence of stratification. At Tikal, skeletons from elaborate tombs indicate that the subjects of these tombs had longer life expectancy, ate better food, and enjoyed better health than the bulk of that city's population. In stratified societies, the elite usually live longer, eat better, and enjoy an easier life than other members of society.

2. Size of dwellings. In early Neolithic sites, dwellings tended to be uniformly small in size. in the oldest excavated cities, however, some dwellings were notably larger than others, well spaced, and located together in one district, whereas dwellings in other parts of the city were much smaller, sometimes little more than hovels. In the city of Eshnunna in Mesopotamia, archaeologists excavated houses that occupied an area of 200 meters situated on main thoroughfares, and huts of but 50 meters located along narrow back alleys. The rooms in the larger houses often contained impressive art work, such as friezes or murals. At Tikal, and other Maya cities, the elite lived in large masonry, multiroomed houses, mostly in the city's center, while lower-class people lived in small, peripherally scattered houses of one or two rooms, built partly or wholly of pole and thatch materials (Figure 10.3).

3. Written documents. Preserved records of business transactions, royal chronicles, or law codes of a civilization reveal much about the social status of

its inhabitants. Babylonian and Assyrian texts reveal three main social classes — aristocrats, commoners, and slaves. The members of each class had different rights and privileges. This stratification was clearly reflected by the law. If an aristocrat put out another aristocrat's eye, then the first aristocrat's eye was to be put out too. Hence, the saying "an eye for an eye." If the aristocrat broke another's bone, then that aristocrat's bone was to be broken in return. If the aristocrat put out the eye or broke the bone of a commoner, however, the punishment was to pay a mina of silver.[4]

4. Correspondence. European documents describing the aboriginal cultures of the New World as seen by visitors and explorers also offer evidence of social stratification. Letters written by the Spanish Conquistadors about the Aztec empire indicate that they found a social order divided into three main classes: nobles, commoners, and serfs. The nobles operated outside the lineage system on the basis of land and serfs allotted them by the ruler from conquered peoples. The commoners were divided into lineages, on which they were dependent for land. Within each of these, individual status depended on the degree of descent from the founder; those more closely related to the lineage founder had higher status than those whose kinship was more distant. The third class in Aztec society consisted of serfs bound to the land and porters employed as carriers by merchants. Lowest of this class were the slaves. Some had voluntarily sold themselves into bondage; others were captives taken in war (for more on the Aztecs, see Chapter 15).

THE MAKING OF CIVILIZATION

From Mesopotamia to China to the South American Andes, we witness the enduring achievements of the human intellect: magnificent palaces built high above ground; sculptures so perfect as to be

---

[4]Sabatino Moseati, *The Face of the Ancient Orient* (New York: Doubleday, 1962), p. 90.

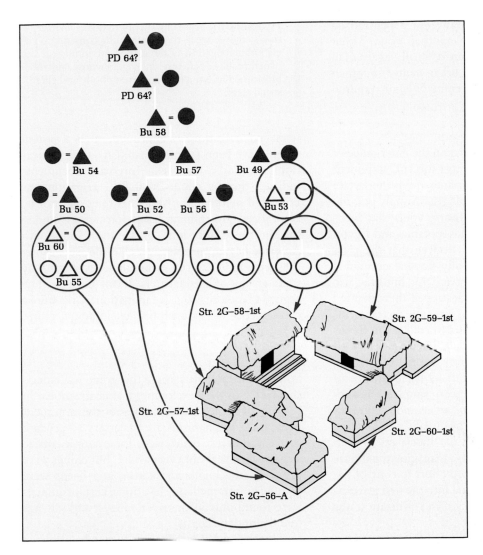

FIGURE 10.3 This drawing is a reconstruction of a lower-class household at Tikal, which may be compared with the elite class palace shown below. The diagram shows the relationships of the people living in the houses: triangles, men; circles, women; double horizontal lines, a marital bond; vertical lines, descent; and single horizontal lines, brothers and sisters.

unrivaled by those of contemporary artists; engineering projects so vast and daring as to awaken in us a sense of wonder. Looking back to the beginnings of history, we can see a point at which humans transform themselves into "civilized" beings; they begin to live in cities and to expand the scope of their achievements at a rapid pace. How is it, then, that humans at a certain moment in history became master builders, harnessing mighty rivers so that they could irrigate crops, developing a system whereby their thoughts could be preserved in writing? The fascinating subject of the development of civilization has occupied the minds of philosophers and anthropologists alike for a long time. We do not yet have the answers, but a number of theories have been proposed.

THEORIES OF CIVILIZATION'S EMERGENCE

Each of the theories sees the appearance of centralized government as the point at which there is no longer any question whether or not a civilization exists. So, the question they pose is: What brought about the appearance of a centralized government? Or, stated another way: What caused the transition from a small, egalitarian farming village to a large urban center in which population density and diversity of labor required a centralized government?

Irrigation Systems

One popular theory concerning the emergence of civilization was given its most forceful statement by Karl Wittfogel,[5] and variants of this theory are still held by some anthropologists. Simply put, the irrigation, or **hydraulic theory,** holds that Neolithic farmers in ancient Mesopotamia and Egypt, and later in the Americas, noticed that the river valleys that were periodically flooded contained better soils than those that were not, but they also noted that violent floods destroyed their planted fields and turned them into swamps. So the farmers built dikes and reservoirs to collect the floodwater and save it until needed. Then they released it into canals and ran it over the fields. At first, these dikes and canals, built by small groups of neighboring farmers, were very simple. The success of this measure led to larger, more complex irrigation systems, which eventually necessitated the emergence of a group of "specialists" — men whose sole responsibility was managing the irrigation system. The centralized effort to control the irrigation process blossomed into the first governing body and elite social class, and civilization was born.

There are several objections to this theory. One of them is that some of the earliest large-scale irrigation systems we know about anywhere in the world developed in highland New Guinea, where strong centralized governments never emerged. Another is that actual field studies of ancient Mesopotamian irrigation systems reveal that by the year 2000 B.C., by which time many cities had already flourished, irrigation was still carried out on a small scale, consisting of small canals and diversions of natural waterways. If there were state-

[5]Karl A. Wittfogel, *Oriental Despotism, A Comparative Study of Total Power* (New Haven: Yale University Press, 1957).

Hydraulic theory: The theory that sees civilization's emergence as the result of the construction of elaborate irrigation systems, the functioning of which required full-time managers whose control blossomed into the first governing body and elite social class.

managed irrigation, it is argued, such a system would have been far more extensive than excavations show it really was. Moreover, documents indicate that by about 2000 B.C. irrigation was regulated by officials of local temples and not by centralized government. Irrigation systems among the Indian civilizations of Central and South America began on a very small scale, suggesting they were built and run by families, or, at most, by small groups of local farmers. It can just as well be argued that more extensive irrigation works were a consequence of civilization's development, rather than a cause.

Trade Networks

Some anthropologists argue that trade was a decisive factor in the development of civilizations. In regions of ecological diversity, so the argument goes, trade mechanisms are necessary to procure scarce resources. In Mexico, for example, maize was grown just about everywhere; but chilies were grown in the highlands; cotton and beans were planted at intermediate elevations; certain animals were found only in the river valleys; and salt was found along the coasts.

This theory holds that some form of centralized authority was necessary in order to organize trade for the procurement of these and other commodities. Once procured, some system was necessary in order to redistribute commodities throughout the population. Redistribution, like procurement, must have required a centralized authority, promoting the growth of a centralized government.

While trade may have played an important role in the development of some civilizations, it did not invariably do so. For example, the Indians of northeastern North America traded widely with each other for at least 6000 years without developing civilizations comparable to those of Mexico or

Peru. In the course of this trade, copper from deposits around Lake Superior wound up in such faraway places as New England, as did chert from Labrador and marine shells from the seacoasts of the southeast. Wampum, made on the shores of Long Island Sound, was carried westward, and obsidian from the Yellowstone region has been found in mounds in Ohio.[6]

Environmental and Social Circumscription

In a series of papers, Robert Carneiro[7] has advanced the theory that civilization develops where populations are hemmed in by such things as mountains, seas, or other human populations. As such populations grow, they have no space in which to expand, and so they begin to compete for increasingly scarce resources. Internally, this results in the development of social stratification, in which an elite controls important resources to which lower classes have limited access. Externally, this leads to warfare and conquest, which, to be successful, require elaborate organization under a centralized authority.

Religion

The three theories just summarized exemplify ecological approaches to explaining the development of civilization. Such theories emphasize the interrelation between people and what they do on the one hand and their environment on the other. Most recent theories of the emergence of civilization take some such approach. While few anthropologists would deny the importance of the human–environment interrelationship, a growing number of them are dissatisfied with theories that do not take into account the beliefs and values which regulate the interaction between people and their environment.[8]

An example of a theory that does take into account the role of beliefs is one which seeks to explain the emergence of Maya civilization in Mesoamerica.[9] This theory holds that Maya civilization was the result of a process of urbanization which took place at Tikal and a few other settlements. In the case study on Tikal earlier in this chapter, it is suggested that Maya religion probably developed as a means of coping with the uncertainties of agriculture. In the last millennium B.C., Tikal seems to have been an important religious center. Because of its religious importance, people sought to settle there, with the result that its population grew in size and density. Because this was incompatible with the prevailing slash-and-burn agriculture, which tends to promote dispersed settlement, new subsistence techniques were developed. By chance, these were sufficiently productive to permit further population growth and, by A.D. 600, Tikal had become an urban settlement of at least 50,000 people. Craft specialization also developed, at first in the service of religion but soon in the service of an emerging social elite as well. This social elite was concerned at first with calendrical ritual, but it soon developed into the centralized governing elite needed to control a population growing larger and more diversified in its interests.

Developing craft specialization served as another factor to pull people into Tikal, where their crafts were in demand. It also required further development of trade networks, if only to provide exotic raw materials. More long-distance trade contacts, of course, brought more contact with outside ideas. In other words, what we seem to have is a complex system with several factors acting upon each other, with religion playing a central role in getting the system started in the first place.

In their search for explanations for civilization's emergence, anthropologists have generally sought to find one theory to explain all cases. Yet, we may have here the cultural equivalent of what biologists

[6]William A. Haviland and Marjory W. Power, *The Original Vermonters* (Hanover, N.H.: University Press of New England, 1981), pp. 213, 273.
[7]Robert L. Carneiro, "A Theory of the Origin of the State," *Science* 169 (1970): 733–738.
[8]Kent V. Flannery and Joyce Marcus, "Formative Oaxaca and the Zapotec Cosmos," *American Scientist* 64 (1976): 374, 375.

[9]William A. Haviland, "The Ancient Maya and the Evolution of Urban Society," *University of Colorado Museum of Anthropology, Miscellaneous Series*, 1975, no. 37.

call convergent evolution, where somewhat similar forms come about in quite different ways. Thus, a theory that accounts for the rise of civilization in one place may not account for its rise in another.

CIVILIZATION AND STRESS

Living in the context of civilization ourselves, we are inclined to view its development as a great step upward on some sort of ladder of progress. Whatever benefits civilization has brought, though, the cultural changes it represents seem to have produced new sorts of problems. Among them is the problem of waste disposal. Actually, waste disposal probably began to be a problem in settled, farming communities even before the emergence of civilization. But as villages grew into towns and towns grew into cities, the problem became far more serious, because the buildup of waste created optimum environments for such diseases as bubonic plague.

Quite apart from sanitation problems, the rise of towns and cities brought with it a problem of acute, infectious diseases. In a small population, such diseases, which include influenza, measles, mumps, polio, rubella, and smallpox, will kill or immunize so high a proportion of the population that the virus cannot continue to propagate. Hence, such diseases, when introduced into small populations, spread immediately to the whole population and then die out. Their continued existence depends on the presence of large population aggregates, such as those provided by towns and cities.

Early cities faced social problems strikingly similar to those found in modern North America. Dense population, class systems, and a strong centralized government created internal stress. The slaves and the poor saw that the wealthy had all the things that they themselves lacked. It was not just a question of luxury items; the poor did not have enough space in which to live with comfort and dignity.

Signs of warfare are common in ancient civilizations. Shown here are some of the 7000 life-sized terra cotta figures of warriors that were placed in the tomb of China's first emperor.

Evidence of warfare in early civilizations is common. Cities were fortified; documents list many battles, raids, and wars between groups; cylinder seals, paintings, and friezes depict battle scenes, victorious kings, and captured prisoners of war. Increasing population and the accompanying scarcity of good farming land often led to boundary disputes and quarrels over land between civilized states or between tribal peoples and a state. Open warfare often developed. People tended to crowd into walled cities for protection and to be near irrigation systems.

The class system also caused internal stress. As time went on, the rich became richer and the poor, poorer. In early civilizations, one's place in society was relatively fixed. Wealth was based on free slave labor. For this reason there was little or no impetus for social reform. Records from the Mesopotamian city of Lagash indicate that social unrest due to exploitation of the poor by the rich grew during this period. Members of the upper class received tracts of farmland some 20 times larger than those granted to members of the lower class. An upper-class reformer, Urukaginal, saw the danger and introduced changes to protect the poor from exploitation by the wealthy, thus preserving the stability of the city.

The rise of cities and civilization laid the basis for modern life. It is distressing to note that many of the problems associated with the first civiliza-tions are still with us. Waste disposal, health problems associated with pollution, crowding, social inequities, and warfare continue to be serious problems. Through the study of past civilizations, we now stand a chance of understanding why such problems persist. Such an understanding will be required if the problems are ever to be overcome. It would be nice if the next cultural revolution saw the human species transcending these problems. If this comes about, anthropology, through its comparative study of civilizations, will have played a key role.

CHAPTER SUMMARY

The world's first cities grew out of Neolithic villages between 6000 and 4500 years ago, first in Mesopotamia, then in Egypt and the Indus Valley. Four basic culture changes mark the transition from Neolithic village life to life in civilized urban centers. The first culture change is agricultural innovation as new farming methods were developed. For example, the ancient Sumerians built an irrigation system that enabled them to control their water resources and thus increase crop yields.

The second culture change is diversification of labor. With the growth of large populations in cities, some people were freed from agricultural activities to develop skills as artisans and craftspeople. With specialization came the development of new technologies, leading to the beginnings of extensive trade systems. An outgrowth of technological innovation and increased contact with foreign people through trade was new knowledge; within the early civilizations, sciences such as geometry and astronomy were first developed.

The third culture change that characterized urban life is the emergence of central government with authority to deal with the complex problems associated with cities. Evidence of a central governing authority comes from such sources as law codes, temple records, and royal chronicles. With the invention of writing, governments could keep records of their transactions and could boast of their own glory. Further evidence of centralized government comes from archeological excavations of city structures.

Typically, the first cities were headed by a king and his special advisers. The reign of the Babylonian King Hammurabi, sometime between 1950 and 1700 B.C., is well known for its efficient government organization and the standardization of its legal system. In the New World, in Peru, the Inca empire reached its culmination in the sixteenth century A.D. With a population of several million people, the Inca state, headed by an emperor, possessed a widespread governing bureaucracy that functioned with great efficiency at every level.

The fourth culture change characteristic of civilization is social stratification, or the emergence of social classes. In the early cities of Mesopotamia, symbols of status and privilege appeared for the first time, and individuals were ranked according to the work roles they filled or the position of their families. Archaeologists have been able to verify that social classes existed in ancient civilizations in four ways: by studying burial customs, as well as skeletons, through grave excavations; by noting the size of dwellings in excavated cities; by examining preserved written documents; and by studying the correspondence of Europeans who described the great civilizations that they destroyed in the New World.

A number of theories have been proposed to

explain why civilizations developed. The irrigation, or hydraulic, theory holds that the effort to build and control an irrigation system required a degree of social organization that eventually led to the formation of a civilization. There are several objections to this theory, however; one might argue that sophisticated irrigation systems were a result of the development of civilization rather than a cause. Another theory suggests that in the multicrop economies of both the Old and the New Worlds, some kind of system was needed to distribute the various food products throughout the population. Such a procedure would have required a centralized authority, leading to the emergence of a centralized government. A third theory holds that civilization develops where populations are circumscribed by environmental barriers or other societies. As such populations grow, competition for space and scarce resources leads to the devel-

opment of centralized authority to control resources and organize warfare.

These theories all emphasize the interaction of people's activities and their environment. A theory that lays greater stress on the beliefs and values which regulate the interaction between people and their environment seeks to explain the emergence of Maya civilization in terms of the role religion may have played in keeping the Maya in and about cities like Tikal.

Sanitation problems in early cities created environments in which infectious diseases were rampant. Early urban centers also faced problems strikingly similar to our own. Dense population, class systems, and a strong centralized government created internal stress. Warfare was a common occurrence; cities were fortified, and armies served to protect the state.

SUGGESTED READINGS

Adams, Richard E. W. *Prehistoric Mesoamerica*. Boston: Little, Brown, 1977. Urban societies have arisen independently in more than one place, and one of those places was Mesoamerica. This book describes the Mesoamerican case, and tries to explain the processes at work that caused urban societies to develop there.

Hamblin, Dora Jane, and the Editors of Time-Life Books. *The First Cities*. Boston: Little, Brown, 1973. This well-illustrated volume in the Time-Life *Emergence of Man* series deals with the earliest cities in the Middle East and the Indus River Valley. Written for a popular audience, it is a good survey of the data and theories relating to these early civilizations.

Melter, David, Don Fowler, and Jeremy Sabloff, eds. *American Archaeology: Past and Future*. Washington: Smithsonian Institution Press, 1986. This collection of articles contains one by Henry Wright, "The Evolution of Civilization," an excellent, up-to-date comparative consideration of the subject.

Pfeiffer, John E. *The Emergence of Society*. New York: McGraw-Hill, 1977. This is a comprehensive survey of the origins of food production and the world's first cities. In order to write this book, the author traveled to archaeological sites throughout the world and consulted with numerous investigators. The book is notable for its inclusion of much data as yet unpublished elsewhere as well as its readability.

Redman, Charles E. *The Rise of Civilization: From Early Farmers to Urban Society in the Ancient Near East*. San Francisco: Freeman, 1978. One of the best-documented examples of the rise of urban societies is that of Greater Mesopotamia in the Middle East. This clearly written textbook focuses on that development, presenting the data, discussing interpretations of those data, as well as problems.

Sabloff, J. A., and C. C. Lamberg-Karlovsky, eds. *The Rise and Fall of Civilizations, Modern Archaeological Approaches to Ancient Cultures*. Menlo Park, Calif., 1974. The emphasis in this collection of articles is theoretical or methodological rather than purely descriptive. Special emphasis is on Mesopotamia and Mesoamerica, but papers are included on Peru, Egypt, the Indus Valley, China, and Europe.

11

HUMAN DIVERSITY

One of the notable characteristics of the human species today is its great physical variability, as suggested by this group of children. Human diversity has long fascinated people, but unfortunately, it has also led to discrimination and even bloodshed.

CHAPTER

PREVIEW

What Are the Causes of Physical Variability in Modern Animals?
In the gene pool of a species like *Homo sapiens,* there are various alleles for any given physical characteristic. When such a species is divided into geographically dispersed populations, as is the human species, forces such as drift and natural selection operate in slightly different ways, causing the store of genetic variability to be unevenly expressed. Thus, for example, genes for dark skin pigmentation are found in high frequency in human populations native to regions of heavy ultraviolet radiation, while genes for light skin pigmentation have a high incidence in populations native to regions of reduced ultraviolet radiation.

Is the Concept of Race Useful for Studying Human Physical Variation?
No. Because races are arbitrarily defined, it is difficult to agree on any specific classification. The problem is compounded by the tendency for "racial" characteristics to occur in gradations from one population to another, without sharp breaks. Furthermore, while one characteristic may be distributed in a north–south gradient, another may occur in an east–west gradient. For these and other reasons, most anthropologists have found it most productive to study the distribution and significance of specific characteristics.

Are There Differences in Intelligence from One Population to Another?
Probably not, despite the fact that some populations receive lower average scores on IQ tests than others. Even so, many individuals in "low-scoring" populations score higher than some in the "higher-scoring" populations. Part of the problem is that there is no agreement on what intelligence really is, except that it is made up of several different talents and abilities. Certainly, there are genes affecting these, but they may be independently assorted, and their expression is known to be affected significantly by environmental factors.

"What a piece of work is man," said Hamlet. "How noble in reason, how infinite in faculties, in form and moving how express and admirable, in action how like an angel, in apprehension how like a god: the beauty of the world, the paragon of animals! And yet to me what is this quintessence of dust?"

What people are to each other is the province of anthropology: physical anthropology reveals what we are; cultural anthropology reveals what we think we are. The modern anthropologist Claude Lévi-Strauss systematically describes human cultures in terms of their rituals and myths. Our dreams of ourselves are as varied as our languages and our physical bodies. We are the same, but we differ. We speak English or French, our hair is curly or straight, our skin is lightly to heavily pigmented, and our height ranges from short to tall. Human genetic variation generally is distributed in such a continuous range, with varying clusters of frequency. The significance we give our variations, the way we perceive them — in fact, whether or not we perceive them at all — is determined by our culture. For example, in many Polynesian countries, where skin color is not a determinant of social status, people really do not notice this physical characteristic; in South Africa, it is the first thing people do notice.

VARIATION AND EVOLUTION

Many behavioral traits — reading, for instance — are learned or acquired by living in a society; other characteristics, such as blue eyes, are passed on physically by heredity. Environment affects both. A person growing up surrounded by books learns to read. If the culture insists that brown-eyed people watch television and blue-eyed people read, the brown-eyed people may end up making videotapes while the blue-eyed people are writing books. These skills or tastes are acquired characteristics. Changes in such things within one population but not another are capable of making the two distinct in learned behavioral characteristics within relatively few generations.

Polymorphic: A species in the gene pool of which there are alternative forms (alleles) for particular genes.

PHYSICAL VARIABILITY

The physical characteristics of both populations and individuals, as we saw in Chapter 2, are a product of the interaction between genes and environments. Thus, one's genes predispose one to a particular skin color, for example, but the skin color one actually has is strongly affected by environmental factors such as the amount of solar radiation. In this case, phenotypic expression is strongly influenced by environment; in some others, such as one's A-B-O blood type, phenotypic expression closely reflects genotype.

For most characteristics, there are within the gene pool of *Homo sapiens* various alternative genes, or alleles. In the color of an eye, the shape of a hand, the texture of skin, many variations can occur. This kind of variability, found in many animal species, signifies a rich potential for new combinations of characteristics in future generations. Such a species is called **polymorphic.** Our blood types, determined by the alleles for A, B, and O blood, are an example of a polymorphic trait, which in this case may appear in any of four distinct phenotypic forms. A polymorphic species faced with changing environmental conditions has within its gene pool the possibility of producing individuals with traits appropriate to its altered life. Many may not achieve reproductive success, but those whose physical characteristics enable them to do well in the new environment will usually reproduce so that their genes will show up more frequently in subsequent generations. Thus, humankind, being polymorphic, has been able to occupy a variety of environments.

An expansion into new environments began with the appearance of the genus *Homo*. With *H. erectus* (Chapter 7), human populations were living in Africa, Southeast Asia, Europe, and China. Each of these places constitutes a different

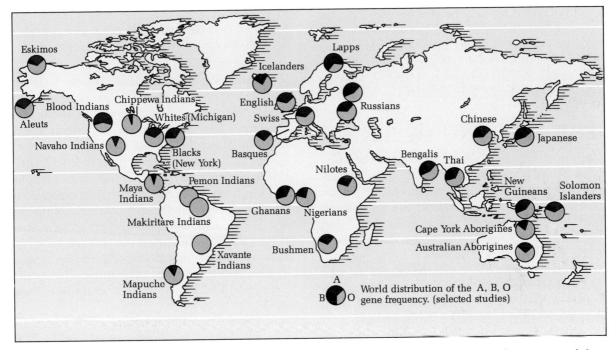

FIGURE 11.1 Frequencies of the three alleles for the A, B, and O blood groups for selected populations around the world.

faunal region, which is to say that each possesses its own distinctive assemblage of animal life, not precisely like that of other regions. This differentiation of animal life is the result of selective pressures that, through the Pleistocene, differed from one region to another. For example, the conditions of life were quite different in China, which lies in the temperate zone, than they were in tropical Southeast Asia. Coupled with differing selective pressures were geographical features that restricted or prevented gene flow between populations of different faunal regions.

When a polymorphic species is divided into geographically dispersed populations, it usually is **polytypic;** that is, the store of genetic variability is unevenly expressed. For example, in the Old World, populations of *H. sapiens* living in the tropics have a higher frequency of genes for dark skin color than do those living farther north. In blood type, *H. sapiens* is polymorphic, with four distinct

Faunal region: A geographic region with its own distinctive assemblage of animal life, not precisely like that of other regions.

Polytypic: A species in which genetic variability is unevenly expressed.

groups (A, B, O, and AB). In the distribution of these types, the polytypic nature of the species is again revealed. The frequency of the O allele is highest in American Indians, especially among some populations native to South America; the highest frequencies of the allele for Type A blood tend to be found among certain European populations (although the highest frequency of all is found among the Blackfoot and Blood Indians of North America); the highest frequencies of the B allele are found in some Asian populations (Figure 11.1). We would expect the earlier species, *H. erectus*, with populations in the four faunal regions of the Old World, to have been polytypic. This appears to have been the case, for the fossils from each of the four regions show some differences from those in the others. It seems, then, that the human species has been polytypic since at least the time of *H. erectus*.

THE MEANING OF RACE

Early anthropologists tried to explore the polytypic nature of the human species by systematically classifying *H. sapiens* into subspecies, or **races,** based on geographic location and phenotypic (physical) features such as skin color, body size, head shape, and hair texture. Such classifications were continually being challenged by the presence of individuals who did not fit the categories, such as light-skinned Africans or dark-skinned "Caucasoids"; to get around the problem, it was assumed that these individuals were hybrids or racial mixtures. Generalized references to human types such as "Asiatic" or "Mongoloid," "European" or "Caucasoid," and "African" or "Negroid" were at best mere statistical abstractions about populations in which certain physical features appeared in higher frequencies than in other populations; no example of "pure" racial types could be found. These categories turned out to be neither definitive nor particularly helpful. The visible traits were found to occur not in abrupt shifts from population to population, but in a continuum that changed gradually, with few sharp breaks. To compound the problem, one trait might change gradually over a north–south gradient, while another might show a similar change over an east–west gradient. Human skin color, for instance, becomes progressively darker as one moves from northern Europe to central Africa, while blood Type B becomes progressively more common as one moves from western to eastern Europe. Finally, there were many variations within each group, and those within groups were often greater than those between groups. In Africa, the skin color of someone from the Kalahari Desert might more closely resemble that of a person of East In-

> **Race:** A population of a species that differs in the frequency of the variants of some gene or genes from other populations of the same species.

dian extraction than the black Nilotic Sudanese who was supposed to be of the same race.

The Negroid was characterized as having dark skin, thick lips, a broad nose, and tightly curled hair; the Mongoloid, a flat face, a flat nose with spread nostrils, and straight hair; and the Caucasoid, pale skin, a narrow nose, and varied eye color and hair form. The classification then expanded to take in American Indians, Australian Aborigines, and Polynesians, but even the expanded system failed to account for dramatic differences in appearance among individuals, or even populations, in each racial category; for example, Europeans, Arabs, and East Indians were all considered Caucasoid.

In an attempt to encompass such variations, schemes of racial classification multiplied. In 1926, J. Deniker classified 29 races according to texture of hair, presumably improving on Roland B. Dixon's 1923 classification based on three indexes of body measures. Hair texture and body build were the characteristics used for another set of racial categories proposed in 1930. By 1947, Earnest Hooton had proposed three new composite races resulting from the interbreeding of "primary" races. Despite these attempts at classification on the part of Western anthropologists, no definitive grouping of distinct, discontinuous biological groups was found for modern humanity.

A turning point is represented by the publication in 1950 of a book called *Races* by Carleton Coon, Stanley Garn, and Joseph Birdsell. Like their predecessors, they too tried to classify modern humans into a number of racial groups — 30 in this case — but they rejected a trait-list approach. Instead, they recognized races as populations that owed certain common characteristics to environmental, primarily climatic, adaptation, which continued to change in response to evolutionary forces such as gene flow and altered selective pressures. While this book certainly had its weak-

These pictures of people from various parts of Africa show the wide range of variation that can be seen within a supposedly single racial category.

nesses, it represented a significant departure from previous attempts at racial classification and was influential in paving the way for our more recent understanding of human variation.

RACE AS A BIOLOGICAL CONCEPT

To understand why the racial approach to human variation has been so unproductive, we must first understand the race concept in strictly biological terms. Briefly, a race may be defined as a population of a species that differs in the frequency of different states of some gene or genes from other populations of the same species. Simple and straightforward though such a definition may

seem, there are three very important things to note about it. First, it is arbitrary; there is no agreement on how many genetic differences it takes to make a race. For some who are interested in the topic, different frequencies in the variants of one gene are sufficient; for others, differences in frequencies involving several genes are necessary. The number of genes and precisely which ones are more important for defining races are still open to debate.

The second thing to note about the biological definition of race is that it does not mean that any one race has exclusive possession of any particular variant of any gene or genes. In human terms, the frequency of the allele for blood group O may be high in one population and low in another, but it is

The "openness" of races to gene flow is illustrated by this picture of a couple with their Asian–American daughter.

present in both. Races are genetically "open," meaning that gene flow takes place between them. Thus, one can easily see the fallacy of any attempt to identify "pure" races; if gene flow cannot take place between two populations, either directly or indirectly through intermediate populations, then they are not races, but are separate species.

The third thing to note about the biological definition of race is that individuals of one race will not necessarily be distinguishable from those of another. In fact, as we have just noted with respect to humans, the differences between individuals within a population may be greater than the differences among populations. This follows from the genetic "openness" of races; no one race has an exclusive claim to any particular gene or allele.

THE CONCEPT OF HUMAN RACES

As a device for understanding polytypic variation in humans, the biological race concept has serious drawbacks. One is that the category is arbitrary to begin with, which makes agreement on any given classification difficult. For example, if one researcher emphasizes skin color, while another emphasizes blood group differences, it is unlikely that they will classify people in the same way. Perhaps if the human species were divided into a number of relatively discrete breeding populations, this

would not be such a problem, but even this is open to debate. What has happened, though, is that human populations have grown in the course of human evolution, and with this growth have come increased opportunities for contact and gene flow among populations. Since the development of food production, the process has accelerated as periodic food shortages have prompted the movement of farmers from their homelands to other places (see Chapter 9). Thus, differences between human populations today are probably less clearcut than back in the days of *H. erectus*, or even the Neandertals.

If this is not enough of a problem, things are complicated even more because humans are so complicated genetically. Thus, the genetic underpinnings of phenotypic traits on which traditional racial classifications are usually based are poorly understood. To compound the problem, "race" exists as a cultural, as well as a biological, category. In various different ways, cultures define religious, linguistic, and ethnic groups as races, thereby confusing linguistic and behavioral traits with physical traits. For example, in many Central and South American countries, people are commonly classified as "Indian," "Mestizo" (mixed), or "Ladino" (of Spanish descent). But despite the biological connotations of these terms, the criteria used for assigning individuals to these categories consist of such things as whether they wear shoes, sandals, or go barefoot; speak Spanish or some Indian language; live in a thatched hut or a European-style house; and so forth. Thus, an Indian, by speaking Spanish, wearing Western-style clothes, and living in a house in a non-Indian neighborhood, ceases to be an Indian, no matter how many "Indian genes" he or she may possess.

This sort of confusion of nonbiological characteristics with what are spoken of as biological categories is by no means limited to Central and South American societies. To one degree or another, such confusion is found in most Western societies, including those of Europe and North America. What makes it worse is that it is frequently combined with attitudes that are then taken as excuses to exclude whole categories of people from certain roles or positions in society. In the United States, for example, it has frequently been asserted that "blacks are born with rhythm," which somehow is thought to give them a "natural affinity" for jazz, "soul music," and similar forms of musical expression. The corollary of this is that blacks are unsuited "by nature" for symphonic music. Hence, one does not find a black at the head of any major symphony orchestra in the United States, even though black conductors such as James de Priest, Paul Freeman, and Dean Dixon have had distinguished careers in Canada and Europe.

Another example of the evil consequences of misconstruction of race occurred when the Nazis declared the superiority of the "Aryan race" (which is really a linguistic grouping and not a race at all), and the inferiority of the "Jewish race" (really an ethnic and religious category), and then used this distinction as an excuse to exclude Jews from life altogether. Tragically, such programs of extermination of one group by another continue to occur in many parts of the world today, including parts of South America, Africa, and Asia. "Holocausts" are by no means things of the past, nor are Jews their only victims.

Considering all the problems, confusion, and evil consequences, it is small wonder that there has been a lot of debate not just about how many human races there may be, but about what "race" is and is not. Often forgotten is the fact that a race, even if it can be defined, is the result of the operation of evolutionary processes. Because it is these processes rather than racial categories themselves in which we are really interested, most anthropologists have abandoned the race concept as being of no particular utility. Instead, they prefer to study the distribution and significance of specific, genetically based characteristics, or else the characteristics of small breeding populations that are, after all, the smallest units in which evolutionary change occurs.

SOME PHYSICAL VARIABLES

Despite all the debate about the reality of human races, human biological variation is a fact of life, and physical anthropologists have learned a great deal about it. Much of it seems related to climatic adaptation. For example, a correlation has been noted between body build and climate. Generally, people native to regions with cold climates tend to have greater body bulk (not to be equated with fat) relative to their extremities (arms and legs) than do people native to regions with hot climates, who tend to be long and slender. Anthropologists generally argue that such differences of body build represent a climatic adaptation; certain body builds are better suited to particular living conditions than others. A person with larger body bulk and shorter extremities may suffer more from summer heat than someone whose extremities are long and whose body is slender. But they will conserve needed body heat under cold conditions. The reason is that a bulky body tends to conserve more heat than a less bulky one, since it has less surface relative to volume. People living in hot, open country, by contrast, benefit from a body build that can get rid of excess heat quickly so as to keep from overheating; for this, long extremities and a slender body, which increase surface area relative to volume, are advantageous.

Studies of body build and climatic adaptation are complicated by the intervening effects on physique of diet, since dietary differences will cause variation in body build. Another complicating factor is clothing. For example, Inuit peoples (the proper name for "Eskimos") live in a region where it is cold much of the year. To cope with this, they long ago developed efficient clothing to keep the body warm. Because of this, the Inuit are provided with what amount to artificial tropical environments inside their clothing. Despite such considerations, it remains true that in northerly regions of the world, bulky body builds predominate, whereas the reverse is true in the tropics.

Anthropologists have also studied such body features as nose, eye shape, and hair textures in relation to climate. A wide flaring nose, for example, is common in populations living in tropical forests; here the air is warm and damp, and so the warming and humidifying functions of the nose are secondary. Longer, more prominent noses, common among cold dwellers, are helpful in humidifying

The epicanthic eyefold is common among peoples native to east Asia.

and warming cold air before it reaches the lungs. Coon, Garn, and Birdsell once proposed that the "Mongoloid face," common in populations native to East and Central Asia, as well as arctic North America, exhibits features adapted to life in very cold environments. The **epicanthic eye fold,** which reduces eye exposure to the cold to a minimum, a flat facial profile, and extensive fatty deposits may help to protect the face against frostbite. Although experimental studies have failed to sustain the frostbite hypothesis, it is true that a flat facial profile generally goes with a round head. A significant percentage of body heat may be lost from the head; however, a round head, having less surface area relative to volume, loses less heat than a longer, more elliptical head. As one would pre-

Epicanthic eye fold: A fold of skin at the inner corner of the eye that covers the true corner of the eye; common in Asiatic populations.

Melanin: The chemical responsible for dark skin pigmentation which helps protect against damage from ultraviolet radiation.

dict from this, long-headed populations are generally found in hotter climates; round-headed ones are more common in cold climate areas.

SKIN COLOR: A CASE STUDY IN ADAPTATION

In the United States, race is most commonly associated with skin color. Perhaps this is inevitable, since it is such an obvious physical trait. Skin color is subject to great variation, and there are at least four main factors associated with it: transparency or thickness of the skin, the copper-colored pigment carotene, reflected color from the blood vessels, and the amount of **melanin** found in a given area of skin. Exposure to sunlight increases the amount of melanin and, hence, the skin darkens. Melanin is known to protect skin against damaging ultraviolet solar radiation[1]; consequently, heavily pigmented peoples are less susceptible to skin cancers and sunburning than are those whose skin has less melanin. They may also be less susceptible to photodestruction of certain vitamins. Since the highest concentration of dark-skinned people tends to be found in the tropical regions of the world, it appears that natural selection has favored heavily pigmented skin as a protection against the strong solar radiation of equatorial latitudes, where ultraviolet radiation is most intense. Because skin cancers generally do not develop until later in life, they are unlikely to have interfered with the reproductive success of lightly pigmented individuals in the tropics, and so are unlikely to have been the agent of selection. On the other hand, severe sunburn, which is especially

[1]Robert M. Neer, "The Evolutionary Significance of Vitamin D, Skin Pigment, and Ultraviolet light," *American Journal of Physical Anthropology* 43 (1975): 409–416.

dangerous to infants, causes the body to overheat and interferes with its ability to sweat, by which it might rid itself of excess heat. Furthermore, it makes one susceptible to other kinds of infection. In addition to all this, decomposition of folate, a vitamin sensitive to heavy doses of ultraviolet radiation, can cause anemia, spontaneous abortion, and infertility.[2]

While dark skin pigmentation has enjoyed a selective advantage in the tropics, the opposite is true in northern latitudes, where skins have gener-

[2]Richard F. Branda and John W. Eatoil, "Skin Color and Photolysis: An Evolutionary Hypothesis," *Science* 201 (1978): 625–626.

ally been lightly pigmented. This lack of heavy amounts of melanin enables the weak ultraviolet radiation of northern latitudes to penetrate the skin and stimulate formation of Vitamin D. Dark pigmentation interferes with this. Without access to external sources of Vitamin D, once provided by cod liver oil but now more often provided in Vitamin D fortified milk, individuals incapable of synthesizing enough of this vitamin in their own bodies were selected against, for they contracted rickets, a disease that seriously deforms children's bones. At its worst, rickets prevents children from reaching reproductive age; at the least, it interferes with a woman's ability to give birth if she does reach reproductive age (Figure 11.2).

Given what we know about the adaptive significance of human skin color, and the fact that, until 700,000 years ago, hominids were exclusively creatures of the tropics, it is likely that lightly pigmented skins are a recent development in human history. Darkly pigmented skins likely are quite ancient. Human skin is more liberally endowed with sweat glands than is the skin of other mam-

These photos of people from Spain, Scandinavia, Senegal, and Indonesia illustrate the range of variation in human skin color. Generally, the closer to the equator populations live, the darker their skin color.

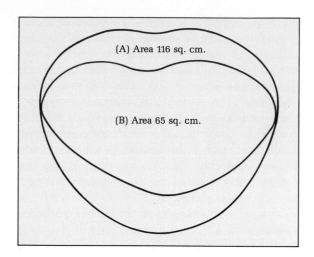

FIGURE 11.2 Outline of a normal pelvic inlet
(*A*) compared with that of a woman with rickets (*B*),
which would interfere with her capacity to give birth.
Rickets is caused by a deficiency of Vitamin D. In the
absence of artificial sources of the vitamin among
people living in northern latitudes, lightly pigmented
people are least likely to contract rickets.

mals; in combination with our lack of much in the way of body hair, this makes for effective elimination of excess body heat in a hot climate. This would have been especially advantageous to early hominids on the savanna, who could have avoided confrontations with carnivorous animals by carrying out most of their activities in the heat of the day. For the most part, carnivores rest then, being active from dusk until early morning. Without much hair to cover early hominid bodies, selection would have favored dark skins; hence, all humans appear to have had a "black" ancestry, no matter how "white" some may be today.

One should not conclude that, because it is newer, lightly pigmented skin is better, or more highly evolved, than heavily pigmented skin. The latter is clearly more highly evolved to the conditions of life in the tropics, although with protective clothing, hats, and sunscreen lotions, lightly pigmented peoples can get along there. But then, the availability of supplementary sources of Vitamin D allows heavily pigmented peoples to do quite well

FIGURE 11.3 Distribution of human skin color before 1492.

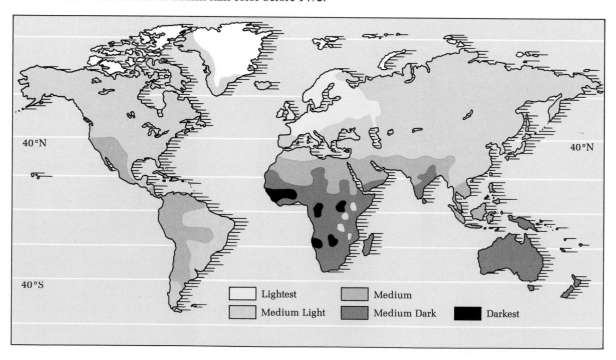

away from the tropics. In both cases, culture has rendered skin color differences largely irrelevant.

The inheritance of skin color is not well understood, except that several genes (rather than variants of a single gene) must be involved. Nevertheless, its geographical distribution, with few exceptions, tends to be continuous, like that of other human traits (Figure 11.3). The exceptions have to do with the movement of certain populations from their original homelands to other regions, and/or the practice of selective mating. For example, there have been repeated invasions of the Indian subcontinent by peoples from the north, who were then incorporated into the Hindu caste system. Still today, the higher the caste, the lighter its skin color. This skin-color gradient is maintained by strict in-group marriage rules. In the United States, statistical studies have shown that there has been a similar trend among blacks, with black women of higher status choosing to marry lighter-skinned males, reflecting the culture's emphasis on light skin as a status symbol. It is quite possible that the black pride movement, which places positive value on features common among those of African descent, such as dark skins, tightly curled hair, and broad flat noses, is leading to a reversal of this cultural selection factor.

THE SOCIAL SIGNIFICANCE OF RACE: RACISM

Scientific facts do not seem to change what people think about race. **Racism** can be viewed solely as a social problem, although at times it has been used by politicians as a purportedly "scientific" tool. It is an emotional phenomenon best explained in terms of collective psychology. Racial conflict results from long-suppressed resentments and hostilities. The racist responds to social stereotypes, not to known scientific facts.

RACE AND BEHAVIOR

The assumption that there are behavioral differences among human races remains an issue of contemporary society, not easily argued away.

Racism: A doctrine of racial superiority by which one group asserts its superiority over another.

Throughout history, certain "races" have been attributed certain characteristics, which assume a variety of names — "national character," "spirit," "temperament" — all of them vague and standing for a number of concepts totally unrelated to the biological concept of race. Common myths involve the "coldness" of the Scandinavians or the "martial" character of the Germanic peoples or the "indolent" nature of blacks. These generalizations serve to characterize a people unjustly; German citizens do not necessarily advocate genocide, nor do blacks necessarily hate to work. The term "race" has a precise biological meaning, but in popular usage, as we have already seen, the term often acquires a meaning unrelated to that given by scientists, often with disastrous results.

To date, no innate behavioral characteristic can be attributed to any group of people that the nonscientist would most probably term a "race" — that cannot be explained in terms of cultural practices. If the Chinese happen to be especially successful mathematicians, it can probably be explained in terms of emphasis within their culture on abstract concepts, learned ways of perceiving the universe, and their philosophies. If U.S. blacks are not as well represented in managerial positions as their fellow citizens, it is because they have been an oppressed minority lacking in opportunities. The list could go on, and all such differences or characteristics can be explained in terms of culture.

Similarly, high crime rates among certain groups can be explained with reference to culture and not biology. Individuals alienated and demoralized by poverty, injustice, and inequality of opportunity tend to display what the dominant members of society regard as antisocial behavior more frequently than those culturally well integrated. For example, American Indians, when they have been equipped and allowed to compete on equal footing with other Americans, have not suffered from the high rate of alcoholism and criminal behavior exhibited by Indians living under conditions of poverty on and off reservations.

RACE AND INTELLIGENCE

A question frequently asked by those unfamiliar with the deficiencies of the race concept is whether or not some races are inherently more intelligent than others. Intelligence tests carried on in the United States by white investigators among whites and blacks have often shown that whites attain higher scores. During World War I, a series of tests known as Alpha and Beta IQ tests, were regularly given to draftees. The results showed that the average score attained by whites was higher than that obtained by blacks. Even though many blacks scored higher than some whites, and some blacks scored higher than most whites, many people took this as proof of white intellectual superiority. But all the tests really showed was that, on the average, whites outperformed blacks in certain social situations. The tests did not measure "intelligence" per se, but the ability, conditioned by culture, of certain individuals to respond to certain socially conditioned problems. These tests had been conceived by whites for fellow middle-class whites. While nonwhites coming from similar backgrounds generally did well, whites as well as nonwhites coming from other backgrounds to meet the challenge of these tests were clearly at a disadvantage. It would be unrealistic to expect individuals unfamiliar with white middle-class values and linguistic behavior to respond to a problem based on a familiarity with these.

Many large-scale intelligence tests continue to be administered in this country. Notable among these are several series in which environmental factors are held constant. Where this is done, blacks and whites tend to score equally well.[3] This is not surprising, since there is no reason to suppose that whatever alleles may be associated with intelligence are likely to be correlated with the ones for skin pigmentation. Intelligence tests, however, have increasingly become the subject of controversy. There are many psychologists as well as anthropologists who believe that their use is

overdone. Intelligence tests, they say, are of limited use, since they are applicable only to particular cultural circumstances. Only when these circumstances are carefully met can any meaningful generalizations be derived from the use of tests.

Notwithstanding the foregoing, there continue to be some who wonder whether or not there are any significant intellectual differences between human populations. On a purely theoretical basis, it could be assumed that just as we see a spectrum of inherited variations in physical traits — skin color, hair texture, height — there could be similar variation in innate intellectual potential of different populations. It is likely that just as there are genes affecting the development of blue eyes, curly hair, or heavily pigmented skin, there are others affecting the development of intelligence. One person who supports that view is the North American psychologist Arthur Jensen. Basing his conclusions on statistical data from tests given to U.S. blacks and whites, Jensen believes that such intellectual differences exist.

From a number of studies it is now clear that there is indeed an appreciable degree of hereditary control of intelligence. First, there is a general tendency for those pairs of individuals who are most genetically similar (identical twins) to be most similar in intelligence, even when reared in different environments. Furthermore, the scores on IQ tests of biological parents and their children are correlated and tend to be similar, while foster parents and their foster children show little of this tendency.

Equally clear are the effects of environment on intelligence. A number of studies consistently show that, in the United States, children reared in rural areas on the average get IQ scores about 15 points lower than children from urban areas; that children deprived of frequent verbal and tactile interaction with adults get significantly lower IQ scores than those who are not; that children in large families score lower on IQ tests than children who have few brothers and sisters; that in large families, the later born have lower IQ scores than the first born; that special training can raise IQ scores by as much as 30 points; and so forth. So,

[3]Peggy R. Sanday, "On the Causes of IQ Differences between Groups and Implications for Social Policy," in Ashley Montagu, ed., *Race and IQ* (New York: Oxford, 1975), pp. 232–238.

like all inherited traits, intelligence is expressed as an interaction between genes and environment.

That one's IQ is to some degree heritable is at the root of an all too common fallacy, the subject of the following Original Study by Stephen Jay Gould.

ORIGINAL STUDY
The Hereditarian Fallacy[4]

The hereditarian fallacy is not the simple claim that IQ is to some degree "heritable." I have no doubt that it is, though the degree has clearly been exaggerated by the most avid hereditarians. It is hard to find any broad aspect of human performance or anatomy that has no heritable component at all. The hereditarian fallacy resides in two false implications drawn from this basic fact:

1. The equation of "heritable" with "inevitable." To a biologist, heritability refers to the passage of traits or tendencies along family lines as a result of genetic transmission. It says little about the range of environmental modification to which these traits are subject. In our vernacular, "inherited" often means "inevitable." But not to a biologist. Genes do not make specific bits and pieces of a body; they code for a range of forms under an array of environmental conditions. Moreover, even when a trait has been built and set, environmental intervention may still modify inherited defects. Millions of Americans see normally through lenses that correct innate deficiencies of vision. The claim that IQ is so-many percent "heritable" does not conflict with the belief that enriched education can increase what we call, also in the vernacular, "intelligence." A partially inherited low IQ might be subject to extensive improvement through proper education. And it might not. The mere fact of its heritability permits no conclusion.

2. The confusion of within- and between-group heredity. The major political impact of hereditarian theories does not arise from the inferred heritability of tests, but from a logically invalid extension. Studies of the heritability of IQ, performed by such traditional methods as comparing scores of relatives, or contrasting scores of adopted children with both their biological and legal parents, are all of the "within-group" type—that is, they permit an estimate of heritability within a single, coherent population (white Americans, for example). The common fallacy consists in assuming that if heredity explains a certain percentage of variation among individuals within a group, it must also explain a similar percentage of the difference in average IQ between groups—whites and blacks, for example. But variation among individuals within a group and differences in mean values between groups are entirely separate phenomena. One item provides no license for speculation about the other.

A hypothetical and noncontroversial example will suffice. Human height has a higher heritability than any value ever proposed for IQ. Take two separate groups of males. The first, with an average height of 5 feet 10 inches, live in a prosperous American town. The second, with an average height of 5 feet 6 inches, are starving in a third-world village. Heritability is 95 percent or so in each place — meaning only that relatively tall fathers tend to have tall sons and relatively short fathers short sons. This high within-group heritability argues neither for nor against the possibility that better nutrition in the next generation might raise the average height of third-world villagers above that of prosperous Americans. Likewise, IQ could be highly heritable within groups, and the average difference between whites and blacks in America might still only record the environmental disadvantages of blacks.

I have often been frustrated with the following response to this admonition: "Oh well, I see what you mean, and you're right in theory. There may be no necessary connection in logic, but isn't it more likely all the same that mean differences between groups would have the same causes as variation within groups?" The answer is still "no." Within- *and* between-group heredity are not tied by rising degrees of probability as heritability increases within groups and differences enlarge between them. The two phenomena are simply separate. Few arguments are more dangerous than the ones that "feel" right but can't be justified.

[4]Stephen Jay Gould, *The Mismeasure of Man* (New York: W.W. Norton, 1981), pp. 155–157.

INTELLIGENCE: WHAT IS IT?

A question that must now be asked is: What do we mean by the term "intelligence?" The answer, quite simply, is that which is measured by IQ tests. Unfortunately, there is no general agreement as to what abilities or talents actually make up the trait of intelligence, except that it is not a single scalable thing in the head comparable to one's height or blood type. Rather, it is made up of a great many talents or abilities. Furthermore, no matter how closely related these are (whatever they are), they must be independently inherited, just as height and blood type are independently inherited. Thus, the various traits that constitute "intelligence" may be independently distributed as are, for example, skin color and blood type. In European populations, the frequency of heavy skin pigmentation increases as one goes from north to south, whereas the frequency of the allele for Type B blood increases as one goes from west to east (Figure 11.4).

The next question is: If we are not exactly sure what IQ tests are measuring, how can we be sure of the validity of such tests — that is, can we be sure an IQ test measures what it is supposed to measure? The answer, of course, is that we cannot be sure. But even at best, an IQ test measures performance (something that one does) rather than genetic disposition (something that lies within the individual). Reflected in one's performance are one's past experiences and present motivational state, as well as one's innate ability. In sum, it is fair to say that an IQ test is not a reliable measure of innate intelligence.

At present, the case for significant differences in intelligence between human populations remains unproven. Nor is it ever likely to be proven, in view of what we saw in Chapter 8 as the major thrust in the evolution of the genus *Homo*. Over the past 2 million years, in all populations of the genus, the emphasis has been on cultural adapta-

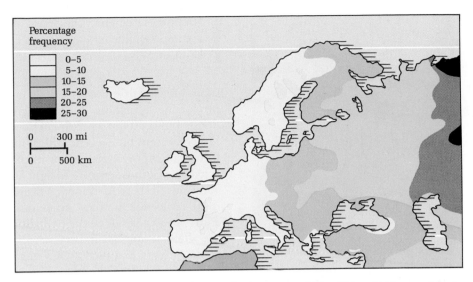

FIGURE 11.4 The east–west gradient in the frequency of blood Type B (shown above) in Europe contrasts with the north–south gradient in skin pigmentation (shown in Figure 11.3). Whatever genes are involved in the various talents that are lumped under the heading "intelligence" must also be independently assorted.

tion — actively inventing solutions to the problems of existence rather than passively relying on biological adaptation. Thus, we would expect a comparable degree of intelligence in all present-day human populations. But even if this were not the case, it would mean only that "dull" and "bright" people are to be found in all human populations, though in different frequencies. Thus, geniuses can and do appear in any population, regardless of what that population's "average" intelligence may be. The fact of the matter is that the only way to be sure that individual human beings develop their innate abilities and skills, whatever they may be, to the fullest is to give them the opportunity to do so. This certainly cannot be accomplished if whole populations are deprived of equal opportunity.

CONTINUING HUMAN BIOLOGICAL EVOLUTION

In the course of their evolution, humans in all parts of the world have come to rely on cultural rather than biological adaptation for their survival. Nevertheless, as they moved from their tropical homeland into other parts of the world, they did develop considerable physical variation from one population to another. The forces responsible for this include genetic drift and biological adaptation to differing climates.

Although much of this physical variation can still be seen in human populations today, the increasing effectiveness of cultural adaptation has often reduced its importance. For instance, the consumption of cod liver oil or vitamin D-fortified milk has canceled out the selective advantage of lightly pigmented skins in northern peoples. At the same time, culture has also imposed its own selective pressures, as we have seen in preceding chapters. Just as the invention of the spear-thrower was followed by a reduction in overall muscularity, or just as the transition to food production was followed by worsened health and mortality, cultural practices today are affecting the human organism in important, often surprising, ways.

The probability of alterations in human biological makeup induced by culture raises a number of important questions. By trying to eliminate ge-

Racist policies, such as apartheid in South Africa, have no basis in scientific fact. Here, residents of a South African squatter camp hold up their passbooks.

Lactose: The primary constituent of fresh milk.

Lactase: An enzyme in the small intestine which enables humans to assimilate lactose.

netic variants for balanced polymorphic traits, such as the sickle-cell trait discussed in Chapter 3, are we also removing alleles that have survival value? Are we weakening the gene pool by allowing people with hereditary diseases and defects to reproduce? Are we reducing chances for genetic variation by trying to control population size?

We are not sure of the answers to all of these questions. If we are able to wipe out sickle-cell anemia, we also may be able to wipe out malaria; thus, we would have eliminated the condition that made the sickle-cell trait advantageous. Nor is it strictly true that medical science is weakening the gene pool by letting those with disorders for which there may be a genetic predisposition, such as diabetes, reproduce. In the present environment, where medication is easily available, such people are as fit as anyone else. However, if such people are denied access to the needed medication, their biological fitness is lost and they die out. In fact, one's financial status affects one's access to medication, and so, however unintentional it may be, one's biological fitness in North American society may be decided by one's financial status.

The effects of culture in enabling individuals to reproduce even though they suffer from genetic disorders are familiar. Perhaps less familiar are the cases in which medical technology selects against some individuals by removing them from the reproducing population. One example can be seen in South Africa. About 1 percent of South Africans of Dutch descent have a gene which, in its dominant form, causes porphyria, a disorder that renders the skin of its victims sensitive to light and causes skin abrasions. If these Afrikaners remain in their quiet rural environment, they suffer only minor skin abrasions as a result of their condition. However, the allele renders them very sensitive to modern medical treatment, such as they might receive in a large urban center like Johannesburg. If they are treated for some unrelated problem with barbiturates or similar drugs, they suffer acute attacks and very often die. In their relatively quiet rural environment where medical services are less readily accessible, the Afrikaners with this peculiar condition are able to live normal lives; it is only in an urban context, where they are more likely to receive medical attention, that they suffer physical impairment or loss of life.

Another example of cultural selection has to do with the ability to assimilate **lactose,** the primary constituent of fresh milk. The ability to assimilate lactose depends on the presence of a particular enzyme, **lactase,** in the small intestine. Failure to retain lactase into adulthood, although it is a recessive trait, is characteristic of most human populations, especially Asian, native Australian, and African populations. Hence, only 10 to 30 percent of Americans of African descent, and 0 to 30 percent of adult Orientals, retain lactase into adulthood.[5] By contrast, lactase retention is normal for over 80 percent of adults of northern European descent. Eastern Europeans, Arabs, and some East Africans are closer to northern Europeans in lactase retention than they are to Asians and other Africans. Generally speaking, a high retention of lactase is

[5]Gail G. Harrison, "Primary Adult Lactase Deficiency: A Problem in Anthropological Genetics," *American Anthropologist* 77 (1975): 815–819.

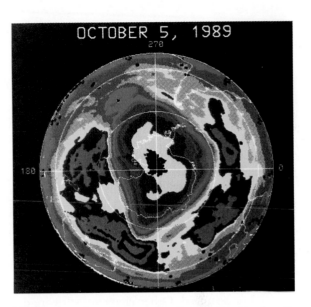

NASA plot of total ozone distribution for October 5, 1989, showing an "ozone hole" larger than the Antarctic continent. As ozone depletion continues, the incidence of skin cancer in humans will increase, with lightly pigmented people being the most severely affected.

The things we do often affect what we are in unexpected ways. Despite this, we often view new innovations as harmless, until evidence convinces us otherwise. For example, power lines are generally viewed as harmless, so long as one does not touch them; nevertheless, recent studies are finding a correlation between certain kinds of cancers and residence in proximity to such lines.

found in populations with a long tradition of fresh milk as an important dietary item. In such populations, selection has in the past favored those individuals with the ability to assimilate lactose, selecting out those who lacked this ability.

In developing countries, milk supplements are used in the treatment of acute protein–calorie malnutrition. Tube-fed diets of milk are used in connection with other medical procedures. Quite apart from medical practices, powdered milk has long been a staple of economic aid to other countries. Such practices in fact discriminate against

the members of populations in which lactase is not commonly retained into adulthood. At the least, those individuals without lactase will fail to utilize the nutritive value of milk; frequently, they will suffer diarrhea, abdominal cramping, and even bone degeneration, with serious results. In fact, the shipping of powdered milk to victims of South American earthquakes in the 1960s caused many deaths among them.

In recent years, there has been considerable concern about human activities that are having an adverse effect on the earth's ozone layer. A major contributor to the ozone layer's deterioration is the use of chlorofluorocarbons in aerosol sprays, refrigeration and air conditioning, and the manufacture of styrofoam. Since the ozone layer screens out some of the sun's ultraviolet rays, its continued deterioration will expose humans to increased ultraviolet radiation. As we saw earlier in this chapter, some ultraviolet radiation is necessary for the production of Vitamin D, but excessive amounts lead to an increased incidence of skin cancers.

Hence, a rising incidence of skin cancers can be predicted as the ozone layer continues to deteriorate. Although a ban on the use of chlorofluorocarbons in aerosol sprays was imposed a few years ago, the destruction of the ozone layer has continued about twice as fast as scientists had predicted it would, even without the ban. More recently, an international treaty further limiting the use of chlorofluorocarbons has been negotiated, but this will merely slow down, rather than halt, further deterioration. Most immediately affected by the consequent increase in ultraviolet radiation will be the world's lightly pigmented peoples, but ultimately, all will be affected.

Clearly, then, cultural practices are presently acting to change the frequencies of genes in human gene pools. Unquestionably, this is deleterious to those individuals who suffer the effects of negative selection. It remains to be seen just what the long-term effects on the human species as a whole will be.

CHAPTER SUMMARY

In humans, most behavioral attitudes are culturally learned or acquired. Other characteristics are determined by an interaction between genes and environment. The gene pools of populations contain various alternative alleles. When the environment changes, their gene pool gives them the possibility of the appropriate physical alteration to meet the change.

When a polymorphic species is separated into different faunal regions, it is usually polytypic — that is, the store of genetic variability is unevenly expressed. It appears that the human species has been polytypic at least since the time of *Homo erectus*.

Early anthropologists classified *Homo sapiens* into subspecies, or races, based on geographical location and such phenotypic features as skin color, body size, head shape, and hair texture. The presence of atypical individuals continually challenged these racial classifications. No examples of "pure" racial types could be found. The visible traits were found to occur in a worldwide continuum. No definite grouping of distinct, discontinuous biological groups has been found in modern humans.

A biological race is a population of a species that differs in the frequency of genetic variants from other populations of the same species. Three observations need to be made concerning this biological definition: (1) It is arbitrary; (2) it does not mean that any one race has exclusive possession of any particular allele(s); and (3) individuals of one race will not necessarily be distinguishable from those of another. As a means for understanding human variation, the concept of race has several limitations. First, race is an arbitrary category, making agreement on any particular classification difficult; second, humans are so complex genetically that often the genetic basis of traits on which racial studies are based is itself poorly understood; and finally, race exists as a cultural as well as a biological category. Most anthropologists now view the race concept as useless, preferring to study the distribution and significance of specific, genetically based characteristics, or else the characteristics of small breeding populations.

Physical anthropologists have determined that much of human physical variation appears related to climatic adaptation. People native to cold climates tend to have greater body bulk relative to their extremities than individuals who live in hot climates; the latter tend to be long and slender. Studies involving body build and climate are complicated by such other factors as the effects on physique of diet and of clothing.

In the United States, race is commonly thought of in terms of skin color. Subject to tremendous variation, skin color is a function of four factors: transparency or thickness of the skin, distribution of blood vessels, and amount of carotene and melanin in a given area of skin. Exposure to sunlight increases the amount of melanin, darkening the skin. Natural selection seems to have favored heavily pigmented skin as protection against the strong solar radiation of equatorial latitudes. In northern latitudes, natural selection has favored relatively depigmented skins, which can utilize relatively weak solar radiation in the production of vitamin D. Selective mating, as well as geographical location, plays a part in skin color distribution.

Racism can be viewed solely as a social problem. It is an emotional phenomenon best explained in terms of collective psychology. The racist individual reacts on the basis of social stereotypes and not established scientific facts.

Many people have assumed that there are behavioral differences among human races. The innate behavioral characteristics attributed by these people to race can be explained in terms of enculturation rather than biology. Those intelligence tests that have been taken to indicate whites are intellectually superior to blacks are designed by whites for whites from similar backgrounds. It is not realistic to expect individuals who are not familiar with white middle-class values to respond to items based on knowledge of these values. Blacks and whites both, if they come from different types of backgrounds, are thus at a disadvantage. At the present, it is not possible to separate the inherited components of intelligence from those that are culturally acquired. Furthermore, there is still no agreement on what intelligence really is, except that it is made up of several different talents and abilities.

Although the human species has come to rely on cultural rather than biological adaptation for survival, human gene pools still continue to change in response to external factors. Many of these changes are brought about by cultural practices; for example, the shipment of powdered milk to human populations which are low in the frequency of the allele for lactase retention into adulthood may contribute to the death of large numbers of people. Those who survive are most likely to be those with the allele for lactase retention. Unquestionably, this kind of selection is deleterious to those individuals who are "selected out" in this way. Just what the long-term effects will be on the human species as a whole remains to be seen.

SUGGESTED READINGS

Brace, C. L., and Ashley Montagu. *Human Evolution*, 2d ed. New York: Macmillan, 1977. Part 3 of this textbook serves as a good introduction to the nonracial approach to human variation.

Brues, Alice M. *People and Races*. New York: Macmillan, 1977. This is a book about the physical differences that distinguish populations of geographically different ancestry. It does not take for granted a background in genetics or any other special field; everything necessary to understand the subject beyond a high school level is here.

Molnar, Stephen. *Human Variation: Races, Types, and Ethnic Groups*, 2d ed. Englewood Cliffs, N.J.: Prentice Hall, 1983. The important key questions examined here are: How does biological diversity relate to the classical racial divisions? Are these divisions useful in the study of our species? How would human environmental relationships affect humanity's future?

Montagu, Ashley, ed. *Race and IQ*. New York: Oxford, 1975. This book is a response to the claims of Jensen, Shockley, and others that there is a link between race and intelligence. Its aim, simply stated, is to debunk such claims. To do this, the editor has assembled articles by 15 authorities on various aspects of the problem.

Weiss, Mark L., and Alan E. Mann. *Human Biology and Behavior*, 4th ed. Boston: Little, Brown, 1985. This recent textbook is notable for its chapters on variability, races, microevolution, traits of complex inheritance, and human adaptability. The authors use a minimum of jargon without oversimplification.

Wooden figure of a Yombe woman from Zaire with her child, made sometime after 1800 A.D. The childhood years are critical ones for all cultures; children must learn a language, which permits them to be given their basic orientation to the world and to be taught appropriate ways of behaving.

PART IV

CULTURE AND SURVIVAL
Communicating, Raising Children, and Staying Alive

INTRODUCTION

All living creatures, be they great or small, fierce or timid, active or inactive, face a fundamental problem in common — that of survival. Simply put, unless they adapt themselves to some available environment, they cannot survive. Adaptation requires the development of behaviors that will help an organism use the environment to its advantage — to find food and sustenance, avoid hazards, and (if the species is to survive) reproduce. In turn, organisms need to have biological equipment that allows the development of appropriate patterns of behavior. For the hundreds of millions of years of life on earth, biological adaptation has been the primary means by which the problem of survival has been solved. This is accomplished as individuals of a particular organism, whose biological equipment is well suited to a particular adaptive way of life, produce more offspring than those whose equipment is not so well suited. In this way, advantageous characteristics become more common in succeeding generations, while less advantageous ones become less common.

By about 2 million years ago, some time after the line of human evolution had branched off from apes, a new means of dealing with the problems of existence came into being. Early hominids began to rely more on what their minds could invent, rather than on what their bodies were capable of doing. Although the human species has not freed itself entirely, even today, from the forces of biological adaptation, it has come to rely primarily on culture — a body of learned traditions that, in essence, tells people how to live — as the medium through which the problems of human existence are solved. The consequences of this are profound. As evolving hominids developed cultural rather than biological solutions to their problems, their chances of survival improved. For example, when hominids added scavenging to their subsistence activities over 2 million years ago, the resources available to them increased substantially. Moreover, the tools and techniques that made this new way of life possible made hominids somewhat less vulnerable to predators than they had been before. Thus, life became a bit easier. With humans, as with other animals, an easier life generally makes for easier reproduction; and with more offspring surviving than before, populations grow. As the archaeological record clearly shows, a slow but steady population growth followed the addition of scavenging to hominid foraging practices.

Among most mammals, population growth frequently leads to the dispersal of fringe populations into regions previously uninhabited by the species. There they find new environments, to which they must adapt or face extinction. This pattern of dispersal seems to have been followed by the evolving human species, for with the emergence of hunting and gathering, humans began to spread geographically, inhabiting new and even harsh environments. As they did so, they devised cultural rather than biological solutions to their new problems of existence. This is illustrated by human habitation of cold regions of the world, which was not dependent on the evolution of humans capable of growing heavy coats of fur, as do other mammals that live in such regions. Instead, humans devised forms of clothing and shelter that, coupled with the use of fire, enabled them to overcome the cold. Moreover, this "cold adaptation" could be rapidly changed in the face of different circumstances. The fact is that cultural equipment and techniques can be changed drastically in less than a single generation, whereas biological change takes many generations to accomplish.

As the medium through which humans handle the problems of existence, culture — the subject of Chapter 12 — is basic to human survival. It cannot do its job, though, unless it deals successfully with certain basic problems. Because culture is learned and not inherited biologically, its transmission from one person to another, and from one generation to the next, depends on an effective system of communication that must be far more complex than that of any other animal. Thus, a first requirement for any culture is to provide a means of communication among individuals. All cultures do this through some form of language, the subject of Chapter 13.

In human societies each generation learns its culture anew. The learning process itself is thus crucial to a culture's survival. A second requirement of culture, then, is the development of reliable means by which individuals learn to behave as members of their community expect them to behave. And how children learn appears to be as important as what they learn. Since to a large extent adult personality is the product of life experiences, the ways children are raised and educated play a major part in the shaping of their later selves: The ability of individuals to function properly as adults depends, to a degree, on how effectively their personalities have been shaped to fit their culture. As we see in Chapter 14, from anthropological investigations into these areas have emerged findings that have implications for human behavior that go beyond anthropology.

As important as effective communication and education are for the survival of a culture, they are of no avail unless the culture is able to satisfy the basic needs of the individuals who live by its rules. A third requirement of culture, therefore, is the ability to provide its members with food, water, and protection from the elements. Chapter 15 discusses the ways in which cultures handle people's basic needs and the ways societies adapt through culture to the environment. Since this leads to the production, distribution, and consumption of goods — the subject matter of economic anthropology — we conclude this section with a chapter (Chapter 16) on economic systems.

12

THE NATURE OF CULTURE

These Bedouin women, shown in their tent, live in Africa's Sahara Desert. All over the world, people have worked out their own cultural solutions to particular problems of existence. Although sometimes construed as old fashioned, traditional ways may offer more in the way of human satisfaction than so-called modern ways.

PREVIEW

What Is Culture?

Culture consists of the abstract values, beliefs, and perceptions of the world that lie behind people's behavior and that their behavior reflects. These are shared by the members of a society, and when acted upon, they produce behavior considered acceptable within that society. Cultures are learned, largely through the medium of language, rather than inherited biologically, and the parts of a culture function as an integrated whole.

How Is Culture Studied?

Anthropologists, like children, learn about a culture by experiencing it and talking about it with those who live by its rules. Of course, anthropologists have less time to learn, but are more systematic in the way they learn. Through careful observation and discussion with informants who are particularly knowledgeable in the ways of their culture, the anthropologist abstracts a set of rules in order to explain how people behave in a particular society.

Why Do Cultures Exist?

People maintain cultures to deal with problems or matters that concern them. To survive, a culture must satisfy the basic needs of those who live by its rules, provide for its own continuity, and provide an orderly existence for the members of a society. In doing so, a culture must strike a balance between the self-interests of individuals and the needs of society as a whole. And finally, a culture must have the capacity to change in order to adapt to new circumstances or to altered perceptions of existing circumstances.

Students of anthropology are bound to find themselves studying a seemingly endless variety of human societies, each with its own distinctive system of politics, economics, and religion. Yet for all this variation, these societies have one thing in common. Each is a collection of people cooperating to ensure their collective survival and well-being. In order for this to work, some degree of predictable behavior is required of each individual within the society, for group living and cooperation are impossible unless individuals know how others are likely to behave in any given situation. In humans, it is culture that sets the limits of behavior and guides it along predictable paths.

THE CONCEPT OF CULTURE

The **culture** concept was first developed by anthropologists toward the end of the nineteenth century. The first really clear and comprehensive definition was that of the British anthropologist Sir Edward Burnett Tylor. Writing in 1871, Tylor defined culture as that complex whole which includes knowledge, belief, art, law, morals, custom and any other capabilities and habits acquired by man as a member of society. Since Tylor's time, definitions of culture have proliferated. In the 1950s, the late A. L. Kroeber and Clyde Kluckhohn combed the literature and collected over a hundred definitions of culture. Recent definitions tend to distinguish more clearly between actual behavior on the one hand and the abstract values, beliefs, and perceptions of the world that lie behind that behavior on the other. To put it another way, culture is not observable behavior, but rather the values and beliefs that people use to interpret experience and generate behavior, and that is reflected in their behavior. An acceptable modern definition of culture, then, runs as follows: Culture is a set of rules or standards that, when acted upon by the members of a society, produce behavior that falls within a range of variance the members consider proper and acceptable.

Culture: A set of rules or standards shared by members of a society, which when acted upon by the members, produce behavior that falls within a range of variation the members consider proper and acceptable.

Society: A group of people who occupy a specific locality and who share the same cultural traditions.

CHARACTERISTICS OF CULTURE

Through the comparative study of many different cultures, anthropologists have arrived at an understanding of the basic characteristics that all cultures share. A careful study of these helps us to see the importance and the function of culture itself.

CULTURE IS SHARED

Culture is a set of shared ideals, values, and standards of behavior; it is the common denominator that makes the actions of individuals intelligible to the group. Because they share a common culture, people can predict how others are most likely to behave in a given circumstance and react accordingly. A group of people from different cultures, stranded over a period of time on a desert island, might appear to become a society of sorts. They would have a common interest — survival — and would develop techniques for living and working together. Each of the members of this group, however, would retain his or her own identity and cultural background, and the group would disintegrate without further ado as soon as its members were rescued from the island. The group would have been merely an aggregate in time and not a cultural entity. **Society** may be defined as a group of people occupying a specific locality, who are dependent on each other for survival and who share a common culture. The way in which these people depend upon each other can be seen in such things as their economic systems and their family relationships; moreover, members of a society are held together by a sense of group identity. The relationships that hold a society together are known as its **social structure.**

Culture and society are two closely related concepts, and anthropologists study both. Obviously, there can be no culture without a society, just as there can be no society without individuals. Conversely, there are no known human societies that do not exhibit culture. Some other species of animals, however, do lead a social existence. Ants and bees, for example, instinctively cooperate in a manner that clearly indicates a degree of social organization; yet this instinctual behavior is not a culture. One can, therefore, have a society without a culture, even though one cannot have a culture without a society. Whether or not there exist animals other than humans that are capable of culture is a question that will be dealt with shortly.

> **Social structure:** The relationships of groups within a society that hold it together.

While a culture is shared by the members of a society, it is important to realize that all is not uniformity. In any human society, at the very least there is some difference between the roles of men and women. This stems from the fact that women give birth but men do not, and that there are obvious differences between male and female anatomy. What every culture does is to give meaning to these differences by explaining them and specifying what is to be done about them as well as how the two kinds of people resulting from the differences should relate to one another and to the world at large. Since each culture does this in its own way, there is tremendous variation from one society to another. Anthropologists use the term

In all human societies, children's play is used both consciously and unconsciously to teach gender roles.

gender to refer to the cultural elaborations and meanings assigned to the biological differentiation between the sexes.

The distinction between sex, which is biological, and gender, which is cultural, is an important one. Presumably, gender differences are as old as human culture — about 2.5 million years — and arose from the biological differences between early human males and females. Back then, males were about twice the size of females, as they are today among such species as gorillas, orangutans, and baboons. As humans evolved, however, the biological differences between the two sexes were radically reduced. Thus, whatever biological basis there once was for gender role differences has largely disappeared. In spite of this, cultures have maintained some differentiation of gender roles ever since, although these differences are far greater in some societies than in others. Paradoxically, gender differences were far more extreme among our own ancestors of the late nineteenth and early twentieth centuries than they are among most historically known food-foraging peoples whose ways of life, though not unchanged, are more like those of our late Stone Age ancestors. In other words, differences between the behavior of men and women in our society today, which are thought by many to be rooted in human biology, are not so rooted at all. Rather, they appear to have been recently elaborated in the course of our own history.

In addition to cultural differences along lines of sex, there will also be some age variation. In any society, children are not expected to behave as adults, and the reverse is equally true. Besides age and sex variation, there may be variation among subgroups in societies. These may be occupational groups, where there is a complex division of labor, or social classes in a stratified society, or ethnic groups in some other societies. When such groups exist within a society, each functioning by its own distinctive standards of behavior, we speak of **subcultural variation.** The degree to which subcultures are tolerated varies greatly from one society to another. Consider, for example, the following

Gender: The elaborations and meanings assigned by cultures to the biological differentiation of the sexes.

Subcultural variation: A distinctive set of standards and behavior patterns by which a group within a larger society operates.

Pluralistic societies: Societies in which there exist a diversity of subcultural patterns.

case from the *Wall Street Journal* of May 13, 1983:

> Salt Lake City — Police called it a cross-cultural misunderstanding. When the man showed up to buy the Shetland pony advertised for sale, the owner asked what he intended to do with the animal.
>
> "For my son's birthday," he replied, and the deal was closed.
>
> The buyer thereupon clubbed the pony to death with a two-by-four, dumped the carcass in his pickup truck and drove away. The horrified seller called the police, who tracked down the buyer. At his house they found a birthday party in progress. The pony was trussed and roasting in a luau pit.
>
> We don't ride horses, we eat them, explained the buyer, a recent immigrant from Tonga.

Raised here is the issue of so-called **pluralistic societies** in which subcultural variation is especially marked. They are characterized by a particular problem: The groups within them, by virtue of their marked degree of subcultural variation, are all essentially operating by different sets of rules. This can create problems, given the fact that social living demands predictable behavior. In a culturally plural society, it may become difficult to comprehend the different standards by which the various subgroups operate. At the least, this can lead to major misunderstandings, as in the case of the Utah Tongans cited above.

It can, however, go far beyond mere misunderstanding, in which case violence and bloodshed may result. Many cases might be cited, but one that we shall look at in some detail in a later chapter (Chapter 25) is Guatemala, where a government distrustful of its Indian population has been killing it off.

Funerals have become commonplace in Guatemala, a prime example of a pluralistic society in which cultural differences have escalated into bloodshed and violence. Thousands of Indian men, women, and children have been killed by the forces of a government controlled by a non-Indian minority. Those not killed are still being systematically deprived of the means of providing for their own well-being.

An example of a subculture in the United States can be seen in the Amish.[1] The old-order Amish originated in Austria and Moravia during the Reformation; today members of this order number about 60,000 and live mainly in Pennsylvania, Ohio, and Indiana. They are pacifistic, agrarian people, whose lives focus on their religious beliefs. They value simplicity, hard work, and a high degree of neighborly cooperation. They dress in a distinctive, plain garb, and even today rely on the horse for transportation as well as agricultural work. They rarely mingle with non-Amish.

The goal of Amish education is to teach reading, writing, and arithmetic and to instill Amish values in their children. They reject "worldly" knowledge and the idea of schools producing good

citizens for the state. The Amish insist that their children attend school near home and that teachers be committed to Amish values. Their nonconformity to the standards of the larger culture has caused frequent conflict with state authorities, as well as legal and personal harassment. The Amish have resisted all attempts to force their children to attend regular public schools. Some compromise has been necessary, and "vocational training" has been introduced beyond the elementary school level to fulfill state requirements. The Amish have succeeded in gaining control of their schools and maintaining their way of life, but they are a beleaguered, defensive culture, more distrustful than ever of the larger culture around them.

The experience of the Amish is one example of the way a subculture may be tolerated by the larger culture within which it functions. Different as they are, the Amish actually practice many values that

[1]John Hostetler and Gertrude Huntington, *Children in Amish Society* (New York: Holt, Rinehart and Winston, 1971).

The Amish people have maintained a distinctive agrarian way of life in the midst of industrialized, North American society. By maintaining their own schools to instill Amish values in their children, prohibiting mechanized vehicles and equipment, and dressing in their distinctive plain clothing, they proclaim their own special identity.

our nation respects in the abstract: thrift, hard work, independence, a close family life. The degree of tolerance accorded to them may also be due in part to the fact that the Amish are white Europeans. American Indian subcultures have been treated differently by whites, who came as conquerors and who defined Indian values as "savage." For over 400 years, Europeans and their descendants in what is now the United States have generally accepted the notion that the Indian cultures were doomed to disappear; yet they are still with us, even if in altered form.

In every culture, there are persons whose idiosyncratic behavior has earned them the terms of "eccentric," "crazy," or "queer." Such persons are looked upon suspiciously by society and are sooner or later excluded from participating in the activities of the group, if their behavior becomes too idiosyncratic. Such exclusion acts to keep what is defined as deviant behavior outside the group. On

the other hand, what is regarded as deviant in one society may not be in another. In traditional Mohave Indian culture, for example, transvestism was accepted so long as the transvestite underwent an initiation ceremony; the person then assumed for life the role of someone of the opposite sex and was permitted to marry.

Because individuals who share a culture tend to marry within their society and thus to share certain physical characteristics, some people mistakenly believe that there is a direct relationship between culture and race. Research has shown that racial characteristics represent biological adaptations to climate and have nothing to do with differences in intelligence or cultural superiority. Some North American blacks have concluded that they have more in common with black Africans than they do with those North Americans who are light-skinned and straight-haired. Yet if they suddenly had to live in a Bantu tribal society, they would

A P P L I C A T I O N
New Houses for Apache Indians

The United States, in common with the other industrialized countries of the world, has within it a number of more or less separate subcultures. Those who live by the standards of one particular subculture have their closest relationships with one another, receiving constant reassurance that their perceptions of the world are the only correct ones, and coming to take it for granted that the whole culture is as they see it. As a consequence, members of one subcultural group frequently have trouble understanding the needs and aspirations of other such groups. For this reason anthropologists, with their special understanding of cultural differences, are frequently employed as go-betweens in situations requiring interaction between peoples of differing cultural traditions.

As an example, George S. Esber, Jr., while still a graduate student in anthropology, was hired to work with architects and a band of Apache Indians in designing a new community for the Apaches. Although architects began with an awareness that cross-cultural differences in the use of space exist, they had no idea of how to get relevant information from the Indians. For their part, the Apaches had no explicit awareness of their needs, for these were based on unconscious patterns of behavior. Moreover, the idea that patterns of behavior could be acted out unconsciously was an alien idea to them.

Esber's task was to persuade the architects to hold back on their planning long enough for him to gather, through fieldwork and review of written records, the

kind of data from which Apache housing needs could be abstracted. At the same time, he had to overcome Apache anxieties over an outsider coming into their midst to learn about matters as personal as their daily lives. With these things accomplished, Esber was able to identify and successfully communicate features of Apache life with important implications for community design to the architects. At the same time, discussions of findings with the Apaches themselves enhanced awareness of their own unique needs.

The outcome of Esber's work was that, in 1981, the Apaches were able to move into houses that had been designed with *their* participation, for *their* specific needs. Among other things, account was taken of the Indians' need to ease into a social situation, rather than to jump right in. Apache etiquette requires that all people be in full view of each other, so each can assess from a distance the behavior of others, in order to act appropriately with them. This requires a large, open living space. At the same time, hosts must be able to offer food to guests as a prelude to further social interaction. Thus, cooking and dining cannot be separated from it. Nor can standard middle-class Anglo kitchen equipment be installed; the need for handling large quantities of food requires large pots and pans, for which extra-large sinks and cupboards are necessary. In such ways were the new houses made to accommodate long-standing native traditions.

---

find themselves lacking the cultural knowledge to be successful members of this group. The culture they share with white North Americans is more significant than the physical traits they share with the Bantu.

CULTURE IS LEARNED

All culture is learned rather than biologically inherited, prompting the anthropologist Ralph Linton to refer to it as humanity's "social hered-

Enculturation: The process by which a society's culture is transmitted from one generation to the next.

ity." One learns one's culture by growing up with it, and the process whereby culture is transmitted from one generation to the next is called **enculturation.**

Most animals eat and drink whenever the urge arises. Humans, however, do most of their eating and drinking at certain culturally prescribed times

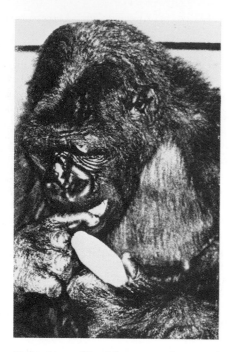

Koko the gorilla picks up a toy banana, signs "toothbrush" (left), and then uses it to brush her teeth (right). Human children, in play, perform similar mental transformations on objects.

and feel hungry as those times approach. These eating times vary from culture to culture. Similarly, a North American's idea of a comfortable way to sleep will vary greatly from that of a Japanese. The need to sleep is determined by biology; the way it is satisfied is cultural.

Through enculturation one learns the socially appropriate way of satisfying one's biologically determined needs. It is important to distinguish between the needs themselves, which are not learned, and the learned ways in which they are satisfied. The biological needs of humans are the same as those of other animals: food, shelter, companionship, self-defense, and sexual gratification. Each culture determines in its own way how these needs will be met.

Not all learned behavior is cultural. A dog may learn tricks, but this behavior is reflexive, the result of conditioning by repeated training, not the prod-

uct of enculturation. On the other hand, non-human primates are capable of forms of cultural behavior. A chimpanzee, for example, will take a twig and strip it of all leaves in order to make a tool with which termites may be extracted from a hole. Such toolmaking, learned by imitating other chimpanzees, is unquestionably a form of cultural behavior until recently thought to be exclusively human. Even more impressive indications of ape capabilities are afforded by long-term studies of young captive apes who have been taught how to "talk" with humans through American Sign Language or some other system. What these reveal is a degree of intelligence and capacity for conceptual thought hitherto unsuspected for nonhuman animals.

There has been a good deal of debate among scientists about the validity of studies of the linguistic and conceptual abilities of captive apes.

Leslie A. White (1900–1975)

Leslie White was a major theoretician in North American anthropology who saw culture as consisting of three essential components. He referred to these components as the techno-economic, the social, and the ideological. White defined the techno-economic aspect of a culture as the way in which the members of the culture deal with their environment, and it is this aspect that then determines the social and ideological aspects of the culture. Because White con-sidered the manner in which culture adapts to its environment to be the most significant factor in its development, his approach has been labeled the **cultural materialist approach.** In *The Evolution of Culture* (1959), White stated his basic law of evolution, that culture evolves in proportion to the increased output of energy on the part of each individual, or to the increased efficiency with which that energy is put to work. In other words, culture develops in direct response to technological "progress." A problem with White's position is his failure to account for the fact that "technological progress" may occur in response to purely cultural stimuli. In this respect, his theories were heavily influenced by eighteenth-century notions of human progress.

(The issues will be more fully discussed in Chapter 13.) Those who are skeptical of the studies feel that the researchers are projecting too much of themselves into their interpretations, ascribing human attributes to nonhuman animals. To be sure, it is easy to see animals as pseudohuman (Garfield the cat, Kermit the frog, and Miss Piggy illustrate the point); on the other hand, the idea that there is supposed to be a deep and unbridgeable gap between humans and animals is deeply embedded in Western culture, as exemplified by Judaic and Christian beliefs. Scientists are, after all, products of their own culture, and it seems likely that much of the resistance to what studies of captive apes seem to be telling us — that the differences between us and them are more of degree than kind — stems from this cultural bias.

What seems to be true, then, is that the cultural capacity of apes is more impressive than was once thought. This should not be surprising, though, given the degree of biological similarity between apes and humans (discussed in Chapter 4). One should not conclude from this, however, that humans are no more than some kind of "naked

Cultural materialist approach: The approach to anthropology that regards the manner in which a culture adapts to its environment as the most significant factor in its development.

ape." Let us not forget that languages used by captive apes were not thought up by, nor learned from, some other ape. The differences between apes and humans *are* of degree, rather than kind, but the degree does make a difference.

CULTURE IS BASED ON SYMBOLS

The anthropologist Leslie White insisted that all human behavior originates in the use of symbols. Art, religion, and money involve the use of symbols. We are all familiar with the fervor and devotion that religion can elicit from a believer; a cross, an image, any object of worship may bring to mind centuries of struggle and persecution or may stand for a whole philosophy or creed. The most important symbolic aspect of culture is language — the substitution of words for objects.

A. R. Radcliffe-Brown (1881–1955)

The British anthropologist A. R. Radcliffe-Brown was the originator of the structural–functionalist school of thought. He and his followers maintained that each custom and belief of a society has a specific function that serves to perpetuate the structure of that society — its ordered arrangement of parts — so that the society's continued existence is possible. The work of the anthropologist, then, was to study the ways in which customs and beliefs function to solve the problem of maintaining the system. From such laws should emerge universal laws of human behavior.

The value of the structural–functionalist approach is that it caused anthropologists to analyze cultures as systems, and to examine the interconnections between their various parts. It also gave a new dimension to comparative studies, as present-day societies were compared in terms of structural–functional similarities and differences rather than their presumed historical connections. Radcliffe-Brown's universal laws have not emerged, however, and the questions remain: Why do particular customs arise in the first place, and how do cultures change?

It is through language that humans are able to transmit culture from one generation to another. We shall consider the important relationship between language and culture in greater detail in Chapter 13.

CULTURE IS INTEGRATED

For purposes of comparison and analysis, anthropologists customarily break a culture down into many seemingly discrete parts, even though such distinctions are arbitrary. The anthropologist who examines one aspect of a culture invariably finds it necessary to examine others as well. This tendency for all aspects of a culture to function as an interrelated whole is called **integration.**

The integration of the economic, political, and social aspects of a culture can be illustrated by the Kapauku Papuans, a mountain people of western New Guinea studied in 1955 by the North American anthropologist Leopold Pospisil.[2] Their economy relies on plant cultivation, along with pig

[2]Leopold Pospisil, *The Kapauku Papuans of West New Guinea* (New York: Holt, Rinehart and Winston, 1963).

> **Integration:** The tendency for all aspects of a culture to function as an interrelated whole.

breeding, hunting, and fishing. Although plant cultivation provides most of the people's food, it is through pig breeding that men achieve political power and positions of legal authority.

Among the Kapauku, pig breeding is a complex business. Raising lots of pigs, obviously, requires lots of food to feed them. This consists primarily of sweet potatoes, grown in garden plots. Some essential gardening activities, however, can be performed only by women; not only this, but pigs must be cared for by women. So, to raise lots of pigs, a man has to have lots of women in the household. The way he gets them is by marrying them; in Kapauku society, multiple wives (polygyny) not only are permitted, but are highly desired. To get them, however, requires payment of bride prices, which can be expensive. Furthermore, wives have to be compensated for their care of pigs. Put simply, it takes pigs, by which wealth is measured, to get wives, which are necessary to raise pigs in the first place. Needless to say, this requires considerable entrepreneurship. It is this ability that produces leaders in Kapauku society.

The interrelatedness of the various parts of Kapauku culture is even more complex than this. For example, the practice of polygyny works best if there are considerably more adult women than men. In the Kapauku case, warfare is endemic, regarded as a necessary evil. By the rules of Kapauku warfare, men get killed but women do not. This system works to promote the kind of imbalance of sexes that facilitates polygyny. Polygyny also tends to work best if wives come to live in their husband's village, rather than the other way around, and that is the case among the Kapauku. Thus, the men of a village are "blood" relatives of one another. Given this, a patrilineal (descent reckoned through men) emphasis in Kapauku culture is not unexpected.

These examples by no means exhaust the interrelationships to be found in Kapauku culture. For example, both patrilineality and endemic warfare tend to promote male dominance, and so it is not surprising to find that positions of leadership in Kapauku society are held exclusively by men, who appropriate the products of women's labor in order to play their political "games." Assertions to the contrary notwithstanding, male dominance is by no means characteristic of all human societies. Rather, as in the Kapauku case, it arises only under particular sets of circumstances, which if changed, will alter the way in which men and women relate to one another.

From what has been said so far, one might suppose that the various parts of a culture must operate in perfect harmony at all times. The analogy would be that of a machine; the parts must all be consistent with one another or it won't run. Try putting diesel fuel in the tank of a car that runs on gasoline and you've got a problem; one part of the system is no longer compatible with the rest. To a degree, this is true of all cultures. A change in one part of a culture usually will affect other parts sometimes in rather dramatic ways. This point, to which we will return later in this chapter, is of particular importance today as diverse agents seek to introduce changes of all sorts into societies all around the world.

At the same time that we must recognize that a degree of harmony is necessary in any properly functioning culture, we should not assume that complete harmony is required. Because no two individuals experience the enculturation process in precisely the same way, no two individuals perceive their culture in exactly the same way, and so there is always some potential for change in any culture. Thus we should speak, instead, of a strain to consistency in culture. So long as the parts are reasonably consistent, a culture will operate reasonably well. If, however, that strain to consistency breaks down, a situation of cultural crisis ensues.

STUDYING CULTURE IN THE FIELD

Armed, now, with some understanding of what culture is, the question arises, How does an anthropologist study culture in the field? Culture, being a set of rules or standards, cannot itself be directly observed; only actual behavior is observable. What must be done is to abstract a set of rules from what is observed and heard in order to explain social behavior, much as a linguist, from the way people speak a language, tries to develop a set of rules to account for the ways those speakers combine sounds into meaningful phrases.

To pursue this further, consider the following discussion of exogamy — marriage outside one's own group — among the Trobriand Islanders, as described by Bronislaw Malinowski.

If you were to inquire into the matter among the Trobrianders, you would find that . . . the natives show horror at the idea of violating the rules of exogamy and that they believe that sores, diseases, even death might follow clan incest. [But] from the viewpoint of the native libertine, *suvasova* (the breach of exogamy) is indeed a specially interesting and spicy form of erotic experience. Most of my informants

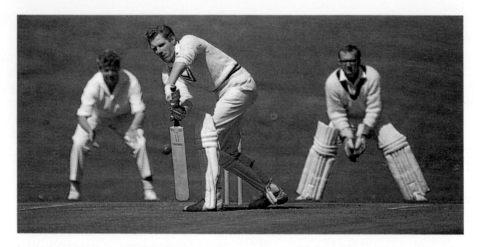

Describing another culture is like trying to describe a new game. The people in this picture may look as though they are playing baseball, but they are playing cricket. To describe cricket in the language of baseball would be at best a caricature of the game as the British know it. The problem in anthropology is how to describe another culture for an audience unfamiliar with it, so that the description is not a caricature.

would not only admit but did actually boast about having committed this offense.[3]

Malinowski himself determined that although such breaches did occasionally occur, they were much less frequent than gossip would have it. Had Malinowski relied solely on what the Trobrianders told him, his description of their culture would have been inaccurate. The same sort of discrepancy between cultural ideals and the way people really do behave can be found in any culture. In Chapter 1 we saw another example from contemporary North America in our discussion of the Garbage Project.

From these examples, it is obvious that an anthropologist must be cautious, if a realistic description of a culture is to be given. To play it safe, data drawn in three different ways ought to be considered. First, the people's own understanding of the rules they share — that is, their notion of the way their society *ought* to be — must be examined. Second, the extent to which people believe they are observing those rules — that is, how they think they actually do behave — needs to be looked at. Third, the behavior that can be directly observed should be considered — in the example of the Trobrianders, whether or not the rule of *suvasova* is actually violated. As we see here, and as we saw in our discussion of the Garbage Project, the way people think they should behave, the way in which they think they do behave, and the way in which they actually behave may be three distinctly different things. By carefully evaluating these elements, the anthropologist can draw up a set of rules that actually may explain the acceptable behavior within a culture.

Of course, the anthropologist is only human. It is difficult to completely cast aside one's personal feelings and biases, which have been shaped by one's own culture. Yet it is important to make every effort to do just this, for otherwise one may seriously misinterpret what one sees. As a case in point, we may see how the male bias of Western culture caused Malinowski to miss important things in his pioneering study of the Trobriand Islanders.

[3]Bronislaw Malinowski, *Argonauts of the Western Pacific* (New York: Dutton, 1922).

Bronislaw Malinowski (1884–1942)

The Polish-born Bronislaw Malinowski argued that people everywhere share certain biological and psychological needs and that the ultimate function of all cultural institutions is to fulfill those needs. Everyone, for example, needs to feel secure in relation to the physical universe. Therefore, when science and technology are inadequate to explain certain natural phenomena — such as eclipses or earthquakes — people develop religion and magic to account for those phenomena and to restore a feeling of security. The nature of the institution, according to Malinowski, is determined by its function.

Malinowski outlined three fundamental levels of needs which he claimed had to be resolved by all cultures:

1. A culture must provide for biological needs, such as the need for food and procreation.
2. A culture must provide for instrumental needs, such as the need for law and education.
3. A culture must provide for integrative needs, such as religion and art.

If anthropologists could analyze the ways in which a culture fills these needs for its members, Malinowski believed that they could also deduce the origin of cultural traits. Although this belief was never justified, the quality of data called for by Malinowski's approach set new standards for ethnographic fieldwork. He himself showed the way with his work in the Trobriand Islands between 1915 and 1918. Never before had such in-depth work been done, nor had such insights been gained into the workings of another culture. Such was the quality of Malinowski's Trobriand research that, with it, ethnography can be said to have come of age as a scientific enterprise.

ORIGINAL STUDY
The Importance of Trobriand Women[4]

Walking into a village at the beginning of fieldwork is entering a world without cultural guideposts. The task of learning values that others live by is never easy. The rigors of fieldwork involve listening and watching, learning a new language of speech and actions, and most of all, letting go of one's own cultural assumptions in order to understand the meanings others give to work, power, death, family, and friends. As my fieldwork in the Trobriand Islands of Papua New Guinea was no exception, I wrestled doggedly with each of these problems. Doing research in the Trobriand Islands created one additional obstacle. I was working in the footsteps of a celebrated anthropological ancestor, Bronislaw Kasper Malinowski. . . .

In 1971, before my first trip to the Trobriands, I thought I understood many things about Trobriand customs and beliefs from having read Malinowski's exhaustive writings. Once there, however, I found that I had much more to discover about what I thought I already knew. For many months I worked with these discordant realities, always conscious of Malinowski's shadow, his words, his explanations. Although I found significant differences in areas of importance, I gradually came to understand how he reached certain conclusions. The answers we both received from informants were not so dissimilar, and I could actually trace how Malinowski had analyzed what his informants told him in a way that made sense and was scientifically significant — given what anthropologists generally then recognized about such societies. Sixty years separate our fieldwork, and any comparison of our studies illustrates not so much Malinowski's mistaken interpretations but the developments in anthropological knowledge and inquiry from his time to mine.

This important point has been forgotten by those anthropologists who today argue that ethnographic writing can never be more than a kind of fictional account of an author's experiences. Although Malinowski and I were in the Trobriands at vastly different historical moments and there also are many areas in which our analyses differ, a large part of what we learned in the field was similar. From the vantage point that time gives to me, I can illustrate how our differences, even those that are major, came to be. Taken together, our two studies profoundly exemplify the scientific basis that underlies the collection of ethnographic data. Like all such data, however, whether researched in a laboratory or a village, the more we learn about a subject, the more we can refine and revise earlier assumptions. This is the way all sciences create their own historical developments. Therefore, the lack of agreement between Malinowski's ethnography and mine must not be taken as an adversarial attack against an opponent. Nor should it be read as an example of the writing of ethnography as "fiction" or "partial truths." Each of our differences can be traced historically within the discipline of anthropology.

My most significant point of departure from Malinowski's analyses was the attention I gave to women's productive work. In my original research plans, women were not the central focus of study, but on the first day I took up residence in a village I was taken by them to watch a distribution of their own wealth — bundles of banana leaves and banana fiber skirts — which they exchanged with other women in commemoration of someone who had recently died. Watching that event forced me to take women's economic roles more seriously than I would have from reading Malinowski's studies. Although Malinowski noted the high status of Trobriand women, he attributed their importance to the fact that Trobrianders reckon descent through women, thereby giving them genealogical significance in a matrilineal society. Yet he never considered that this significance was underwritten by women's own wealth because he did not systematically investigate the women's productive activities. Although in his field notes he mentions Trobriand women making these seemingly useless banana bundles to be exchanged at a death, his published work only deals with men's wealth.

In the Trobriand Islands, women's wealth consists of skirts and banana leaves, large quantities of which must be given away upon the death of a relative.

My taking seriously the importance of women's wealth not only brought women as the neglected half of society clearly into the ethnographic picture but also forced me to revise many of Malinowski's assumptions about Trobriand men. For example, Trobriand kinship as described by Malinowski has always been a subject of debate among anthropologists. For Malinowski, the basic relationships within a Trobriand family were guided by the matrilineal principle of "mother-right" and "father-love." A father was called "stranger" and had little authority over his own children. A woman's brother was the commanding figure and exercised control over his sister's sons because they were members of his matrilineage rather than their father's matrilineage.

According to Malinowski, this matrilineal drama was played out biologically by the Trobrianders' belief that a man has no role as genitor. A man's wife is thought to become pregnant when an ancestral spirit enters her body and causes conception. Even after a child is born, Malinowski reported, it is the woman's brother who presents a harvest of yams to his sister so that her child will be fed with food from its own matrilineage, rather than its father's matrilineage. In this way, Malinowski conceptualized matrilineality as an institution in which the father of a child, as a member of a *different* matrilineage, was excluded not only from participating in procreation but also from giving any objects of lasting value to his children, thus provisioning them only with love.

In my study of Trobriand women and men, a different configuration of matrilineal descent emerged. A Trobriand father is not a "stranger" in Malinowski's definition, nor is he a powerless figure as the third party to the relationship between a woman and her brother. The father is one of the most important persons in his child's life, and remains so even after his child grows up and marries. Even a father's procreative importance is incorporated into his child's growth and development. A Trobriand man gives his child many opportunities to gain things from his matrilineage, thereby adding to the available resources that he or she can draw upon. At the same time, this giving creates obligations on the part of a man's children toward him that last even beyond his death. Therefore, the roles that men and their children play in each other's lives are worked out through extensive cycles of exchanges, which define the strength of their relationships to each other and eventually benefit the other members of both their matrilineages. Central to these exchanges are women and their wealth.

To understand Trobriand kinship from this perspective has broader implications because kinship relations form the basis of chiefly power. Malinowski's studies never made clear whether Trobriand chiefs had supreme autonomy that made them "paramount" chiefs, as he called them, or whether, like most other societies in New Guinea, Trobrianders were more egalitarian in their relationships with each other and chiefs were merely first among equals. From my own and other recent research, we now know that of all the Trobriand Islands, only on Kiriwina are chiefs granted extensive authority and power; on Vakuta Island, to the south of Kiriwina, a chief had little advantage over anyone else; similarly, on Kaileuna Island, to the west, a chief is much less powerful than Kiriwina chiefs; and on Kitava Island, to the east, inherited positions of chieftaincy are absent. Malinowski did most of his fieldwork on Kiriwina, and therefore, he could not have known about these variations. But he also never recognized the profound extent to which Kiriwina women enter into the public world of politics. Only on the island of Kiriwina do exchanges of women's wealth reach such large proportions and involve men in such critical ways. For these reasons, exchanges of women's wealth establish stability in the exchange relationships between men, and the necessity for women's wealth each time someone dies requires the expenditure of certain kinds of men's resources. At the same time, the presence of women's wealth means that men are not totally dependent upon their own shell and stone valuables at a death.

These aspects of women's wealth, that is, stabilizing relationships and leveling some kinds of men's resources while keeping other kinds free, determine the level of hierarchy that chiefs are able to maintain, while alternately showing the limitations chiefs face in gaining additional powers that would bring them greater autonomy.

That Malinowski never gave equal time to the women's side of things, given the deep significance of their role in societal and political life, is not surprising. Only recently have anthropologists begun to understand the importance of taking women's work seriously. In some cultures, such as the Middle East or among Australian aborigines, it is extremely difficult for ethnographers to cross the culturally bounded ritual worlds that separate women from men. In the past, however, both women and men ethnographers generally analyzed the societies they studied from a male perspective. The "women's point of view" was largely ignored in the study of gender roles, since anthropologists generally perceived women as living in the shadows of men — occupying the private rather than the public sectors of society, rearing children rather than engaging in economic or political pursuits.

[4]Annette B. Weiner, *The Trobrianders of Papua New Guinea*, pp. 4–7; © 1987 by Holt, Rinehart and Winston, Inc., reprinted by permission of the publisher.

CULTURE AND PROCESS

In the course of their evolution humans, like all animals, have been continually faced with the problem of adapting to their environment. The term **adaptation** refers to a process by which organisms achieve a beneficial adjustment to an available environment, and the results of that process — the possession of characteristics that permit organisms to overcome the hazards, and secure the resources that they need, in the particular environments in which they live. With the exception of humans, organisms have generally adapted by developing advantageous anatomical and physiological characteristics. For example, a body covering of hair, coupled with certain other physiological mechanisms, protects mammals from extremes of temperature; specialized teeth help them to procure the kinds of food they need; and so on. Humans, however, have come to depend more and more on cultural adaptation. For example, they have not relied on biology to provide them with built-in fur coats to protect them in cold climates. Instead, they make their own coats, build fires, and erect shelters to protect themselves against the cold. More than this, culture enables people to utilize a wide diversity of environments; by manipulating environments through cultural means, people have been able to move into the Arctic and the Sahara and have even gotten to the moon. Through culture the human species has secured not just its survival but its expansion as well.

> **Adaptation:** A process by which organisms achieve beneficial adjustment to an available environment and the results of that process — the characteristics of organisms that fit them to the particular set of conditions of the environment in which they are generally found.

What is adaptive at one time may not be at another. In the United States, the principle source of fruits, vegetables, and fiber is the Central Valley of California, where vast irrigation works have made the desert bloom. As happened in ancient Mesopotamia, evaporation concentrates salts in the water, but here pollution is made even worse by the use of chemical fertilizers. These poisons are now accumulating in the soil and threaten to make the valley a desert again.

This is not to say that everything that humans do they do *because* it is adaptive to a particular environment. For one thing, people don't just react to an environment as given; rather, they react to it as they perceive it, and different groups of people may perceive the same environment in radically different ways. They also react to things other than the environment: their own biological natures, for one, and their beliefs, attitudes, and the consequences of their own behavior, for others. All of these things present them with problems, and people maintain cultures to deal with problems, or matters that concern them. To be sure, their cultures must produce behavior that is generally adaptive, or at least not maladaptive, but this is not the same as saying that cultural practices necessarily arise because they are adaptive in a given environment. The fact is, current utility of a custom is an unreliable guide to its origin.

A further complication is the relativity of any given adaptation: what is adaptive in one context may be seriously maladaptive in another. For example, the sanitation practices of food-foraging peoples are appropriate to contexts of low population levels and some degree of residential mobility, but become serious health hazards in the context of large, fully sedentary populations. Similarly, behavior that is adaptive in the short run may be maladaptive over the long run. Thus, the development of irrigation in ancient Mesopotamia (modern-day Iraq) made it possible over the short run to increase food production, but over the long run it favored the gradual accumulation of salts in the soils. This, in turn, contributed to the collapse of civilization there after 2000 B.C. Similarly, the "development" of prime farmland today in places like the eastern United States for purposes other than food production makes us increasingly dependent on food raised in marginal environments. High yields are presently possible through the application of expensive technology, but continuing loss of topsoil, increasing salinity of soils through evaporation of irrigation waters, and silting of irrigation works, not to mention impending shortages of water and fossil fuels, make continuing high yields over the long term unlikely.

CULTURAL ADAPTATION

A good example of the way cultural factors are involved in a people's adaptation is afforded by the Yanomamö, a people who inhabit the tropical forests of Venezuela and Brazil.[5] Their adaptation to their sociopolitical environment is as important as their adaptation to nature, and their adjustment to it affects the way they are distributed over the land, their patterns of migration, and the kinds of relationships they maintain with their neighbors.

The Yanomamö are a fiercely combative people who inhabit villages of 40 to 250 persons. Village life revolves around the cultivation of a plantain garden and warring against other villages. Because peace is so uncertain, a village must be prepared to evacuate, either to a new location or to the parent village, on very short notice. Since the garden is of such economic importance, however, abandoning it to start a new one elsewhere is seen as a formidable task, and is resisted except in the most extreme situations. Alliances are therefore made with neighboring villages, so that one village joins another's war parties, or takes in the inhabitants of another village during times of need.

The Yanomamö are so combative that in a village of 100 people there is bound to be feuding and bloodshed, necessitating a split, with the dissident faction going off to establish a new garden. Although Yanomamö try to avoid the establishment of a new garden because of the labor and uncertainty of the first harvest, their conflicts force them to this decision frequently. While they are a gardening people, their choice of a garden site is based on political considerations.

FUNCTIONS OF CULTURE

A culture cannot survive if it does not successfully deal with basic problems. A culture must provide for the production and distribution of goods and services considered necessary for life. It must provide for biological continuity through the reproduction of its members. It must enculturate new members so that they can become functioning adults. It must maintain order among its members, as well as between them and outsiders. Finally, it must motivate its members to survive and engage in those activities necessary for survival.

CULTURE AND CHANGE

All cultures change over a period of time, although not always as rapidly or as massively as many are doing today. Changes take place in response to such events as environmental crises, intrusion of outsiders, or modification of behavior and values within the culture. In our own culture, clothing fashions change frequently. In the past few decades it has become culturally permissible for men and women alike to bare more of their bodies, not just in swimming but in dress as well. Along with this has come greater permissiveness about the body in photographs and movies. Finally, the sexual attitudes and practices of North Americans have become more permissive. Obviously these changes are interrelated, reflecting an underlying change in attitudes toward cultural rules regarding sex.

Culture change can bring unexpected and often disastrous results. A case in point is the drought that afflicted so many peoples living in Africa just south of the Sahara Desert in the mid-1980s. Native to this region are a number of pastoral nomadic peoples, whose lives are centered on cattle and other livestock, which are herded from place

[5]Napoleon A. Chagnon, *Yanomamö: The Fierce People*, 2d ed. (New York: Holt, Rinehart and Winston, 1988).

Clothing fashions change frequently in the United States, as illustrated by these two photos. The bathing suits worn in 1906 contrast markedly with those worn in the 1980s.

to place as required for pasturage and water. For thousands of years these people have been able to go about their business, efficiently utilizing vast areas of arid lands in ways that allowed them to survive severe droughts many times in the past. Unfortunately for them, their nomadic life-style, which makes it difficult to impose controls upon them and takes them across international boundaries at will, makes them anathema to the governments of the newly emerged states of the region. Seeing nomads as a challenge to their authority, these governments have gone all out to convert them into sedentary villagers. Overgrazing has been a result of this loss of mobility, and the problem has been compounded by government efforts to involve the pastoralists in a market economy by raising many more animals than required for their own needs, in order to have a surplus to sell. The resultant devastation, where there had previously been no significant overgrazing or erosion, now makes droughts far more disastrous than they would otherwise be, and places the former nomads' very existence in jeopardy.

CULTURE, SOCIETY, AND THE INDIVIDUAL

Ultimately, a society is no more than a union of individuals, all of whom have their own special needs and interests. If a society is to survive, it must succeed in balancing the self-interest of its members against the demands of the society as a whole. To accomplish this, a society offers rewards for adherence to its cultural standards. In most cases, these rewards assume the form of social acceptance. In contemporary North American society, a man who holds a good job, is faithful to his wife, and goes to church, for example, may be elected "Model Citizen" by his neighbors. In order to ensure the survival of the group, each individual must learn to postpone certain immediate satisfactions. Yet the needs of the individual cannot be suppressed too far, lest levels of stress become too much to bear. Hence, a delicate balance

A "drug bust" in New York City. Increasing substance abuse is one symptom of a culture's failure to satisfy the needs of individuals who live by its rules.

always exists between an individual's personal interests and the demands made upon each individual by the group. Take, for example, the matter of sex, which, like anything that people do, is shaped by culture. Sex is important in any society, for it helps to solidify cooperative bonds between men and women, as well as to ensure the perpetuation of the society itself. Yet sex can be disruptive to social living; if who has sexual access to whom is not clearly spelled out, competition for sexual privileges can destroy the cooperative bonds on which human survival depends. Uncontrolled sexual activity, too, can result in reproductive rates that cause a society's population to outstrip its resources. Hence, as it shapes sexual behavior, every culture must balance the needs of society against the need for sufficient individual gratification, lest frustration build up to the point of being disruptive in itself.

Not just in sex, but in all things, cultures must strike a balance between the needs of individuals and those of society. When those of society take precedence, then individuals experience excessive stress. Symptomatic of this are increased levels of mental illness and behavior regarded as antisocial: violence, crime, abuse of alcohol and other drugs, suicide, or simply alienation. If not corrected, the situation can result in cultural breakdown.

Just as problems develop if the needs of society take precedence over those of the individual, so also do they develop if the balance is upset in the other direction. This is precisely what has happened among the Ik, a Ugandan people who at one time were removed from their homeland in order to create a national park.[6] As a consequence, their

[6]Colin M. Turnbull, *The Mountain People* (New York: Simon & Schuster, 1972).

An Ik child in the unused kitchen of her family compound. She made the mistake of thinking of it as home. Her parents were unable to feed her, and when she persisted in her demands, they shut her in. Being too weak to break out, she died there; a few days later, her body was unceremoniously thrown out. Such acts are "standard" among the Ik.

traditional ways were severely disrupted, and resources are no longer adequate to meet their needs. Among the Ik today, every individual past the age of three is responsible for his or her own well-being; no one is expected to do anything for anyone else. Once they are weaned, children are turned loose to find their own food, and no child expects to be fed by a parent, any more than the aged or infirm expect to be fed by their children. Any who are unable to find their own food die. In this society people have died, while their husbands or wives are plump and healthy; those who go out and get food, returning well fed at the end of the

Ethnocentrism: The belief that one's own culture is superior in every way to all others.

day, wouldn't dream of bringing any back to share with a sick wife, husband, or child. The Ik show us what can happen to a people where individuals are required to fend for themselves. They are dying out morally as well as physically, and there is now no one alive among them who can remember a single act of kindness.

EVALUATION OF CULTURE

We have knowledge of diverse cultural solutions to the problems of human existence. The question often arises, Which is best? In the nineteenth century Western peoples had no doubts about the answer — Western civilization was obviously the peak of human development. At the same time, though, anthropologists were intrigued to find that all cultures with which they had any familiarity saw themselves as the best of all possible worlds. Often this was reflected in a name for the society, which roughly translated meant "we human beings" as opposed to "you subhumans." We now know that any culture that is functioning adequately regards itself as the best, a view reflecting the phenomenon known as **ethnocentrism.** Hence, the nineteenth-century Westerners were merely displaying their own ethnocentrism.

Anthropology's reaction against ethnocentrism began when anthropologists started to live among so-called savage peoples and discovered that they were just as human as anyone else. They have been actively engaged in the fight against ethnocentrism ever since. In reaction against ethnocentrism, anthropologists began to examine each culture on its own terms, asking whether or not the culture satisfied the needs and expectations of the people themselves. If a people practiced human sacrifice, for example, they asked whether or not the taking of human life was acceptable according to native values. The idea that a culture must be evaluated according to its own standards, and those alone, is called **cultural relativism.** One could say, for instance, that the ritual killing of other human beings may be acceptable in some societies, and yet it is a custom North Americans, among other peoples, would not wish to emulate, no matter how functional it may be to some other group of people.

While cultural relativism is vastly preferable to the ethnocentric approach, both positions represent extreme viewpoints. These may be characterized as, on the one hand, "we are right and everyone else is wrong," and on the other as "anything goes." A formula for evaluating cultures that avoids the use of ethnocentric criteria, while retaining the essential elements of cultural relativism, was proposed more than 30 years ago by the anthropologist Walter Goldschmidt. In his approach the important question to ask is, How well does a given culture satisfy the physical and psychological needs of those whose behavior it guides. Specific indicators are to be found in the nutritional status and general physical and mental health of its population, the incidence of crime and delinquency, the demographic structure, stability and tranquility of domestic life, and the group's relationship to its resource base. The culture of a society in which one finds high rates of malnutrition, crime, delinquency, suicide, emotional disorders and despair, and environmental degradation may be said to be operating less well than that

> **Cultural relativism:** The thesis that because cultures are unique, they can be evaluated only according to their own standards and values.

of another society where few such problems exist. In a well-working culture, people "can be proud, jealous, and pugnacious, and live a very satisfactory life without feeling '*angst*,' 'alienation,' 'anomie,' 'depression,' or any of the other pervasive ills of our own inhuman and civilized way of living."[7] It is when people feel helpless to effect their own lives in their own societies, when traditional ways of coping no longer seem to work, that the symptoms of cultural breakdown become prominent.

A culture is essentially a system to ensure the continued well-being of a group of people; therefore, it may be termed successful so long as it secures the survival of a society in a way that its members recognize as reasonably fulfilling. What complicates matters is that any society is made up of groups with different interests, raising the possibility that some peoples may be served better than others. Therefore, a culture that is quite fulfilling for one group within a society may be less so for another. For this reason, the anthropologist must always ask: Whose needs, and whose survival, is best served by the culture in question? Only then can a reasonably objective judgment be made about how well a culture is working.

CHAPTER SUMMARY

Culture, to the anthropologist, is a set of rules or standards that, when acted upon by the members of a society, produce behavior that falls within a range of variance the members consider proper and acceptable.

All cultures share certain basic characteristics; study of these sheds light on the nature and function of culture itself. Culture is a set of shared ideals, values, and standards of behavior. It cannot exist without society — a group of people occupying a specific locality who are dependent on each

other for survival. Society is held together by relationships determined by social structure or social organization. Although culture cannot exist without society, one can have society, as do creatures like ants and bees, without culture. All is not uniformity within a culture, as there is some difference between male and female roles in any human society. Anthropologists use the term gender to

[7]Robin Fox, *Encounter with Anthropology* (New York: Dell, 1968), p. 290.

refer to the elaborations or meanings cultures assign to the biological differences between men and women. Age variation is also universal, and in some cultures there is subcultural variation as well. A subculture shares certain broad assumptions of the larger culture, while observing a set of rules that is somewhat different. Pluralistic societies are those in which subcultural variation is particularly marked. They are characterized by a number of groups operating under different sets of rules. A subculture in the United States can be seen in the Amish.

A second basic characteristic of all cultures is that they are learned. Individual members of a society learn the accepted norms of social behavior through the process of enculturation. A third characteristic is that culture is based on symbols. It is transmitted through the communication of ideas, emotions, and desires expressed in language. Finally, culture is integrated, so that all aspects of a culture function as an integrated whole. In a properly functioning culture, though, total harmony of all elements is approximated, rather than completely achieved.

The job of the anthropologist is to abstract a set of rules from what he or she observes in order to explain the social behavior of people. To arrive at a realistic description of a culture free from personal and cultural biases, the anthropologist must (1) examine a people's notion of the way their society ought to function, (2) determine how a people think they behave, and (3) compare these with how a people actually do behave. The anthropologist must also be as free as possible of the biases of his or her own culture.

Cultural adaptation has enabled humans, in the course of evolution, to survive and expand in a variety of environments. Sometimes, though, what is adaptive in one set of circumstances, or over the short run, is maladaptive in another set of circumstances, or over the long run.

To survive, a culture must satisfy the basic biological needs of its members, provide for their continuity, and maintain order among its members and between its members and outsiders.

All cultures change over time, sometimes because the environment to which they were adapted has changed, sometimes because outsiders have intruded, and sometimes because values within the culture have undergone modification. Sometimes the unforeseen consequences of change are disastrous for a society.

A society must strike a balance between the self-interest of individuals and the needs of the group. If one or the other becomes paramount, the result may be cultural breakdown.

A recurring question asked by nonanthropologists has been, Which culture is best? Ethnocentrism is the tendency to regard one's own culture as better than all others. One concept that anthropologists use to counter ethnocentrism is cultural relativism, which involves examining each culture on its own terms, according to its own standards. The least biased measure of a culture's success, however, employs criteria indicative of its effectiveness at securing the survival of a society in a way that its members see as being reasonably fulfilling.

SUGGESTED READINGS

Gamst, Frederick C., and Edward Norbeck. *Ideas of Culture: Sources and Uses.* New York: Holt, Rinehart and Winston, 1976. This is a book of selected writings, with editorial comments, about the culture concept. From these selections one can see how the concept has grown, as well as how it has given rise to narrow specializations within the field of anthropology.

Goodenough, Ward H. *Description and Comparison in Cultural Anthropology.* Chicago: Aldine, 1970. The major question to which Goodenough addresses himself is how the anthropologist is to avoid ethnocentric bias when studying culture. His approach relies on models of descriptive linguistics. A large part of the book is concerned with kinship and terminology, with a discussion of the problems of a universal definition of marriage and the family. This is a particularly lucid discussion of culture, its relation to society, and the problem of individual variance.

Keesing, Roger M. *Cultural Anthropology: A Contemporary Per-spective.* New York: Holt, Rinehart and Winston, 1976. This book approaches anthropology by tackling the important problems of cultural anthropology, discussing them through ethnographic examples and theoretical considerations. In the process the author takes a critical stance toward conventional anthropological thinking and practice.

Kroeber, Alfred L. *Anthropology: Culture Processes and Patterns.* New York: Harcourt, 1963. This volume consists of chapters dealing specifically with matters of culture patterns and processes. The chapters are selected from Kroeber's major work, *Anthropology.*

Linton, Ralph. *The Study of Man: An Introduction.* New York: Appleton, 1963. Linton wrote this book in 1936 with the intention of providing a general survey of the field of anthropology. His study of social structure is illuminating. This book is regarded as a classic and is an important source historically.

13

LANGUAGE AND COMMUNICATION

Although humans rely primarily on language for conversation, it is by no means the only system used. These girls in a Parisian amusement park are expressing their emotions through a combination of facial expression and body gestures.

PREVIEW

What Is Language?

Language is a system of sounds that, when put together according to certain rules, results in meanings that are intelligible to all speakers. Although humans rely primarily on language to communicate with one another, it is not their sole means of communication. Others are paralanguage, a system of extralinguistic noises that accompany language, and kinesics, a system of body motions used to convey messages.

How Is Language Related to Culture?

Languages are spoken by people, who are members of societies, each of which has its own distinctive culture. Social variables, such as class, gender, and status of the speaker, will influence people's use of language. Moreover, people communicate what is meaningful to them, and what is or is not meaningful is defined by their particular culture. In fact, our use of language affects, and is affected by, our culture.

How Did Language Begin?

Many theories have been proposed to account for the origin of language, several of them quite farfetched. One theory held by some anthropologists today is that human language began as a system of gestures. Various biological changes associated with toolmaking and tool using, in early hominids, set the stage for speech, with mouth gestures perhaps playing an important role in this transformation.

All normal humans have the ability to talk, and in many societies they may spend a considerable part of each day doing so. Indeed, so involved with our lives is **language** that it permeates everything we do, and everything we do permeates language. There is no doubt that our ability to speak rests squarely upon our biological organization. We are "programmed" to speak, although only in a general sort of way. Beyond the cries of babies, which are not learned but which do communicate, humans must learn how to speak. We must be taught to speak a particular language, and any normal child who begins early enough can learn any particular language.

Language is a system for the communication, in **symbols,** of any kind of information. In the sense that nonhuman animals also communicate certain kinds of information systematically, we may speak of animal language. "Symbol" in our definition, however, means any kind of sound or gesture to which cultural tradition has given meaning as standing for something, and not one that has a natural or self-evident meaning, which we call a **signal.** A tear is a signal of crying, and crying is a signal of some kind of emotional or physical state; the word "crying," however, is a symbol, a group of sounds to which we have learned to assign the meaning of a particular action, and which we can use to communicate that meaning whether or not anyone around us is actually crying.

At the moment language experts are not certain whether to give credit to animals — bees, dolphins, or chimpanzees — for the ability to use symbols as well as signals, even though these animals and many others have been found to communicate in remarkable ways. Some apes have been taught the American Sign Language for the Deaf, with results such as those described in Chapters 4 and 12. What are the implications of this for our understanding of the nature and evolution of language? No certain answer can be given until we have a better understanding of animal communication than we now have. What we can be sure of is that human culture, as we know it, is ultimately dependent on a system of communication far more com-

> **Language:** A system of communication using sounds that are put together in meaningful ways according to a set of rules.
>
> **Symbols:** Sounds or gestures that stand for meanings among a group of people.
>
> **Signal:** A sound or gesture that has a natural or self-evident meaning.

plex than that of any other animal. The reason for this is that culture must be learned; each individual has to be taught by other individuals the knowledge and rules for behavior that are appropriate for full participation in his or her society. While learning can and does take place in the absence of language by observation and imitation, guided by just a few signs or symbols, all known cultures are so rich in their content that they require systems of communication that not only can give precise labels to various classes of phenomena, but also permit people to range over their experiences in the past and future, as well as the present. The central and most highly developed human system of communication is language. Knowledge of the workings of language, then, is essential to a full understanding of culture.

THE NATURE OF LANGUAGE

Any human language — English, Chinese, Swahili — is obviously a means of transmitting information and sharing with others both cultural and individual experiences. Because we tend to take language for granted, it is perhaps not so obvious that language is also a system that enables us to translate our concerns, beliefs, and perceptions into symbols that can be understood and interpreted by others. This is done by taking a few sounds — no language uses more than about 50 — and developing rules for putting them together in meaningful ways. The many such languages presently in existence all over the world — an estimated 3,000 different ones — may well astound and mystify us by their great variety and complexity; but this should not blind us to the fact that all languages, as far back as we can trace them, are organized on the same basic plan.

Linguistics, the modern scientific study of language, began as early as the seventeenth century, in the age of exploration and discovery, with the accumulation of facts: the collecting of sounds, words, and sentences from as many different languages as possible, chiefly those encountered in exotic lands by European explorers, invaders, and missionaries. The great contribution of the nineteenth century was the discovery of system, regularity, and relationships in the data and the tentative formulation of some laws and regular principles. In the twentieth century, while we are still collecting data, we have made considerable progress in the reasoning process, testing and working from new and improved theories. Insofar as theories and facts of language are verifiable by independent researchers looking at the same materials, there may now be said to be a science of linguistics.

THE SOUND AND SHAPE OF LANGUAGE

How can an anthropologist, a missionary, a social worker, or a medical worker approach and make sense of a language that has not already been analyzed and described, or for which there are no immediately available materials? There are hundreds of such languages in the world; fortunately, some fairly efficient methods have been developed to help with the task. It is a painstaking process to unravel a language, but it is ultimately rewarding and often even fascinating for its own sake.

The process requires first a trained ear and a thorough understanding of the way speech sounds are produced. Otherwise, it will be extremely difficult to write out or make intelligent use of any data. To satisfy this preliminary requirement, most people need special training in **phonetics,** or the systematic study of the production, transmission, and reception of speech sounds.

Linguistics: The modern scientific study of all aspects of language.

Phonetics: The study of the production, transmission, and reception of speech sounds.

Phonology: The study of the sound patterns of language.

Phonemes: In linguistics, the smallest classes of sound that make a difference in meaning.

Allophones: In linguistics, different sounds belonging to the same sound class, or phoneme.

Phonology

In order to analyze and describe any new language, an inventory of all of its sounds and an accurate way of writing them down are needed. Some sounds of other languages may be very much like the sounds of English; others may be sounds that we have never consciously produced. But since we all have the same vocal equipment, there is no reason why we should not be able, with practice, to reproduce all the sounds that anyone else makes. Once this is accomplished, the sound patterns of language can be studied to discover the abstract rules that tell us which combinations of sounds are permissible and which are not. This study is known as **phonology.**

The first step in studying any particular language, once a number of utterances have been collected, is to isolate the smallest classes of sound that make a difference in meaning, called **phonemes,** and to analyze the actual sounds that belong to each of these classes, called **allophones.** This isolation and analysis may be done by a process called the minimal-pair test: The linguist tries to find two short words that appear to be exactly alike except for one sound, such as *bit* and *pit* in English. If the substitution of [b] for [p] in this minimal pair makes a difference in meaning, which it does in English, then those two sounds have been identified as members of distinct phonemes of the language and will require two different symbols to record. If, however, the linguist finds two different pronunciations, and then finds that there

allophones → /p/ or /pᵃ/ in other lang., /t/ or /tɬ/ in English

An important tool for the modern linguist is a good, portable tape recorder. Here, a group of !Kung listen to playback of stories recorded in the field.

is no difference in their meaning for a native speaker, the sounds represented will be considered allophones of the same phoneme, and for economy of representation just one of the two symbols will be used to record that sound wherever it is found. For greater accuracy and to avoid confusion with the various sounds of our own language, the symbols of a phonetic alphabet, such as was developed by Edward Sapir for the American Anthropological Association (Table 13.1), can be used to distinguish between the sounds of most languages in a way comprehensible to anyone who knows the system.

Morphology
The process of making and studying an inventory of sounds may, of course, be a long task; concurrently, the **morphologist** may begin to work out

Morphologist: In linguistics, a person who studies sound combinations.

Morphemes: In linguistics, the smallest units of sound that carry a meaning.

all groups or combinations of sounds that seem to have meaning. These are called **morphemes,** and they are the smallest units that have meaning in the language (unlike phonemes, which, while making a difference in meaning, have no meaning by themselves). They may consist of words or parts of words. A field linguist can abstract morphemes and their meanings from speakers of a language by means of pointing or gesturing to elicit words and their meanings, but the ideal situation is to have an *informant*, a person who knows enough of a common second language, so that approximate transla-

TABLE 13.1

Phonetic vowel symbols (Sapir System)*

i (Fr. *fini*)	*ü* (Fr. *lune*)	*i*	*u* (Swed. *hus*)	*ï*	*u* (Ger. *gut*)
ι (Eng. *bit*)	*ü̇* (Ger. *Mütze*)	*ι*	*u̇*	*i̇*	*v* (Eng. *put*)
e (Fr. *été*)	*ö* (Fr. *peu*)	—	*ȯ*	*α* (Eng. *but*)	*o* (Ger. *so*)
ε (Eng. *men*)	*ö̈* (Ger. *Götter*)	—	*ɔ̇*	*a* (Ger. *Mann*)	*ɔ* (Ger. *Volk*)
—	*ω̈* (Fr. *peur*)	—	*ω̇*	—	*ω* (Eng. *law*)
ä (Eng. *man*)	—	*à* (Fr. *patte*)	—	—	—

*The symbol *ə* is used for an "indeterminate" vowel.

Source: George L. Trager, *Language and Languages* (San Francisco: Chandler Publishing Company, 1972), p. 304.

tions can be made more efficiently and confidently. It is pointless to write down data without any suggestion of meaning for them. *Cat* and *dog* would, of course, turn out to be morphemes, or meaningful combinations of sounds, in English. By pointing to two of either of them, the linguist could elicit *cats* and *dogs*. This indicates that there is another unit that carries meaning, an *s*, that may be added to the original morpheme to mean "plural." When the linguist finds that this *s* cannot occur in the language unattached, it will be identified as a **bound morpheme;** because *dog* and *cat* can occur unattached to anything, they are called **free morphemes.** Because the sound represented as *s* is actually different in the two words (*s* in *cats* and *z* in *dogs*), the linguist will conclude that the sounds *s* and *z* are **allomorphs** of the plural morpheme; that is, they are two varieties of the same morpheme (even though they may be two different phonemes), occurring in different contexts but with no difference in meaning.

Bound morpheme: A sound that can occur in a language only in combination with other sounds, as *s* in English to signify the plural.

Free morphemes: Morphemes that can occur unattached in a language; for example, *dog* and *cat* are free morphemes in English.

Allomorphs: Variants of a single morpheme.

Frame substitution: A method used to identify the syntactic units of language. For example, a category called "nouns" may be established as anything that will fit the substitution frame "I see a _____."

Grammar and Syntax

The next step is to put morphemes together to form phrases or sentences. This process is known as identifying the syntactic units of the language, or the meaningful combination of morphemes in larger chains or strings. One way to do this is to use a method called **frame substitution.** By proceeding slowly at first, and relying on pointing or gestures, the field linguist can elicit such strings as *my cat, your cat,* or *her cat,* and *I see your cat, she sees my cat.* This begins to establish the rules or principles of phrase and sentence making, the **syntax** of the language.

Further success of this linguistic study depends greatly on individual ingenuity, tact, logic, and experience with language. A language may make extensive use of kinds of utterances that are not found at all in English and that an English-speaking linguist might not, therefore, even think of asking for. Furthermore, certain speakers may pretend not to be able to say (or may truly not be able to say) certain things considered by their culture to be impolite, taboo, or inappropriate for mention to outsiders. It may even be unacceptable to point, in which case the linguist will have to devise roundabout ways of eliciting words for objects.

The **grammar** of the language will ultimately consist of all observations about its morphemes and syntax. Further work may include the establishment, by means of substitution frames, of all the **form classes** of the language, that is, the parts of speech or categories of words that work the same way in any sentence. For example, we may establish a category we call "nouns," defined as anything that will fit the substitution frame "I see a _____." We simply make the frame, try out a number of words in it, and have a native speaker indicate yes or no for whether the words work. In English, the words *house* and *cat* will fit this frame and will be said to belong to the same form class, but the word *think* will not. Another possible substitution frame for nouns might be "The _____ died," in which the word *cat* will fit, but not the word *house.* Thus we can identify subclasses of our nouns — in this case, what we can call "animate" and "inanimate" subclasses. The same procedure may be followed for all the words of the language, using as many different frames as necessary, until we have a lexicon, or dictionary, that accurately describes the possible uses of all the words in the language.

Syntax: In linguistics, the rules or principles of phrase and sentence making.

Grammar: The entire formal structure of a language consisting of all observations about the morphemes and syntax.

Form classes: The parts of speech or categories of words that work the same way in any sentence.

Paralanguage: The extralinguistic noises that accompany language, for example, those of crying or laughing.

Voice qualities: In paralanguage, the background characteristics of a speaker's voice.

One of the strengths of modern descriptive linguistics is the objectivity of its methods. A descriptive linguist will not approach a language with the idea that it must have nouns, verbs, prepositions, or any other of the form classes identifiable in English. The linguist instead sees what turns up in the language and makes an attempt to describe it in terms of its own inner workings. For convenience, morphemes that behave approximately like English nouns and verbs may be labeled as such, but if it is thought that the terms are misleading, the linguist may instead call them "x-words" and "y-words," or "form class A" and "form class B."

PARALANGUAGE

Voice Qualities

Although humans rely primarily on language for their communication, it is by no means the only system used. How often has it been remarked, "It's not what he said so much as how he said it"? What the speaker is concerned with in this phrase is **paralanguage,** a less developed system of communication than language, which always accompanies it. Paralanguage may be defined as a system of extralinguistic noises that generally accompany language. While it is not always easy for the linguist to distinguish between the sounds of language and paralinguistic noises, two different kinds of the latter have been identified. The first has to do with **voice qualities,** which operate as the background characteristics of a speaker's voice. These involve pitch range, or spread upward or downward; vocal lip control, ranging from hoarseness to openness; glottis control, or sharp to smooth transitions in pitch; articulation control, or forceful and relaxed speech; rhythm control, or smooth and jerky setting off of portions of vocal activity; resonance, ranging from resonant to thin; and tempo, an increase or decrease from the norm.

Voice qualities are capable of communicating much about the state of being of the person who is speaking, quite apart from what is being said. An obvious example of this is slurred speech, which may indicate that the speaker is intoxicated. Or if someone says with a drawl, coupled with a restricted pitch range, that they are delighted with something, it probably indicates that they aren't delighted at all. The same thing said more rapidly, with increasing pitch, might indicate that the speaker really is genuinely excited about the matter. While the speaker's state of being is affected by his or her anatomical and physiological status, it is also markedly affected by the individual's overall self-image in the given situation. If an individual is made to feel anxious by being crowded in some way, or by some aspects of the social situation, for example, this anxiety will probably be conveyed by certain voice qualities.

Vocalizations

The second kind of paralinguistic noises consists of **vocalizations.** Instead of being background characteristics, these are actual identifiable noises that, unlike voice qualities, are turned on and off at perceivable and relatively short intervals. They are, nonetheless, separate from language sounds. One category of vocalizations consists of **vocal characterizers:** laughing or crying, yelling or whispering, yawning or belching, and the like. One "talks through" vocal characterizers, and they are generally indicative of the speaker's attitude. If one yawns while speaking to someone, for example, this may indicate an attitude of boredom on the part of the speaker. Breaking, an intermittent tensing and relaxing of the vocal musculature pro-

Vocalizations: Identifiable paralinguistic noises that are turned on and off at perceivable and relatively short intervals.

Vocal characterizers: In paralanguage, sound productions such as laughing or crying that humans "speak through."

Vocal qualifiers: In paralanguage, sound productions of brief duration that modify utterances in terms of intensity.

Vocal segregates: In paralanguage, sound productions that are similar to the sounds of language but do not appear in sequences that can properly be called words.

Kinesics: A system of postures, facial expressions, and body motions that convey messages.

ducing a tremulousness while speaking, may indicate great emotion on the part of the speaker.

Another category of vocalizations consists of **vocal qualifiers.** These are of briefer duration than vocal characterizers, being limited generally to the space of a single intonation pattern of language. They modify utterances in terms of intensity—loud versus soft; pitch—high versus low; and extent—drawl versus clipping. These indicate the speaker's attitude to specific phrases such as "get out." The third category consists of **vocal segregates.** These are somewhat like the actual sounds of language, but they don't appear in the kinds of sequences that can be called words. Examples of vocal segregates familiar to English-speaking peoples are such substitutes for language as *shh, uh-uh,* or *uh-huh.*

KINESICS

Kinesics may be thought of as a system for communication through motion. Familiar to many through the phrase "body language," kinesics is a system of postures, facial expressions, and bodily motions that convey messages. These messages may be communicated directly, as in the case of gestures. For example, in North America scratching one's scalp, biting one's lip, and knitting one's brows are ways of conveying doubt. A more com-

Shown here are different gender signals sent by men and women in North America.
While women tend to hold their arms and legs together, men hold theirs apart.

plex example is afforded by the gender signals sent by North American men and women. Although there is some regional and class variation, women generally bring their legs together, at times to the point that the upper legs cross, either in a full leg cross with feet still together, the outer sides of the feet parallel to one another, or in standing knee over knee. The pelvis is carried rolled slightly forward. The upper arms are held close to the body, and in movement, the entire body from neck to ankle is presented as a moving whole. Men, by contrast, hold their legs apart, with the upper legs at a 10 or 15° angle. Their pelvis is carried in a slightly rolled back position. The arms are held out at 10 to 15° from the body, and they are moved independently of the body. Finally, a man may subtly wag his hips with a slight right and left presentation, with a movement involving a twist at the base of the rib cage and at the ankles.

Such gender markers are not the same as invitations to sexual activity. Rather, they are conventions inscribed on the body through imitation and subtle training. In any culture, as little girls grow up, they imitate their mothers or other older women; little boys do the same with their fathers or other older men. In our own culture, by the time we become adults, we have acquired a host of gender markers that intrude into every moment of our lives, so much so that we are literally at a loss if we do not know the sex of someone with whom we must interact. This is easily verified, as the philosopher Marilyn Frye suggests:

To discover the differences in how you greet a woman and how you greet a man, for instance, just observe yourself, paying attention to the following sorts of things: frequency and duration of eye contact, frequency and type of touch, . . . physical distance maintained between bodies, how and whether you smile . . ., whether your body dips into a shadow curtsey or bow. That I have two repertories for handling introductions to people was vividly confirmed for me when a student introduced me to his friend, Pat, and I really could not tell what sex Pat was. For a moment I was stopped cold, completely incapable of

Some kinesic gestures that humans use are also used by other primates.

action. I felt myself helplessly caught between two paths — the one I would take if Pat were female and the one I would take if Pat were male. Of course the paralysis does not last. One is rescued by one's ingenuity and good will: one can invent a way to behave as one says "How do you do?" to a human being. But the habitual ways are not for humans: they are one way for women and another for men.[1]

Often, kinesic messages complement spoken messages, as by nodding the head while affirming something verbally. Other examples are punching the palm of the hand for emphasis, raising the head and brows when asking a question, and using the hands to illustrate what is being talked about. Such gestures are rather like bound morphemes — they have meaning but don't stand alone, except in particular situations, such as a nodded response to a question.

Although little scientific notice was taken of kinesics before the 1950s, there has since been a great deal of research, particularly among North Americans. Cross-cultural research has shown, however, that there is a good deal of similarity around the world in such basic expressions as smiling, laughing, crying, and the facial expressions of anger. More specifically, there is great similarity in the routine for greeting over a distance around the world. Europeans, Balinese, Papuans, Samoans, !Kung, and at least some South American Indians all smile and nod, and if the individuals are especially friendly, they will raise their eyebrows with a rapid movement, keeping them raised for a fraction of a second. All of this signals a readiness for contact. The Japanese, however, suppress the eyebrow flash, regarding it as indecent, which goes to show that there are important differences, as well as similarities, cross-culturally. This can be seen in kinesic expressions for yes and no. In our culture, one nods the head for yes and shakes it for no. The people of Sri Lanka, like us, will nod to answer yes to a factual question, but if asked to do something, a slow sideways movement of the head means yes. In Greece, the nodded head means yes, but no is indicated by jerking the head back so as to lift the

[1]Marilyn Frye, "Sexism," in *The Politics of Reality* (New York: The Crossing Press, 1983), p. 20.

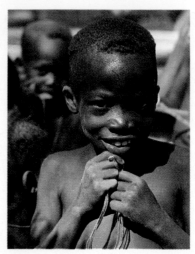

There is a great deal of similarity around the world in such basic expressions as smiling, laughing, crying, and the facial expressions of anger. Shown here are smiling children from Soviet Central Asia (left), Senegal (middle), and Brazil (right).

face; at the same time, the eyes are often closed and the eyebrows lifted.

LINGUISTIC CHANGE

In our discussion of the sound and shape of language, we looked briefly at the internal organization of language — its phonology, morphology, syntax, and grammar. It is the descriptive approach to language that is concerned with registering and explaining all the features of any one particular language at any one time in its history. **Descriptive linguistics** concentrates, for example, on the way modern French, or Spanish, functions now, as if the language were a separate system, consistent within itself, without any reference to historical reasons for its development. Yet languages, like cultures, have histories. The Latin *ille* ("that") is identifiable as the origin of both the French *le* ("the") and the Spanish *el* ("the"), even though the descriptive linguist treats *le* and *el* only as they function in the modern language, where the meaning "that" is no longer relevant and very few native speakers are aware that they are speaking modern derivatives of Latin. **Historical linguistics**, by contrast, investigates relationships between earlier

Descriptive linguistics: The study of language concerned with registering and explaining all the features of a language at one point in history.

Historical linguistics: The study of relationships between earlier and later forms of a language, antecedents in older languages of developments in modern languages, and relationships among older languages.

and later forms of the same language, antecedents in older languages for developments in modern languages, and questions of relationships between older languages. Historical linguists, for example, attempt to identify and explain the development of early medieval spoken Latin into later medieval French and Spanish by investigating both natural change in the original language and the influence of contacts with the "barbarian" invaders from the north. There is no conflict between historical and descriptive linguists, the two approaches being recognized as interdependent. Even a modern language is constantly changing, and it changes according to principles that can be established only historically.

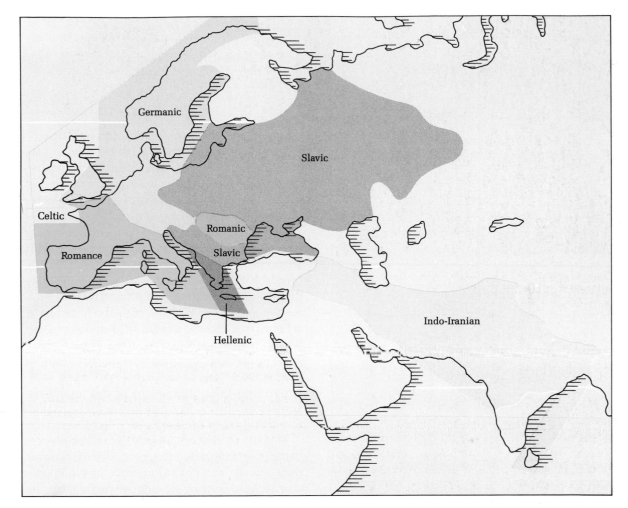

FIGURE 13.1 The Indo-European languages.

Historical linguists have achieved considerable success in working out the genealogical relationships between different languages, and these are reflected in schemes of classification. For example, English is one of a number of languages classified in the Indo-European **language family** (Figure 13.1). This family is subdivided into some 11 **language subgroups,** which reflect the fact that there has been a long period of **linguistic divergence** from an ancient unified language (referred to as Proto-Indo-European) into separate languages. English is one of a number of languages in the

Language family: A group of languages that are ultimately descended from a single ancestral language.

Language subgroups: Languages of a family that are more closely related to one another than they are to other languages of the same family.

Linguistic divergence: The development of different languages from a single ancestral language.

Germanic subgroup (Figure 13.2). These languages are the result of further linguistic divergence, but they are all more closely related to one

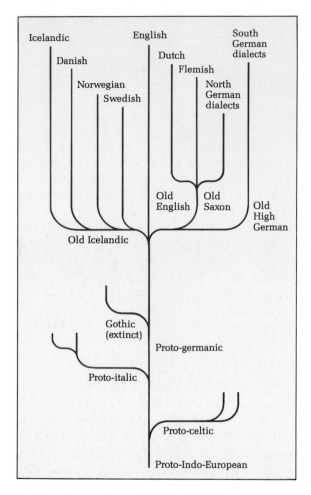

FIGURE 13.2 English is one of a group of languages in the Germanic subgroup of the Indo-European family. This diagram shows its relationship to other languages in the same subgroup. The root was proto-Indo-European, a language spoken by a people who spread westward over Europe, bringing with them both their customs and their language.

than they are to the languages of other subgroups of the Indo-European family.

Historical linguists have been successful in describing the changes that have taken place as languages have diverged from more ancient parent languages. They have also developed means of estimating when certain migrations, invasions, and contacts of peoples have taken place, on the basis

Glottochronology: In linguistics, a method of dating divergence in branches of language families.

Core vocabulary: In language, pronouns, lower numerals, and names for body parts and natural objects.

of linguistic similarities and differences. The concept of linguistic divergence, for example, is used to suggest the time at which one group of speakers of a language separated from another group. A more complicated technique, known as **glottochronology,** was developed by Swadesh and Lees in the early 1950s to try to date the divergence of related languages, such as Latin and Greek, from an earlier common language. The technique is based on the assumption that changes in a language's **core vocabulary** — pronouns, lower numerals, and names for parts of the body and natural objects — occur at a more or less constant rate. By applying a logarithmic formula to two related core vocabularies, one should be able to determine how many years the languages have been separated. Although not as precise as this might suggest, glottochronology provides a useful way of estimating when languages may have separated.

If many of the changes that have taken place in the course of linguistic divergence are well known, their causes are not. One force for linguistic change is borrowing by one language from another, and languages do readily borrow from one another; but if borrowing were the sole force for change, linguistic differences would be expected to become less pronounced through time. It is by studying modern languages in their cultural settings that one can begin to understand the forces for change. One such force is novelty, pure and simple. There seems to be a human tendency to admire the person who comes up with a new and clever idiom, a new and useful word, or a particularly stylish pronunciation, so long as these do not seriously interfere with communication. Indeed, in linguistic matters, complexity tends to be admired, while simplicity seems dull. Hence, about as fast as a language may be simplified, purged of needlessly complex constructions or phrases, new ones will arise.

Group membership also plays a role in linguistic change. Part of this is functional: professions, sects, or other groups in a society often have need of special vocabularies to be able to communicate effectively about their special interests. Beyond this, special vocabularies may serve as labeling devices; those who use such vocabularies are set off as a group from those who do not, and this helps to create a strong sense of group identity.

> When a linguist writes of "morphophonic alteration in the verb paradigm" or an anthropologist writes of "the structural implications of matrilateral cross-cousin marriage," they express, in part at least, their membership in a profession and their ability to use its language. To those on the inside, professional terminology may connote the comforting security of their familiar in-group; to those on the outside, it may seem an unneeded and pretentious use of mumbo-jumbo where perfectly adequate and simple words would do as well. But whether needed or not, professional terminology does serve to differentiate language and to set the speech of one group apart from that of others. To that degree it is a force for stylistic divergence.[2]

Phonological differences between groups may be regarded in the same light as vocabulary differences. In a class-structured society, for example, members of the upper class may try to keep their pronunciation distinct from that of lower classes. An example of a different sort is afforded by coastal communities in the state of Maine, in particular, though it may be seen to varying degrees elsewhere along the New England coast. In the past, people in these communities developed a style of pronunciation quite distinct from the styles of "inlanders." More recently, as outsiders have moved into these coastal communities, either as summer people or as permanent residents, the traditional coastal style has come to identify those who adhere to traditional coastal values, as opposed to those who do not.

[2]Robbins Burling, *Man's Many Voices: Language in Its Cultural Context* (New York: Holt, Rinehart and Winston, 1970), p. 192.

> **Linguistic nationalism:** The attempt by nations to proclaim independence by purging their languages of foreign terms.
>
> **Ethnolinguistics:** The study of the relation between language and culture.

One other far-reaching force for linguistic change is **linguistic nationalism,** an attempt by whole nations to proclaim their independence by purging their vocabularies of "foreign" terms. This phenomenon is particularly characteristic of the former colonial countries of Africa and Asia today. It is by no means limited to those countries, however, as one can see by periodic French attempts to purge their language of such Americanisms as *le hamburger.* Also in the category of linguistic nationalism are revivals of languages long out of common use, such as Gaelic and Hebrew.

LANGUAGE IN ITS CULTURAL SETTING

Rewarding though it is to analyze language as a system in which linguistic variables dependent upon other linguistic phenomena operate, it is important to realize that languages are spoken by people, who are members of societies, each of which has its own distinctive culture. Individuals tend to vary in the ways they use language, and as the preceding discussion suggests, social variables such as class and status of the speaker will also influence their use of language. Moreover, people choose words and sentences so as to communicate meaning, and what is meaningful in one culture may not be in another. The fact is that our use of language affects, and is affected by, our culture.

The whole question of the relationships between language and culture is the province of **ethnolinguistics,** an outgrowth of both ethnology and descriptive linguistics, which has become almost a separate field of inquiry. Ethnolinguistics is concerned with every aspect of the structure and

Language Renewal among the Northern Ute

On April 10, 1984, the Northern Ute Tribe became the first community of American Indians in the United States to affirm the right of its members to regain and maintain fluency in their ancestral language and their right to use it as a means of communication throughout their lives. Like many other Native Americans, these people had experienced a decline in fluency in their native tongue, as they were forced to interact more and more intensively with outsiders who spoke only English. Once the on-reservation boarding school was closed in 1953, Ute children had to attend schools where teachers and most other students were ignorant of the Ute language. Outside the classroom as well, children and adults alike were increasingly bombarded by English as they sought employment off the reservation, traded in non-Indian communities, or were exposed to television and other popular media. By the late 1960s, although Ute language fluency was still highly valued, many members of the community could no longer speak it.

Alarmed by this situation, the group of Ute parents and educators that supervises federally funded tutorial services to Indian students decided that action needed to be taken, lest their native language be lost altogether. With the assistance of other community leaders, they launched discussions into what might be done about the situation, and invited anthropologist William L. Leap to join in these discussions. Previously, Leap had worked on language education with other tribes, and he was subsequently hired by the Utes to assist them in their efforts at linguistic renewal. One result of his work was the official statement of policy, by the tribe's governing body, noted above.

Leap began work for the Northern Utes in 1978, and his first task was to carry out a first-ever reservation-wide language survey. This found, among other things, that inability to speak Ute did not automatically imply loss of skill; evidently, many nonspeakers retained a "passive fluency" in the language and could understand it, even though they couldn't speak it. Furthermore (and quite contrary to expectations), children who were still able to speak Ute had fewer problems with English in school than did nonspeakers.

Over the next few years, Leap helped set up a Ute language renewal program within the tribe's Division of Education, wrote several grants to provide funding, led staff training workshops in linguistic transcription and grammatical analysis, provided technical assistance in designing a practical writing system for the language, and supervised data-gathering sessions with already-fluent speakers of the language. With the establishment in 1980 of an in-school program to provide developmental Ute and English instruction to Indian and other interested children, he became staff linguist. In this capacity he helped train the language teachers (all of whom were Ute, and none of whom had degrees in education); carried out research that resulted in numerous technical reports, publications, and in-service workshops; helped prepare a practical Ute language handbook for home use so that parents and grandparents might enrich the children's language learning experience; prepared the preliminary text for the tribe's statement of policy on language, and helped persuade the governing body into acceptance of this. By 1984, not only did this policy become "official," but several (not just one) language development projects were in place on the reservation, all monitored and coordinated by a tribally sanctioned language and culture committee. Supported by both tribal and federal funds, the projects involved the participation of persons with varying degrees of familiarity with the language. Although literacy was not a goal, practical needs resulted in development of practical writing systems, and a number of people in fact became literate in Ute. One important reason for all this success was the involvement of the Ute people in all stages of development; not only did these projects originate in response to their own expressed needs, but they were active participants in all discussions and made decisions at each stage of activities, participating not just as individuals, but as members of family, kin, community, and band.

use of language that has anything to do with society, culture, and human behavior.

LANGUAGE AND THOUGHT

An important ethnolinguistic concern of the 1930s and 1940s was the question of whether language might indeed determine culture. Do we see and react differently to the colors blue and green, with different cultural symbolism for the two different colors, only because our language has different names for these two neighboring parts of the unbroken color spectrum? When anthropologists noticed that some cultures lump together blue and green with one name, they began to wonder about this question. The American linguist Edward Sapir first formulated the problem, and his student Benjamin Lee Whorf, drawing on his experience with the language of the Hopi Indians, developed a full-fledged theory, sometimes called the **Whorfian hypothesis.** Whorf proposed that a language is not simply an encoding process for voicing our ideas and needs but is rather a shaping force, which, by providing habitual grooves of expression that predispose people to see the world in a certain way, guides their thinking and behavior. The problem is a little like the old question of the chicken or the egg, and some later formulations of Whorf's theory about which came first, thinking and behavior or language, have since been criticized as both logically unsound and not amenable to any experimentation or proof. Its primary value is that it did begin to focus attention on the relationships between language and culture.

The opposite point of view is that language reflects reality. In this view, language mirrors cultural reality, and as the latter changes, so too will language. Some support for this is provided by studies of blue–green color terms. It has been shown that eye pigmentation acts to filter out the shorter wavelengths of solar radiation. Color vision is thus limited through a reduced sensitivity to blue and confusion between the short visible wavelengths. The effect shows up in color-naming behavior, where green may be identified with blue,

Whorfian hypothesis: The hypothesis, proposed by the linguist B. L. Whorf, which states that language, by providing habitual grooves of expression, predisposes people to see the world in a certain way and so guides their thinking and behavior.

blue with black, or both green and blue with black. The severity of visual limitation, as well as the extent of lumping of color terms, depends on the density of eye pigmentation characteristic of the people in a given society.

These findings do not mean that language merely reflects reality, any more than thinking and behavior are determined by language. The truth of the matter is more as anthropologist Peter Woolfson has put it:

> Reality should be the same for us all. Our nervous systems, however, are being bombarded by a continual flow of sensations of different kinds, intensities, and durations. It is obvious that all of these sensations do not reach our consciousness; some kind of filtering system reduces them to manageable propositions. The Whorfian hypothesis suggests that the filtering system is one's language. Our language, in effect, provides us with a special pair of glasses that heightens certain perceptions and dims others. Thus, while all sensations are received by the nervous system, only some are brought to the level of consciousness.[3]

Linguists are finding that although language is generally flexible and adaptable, once a terminology is established, it tends to perpetuate itself and to reflect and reveal the social structure and the common perceptions and concerns of a group. For example, English is richly endowed with words having to do with war, the tactics of war, and the hierarchy of officers and fighting men. It is rich, too, in militaristic metaphors, as when we speak of "conquering" space, "fighting" the "battle" of the budget, carrying out a "war" on poverty, making a "killing" on the stock market, "shooting down" an

[3]Peter Woolfson, "Language, Thought, and Culture," in *Language*, ed. Virginia P. Clark, Paul A. Escholz, and Alfred F. Rosa (New York: St. Martin's, 1972), p. 4.

computer langs

Nuer cattle resting outside their "barn." So important are cattle to these people that they have more than 400 names to describe them.

argument, or "bombing" out on an exam, to mention just a few. An observer from an entirely different and perhaps warless culture could understand a great deal about the importance of warfare in our lives, as well as how we go about conducting it, simply from what we have found necessary to name and how we talk. Similarly, anthropologists have noted that the language of the Nuer, a nomadic people of Africa, is rich in words and expressions having to do with cattle; not only are more than 400 words used to describe cattle, but Nuer boys actually take their names from them. Thus, by studying the language we can determine the importance of cattle to Nuer culture, attitudes to cattle, and the whole etiquette of human and cattle

relationships. A people's language does not, however, prevent them from thinking in new and novel ways. If this leads to important changes in common perceptions and concerns, then language can be expected to change accordingly.

Kinship Terms

In the same connection, anthropologists have paid considerable attention to the way people name their relatives in various societies (further observations on the question of kinship terms will be found in Chapter 19). In English we have terms to identify brother, sister, mother, father, grandmother, grandfather, granddaughter, grandson, niece, nephew, mother-in-law, father-in-law, sister-in-law, and brother-in-law. Some people also distinguish first and second cousin and great-aunt and great-uncle. Is this the only possible system for naming relatives and identifying relationships? Obviously not. We could have separate terms, as some cultures do, for younger brother and older brother, for mother's sister and father's sister, and so on. What we can describe in English with a phrase, if pressed to do so, other languages make explicit from the outset, and vice versa: a number of languages use the same word to denote both a brother and a cousin, and a mother's sister may also be called by the same term as one's mother.

What do kinship terms reveal? From them, we can certainly gain a good idea of how the family is structured, what relationships are considered especially important, and sometimes what attitudes toward relationships may prevail. Caution is required, however, in drawing conclusions from kinship terms. Just because we do not distinguish linguistically in English between our mother's parents and our father's parents (both are simply grandmother and grandfather), does that mean that we do not know which is which? Certainly not. Nevertheless, nonanthropologists, when confronted with a kinship system in which the same term is applied to father's brother as to father, frequently make the mistake of assuming that "these people don't know who their own father is."

LANGUAGE AND GENDER

Throughout history, human beings have handled the relationship between men and women in many different ways, and here again language can be revealing. In English-speaking societies, for example, men and women use the language in different ways, revealing a deep-seated bias against women, as the following Original Study demonstrates.

ORIGINAL STUDY
Sexism in the English Language[4]

"Women's language" is that pleasant (dainty?), euphemistic never-aggressive way of talking we learned as little girls. Cultural bias was built into the language we were allowed to speak, the subjects we were allowed to speak about, and the ways we were spoken of. Having learned our linguistic lesson well, we go out in the world, only to discover that we are communicative cripples — damned if we do, and damned if we don't.

If we refuse to talk "like a lady," we are ridiculed and criticized for being unfeminine. ("She thinks like a man," is, at best, a left-handed compliment.) If we do learn all the fuzzy-headed, unassertive language of our sex, we are ridiculed for being unable to think clearly, unable to take part in a serious discussion, and therefore unfit to hold a position of power. . . .

In the same way as words and speech patterns used *by* women undermine her image, those used to *describe* women make matters even worse. Often a word may be used of both men and women (and perhaps of things as well); but when it is applied to women, it assumes a special meaning that, by implication rather than outright assertion, is derogatory to women as a group.

The use of euphemisms has this effect. A euphemism is a substitute for a word that has acquired a bad connotation by association with something unpleasant or embarrassing. But almost as soon as the new word comes into common usage, it takes on some of the old bad connotations, since feelings about the things people referred to are not altered by a change of name; thus new euphemisms must be constantly found.

There is one euphemism for *woman* still very much alive. The word, of course, is *lady*. *Lady* has a masculine counterpart, namely *gentleman*, occasionally shortened to *gent*. But for some reason *lady* is very much commoner than *gent(leman)*.

The decision to use *lady* rather than *woman*, not vice versa, may considerably alter the sense of a sentence, as the following examples show:

(a) A woman (lady) I know is a dean at Berkeley.
(b) A woman (lady) I know makes amazing things out of shoelaces and old boxes.

The use of *lady* in (a) imparts a frivolous, or nonserious, tone to the sentence: the matter under discussion is not one of great moment. Similarly, in (b), using *lady* here would suggest that the speaker considered the "amazing things" not to be serious art, but merely a hobby or an aberration. If *woman* is used, she might be a serious sculptor. To say *lady doctor* is very condescending, since no one ever says *gentleman doctor* or even *man doctor*. For example, mention in the San Francisco *Chronicle* of January 31, 1972, of Madalyn Murray O'Hair as the *lady atheist* reduces her position to that of scatterbrained eccentric. Even *woman atheist* is scarcely defensible: sex is irrelevant to her philosophical position.

Many women argue that, on the other hand, *lady* carries with it overtones recalling the age of chivalry: conferring exalted stature on the person so referred to. This makes the term seem polite at first, but we must also remember that these implications are perilous: they suggest that a "lady" is helpless, and cannot do things by herself.

Lady can also be used to infer frivolousness, as in titles of organizations. Those that have a serious purpose (not merely that of enabling "the ladies" to spend time with one another) cannot use the word *lady* in their titles, but less serious ones may. Compare the *Ladies' Auxiliary* of a men's group, or the *Thursday Evening Ladies' Browning and Garden Society* with *Ladies' Liberation* or *Ladies' Strike for Peace*.

What is curious about this split is that *lady* is in origin a euphemism — a substitute that puts a better face on something people find uncomfortable — for *woman*. What kind of euphemism is it that subtly denigrates the people to whom it refers? Perhaps *lady* functions as a euphemism for *woman* because it does not contain the sexual implications present in *woman*: it is not "embarrassing" in that way. If this is so, we may expect that, in the future, *lady* will replace *woman* as the primary word for the human female, since *woman* will become too blatantly sexual. That this distinction is already made in some contexts is shown in the following examples, where you can try replacing *woman* with *lady*:

(a)   She's only twelve; but she's already a woman.
(b)   After ten years in jail, Harry wanted to find a woman.
(c)   She's my woman, see, so don't mess around with her.

Another common substitute for *woman* is *girl*. One seldom hears a man past the age of adolescence referred to as a boy, save in expressions like "going out with the boys," which are meant to suggest an air of adolescent frivolity and irresponsibility. But women of all ages are "girls": one can have a man — not a boy — Friday; women have girlfriends, but men do not — in a nonsexual sense — have boyfriends. It may be that this use of *girl* is euphemistic in the same way the use of *lady* is: in stressing the idea of immaturity, it removes the sexual connotations lurking in *woman*. *Girl* brings to mind irresponsibility: you don't send a girl to do a woman's errand (or even for that matter, a boy's errand). She is a person who is both too immature and too far from real life to be entrusted with responsibilities or with decisions of any serious or important nature.

Now let's take a pair of words which, in terms of the possible relationships in an earlier society, were simple male–female equivalents, analogous to bull:cow. Suppose we find that, for independent reasons, society has changed in such a way that the original meanings now are irrelevant. Yet the words have not been discarded, but have acquired new meanings, metaphorically related to their original senses. But suppose these new metaphorical uses are no longer parallel to each other. By seeing where the parallelism breaks down, we discover something about the different roles played by men and women in this culture. One good example of such a divergence through time is found in the pair *master:mistress*. Once used with reference to one's power over servants, these words have become unusable today in their original master–servant sense as the relationship has become less prevalent in our society. But the words are still common.

Unless used with reference to animals, *master* now generally refers to a man who has acquired consummate ability in some field, normally nonsexual. But its feminine counterpart cannot be used in this way. It is practically restricted to its sexual sense of "paramour." We start out with two terms, both roughly paraphrasable as "one who has power over another." But the masculine form, once a person is no longer able to have absolute power over another, becomes usable metaphorically in the sense of "having power over *something*." *Master* requires as its object only the name of some activity, something inanimate and abstract. But *mistress* requires a masculine noun in the possessive to precede it. One cannot say: "Rhonda is a mistress." One must be *someone's* mistress. A man is defined by what he does, a woman by her sexuality, that is, in terms of one particular aspect of her relationship to men. It is one thing to be an *old master* like Hans Holbein, and another to be an *old mistress*.

The same is true of words like *spinster* and *bachelor* — gender words for "one who is not married." The resemblance ends with the definition. While *bachelor* is a neutral term, often used as a compliment, *spinster* is often used pejoratively, with connotations of prissiness, fussiness, and so on. To be a bachelor implies that one has the choice of marrying or not, and this is what makes the idea of a bachelor existence attractive, in the popular literature. He has been pursued and has successfully eluded his pursuers. But a spinster is one who has not been pursued, or at least not seriously. She is old, unwanted goods. The metaphorical connotations of bachelor generally suggest sexual freedom; of spinster, puritanism or celibacy.

These examples could be multiplied. It is generally considered a *faux pas*, in society, to congratulate a woman on her engagement, while it is correct to congratulate her fiancé. Why is this? The reason seems to be that it is impolite to remind people of things that may be uncomfortable to them. To congratulate a woman on her engagement is really to say, "Thank goodness! You had such a close call!" For the man, on the other hand, there was no such danger. His choosing to marry is viewed as a good thing, but nothing essential.

The linguistic double standard holds throughout the life of the relationship. After marriage a bachelor and spinster become man and wife, not man and woman. The woman whose husband dies remains "John's widow"; John, however, is never "Mary's widower."

Finally, why is it that sales clerks and others are so quick to call women customers "dear," and "honey," and other terms of endearment they really have no business using? A male customer would never put up with it. But women, like children, are supposed to enjoy these endearments, rather than being offended by them.

In more ways than one, it's time to speak up.

[4]Robin Lakoff, "You Are What You Say," *MS Magazine*, July 1974. Reprinted with permission of the author.

SOCIAL DIALECTS

In our previous discussion of linguistic change, phonological and vocabulary differences between groups were noted as important forces for linguistic change. Varying forms of a language that are similar enough to be mutually intelligible are known as **dialects,** and the study of dialects is a concern of **sociolinguistics.** Technically, all dialects are languages—there is nothing partial or sublinguistic about them—and the point at which two different dialects become distinctly different languages is roughly the point at which speakers of one are almost totally unable to communicate with speakers of the other. Boundaries may be psychological, geographical, social, or economic, and they are not always very clear. There is usually a transitional territory, or perhaps a buffer zone, where features of both are found and understood, as between central and southern China. The fact is that if you learn the Chinese of Beijing, you cannot communicate with the waiter in your local Chinese restaurant who comes from Canton or Hong Kong, although both languages—or dialects—are conventionally called Chinese.

> **Dialects:** Varying forms of a language that reflect particular regions or social classes and that are similar enough to be mutually intelligible.
>
> **Sociolinguistics:** The study of the structure and use of language as it relates to its social setting.

A classic example of the kind of dialect that may set one group apart from others within a single society is one spoken by many inner-city blacks. Educator Dorothy Seymour provides the following example:

"Cmon, man, les git goin'!" called the boy to his companion. "Dat bell ringin'. It say, 'Git in rat now!'" He dashed into the school yard.

"Aw, f'get you," replied the other. "Whe' Richuh? Whe' da' muvvah? He be goin' to schoo'."

"He in de' now, man!" was the answer as they went through the door.

In the classroom they made for their desks and opened their books. The name of the story they tried to read was "Come." It went:

Come, Bill, come
Come with me.

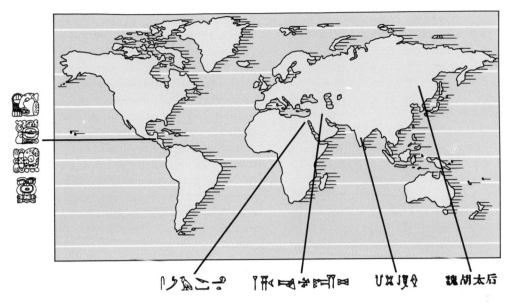

FIGURE 13.3 The impermanence of spoken words contrasts with the relative permanence of written records. In all of human history, writing has been independently invented no more than five times, in the places shown on this map.

Come and see this.
See what is here.

The first boy poked the second. "Wha' da' wor'?"
"Da' wor' *is*, you dope."
"*Is*? Ain't no wor' *is*. You jivin' me? Wha' da wor' mean?"
"Ah dunno. Jus' *is*."[5]

Unfortunately, there is a widespread perception among middle-class whites and blacks alike that this dialect is somehow substandard or defective, which it is not. Rather, it is a highly structured mode of speech, capable of expressing anything its speakers care to express, often in extremely creative ways (as in "rapping"). Many of its distinctive features stem from retention of sound patterns, grammatical devices, and even words of the West African languages spoken by the ancestors of today's black Americans. Compared to Black English, the Standard dialect lacks certain sounds; contains some sounds that are unnecessary for which others may serve just as well; doubles and drawls some of its vowel sounds in sequences that are unusual and difficult to imitate; lacks a method of forming an important tense (the habitual); requires too many ways of indicating tense, plurality, and gender; and doesn't mark negatives in such a way as to make a strong negative statement.

Because their dialect differs so much from Standard English, and has been stigmatized so often, speakers of Black English frequently find themselves at a disadvantage outside of their own communities. In schools, for example, black children may be seen by teachers as deficient in verbal skills and may even be diagnosed — quite wrongly — as "learning impaired." The great challenge for the schools is to find ways of teaching these children how to use Standard English in those situations

[5]Dorothy Z. Seymour, "Black Children, Black Speech," in *Language Awareness*, 4th ed., ed. Paul Escholz, Alfred Rosa, and Virginia Clark (New York: St. Martin's, 1986), p. 74.

Because they are culture bound, standardized tests devised by people from one subcultural background usually fail to measure what they are supposed to measure when administered to those from another background.

where it is to their advantage to do so, without denigrating or affecting their ability to use the dialect of their own community. Martin Luther King was particularly skilled at switching back and forth between the two dialects, depending on the situation in which he was speaking. Less consciously, we all do the same sort of thing when we switch from formality to informality in our speech, depending upon where we are and to whom we are talking. The process of changing from one level of language to another as the situation demands, whether from one language to another or from one dialect of a language to another, is known as **code switching,** and it has been the subject of a number of sociolinguistic studies.

Other Sociolinguistic Concerns

Of the many other concerns of sociolinguistics today we can only mention that we also find investigations of children's languages and word games, the structure of folktales and folk songs, bilingualism and multilingualism, pidgin languages and creoles ("trade languages" with simple grammars and mixed vocabularies, developed to enable peo-

> **Code switching:** The process of changing from one level of language to another.

ples of widely different languages to communicate), linguistic borrowing and innovation, forms of address and politeness, secret languages, magic languages, and myth. The list increases and has begun to duplicate many of the concerns of other fields or disciplines. Almost every aspect of anthropology and sociology has a linguistic side or a relevance to linguistics. This new field of sociolinguistics proves to be not one field but many, and it is providing an opportunity for some productive cooperation and sharing between disciplines.

THE ORIGINS OF LANGUAGE

A realization of the central importance of language for human culture leads inevitably to speculation about how language might have started in the first place. The question of the origin of language has long been a popular subject, and some reasonable and many not so reasonable theories have been proposed: exclamations became words, sounds in nature were imitated, or people simply got together and assigned sounds to objects and actions. The main trouble with past theories is that there was so little in the way of evidence that theorizing often reached the point of wild speculation. The result was a reaction against such theorizing, exemplified by the ban imposed in 1866 by the Société de Linguistique de Paris against papers on linguistic origins. Now there is more evidence to work with — better knowledge of primate brains, new studies of primate communication, more human fossils that can be used to tentatively reconstruct the brain's evolution, and a better understanding of early hominid ways of life. We still can't prove how and when human language developed, but we can speculate much less wildly than was once the case.

Attempts to teach other primates to talk like humans have not been successful. In a lengthy experiment in communication, the chimpanzee Viki

Multilinguism is likely to be important in pluralistic societies. Because a people's language is attuned to their traditional ways of thinking about themselves and the world around them, retention of their language helps preserve cultural traditions. It also helps to proclaim their distinctive identity within the wider society.

learned to voice only a few words, such as *up*, *mama*, and *papa*. Clearly, apes are incapable of spoken language, and the main reason for this seems to be a lack of connection in the nonhuman primate brain between auditory and motor speech areas.

Better results have been achieved through nonvocal methods. Chimpanzees and gorillas in the wild make a variety of vocalizations, but these are mainly emotional, rather than propositional. In this sense, they are equivalent to human paralanguage. Much of their communication takes place by kinesic means — the use of specific gestures and postures. Indeed, some of these, such as kissing and embracing, are in virtually universal use today among humans, as well as apes. Allen and Beatrice Gardner began teaching the American Sign Language, used by the deaf, to their young chimpanzee Washoe in 1966. After 22 months, Washoe had a vocabulary of 30 signs, and her rate of acquisition was accelerating. By the time she was four

years old she had a vocabulary of 132 signs. The first signs she learned were for nouns. She was able to transfer each sign from its original referent to other appropriate objects and even pictures of objects. Her vocabulary includes verbs, adjectives, and words like *sorry* and *please*. Washoe can string signs together properly to produce original sentences. Even more impressive, Washoe has been observed spontaneously teaching her own offspring how to sign.

The chimpanzee Sarah has learned to converse by means of pictographs — designs such as squares and triangles — on brightly colored plastic chips. Each pictograph stands for a noun or a verb. Sarah can also produce new sentences of her own. Another chimpanzee, Lana, converses by means of a computer with a keyboard somewhat like that of a typewriter, but with symbols rather than letters.

One of the most fascinating experiments of this kind has been the teaching of the American Sign Language to a young gorilla named Koko. Koko's

Humans talk, but other primates communicate largely through gestures. Still, humans have not abandoned gestural language altogether, as we see here. The human and the rhesus monkey are using the same open-mouth threat.

working vocabulary — those signs used regularly and appropriately — now consists of over 500 signs. She knows about 500 more, however, and has used as many as 251 of them in a single hour. Not only does she respond to and ask questions, but she also refers to events removed in time and space. This last characteristic, **displacement,** is one of the distinctive characteristics of human speech. Koko has now been joined by a young gorilla named Michael, and the two regularly converse with one another.

Washoe, Sarah, Lana, and Koko are only a few of the apes whose abilities to communicate have been investigated in recent years. Not everyone is convinced that they are capable of true language. The basic question seems to be, Do they *know* that a sign can stand for an object in time and space,

Displacement: The ability to refer to things and events removed in time and space.

and that a name can be used to convey information to other animal beings? After all, say the critics, even pigeons can be taught to peck selectively at red keys to obtain food and green keys to obtain water. Might not the apes be doing a very clever version of this?

Part of the problem here seems to be an "either–or" aspect of the debate: either apes have language capabilities comparable to those of humans, or they do not. What gets lost in the arguments is the possibility that apes may have *some* language capabilities, even if they are not on a par with those of humans. Certainly, studies such as that of Koko are strong evidence.

[handwritten: Diff. to believe they were making tools 24 hrs a day]

One can argue reasonably that the early hominids, which shared a common ancestry with the African apes, probably had a system of communication not unlike what we see among modern chimpanzees and gorillas, and that human paralanguage and kinesics are altered survivals of that system. The experiments with Washoe, Koko, and other apes show the potential represented by this kind of system. Working from information such as this, Gordon W. Hewes has revived and refined the hypothesis that human language began as a gestural, rather than vocal, system.[6] That the earliest representatives of the genus *Homo* were making stone tools and exhibited the beginnings of human culture (Chapter 6) suggests that their communicative abilities surpassed those of wild apes and may have been comparable to Koko's. Such a sign language would probably have sufficed for their purposes.

While no evolution of the mouth, tongue, or larynx was necessary to the origin of true spoken language in early *Homo*, changes in brain organization were. In accomplishing these, toolmaking and tool use may have played a key role. The need to have in mind an abstract image of the finished tool before striking the first flake, for example, would have favored the ability to form associations between abstract concepts and tangible objects, a necessary precondition for human speech. Furthermore, the increasing importance of precise hand movements in toolmaking would have favored cerebral lateralization (right-handedness with left-hemisphere dominance) and cross-modal transfer of learning, making for easy integration of vocal–auditory and visual–tactile experience, also necessary for spoken language. Once these biological underpinnings were sufficiently developed, the changeover from gestural to spoken language could have taken place, with mouth gestures perhaps playing an important role.

The advantage of spoken over gestural language to a species increasingly dependent on tool use for survival is obvious. To "talk with your hands," you must stop whatever else you are doing with them; speech, however, does not interfere with that. Thus, we might expect the switch from gestural to spoken language to have taken place not long after the appearance of toolmaking *Homo*. Many anthropologists believe that the *Homo erectus'* use of more complex tools, control of fire, and effective hunting of sometimes large game through strategies such as cooperative fire drives could not have occurred without some sort of spoken language. Others have argued that the vocal apparatus of *H. erectus* was not adequate for speech. What such arguments fail to take into account, however, is that spoken language, when it first evolved, may have been based on a range of sounds different from those used today. Indeed, the appearance of evidently symbolic objects in deposits left by *Homo erectus* strongly implies more than a rudimentary linguistic ability, for such objects can have no shared meaning in the absence of explanation.

[handwritten: little evidence]

The search for a truly primitive language spoken by a living people that might show the processes of language just beginning or developing has been abandoned, no doubt permanently. Is there such a thing as a primitive language? So far, all human languages that have been described and studied, even among people with something approximating a Stone Age culture, are highly developed, complex, and capable of expressing infinite meanings. The truth is that people have been talking in this world for an extremely long time, and every known language, wherever it is, now has a long history and has developed subtleties and complexities that strongly resist any label of "primitivism." What a language may or may not express is not a measure of its age, but of its speakers' kind of life, reflecting what they want or need to share and communicate with others.

[6]Gordon W. Hewes, "Primate Communication and the Gestural Origin of Language," *Current Anthropology*, 14 (1973): 5–24.

CHAPTER SUMMARY

Anthropologists need to understand the workings of language, because it is through language that people in every culture are able to share their experiences, concerns, and beliefs, over the past and in the present, and to communicate these to the next generation. Language makes communication of infinite meanings possible by employing a few sounds that, when put together according to certain rules, result in meanings that are intelligible to all speakers.

Linguistics is the modern scientific study of all aspects of language. Phonetics focuses on the production, transmission, and reception of speech sounds. Phonology studies the sound patterns of language in order to extract the rules that govern the way sounds are combined. Morphology is concerned with the smallest units of meaningful combinations of sounds — morphemes — in a language. Syntax refers to the principles according to which phrases and sentences are built. The entire formal structure of a language, consisting of all observations about the morphemes and syntax, constitutes the grammar of a language.

Paralanguage, which always accompanies language, is a less developed means of communication than language and involves such noises as voice qualities and vocalizations. Another means of communication is kinesics, a system of body motions used to convey messages.

Descriptive linguistics registers and explains the features of a language at a particular time in its history. Historical linguistics investigates relationships between earlier and later forms of the same language. A primary concern of historical linguists is to identify the forces behind the changes that have taken place in languages in the course of linguistic divergence. Historical linguistics also provides a means of roughly dating certain migrations, invasions, and contacts of people.

Ethnolinguistics deals with language as it relates to society, culture, and human behavior. Some linguists, such as Benjamin Lee Whorf, have proposed that language shapes the way people think and behave. Others argue that language reflects reality. Although linguists find language flexible and adaptable, they have found that once a terminology is established, it tends to perpetuate itself and to reflect much about the speakers' beliefs and social relationships. Kinship terms, for example, help reveal how a family is structured, what relationships are considered close or distant, and what attitudes toward relationships are held. Similarly, gender language reveals how the men and women in a society relate to one another.

A social dialect is the language of a group of people within a larger one, all of whom may speak more or less the same language. Sociolinguists are concerned with whether dialect differences reflect cultural differences. They also study code switching — the process of changing from one level of language to another as the situation demands — for much the same reason.

Some anthropologists believe that human language began as a gestural rather than a vocal system. Various biological changes associated with toolmaking and tool using among early hominids set the stage for speech, with mouth gestures perhaps playing an important role in this transformation.

For some time, linguists searched for a truly primitive language spoken by a living group that would reveal language in its very early state. This search has been abandoned. All languages that have been studied, including those of people with "primitive" cultures, are complex, sophisticated, and able to express a wide range of experiences. What a language is capable of expressing has nothing to do with its age, but with the kind of culture its speakers share and wish to communicate.

SUGGESTED READINGS

Birdwhistell, Ray L. *Kinesics and Context.* Philadelphia: University of Pennsylvania Press, 1970. Kinesics was first delineated as an area for anthropological research by Birdwhistell, so this book is particularly appropriate for those who wish to know more about the phenomenon.

Burling, Robbins. *Man's Many Voices: Language in Its Cultural Context.* New York: Holt, Rinehart and Winston, 1970. An investigation into the nonlinguistic factors that affect the use of language, such as kinship systems and the wider cultural context. It relies heavily on examples from southern and Southeast Asia.

Crane, L. Ben, Edward Yeager, and Randal L. Whitman. *An Introduction to Linguistics.* Boston: Little, Brown, 1981. A book that gives balanced coverage to all subfields of linguistics, including topics traditionally ignored in textbooks.

Gelb, Ignace J. *A Study of Writing.* London: Routledge, 1952. The aim of this study is to lay a foundation for a new science of writing, grammatology. It attempts to establish general principles governing the use and evolution of writing on a comparative basis, and is the first systematic presentation of the history of writing based on these principles.

Hickerson, Nancy Parrot. *Linguistic Anthropology.* New York: Holt, Rinehart and Winston, 1980. A description and explanation of what anthropological linguistics is all about, written so as to be understood by beginning students.

Lehmann, Winifred P. *Historical Linguistics, An Introduction,* 2d ed. New York: Holt, Rinehart and Winston, 1973. In recent years, historical linguistics has tended to be overshadowed by descriptive linguistics. Historical linguistics, however, remains an active and changing field, and this book is a good introduction to it.

Patterson, Francine, and Eugene Linden. *The Education of Koko.* New York: Holt, Rinehart and Winston, 1981. A fascinating and readable account of the longest continuing study of an ape's linguistic abilities ever undertaken. In it, Patterson deals with the various criticisms that have been leveled at ape-language studies.

Trager, George L. "Paralanguage: A First Approximation," in *Language in Culture and Society,* edited by Dell Hymes. New York: Harper & Row, 1964, pp. 274–279. The author is the pioneer in paralinguistic research, and in this article he discusses what paralanguage is, why it should be studied, and how.

14

CULTURE AND PERSONALITY

Among some Malaysian people, men play a major role in the everyday care of infants and toddlers. In some other societies, children below the age of puberty are all but ignored by the men. These and other differences in child-rearing practices around the world, and their possible effects on personality development, have long been of interest to anthropologists.

PREVIEW

What Is Enculturation?

Enculturation is the process by which culture is passed from one generation to the next. It begins soon after birth, as self-awareness — the ability to perceive oneself as an object in time and space and to judge one's own actions — starts to develop. For self-awareness to function, the individual must be provided with a behavioral environment. First, one learns about a world of objects other than self, and these are always perceived in terms that are specified by the culture in which one grows up. Along with this, one is provided with spatial, temporal, and normative orientations.

What Is the Effect of Enculturation on Adult Personality?

Studies have shown that there is some kind of nonrandom relationship between enculturation and personality development, although it is also clear that each individual begins with certain broad potentials and limitations that are genetically inherited. In some cultures certain child-rearing practices seem to promote the development of compliant personalities, while in others different practices seem to promote more independent, self-reliant personalities.

Are Different Personalities Characteristic of Different Cultures?

Although cultures vary a great deal in terms of the personality traits that are looked upon with admiration or disapproval, it is difficult to characterize cultures in terms of particular personalities. Of the several attempts that have been made, the concept of modal personality is the most satisfactory. This recognizes that in any human society there will be a range of individual personalities, but that some will be more "typical" than others.

Do Cultures Differ in What They Regard as Abnormal Personalities?

A normal personality may be thought of as one that approximates the modal personality of a particular culture. Since modal personalities may differ from one culture to another, and since cultures may differ in the range of variation they will accept, it is clear that abnormal personality is a relative concept. A particular personality regarded as abnormal in one culture may not be so regarded in another.

In 1690 John Locke presented his *tabula rasa* theory in his book, *An Essay Concerning Human Understanding*. This notion held that the newborn human was like a blank slate, and what the individual became in life was written on the slate by his or her life experiences. The implication is that all individuals are biologically identical at birth in their potential for personality development and that their adult personalities are exclusively the products of their postnatal experiences, which will differ from culture to culture. Stated in these terms, the theory is not acceptable, for we know that each person is born with unique inherited tendencies that will influence his or her adult personality. It is also known, however, that genetic inheritance sets rather broad potentials and limitations and that life experiences, particularly in the early years, are critically important in the shaping of individual personalities. Since different cultures handle the raising and education of children in different ways, these practices and their effects on personalities are important subjects of anthropological inquiry. Such studies gave rise to the sub-

Enculturation: The process by which a society's culture is transmitted from one generation to the next.

field of psychological anthropology, and are the subjects of the present chapter.

THE SELF AND ITS BEHAVIORAL ENVIRONMENT

Since culture is created and learned rather than biologically inherited, all societies must somehow ensure that culture is adequately transmitted from one generation to the next. This process of transmission is known as **enculturation,** and it begins soon after birth. The first agents of enculturation in all societies are the members of the household into which a person is born. At first, the most important member of this household is the newborn's mother, but other members of the house-

Shown here is a chimpanzee mother with three of her offspring. The basic primate child-rearing unit consists of a mother and her offspring; to this humans have added an adult male. In some societies, this is the mother's husband; in others, it is her brother.

hold soon come to play roles in the process. Just who these others are depends on how households are structured in the particular society (Chapter 18). In our own, they usually include the father or stepfather and the child's siblings. In other societies the father may have little contact with his children in their early years; indeed, there are societies where men do not even live with the mothers of their children. In such instances, brothers of the child's mother usually have important responsibilities toward their nieces and nephews. In many societies, grandparents, other wives of the father, or brothers of the father or sisters of the mother, not to mention their children, are also likely to be key players in the enculturation process.

As the young person matures, individuals outside the household are brought into the process. These usually include other kin, and certainly the individual's peers. The latter may be included informally in the form of play groups or formally in age associations, where children actually teach other children. In some societies, and our own is a good example, professionals are brought into the process of enculturation to provide formal instruction, although in many societies, children are pretty much allowed to learn through observation and participation, at their own speed.

THE SELF

Enculturation begins with the development of **self-awareness** — the ability to identify oneself as an object, to react to oneself, and to appraise or evaluate oneself. People do not have this ability at birth, even though it is essential for existence in human societies. It is self-awareness that permits one to assume responsibility for one's conduct, to learn how to react to others, and to assume a variety of roles. An important aspect of self-awareness is the attachment of positive value to the self. This is necessary in order to motivate individuals to act to their advantage rather than disadvantage. Self-identification by itself is not sufficient for this.

Self-awareness does not come all at once. In our own society, for example, self and nonself are not clearly distinguished until about two years of age.

Self-awareness: The ability to identify oneself as an object, to react to oneself, and to appraise oneself.

The development of self-awareness in our society, however, may lag somewhat, since the neuromotor development of our infants, which proceeds in concert with it, has been shown to lag behind that of infants in many, perhaps even most, non-Western societies. The reasons for this are not yet clear, although the amount of human contact and stimulation that infants receive probably plays an important role. For example, at 15 weeks of age, the home-reared infant in North America is in contact with its mother for about 20 percent of the time, on the average. At the same age, infants in the traditional !Kung (the ! refers to a click, made by pressing the tip of the tongue against the roof of the mouth, from which it is then drawn sharply away) society of South Africa's Kalahari Desert are in close contact with their mothers about 70 percent of the time. Moreover, their contacts are not usually limited to their mothers; they include numerous other adults and children of virtually all ages. In the United States and Canada, something approximating these same conditions is now being provided by day care centers. So long as their personnel remains stable and (ideally) is recruited from the same neighborhood, these centers should have a positive effect on the cognitive and social development of the very young children enrolled in them.

In the development of self-awareness, perception, or a kind of vague awareness of one's existence, precedes conception, or more specific knowledge of the interrelated needs, attitudes, concerns, and interests that define what one is, and this involves a cultural definition of self. In this definition, language plays a crucial role. So it is that in all cultures individuals master personal and possessive pronouns at an early age. Personal names, too, are important devices for self-identification in all cultures. Then, as infancy gives way to early childhood, the "I" or "me" is increasingly separated from the environment.

The Ituri forest in the geographical heart of Africa, is viewed in two very different ways by the people who live there. Mbuti foragers view it with affection; like a benevolent parent, it provides them with all they ask in the way of sustenance, protection, and security. Village-dwelling farmers, by contrast, view the forest with a mixture of fear, hostility, and mistrust — something they must constantly struggle to control.

THE BEHAVIORAL ENVIRONMENT

In order for self-awareness to emerge and function, basic orientations are necessary to structure the psychological field in which the self is prepared to act. Thus, each individual must learn about a world of objects other than self. The basis of this world of other-than-self is what we would think of as the objective environment of things. The objective environment, though, is organized culturally and mediated symbolically through language. Putting this another way, we might say that the objective world is perceived through cultural glasses. Those attributes of the environment that are culturally significant are singled out for attention and labeled; those that are not may be ignored or lumped together in broad categories. Culture, however, also *explains* the perceived environment. This is important, for it provides the individual with an orderly, rather than chaotic, universe within which to act. Behind this lies a powerful psychological drive to reduce uncertainty, the product of a universal human need for a balanced and integrated perspective on the relevant universe. When confronted with ambiguity and uncertainty, people invariably strive to clarify and give structure to the situation; they do this, of course, in ways that their particular culture tells them are appropriate. Indeed, the greater the lack of structure and certainty, the greater individual suggestibility and persuadability tend to be. Thus, we should not be surprised to find that explanations of the universe are never entirely objective in nature.

The behavioral environment in which the self acts involves more than object orientation alone. Action requires spatial orientation, or the ability to get from one object, or place, to another. In all societies, names and significant features of places are important means of discriminating and representing points of reference for spatial orientation. Individuals must know where they have been and will be in order to get from one place to another. They also need to maintain a sense of self-continuity, so that past actions are connected with those in the present and future. Hence, temporal orientation is also part of the behavioral environment. Just as the perceived environment is organized in cultural terms, so too are time and space.

A final aspect of the behavioral environment is the normative orientation. Values, ideals, and standards, which are purely cultural in origin, are as much a part of the individual's behavioral environment as are trees, rivers, and mountains. Without them one would have nothing by which to judge either one's own actions or those of others. In short, the self-appraisal aspect of self-awareness could not be made functional.

Like any aspect of culture, conceptions of the self vary considerably from one society to another. The Penobscot Indians, who at one time relied on fishing, hunting, and the gathering of wild plants (food foraging) for subsistence, and people whose descendants still live today in the woodlands of northeastern North America, serve as an example.[1]

The Penobscot

When first encountered by Europeans, the Penobscot conceived of each individual as being made up of two parts — the body and a "vital self." The latter was dependent on the body, yet was able to disengage itself from the body and travel about for short periods of time, to perform overt acts and to interact with other "selves." It was activity on the part of the vital self that was thought to occur in dreams. So long as the vital self returned to the body in a reasonable period of time, the individual remained in good health; but if the vital self was prevented from returning to the body, then the individual sickened and died. Along with this dual nature of the self went a potential for every individual to work magic. Theoretically, it was possible to send one's own vital self out to work mischief on others, just as it was possible for others to lure one's vital self away from the body, resulting in sickness and eventual death.

To many people today, the traditional Penobscot concept of self may seem strange. The British colonists of New England regarded such ideas as false and shot through with superstition, even though their own concept of self at the time was every bit as supernaturalistic. To the Indians their concept made sense, for it adequately accounted for their experience, regardless of its rightness or wrongness in any objective sense. Furthermore, the Penobscot view of self is relevant for anyone who wishes to understand Penobscot behavior in the days when the British and French first tried to settle in North America. For one thing, it was re-

[1]Frank G. Speck, "Penobscot Shamanism," *Memoirs of the American Anthropological Association*, 6 (1920): 239–288.

sponsible for an undercurrent of suspicion and distrust of strangers, as well as the individual secretiveness that characterized Penobscot society at the time. This propensity for individual secretiveness made it difficult for a potentially malevolent stranger to gain control of an individual's vital self. Also, the belief that dreams are real experiences, rather than expressions of unconscious desires, could impose burdens of guilt and anxiety on individuals who dreamed of doing things not accepted as proper. Finally, individuals indulged in acts that would strike many people today as quite mad. A case in point is a Penobscot Indian who spent the night literally fighting for his life with a fallen tree. To the Indian, this was a metamorphosed magician who was out to get him, and it would have been madness *not* to try to overcome his adversary.

The behavioral environment in which the Penobscot self operated consisted of a flat world, which these people conceived as being surrounded on all sides by salt water. They could actually see the latter downstream, where the Penobscot River reached the sea. The river itself was the spatial reference point and was as well the main artery for canoe travel in the region. The largest of a number of watercourses, it flowed through forests abounding with game. Like humans, each animal was also composed of a body and a vital self. Along with the animals were various quasi-human supernatural beings that inhabited bodies of water and mountains or roamed freely through the forest. One of these, Gluskabe, created the all-important Penobscot River by killing a greedy giant frog that had monopolized the world's water supply. Gluskabe was also responsible for a number of other natural features of the world, often as a by-product of punishment, such as that of the giant frog, for transgressions of the moral code. Indeed, individuals had to worry about their behavior vis-à-vis both animals and these quasi-human beings, or they, too, would come to various kinds of grief. Hence, these supernaturals not only "explained" many otherwise unexplainable natural phenomena to the Penobscot but were also important in structuring the Penobscot moral order. To the Penobscot, all

Patterns of affect: How people feel about themselves and others.

of this was quite believable; the lone hunter, for example, off for extended periods in the forest, knew he would hear in the night the cry of Pskedemus, the swamp woman. And a Penobscot accepted the fact that his or her vital self routinely traveled about while the body slept, interacting with various of these supernatural beings.

Penobscot concepts of the self and behavioral environment have changed considerably since the seventeenth century, just as have those of the descendants of the early Europeans who first came to New England. Both groups may now be said to hold modern beliefs about the nature of their selves and the world they live in. The old beliefs were associated with **patterns of affect** — how people *feel* about themselves and others — which differed considerably in Indian and European cultures. This is significant, for as the Chinese-American anthropologist Francis Hsu has pointed out, patterns of affect are likely to persist over thousands of years, even in the face of far-reaching changes in all other aspects of culture.[2] A failure to understand this point seems to be at least partially responsible for the generally negative attitude, on the part of many non-Indians, to the land-claims suit, which the Penobscots recently won against the state of Maine, the largest ever brought by an Indian tribe in the lower 48 states.

PERSONALITY

In the process of enculturation we have seen that each individual is introduced to the concepts of self and the behavioral environment characteristic of his or her culture. The result is that a kind of cognitive map of the operating world is built up, in terms of which the individual will think and act. This cognitive map is an integrated, dynamic system of perceptual assemblages, including the self

[2]Francis L. K. Hsu, "Role, Affect, and Anthropology," *American Anthropologist*, 79 (1977): 807.

and its behavioral environment. When we speak of an individual's **personality,** we are generalizing about that individual's cognitive map over time. Hence, personalities are products of enculturation, as experienced by individuals, each with a particular genetic makeup. The term *personality* does not lend itself to a formal definition, but for our purposes we may take it as the distinctive way a person thinks, feels, and behaves.

THE DEVELOPMENT OF PERSONALITY

Although what one learns is important to personality development, most anthropologists assume that how one learns is no less important. With the psychoanalytic theorists, they view adult personality as having been strongly influenced by early childhood experiences. Indeed, many anthropologists have been strongly attracted by psychoanalytic theory, but with a difference. The psychoanalytic literature tends to be long on concepts, speculation, and clinical data, but short on less culture-bound studies. Anthropologists, for their part, are most interested in careful field studies that seek to shed light on personality development. For example, in Western society, men have traditionally been expected to be tough, aggressive, assertive, dominant, self-reliant, and achievement-oriented, whereas women have been expected to be passive, obedient, compliant, loyal, and caring. To many, these personality differences between the sexes seem so "natural" that they must be biologically grounded and therefore inescapable, unchangeable, and universal. But are they? Have anthropologists identified any psychological or personality characteristics which universally differentiate men and women?

As Margaret Mead's pioneering studies suggested, and subsequent cross-cultural studies have confirmed, there are no absolute personality differences between men and women. Among the Arapesh of New Guinea it is not just the women, but the men, too, who are gentle and nonaggressive, while among the Mundugamor (also of New

Personality: The distinctive way a person thinks, feels, and behaves.

Guinea), both sexes are angry and aggressive. In yet another New Guinea society, the Tchambuli, it is the men who decorate themselves, are vain, and are interested in art, theater, and petty gossip, whereas the women are unadorned, brisk, and efficient in such practical tasks as raising children, fishing, and marketing. Clearly, although each culture has different expectations for male–female behavior, the criteria of differentiation in one may bear no relation to those in another, and may in fact be poles apart. From this we may conclude there is no inevitability to the physical, political, and economic dominance that men have exerted over women in Western society, and that other arrangements are possible.

To understand the importance of child-rearing practices for the development of gender-related personality characteristics, we may look briefly at how children grow up among !Kung food foragers of Africa's Kalahari Desert, as compared with how they grow up in sedentary villages in the same region, where people tend small herds of goats and plant gardens for their livelihood.[3] In the former instance, dominance and aggressiveness are not tolerated in either sex; men are as mild-mannered as the women, while women are as energetic and self-reliant as the men. In the villages, by contrast, men and women exhibit personality characteristics approximating those that have traditionally been thought of as typically masculine and feminine in our own society. Among the food foragers, children of both sexes receive lengthy, intensive care from their mothers, whose attention is not diverted by the birth of new offspring until after the passage of many years. This is not to say that they are constantly with their children, for they are not; when they go gathering in the bush, they do not

[3]Patricia Draper, "!Kung Women: Contrasts in Sexual Egalitarianism in Foraging and Sedentary Contexts," in *Toward an Anthropology of Women*, ed. Rayna Reiter (New York: Monthly Review Press, 1975), pp. 77–109.

Margaret Mead (1901–1978)

Although all of the natural and social sciences are able to look back and pay homage to certain "founding fathers," anthropologists take pride in the fact that they have a number of "founding mothers" to whom they pay homage. One is Margaret Mead, who was encouraged by her teacher Franz Boas to pursue a career in anthropology at a time when most other academic disciplines rarely accepted women into their ranks. In 1925, she set out for Samoa, in order to test the theory, widely accepted at the time, that the biological changes of adolescence could not be accomplished without a great deal of stress, both social and psychological. In her book *Coming of Age in Samoa: A Psychological Study of Primitive Youth for Western Civilization*, she concluded that adolescence does not have to be a time of stress and strain, but that cultural conditions may make it so. Published in 1928, this book is generally credited as marking the beginning of the field of culture and personality.

Pioneering works are never without their faults, and *Coming of Age* is no exception, as Mead herself recognized. It would be strange indeed had we not learned things about becoming adults, both on and off Samoa, over the 60+ years that have passed since 1928. Highly publicized criticism of Mead's Samoa study that began after her death, however, was more a "media event" than a scientific discourse; among other things, it misrepresented both her work and anthropology itself.

While not the "last word" on Samoan youth, Mead's book stands as a landmark for several reasons: Not only was it a deliberate test of a Western psychological hypothesis; it also showed psychologists the value of modifying intelligence tests so as to be appropriate for the population under study; and by emphasizing the lesson to be drawn for Mead's own society, it laid the groundwork for the popularization of anthropology and advanced the cause of applied anthropology.

always take their offspring with them. At such times, the children will be supervised by their fathers or other adults of the community, one-third to one-half of whom are always to be found in camp on any given day. Because these include men as well as women, children are as much habituated to the male as to the female presence.

Fathers, too, spend much time with their offspring, interacting with them in nonauthoritarian ways. Although they may correct their children's behavior, so may women, who neither defer to male authority nor use the threat of paternal anger. Thus, no one grows up to respect or fear male authority any more than that of women. In fact, a child who misbehaves, instead of being punished, will simply be carried away and interested in some other more inoffensive activity. Nor are boys or girls assigned tasks to do; both sexes do equally little work, instead spending much of their time in play groups that include members of both sexes of widely different age. Thus, !Kung children have few experiences that set one sex apart from another. While older ones do amuse and monitor younger ones, this is done spontaneously rather than as an assigned chore, and the burden does not fall any more heavily on girls than boys.

Among the sedentary villagers, women spend much of their time in and around the home preparing food and attending to other domestic chores, as well as tending the children. The work of men, by contrast, requires them to spend many hours outside the household. As a result, children are less habituated to their presence. This remoteness, coupled with their more extensive knowledge

Among traditional !Kung, fathers spend much time with their children, interacting with them in nonauthoritarian ways, and no one grows up to respect or fear male authority any more than female authority.

of the outside world, tends to enhance their influence within the household.

Within the household, sex-role typing begins early, as girls, as soon as they are old enough, are expected to attend to many of the needs of their younger siblings, thereby allowing the mother more time to attend to her other domestic tasks. This not only shapes, but limits, the behavior of girls, who cannot range as widely or explore as freely and independently as they could without little brothers and sisters in tow. Indeed, they must stay close to home and be more careful, more obedient, and more sensitive to the wishes of others than they otherwise might be. Boys, by contrast, have little to do with the handling of infants, and when they are assigned work, it generally takes them away from the household. Thus, the space that girls occupy becomes restricted, and they are trained in behaviors that promote passivity and nurturance, whereas boys begin to become the distant, controlling figures they will be as adults.

From this comparison, we may begin to understand how a society's economy helps structure the way a child is brought up, and how this, in turn, influences the adult personality. It also shows that there are alternatives to the way that children are raised in Western societies and that by changing the conditions in which our children grow up, we might make it significantly easier for men and women to interact on an equal basis than has been the case so far. Thus, child rearing emerges as not only an anthropological problem, but a practical one as well.

Dependence Training

Although Margaret Mead compared sex and temperament in three different societies in the early 1930s, most cross-cultural studies of the effects of child rearing on personality have been carried out more recently by John and Beatrice Whiting and Irving L. Child, or their associates. Their work has demonstrated a number of apparent regularities.

For example, it is possible to distinguish at a broad level of generalization between two different patterns of child rearing, which we may label for convenience "dependence training" and "independence training."[4]

Dependence training tends to ensure compliance in the performance of assigned tasks and to keep individuals within the group. This pattern is typically associated with extended families, which consist of several husband–wife–children groups within the same household, and which are most apt to be found in societies in which the economy is based on subsistence farming. Such families are important, for they provide the large labor force necessary to till the soil, tend whatever flocks are kept, and carry out other part-time economic pursuits considered necessary for existence. Such large families, however, have built into them certain tensions that are potentially disruptive. For example, one of the adults typically makes the important family decisions, which must be followed by all other family members. In addition, the in-marrying spouses — husbands and/or wives — must subordinate themselves to the will of the group, which may be quite difficult for them. Dependence training helps to keep these potential problems under control, and involves both positive and negative aspects. On the positive side, indulgence is shown to young children, particularly in the form of prolonged oral gratification. Nursing continues for several years and is virtually on demand. This may be interpreted as rewarding the child for seeking support within the family, the main agent in meeting the child's needs. Also on the positive side, children at a relatively early age are assigned a number of child-care and domestic tasks, all of which make significant and obvious contributions to the family's welfare. Thus, family members all actively work to help and support one another. On the negative side, behavior that is interpreted by the adults as aggressive or sexual is apt to be actively discouraged. Moreover, the adults tend to be quite insistent on overall obedience,

> **Dependence training:** Child-rearing practices that foster compliance in the performance of assigned tasks and dependence on the family, rather than reliance on oneself.
>
> **Independence training:** Child-rearing practices that promote independence, self-reliance, and personal achievement on the part of the child.

which is seen as rendering the individual subordinate to the group. This combination of positive and negative reinforcement ideally produces individuals who are obedient, supportive, noncompetitive, and generally responsible, who will stay within the fold and not do anything potentially disruptive. Indeed, their very definition of "self" comes from their affiliation with a group, rather than from the mere fact of their individual existence.

Independence Training

By contrast, **independence training** emphasizes individual independence, self-reliance, and personal achievement. It is typically associated with societies in which nuclear families, consisting of a husband, wife, and their offspring, are independent rather than a part of some larger household group. Independence training is particularly characteristic of industrial societies such as our own, where self-reliance and personal achievement, especially on the part of men, are important traits for survival. Again, this pattern of training involves both positive and negative reinforcement. On the negative side, little emphasis is placed on prolonged oral gratification, and feeding is more by schedule than on demand. In the United States, for example, we like to establish a schedule as soon as possible, and it is not long before we start feeding infants baby food, and even try to get them to feed themselves. This has reached the point where many parents are delighted if they can prop their infants up in the crib or playpen so that they can hold their own bottles. In fact, infants do not receive the amount of attention they so often do in nonindustrialized societies. In the United States, mothers may be very affectionate with their 15-

[4]Eric Wolf, *Peasants* (Englewood Cliffs, N.J.: Prentice-Hall, 1966), pp. 69–70.

In the 1950s, in an effort to end its special relationship with Native Americans, the federal government began to relocate Indians to urban areas. For a people whose very definition of *self* springs from the group into which they were born, separation from family and kin often leads to severe mental depression.

week-old infants during the 20 percent of the time they are in contact with them but for the other 80 percent of the time the infants are more or less on their own. Collective responsibility is not encouraged in children; they are not given responsible tasks to perform until later in childhood, and these are generally few in number. Furthermore, their contribution to the welfare of the family is often not immediately apparent to the child, to whom the tasks appear arbitrary as a result.

Positive reinforcement is given to displays of aggression and sexuality, or at least they are tolerated to a greater degree than where dependence training is the rule. In schools, and even in the family, competition is emphasized. In our society we have gone to the extreme of turning the biological functions of infancy — eating, sleeping, crying, and elimination — into contests between parents and offspring. In our schools, considerable resources are devoted to competitive sports, but competition is fostered within the classroom as

well: overtly, through such devices as spelling bees and competition for prizes, covertly through such devices as grading on a curve. The latter practice, widely utilized for certain heavily enrolled courses on some college campuses, condemns some students to failure, irrespective of how well they actually do, so long as most of the class does better. This puts students in competition with each other, for one soon learns that one's own chances for a decent grade depend, as much as anything, on other members of the class not doing well themselves. If the stakes are high, students may devote considerable effort to placing obstacles in the way of classmates, so that they are prevented from doing too well. Thus, by the time one has grown up in our society, regardless of what one may think about it, one has received a clear message: Success is something that comes at someone else's expense. "Even the team spirit, so loudly touted" in school athletics (or out of school in Little League baseball and the like), "is merely a more efficient way,

In North American society, independence training pits individuals against one another through games and other forms of competition.

through limited cooperation, to 'beat' a greater number of people more efficiently."[5]

In sum, independence training generally encourages individuals to seek help and attention, rather than to give it, and to try to exert individual dominance. Such qualities are useful in societies with social structures that emphasize personal achievement and in which individuals are expected to look out for their own interests.

In food-foraging societies, child-rearing practices combine elements of independence and dependence training. "Share and share alike" is the order of the day, and so competitive behavior, which can interfere with the cooperation on which all else depends, is discouraged. Thus, infants receive much in the way of positive, affectionate attention from adults, along with prolonged oral gratification. This, as well as low pressure for compliance and a lack of emphasis on competition, encourages individuals to be more supportive of one another than is often the case in modern industrial societies. At the same time, personal achievement and independence are encouraged, for those individuals most capable of self-reliance are apt to be the most successful in the food quest.

[5]Colin M. Turnbull, *The Human Cycle* (New York: Simon & Schuster, 1983), p. 74.

In the United States the argument has sometimes been made (not by anthropologists) that "permissive" child rearing produces irresponsible adults. Since the practices of food foragers seem to be about as "permissive" as they can get, and yet socially responsible adults are produced, it is worth taking a closer look at how this is achieved. In the following Original Study, we see how children grow up among the Mbuti, hunters and gatherers who live in Zaire's Ituri forest.

It must be stressed that no particular system of child rearing is inherently better or worse than any other; what matters is whether the system is functional or dysfunctional in the context of a particular society. If compliant adults, who are accepting of authority, are required, then independence training will not work well in that society. Nor will dependence training serve very well a society in which adults are expected to be independent, self-reliant, and questioning of authority. Sometimes, however, inconsistencies develop, and here we may look again at our own situation. As we have seen, independence training generally tends to be stressed in the United States, and we often speak in glowing terms of the worth of personal independence, the dignity of the individual, and so on. Our pronouncements, however, do not always suit our actions. In spite of our professed desire for personal independence, there seems to be a strong underlying desire for compliance. This is reflected, for example, in the decisions handed down over the past 15 years or so by the Supreme Court, which, as observers of the Court have noted, have increasingly favored the rights of authority over those of individuals. It is reflected as well by the way the federal government in the early 1980s, at a time when it was working to ease up on enforcement of legislation dealing with civil rights, aggressively sought to prosecute to the fullest extent young men who, for whatever reason, did not register for the draft. Finally, it is reflected by the fate of "whistle-blowers" in government bureaus, who, if they don't lose their jobs, are at least shunted to one side and passed by when the rewards are handed out. In business as well as in government,

---

ORIGINAL STUDY
Growing Up among the Mbuti[6]

In the first three years of life every Mbuti alive experiences almost total security. The infant is breast-fed for those three years, and is allowed almost every freedom. Regardless of gender, the infant learns to have absolute trust in both male and female parents. If anything, the father is just another kind of mother, for in the second year the father formally introduces the child to its first solid food. There used to be a beautiful ritual in which the mother presented the child to the father in the middle of the camp, where all important statements are made (anyone speaking from the middle of the camp must be listened to). The father took the child and held it to his breast, and the child would try to suckle, crying *"ema, ema,"* or "mother." The father would shake his head, and say "no, father . . . *eba,"* but like a mother (the Mbuti said), then give the child its first solid food.

At three the child ventures out into the world on its own and enters the *bopi*, what we might call a playground, a tiny camp perhaps a hundred yards from the main camp, often on the edge of a stream. The *bopi* were indeed

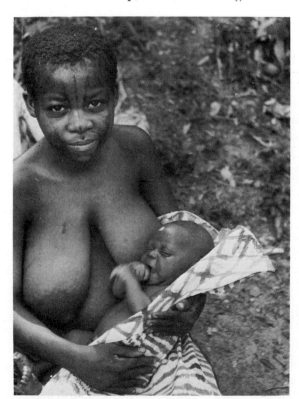

For the Mbuti, education into social consciousness begins at the mother's breast. Here the infant is wrapped in a freshly cut and decorated piece of bark cloth, symbolizing its ultimate dependence on the forest, the mother and father of them all.

playgrounds, and often very noisy ones, full of fun and high spirits. But they were also rigorous training grounds for eventual economic responsibility. On entry to the *bopi*, for one thing, the child discovers the importance of age as a structural principle, and the relative unimportance of gender and biological kinship. The *bopi* is the private world of the children. Younger youths may occasionally venture in, but if adults or elders try, as they sometimes do when angry at having their afternoon snooze interrupted, they invariably get driven out, taunted, and ridiculed. Children, among the Mbuti, have rights, but they also learn that they have responsibilities. Before the hunt sets out each day it is the children, sometimes the younger youths, who light the hunting fire.

Ritual among the Mbuti is often so informal and apparently casual that it may pass unnoticed at first. Yet insofar as ritual involves symbolic acts that represent unspoken, perhaps even unthought, concepts or ideals, or invoke other states of being, alternative frames of mind and reference, then Mbuti life is full of ritual. The hunting fire is one of the more obvious of such rituals. Early in the morning children would take firebrands from the *bopi*, where they always lit their own fire with embers from their family hearths, and set off on the trail by which the hunt was to leave that day (the direction of each day's hunt was always settled by discussion the night before). Just a short distance from the camp they lit a fire at the base of a large tree, and covered it with special leaves that made it give off a column of dense smoke. Hunters leaving the camp, both men and women, and such youths and children as were going with them, had to pass by this fire. Some did so casually, without stopping or looking, but passing through the smoke. Others reached into the smoke with their hands as they passed, rubbing the smoke into their bodies. A few always stopped, for a moment, and let the smoke envelop them, only then almost dreamily moving off.

And indeed it *was* a form of intoxication, for the smoke invoked the spirit of the forest, and by passing through it the hunters sought to fill themselves with that spirit, not so much to make the hunt successful as to minimize the sacrilege of killing. Yet they, the hunters, could not light the fire themselves. After all, they were already contaminated by death. Even youths, who daily joined the hunt at the edges, catching any game that escaped the nets, by hand, if they could, were not pure enough to invoke the spirit of forestness. But young children were uncontaminated, as yet untainted by contact with the original sin of the Mbuti. It was their responsibility to light the fire, and if it was not lit then the hunt would not take place, or as the Mbuti put it, the hunt *could* not take place.

In this way even the children in Mbuti society, at the first of the four age levels that dominate Mbuti social structure, are given very real social responsibility and see themselves as a part of that structure, by virtue of their purity. After all, they have just been born from the source of all purity, the forest itself. By the same reasoning, the elders, who are about to return to that ultimate source of all being, through death, are at least closer to purity than the adults, who are daily contaminated by killing. Elders no longer go on the hunt. So, like the children, the elders have important sacred ritual responsibilities in the Mbuti division of labor by age. In the *bopi* the children play, but they have no "games" in the strict sense of the word. Lévi-Strauss has perceptively compared games with rituals, suggesting that whereas in a game the players start theoretically equal but end up unequal, in a ritual just the reverse takes place. All are equalized. Mbuti children could be seen every day playing in the *bopi*, but not once did I see a game, not one activity that smacked of any kind of competition, except perhaps that competition that it is necessary for us all to feel from time to time, competition with our own private and personal inadequacies. One such pastime (rather than game) was tree climbing. A dozen or so children would climb up a young sapling. Reaching the top, their weight brought the sapling bending down until it almost touched the ground. Then all the children leapt off together, shrieking as the young tree sprang upright again with a rush. Sometimes one child, male or female, might stay on a little too long, either out of fear, or out of bravado, or from sheer carelessness or bad timing. Whatever the reason, it was a lesson most children only needed to be taught once, for the result was that you got flung upward with the tree, and were lucky to escape with no more than a few bruises and a very bad fright.

Other pastimes taught the children the rules of hunting and gathering. Frequently elders, who stayed in camp when the hunt went off, called the children into the main camp and enacted a mock hunt with them there. Stretching a discarded piece of net across the camp, they pretended to be animals, showing the children how to drive them into the nets. And, of course, the children played house, learning the patterns of cooperation that would be necessary for them later in life. They also learned the prime lesson of egality, other than for purposes of division of labor making no distinction between male and female, this nuclear family or that. All in the *bopi* were *apua'i* to each other, and so they would remain throughout their lives. At every age level — childhood, youth, adulthood, or old age — everyone of that level is *apua'i* to all the others. Only adults sometimes (but so rarely that I think it was only done as a kind of joke, or possibly insult) made the distinction that the Bira do, using *apua'i* for male and *amua'i* for female. Male or female, for the Mbuti, if you are the same age you are *apua'i*, and that means that you share everything equally, regardless of kinship or gender.

Sometime before the age of puberty boys or girls, whenever they feel ready, move back into the main camp from the *bopi* and join the youths. This is when they must assume new responsibilities, which for the youths are primarily political. Already, in the *bopi*, the children become involved in disputes, and are sometimes instrumental in settling them by ridicule, for nothing hurts an adult more than being ridiculed publicly by children. The art of reason, however, is something they learn from the youths, and it is the youths who apply the art of reason to the settlement of disputes.

When puberty comes it separates them, for the first time in their experience, from each other as *apua'i*. Very plainly girls are different from boys. When a girl has her first menstrual period the whole camp celebrates with the wild *elima* festival, in which the girl, and some of her chosen girl friends, are the center of all attention, living together in a special *elima* house. Male youths sit outside the *elima* house and wait for the girls to come out, usually in the afternoon, for the *elima* singing. They sing in antiphony, the girls leading, the boys responding. Boys come from neighboring territories all around, for this is a time of courtship. But there are always eligible youths within the camp as well, and the *elima* girl may well choose girls from other territories to come and join her, so there is more than enough excuse for every youth to carry on several flirtations, legitimate or illegitimate. I have known even first cousins to flirt with each other, but learned to be prudent enough not to pull out my kinship charts and point this out—well, not in public anyway.

The *elima* is more than a premarital festival, more than a joint initiation of youth into adulthood, and more than a rite of passage through puberty, though it is all those things. It is a public recognition of the opposition of male and female, and every *elima* is used to highlight the *potential* for conflict that lies in that opposition. As at other times of crisis, at puberty, a time of change and uncertainty, the Mbuti bring all the major forms of conflict out into the open. And the one that evidently most concerns them is the male/female opposition.

The adults begin to play a special form of "tug of war" that is clearly a ritual rather than a game. All the men are on one side, the women on the other. At first it looks like a game, but quickly it becomes clear that the objective is for *neither* side to win. As soon as the women begin to win, one of them will leave the end of the line and run around to join the men, assuming a deep male voice and in other ways ridiculing manhood. Then, as the men begin to win, a male will similarly join the women, making fun of womanhood as he does so. Each adult on changing sides attempts to outdo all the others in ridiculing the opposite sex. Finally, when nearly all have switched sides, and sexes, the ritual battle between the genders simply collapses into hysterical laughter, the contestants letting go of the rope, falling onto the ground, and rolling over with mirth. Neither side wins, both are equalized very nicely, and each learns the essential lesson, that there should be *no* contest.

[6]From Colin M. Turnbull, *Mbuti Pygmies: Change and Adaptation*, pp. 39–47; copyright © 1983 by Holt, Rinehart and Winston, Inc. Reprinted by permission of the publisher.

there is a tendency for the rewards to be given to those who go along with the system, while criticism, no matter how constructive, is a risky business. In corporate as well as government bureaucracies, the ability to please, not shake up the system, is what is required for success. Yet in spite of pressures for compliance, which would be most effectively served by dependence training, we continue to raise our children to be independent, and then wonder why they so often refuse to behave the way adults would have them behave.

GROUP PERSONALITY

From studies such as those reviewed here, it is clear that personality, child-rearing practices, and other aspects of culture are interrelated in some kind of nonrandom way. Whiting and Child have argued that the child-rearing practices of a society originate in basic customs surrounding nourishment, shelter, and protection, and that these child-rearing practices in turn produce particular kinds of adult personalities.[7] The trouble is that correlations do not prove cause and effect. We are still left with the fact that, however logical it may seem, such a causal chain remains an unproven hypothesis.

The existence of a close, if not causal, interrelationship between child-rearing practices and personality, coupled with variation in child-rearing practices from one society to another, has led to a number of attempts to characterize groups in terms of particular kinds of personalities. Indeed, common sense suggests that personalities appropriate for one culture may be less appropriate for some others. For example, an egocentric, aggressive personality would be out of place where cooperation and sharing are the keys to success. Or, in the context of traditional Penobscot Indian culture, which we examined briefly earlier in this chapter, an open and extroverted personality would seem inappropriate, for it would be inconsistent with the prevailing conception of the self.

Unfortunately, common sense, like conventional wisdom in general, isn't always true. The question is worth asking: Can we describe a group personality without falling into stereotyping? The answer appears to be a qualified yes; in an abstract way, we may speak of a generalized "cultural personality" for a society, so long as we do not expect to find a uniformity of personalities within that society. Put another way, each individual develops certain personality characteristics that, from common experience, resemble those of other people. Yet because each individual is exposed to unique experiences as well, may react to common experiences in novel ways, and brings to these experiences a unique (except for the case of identical twins) genetic potential, each also acquires distinct personality traits. Because individual personalities differ, the organization of diversity is important to all cultures.

As an example of the fact that individual personalities in traditional societies are far from uniform, consider the case of the Yanomamö, whom we discussed in Chapter 12. Among them, individual men strive to achieve a reputation for fierceness and aggressiveness that they are willing to defend at the risk of serious personal injury and death. And yet there are men among the Yanomamö who are quiet and somewhat retiring. In any gathering of these people, the quiet ones are all too easily overlooked by outsiders, when almost everyone else is in the front row pushing and demanding attention. Not only do traditional societies include a range of personalities, but some of those personalities may differ in no important way from those of some individuals in our own society. As Ruth Landes once observed, an Ojibwa Indian shaman she knew at Emo, Ontario, displayed the same "cold, moralistic, driven personality" as does ex-President Nixon.[8]

MODAL PERSONALITY

Obviously, any fruitful approach to the problem of group personality must recognize that each individual is unique to a degree in both inheritance and

[7]John W. M. Whiting and Irvin L. Child, *Child Training and Personality: A Cross-cultural Study* (New Haven, Conn.: Yale University Press, 1953).

[8]Ruth Landes, "Comment," *Current Anthropology*, 23 (1982): 401.

A Yanamamö man shows his fierceness in a warfare stance. While flamboyant, belliger-
ent personalities are especially compatible with the Yanamamö ideal that men should be
fierce, some are quiet and retiring.

life experiences, and that we should expect a range of personality types in any society. In addition, personality traits that may be regarded as appropriate in men may not be so regarded in women, and vice versa. Given all this, we may focus our attention on the **modal personality** of a group, defined as the personality typical of a culturally bounded population, as indicated by the central tendency of a defined frequency distribution. Modal personality is a statistical concept, and as such, it opens up for investigation the questions of how societies organize diversity and how diversity relates to culture change. Such questions are easily overlooked if one associates one particular type of personality with one particular culture, as older approaches (like that of Ruth Benedict, described in the box on p. 351) tended to do. At the same time, modal personalities of different groups can be compared.

Data on modal personality are best gathered by means of psychological tests administered to a sample of the population in question. Those most often used include the Rorschach, or "ink-blot," test and the Thematic Apperception Test (TAT). The latter consists of pictures, which the individual being tested is asked to explain or tell what is

Modal personality: The personality typical of a society as indicated by the central tendency of a defined frequency distribution.

going on. There are, as well, other sorts of projective tests that have been used at one time or another; all have in common a purposeful ambiguity, so that the individual tested has to structure the situation before responding. The idea is that one's personality is projected into the ambiguous situation. Along with the use of such tests, observations recording the frequency of certain behaviors, the collection and analysis of life histories and dreams, and the analysis of oral literature are also helpful in eliciting data on modal personality.

It is clear that the concept of modal personality as a means of dealing with group personality, while having much to recommend it, presents certain difficulties. One of these is the complexity of the measurement techniques themselves, which may be difficult to carry out in the field. For one thing, an adequate representative sample of subjects is necessary. The problem here is twofold: making sure that the sample is genuinely representative

Ruth Fulton Benedict (1887–1947)

Ruth Benedict came late to anthropology; upon her graduation from Vassar College, she taught high school English, published poetry, studied dancing, and tried her hand at social work. In anthropology, she developed the idea that culture was a projection of the personality of those who created it. In her most famous book, *Patterns of Culture* (1934), she compared the cultures of three peoples — the Kwakiutl of western Canada, the Zuni of the southwestern United States, and the Dobuans of Melanesia. She held that each was comparable to a great work of art, with an internal coherence and consistency of its own. Seeing the Kwakiutl as egocentric, individualistic, and ecstatic in their rituals, she labeled their cultural configuration

"Dionysian"; the Zuni, whom she saw as living by the golden mean, wanting no part of excess or disruptive psychological states, and distrusting of individualism, she characterized as "Apollonian." The Dobuans, whose culture seemed magic-ridden, with everyone fearing and hating everyone else, she characterized as "paranoid."

Although *Patterns of Culture* still enjoys popularity in some nonanthropological circles, anthropologists have long since abandoned its approach as impressionistic and not susceptible to replication. To compound the problem, Benedict's characterizations of cultures are misleading (the supposedly "Apollonian" Zunis, for example, sometimes indulge in such seemingly "Dionysian" practices as sword swallowing and walking over hot coals), and the use of such value-laden terms as "paranoid" prejudices others toward it. Nonetheless, the book did have an enormous and valuable influence in focusing attention on the problem of the interrelation between culture and personality, and in popularizing the reality of cultural variation.

---

and having the time and personnel necessary to administer the tests, conduct interviews, and so on, all of which can be lengthy proceedings. Also, the tests themselves constitute a problem, for those devised in one cultural setting may not be appropriate in another. This is more of a problem with the TAT than with some other tests, although different pictures have been devised for other cultures. Still, to minimize any hidden cultural bias, it is best not to rely on projective tests alone. In addition to all this, there are often language problems, which may lead to misinterpretation. Then, too, the field investigator may be in conflict with cultural values. A people like the Penobscot, whose concept of self we surveyed earlier, would not take kindly to revealing their dreams to strangers. Finally, there is the question of what is being measured. Just what, for example, is aggression? Does everyone define it the same way? Is it a legitimate entity, or does it involve other variables?

NATIONAL CHARACTER

No discussion of group personality would be complete without a consideration of national character, which popular thought all too often ascribes to the citizens of many different countries. Henry Miller epitomizes this view when he says, "Madmen are logical — as are the French," suggesting that Frenchmen, in general, are overly rational. A Parisian, on the other hand, might view North Americans as maudlin and unsophisticated. Similarly, we all have in mind some image, perhaps not well defined, of the "typical" Russian or Japanese or Englishman. Essentially, these are simply stereotypes. We might well ask, however, if these stereotypes have any basis in fact. Is there, in reality, such a thing as national character?

Some anthropologists have thought that maybe the answer was yes. Accordingly, national character studies were begun that sought to discover basic personality traits shared by the majority of

Gentleness at home, but brutality and sadism in war, were portrayed as important aspects of Japanese national character by North Americans at the height of World War II. Such stereotypes of Japanese character were as much a reflection of North American wartime attitudes and passions as anything else.

the peoples of modern countries. Along with this went an emphasis on child-rearing practices and education as the factors theoretically responsible for such characteristics. Margaret Mead, Ruth Benedict, Weston LaBarre, and Geoffrey Gorer conducted pioneering studies of national character, using relatively small samples of informants. During World War II, techniques were developed for studying "culture at a distance" through the analysis of newspapers, books, and photographs. By investigating memories of childhood and cultural attitudes, and by examining graphic material for the appearance of recurrent themes and values, researchers tried to portray national character.

The Japanese

At the height of World War II, Geoffrey Gorer attempted to determine the underlying reasons for the "contrast between the all-pervasive gentleness

of Japanese family life in Japan, which has charmed nearly every visitor, and the overwhelming brutality and sadism of the Japanese at War." Strongly under the influence of Freud, Gorer sought his causes in the toilet-training practices of the Japanese, which he believed were severe and threatening. He suggested that because Japanese infants were forced to control their sphincters before they had acquired the necessary muscular or intellectual development, they grew up filled with repressed rage. As adults, the Japanese were able to express this rage in their brutality in war.[9]

In the midst of war Gorer was not able to do fieldwork in Japan. After the war was over, though, the toilet-training hypothesis could be tested, at which time it was found that the severity of Japa-

[9]Geoffrey Gorer, "Themes in Japanese Culture," *Transactions of the New York Academy of Sciences*, Series II, 5 (1943).

nese toilet training was a myth. Children were not subject to severe threats of punishment. Nor were all Japanese soldiers brutal and sadistic in war; some were, but then so were some North Americans. Also, the fact that the postwar Japanese took the lead in peace movements in the Far East hardly conformed to the wartime image of brutality.

Gorer's study, along with others by Benedict and LaBarre, was most important, not in revealing the importance of Japanese sphincters on the national character, but in pointing out the dangers of generalizing from insufficient evidence and employing simplistic individual psychology to explain complex social phenomena.

Objections to National Character Studies

Critics of national character theories have emphasized the tendency for such work to be based on unscientific and overgeneralized data. The concept of modal personality has a certain statistical validity, they argue, but to generalize the qualities of a complex nation on the basis of such limited data is to lend insufficient recognition to the countless individuals who vary from the generalization. Further, such studies tend to be highly subjective; for example, the tendency during the late 1930s and 1940s for anthropologists to characterize the German people as aggressive paranoids was obviously a reflection of wartime hostilities and not of scientific objectivity.

It has also been pointed out that occupational and social status tends to cut across national boundaries. A French farmer may have less in common with a French factory worker than he does with a German farmer. Yet in spite of all the difficulties, and the valid criticisms of past studies, Francis Hsu, in his presidential address to the American Anthropological Association in 1978, asserted that there is a new urgency to studies of national character, and that without them, we will probably never really understand what motivates the leaders and civil servants of modern nations.[10]

[10]Francis L. K. Hsu, "The Cultural Problem of the Cultural Anthropologist," *American Anthropologist*, 81 (1979): 528.

Core values: Those values especially promoted by a particular culture.

Hsu's approach has been to study the **core values** of a nation's culture and related personality traits. The Chinese, he suggests, value kin ties and cooperation above all else. To them, mutual dependence is the very essence of personal relationships, and has been for thousands of years. Compliance and subordination of one's will to that of family and kin transcends all else, while self-reliance is neither promoted nor a source of pride. Following the 1949 revolution, Mao Tse Tung sought to expand the sphere of affect to the nation as a whole, with himself as the "father" of all citizens.

Perhaps the core value held in highest esteem by North Americans of European descent is that of "rugged individualism," at least for men (only recently has this become recognized as a valid ideal for women). Nowadays, the single individual is supposed to be able to achieve anything he or she likes, given a willingness to work hard enough. From their earliest years, individuals are subjected to relentless pressures to excel, and as we have already noted, competition and winning are seen as crucial to this. Undoubtedly, this contributes to the "restlessness" and "drivenness" of North American society, and to the degree that it motivates individuals to work hard and to go where the economy needs them, it fits well with the needs of an industrial society. Thus, while the Chinese are firmly bound into a larger group to which they have lifelong obligations, North Americans are isolated from all other kin save husband or wife (and something like 50 percent of marriages end in divorce). Even parents and children have no legal obligations to one another, once the latter have reached the age of majority. This isolation of the individual has been suggested as one reason for the North American obsession with pets. A dog or a cat may partially compensate for limited opportunities to maintain close affective ties with other human beings.

The core values of Chinese culture promote the integration of the individual into a larger group, as in the case of these workers exercising together. The core values of Anglo-American culture, by contrast, promote the separation of the individual from the group.

ABNORMAL PERSONALITY

The concept of modal personality holds that a range of personalities will exist in any society. The modal personality itself may be thought of as normal for that society, but may in fact be shared by less than half the population. What of those personalities that differ from this? The Dobuans of New Guinea and certain Plains Indians furnish examples of normal and abnormal behavior strikingly different from our own.

NORMAL AND ABNORMAL BEHAVIOR

The individual man in Dobu whom the other villagers considered neurotic and thoroughly disoriented was a man who was naturally friendly and found activity an end in itself. He was a pleasant fellow who did not seek to overthrow his fellows or to punish them. He worked for anyone who asked him, and he was tireless in carrying out their commands. In any other Dobuan, this would have been scandalous behavior, but in him it was regarded as merely silly. The village treated him in a kindly fashion, not taking advantage of him, nor making sport of or ridiculing him, but he was definitely regarded as one who stood outside the normal conventions of behavior.

Among certain Plains Indians, a man, compelled by supernatural spirits, could assume woman's attire and perform woman's work; he could even marry another man, although not all men who assumed a woman's identity were homosexuals, nor did all homosexuals behave in this way. Under this institution of the "berdache," an individual would find himself living in a dramatically different manner from most men; yet, although the berdache was rare among Indians, it was *not*

Among Indians of North America's Great Plains, men like the one shown here could dress and act like women without being regarded as abnormal. By contrast, such behavior in Western society traditionally has been regarded as abnormal.

looked upon as the behavior of an abnormal individual. Quite the contrary, for the berdache was often sought out as a curer, artist, matchmaker, and companion of warriors, because of the great spiritual power he was thought to possess.

In Western societies like the United States, behavior like that of the Plains Indian berdaches has traditionally been regarded as abnormal. If a man dresses as a woman, it is generally regarded as a cause for concern and is likely to lead to psychiatric intervention. Nor have jobs traditionally filled by women been seen as desirable for men. By con-

trast, women are much more free to wear masculine-style clothing and to assume jobs more usually held by men, even though to do so may cause them to be branded as somehow "unfeminine." What lies behind this are traditional values (jobs traditionally associated with men have been more highly valued then those associated with women) and a pattern of child rearing that creates problems of gender identity for both sexes, although of a different sort for each sex.

As Nancy Chodorow has argued, in our society, girls have traditionally been raised by women, usually their mothers, and most still are. Thus, feminine role models are constantly available and easily understandable. Very early, girls begin to do the things that women do, and gradually and continuously acquire the identity deemed appropriate for their sex. Once they enter school, however, they learn that women are not all-powerful and prestigious, that it is men who generally run things and who are portrayed as the ones who have most advanced human progress. As a consequence, a girl finds that the feminine identity, which has become so easy for her, leaves much to be desired. Under the circumstances, she is bound to feel a certain resentment toward it.

Boys have a different problem; like girls they too begin their lives in a feminine world. With adult men out of the house working, not only is a male model rarely present, but it is the mother who seems to be all-powerful. Under these conditions, boys begin to develop a feminine identity with its expected compliant personality. In keeping with all this, it used to be that boys were even dressed as girls (dresses for little boys were not dropped from the Sears catalog until 1940) until the age thought proper to "graduate" into less feminine attire arrived. Once out of the house and in school, boys learn that they must switch from a female to a male identity; in a sense, they must renounce femininity and prove their maleness, in a way that girls do not have to prove their femaleness. Generally speaking, the more distant is a boy's father (or other male companion of his mother), the greater the boy's insecurity in his male identity and the greater his compulsion to be seen as really masculine. To do this, he must strive all the harder to be aggressive and assert his dominance, particularly over women.

Nancy Chodorow sums up the situation as follows:

> Sex-role ideology and socialization for these roles seem to ensure that neither boys nor girls can attain both stable identity and meaningful roles. The tragedy of woman's socialization is not that she is left unclear, as is the man, about her basic sexual identity. This identity is ascribed to her, and she does not need to prove to herself or to society that she had earned it or continues to have it. Her problem is that this identity is clearly devalued in the society in which she lives. This does not mean that women too should be required to compete for identity, to be assertive and to need to achieve — to "do" like men. Nor does it suggest that it is not crucial for everyone, men and women alike, to have a stable sexual identity. But until male "identity" does not depend upon men's proving themselves, their "doing" will be a reaction to insecurity, not a creative exercise of their humanity, and woman's "being," far from being an easy and positive acceptance of self, will be a resignation to inferiority. And as long as women must live through their children, and men do not genuinely contribute to socialization and provide easily accessible role models, women will continue to bring up sons who's sexual identity depends upon devaluing femininity inside and outside themselves, and daughters who must accept this devalued position and resign themselves to producing more men who will perpetuate the system that devalues them.[11]

What this example shows us is how a culture may itself actually induce certain kinds of psychological conflicts, with important consequences for the entire society. Although the conditions under which children are raised in our society are now changing, we have a long way to go before the conflicts just described become things of the past. But

what has seemed to be "normal" in the past may become "abnormal" in the future.

The standards that define normal behavior for any culture are determined by that culture itself. Obviously, no society could survive if suicide were looked upon as normal behavior; yet each culture determines for itself the circumstances under which suicide may be acceptable. The Aymara of the Bolivian Andes, for example, disapprove of suicide, but a man possessed by spirits of the dead, which cannot be exorcised, may take his own life and yet be remembered with respect. Given his affliction, suicide is considered to be perfectly reasonable. Moral acts are those that conform to cultural standards of good and evil, and each society determines those standards for itself. Morality is thus based on culturally determined ideals.

Is all this to suggest that "normality" is a meaningless concept as it is applied to personality? Within the context of a given culture, the concept of normal personality is quite meaningful. A. I. Hallowell somewhat ironically observed that it is normal to share the delusions traditionally accepted by one's society. Abnormality involves the development of a delusional system not sanctioned by the culture. When an individual is disturbed because he or she cannot adequately measure up to the norms of society and yet be happy, the individual may be termed neurotic. When an individual's delusional system is significantly different from that of his or her society and in no way reflects its norms, the individual may be termed psychotic.

Culturally induced conflicts not only can, if severe enough, produce psychosis but can determine the form of the psychosis as well. In a culture that encourages aggressiveness and suspicion, the madman is that individual who is passive and trusting. In a culture that encourages passivity and trust, the madman is that individual who is aggressive and suspicious. Just as each society establishes its own norms, each individual is unique in his or her perceptions. Many anthropologists see the only meaningful criterion for personality evaluation as the correlation between personality and social conformity.

---

[11]Nancy Chodorow, "Being and Doing: A Cross-cultural Examination of the Socialization of Males and Females," in *Woman in Sexist Society*, Vivian Gornick and Barbara K. Moran, eds. (New York: Basic Books, 1971), p. 193.

Anthropologists and Mental Health

One consequence of "development" in the newly emerged states of Africa, Asia, and Central and South America is a rising incidence of mental disturbances among their people. Similarly, mental health problems abound among ethnic minorities living within industrialized countries. Unfortunately, orthodox approaches to mental health have not been successful at dealing with these problems, for a number of reasons. For one, different ethnic groups have different attitudes toward mental disorders than do medical practitioners (who are products of Western culture). For another, the diverse conditions under which different ethnic groups live produce culturally patterned health conditions, including culture-bound syndromes not recognized by the orthodox medical profession. Among Puerto Ricans, for example, a widely held belief is that spirits are active in the world and that they influence human behavior. Thus, for someone with a psychiatric problem, it makes sense to go to a native spiritist for help, rather than to a psychiatrist. In a Puerto Rican community, going to a spiritist is "normal." Not only does the client not understand the symbols of psychiatry, but to go to a psychiatrist implies that he or she is "crazy" and requires restraint, or removal from the community.

Although practitioners of Western medicine have traditionally regarded spiritists and other folk healers as ignorant people, if not charlatans, experiments were begun in the 1950s to provide community-based treatment in which psychiatrists cooperated with traditional healers. Since then, this approach has gained widespread acceptance in many parts of the world, as when (in 1977) the World Health Organization advocated cooperation between health professionals and native specialists (including herbalists and midwives). As a consequence, many anthropologists have found work as cultural brokers, studying the cultural system of the client population and explaining this to the health professionals, while at the same time explaining the world of the psychiatrists to the folk healers and the client population.

As an example, as a part of the Miami Community Mental Health Program, a field team led by an anthropologist was set up to work with the Puerto Rican community of Dade County. Like other ethnic communities in the area, this one was characterized by low incomes, high rents, and a plethora of health (including mental health) problems, yet health facilities and social service agencies were underutilized. Working in the community, the team successfully built up support networks among the Puerto Ricans, involving extended families, churches, clubs, and spiritists. At the same time, they gathered information about the community, which was provided to appropriate social service agencies. At the Dade County Hospital, team members acted as brokers between the psychiatric personnel and their Puerto Rican clients, and a training program was implemented for the mental health staff.

While it is true that culture defines what is and is not normal behavior, the situation is complicated by findings suggesting that major categories of mental disorders may be universal types of human affliction. Take, for example, the case of schizophrenia, probably the most common of all psychoses. Individuals afflicted by schizophrenia experience distortions of reality that impair their ability to function adequately, and so they withdraw from the social world into their own psycho-

Ethnic psychoses: Mental disorders specific to particular ethnic groups.

logical shell, from which they do not emerge. Although environmental factors play a role, there is evidence that schizophrenia is caused by a biochemical disorder for which there is an inherited tendency. One of its more severe forms is paranoid schizophrenia. Those suffering from it fear and mistrust almost everyone; they hear voices that whisper dreadful things to them, and they are convinced that someone is out to get them. Acting on this conviction, they engage in bizarre types of behavior, which leads to their removal from society, usually to a mental institution.

A precise image of paranoid schizophrenia is one of the so-called **ethnic psychoses** known as *Windigo*. Such psychoses involve symptoms of mental disorder specific to particular ethnic groups. Windigo psychosis is limited to northern Algonkian Indian groups such as the Chippewa, Cree, and Ojibwa. In their traditional belief systems, these northern Indians recognized the existence of cannibalistic monsters called Windigos. Individuals afflicted by the psychosis developed the delusion that falling under control of these monsters, they themselves were being transformed into Windigos, with a craving for human flesh. At the same time, they saw people around them turning into various edible animals — fat, juicy beavers, for instance. Although the victim of Windigo psychosis developed the exaggerated fear of actually indulging in cannibalism, there are no known instances of human flesh being actually eaten, at least as the result of the psychosis alone. For this reason, some anthropologists have doubted the existence of the psychosis, but the fear of cannibalism was real enough to the Indians.

At first, Windigo psychosis seems quite different from Western clinical cases of paranoid schizophrenia, but a closer look suggests otherwise; the disorder was merely being expressed in ways compatible with traditional northern Algonkian culture. Ideas of persecution, instead of being directed toward other humans, are directed toward supernatural beings (the Windigo monsters); cannibalistic panic replaces homosexual panic, and the like. The northern Algonkian Indian, like the Westerner, expresses his or her problem in terms compatible with the appropriate view of the self and its behavioral environment. The northern Algonkian, though, was removed from society, not by being committed to a mental institution, but by being killed.

Windigo behavior has seemed exotic and dramatic to the Westerner. When all is said and done, however, the imagery and symbolism that a psychotic person has to draw upon is that which his or her culture has to offer, and in northern Algonkian culture, these involve myths in which cannibal giants figure prominently. By contrast, the delusions of Irish schizophrenics draw upon the images and symbols of Irish Catholicism, and feature Virgin and Savior motifs. Anglo-Americans, on the other hand, tend toward secular or electromagnetic persecution delusions. The underlying structure of the mental disorder is the same in all cases, but its expression is culturally specific.

CURRENT TRENDS IN PSYCHOLOGICAL ANTHROPOLOGY

Although they may now be criticized for being impressionistic and not susceptible to replication, rather than scientific, the classic studies of Benedict, Mead, and other pioneers in the investigation of culture and personality remain important for their contribution to the realization that human behavior is relative. The theory of cultural relativity resulting from the study of many societies undermined the ethnocentrism common to all human groups. Anthropologists have established that cultures are indeed different and that these differences are associated with personality differences.

By 1960, however, there was a sense that a point of diminishing returns had been reached in the study of personality differences between cultures. Instead of looking at individual differences within cultures as annoying distortions of norms, many culture and personality specialists began to look more closely at such differences in order to understand better such behavior as the altered states of consciousness employed by religious practitioners in many of the world's societies. Others began to devote more attention to the study of cognitive

Of interest to anthropologists are the effects of day-care centers on child development. Among monkeys and apes, infants deprived of maternal attention and affection, if they manage to survive at all, will not develope normally. Among humans, substitutes who are not strangers to the child may take over for the mother, with no ill effects on the child's development. However, if personnel are not recruited from the same neighborhood and there is staff turnover, eight to ten hours a day spent in a child-care center may produce children who cannot form social bonds.

processes — how people think and perceive the world in which they live. By observing how individual members of particular societies segment, interpret, and express reality through language, anthropologists should be able to draw general conclusions about the implicit mental representations of reality in the minds of these individual culture bearers — their cognitive "models" of the world around them. This, of course, continues an interest in the self and its behavioral environment, as discussed earlier in this chapter.

An interest in psychoanalytical theory has always characterized culture and personality studies, but current investigators are combining psychoanalytically based theories with biological and social variables to discover, analyze, and explain the laws of cultural dynamics. Thus, current studies are examining human genetic and ecological processes that are entirely independent of culture, but that cause change in the human biological system upon which culture depends.

Studies of child-rearing practices, a central concern of culture and personality studies from their earliest days, have burgeoned into a specialized field in their own right. Today the emphasis is on cross-cultural studies of physiological maturation, interpersonal contacts, group composition, and the like, often to test the theories developed in the other social and behavioral sciences. They have been broadened, however, to embrace the new subfield of educational anthropology. Similarly, the old interest in abnormal personality has given birth to numerous cross-cultural studies of mental health and illness, which are now part of the new specialty called medical anthropology.

In sum, the field of culture and personality has expanded and become a highly varied field. As a reflection of this, specialists began in the 1960s to refer to their field as psychological anthropology. This anthropological specialty is flourishing today, and we shall deal with some of its findings in later chapters of this book, as in our discussion of revitalization movements in Chapters 22 and 24.

CHAPTER SUMMARY

Enculturation, the process by which culture is passed from one generation to the next, begins soon after birth. Its first agents are the members of an individual's household, but later, in some societies, this role is assumed by professionals. For enculturation to proceed, individuals must possess self-awareness, or the ability to perceive themselves as objects in time and space and to judge their own actions. A major facet of self-awareness is a positive view of the self, for it is this that motivates persons to act to their advantage rather than disadvantage.

Several requirements involving one's behavioral environment need to be met in order for emerging self-awareness to function. The individual first needs to learn about a world of objects other than self; this environment is perceived in terms compatible with the values of the culture into which one is born. Also required is a sense of both spatial and temporal orientation. Finally, the growing individual needs a normative orientation, or an understanding of the values, ideals, and standards that constitute the behavioral environment.

Personality is a product of enculturation and refers to the distinctive ways a person thinks, feels, and behaves. With the psychoanalysts, most anthropologists believe that adult personality is shaped by early childhood experiences. A prime goal of anthropologists has been to produce objective studies that test this theory. Cross-cultural studies of gender-related personality characteristics, for example, show that there are no absolute personality differences between men and women. Instead, a society's economy helps structure the way children are brought up, which in turn influences their adult personalities.

Anthropologists John and Beatrice Whiting and Irvin Child, on the basis of cross-cultural studies, have established the interrelation of personality, child-rearing practices, and other aspects of culture. One may speak, for example, of dependence training. Usually associated with traditional farming societies, it tries to ensure that members of society will willingly and routinely work for the benefit of the group, performing the jobs assigned to them. At the opposite extreme, independence training, typical of societies characterized by independent nuclear families, puts a premium on self-reliance and independent behavior. Although a society may emphasize one sort of behavior over the other, it may not emphasize it to the same degree in both sexes. John Whiting and Child believe that child-rearing practices have their roots in a society's customs surrounding the meeting of the basic physical needs of its members; these practices, in turn, develop particular kinds of adult personalities.

Anthropologists have long worked on the problem of whether it is possible to delineate a group personality without falling into stereotyping. Each culture chooses, from the vast array of possibilities, those traits that it sees as normative or ideal. Individuals who conform to these traits are rewarded; the rest are not. The modal personality of a group is the personality typical of a culturally bounded population, as indicated by the central tendency of a defined frequency distribution. As a statistical concept, it opens up for investigation how societies organize the diverse personalities of their members, some of which conform more than others to the model "type."

National character studies have focused on the modal characteristics of modern countries. They have then attempted to determine the child-rearing practices and education that shape such a personality. Investigators during World War II interviewed foreign-born nationals and analyzed other sources in an effort to depict national character. Many anthropologists believe that national character theories are based on unscientific and overgeneralized data. Others believe that new studies of national character, without the flaws of past studies, are needed if we are really to understand what motivates the leaders and civil servants of modern states.

What defines normal behavior in any culture is determined by the culture itself, and morality is defined by culturally determined ideals. Abnormality involves developing a delusional system not accepted by the culture. Culturally induced conflicts not only can produce psychosis but can determine the form of the psychosis as well.

Current studies in psychological anthropology are combining traditional psychoanalytically based theories with biological and social factors to explain culture and cultural dynamics. Attention is also being given to cognitive processes of the mind, which are the basic mechanisms responsible for such cultural expression as language, myth, and art. At the same time, cross-cultural studies of child rearing and mental health have become established as anthropological subfields in their own right.

SUGGESTED READINGS

Barnouw, Victor. *Culture and Personality*, 4th ed. Homewood, Ill.: Dorsey Press, 1985. A recent revision of a well-respected text designed to introduce students to psychological anthropology.

Hunt, Robert C., ed. *Personalities and Cultures: Readings in Psychological Anthropology*. Garden City, N.Y.: Natural History Press, 1967. The 18 articles included in this book focus on various aspects of culture and personality. Attention is given to psychological and sociocultural variables and the relationships between them.

Norbeck, Edward, Douglas Price Williams, and William McCord, eds. *The Study of Personality: An Interdisciplinary Appraisal*. New York: Holt, Rinehart and Winston, 1968. The volume contains addresses given at Rice University in 1966. Its objective is to review and appraise knowledge and theories concerning personality in several scholarly fields (psychology, anthropology, sociology, philosophy of science, and so forth). It also discusses factors that influence the formation of personality, and the personalities of social and psychiatric deviates.

Wallace, Anthony F. C. *Culture and Personality*, 2d ed. New York: Random House, 1970. The logical and methodological foundations of culture and personality as a science form the basis of this book. The study is guided by the assumptions that anthropology should develop a scientific theory about culture, and that a theory pretending to explain or predict cultural phenomena must reckon with noncultural phenomena (such as personality) as well.

Whiting, John W. M., and I. Child. *Child Training and Personality: A Cross-cultural Study*. New Haven, Conn.: Yale University Press, 1953. How culture is integrated though the medium of personality processes is the main concern of this study. It covers both the influence of culture on personality and the influence of personality on culture. It is oriented toward testing general hypotheses about human behavior in any and all societies, rather than toward a detailed analysis of a particular society.

15

PATTERNS OF SUBSISTENCE

Ecuadorians with chickens they have raised for market. The basic business of culture is securing the survival of those who live by its rules, and so the study of subsistence activities is an important aspect of anthropological study.

PREVIEW

What Is Adaptation?

Adaptation refers to the process of interaction between changes made by an organism on its environment and changes induced by the environment in the organism. This kind of two-way adjustment is necessary for the survival of all life forms, including human beings.

How Do Humans Adapt?

Humans adapt through the medium of culture, as they develop ways of doing things that are compatible with the resources they have available to them and within the limitations of the environment in which they live. In a particular region, people living in similar environments tend to borrow from one another customs that seem to work well in those environments. Once achieved, adaptations may be remarkably stable for long periods of time, even thousands of years.

What Sorts of Adaptations Have Humans Achieved through the Ages?

Food foraging is the oldest and most universal type of human adaptation. To it, we owe such important elements of social organization as the sexual division of labor, food sharing, and a home base as the center of daily activity and the place where food sharing is accomplished. Quite different adaptations, involving farming and animal husbandry, began to develop in some parts of the world between 9,000 and 11,000 years ago. Horticulture — the cultivation of domestic plants by means of simple hand tools — made possible more permanent settlements and a reorganization of the division of labor. Under pastoralism — reliance on raising herds of domestic animals — nomadism continued, but new modes of interaction with other peoples were developed. Urbanism began to develop as early as 5,000 years ago in some places, as intensive agriculture produced sufficient food to support full-time specialists of various sorts. With this went a further transformation of the social fabric.

Several times today you will interrupt your activities to eat or drink. You may take this very much for granted, but if you went totally without food for as long as a day, you would begin to feel the symptoms of starvation: weakness, fatigue, headache. After a month of starvation, your body would probably never repair the damage. A mere week to 10 days without water would be enough to kill you.

All living beings, and people are no exception, must satisfy certain basic needs to stay alive. Among these needs are food, water, and shelter. Humans may not live by bread alone, but nobody can live long without any bread at all; and no creature could long survive if its relations with its environment were random and chaotic. Living beings must have regular access to a supply of food and water and a reliable means of obtaining and using it. A lion might die if all its prey disappeared, if its teeth and claws grew soft, or if its digestive system failed. Although people face these same sorts of problems, they have an overwhelming advantage over other creatures; people have culture. If our meat supply dwindles, we can turn to some vegetable, like the soybean, and process it to taste like meat. When our tools fail, we replace them or invent better ones. Even when our stomachs are incapable of digesting food, we can "predigest" it by boiling or pureeing. We are, however, subject to the same needs and pressures as all living creatures, and it is important to understand human behavior from this point of view. The crucial concept that underlies such a perspective is adaptation, that is, how humans manage to deal with the contingencies of daily life (for a formal definition of adaptation, see Chapter 3). Dealing with these contingencies is the basic business of all cultures.

ADAPTATION

The process of adaptation establishes a moving balance between the needs of a population and the potential of its environment. One illustration of this process can be seen in the case of the Tsembaga, highlanders of New Guinea, who support themselves chiefly through **horticulture** — the

> **Horticulture:** Cultivation of crops with hand tools such as digging sticks or hoes.

cultivation of crops with simple hand tools.[1] Although they also raise pigs, they eat them only under conditions of illness, injury, warfare, or celebration. At such times the pigs are sacrificed to ancestor spirits, and their flesh is ritually consumed by those people involved in the crisis. (This guarantees a supply of high-quality protein when it is most needed.)

In precolonial times, the Tsembaga and their neighbors were bound together in a unique cycle of pig sacrifices that served to mark the end of hostilities between groups. Frequent hostilities were set off by a number of ecological pressures, in which pigs were a significant factor. Since very few pigs were normally slaughtered and their food requirements were great, they could very quickly literally eat a local group out of house and home. The need to expand food production in order to support the prestigious but hungry pigs put a strain on the land best suited for farming. Therefore, when one group had driven another off its land, hostilities ended, and the new residents celebrated their victory with a pig festival. Many pigs were slaughtered, and the pork was widely shared among allied groups. Even without hostilities, festivals were held whenever the pig population became unmanageable, every 5 to 10 years, depending on the groups' success at farming. Thus, the cycle of fighting and feasting kept the balance among humans, land, and animals.

The term "adaptation" also refers to the process of interaction between changes made by an organism to its environment and changes made in the organism by the environment. The spread of the allele for sickle-cell anemia, discussed in Chapter 3, is a case in point. It is also a neat illustration of the relativity of any adaptation. In malarial areas, the allele responsible for this condition is

[1]Roy A. Rappaport, "Ritual Regulation of Environmental Relations among a New Guinea People," in *Environment and Cultural Behavior*, ed. Andrew P. Vayda (Garden City, N.Y.: Natural History Press, 1969), pp. 181–201.

A Tsembaga tends an oven in which a pig, dedicated to the red spirits, is cooked. Such pig feasts help control the size of the pig population and ensure that people have access to high-quality protein at times of crisis.

adaptive for human populations, even though some individuals suffer as a result of its presence. In nonmalarial regions, however, it is positively maladaptive, for it confers no advantage at all on human populations living under such conditions, while some individuals die as a result of its presence.

THE UNIT OF ADAPTATION

The unit of adaptation includes both organisms and environment. Organisms exist as members of populations, which as populations must have the flexibility to cope with variability and change within the environment. In biological terms, this means that different organisms within the popula-

Ecosystem: A system, or a functioning whole, composed of both the physical environment and the organisms living within it.

tion have somewhat differing genetic endowments. In cultural terms, it means that there is variation among individual skills, knowledge, and personalities. Organisms and environments form interacting systems. People might as easily be farmers as fisherfolk, but we do not expect to find farmers north of the Arctic Circle or fisherfolk in the Sahara Desert.

We might consider the example of a group of lakeside fisherfolk. The people live off fish, which, in turn, live off smaller organisms. Those animals, in turn, consume green plants; plants liberate minerals from water and mud, and, with energy from sunlight, transform them into proteins and carbohydrates. Dead plant and animal matter is decomposed by bacteria, and chemicals are returned to the soil and water. Some energy escapes from this system in the form of heat. Evaporation and rainfall constantly recirculate the water. People add chemicals to the system in the form of their wastes, and if people are careful, they may help to regulate the balance of animals and plants.

Some anthropologists have borrowed the ecologists' concept of **ecosystem.** An ecosystem is composed of both the physical environment and the organisms living within it. The system is bound by the activities of the organisms as well as by such physical processes as erosion and evaporation.

Human ecologists are generally concerned with detailed microstudies of particular human ecosystems; they emphasize that all aspects of human culture must be considered, not just the most obvious technological ones. The Tsembaga's attitude toward pigs and the cycle of sacrifices have important economic functions; we see them in this way, but the Tsembaga do not. They are motivated by their belief in the power and needs of their ancestral spirits. Although the pigs are consumed *by* the living, they are sacrificed *for* ancestors. Human ecosystems must often be interpreted in cultural terms.

EVOLUTIONARY ADAPTATION

Adaptation must also be understood from a historical point of view. For an organism to fit into an ecosystem, it must have the potential ability to adjust to or become a part of it. The Comanche, whose history began in the harsh, arid country of southern Idaho, provide a good example.[2] In their original homeland, they subsisted on wild plants, small animals, and occasionally larger game. Their material equipment was simple and limited to what could be transported by the women of the tribe. The size of their groups was restricted, and what little social power could develop was in the hands of the shaman, who was a combination of medicine man and spiritual guide.

At some point in their nomadic history, the Comanche moved onto the Great Plains, where buffalo were abundant and the Indians' potential as hunters could be fully developed. As larger groups could be supported by the new food supply, the need arose for a more complex political organization. Hunting ability thus became a means to acquire political power.

Eventually, the Comanche acquired horses and guns from whites, which greatly enhanced their hunting prowess, and the great hunting chiefs became powerful indeed. The Comanche became raiders in order to get horses, which they did not breed for themselves, and their hunting chiefs evolved into war chiefs. The once "poor" and peaceful food foragers of the Great Basin became wealthy pirates, dominating the Southwest from the borders of New Spain (Mexico) in the south to those of New France (Louisiana) and the fledgling United States in the east and north. In moving from one environment to another, and in evolving from one way of life to a second, the Comanche made the most of their developing potentials, or cultural **preadaptations.**

Sometimes societies that have developed independently find similar solutions to similar problems. For example, another group that moved out onto the Great Plains and took up a form of Plains

> **Preadaptations:** In culture, existing customs which, by chance, have potential for a new cultural adaptation.
>
> **Parallel evolution:** In cultural evolution, the development of similar adaptations to similar environmental conditions by peoples of similar cultural backgrounds.

Indian culture, similar in many ways to that of the Comanche, was the Cheyenne. Yet their cultural background was quite different; formerly, they were settled farmers with social, political, and religious institutions quite unlike those of the Comanche back in their ancestral homeland. The development of similar cultural adaptations to similar environmental conditions by peoples of quite different cultural backgrounds is the cultural equivalent of convergent evolution (Chapter 3).

Somewhat similar to the phenomenon of convergent evolution is **parallel evolution,** the difference being that similar adaptations are achieved by peoples of somewhat similar cultural backgrounds. For example, the development of farming in Southwest Asia and Mesoamerica took place independently, among people in both places, whose ways of life were already similar (Chapter 9).

It is important to recognize that stability as well as change is involved in evolutionary adaptation, and that once a satisfactory adaptation is achieved, too much in the way of change may cause it to break down.

Thus, episodes of major change may be followed by long periods of relative stability. For example, by 3500 B.C., a way of life had evolved in northwestern New England and southern Quebec that was well attuned to the environmental conditions of the times.[3] Since those conditions remained more or less the same over the next 5000 years or so, it is understandable that people's lifeways remained so as well. This is not to say that change was entirely absent, for it was not. ("Stable" does not mean "static.") From time to time,

---

[2]Ernest Wallace and E. Adamson Hoebel, *The Comanches* (Norman: University of Oklahoma Press, 1952).

[3]William A. Haviland, "The First Vermonters," in *Sesqui-Centennial History of Vermont*, ed. H. N. Muller (Montpelier, Vt.: Vermont Historical Society, in press).

The Indian tribes of the North American plains, such as the Sioux, Crow, and Comanche, show a great deal of cultural similarity because they have had to adapt to similar environmental conditions. For a map of Native American culture areas, see Figure 15.1.

Abenakis at work at 91 years
Abénakis au travail à 91 ans

To say that a society is stable is not to say that it is changeless. This western Abenaki from Quebec is a descendant of people who maintained a stable way of life in the region for 5000 years, even though they frequently incorporated new elements into their culture. Many of these, such as birchbark canoes, which largely replaced the older dugouts, made life a bit easier.

people refined and improved their way of life, as when hunting methods were improved first by adoption of the spear-thrower and later by adoption of the bow and arrow; when cooking was improved by the substitution of pottery vessels for containers made from animal hide, wood, or bark; when transport was improved by the replacement of heavy and cumbersome dugouts by sturdy yet lightweight birchbark canoes; or when people began to supplement the products of hunting, gathering, and fishing with limited cultivation of corn, beans, and squash. Despite these changes, however, the native peoples of the region still basically retained the unique structure of their culture,

and tended toward a balance with their resource base, well into the seventeenth century, when the culture began to be affected by pressures associated with the European invasion of North America. Such long-term stability by no means implies "stagnation," "backwardness," or "failure to progress"; rather, it is indicative of success. Had this culture not effectively satisfied people's physical and psychological needs, it never would have endured as it did for thousands of years.

CULTURE AREAS AND CULTURE TYPES

The aboriginal **culture area** of the Great Plains (Figure 15.1) was a geographical region in which there existed a number of societies with similar patterns of life. Thirty-one politically independent tribes (of which the aforementioned Cheyenne and Comanche were but two) faced a common environment, in which the buffalo was the most obvious and practical source of food as well as of materials for clothing and shelter. Living close by each other, different people were able to share new inventions and discoveries. They reached a common and shared adaptation to a particular ecological zone.

The Indians of the Great Plains were, at the time of contact with Europeans, invariably buffalo hunters, dependent on this animal for food, clothing, shelter, and bone tools. Each tribe was organized into a number of warrior societies, and prestige came from hunting and fighting skills. Their camps were typically arranged in a distinctive circular pattern. Many religious rituals, such as the Sun Dance, were practiced throughout the plains region.

Sometimes geographical regions are not uniform in climate and topography, and so new discoveries do not always spread from one group to another. Moreover, within a culture area, there are variations between local environments, and these favor variations in adaptation. The Great Basin of the western United States — an area embracing the states of Nevada and Utah, with adjacent portions of California, Oregon, Wyoming, and Idaho — is a case in point.[4] The Great Basin Shoshone Indians were divided into a northern and a western group, both primarily nomadic hunters and gatherers. In the north, a relative abundance of game animals provided for the maintenance of larger populations, requiring a great deal of cooperation among local groups. The western Shoshone, on the other hand, were almost entirely dependent on the gath-

> **Culture area:** A geographical region in which a number of different societies follow a similar pattern of life.
>
> **Culture type:** The view of a culture in terms of the relation of its particular technology to the environment exploited by that technology.

ering of wild plants for their subsistence, and as these varied considerably in their seasonal and local availability, the western Shoshone were forced to cover vast distances in search of food. Under such conditions, it was most efficient to travel in groups of but a few families, only occasionally coming together with other groups, and not always with the same ones.

The Shoshone were not the only inhabitants of the Great Basin. To the south lived the closely related Paiutes. They, too, were food foragers living under the same environmental conditions as the Shoshone, but the Paiutes managed their food resources more actively by diverting small streams to irrigate wild crops. They did not plant and cultivate these, but they were able to secure higher yields than their northern neighbors. Hence, their populations were larger than those of the Shoshone, and they led a more settled existence.

To deal with variations within a given region, Julian Steward proposed the concept of **culture type,** a culture considered in terms of a particular technology and its relationship with those environmental features that the technology is equipped to deal with. The example of the Great Plains shows how technology helps decide just which environmental features will be useful. Those same prairies that once supported buffalo hunters now support grain farmers. The Indians were prevented from farming the plains not for environmental reasons, nor for lack of knowledge about farming, since some of them, like the Cheyenne, had been farmers before they moved on to the plains. They did not farm because the buffalo herds provided abundant food without farming, and because farming would have been difficult without the steel-tipped plow that was needed to break up the compacted prairie sod. The farming

[4]Julian H. Steward, *Theory of Culture Change: The Methodology of Multilinear Evolution* (Urbana: University of Illinois Press, 1972).

North America:
1. Plains Area
2. Plateau Area
3. California Area
4. North Pacific Coast Area
5. Eskimo Area

6. Mackenzie Area
7. Eastern Woodland Area
8. Southeastern Area
9. Southwestern Area
10. Mesoamerica

South America:
11. Chibcha Area
12. The Inca Area
13. Guanaco Area
14. Amazon Area
15. The Antilles

FIGURE 15.1 The culture area concept was developed by North American anthropologists in the early part of the twentieth century. The map shows culture areas that have been defined for the Americas. Within each numbered area there is an overall similarity of native cultures, compared with the differences that exist between areas.

Julian H. Steward (1902–1972)

This North American developed an approach that he called **cultural ecology** — that is, the interaction between specific cultures with their environments. Initially, Steward was struck by a number of similarities in the development of urban civilizations in both Peru and Mesoamerica, and noted that certain developments were paralleled in the urban civilizations of the Old World. He identified the constants and abstracted from these his laws of cultural development. Steward proposed three fundamental procedures for cultural ecology:

1. The interrelationship of a culture's technology and its environment must be analyzed. How effectively does the culture take advantage of available resources to provide food and housing for its members?
2. The pattern of behavior associated with a culture's technology must be analyzed. How do members of the culture go about performing the work that is necessary for their survival?
3. The relation between those behavior patterns and the rest of the cultural system must be determined. How does the work they do to survive affect the people's attitudes and outlooks? How is their survival behavior linked to their social activities and their personal relationships?

potential of the Great Plains was simply not a relevant feature of the environment, given the available resources and technology before the coming of the Europeans.

CULTURE CORE

Environment and technology are not the only factors that determine a society's way of subsistence; social and political organization also affect the application of technology to the problem of staying alive. To understand the rise of irrigation agriculture in the great centers of ancient civilization, such as China, Mesopotamia, and Mesoamerica, it is important to note not only the technological and environmental factors that made possible the building of large scale irrigation works but also the social and political organization needed to mobilize the many workers necessary to build and maintain the systems. One must examine the monarchies and priesthoods that organized the work and decided where the water would be used and how the agricultural products of this joint venture would be distributed.

Cultural ecology: The study of the interaction of specific human cultures with their environment.

Culture core: The features of a culture that play a part in matters relating to the society's way of making a living.

Those features of a culture that play a part in the society's way of making its living are called its **culture core.** This includes the society's productive techniques and its knowledge of the resources available to it. It encompasses the patterns of labor involved in applying those techniques to the local environment. For example, do people work every day for a fixed number of hours, or is most work concentrated during certain times of the year? The culture core also includes other aspects of culture that bear on the production and distribution of food. An example of the way ideology can indirectly affect subsistence can be seen in a number of cultures where religion may place restrictions on the use of foods that are both locally available and nutritionally valuable. One reported example of this is a taboo that some Inuit of the Canadian Arctic follow; it forbids the hunting of seals in the summer. It has been said that if land game fails, a whole group will starve, even though seals are available to them.[5]

A number of anthropologists, known as **ethnoscientists,** are actively attempting to understand the principles behind folk ideologies and the way those principles usually help keep a people alive. The Tsembaga, for example, avoid certain low-lying, marshy areas, because they believe those areas are inhabited by red spirits who punish trespassers. Western science, by contrast, interprets those areas as the home of mosquitos, and the "punishment" as malaria. Whatever Westerners may think of the Tsembaga's belief in red spirits, it is a perfectly useful and reasonable one; it keeps them away from marshy areas just as surely as does a belief in malaria. If we want to understand why people in other cultures behave the way they do, we must understand their system of thought from their point of view as well as our own. Not all such beliefs are as easy to translate into our terms as are those of the Tsembaga red spirits.

THE FOOD-FORAGING WAY OF LIFE

At the present time, perhaps a quarter of a million people — less then 0.003 percent of a world population of over four billion — support themselves chiefly through hunting, fishing, and the gathering of wild plant foods. Yet, before the domestication of plants and animals, which began a mere 10,000 years ago, all people supported themselves through some combination of plant gathering, hunting, and fishing. Of all the people who have *ever* lived, 90 percent have been food foragers, and it was as food foragers that we became truly human, acquiring the basic habits of dealing with one another and with the world around us that still guide the behavior of individuals, communities, and nations. Thus, if we would know who we are

[5]Annemarie deWaal Malefijt, *Religion and Culture: An Introduction to Anthropology of Religion* (London: Macmillan, 1969), pp. 326–327.

Ethnoscientists: Anthropologists who seek to understand how natives perceive their universe.

and how we came to be, if we would understand the relationship between environment and culture, and if we would comprehend the institutions of the food-producing societies that have arisen since the development of farming and animal husbandry, we should turn first to the oldest and most universal of fully human life-styles, the food-foraging adaptation. The beginnings of this we examined in Chapters 6, 7, and 8.

When food foragers had the world to themselves some 10,000 years ago, they had their pick of the best environments. These have long since been appropriated by farming and, more recently, by industrial societies. Today, most food foragers are to be found only in the world's marginal areas — frozen Arctic tundra, deserts, inaccessible forests. These habitats, although they may not support large or dense agricultural societies, provide a good living for food-foraging peoples.

Until recently it was assumed that a food-foraging life in these areas was difficult and that one had to work hard just to stay alive. Behind this view lies the Western notion of progress, which, although widely accepted as being a fact of nature, is actually nothing more than a culturally conditioned bias. This predisposes us to see what is new as generally preferable to what is old, and to read human history as a more or less steady climb up an evolutionary ladder of progress. Thus, if food foraging as a way of life is much older than industrial civilization (which it is), the latter must be intrinsically better than the former. Hence, food-foraging societies are referred to as "primitive," "backward," or "undeveloped," by which labels economists, politicians, and other members of industrial or would-be industrial societies express their disapproval. In reality, food-foraging societies are very highly developed, but in a way very different from industrial societies.

Detailed studies have revealed that life in food foraging societies is far from being "solitary, poor, nasty, brutish, and short," as the philosopher

Scene from the film *The Gods Must Be Crazy*. Such films perpetuate the inaccurate stereotype of food-foraging peoples as "living fossils" out of a changeless past.

Thomas Hobbes claimed over 300 years ago. Rather, their diets are well balanced and ample, and they are less likely to experience severe famine than are farmers. While their material comforts are limited, so are their desires. On the other hand, they have plenty of leisure time in which to concentrate on family ties, social life, and spiritual development. The !Kung of South Africa's Kalahari Desert—scarcely what one would call a "lush" environment—obtain a better than adequate diet in an average workweek of about 20 hours. Their lives are rich in human warmth and aesthetic experience, displaying a balance of work, love, ritual, and play that many of us might envy. Small wonder that some anthropologists have gone so far as to label this "the original affluent society." The !Kung are not exceptional among food foragers today; one can only wonder about the level of affluence achieved by their ancient counterparts who lived in lusher environments with more secure and plentiful supplies of food.

All modern food foragers have had some degree of exposure to neighbors whose ways of life often differ radically from their own. The Mbuti of Zaire's Ituri rainforest (see the Original Study in Chapter 14), for example, live in a complex patron–client relationship with their neighbors, Bantu- and Sudanic-speaking peoples who are farmers. They exchange meat and other products of the forest for farm produce and manufactured goods. During part of the year, they live in their patron's village and are incorporated into his kin group, even to the point of allowing him to initiate their sons.

While some modern food foragers, like the Mbuti, have continued to maintain traditional ways, while adapting to neighbors and traders, various others have reverted to this way of life after giving up other modes of subsistence. Some, like the Cheyenne of the Great Plains, were once farmers, while others, like many of the !Kung of Southern Africa, were once pastoral nomads. Nor

The members of industrialized societies are not immune to the lure of food foraging. Many find pleasure in occasional foraging for wild foods, as the author is doing here for clams. Some — as in commercial fishing — forage full time.

Human groups, including food foragers, do not exist in isolation, except occasionally, and then not for long. The snowmobile this Alaskan native is using is indicative of his links with the wider world. In the past, Alaskan natives were regular participants in a trade network of such vast extent that Alaskan furs, walrus ivory, and hides were reaching Europe before people living there had any inkling that the lands of the western hemisphere even existed.

are such reversions things of the past. In the 1980s, when a world economic recession led to the abandonment of many sheep stations in the Australian "Outback," a number of aboriginal peoples returned to a food-foraging way of life, thereby emancipating themselves from a dependency on the government into which they had been forced.

An important point that emerges from the preceding discussion is this: People in the world today who subsist by hunting, fishing, and gathering wild plants are not following an ancient way of life because they do not know any better; they are doing it through deliberate choice. In many cases, they find such satisfaction in living the way they do that they often go to great lengths to avoid adopting other ways of life.

CHARACTERISTICS OF THE FOOD-FORAGING LIFE

Food foragers are by definition people who do not farm or practice animal husbandry. Hence, they must accommodate their places of residence to naturally available food sources. This being the case, it is no wonder that they move about a great deal. Such movement is not aimless wandering, but is done within a fixed territory or home range. Some, like the !Kung who depend on the reliable and highly drought-resistant Mongongo nut, may keep to fairly fixed annual routes and cover only a restricted territory. Others, such as the Great Basin Shoshone, must cover a wider territory; their course is determined by the local availability of the erratically productive pine nut. A crucial factor in this mobility is the availability of water. The distance between the food supply and water must not be so great that more energy is required to fetch water than can be obtained from the food.

Another characteristic of the food-foraging adaptation is the small size of local groups, 25 to 50 being the average number. Although no completely satisfactory explanation of group size has yet been offered, it seems certain that both ecological and social factors are involved. Among those suggested are the **carrying capacity** of the land, the number of people who can be supported by the available resources at a given level of food-getting techniques, and the **density of social relations,** roughly the number and intensity of interactions between camp members. More people means a higher social density, which, in turn, means more opportunities for conflict.

Both carrying capacity and social density are complex variables. Carrying capacity involves not only the immediate presence of food and water but the tools and work necessary to secure them, as well as short- and long-term fluctuations in their availability. Social density involves not only the number of people and their interactions but also the circumstances and quality of those interactions and the mechanisms for regulating them. A mob of a hundred angry strangers has a different social density than the same number of neighbors enjoying themselves at a block party.

Among food-foraging populations, social density seems always to be in a state of flux, as people spend more or less time away from camp and as they move to other camps, either on visits or more permanently. Among the !Kung, for example, exhaustion of local food resources, conflict within the group, or the desire to visit friends or relatives living elsewhere, cause people to leave one group for another. As Richard Lee notes: "The !Kung love to go visiting, and the practice acts as a safety valve when tempers get frayed. In fact, the !Kung usually move, not when their food is exhausted, but rather when only their patience is exhausted.[6]

If a camp has so many children that it creates a burden for the working adults, some young families may be encouraged to join others where there are fewer children. Conversely, groups with few children may actively recruit families with young children in order to ensure the group's survival. Redistribution of people, then, is an important

Carrying capacity: The number of people who can be supported by the available resources at a given level of technology.

Density of social relations: Roughly, the number and intensity of interactions among the members of a camp or other residential unit.

mechanism for regulating social density as well as for assuring that the size and composition of local groups is suited to local variations in resources. Thus, cultural adaptations serve to help transcend the limitations of the physical environment.

In addition to seasonal or local adjustments, long-term adjustments to resources must be made. Most food-foraging populations seem to stabilize in numbers well below the carrying capacity of their land. In fact, the home ranges of most food foragers can support from three to five times as many people as they typically do. In the long run, though, it may be more adaptive for a group to keep its numbers low rather than to expand indefinitely and risk being cut down by a sudden and unexpected natural reduction in food resources. The population density of food-foraging groups rarely exceeds one person per square mile, a very low density; yet their resources could support greater numbers.

Just how food-foraging peoples regulate population size has come to be understood only recently. Typically, such peoples nurse their infants several times each hour over a period of as many as 4 or 5 years. The constant stimulation of the mother's nipple is known to suppress the level of hormones that promote ovulation, making conception unlikely. By prolonging this over several years, women avoid giving birth except at widely spaced intervals, and the total number of offspring remains low.

THE IMPACT OF FOOD FORAGING ON HUMAN SOCIETY

Although much has been written on the theoretical importance of hunting in shaping the supposedly competitive and aggressive nature of the

[6]Richard Lee, *The Dobe !Kung: Foragers in a Changing World* (New York: Holt, Rinehart and Winston, 1984), p. 60.

human species, most anthropologists are unconvinced by these arguments. The fact is that most known food-foraging peoples are remarkably unaggressive and place more emphasis on cooperation than they do on competition. It does seem likely that three crucial elements of human social organization did develop along with food foraging. The first of these is the sexual division of labor. Some form of division of labor by sex, however modified, has been observed in all human societies, and is probably as old as human culture (see Chapter 12). There is some tendency in contemporary Western society to do away with such division, as we shall see in the next chapter. One may ask what the implications are for future cooperative relationships between men and women, a problem we will discuss further in Chapters 17 and 18.

Sexual Division of Labor

The hunting and butchering of large game as well as the processing of hard or tough raw materials are almost universally masculine occupations. Women's work, by contrast, usually consists of gathering and processing a variety of vegetal foods and of various other domestic chores. Historically, this pattern appears to have its origin in an earlier era, in which males, who were twice the size of females, got meat by scavenging from the carcasses of dead animals, butchered it with stone tools, and shared it with females (see Chapter 6). Females, for their part, gathered wild plant foods, probably using digging sticks and carrying devices made of soft, perishable materials. As the hunting of live animals replaced scavenging as a source of meat, and the biological differences between the sexes were reduced to minor proportions, the essence of the original division of labor was maintained nonetheless.

Among food foragers today, the work of women is no less arduous than that of men. !Kung women, for example, may walk as many as 12 miles a day two or three times a week to gather food, carrying not only their children, but on the return home, anywhere from 15 to 33 pounds of food. Still, they do not have to travel quite so far afield as do men

on the hunt, nor is their work usually quite so dangerous. Finally, their tasks require less rapid mobility, do not require complete and undivided attention, and are readily resumed after interruption. All of this is compatible with those biological differences which do remain between the sexes. Certainly women who are pregnant, or have infants to nurse, cannot as easily travel long distances in pursuit of game as can men. In addition to wide-ranging mobility, the successful hunter must also be able to mobilize rapidly high bursts of energy. Although some women can certainly run faster than some men, it is a fact that in general men can run faster than women, even if the latter are not pregnant or encumbered with infants. Because human females must be able to give birth to infants with relatively large heads, their pelvic structure differs from that of human males to a greater degree than among most other species of mammals. As a consequence, the human female is not as well equipped as is the human male when rapid and prolonged mobility are required.

To say that the sexual division of labor among food foragers is compatible with the biological differences between men and women is *not* to say that it is biologically determined. Among the Indians of the Great Plains of North America, for example, there are numerous reported cases of women who gained fame as hunters and warriors, both regarded as men's activities. There is even one case of a Gros Ventre girl captured by the Crow who became one of their chiefs, so accomplished was she at what were considered to be masculine pursuits. In fact, the sexual division of labor is nowhere near as rigid among food foragers as it is in most other types of society. Thus, !Kung men willingly and without embarrassment, as the occasion demands, will gather wild plant foods, build huts, and collect water, all clearly regarded as women's work. To return to the Plains Indians, any young man for whom masculine pursuits seemed uncongenial could assume the dress and demeanor of women, providing he had the necessary skills to achieve success in feminine activities. Although sexual preferences might enter into the decision to assume a feminine identity, not all such individu-

Food foragers always have a division of labor in which women prepare food and men hunt, as shown here among the !Kung.

als were homosexuals, nor did all homosexuals assume a woman's role. Clearly, sexual preference was of lesser importance than occupation and appearance.

The nature of women's work in food-foraging societies is such that it can be done while taking care of children. It can also be done in company with other women, which helps alleviate somewhat the monotony of the work. In the past, there has been a tendency to underestimate the contribution made by the food-gathering activities of women to the survival of their group. Most modern food foragers obtain 60 to 70 percent of their diets from plant foods, with perhaps some fish and shellfish provided by women.

Although women in food-foraging societies

may spend a good deal of their time gathering food, men do not spend all or even the greatest part of their time in hunting. The amount of energy expended in hunting, especially in hot climates, is often greater than the energy return from the kill. Too much time spent at hunting might actually be counterproductive. Energy itself is derived primarily from plant carbohydrates, and it is the woman gatherer who brings in the bulk of the calories. A certain amount of meat in the diet, though, guarantees high-quality protein that is less easily obtained from plant sources, for meat contains all of the amino acids, the building blocks of protein, and in exactly the right balance, that are required by the human body. This is important, for the entire spectrum must be provided in the proper balance at the same meal, if their full value is to be realized, and the lack of just one prevents full utilization of the others. No one plant food does this by itself, and in order to get by without meat, one must hit on exactly the right combination of plants together to provide the essential amino acids in the right proportions.

Food Sharing

A second important feature of human social organization associated with food foraging is the sharing of food between adults, something that is very rare among nonhuman primates. It is easy enough to see why sharing takes place, with women supplying one kind of food and men another. Among the !Kung, women have control over the food that they collect, and can share it with whoever they choose. Men, by contrast, are constrained by rules which specify how much meat is to be distributed. Thus, a hunter has little effective control over the meat he brings into camp. For the individual hunter, meat sharing is really a way of storing it for the future; his generosity, obligatory though it might be, gives him a claim on the future kills of other hunters. As a cultural trait, food sharing has the obvious survival value of distributing resources needed for subsistence.

Although carnivorous animals often share food, the few examples of food sharing among nonhuman primates all involve groups of male chimpanzees cooperating in a hunt and later sharing the spoils, frequently with females and juveniles. What this suggests is that the origins of food sharing and the division of labor are related to a shift in food habits from infrequent to more frequent meat eating. This seems to have occurred with the appearance of the earliest members of the genus *Homo* some 2.5 million years ago.

A final distinctive feature of the food-foraging economy is the importance of the camp as the center of daily activity and the place where food sharing actually occurs. Among nonhuman primates, activities tend to be divided between feeding areas and sleeping areas, and the latter tend to be shifted each evening. Food-foraging people, however, live in camps of some permanence, for example the dry-season camps of the !Kung that serve for the entire winter or the dry-season camps of the Hadza of Tanzania that are oriented to the hunt and serve for several days but never more than a week or two. Moreover, human camps are more than sleeping areas; people are in and out all day, eating, working, and socializing in camps to a greater extent than any other primates.

Cultural Adaptations and Material Technology

The mobility of food-foraging groups may depend on the availability of water, as in the case of the !Kung; of pine nuts, as for the Shoshone; or of game animals, as for the Hadza. Hunting styles and equipment may also play a role in determining population size and movement. Some Mbuti hunt with nets. This requires the cooperation of 7 to 30 families; consequently, their camps are relatively large. The camps of those who hunt with bow and arrow number from three to six families. Too many archers in the same locale means that each must travel a great distance daily to keep out of another's way. Only during midsummer do the archers collect into larger camps for religious ceremonies, matrimonial arrangements, and social exchange. At this time, the bowmen turn to communal beat hunts. Without nets, they are less effective than their neighbors, so it is only when the net hunters are widely dispersed in the pursuit of honey that the archers can come together.

Egalitarian Society

An important characteristic of the food-foraging society is its egalitarianism. food foragers are usually highly mobile; and lacking animal or mechanical means of transportation, they must be able to travel without many encumbrances, especially on food-getting expeditions. Their material goods must be limited to the barest essentials, which include implements that serve for hunting; gathering; fishing; building; and making tools, cooking utensils, traps, and nets. There is little chance for the accumulation of luxuries or surplus goods, and the fact that no one owns significantly more than another helps to limit status differences. Age and sex are usually the only sources of important status differences in food-foraging societies.

It is important to realize that status differences by themselves do not imply any necessary inequality, a point that has all too often been misunderstood, especially where relations between men and women are concerned. In the following Original Study, Anthropologist Eleanor Leacock argues that, in egalitarian societies, egalitarianism applies as much to women as to men.

ORIGINAL STUDY
Men and Women in Egalitarian Societies[7]

With regard to the autonomy of women, nothing in the structure of egalitarian band societies necessitated special deference to men. There were no economic and social liabilities that bound women to be more sensitive to men's needs and feelings than vice versa. This was true even in hunting societies, where women did not furnish a major share of the food. The record of seventeenth-century Montagnais–Naskapi life in *The Jesuit Relations* makes this clear. [The Montagnais and Naskapi live in Labrador.] Disputes and quarrels among spouses were virtually nonexistent, Le Jeune reported, since each sex carried out its own activities without "meddling" in those of the other. Le Jeune deplored the fact that the Montagnais "imagine that they ought by right of birth, to enjoy the liberty of wild ass colts, rendering no homage to any one whomsoever." Noting that women had "great power," he expressed his disapproval of the fact that men had no apparent inclination to make their wives "obey" them or to enjoin sexual fidelity upon them. He lectured the Indians of this failing, reporting in one instance, "I told him then that he was the master, and that in France women do not rule their husbands." Le Jeune was also distressed by the sharp and ribald joking and teasing into which women entered along with the men. "Their language has the foul odor of the sewers," he wrote. The *Relations* reflect the program of the Jesuits to "civilize" the Indians, and during the course of the seventeenth century they attempted to introduce principles of formal authority, lectured the people about obeying newly elected tribal chiefs, and introduced disciplinary measures in the effort to enforce male authority upon women. No data are more illustrative of the distance between hierarchical and egalitarian forms of organization than the Jesuit account of these efforts.

Nonetheless, runs the argument for universal female subservience to men, the hunt and war, male domains, are associated with power and prestige to the disadvantage of women. What about this assumption?

Answers are at several levels. First, it is necessary to modify the exaggerations of male as hunter and warrior. Women did some individual hunting . . . and they participated in hunting drives that were often of great importance. Men did a lot of non-hunting. Warfare was minimal or nonexistent.

The association of hunting, war, and masculine assertiveness is not found among hunter–gatherers except, in a limited way, in Australia. Instead, it characterizes horticultural societies in certain areas, notably Melanesia and the Amazon lowlands.

It is also necessary to reexamine the idea that these male activities were in the past more prestigious than the creation of new human beings. I am sympathetic to the skepticism with which women may view the argument that their gift of fertility was as highly valued as or more highly valued than anything men did. Women are too commonly told today to be content with the wondrous ability to give birth and with the presumed propensity for "motherhood" as defined in saccharine terms. They correctly read such exhortations as saying, "Do not fight for a change in status." However, the fact that childbearing is associated with women's present oppression does not mean this was the case in earlier social forms. To the extent that hunting and warring (or, more accurately, sporadic raiding, where it existed) were areas of male ritualization, they were just that: areas of male ritualization. To a greater or lesser extent women participated in the rituals, while to a greater or lesser extent they were also involved in ritual elaborations of generative power, either along with men or separately. To presume the greater importance of male than female participants, or to casually accept the statements to this effect of later-day male informants, is to miss the basic function of dichotomized sex-symbolism in egalitarian society. Dichotomization made it possible to ritualize the reciprocal roles of females and males that sustained the group. As ranking began to develop, it became a means of asserting male dominance, and with the full-scale development of classes sex ideologies reinforced inequalities that were basic to exploitative structures.

Much is made of Australian Aboriginal society in arguments for universal deference of women toward men. The data need ethnohistorical review, since the vast changes that have taken place in Australia over the last two centuries cannot be ignored in the consideration of ritual life and of male brutality toward women. Disease, outright genocidal practices, and expulsion from their lands reduced the population of native Australians to its lowest point in the 1930s, after which the cessation of direct genocide, the mission distribution of foods, and the control of infant mortality began to permit a population increase. The concomitant intensification of ceremonial life is described as follows by Godelier

> This . . . phenomenon, of a politico-religious order, of course expresses the desire of these groups to reaffirm their cultural identity and to resist the destructive pressures of the process of domination and acculturation they are undergoing, which has robbed them of their land and subjected their ancient religious and political practices to erosion and systematic extirpation.

Thus ceremonial elaboration was oriented toward renewed ethnic identification, in the context of oppression. Furthermore, on the reserves, the economic autonomy of women vis-à-vis men was undercut by handouts to men defined as heads of families and by sporadic opportunities for wage labor open to men. To assume that recent ritual data reflect aboriginal Australian symbolic structures as if unchanged is to be guilty of freezing these people in some timeless "traditional culture" that does not change or develop, but only becomes lost; it is to rob them of their history. Even in their day [the nineteenth century], Spencer and Gillen noted the probable decline in women's ceremonial participation among the Arunta.

Allusions to male brutality toward women are common for Australia. Not all violence can be blamed on European colonialism, to be sure, yet it is crass ethnocentrism, if not outright racism, to assume that the grim brutality of Europeans toward the Australians they were literally seeking to exterminate was without profound effect. A common response to defeat is to turn hostility inward. The process is reversed when people acquire the political understanding and organizational strength to confront the source of their problems, as has recently been happening among Australian Aborigines.

References to women of recent times fighting back publicly in a spirited style, occasionally going after their husbands with both tongue and fighting club, and publicly haranguing both men and women bespeak a persisting tradition of autonomy. In relation to "those reciprocal rights and duties that are recognized to be inherent in marriage," Kaberry writes:

> I, personally, have seen too many women attack their husbands with a tomahawk or even their own boomerangs, to feel that they are invariably the victims of ill treatment. A man may perhaps try to beat his wife if she has not brought in sufficient food, but I never saw a wife stand by in submission to receive punishment for her culpable conduct. In the quarrel she might even strike the first blow, and if she were clearly in danger of being seriously hurt, then one of the bystanders might intervene, in fact always did within my experience.

Nor did the man's greater strength tell in such a struggle, for the wife "will pack up all her goods and chattels and move to the camp of a relative . . . the loss of an economic partner . . . brings the man to his senses and he attempts a reconciliation." Kaberry concludes that the point to stress about this indispensability of a woman's economic contribution is "not only her great importance in economics, but also her power to utilize this to her own advantage in other spheres of marital life."

A further point also needs stressing: such quarrels are not, as they may first appear, structurally at the same level as similar quarrels in our own society. In our case, reciprocity in marital rights and duties is defined in terms of a social order in which subsistence is gained through paid wage labor, while women supply socially essential but unpaid services within a household. A dichotomy between "public" labor and "private" household service marks the household "slavery" of women. In all societies, women use the resources available to them to manipulate their situation to their advantage as best they can, but they are in a qualitatively different position, structurally, in our society from that in societies where what has been called the "household economy" is the *entire* economy. References to the autonomy of women when it comes to making decisions about their own lives are common for such societies. Concomitant autonomy of attitude is pointed out by Kaberry, again, for the Kimberly peoples: "The women, as far as I could judge from their attitudes," she writes, "remained regrettably profane in their attitude towards the men." To be sure, they much admired the younger men as they paraded in their ceremonial finery, but "the praise uttered was in terms that suggested that the spectators regarded the men as potential lovers, and not as individuals near unto gods." In summary, Kaberry argues that "there can be no question of identifying the sacred inheritance of the tribe only with the men's ceremonies. Those of the women belong to it also." As for concepts of "pollution," she says, "the women with regard to the men's rituals are profane and uninitiated; the men with regard to the women's ritual are profane and uninitiated."

The record on women's autonomy and lack of special deference among the seventeenth-century Montagnais-Naskapi is unambiguous. Yet this was a society in which the hunt was overwhelmingly important. Women manufactured clothing and other necessities, but furnished much less food than was the usual case with hunter–gatherers. In the seventeenth century, women as well as men were shamans, although this is apparently no longer remembered. As powerful shamans, they might exhort men to battle. Men held certain feasts to do with hunting from which women were excluded. Similarly, men were excluded from women's feasts about which we know nothing but that they were held. When man needed more than public teasing to ensure his good conduct, or in times of crisis, women held their own councils. In relation to warfare, anything but dominance–deference behavior is indicated. In historic times, raids were carried on against the Iroquois, who were expanding their territories in search of furs. The fury with which women would enjoin men to do battle and the hideous and protracted intricacies of the torture of captives in which they took the initiative boggle the mind. Getting back at the Iroquois for killing their menfolk was central, however, not "hailing the conquering hero."

[7]Eleanor Leacock, "Women's Status in Egalitarian Society: Implications for Social Evolution," in *Myths of Male Dominance: Collected Articles on Women Cross Culturally* (New York: Monthly Review Press, 1981) pp. 140–145. Copyright © 1981 by Eleanor Leacock. Reprinted by permission of Monthly Review Foundation.

Food foragers make no attempt to accumulate surplus foodstuffs, often an important source of status in agrarian societies. To say that they do not accumulate food surpluses, however, is not to say that they live constantly on the verge of starvation. Their environment is their storehouse, and, except in the coldest climates (where a surplus is put by to see people through the lean season), or in times of acute ecological disaster, there is always some food to be found in a group's territory. Because food resources are typically distributed equally throughout the group (share and share alike is the order of the day), no one achieves the wealth or status that hoarding might bring. In such a society, wealth is a sign of deviance rather than a desirable characteristic.

The food forager's concept of territory contributes as much to social equality as it does to the equal distribution of resources. Most groups have home ranges, within which access to resources is open to all members: What is available to one is available to all. If a Mbuti hunter discovers a honey tree, he has first rights; but when he has taken his share, others have a turn. In the unlikely possibility that he does not take advantage of his discovery, others will. No one owns the tree; the system is first come, first served. Therefore, knowledge of the existence of food resources circulates quickly throughout the entire group.

Families move easily from one group to another, settling in any group where they have a previous kinship tie. The composition of groups is always shifting. This loose attitude toward group membership promotes the widest access to resources and, at the same time, is a device that maintains a balance between populations and resources.

The food forager pattern of generalized exchange, or sharing without any expectation of a direct return, also serves the ends of resource distribution and social equality. A !Kung man or woman spends as much as two-thirds of his or her day visiting others or receiving guests; during this time, many exchanges of gifts take place. To refuse to share — to hoard — would be morally wrong. By sharing whatever is at hand, the !Kung achieve social leveling and assure their right to share in the windfalls of others.

FOOD-PRODUCING SOCIETY

As we saw in Chapters 6, 7, and 8, it was toolmaking that allowed humans to become meat eaters as well as consumers of plant foods. The next truly momentous event in human history was the domestication of plants and animals. As we saw in Chapter 9, by changing the way they provided for their subsistence, people changed the very nature of human society itself.

Humans adapted to their new way of life in a number of ways. For example, some societies became horticultural — small communities of gardeners working with simple hand tools and using neither irrigation nor the plow. Horticulturists typically cultivate several varieties of crops together in small gardens they have cleared by hand. Technologically more complex than the horticulturists are the intensive agriculturalists, who employ such techniques as irrigation, fertilizers, and the wooden or metal plow pulled by harnessed draft animals, to produce food on larger plots of land. The distinction between horticulturalist and agriculturalist is not always an easy one to make. For example, the Hopi Indians of the North

These Chinese farmers are planting rice in their traditional way. While supporting larger and more sedentary populations than can food foraging, farming generally requires longer and more monotonous work.

American Southwest traditionally used irrigation in their farming, while at the same time using simple hand tools.

As food producers, people have developed several major crop complexes: two adapted to seasonal uplands and two to tropical wetlands. In the dry uplands of Southwest Asia, for example, they time their agricultural activities with the rhythm of the changing seasons, cultivating wheat, barley, flax, rye, and millet. In the tropical wetlands of the Old World, rice and tubers such as yams and taro are cultivated. In the New World, people have adapted to environments similar to those of the Old World, but have cultivated different plants. Maize, beans, squash, and the potato are typically grown in drier areas, whereas manioc is extensively grown in the tropical wetlands.

HORTICULTURE: THE GURURUMBA

A good example of a horticultural society that has adapted to its environment successfully are the Gururumba, numbering about 1121 people who live in six villages spread over 30 square miles in the Upper Asaro valley of New Guinea. Because of the elevation, the climate is cool and damp, and the area receives about 100 inches of rain a year.[8]

Each Gururumba village has a number of gardens separated by fences; several small families may have plots inside each fenced area. Every adult is involved in food production, with a strict division of labor according to sex. Men plant and tend sugarcane, bananas, taro, and yams, while women cultivate sweet potatoes and a variety of green vegetables. A family's social prestige is partially based on the neatness and productivity of its garden. Crops are rotated, but fertilizers are not used. Each gardener maintains more than one plot and uses different soils and different ecological zones for different crops; thus, the gardens are ready for

harvesting at different times of the year, assuring a constant food supply. (Another technologically simple cultivating technique used by many horticultural societies, but not the Gururumba, is the slash-and-burn method, in which trees are cut, allowed to dry for several months, then set afire. The ashes provide nutrients for the soil, which is then seeded and cultivated.) Since rainfall is plentiful, the Gururumba do not irrigate their gardens, and although some plots are planted on slopes with angles of 45 degrees, terracing is not practiced. Simple hand tools, such as digging sticks made of wood or ground stone, are used by the men to break the soil.

Like many such societies in New Guinea and the nearby islands of Melanesia, Gururumba society is knit together through a complex system of gift exchange, in which men lavish gifts on one another and so accumulate a host of debtors. The more a man gives away, the more is owed him, and hence the more prestige he has. For this reason, every man keeps two gardens, one with crops to fulfill his everyday needs and one with "prestige" crops for his exchange needs. Although the crops planted in the latter gardens are not special, particular care is given to this garden to assure crops of the finest quality. A man anticipates a major occasion when he will have to give a feast, such as a daughter's wedding or a son's initiation, by planting his prestige garden a year in advance.

The second major feature of the Gururumba subsistence pattern, also common throughout this culture area, is the keeping of pigs. Pigs are raised not primarily for food but as gift-exchange items to enhance social prestige. Every 5 to 7 years, a huge pig feast, called an *idzi namo* ("pig flute") is held. Hundreds of pigs are killed, cooked, and distributed, simultaneously abolishing old obligations and creating new ones for the clan that gives the feast. As was the case among the Tsembaga whom we met earlier in this chapter, the pig feast helps the Gururumba get rid of a pig population that has grown too large to continue feeding; it also provides occasional animal protein in their diet.

[8]Most of the following information is taken from Philip L. Newman, *Knowing the Gururumba* (New York: Holt, Rinehart and Winston, 1965).

Gururumba men carrying away gifts from a food distribution. A complex system of gift exchanges helps to knit Gururumba society together.

PASTORALISM: THE BAKHTIARI

One of the more striking examples of human adaptation to the environment is the **pastoralist,** who lives in societies in which animal husbandry is viewed as the ideal way of making a living and in which movement of all or part of the society is considered a normal and natural part of life. This cultural aspect is vitally important, for while economic analysis of some groups may show that they earn more from nonpastoral sources, the concept of nomadic pastoralism remains central to their own identities. These societies are built around a pastoral economic specialization, but imbued with values far beyond just doing a job. This distinguishes them from American ranchers, who likewise have a pastoral economic specialization but identify culturally with a larger society.[9] It also sets

[9]Thomas J. Barfield, "Introduction," *Cultural Survival Quarterly* 8 (Spring 1984): 2.

Pastoralist: Member of a society in which animal husbandry is regarded as the ideal way of making a living, and in which movement of all or part of the society is considered a normal and natural way of life.

them apart from food foragers, migrant farm workers, corporate executives, and others who are nomadic without being pastoralists.

Pastoralism is an effective way of living in arid grasslands and deserts, such as those that stretch eastward from the dry country of North Africa through the Arabian Desert, across the plateau of Iran and into Turkestan and Mongolia. One group of people living in this belt of arid lands is the Bakhtiari, a fiercely independent tribe who live in the south Zagros mountains of western Iran, where they tend herds of goats and fat-tailed sheep.[10] Although some of the tribesmen own horses and most own donkeys, these are used only for transport; the animals around which Bakhtiari life revolves are the sheep and goat.

The harsh, bleak environment dominates the lives of these people: It determines when and where they move their flocks, the clothes they wear, the food they eat, and even their dispositions — they have been called "mountain bears" by Iranian townspeople. In the Zagros are ridges that reach altitudes of 12,000 to 14,000 feet. Their steep, rocky trails and escarpments challenge the hardiest and ablest climbers; jagged peaks, deep chasms, and watercourses with thunderous torrents also make living and traveling hazardous.

The pastoral life of the Bakhtiari revolves around two seasonal migrations to find better grazing lands for the flocks. Twice yearly, the tribe moves: in the fall, from their *sardsir*, or summer quarters in the mountains, and in the spring, from their *garmsir*, or winter quarters in the lowlands. In the fall, before the harsh winter comes to the mountains, the nomads load their tents and other belongings on donkeys and drive their flocks down to the warm plains that border Iraq in the west; grazing land here is excellent and well watered in the winter. In the spring, when the low-lying pastures dry up, the Bakhtiari return to the mountain valleys, where a new crop of grass is sprouting. For this trek, they split into five groups, each containing about 5,000 individuals and 50,000 animals.

The return trip north is the more dangerous because the mountain snows are melting and the gorges are full of turbulent, ice-cold water rushing down from the mountain peaks. This long trek is further impeded by the kids that are born in the spring, just before migration. Where the water courses are not very deep, the nomads ford them. Deeper channels, including one river that is a half-

mile wide, are crossed with the help of inflatable goatskin rafts, on which are placed infants, the elderly and infirm, and lambs and kids; the rafts are then pushed by the men swimming alongside in the icy water. If they work from dawn to dusk, the nomads can get all of the people and animals across the river in 5 days. Not surprisingly, dozens of sheep are drowned each day at the river crossing.

In the mountain passes, where a biting wind numbs the skin and brings tears to the eyes, the Bakhtiari must make their way through slippery unmelted snow. Climbing the steep escarpments is dangerous, and the stronger men must often carry their own children and the newborn kids on their

Bakhtiari women filling water containers made of goat skin. In the spring, waterskins are filled with air to float people, young animals and belongings across rivers as they move to higher pastures.

[10]Material on the Bakhtiari is drawn mainly from Frederik Barth, "Nomadism in the Mountain and Plateau Areas of South West Asia," *The Problems of the Arid Zone* (UNESCO, 1960), pp. 341–355; Carleton S. Coon, *Caravan: The Story of the Middle East*, 2d ed. (New York: Holt, Rinehart and Winston, 1958), chap. 13; Philip C. Salzman, "Political Organization among Nomadic Peoples," *Proceedings of the American Philosophical Society* 111 (1967): 115–131.

shoulders as they make their way over the ice and snow to the lush mountain valley that is their goal. During each migration the tribe may cover as many as 200 miles, and the trek can take weeks, because the flocks travel slowly and require constant attention. The nomads have fixed routes and a somewhat definite itinerary; generally, they know where they should be and when they should be there. On the drive, the men and boys herd the sheep and goats, while the women and children ride the donkeys along with the tents and other equipment.

When they reach their destination, the Bakhtiari live in black tents of goat's-hair cloth woven by the women. The tents have sloping tops and vertical sides, held up by wooden poles. Inside, the furnishings are sparse: rugs woven by the women or heavy felt pads cover the floor. Against one side of the tent are blankets; containers made of goatskin, copper utensils, clay jugs, and bags of grain line the opposite side. Bakhtiari tents provide an excellent example of adaptation to a changing environment. The goat's-hair cloth retains heat and repels water during the winter and keeps out heat during the summer. These portable homes are very easy to erect, take down, and transport.

Sheep and goats are central to Bakhtiari subsistence. The animals provide milk, cheese, butter, meat, hides, and wool, which is woven into clothes, tents, storage bags, and other essentials by the women or sold in towns. The tribe also engages in very limited horticulture; it owns lands that contain orchards, and the fruit is consumed by the nomads or sold to townspeople. The division of labor is according to sex. The men, who take great pride in their marksmanship and horsemanship, engage in a limited amount of hunting on horseback, but their chief task is the tending of the flocks. The women cook, sew, weave, care for the children, and carry fuel and water.

The Bakhtiari have their own system of justice, including laws and a penal code. They are governed by tribal leaders, or *khans*, who are elected or inherit their office. Most of the *khans* grew wealthy when oil was discovered on tribal lands around the

turn of the last century, and many of them are well educated, having attended Iranian or foreign universities. Despite this, and although some of them own houses in cities, the *khans* spend much of their lives among their people.

URBAN LIFE AMONG NONINDUSTRIAL PEOPLES

With the intensification of agriculture, some farming communities grew into cities, in which individuals who had previously been engaged in agriculture were freed to specialize in other activities. Thus, such craftsmen as carpenters, blacksmiths, sculptors, basketmakers, and stonecutters contribute to the vibrant, diversified life of the city (Chapter 10).

Unlike horticulturalists and pastoralists, city dwellers are only indirectly concerned with adapting to their natural environment. Far more important is the need to adapt to living and getting along with their fellow urbanites. Urbanization brings with it a new social order: Marked inequality develops as society becomes stratified as people are ranked according to the kind of work they do, or the family they are born into. As social institutions cease to operate in simple, face-to-face groups of relatives, friends, and acquaintances, they become more formal and bureaucratic, with specialized political institutions.

AZTEC CITY LIFE

The Aztec empire, which flourished in Mexico in the sixteenth century, is a good example of a highly developed urban society among non-Western peoples.[11] The capital city of the empire, Tenochtitlán (modern-day Mexico City), was located in a fertile valley 7,000 feet above sea level. Its population, along with that of its sister city, Tlatelolco, was about 200,000 in 1519, when Cortés first saw it. This makes it five times more populous than the city of London at the same time. The Aztec metropolis sat on an island in the middle of a salt lake,

[11]Most of the following information is taken from Frances F. Berdan, *The Aztecs of Central Mexico* (New York: Holt, Rinehart and Winston, 1982).

which has since dried up, and two aqueducts brought in fresh water from springs on the mainland. A 10-mile dike rimmed the eastern end of the city to ward off floodwaters originating in the neighboring lakes during the rainy season.

As in the early cities of Southwest Asia, the foundation of Aztec society was agriculture. Corn was the principal crop. Each family, allotted a plot of land by its lineage, cultivated any of a number of crops, including beans, squash, gourds, peppers, tomatoes, cotton, and tobacco. Unlike Old World societies, however, only a few animals were domesticated; these included dogs and turkeys (both for eating).

As Tenochtitlán grew and land became scarce, Aztec farmers made use of an ingenious method to cope with this situation: They created *chinampas*, or reed-walled gardens, out of the marsh that surrounded the capital. Each *chinampa*, actually a small, man-made island whose soil was as fertile as that of the Nile Delta, was tended by farmers who paddled around the interconnecting canals in small dugout canoes. Even today, *chinampas* can be found at Xochimilco, a few miles outside Mexico City.

Aztec agricultural success provided for an increasingly large population and the diversification of labor. Skilled artisans, such as sculptors, silversmiths, stone workers, potters, weavers, feather workers, and painters were able to make good livings by pursuing these crafts exclusively. Since religion was central to the operation of the Aztec social order, these craftsmen were continuously engaged in the manufacture of religious artifacts, clothing, and decorations for buildings and temples. Other nonagricultural specialists included some of the warriors; the traveling merchants, or *pochteca*; the priests; and the government bureaucracy of nobles.

As specialization increased, among both individuals and cities of the Aztec empire, the market became an extremely important economic and social institution. In addition to the daily markets in each city, there were larger markets in the various cities, held at different times of the year. Buyers and sellers traveled to these from the far reaches of the empire. The market at Tlatelolco was so huge that the Spanish compared it to those of Rome and Constantinople. At the Aztec markets, barter was the primary means of exchange. At times, however, cacao beans, gold dust, crescent-shaped knives, and copper were used.

In addition to its obvious economic use, the market served social functions: People went there not only to buy or to sell but to meet other people and to hear the latest news. A law actually required that each person go to market at least once within a specified number of days; this ensured that the citizenry was kept informed of all important news. The other major economic institution, trade networks between the Aztec capital and other cities, brought goods such as chocolate, vanilla beans, and pineapples into Tenochtitlán.

Aztec social order was stratified into three main classes: nobles, commoners, and serfs. The nobles operated outside the lineage system on the basis of land and serfs allotted them by the ruler from conquered peoples. The commoners were divided into lineages, on which they were dependent for land. Within each of these, individual status depended on the degree of descent from the founder: those more closely related to the lineage founder had higher status than those whose kinship was more distant. The third class in Aztec society consisted of serfs bound to the land and porters employed as carriers by merchants. Lowest of this class were the slaves. Some had voluntarily sold themselves into bondage; others were captives taken in war.

The Aztecs were governed by a semidivine king, who was chosen by a council of nobles, priests, and leaders from among candidates of royal lineage. Although the king was an absolute monarch, the councilors advised him on affairs of state. A vast number of government officials oversaw various functions, such as maintenance of the tax system, administration of the courts of justice, management of government storehouses, and control of military training.

The typical Aztec city was rectangular and reflected the way the land was divided among the lineages. In the center was a large plaza containing

Model of the center of Tenochtitlán, the Aztec capital city.

the temple and the house of the city's ruler. At Tenochtitlán, with a total area of about 20 square miles, a huge temple and two lavish palaces stood in the central plaza, also called the "Sacred Precinct." Surrounding this area were other ceremonial buildings belonging to each lineage.

As in a modern city, housing in Tenochtitlán ranged from squalid to magnificent. On the outskirts of the city, on *chinampas*, were the farmers' hovels, huts of thatched straw and wattle smeared with mud. In the city proper were the houses of the middle class — graceful, multi-roomed, single- and two-story stone and mortar buildings, each of which surrounded a flower-filled patio and rested on a stone platform for protection against floods. It is estimated that there were about 60,000 houses in Tenochtitlán. The focal points of the city were the *teocallis*, or pyramidal temples, at which religious ceremonies, including human sacrifice, were held. The 100-foot-high double temple dedicated to the war god and the rain god was made of stone and featured a steep staircase that led to a platform with an altar, a chamber containing shrines, and an antechamber for the priests.

The palace of the emperor Moctezuma boasted numerous rooms for attendants and concubines, a menagerie, hanging gardens, and a swimming

Preindustrial cities: The kinds of urban settlements that are characteristic of nonindustrial civilizations.

pool. Since Tenochtitlán sat in the middle of a lake, it was unfortified and connected to the mainland by three causeways. Communication among different parts of the city was easy, and one could travel either by land or by water. A series of canals, with footpaths running beside them, ran throughout the city. The Spaniards who came to this city reported that thousands of canoes plied the canals, carrying passengers and cargo around the city; these Europeans were so impressed by the communication network that they called Tenochtitlán the "Venice of the New World."

NONINDUSTRIAL CITIES IN THE MODERN WORLD

Tenochtitlán is a good example of the kind of urban settlement that was characteristic of most ancient, nonindustrial civilizations. Commonly termed **preindustrial cities,** they are apt to be thought of as things of the past, or as little more

The modern industrial city is a very recent human invention, although its roots lie in the so-called preindustrial city. The widespread belief that so-called preindustrial cities are things of the past and that industrial cities are things of the future is based on culture-bound assumptions rather than established facts.

than stages in some sort of inevitable progression toward the kinds of industrial cities one finds today in places like Europe and North America. This essentially ethnocentric view obscures the fact that "preindustrial" cities are far from uncommon in the world today — especially in the so-called Third World countries. Furthermore, industrial cities have not yet come close to demonstrating that they have the long-term viability shown by nonindustrial cities, which in some parts of the world have been around for not just hundreds but thousands of years.

CHAPTER SUMMARY

Needs and pressures require people to adjust their behavior to suit their environment. This adjustment, which involves both change and stability, is a part of adaptation. Adaptation means that there is a moving balance between a society's needs and its environmental potential. Adaptation also refers to the interaction of an organism and its environment, with each causing changes in the other. The unit of adaptation includes both the organism and its environment. Adaptation is a continuing process, and it is essential for survival. An ecosystem is bound by the activities of organisms and by physi-

cal forces such as erosion. Human ecosystems must be considered in terms of all aspects of culture.

To fit into an ecosystem an organism must be able to adapt or become a part of it. Once such a fit is achieved, stability may serve the organism's interest more than change.

A culture area is a geographical region in which various societies follow similar patterns of life. Since geographical regions are not always uniform in climate and topography, new discoveries do not always spread to every group. Environmental variation also favors variation in technology, since needs may be quite different from area to area.

Julian Steward used the concept of culture type to explain variations within geographical regions. In this view, a culture is considered in terms of a particular technology and of the particular environmental features that technology is best suited to deal with.

The social and political organization of a society are other factors that influence how technology is to be used to ensure survival. Those features of a culture that play a part in the way the society makes a living are its culture core. Anthropologists can trace direct relationships between types of culture cores and types of environments.

The food-foraging way of life, the oldest and most universal type of human adaptation, requires that people move their residence according to changing food sources. For as yet unknown ecological and social factors, local group size is kept small. One explanation contends that small sizes fit land capacity to sustain the groups. Another states that the fewer the people, the less the chance of social conflict. The primary mechanism for regulation of population size among food foragers is frequent stimulation of the female nipple, which prevents ovulation, because infants nurse several times an hour for several years.

Three important elements of human social organization probably developed along with scavenging and hunting for meat. These are a sexual division of labor, food sharing, and the camp as the center of daily activity and the place where food sharing takes place.

A characteristic of food-foraging societies is their egalitarianism. Since this way of life requires mobility, people accumulate only the material goods necessary for survival so that status differ-

ences are limited to those based on age and sex. Even at that, egalitarianism applies as much to women as to men. Food resources are distributed equally throughout the groups; thus, no individual can achieve the wealth or status that hoarding might bring.

One correlate of the food-producing revolution was the development of permanent settlements, as people practiced simple horticulture, using neither the plow nor irrigation nor intensive agriculture, a more complex activity that requires irrigation, fertilizers, and draft animals. Pastoralism is a means of subsistence that relies on raising herds of domesticated animals, such as cattle, sheep, and goats. Pastoralists are usually nomads, moving to different pastures as required for grass and water.

With the intensification of agriculture, some farming communities grew into cities. Social structure becomes increasingly stratified with the development of cities, and people are ranked according to the work they do and the family they are born into. Social relationships grow more formal and political institutions are formed.

One should not conclude that there is inevitability to the sequence from food foraging, through horticultural/pastoral, to nonindustrial urban and then industrial society, even though these did appear in that order. Where older adaptations continue to prevail, it is because conditions are such that they continue to work so well, and provide such satisfaction, that the people who maintain them prefer them to the alternatives of which they are aware. It is not because of any "backwardness" or ignorance. Modern food-forager, horticultural, pastoral, nonindustrial, and industrial urban societies are all highly evolved adaptations, each in its own particular way.

SUGGESTED READINGS

Lustig-Arecco, Vera. *Technology: Strategies for Survival.* New York: Holt, Rinehart and Winston, 1975. Although the early anthropologists devoted a good deal of attention to technology, the subject fell into neglect early in the twentieth century. This is one of the few recent studies of the subject. The author's particular interest is the technoeconomic adaptation of hunters, pastoralists, and farmers.

Oswalt, Wendell H. *Habitat and Technology*. New York: Holt, Rinehart and Winston, 1972. The author develops a taxonomy that permits precise cross-cultural comparisons of the complexity of manufactures. The research is based on a systematic analysis of the known manufactures of non-Western peoples. Shelters, tools, clothing, implements, and cultivated foodstuffs are considered.

Schrire, Carmel, ed. *Past and Present in Hunter Gatherer Studies*. Orlando, Fla.: Academic Press, 1984. This collection of papers demolishes many a myth (including several held by anthropologists) about food-foraging societies. Especially recommended is the editor's introduction, "Wild Surmises on Savage Thoughts."

Sjoberg, Gideon. *The Preindustrial City*. New York: Free Press, 1960. In this important study, the author draws on cross-cultural research to discuss the nature of "preindustrial" cities everywhere.

Vayda, Andrew, ed. *Environment and Cultural Behavior: Ecological Studies in Cultural Anthropology*. Garden City, N.Y.: Natural History Press, 1969. The focus of the studies collected here is the interrelationship between cultural behavior and environmental phenomena. The writers attempt to make cultural behavior intelligible by relating it to the material world in which it develops. This volume includes articles concerning population, divination, ritual, warfare, food production, climate, and diseases.

16

ECONOMIC SYSTEMS

The most basic characteristic of the market in non-Western societies is that it always means a market place, where actual goods are exchanged. At this Andean market, Indians and non-Indians alike are able to exchange items they have produced for things that they need but can only get from others.

CHAPTER

PREVIEW

How Do Anthropologists Study Economic Systems?

Anthropologists study the means by which goods are produced, distributed, and consumed in the context of the total culture of particular societies. Although they have borrowed theories and concepts from economists, most anthropologists feel that principles derived from the study of Western market economies have limited applicability to economic systems where people do not produce and exchange goods for profit.

How Do the Economies of Nonindustrial Peoples Work?

In non-Western, nonindustrial societies there is always a division of labor by age and sex, with some additional craft specialization. Land and other valuable resources are usually controlled by groups of relatives, such as bands or lineages, and individual ownership is rare. Production takes place in the quantity and at the time required, and most goods are consumed by the group that produces them. Leveling mechanisms ensure that no one accumulates significantly more goods than anyone else.

How and Why Are Goods Exchanged in Nonindustrial Societies?

Nonindustrial peoples exchange goods through the processes of reciprocity, redistribution, and market exchange. Reciprocity involves the exchange of goods and services of roughly equivalent value, and it is often undertaken for ritual purposes or for purposes of gaining prestige. Redistribution requires some sort of government and/or religious elite to collect and then reallocate resources, in the form of either goods or services. Market exchange, which in nonindustrial societies means going to a specific place for direct exchange of goods, also serves as entertainment and as a means of exchanging important information. The latter are frequently primary motivating forces bringing people into the marketplace.

An economic system may be defined as one by which goods are produced, distributed, and consumed. Since a people, in pursuing a particular means of subsistence, necessarily produces, distributes, and consumes things, it is obvious that our earlier discussion of patterns of subsistence (Chapter 15) involved us with economic matters. Yet there is much more to economic systems than we have so far covered. This chapter will look at aspects of economic systems — specifically systems of production, exchange, and redistribution — that require more discussion than we were able to give them in the last chapter.

ECONOMIC ANTHROPOLOGY

It is perhaps in the study of the economies of nonliterate peoples that we are most apt to fall prey to interpreting anthropological data in terms of our own technologies, our own values of work and property, and our own determination of what is rational (Figure 16.1). Take, for example, the following statement from a recent respected textbook in economics: "In all societies, the prevailing reality of life has been the inadequacy of output to fill the wants and needs of the people."[1] What this ethnocentric assertion fails to realize is that in many societies people's wants are maintained at levels that can be fully and continuously satisfied, and without jeopardizing the environment. In such societies, things are produced in the quantity and at the time required, and to do more than this makes no sense at all. Thus, no matter how hard people may work when hard work is called for, at other times they will have available hours, days, or even weeks on end to devote to "unproductive" (in the economic sense) activities. To Western observers, such people are apt to appear lazy; "instead of disciplined workers, they are reluctant and

untrained laborers."[2] If the people happen to be hunters and gatherers, even the hard work is likely to be misinterpreted. In Western culture hunting is defined as a sport; hence, the men in food-foraging societies are often perceived as spending virtually all of their time in "recreational pursuits," while the women are working themselves to the bone.

The point to be made here is that to understand how the schedule of wants or demands of a given society is balanced against the supply of goods and services available, it is necessary to introduce a noneconomic variable — the anthropological variable of culture. In any given economic system, economic processes cannot be interpreted without culturally defining the demands and understanding the conventions that dictate how and when they are satisfied.

As a case in point, we may look briefly at yam production among the Trobriand Islanders, who inhabit a group of coral atolls that lie north of New Guinea's eastern end.[3] Trobriand men spend a great deal of their time and energy raising yams, not for themselves or their own families, but to give others, normally their sisters and married daughters. The purpose of this yam production is not to provision the households of those to whom they are given, as most of what people eat they grow for themselves in gardens in which they plant taro, sweet potatoes, tapioca, greens, beans, and squash, as well as breadfruit and banana trees. The reasons for a man to give yams to a woman are twofold: to show his support for her husband and to enhance his own influence. Once received by the woman, they are loaded into her husband's yam house, symbolizing his worth as a man of power and influence in his community. Some of these yams he may use to purchase a variety of things, including armshells, shell necklaces and earrings, betel nuts, pigs, chickens, and such locally produced goods as wooden bowls, combs, floor mats, lime pots, or even magic spells. Some

[1]Robert L. Heilbroner and Lester C. Thurow, *The Economic Problem*, 6th ed. (Englewood Cliffs, N.J.: Prentice-Hall, 1981), p. 327.

[2]Ibid., p. 609.
[3]Annette B. Weiner, *The Trobrianders of Papua New Guinea* (New York: Holt, Rinehart and Winston, 1988).

The Chief Registrar of Natives,
NAIROBI.

N.A.D. Form No 54/______

COMPLAINT OF DESERTION OF REGISTERED NATIVE.

Native's Certificate No. ____________ Name ____________

The above native deserted from my employ ____________
(date)

He was engaged on ________ on ________ days verbal contract
(date) ________ months written contract

at ________________________
(place) *(Contract No.)*

I wish to prosecute him for this offence and hereby agree to appear as a witness or to produce evidence if and when called upon.

____
Signature of Employer

Address ____________
____

Date ____________

FIGURE 16.1 People with industrial economies frequently misunderstand the work ethic in so-called "tribal" societies. Thus the British, in colonial Kenya, thought it necessary to teach natives "the dignity of labor," and made it a crime for a tribal person to quit work without authorization.

he must use to discharge obligations, as in the presentation of yams to the relatives of his daughter's husband when she marries, or the payments that must be made following the death of a member of his lineage (a group of relatives descended, in this case through women, from a common ancestor). Finally, any man who aspires to high status and power is expected to show his worth by organizing a yam competition, in the course of which huge quantities of yams are given away to invited guests. As anthropologist Annette Weiner explains: "A yam house, then, is like a bank account; when full, a man is wealthy and powerful. Until yams are cooked or they rot, they may circulate as limited currency. That is why, once harvested, the usage of yams for daily food is avoided as much as possible."[4]

[4]Ibid., p. 86.

By giving yams to his sister or daughter, not only does a man express his confidence in the woman's husband, but he also makes the latter indebted to him. Although the recipient rewards the gardener and his helpers by throwing a feast, at which they are fed cooked yams, taro, and—what everyone especially looks forward to—ample pieces of pork, this in no way pays off the debt. Nor does the gift of a stone ax blade (another valuable in the Trobriand system), which may reward an especially good harvest. The debt can only be repaid in women's wealth, which consists of bundles of banana leaves, and skirts made of the same material that have been dyed red. Although the bundles are of no utilitarian value, extensive labor is invested in their production, and large quantities of them, along with skirts, are regarded as essential in paying off all the members of other lineages who were close to a recently deceased relative in

Trobriand men devote a great deal of time and energy to raising yams, not for themselves, but to give to others. These yams, which have been raised by men related through marriage to a chief, are about to be loaded into the chief's yam house.

life and who assisted with the funeral. At the same time, the wealth and vitality of the dead person's lineage are measured by the quality and quantity of the bundles and skirts so distributed. Because a man has received yams from his wife's brother, he is obligated to provide her with yams with which she can purchase the necessary bundles and skirts, over and above those she herself has produced, in order to help with payments following the death of a member of her lineage. Because deaths are unpredictable, and can occur at any time, a man must have yams available for his wife when she needs

them. This, and the fact that she may require all of his yams, acts as an effective check on a man's wealth.

Like people the world over, the Trobriand Islanders assign meanings to objects that make them worth far more than their cost in labor or the materials of which they are made. Yams, for example, establish long-term relationships that lead to other advantages, such as access to land, protection, assistance, and other kinds of wealth. Thus, yam exchanges are as much social and political as they are economic transactions. Banana leaf bundles and skirts, for their part, are symbolic of the political state of lineages, and of their immortality. In their distribution, which is related to rituals associated with death, we see how men in Trobriand society are ultimately dependent on women and their valuables. So important are these matters to the Trobrianders that even in the face of Western money, education, religion, and law, these people remain as committed today as in the past to yam cultivation and the production of women's wealth. Looked at in terms of Western economics, this appears to make little sense, but looked at in terms of Trobriand values and concerns, it makes a great deal of sense.

RESOURCES

In every society there are customs and rules governing what kind of work is done, who does the work, who owns the resources and tools, and how the work is accomplished. Raw materials, labor, and technology are the productive resources that a social group may use to produce desired goods and services. The rules surrounding the use of these are embedded in the culture and determine the way the economy operates.

PATTERNS OF LABOR

In every human society, there has always been a division of labor by both sex and age; such division is an elaboration of patterns found in all higher primates. Dividing labor according to sex increases the chances that the learning of necessary skills will be more efficient, since only half the adult repertoire needs to be learned by any one individual. Dividing labor according to age provides sufficient time for those skills to be developed.

Sexual Division of Labor

Whether men or women do a particular job varies from group to group, but much work has been set apart as the work of either one sex or the other. The sexual division of labor in human societies of all sorts has been studied extensively by anthropologists, and we discussed some aspects of it in the preceding chapter, as well as in Chapter 6. For example, we have seen that the tasks most often regarded as "women's work" tend to be those that can be carried out near home and that are easily resumed after interruption. The tasks most often regarded as "men's work" tend to be those that require physical strength, rapid mobilization of high bursts of energy, frequent travel at some distance from home, and assumption of high levels of risk and danger. There are, however, plenty of exceptions, as in those societies where women regularly carry burdensome loads or put in long hours of hard work cultivating crops in the fields. In some societies, women perform almost three-quarters of all work, and there are even societies where women serve as warriors. In the nineteenth-century kingdom of Dahomey, in West Africa, thousands served in the armed forces of the Dahomean king, and in the eyes of some observers, they were better fighters than their male counterparts. Clearly, the sexual division of labor cannot be explained simply as a consequence of male strength, male expendability, or female reproductive biology.

Instead of looking for biological imperatives to explain the sexual division of labor, a more productive strategy is to examine the kinds of work done by men and women in the context of specific societies, to see how it relates to other cultural and historical factors. What we find are three different configurations, one featuring flexibility and sexual integration, another featuring rigid segregation by sex, and a third combining elements of the other two.[5] The flexible/integrated pattern is exemplified by people like the !Kung, whose practices we examined in Chapter 15, and is seen most often among food foragers and subsistence farmers. In such societies, up to 35 percent of activities are performed by both sexes with approximately equal participation, while those tasks deemed appropriate for one sex may be performed by the other, without loss of face, as the situation warrants. Where these practices prevail, boys and girls grow up in much the same way, learn to value cooperation over competition, and become equally habituated to adult men and women, who interact with one another on a relatively equal basis.

Sexually segregated societies are those in which almost all work is rigidly defined as either masculine or feminine, so that men and women rarely engage in joint efforts of any kind. In such societies, it is inconceivable that someone would even think of doing something considered to be the work of the opposite sex! This pattern is frequently seen in pastoral nomadic, intensive agricultural, and industrial societies, in which men's work keeps them outside the home for much of the time. Thus, boys and girls alike are raised primarily by women, who encourage compliance in their charges. At some point, however, boys must undergo a role reversal to become like men who are supposed to be tough, aggressive, and competitive, and to do this, they must prove their masculinity in ways that women do not have to prove their feminine identity. Commonly, this involves assertions of male superiority, and hence authority, over women. Historically, sexually segregated societies have often imposed their control on those featuring sexual integration, upsetting the egalitarian nature of the latter.

In the third, or dual sex, configuration, men and women carry out their work separately, as in sexu-

[5]Peggy Reeves Sanday, *Female Power and Male Dominance: On the Origins of Sexual Inequality* (Cambridge: Cambridge University Press, 1981), pp. 79–80.

Often, work that is considered appropriate for women in one society is performed by men in another, and vice versa. Shown here is an Aymara Indian man spinning thread, and Guajiro Indian women carrying heavy loads.

ally segregated societies, but the relationship between them is one of balanced complementarity, rather than inequality. Although competition is a prevailing ethic, each sex manages its own affairs, and the interests of both men and women are represented at all levels. Thus, as in sexually integrated societies, neither sex exerts dominance over the other. The dual sex orientation may be seen among certain Native American peoples whose economies were based upon subsistence farming, as well as among several West African kingdoms, such as that of the Dahomeans.

Among the Maya, young boys make a substantial contribution to the work of the fields. Among food foragers, large numbers of children are a burden to women; in agrarian societies, the work they contribute to the family makes them an economic asset.

Age Division of Labor

A division of labor according to age is also typical of human societies. Among the !Kung, for example, children are not expected to contribute significantly to subsistence until they reach their late teens. The !Kung equivalent of "retirement" comes somewhere around the age of 60. Elderly people, while they will usually do some foraging for themselves, are not expected to contribute much food. On the other hand, older men and women alike play an essential role in spiritual matters; being freed from food taboos and other restrictions that apply to younger adults, they may handle ritual substances considered dangerous to those still involved with hunting or having children. By virtue of their old age, they also remember things that happened far in the past. Thus, they are repositories of accumulated wisdom — the "libraries" of a nonliterate people — and are able to suggest solutions to problems that younger adults have never before had to face. Thus, they are far from being unproductive members of society.

In many nonindustrial societies, not just older people, but children as well, may make a greater contribution to the economy in terms of work and responsibility than is common in our own. For instance, in Mayan communities in southern Mexico and Guatemala, young children not only look after their younger brothers and sisters but help with housework as well. Girls begin to make a substantial contribution to the work of the household by the age of 7 or 8, and by the time they are 11, they are constantly busy grinding corn, making tortillas, fetching wood and water, sweeping the house, and so forth. Boys have less to do, but are given small tasks, such as bringing in the chickens or playing with a baby. However, by the time they are 12, they are carrying toasted tortillas to the men out working in the fields and returning from there with loads of corn.[6]

Cooperation

Cooperative work groups can be found everywhere in nonliterate as well as literate and in nonindustrial as well as industrial societies. Often, if the effort involves the whole community, there is a festive spirit to the work. Jomo Kenyatta, the anthropologist who went on to become a respected statesman as well as "father" of an independent Kenya, described the time of enjoyment after a day's labor in his country:

> If a stranger happens to pass by, he will have no idea that these people who are singing and dancing have completed their day's work. This is why most Europeans have erred by not realizing that the African in

[6]Evon Z. Vogt, *The Zinacantecos of Mexico, A Modern Maya Way of Life* (New York: Holt, Rinehart and Winston, 1970), pp. 62–67.

his own environment does not count hours or work by the movement of the clock, but works with good spirit and enthusiasm to complete the tasks before him.[7]

Among the !Kung, women go out to gather wild plant foods about three times a week. Although they may go out alone, they more often go out in groups, talking loudly as they go. This not only turns what might otherwise seem a monotonous task into a social occasion; it also causes large animals — potential sources of danger — to move elsewhere.

In most human societies, the basic unit in which cooperation takes place is the household. It is a unit of production and consumption at one and the same time; only in industrial societies have these two things been separated. The Mayan farmer, for example, unlike his North American counterpart, is not so much running a commercial enterprise as he is a household. He is motivated by a desire to provide for the welfare of his own family; each family, as an economic unit, works as a group for its own good. Cooperative work may be undertaken outside of the household, however, for other reasons, though not always voluntarily. It may be done to fulfill duties to in-laws; it may be performed for chiefs or priests, by command. Thus, institutions of family, kinship, religion, and the state all may act as organizing elements that define the nature and condition of each worker's cooperative obligations.

Craft Specialization

In nonindustrial societies, where division of labor occurs along lines of age and sex, each person in the society has knowledge and competence in all aspects of work appropriate to his or her age and sex. In modern industrial societies, by contrast, there exists a greater diversity of more specialized tasks to be performed, and no individual can even begin to have knowledge of all those appropriate for his or her age and sex. Yet even in nonindustrial societies, there is some specialization of craft. This

In nonindustrial societies, households produce much of what they consume. Among the Maya, men work in the fields to produce food for the household; women prepare the food and take care of other chores that can be performed in or near the house.

[7]Melville Herskovits, *Economic Anthropology: A Study in Comparative Economics*, 2d ed. (New York: Knopf, 1952), p. 103.

is often minimal in food-foraging societies, but even here the arrow points of one man may be in some demand because of his particular skill at making them. Among people who produce their own food, there is apt to be more in the way of specialization. In the Trobriand Islands, for example, if one wanted stone to make ax blades, one had

In industrial societies, people do not have unrestricted access to the means of production, nor do they generally produce directly for their own consumption. Instead, they work for strangers, often at monotonous tasks done in a depersonalized setting. Such conditions contribute to alienation, a major problem in industrial societies.

to travel some distance to one particular island where the appropriate kind of stone was quarried; clay pots, on the other hand, were made by people living on yet another island.

An example of specialization can be seen among Afar tribesmen of Ethiopia's Danakil depression. They are miners of salt, which since ancient times has been widely traded in East Africa. It is mined from the crust of an extensive salt plain in the north part of the depression, and to get it is a risky and difficult business. L. M. Nesbitt, the first European to successfully traverse the depression, labeled it "the hell hole of creation."[8] The heat is extreme during the day, with shade temperatures between 140° and 156° F not unusual. Shade is not to be found on the salt plain, however, unless a shelter of salt blocks is built. Nor is there food or water for man or beast. To add to the difficulty, until recently the Muslim Afars and the Christian Tegreans, highlanders who also mine salt, were mortal enemies.

Successful mining, then, requires skill at planning and organization, as well as physical strength and the will to work under the most trying condi-

[8]L. M. Nesbitt, *Hell-Hole of Creation* (New York: Knopf, 1935).

tions.[9] Pack animals to carry the salt have to be fed in advance, for to carry sufficient fodder for them interferes with their ability to carry out salt. Food and water must be carried for the miners, who usually number 30 to 40 per group. Travel is planned to take place at night to avoid the intense heat of day. In the past, measures to protect against attack had to be taken. Finally, timing is critical; a party has to get back to sources of food and water before its own supplies are too long exhausted, and before its animals are unable to continue farther.

CONTROL OF LAND

All societies have regulations that determine the way valuable land resources will be allocated. Food foragers must determine who can hunt game and gather plants and where these activities take place. Horticulturists must decide how their farmland is to be acquired, worked, and passed on. Pastoralists require a system that determines rights to watering places and grazing land, as well as the right of access to land over which they move their herds. Full-time or intensive agriculturalists must have some means of determining title to land and access to water supplies for irrigation purposes. In our own industrialized Western society, a system of private ownership of land and rights to natural resources generally prevails. Although elaborate laws have been established to regulate the buying, owning, and selling of land and water resources, if individuals wish to reallocate valuable farmland, for instance, for another purpose, they are generally able to do so.

In nonindustrial societies, land is often controlled by kinship groups such as the lineage (discussed in Chapter 19) or band, rather than by individuals. For example, among the !Kung, each band of anywhere from 10 to 30 people lives on roughly 250 square miles of land, which they consider to be their territory — their own country. These territories are defined not in terms of boundaries, but

[9]Haile Michael Mesghinua, "Salt Mining in Enderta," *Journal of Ethiopian Studies* 4, no. 2 (1966); Kevin O'Mahoney, "The Salt Trade," *Journal of Ethiopian Studies* 8, no. 2 (1970).

rather in terms of waterholes that are located within them. The land is said to be "owned" by those who have lived the longest in the band, usually a group of brothers and sisters or cousins. Their ownership, however, is more symbolic than real. They cannot sell (or buy) land, but their permission must be asked by outsiders to enter the territory. To refuse such permission, though, would be unthinkable.

The practice of defining territories on the basis of core features, be they waterholes (as among the !Kung), distinctive features of the landscape where ancestral spirits are thought to dwell (as among Australian aborigines), watercourses (as among Indians of the northeastern United States), or whatever, is typical of food foragers. Territorial boundaries are left vaguely defined, at best. The adaptive value of this is clear; the size of band territories, as well as the size of the bands themselves, can adjust to keep pace with availability of resources in any given place. Such adjustment would be more difficult under a system of individual ownership of clearly bounded land.

Among some West African farmers, a feudal system of landownership prevails, by which all land belongs to the head chief. He allocates it to various subchiefs, who in turn distribute it to lineages; lineage leaders then assign individual plots to each farmer. Just as in medieval Europe, these African people owe allegiance to the subchiefs (or nobles) and the principal chief (or king). The people who work the land must pay taxes and fight for the king when necessary. The people, in a sense, "own" the land and transmit their ownership to their heirs. No one, however, can give away, sell, or otherwise dispose of a plot of land without approval from the elder of the lineage. When an individual no longer needs the land that has been allocated, the lineage head rescinds title to it and reallocates it to someone else in the lineage. The important operative principle here is that the system extends the right of the individual to use land for a certain period of time, but the land is not "owned" outright. This serves to maintain the integrity of valuable farmland as such, preventing

its loss through subdivision and conversion to other uses.

TECHNOLOGY

All societies have some means of creating and allocating the tools and other artifacts used in the production of goods and passed on to succeeding generations. The number and kinds of tools a society uses are related to the life-styles of its members. Food foragers and pastoral nomads, who are frequently on the move, are apt to have fewer and simpler tools than the more sedentary farmer, in part because a great number of complex tools would decrease their mobility.

Food foragers make and use a variety of tools, many of which are ingenious in their effectiveness. Some of these they make for their own use, but codes of generosity are such that a person may not refuse giving or loaning what is requested. Thus, tools may be given or loaned to others in exchange for the products resulting from their use. For example, a !Kung who gives his arrow to another hunter has a right to a share in any animals that the hunter may kill. Game is thought to "belong" to the man whose arrow killed it.

Among horticulturists, the ax, machete, and digging stick or hoe are the primary tools. Since these are relatively easy to produce, every person can make them. Although the maker has first rights to their use, when that person is not using them, any member of the family may ask to use them and usually is granted permission to do so. To refuse would cause the tool owner to be treated with scorn for this singular lack of concern for others. If another relative helps raise the crop that is traded for a particular tool, that relative becomes part owner of the implement, and it may not be traded or given away without his or her permission.

In sedentary communities, which farming makes possible, tools and other productive goods become more complex and more difficult and costlier to make. Where this happens, individual ownership in them usually becomes more abso-

Top ranking cargoholders in the Maya community of Zinacantan (the word "cargo" is from the Spanish word for "burden"). These men will retire from office deeply in debt, but loaded with prestige.

lute, as do the conditions under which persons may borrow and use such equipment. It is easy to replace a knife lost by a relative during palm cultivation, but much more difficult to replace an iron plow or a power-driven threshing machine. Rights to the ownership of complex tools are more rigidly applied; generally the person who has supplied the funds for the purchase of a complex piece of machinery is considered the sole owner and may decide how and by whom it will be used.

LEVELING MECHANISMS
In spite of the increased opportunities that exist in sedentary, farming communities for people to accumulate belongings, limits on property acquisition may be as prominent in them as among nomadic peoples. In such communities, social obligations compel people to divest themselves of wealth, and no one is permitted to accumulate too much more than others. Greater wealth simply brings greater obligation to give. Anthropologists refer to such obligations as **leveling mechanisms.**

Leveling mechanism: A societal obligation compelling a family to distribute goods so that no one accumulates more wealth than anyone else.

Leveling mechanisms are found in communities where property must not be allowed to threaten a more or less egalitarian social order, as in many Mayan villages and towns in the highlands of Mexico and Guatemala. In these communities, cargo systems function to siphon off any excess wealth that people may accumulate. A cargo system is a civil–religious hierarchy, which, on a revolving basis, combines most of the civic and ceremonial offices of a community in a hierarchical sequence, with each office being occupied for one year. All offices are open to all men, and eventually virtually every man has at least one term in office. The scale is pyramidal, which is to say that more offices exist at the lower levels, with progressively fewer at the top. For example, in a community of about 8,000 people, there may be four levels of offices, with 32 on the lowest level, 12 on the next one up, 6 on the next, and 2 at the top. Offices at the lower level include those for the performance of various menial chores, such as sweeping and carrying messages. The higher offices are those of councilmen, judges, mayors, and ceremonial positions. These positions are regarded as burdens, for which one receives no pay. Instead, the office-holder is expected to pay for the food, liquor, music, fireworks, or whatever is required for community festivals or for banquets associated with the transmission of office. After holding a cargo position, a man usually has a period of rest, during which he may accumulate sufficient resources to campaign for a higher office. Each male citizen of the community is socially obligated to serve in the system at least once, and social pressure to do so is such that it drives individuals who have once again accumulated excess wealth to apply for higher offices in order to raise their social status. Thus, while some individuals have appreciably more prestige than others in their community, no one has appreciably more wealth in a material sense than anyone else.

In addition to equalizing wealth, the cargo system accomplishes other things as well. Through its system of offices, it ensures that necessary services within the community are performed. Members are also pressured into investing their resources in their own community, rather than elsewhere. Finally, it keeps goods in circulation, rather than sitting around "gathering dust" somewhere.

DISTRIBUTION AND EXCHANGE

In our own money economy, there is a two-step process between labor and consumption. The money received for labor must be translated into something else before it is directly consumable. In societies with no such medium of exchange, the rewards for labor are usually direct. The workers in a family group consume what they harvest; they

> **Reciprocity:** The exchange of goods and services, of approximately equal value, between two parties.

eat what the hunter or gatherer brings home; they use the tools that they themselves make. But even where there is no formal medium of exchange, some distribution of goods takes place. Karl Polanyi, an economist, classified the cultural systems of distributing material goods into three modes: reciprocity, redistribution, and market exchange.[10]

RECIPROCITY

Reciprocity refers to a transaction between two parties, whereby goods and services of roughly equivalent value are exchanged. This may involve gift giving, but in non-Western societies, pure altruism in gift giving is as rare as it is in our own society. The overriding motive is to fulfill social obligations and perhaps to gain a bit of prestige in the process. It might be best compared in our society to someone who gives a party. He or she may go to great lengths to impress others by the excellence of the food and drink served, not to mention the quality of wit and conversation of those in attendance. The expectation is that, sooner or later, he or she will be invited to similar parties by some, although perhaps not all, of the guests.

Social customs dictate the nature and occasion of exchange. When an animal is killed by a group of hunters in Australia, the meat is divided among the families of the hunters and other relatives. Each person in the camp gets a share, the size depending on the nature of the person's kinship tie to the hunters. The least desirable parts are kept by the hunters themselves. When a kangaroo is killed, for example, the left hind leg goes to the brother of the hunter, the tail to his father's brother's son, the loins and the fat to his father-in-law, the ribs to his

[10]Karl Polanyi, "The Economy as Instituted Process," in *Economic Anthropology: Readings in Theory and Analysis*, ed. Edward E. LeClair, Jr., and Harold K. Schneider (New York: Holt, Rinehart and Winston, 1968), pp. 122–143.

mother-in-law, the forelegs to his father's younger sister, the head to his wife, and the entrails and the blood to the hunter. If there were arguments over the apportionment, it would be because the principles of distribution were not being followed properly. The hunter and his family would seem to fare badly according to this arrangement, but they have their turn when another man makes a kill. The giving and receiving is obligatory, as is the particularity of the distribution. Such sharing of food reinforces community bonds and ensures that everyone eats. It might also be viewed as a way of saving perishable goods. By giving away part of his kill, the hunter gets a social IOU for a similar amount of food in the future. It is a little bit like putting money in a time-deposit savings account.

The food-distribution practice just described for Australian hunters constitutes an example of **generalized reciprocity**. This may be defined as an exchange in which neither is the value of what is given calculated nor is the time of repayment specified. Gift giving, in the altruistic sense, also falls in this category. Most commonly, generalized reciprocity occurs among close kin or people who otherwise have very close ties with one another.

Balanced reciprocity differs, in that it is not part of a long-term process. The giving and receiving, as well as the time involved, are more specific. Examples of balanced reciprocity among the Crow Indians are related by Robert Lowie.[11] A woman skilled in the tanning of buffalo hides might offer her services to a neighbor who needed a new cover for her tepee. It took an expert to design a tepee cover, which required from 14 to 20 skins. The designer might need as many as 20 collaborators, whom she instructed in the sewing together of the skins and whom the tepee owner might remunerate with a feast. The designer herself would be given some kind of property by the tepee owner. In another example from the Crow, Lowie relates that if a married woman brought her brother a present of food, he might reciprocate with a pres-

Generalized reciprocity: A mode of exchange in which neither the value of the gift is calculated nor the time of repayment is specified.

Balanced reciprocity: A mode of exchange in which the giving and the receiving are specific for the value of the goods and the time of their delivery.

Negative reciprocity: A form of exchange in which the giver tries to get the better of the exchange.

ent of 10 arrows for her husband, which rated as the equivalent of a horse.

Giving, receiving, and sharing as so far described constitute a form of social security or insurance. A family contributes to others when it has the means and can count on receiving from others in time of need. A leveling mechanism is at work in the process of generalized or balanced reciprocity, promoting an egalitarian distribution of wealth over the long run.

Negative reciprocity is a third form of exchange, in which the giver tries to get the better of the exchange. The parties involved have opposed interests, usually are members of different communities, and are not closely related. The ultimate form of negative reciprocity is to take something by force. Less extreme forms involve the use of guile and deception, or at the least hard bargaining. Among the Navajo, according to the anthropologist Clyde Kluckhohn, "to deceive when trading with foreign tribes is morally accepted."[12]

Barter and Trade

Exchange that takes place within a group of people generally takes the form of generalized or balanced reciprocity. When it takes place between two groups, there is apt to be at least a potential for hostility and competition. Therefore, such exchange may well be in the form of negative reciprocity, unless some sort of arrangement has been made to ensure at least an approach to balance.

---

[11]Robert Lowie, *Crow Indians* (New York: Holt, Rinehart and Winston, 1956), p. 75; original edition, 1935.

[12]Clyde Kluckhohn, quoted in Marshall Sahlins, *Stone Age Economics* (Chicago: Aldine, 1972), p. 200.

Barter is one form of negative reciprocity by which scarce items from one group are exchanged for desirable goods from another group. Relative value is calculated, and despite an outward show of indifference, sharp trading is more the rule, when compared with the reciprocal nature of the exchanges within a group.

An arrangement that partook partly of balanced reciprocity and partly of barter existed between the Kota, in India, and three neighboring tribes who traded their surplus goods and certain services with the Kota. The Kota were the musicians and artisans for the area. They exchanged iron tools with the other three groups and provided the music essential for ceremonial occasions. The Toda furnished to the Kota *ghee* (a kind of butter) for certain ceremonies and buffalo for funerals; relations between the Kota and the Toda were friendly. The Badaga were agricultural and traded their grain for music and tools. Between the Kota and Badaga there was a feeling of great competition, which sometimes led to one-sided trading practices; it was usually the Kota who procured the advantage. The forest-dwelling Kurumba, who were dreaded sorcerers, had honey, canes, and occasionally fruits to offer, but their main contribution was protection against the supernatural. The Kota feared the Kurumba, and the Kurumba took advantage of this in their trade dealings, so that they always got more than they gave. Thus there was great latent hostility between these two tribes.

Silent trade is a specialized form of barter in which no verbal communication takes place. In fact, it may involve no actual face-to-face contact at all. Such is the case with many forest-dwelling people in the world. Carleton Coon has described how this system works:

> The forest people creep through the lianas to the trading place, and leave a neat pile of jungle products, such as wax, camphor, monkeys' gall bladders, birds' nests for Chinese soup. They creep back a certain distance, and wait in a safe place. The partners to the exchange, who are usually agriculturalists with a more elaborate and extensive set of material posses-

Silent trade: A form of barter in which no verbal communication takes place.

sions but who cannot be bothered stumbling through the jungle after wax when they have someone else to do it for them, discover the little pile, and lay down beside it what they consider its equivalent in metal cutting tools, cheap cloth, bananas, and the like. They too discreetly retire. The shy folk then reappear, inspect the two piles, and if they are satisfied, take the second one away. Then the opposite group comes back and takes pile number one, and the exchange is completed. If the forest people are dissatisfied, they can retire once more, and if the other people want to increase their offering they may, time and again, until everyone is happy.[13]

The reasons for silent trade can only be postulated, but in some situations trade may be silent for lack of a common language. More often it may serve to control hostility so as to keep relations peaceful. In a very real sense, good relations are maintained by preventing relations. Another possibility, which does not exclude the others, is that it makes exchange possible where problems of status might make verbal communication unthinkable. In any event, it provides for the exchange of goods between groups in spite of potential barriers.

THE KULA RING

We tend to think of trade as something undertaken for purely practical purposes, in order to gain access to necessary goods and services. However, not all trade is motivated by economic considerations. A classic example of this is the Kula of the Trobriand Islanders, first described by Malinowski in 1920, but still going strong in the 1980s.[14] From their coral atolls, men periodically set sail in their canoes in order to exchange shell valuables with their Kula partners, who live on far distant islands. These voyages take men away from

[13]Carleton S. Coon, *A Reader in General Anthropology* (New York: Holt, Rinehart and Winston, 1948), p. 594.
[14]Weiner *The Trobrianders*, pp. 139–157.

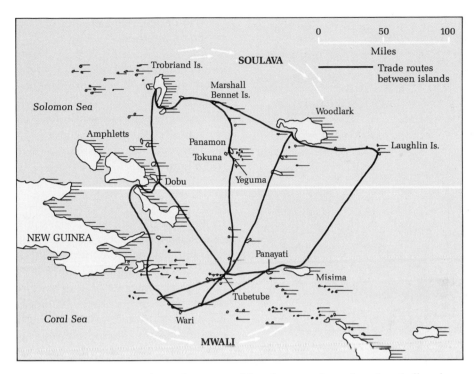

FIGURE 16.2 This map shows the ceremonial trade routes for exchanging shell necklaces and armbands in the Kula ring.

their homes for weeks, even months, at a time, and may expose them to various hardships along the way. The valuables consist of red shell necklaces, which always circulate in a clockwise direction, and ornate white armshells, which move in the opposite direction (Figure 16.2). These objects are ranked according to their size, color, the fineness of their polish, and their particular histories. Such is the fame of some that when they appear in a village, they create a sensation. No one man holds these valuables for very long, at most perhaps ten years. To hold on to an armshell or necklace too long risks disrupting the "path" that it must follow as it is passed from one partner to another.

Although men on Kula voyages may use the opportunity to trade for other things, this is not the reason for such voyages, nor is the Kula necessary for trade to take place. In fact, overseas trade is regularly undertaken without the exchange of shell valuables. Instead, Trobriand men seek to create history through their Kula exchanges. By circulating armbands and necklaces that accumulate the histories of their travels and names of those who have possessed them, men proclaim their individual fame and talent, gaining considerable influence for themselves in the process. Although the idea is to match the size and value of one shell for another, men draw on all their negotiating skills, material resources, and magical expertise to gain access to the strongest partners and most valuable shells; thus, an element of negative reciprocity enters in as a man may divert shells from their proper "paths," or entice others to compete for whatever necklaces and armbands he may have to offer. But when all is said and done, success is limited, for while a man may keep a shell

These photos show Kula valuables, and a canoe used for Kula voyages.

for five or ten years, sooner or later it must be passed on to others.

The Kula is a most elaborate complex of ceremony, political relationships, economic exchange, travel, magic, and social integration. To see it only in its economic aspects is to misunderstand it completely. The Kula demonstrates once more the close interrelationship of economic with other cultural factors, and shows that economics is not a realm unto itself.

REDISTRIBUTION

In nonindustrial societies, where there is a sufficient surplus to support a government, income will flow into the public coffers in the form of gifts, taxes, and the spoils of war; then it will be distributed again. The chief or king has three motives in disposing of this income: The first is to maintain his position of superiority by a display of wealth; the second is to assure those who support him an adequate standard of living; and the third is to establish alliances outside of his territory.

The administration of the Inca empire in Peru was one of the most efficient the world has ever known, both in the collection of taxes and in methods of control.[15] A census was kept of the population and resources. Tributes in goods and, more important, in services were levied. Each craftsman had to produce a specific quota of goods from materials supplied by overseers. Forced labor might be used for agricultural work or work in the mines. Forced labor was also employed in a program of public works, which included a remarkable system of roads and bridges throughout the mountainous terrain, aqueducts that guaranteed a supply of water, and storehouses that held surplus food for use in times of famine. Careful accounts were kept of income and expenditures. A governmental bureaucracy had the responsibility for seeing that production was maintained and that commodities were distributed according to the regulations set forth by the ruling powers.

[15]J. Alden Mason, *The Ancient Civilizations of Peru* (Baltimore: Penguin, 1957).

A protest against conspicuous consumption: fur coats do not keep one any warmer than other kinds of coats that are far less expensive, easier to care for, and less wasteful of the world's wildlife resources. Furthermore, they would be more comfortable to wear with the fur inside rather than outside.

Redistribution: A form of exchange in which goods flow into a central place, such as a market, and are distributed again.

Conspicuous consumption: A term coined by Thorstein Veblen to describe the display of wealth for social prestige.

Through the activities of the government, **redistribution** took place. The ruling class lived in great luxury, but goods were redistributed to the common people when necessary. In redistribution the exchange is not between individuals or between groups. Instead, a certain portion of the products of labor is funneled into one source and is parceled out again as directed by a central administration. Taxes are a form of redistribution in the United States; people pay taxes to the government, some of which support the government itself, while the rest are redistributed either in the form of cash, as in the case of welfare payments, government loans, and subsidies to business, or in the form of services, as in the case of food and drug inspection, construction of freeways, support of the military, and the like. Increasingly with the growth of the federal deficit since 1980, more and more wealth is being redistributed from middle-income taxpayers to wealthy holders of govern-

ment securities in order to finance the debt. For a process of redistribution to be possible, a society must have a centralized system of political organization, as well as an economic surplus over and above people's immediate needs.

DISTRIBUTION OF WEALTH

In societies in which people devote most of their time to subsistence activities, gradations of wealth are small, kept that way through leveling mechanisms and systems of reciprocity, which serve to distribute in a fairly equitable fashion what little wealth exists.

Display for social prestige, what economist Thorstein Veblen called **conspicuous consumption,** is a strong motivating force for the distribution of wealth in societies where some substantial surplus is produced. It has, of course, long been recognized that conspicuous consumption plays a prominent role in our own society, as individuals compete with one another for prestige. Indeed, many North Americans spend much of their lives trying to impress others, and this requires the display of items symbolic of prestigious positions in life. The ultimate in prestigious statuses is that of someone who doesn't have to work for a living, and here lies the irony: people may work long and hard in order to acquire the things that will make it appear as if they belong to a nonworking class of society. This all fits very nicely into an economy based on consumer wants:

In an expanding economy based on consumer wants, every effort must be made to place the standard of living in the center of public and private consideration, and every effort must therefore be lent to remove material and psychological impediments to consumption. Hence, rather than feelings of restraint, feelings of letting-go must be in the ascendant, and the institutions supporting restraint must recede into the background and give way to their opposite.[16]

A form of conspicuous consumption may occur in nonindustrial societies, and a case in point is the potlatch, an important ceremony among the Indi-

ans of the northwest coast of North America. In traditional northwest coast society, potlatches were held when new high-ranking individuals assumed the office of chief; later they became a means by which persons of high status might compete for even higher status through the grandiose display, and even destruction, of wealth. Although outlawed for a while by the Canadian government, potlatching is again legal, and is alive and well today among peoples such as the Kwakiutl Indians, who are the subject of the following Original Study.

[16]Jules Henry, "A Theory for an Anthropological Analysis of American Culture," in *Anthropology and American Life*, ed. Joseph G. Jorgensen and Marcello Truzzi (Englewood Cliffs, N.J.: Prentice-Hall, 1974), p. 14.

ORIGINAL STUDY
The Potlatch[17]

Among the Kwakiutl Indians of British Columbia, the potlatch is the most important public ceremony for the announcement of significant events and the claiming of hierarchical names, hereditary rights, and privileges. Such announcements or claims are always accompanied by the giving of gifts from a host to all guests. The guests are invited to witness, and later to validate, a host's claims, and each receives gifts of varying worth according to his rank.

Potlatches are held to celebrate births, marriages, deaths, adoptions, or the coming of age of young people. They may also be given as a penalty for breaking a taboo, such as behaving frivolously or performing ineptly during a sacred winter dance. A potlatch to save face can be prompted by an accident even as trivial as the capsizing of a canoe or the birth of a deformed child. Among the most extravagant potlatches are those given for rivalry or vengeance.

All potlatches are public. The host, with the support of his family, numima (the next largest tribal subdivision), or tribe, invites other families, numimas, or tribes. The size of the gathering reveals the affluence and prestige of the host. At the ceremony, he traces his line of descent and his rights to the claims he is making. Every name, dance, or song used by the host must be acknowledged and legitimized by the guests. No announcement or claim is made without feasting and the distribution of gifts. Gifts are given to guests in the order of their tribal importance and of a value relative to this prestige. Clearly high-ranking chiefs receive more gifts than lesser men, but the value and quantity of gifts distributed at a potlatch re-

Among the Indians of the northwest coast of North America, a potlatch was necessary to validate the assumption of an important title or status. In the process, the necessary giving of gifts ensured the widespread distribution of goods. Today, potlatches are still important activities among these people.

flect less on the recipients than on the donor. The gifts he gives away — or in some cases the property he publicly destroys — are marks of his wealth, rank, generosity, and self-esteem. Over a period of time, they also measure the power and prestige that he will be able to maintain over others of high status. For, at a later potlatch, each high-ranking guest will try to return as much, or preferably more, than he received. To keep track of the gifts distributed and the precise hierarchy of guests, each donor has the assistance of a "potlatch secretary" whose records are needed to maintain correct social form and avoid offense.

Potlatch gifts vary widely, from money to property. They include boats, blankets, flour, kettles, fish oil, and, in former times, slaves. More recently, gifts have included sewing machines, furniture, even pool tables. Probably the most valuable potlatch material has little intrinsic worth but enormous symbolic value. These are coppers — large pieces of beaten sheet copper shaped like shields with a ridge running down the center of the lower half. They are painted with black lead and a design is incised through the paint. Each copper has a name and its potlatch history determines its value. One copper, called "All other coppers are ashamed to look at it," had been paid for with 7500 blankets; another known as "Making the house empty of wealth" was worth 5000 blankets.

During a potlatch, which can last several days and long into each night, speeches, songs, and dances are mixed with the giving of gifts, snacks, and more lavish feasting. The host is not the only speaker; usually high-ranking guests also speak or supervise the singing, dancing, and drumming. Elaborate ceremonial costumes are worn by the speaker — who holds a "speaker's staff" — by dancers and musicians; the hall where the potlatch is held is decorated with painted hangings and tribal insignia.

All potlatch ceremonies are marked by exacting standards of etiquette and behavior. Impropriety, whether intentional or accidental, requires an immediate response. Mistakes in procedure, public quarreling, or an accident witnessed by others brings a sense of shame and indignity on its perpetrator, who must immediately "cover (or wipe off) the shame," making a payment to re-establish his self-esteem. Often, blankets are torn into strips and each witness is given a piece.

The Kwakiutl respond similarly to insults. Potlatchers sometimes deliberately insult a guest by calling his name out of order, by spilling oil on him, by throwing him his gift, or by presenting him with an inappropriate portion of food. The offended guest retaliates immediately by giving gifts himself, or by destroying something valuable of his own while denouncing the potlatcher. Violence sometimes erupts. On some occasions the host ignores a face-saving gesture of a guest and this may precipitate a rivalry potlatch. If a host mistakenly offends, a guest restores his pride by giving the host a reprimand gift. Embarrassed by his carelessness, the correct host will make restitution in double the amount of the reprimand gift.

Rivalries also develop when two men compete for the same name, song, or other privilege. Each contestant recites his closest genealogical connection with the claim and tries to outdo his rival in the amount of property he can give away. In the heat of such rivalries, contestants sometimes break off a piece of copper, thereby destroying its value, and give the piece to their rival. The rival might then bring out his own copper of at least equal value, break it, and give both pieces back to the opponent. Great merit came to the man who threw his copper into the sea, "drowning it," thus showing his utter contempt for property and implying that his importance was such that what he destroyed was of little concern to him. At times this ostentatious destruction of property included canoes, house planks, blankets, and even slaves, in former days.

The witnesses to these dramatic acts of the potlatch act as judges to the claims; ultimately, they decide the victor. A powerful and prestigious man can sway public opinion by recognizing the claim of one contestant over another at a subsequent potlatch. Indeed, this is a basic principle of the potlatch; a successful potlatch in itself cannot legitimize a claim. It is the behavior of other hosts at later potlatches that validates a claim for once and for all.

In the case of the potlatch, a surplus is created for the express purpose of gaining prestige through a display of wealth and generous giving of gifts. But, unlike conspicuous consumption in our own society, the emphasis is not so much on the hoarding of goods which would make them unavailable to others. Instead, the emphasis is on giving away, or at least getting rid of one's wealth goods. Thus, potlatch serves as a leveling mechanism, preventing some individuals from accumulating too much wealth at the expense of other members of society.

[17]From *The Kwakiutl: Indians of British Columbia*, by Ronald P. Rohner and Evelyn C. Rohner, pp. 95, 97–98, 103–104. Copyright © 1970 by Holt, Rinehart and Winston, Inc. Adapted and reprinted by permission of the publisher.

MARKET EXCHANGE

To an economist, market exchange has to do with the buying and selling of goods and services, with prices set by forces of supply and demand. Just where the buying and selling takes place is largely irrelevant. Although some of our market transactions do take place in a specific identifiable location — much of the trade in cotton, for example, takes place in the New Orleans Cotton Exchange — it is also quite possible for a North American to buy and sell goods without ever being on the same side of the continent. When people talk about a market in today's world, the particular place where something is sold is often not important at all. For example, think of the way people speak of a "market" for certain types of automobiles, or for mouthwash.

Market exchange may also take place in the non-Western world, usually in societies with a state type of political organization. In such cases, an actual market*place* plays far more prominent a role than in our system. The chief goods exchanged in non-Western markets are material items produced by people, who bring to the market the produce and animals they have grown and raised and the handicrafts they have made. These they sell or exchange for items they want and cannot produce themselves. Land, labor, and occupations are not bought and sold as they are through the Western market economy. In other words, what happens in the marketplace has nothing to do with the price of land, the amount paid for labor, or the cost of services. The market is local, specific, and contained. Prices are apt to be set on the basis of face-to-face bargaining, rather than by faceless "market forces" wholly removed from the transaction itself. Nor need some form of money be involved; instead, goods may be directly exchanged between the specific individuals involved.

Some noneconomic aspects of marketplaces in nonindustrial societies overshadow the strictly economic aspects. Social relationships are as important in the marketplace as they are in other aspects of the economy. For example, dancers and other entertainers perform in the marketplace. It is customary for people to gather there to hear news. In ancient Mexico, under the Aztecs, people were required by law to go to market at specific intervals, in order to be informed about what was going on. Government officials held court and settled judicial disputes at the market. Above all, the market is a gathering place where people renew friendships, see relatives, gossip, and keep up with the world.

In the United States, as part of a reaction to the increasingly "face-to-faceless" nature of our economic system, there has been something of a revival and proliferation of "flea markets," where anyone, for a small fee, may display and sell handicrafts, secondhand items, farm produce, and paintings in a face-to-face setting. There is excitement in the search for bargains and an opportunity for haggling. A carnival atmosphere prevails, with eating, laughing, and conversation, and items may even be bartered without any cash passing hands. These flea markets, or farmers' markets, are similar to the markets of non-Western societies.

The Chicago Commodities Exchange, where people are buying and selling, even though no goods are physically present.

ECONOMICS, CULTURE, AND THE WORLD OF BUSINESS

At the start of this chapter, we noted that it is perhaps in the study of the economies of nonliterate

In non-Western societies, the market is an important focus of social as well as economic activity. This photo shows the men socializing while women sell goods in a Peruvian market.

peoples that we are most apt to fall prey to our own ethnocentric biases. The misunderstandings that result from our failure to overcome these biases are of major importance to us in the modern world in at least two ways. For one, they encourage development schemes in Third World countries (that is, the states of Africa, Asia, and Central and South America that by Western economic standards are regarded as "underdeveloped" — a comfortably ethnocentric term) that all too often result in poverty, poor health, discontent, and a host of other ills. In northeastern Brazil, for example, development of large-scale plantations in order to grow sisal for export to the United States took over numerous small farms on which peasants grew food in order to feed themselves. With this, peasants joined the ranks of the unemployed. Being unable to earn enough money to satisfy their minimal nutritional needs, the incidence of malnutri-

tion rose dramatically. Similarly, development projects in Africa, designed to bring about changes in local hydrology, vegetation, and settlement patterns — and even programs aimed at reducing certain diseases — have frequently led directly to *increased* disease rates.[18] Fortunately, there is now a growing awareness on the part of development officials that future projects are unlikely to succeed without the expertise that anthropologically trained people can bring to bear.

Achieving an understanding of the economic systems of other peoples that is not bound by the hopes and expectations of our own culture has also become a matter of import for corporate executives in today's world. At least, recognition of the embeddedness of such systems within the cultures

[18]John H. Bodley, *Victims of Progress*, 2d ed. (Palo Alto, Calif.: Mayfield, 1982), p. 153.

A flea market in the United States — a common weekend event in many areas of the country.

Remains of a "model village," built especially for the Mbuti, to bring them out of the forest and integrate them into Zaire's national life. In these villages, the rectangular shapes and inflexible architecture are so foreign to the Mbuti that even when they stay, they build traditional huts behind the abandoned model homes. Mostly, though, these villages quickly become death traps, breeding malaria, dysentery, yaws, and venereal disease, spread by truckers up and down the road. The Third World is strewn with failed development projects, conceived by well-meaning but uninformed planners.

of which they are parts could avoid problems of the sort experienced by a large New York City–based cosmetics manufacturer. About to come out with an ad in Italy featuring a model holding some flowers, it was discovered that the flowers were the kind traditionally given at Italian funerals. On another occasion, a new product was about to be marketed as a room-and-closet spray. But the name was changed after a manager in England called to say that in his country, "closet" meant toilet.

Anthropologists Edward and Mildred Hall describe another case of the same sort:

José Ybarra and Sir Edmund Jones are at the same party and it is important for them to establish a cordial relationship for business reasons. Each is trying to be warm and friendly, yet they will part with mutual distrust and their business transaction will probably fall through. José, in Latin fashion, moved closer and closer to Sir Edmund as they spoke, and this movement was miscommunicated as pushiness to Sir Edmund, who kept backing away from this intimacy, and this was miscommunicated to José as coldness.[19]

[19]Edward T. Hall and Mildred Reed Hall, "The Sounds of Silence," in *Anthropology 86/87*, ed. Elvio Angeloni (Guilford, Conn.: Dushkin, 1986), p. 65.

APPLICATION
The Anthropologist as a Business Consultant

When people are told that the head of the Cultural Analysis Group at Planmetrics, a Chicago-based consulting firm, is Steve Barnett, holder of a Ph.D. in anthropology from the University of Chicago, their reaction is usually one of surprise. In the public mind, people with advanced degrees in anthropology are supposed to work in exotic, faraway places like remote islands, deep forests, hostile deserts, or arctic wastes — not in the world of business. After all, when anthropology makes the pages of the *New York Times*, is it not to report the "discovery" of a "last-surviving Stone-Age tribe," the uncovering of some ancient "lost city," or the recovery of bones of some remote human ancestor, usually in some out-of-the-way part of the world?

As we saw in the first chapter of this book, anthropologists have had a long-standing interest in their own culture, and many of them, as applied anthropologists, are putting their expertise to work in attempts to find solutions to problems of various sorts. The problems that Steve Barnett solves have to do with consumer behavior, and his clients are some of the country's largest corporations. He is especially sought out to help with problems that traditional techniques of market research have failed to resolve.

Instead of using the polling techniques that market researchers prefer, Barnett relies on participant observation. When Kimberly Clark hired him to help with the redesign of disposable diapers, for example, he recorded on videotape 200 hours of diaper changing at a day care center, which he then analyzed as if it were a ritual in another culture in order to develop meaningful categories by which to understand the diaper-changing process. Similar techniques were used in studies of dishwashing and dusting for Procter and Gamble. For a "teen report" that goes out every few months to fast-food chains and clothing and record companies, Barnett employs anthropology graduate students to "hang out" with teenagers in order to write what amounts to ethnographic reports of them.

According to Barnett, cultural anthropologists have skills in analyzing everyday life that no other social scientists have. Napier Collins, who does corporate planning for Royal Dutch Shell — a firm that used Barnett regularly for nearly eight years — agrees. Speaking of the need to find out how people react to higher energy prices, Collins noted "Economists and public opinion polling groups, with their mechanically derived data, can't answer that kind of question as well as a cultural anthropologist who is trained to analyze how people behave."

Source: Tamar Lewin, "Casting an Anthropological Eye on American Consumers," *New York Times*, May 11, 1986, 6F.

Where Third World countries are involved, the chances for cross-cultural misunderstandings increase dramatically. The executives of major corporations realize their dependency on these countries for raw materials, they are increasingly inclined to manufacture their products in them, and they see their best potential for market expansion as lying in the Third World. That is why business recruiters on college campuses in the United States are on the lookout for job candidates with the kind of understanding of the world that anthropology provides.

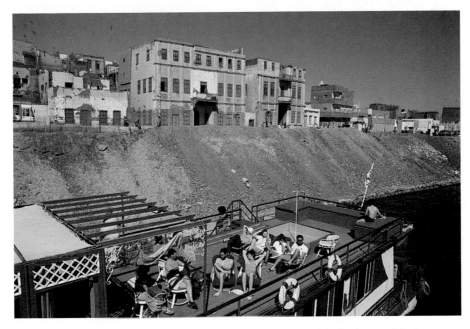

Westerners sunbathing in the Middle East. Such exposure of the body in public is a custom which people in Middle Eastern societies find offensive.

CHAPTER SUMMARY

An economic system is the means by which goods are produced, distributed, and consumed. The study of the economics of nonliterate, nonindustrial societies can be undertaken only in the context of the total culture of each society. Each society solves the problem of getting its living by allocating raw materials, land, labor, and technology and by distributing goods according to its own priorities.

The work that people do is a major productive resource, and the allotment of work is always governed by rules according to sex and age. Only a few broad generalizations can be made covering the kinds of work performed by men and women. Instead of looking for biological imperatives to explain the sexual division of labor, a more productive strategy is to examine the kinds of work done by women in the context of specific societies to see

how it relates to other cultural and historical factors. The cooperation of many people working together is a typical feature of both nonliterate and literate societies. Specialization of craft is important even in societies with a very simple technology.

All societies regulate the way that the valuable resources of land will be allocated. In nonindustrial societies, individual ownership of land is rare; generally land is controlled by kinship groups, such as the lineage or band. This system provides for greater flexibility of land use, since the size of the band territories, or of the bands themselves, can be adjusted according to the availability of resources in any particular place. The technology of a people, in the form of the tools they use, is related to their mode of subsistence. In food-foraging societies, codes of generosity promote free access to tools, even though these may have been made by individuals for their own use. In sedentary, farming communities, there is greater opportunity to accumulate material belongings, and inequalities of wealth may develop. In many such communities, though, a relatively egalitarian social order is maintained through the operation of leveling mechanisms.

Nonliterate people consume most of what they produce themselves, but they do exchange goods. The processes of distribution that may be distinguished are reciprocity, redistribution, and market exchange. Reciprocity is a transaction between individuals or groups, involving the exchange of goods and services of roughly equivalent value. Usually it is prescribed by ritual and ceremony.

Barter and trade take place between groups. There are elements of reciprocity in trading exchanges, but there is a greater calculation of the relative value of goods exchanged. Barter is one form of negative reciprocity, by which scarce goods from one group are exchanged for desirable goods from another group. Silent trade, which need not involve face-to-face contact, is a specialized form of barter in which no verbal communication takes place. It is one means by which the potential dangers of negative reciprocity may be controlled. A classic example of exchange between groups that partook of both reciprocity and sharp trading was the Kula ring of the Trobriand Islanders.

Strong centralized political organization is necessary for redistribution to take place. The government assesses each citizen a tax or tribute, uses the proceeds to support the governmental and religious elite, and redistributes the rest, usually in the form of public services. The collection of taxes and delivery of government services and subsidies in the United States constitute a form of redistribution.

Display for social prestige is a motivating force in societies, including our own, where there is some surplus of goods produced. In our society, goods that are accumulated for display generally remain in the hands of those who accumulated them, whereas in other societies they are generally given away; the prestige comes from publicly divesting oneself of valuables.

Exchange in the marketplace serves to distribute goods in a district. In nonindustrial societies, the marketplace is usually a specific site where material items produced by the people are exchanged. It also functions as a social gathering place and a news medium.

The anthropological approach to economics has taken on new importance in today's world of international development and commerce. Without it, development schemes in the Third World are prone to failure, and international trade is handicapped as a result of cross-cultural misunderstandings.

SUGGESTED READINGS

Bohannan, Paul, and George Dalton, eds. *Markets in Africa.* Evanston, Ill.: Northwestern University Press, 1962. These essays on the market system of African economic life are studies of economic activities ranging in complexity from aboriginal to present-day marketing systems. The noneconomic function of African markets is discussed, and one article deals with current changes in Africa as they affect markets.

Dalton, George. *Traditional Tribal and Peasant Economies: An Introductory Survey of Economic Anthropology.* Reading, Mass.: Addison-Wesley, 1971. This book is just what the title says it is, by one of the major specialists in economic anthropology.

Leclair, Edward E., Jr., and Harold K. Schneider, eds. *Economic Anthropology: Readings in Theory and Analysis.* New York: Holt, Rinehart and Winston, 1968. This is a selection of significant writings in economic anthropology from the past 50 years. In the first section are theoretical papers covering the major points of view, and in the second are case materials selected to show the practical application of the various theoretical positions.

Nash, Manning. *Primitive and Peasant Economic Systems.* San Francisco: Chandler, 1966. This book studies the problems of economic anthropology, especially the dynamics of social and economic change, in terms of primitive and peasant economic systems. The book is heavily theoretical, but draws on the author's fieldwork in Guatemala, Mexico, and Burma.

On the Northwest coast of North America, a distinctive art style developed, based on representative carving in wood as exemplified by this house post. Primarily heraldic in nature, much of this art had to do with the history of family lines and ancestors, all of which were important for Northwest coast social organization.

PART V

THE FORMATION OF GROUPS

Solving the Problem of Cooperation

INTRODUCTION

One of the really important things to emerge from anthropological study is the realization of just how fundamental cooperation is to human survival. Through cooperation, all known humans handle even the most basic problems of existence, the need for food and protection — not only from the elements but from predatory animals and even each other. To some extent, this is true not only for humans, but for monkeys and apes as well. Baboons, for example, protect themselves against predators by traveling about in large troops that include males as well as females with their young. Owing to their much larger size and far more formidable canine teeth, the males are a more credible threat to predators than are the females. Within the troop, females provide themselves and their infants with protection against harassment from other baboons by forming friendships with particular males. Among humans, males still usually bear primary responsibility for their group's defense, even though the anatomical and physiological differences between the sexes have been reduced to relatively minor proportions compared with what we see in most monkeys and apes. Moreover, women are potentially as capable of fighting as are men, and in some societies women do bear arms. But what sets humans apart from other primates even more is some form of cooperation in subsistence activities on a regular basis. At the least, this takes the form of the sexual division of labor as seen among food-foraging peoples. Such cooperation is not customary among nonhuman primates; adult chimpanzees, for example, may cooperate to get meat, and share it when they get it, but they don't get meat very often, and they don't normally share other kinds of food the way humans do.

Just as cooperation seems to be basic to human nature, so the organization of groups is basic to effective cooperation. Humans form many kinds of groups, and each is geared to solving different kinds of problems with which people must cope. Social groups are important to humans also because they give identity and support to their members. The basic building block of human societies is the household, within which economic production, consumption, inheritance, child rearing, and shelter are organized and carried out. Usually, the core of the household consists of some form of family, a group of relatives that stems from the parent–child bond and the interdependence of men and women. Although it may be structured in many different ways, however structured, the family provides for economic cooperation between men and women, while furnishing at the same time the kind of setting within which child rearing may take place. Another problem faced by all human societies is the need to control sexual activity, and this is the job of marriage. Given the close connection between sexual activity and the production of children, who must then be nurtured, a close interconnection between marriage and family is to be expected.

Many different marriage and family patterns exist the world over, but all societies have some form of marriage and most (but not all) have some form of family organization. As we shall see in Chapters 17 and 18, the forms of family and marriage organization are to a large extent shaped by the specific kinds of problems that people must solve in particular situations.

The solutions to some organizational challenges are beyond the scope of the family. These include such matters as defense, allocation of resources, and provision of work forces for tasks too large to be undertaken by a family. Some societies develop formal political systems to perform these functions. Nonindustrial societies frequently meet these challenges through kinship groups, which we discuss in Chapter 19. These large, cohesive groups of individuals base their loyalty to one another on descent from a common ancestor or their relationship to a living individual. In societies where a great number of people are linked by kinship, these groups serve the important function of precisely defining the social roles of their members. In this way they reduce the potential for tension that might arise from the sudden and unexpected behavior of an individual. They also provide their members with material security and moral support through religious and ceremonial activities.

Other important forms of human social groups are the subjects of Chapter 20. Where kinship ties do not provide for all of the organizational needs of a society, grouping by age and/or sex is one force that may be used to create social groups. In North America, as well as in many non-Western countries, today and in the past, the organization of persons by age is common. In many areas of the world, too, social groups based on the common interests of their members serve a vital function. In industrializing countries, they may help to ease the transition of rural individuals into the urban setting. Finally, groups based on social rank are characteristic of the world's civilizations, past and present. Such groups are referred to as social classes, and they are always ranked high versus low relative to one another. Class structure involves inequalities between classes and frequently is the means by which one group may dominate large numbers of other people. To the extent that social-class membership cuts across lines of kinship, residence, age, or other group membership, it may work to counteract tendencies for a society to fragment into discrete special-interest groups. Paradoxically, it does so in a way which is itself divisive, in that class distinctions systematically deprive people of equal access to important resources. Thus, class conflict has been a recurrent phenomenon in class-structured societies, in spite of the existence of political and religious institutions that function to perpetuate the status quo.

17

SEX AND MARRIAGE

Trobriand men cook food for a feast at marriage. In all human societies marriage establishes a continuing sexual relationship between a man and a woman, which is backed by legal, economic, and social forces. Thus, unlike mating, which is biological, marriage is distinctively cultural.

PREVIEW

What Is Marriage?

Marriage is a transaction and resulting contract in which a woman and a man establish a continuing claim to the right of sexual access to one another, and in which the woman involved is eligible to bear children. Although in many societies, husbands and wives live together as members of the same household, this is not true in all societies. And though most marriages around the world tend to be to a single spouse, most societies permit, and regard as most desirable, marriage of a single individual to multiple spouses.

What Is the Difference between Marriage and Mating?

All animals, including humans, mate — that is, they form a sexual bond with individuals of the opposite sex. Some mate for life, and some do not; some mate with a single individual of the opposite sex, and some with several. Only marriage, however, is backed by social, legal, and economic forces. Thus, while mating is biological, marriage is cultural.

Why Is Marriage Universal?

A problem universal to all human societies is the need to control sexual relations, in order that they not introduce a disruptive, combative influence into society. Because the problem is universal, it follows that marriage should be universal. The specific form that marriage takes is related to who has rights to offspring that normally result from sexual intercourse, as well as how property is distributed.

Among the Trobriand Islanders, whose yam exchanges and Kula voyages we examined in Chapter 7, children who have reached the age of seven or eight years begin playing erotic games with each other and imitating adult seductive attitudes. Within another four or five years they begin to pursue sexual partners in earnest, changing partners often, experimenting first with one and then another. By the time they are in their mid-teens, meetings between lovers take up most of the night, and affairs between them are apt to last for several months. Ultimately, lovers begin to meet the same partner again and again, rejecting the advances of others. When the couples are ready, they appear together one morning outside the young man's house, as a way of announcing their intention to be married.

For young Trobrianders, attracting lovers is an important business, and they spend a great deal of time making themselves look as attractive and seductive as possible. Youthful conversations during the day are loaded with sexual innuendos, and magical spells as well as small gifts are employed to entice a prospective sex partner to the beach at

To attract lovers, young Trobriand Islanders must look as attractive and seductive as possible. The young men shown here have decorated themselves with Johnson's Baby Powder, while the young girl's beauty has been enhanced by decorations given her by her father.

night, or to the house in which boys sleep apart from their parents. Because girls, too, sleep apart from their parents, youths and adolescents have considerable freedom in arranging their love affairs. Boys and girls play this game as equals, with neither sex being more dominant than the other.

As anthropologist Annette Weiner points out, all of this sexual activity is not a frivolous, adolescent pastime. Attracting lovers:

> is the first step toward entering the adult world of strategies, where the line between influencing others while not allowing others to gain control of oneself must be carefully learned. . . . Sexual liaisons give adolescents the time and occasion to experiment with all the possibilities and problems that adults face in creating relationships with those who are not relatives. Individual wills may clash, and the achievement of one's desire takes patience, hard work, and determination. The adolescent world of lovemaking has its own dangers and disillusionments. Young people, to the degree they are capable, must learn to be both careful and fearless.[1]

The Trobriand attitude toward adolescent sexuality stands in marked contrast to that of North American society. Theoretically, North Americans are not supposed to have sexual relations outside of wedlock, although as is well known, there is a considerable discrepancy between theory and practice. Nonetheless, premarital sexual activity in our society cannot be conducted with the openness and approval that characterizes the Trobriand situation. As a consequence, it is not subject to the kind of social pressures from the community at large that prepare traditional Trobriand youths for the adult world after marriage.

CONTROL OF SEXUAL RELATIONS

One distinctively human characteristic is the ability for human females, like human males, to engage in sexual relations at any time they want to, or whenever their culture tells them it is appropriate.

While this ability to perform at any time is not unusual on the part of male mammals in general, it is not usual on the part of females. Although female primates, whose offspring are weaned but who have not yet become pregnant again, are likely to engage in sexual activity around the time of ovulation (approximately once a month), they are otherwise little interested in such activity. Only the human female may be willing to engage in sex at any point in her cycle, or even when she is pregnant. In some societies, intercourse during pregnancy is thought to promote the growth of the fetus. Among Trobriand Islanders, for example, a child's identity is thought to come from its mother, but it is the father's job to build up and nurture the child, which he begins to do before birth through frequent intercourse with the mother.

On the basis of clues from the behavior of other primates, anthropologists have speculated about the evolutionary significance of this human female sexuality. The best current explanation is that it arose as a side effect of persistent bipedal locomotion in early hominids.[2] The energetic requirements of this form of locomotion are such that endurance is impossible without a hormone output that is significantly greater than that of other primates. These hormones catalyze the steady release of muscular energy that is required for endurance; at the same time, they make us the "sexiest" of all primates. This is not to say that either men or women are simply at the mercy of their hormones where sex is concerned, for the human species has cortical control over sex. People engage in it when it suits them to do so and when it is deemed appropriate.

Although developed as an accidental by-product of something else, a common phenomenon in evolution, the ability to engage in sex at any time on the part of females as well as males would have been advantageous to early hominids to the extent

[1]Annette B. Weiner, *The Trobrianders of Papua New Guinea* (New York: Holt, Rinehart and Winston, 1988), p. 71.

[2]James N. Spuhler, "Continuities and Discontinuities in Anthropoid–Hominid Behavioral Evolution: Bipedal Locomotion and Sexual Reception," in *Evolutionary Biology and Human Social Behavior*, ed. N. A. Chagnon and William Irons (North Scituate, Mass.: Duxbury Press, 1979), pp. 454–461.

Attempts by males to dominate females may introduce a competitive, combative element into social relations. Among gorillas, male silverbacks like the one on the left maintain absolute breeding rights over females in their group. All other adult males must acknowledge his dominance, or leave the group and attempt to lure females from other groups.

that it acted, not alone but with other factors, to tie members of both sexes more firmly to the social groups so crucial to their survival. At the same time, however, that sexual activity can reinforce group ties, it can also be disruptive. This stems from the basic primate characteristic of male dominance. It is based on the fact that, on the average, males are bigger and more muscular than females, although this differentiation has become drastically reduced in modern *Homo sapiens* compared with the earliest hominids. Among other primates, the males' larger size allows them to try to dominate females when the latter are at the height of their sexuality; this trait can be seen among baboons, gorillas, and, though less obviously, chimpanzees (significantly, the size difference between male and female chimpanzees is not as great as among baboons or gorillas, but it is still greater than among modern humans). With early hominid females potentially ready for sexual intercourse at any time, dominant males may have attempted to monopolize females; an added inducement could have been the prowess of the female at food gathering. In food-foraging societies, the bulk of the food is usually provided by the gathering activities of women. In any event, a tendency to monopolize females would introduce the kind of competitive, combative element into hominid groupings that one sees among many other primate species — one that cannot be allowed to disrupt harmonious social relationships. The solution to this problem is to bring sexual activity under cultural control. Thus, just as a culture tells people what, when, and how they may eat, so does it tell them when, where, how, and with whom they may have sex.

RULES OF SEXUAL ACCESS

We find that everywhere societies have cultural rules controlling sexual relations. In the United States and Canada, the official ideology has been that all sexual activity outside of wedlock is taboo. One is supposed to establish a family, which we do through marriage. With this, a person establishes a continuing claim to the right of sexual access to another person. Actually, very few known societies — only about 5 percent — prohibit all sexual involvement outside of marriage, and even ours has become less restrictive. In other societies, as we have already seen, things are often done quite differently. As a further example, we may look at the Nayar peoples of India.[3]

The Nayar constitute a landowning, warrior caste from southwest India. Among them, estates are held by corporations of sorts, which are made up of kinsmen related in the female line. These kinsmen all live together in a large household, with the eldest male serving as manager.

Three transactions that take place among the Nayar are of concern to us here. The first occurs shortly before a girl undergoes her first menstruation. It involves a ceremony that joins together in a temporary union the girl with a young man. This union, which may or may not involve sexual relations, lasts for a few days and then breaks up. There is no further obligation on the part of either individual, although the woman and her future children will probably mourn for the man when he dies. What this transaction does is to establish the girl's eligibility for sexual activity with men who are approved by her household. With this, she is officially an adult.

The second transaction takes place when a girl enters into a continuing sexual liaison with an approved man. This is a formal relationship, which requires the man to present her with gifts three times each year until such time as the relationship may be terminated. In return, the man may spend the nights with her. In spite of continuing sexual privileges, however, the man has no obligation to support his sex partner economically, nor is her home regarded as his home. In fact, she may have such an arrangement with more than one man at a time. Regardless of how many men are involved with a single woman, this second Nayar transaction, which is their version of marriage, clearly specifies who has sexual access to whom, so as to avoid conflict. We may define **marriage** as a transaction and resulting contract in which a woman

> **Marriage:** A transaction and resulting contract in which a woman and a man establish a continuing claim to the right of sexual access to one another, and in which the woman involved is eligible to bear children.
>
> **Affinal kin:** Relatives by marriage.
>
> **Conjugal bond:** The bond between a man and a woman who are married.

and man establish a continuing claim to the right of sexual access to one another, and in which the woman involved is eligible to bear children.[4] Thus defined, marriage is universal, presumably because the problems with which it deals are universal. As the Nayar case demonstrates, however, marriage need not have anything to do with beginning a new family, or even establishing a cooperative economic relationship between people of opposite sexes.

In the absence of effective birth-control devices, the usual result of sexual activity is that, sooner or later, the woman becomes pregnant. When this happens among the Nayar, some man must formally acknowledge paternity. This is done by his making gifts to the woman and the midwife. Though he may continue to take much interest in the child, he has no further obligations, for the education and support of the child are the responsibility of the child's mother's brothers, with whom the child and the mother live. What we have in this third transaction is one that establishes the legitimacy of the child. In this sense, it is the counterpart of the registration of birth in our own culture, in which motherhood and fatherhood are spelled out. In our society, the father is supposed to be the mother's husband, but in numerous other societies, there is no such necessity.

Before leaving the Nayar, it is important to note that there is nothing here comparable to the family as we know it in our own society. The group that forms the household does not include **affinal kin,** or those individuals joined by a **conjugal bond** established by marriage. As will be seen in Chapter

[3]My interpretation of the Nayar follows Ward H. Goodenough, *Description and Comparison in Cultural Anthropology* (Chicago: Aldine, 1970), pp. 6–11.

[4]Ibid., pp. 12–13.

18, a household doesn't have to be a family as we know it. Among the Nayar the household is composed wholly of what we often call "blood" relatives, which are technically known as **consanguineal kin.** Sexual relations are with those who are not consanguineal kin, and so live in other households. And this brings us to another human universal, the incest taboo.

THE INCEST TABOO

No human society has ever been found to be without a rule, called the **incest taboo,** that prohibits sexual relations between parents and children, or siblings. The universality of this rule, save for a few exceptions involving siblings, has fascinated anthropologists and other students of human behavior. It has become something of a challenge for anthropologists to explain why incest should commonly be regarded as such a loathsome thing.

Many explanations have been given. Of those that have gained some popularity at one time or another, the simplest and least satisfactory is based on "human nature"—that is, some instinctive horror of incest. It is also documented that human beings raised together have less sexual attraction for one another, but by itself this argument may simply substitute the result for the cause. The incest taboo ensures that children and their parents, who are constantly in intimate contact, avoid regarding one another as sexual objects. Besides this, if there were an instinctive horror of incest, we would be hard-pressed to account for the far from rare violations of the incest taboo, such as occur in our own society (an estimated 10–14 percent of our children under 18 years of age have been involved in incestuous relations[5]), or for cases of institutionalized incest, such as that which required the head of the Inca empire in Peru to marry his own sister.

Various psychological explanations of the incest taboo have been advanced at one time or another. Sigmund Freud tried to account for it in his psy-

> **Consanguineal kin:** Relatives by birth; that is, "blood" relatives.
>
> **Incest taboo:** The prohibition of sexual relations between parent and child or siblings.

choanalytic theory of the unconscious. According to him, the son desires the mother, creating a rivalry with the father. (Freud called this the Oedipus complex.) He must suppress these feelings or earn the wrath of the father, who is far more powerful than he. The attraction of the daughter to the father, or the Electra complex, places her in rivalry with her mother. Freud's theory can be viewed as an elaboration of the reasons for a deep-seated aversion to sexual relations within the family. Some other psychologists have endorsed the belief that young children can be emotionally scarred by sexual experiences, which they may have interpreted as violent and frightening acts of aggression. The incest taboo thus protects children against sexual advances by older members of the family. A closely related theory is that the incest taboo helps prevent girls who are socially and emotionally too young for motherhood from becoming pregnant.

Early students of genetics thought that the incest taboo precluded the deleterious effects of inbreeding. While this is so, it is also true that as with domestic animals, inbreeding can increase desired characteristics as well as deleterious ones. Furthermore, deleterious effects will show up sooner than would otherwise be the case, so that whatever genes are responsible for them may be more quickly eliminated from the population. On the other hand, preference for a genetically different mate does tend to maintain a higher level of genetic diversity within a population, and in evolution this generally works to a species' advantage. Without genetic diversity a species cannot adapt biologically to a changed environment when and if this becomes necessary.

A truly convincing explanation of the incest taboo has still to be advanced. Yet there are persistent hints that it may be a cultural elaboration of an underlying biological tendency toward avoid-

[5]Patricia Whelehan, "Review of Incest, a Biosocial View," *American Anthropologist* 87 (1985): 678.

Shown here is Raherka, Chief of Scribes in Egypt's Fifth Dynasty, with his wife. In ancient Egypt, where both men and women inherited, brother-sister marriages served to keep property intact.

Endogamy: Marriage within a particular group or category of individuals.

Exogamy: Marriage outside the group.

the incest taboo after all. Support for this appears to come from studies that show that children raised together on an Israeli kibbutz, although not required or even encouraged to do so, almost invariably marry outside their group. In this case, however, appearances seem to be deceiving, for most Israeli youths leave the kibbutz in their late teens for service in the armed forces. Thus, they are away from the kibbutz just when they are most likely to be involved with outsiders of the opposite sex and ready to consider marriage. An even greater objection to the "biological avoidance" theory, however, is raised by detailed census records made in Roman Egypt that conclusively demonstrate that brother–sister marriages not only were common, but were preferred by ordinary members of the farming class.[6]

If indeed there is a biological basis for inbreeding avoidance among humans, it clearly is far from being completely effective in its operation, nor is its mechanism understood. To say that certain genes program specifically for inbreeding avoidance, as some have argued, is not warranted on the basis of existing evidence, nor is it likely, based upon what we do know about the workings of human genes.

ENDOGAMY AND EXOGAMY

Whatever its cause, the utility of the incest taboo can be seen by examining its effects on social structure. Closely related to prohibitions against incest are rules against **endogamy,** or marriage within a particular group of individuals. If the group is defined as just one immediate family, then almost all societies prohibit endogamy and practice **exogamy,** or marriage outside the group. On the other hand, a society that practices exogamy at one level may practice endogamy at another. Among the

ance of inbreeding. Studies of animal behavior have shown such a tendency to be common among those species that are relatively large, long-lived, slow to mature, and intelligent. Humans qualify for membership in this group on all counts. So do a number of other primates, including those most closely related to humans — chimpanzees. Although they exhibit few sexual inhibitions, chimpanzees do tend to avoid inbreeding between siblings and between females and their male offspring. So perhaps the tendency for human children to look for sex partners outside the group in which they have been raised is not just the result of

[6]Jack Goody, *The Development of the Family and Marriage in Europe* (Cambridge: Cambridge University Press, 1983), p. 43.

Claude Lévi-Strauss (1908–)

Claude Lévi-Strauss is the leading exponent of French Structuralism, which sees culture as a surface representation of underlying mental structures that have been affected by a group's physical and social environment, as well as its history. Thus, cultures may vary considerably, even though the structure of the human thought processes responsible for them is the same everywhere.

Human thought processes are structured, according to Lévi-Strauss, into contrastive pairs of polar opposites, such as light versus dark, good versus evil, nature versus culture, raw versus cooked. The ultimate contrastive pair is that of "self" versus "others," which is necessary for true symbolic communication to take place, and upon which culture depends. Communication is a reciprocal exchange, which is extended to include goods and women. Hence, the incest taboo stems from this fundamental contrastive pair. From this universal taboo stem the many and varied marriage rules that have been described by ethnographers.

Trobriand Islanders, for example, each individual has to marry outside of his or her own clan and lineage (exogamy). However, since eligible sex partners are to be found within one's own community, village endogamy, though not obligatory, is commonly practiced.

Sir Edward Tylor long ago advanced the proposition that alternatives to inbreeding were either "marrying out or being killed out."[7] Our ancestors, he suggested, discovered the advantage of intermarriage to create bonds of friendship. Claude Lévi-Strauss elaborated on this premise. He saw exogamy as the basis of a distinction between early hominid life in isolated endogamous groups and the life of *Homo sapiens* in a supportive society with an accumulating culture. Alliances with other groups, established and strengthened by marriage ties, make possible a sharing of culture.

In a roundabout way, exogamy also helps to explain some exceptions to the incest taboo, such as that of obligatory brother and sister marriage

within the royal families of ancient Egypt, the Inca empire, and Hawaii. Members of these royal families were considered semidivine, and their very sacredness kept them from marrying mere mortals. The brother and sister married so as *not* to share their godliness, thereby maintaining the "purity" of the royal line. By the same token, in Roman Egypt, where property was inherited by women as well as men, and where there was a particularly tight relationship between land and people, brother–sister marriages among the farming class acted to prevent fragmentation of a family's holdings.

THE DISTINCTION BETWEEN MARRIAGE AND MATING

Having defined marriage in terms of sexual access, it is important at this point to make clear the distinction between systems of marriage and mating. All animals, including humans, mate; some for life and some not; some with a single individual of the opposite sex, and some with several. Only marriage, however, is sanctioned by legal, economic, and social forces. Even among the Nayar, where

[7]Quoted in Roger M. Keesing, *Cultural Anthropology: A Contemporary Perspective* (New York: Holt, Rinehart and Winston, 1976), p. 286.

APPLICATION
Anthropology and AIDS

In North America, the 1960s and the 1970s were a time of social foment, involving, among other things, significant changes in sexual values and practices. With this revolution developed new life-styles, including sexual experimentation with different partners as well as with different techniques. Inevitably, these changes were reflected in the health problems of sexually active individuals; in particular, the incidence of sexually transmitted diseases of all kinds has skyrocketed. Among these is acquired immune-deficiency syndrome, or AIDS, which can in addition be transmitted through intravenous drug use and blood transfusions. In the United States, AIDS was unknown before the mid-1970s; since then, it has become probably the most serious menace to public health in the twentieth century. By the beginning of 1986, as many as 1 million people in the United States were probably infected. Since then, many more have become so.

Although AIDS also infects heterosexuals, it is gay men (homosexuals and bisexuals) who have suffered the most in the United States. In San Francisco's gay community, the first cases appeared in 1979, and by 1980, it was evident that a major epidemic was under way. As part of a concerted effort to deal with this situation, a group at the University of California, San Francisco, began a team study to learn more about the disease, and to begin efforts at prevention and health education based on current knowledge of AIDS. Included on the team was E. Michael Gorman, a medical anthropologist who had training as well in epidemiology and infectious disease and had extensive experience working with the city's gay population on health-related issues. Data gathered by the team included information on demography, medical history, sexual history, social factors, alcohol and drug usage, and sexual contacts. Gaining information on history posed a particular challenge, requiring knowledge of and sensitivity to not only various aspects of gay male sexual behavior, but also the cultural themes of gay subcultures.

As Gorman points out, the participation of a medical anthropologist and the use of anthropological methodologies were of great relevance in many respects.

Epidemiological inquiry focuses primarily on the determinants of disease in human population. In this context, anthropological knowledge assisted in the more precise definition of the epidemiological variables of interest: person, time, and place. Specific knowledge of the population at risk and familiarity with the cultural context also aided in the process of investigating the epidemic. Experience with the community and understanding of its mores and history likewise facilitated the research process and brought community needs such as health education, risk reduction information, and prevention generally to the attention of the investigators.*

No less important than the research is prevention for in the absence of either cure or vaccine, the only effective way to deal with AIDS is through education and the development of risk-reduction strategies. Here, the input of anthropologists is especially valuable in designing and implementing prevention programs tailored (as they must be) to the concerns of particular high-risk populations, each of which has its distinctive subculture. Finally, anthropologists are highly qualified to act as culture brokers, clarifying issues and positions to both public health officials and the communities they seek to serve.

*E. Michael Gorman, "The AIDS Epidemic in San Francisco: Epidemiological and Anthropological Perspectives," in *Applying Anthropology, An Introductory Reader*, ed. Aaron Podolefsky and Peter J. Brown (Mountain View, Calif.: Mayfield, 1989), pp. 197–198.

In the United States, as in most Western countries, monogamy is the only legally recognized form of marriage. Nevertheless, about 50% of all marriages end in divorce, and most divorced people remarry at least once. Thus, serial monogamy is far from uncommon.

marriage seems to involve little other than a sexual relationship, a woman's husband is legally obligated to provide her with gifts at specified intervals. Nor may a woman legally have sex with a man to whom she is not married. Thus, while mating is biological, marriage is cultural.

The distinction between marriage and mating may be seen by looking, briefly, at practices in North American society, in which **monogamy** — the taking of a single spouse — is the only legally recognized form of marriage. Not only are other forms not legally sanctioned, but our systems of inheritance, by which property and wealth are transferred from one generation to the next, are predicated upon the institution of monogamous

> **Monogamy:** Marriage in which an individual has a single spouse.

marriage. Mating patterns, by contrast, are frequently *not* monogamous. Not only is adultery far from rare in the United States and Canada, but it has become increasingly acceptable for individuals of the opposite sex — particularly young people who have not yet married — to live together outside of wedlock. None of these arrangements, however, are legally sanctioned. Even married couples who do not engage in sexual activity outside of wedlock frequently mate with one or more individuals of the opposite sex; after all, something like 50 percent of all marriages end in divorce, and most divorced people ultimately remarry.

Among primates in general, monogamous mating patterns are not common. Although some smaller species of South American monkeys, a few island-dwelling populations of leaf-eating Old World monkeys, and all of the smaller apes (gibbons and siamangs) do mate for life with a single individual of the opposite sex, none of these are closely related to human beings, nor do "monogamous" primates ever display the degree of anatomical differences between males and females that is characteristic of our closest primate relatives, or that were characteristic of our own ancient ancestors. Thus it is not likely that the human species began its career as one with monogamous mating patterns. Certainly, one cannot say (as some have tried to assert) that the human species is, by nature, monogamous in its mating behavior.

MARRIAGE AND THE FAMILY

Although, as we saw in our discussion of the Nayar, marriage does not have to result in the formation of a new family, it can easily serve this purpose, in addition to its main function of indicating who has continuing sexual access to whom. This is precisely what is done in most human societies. Consequently, some mention of family organization — otherwise discussed in Chapter 18 — is necessary before we can proceed further with our discussion of marriage. If we were to define the family in terms with which we are familiar, as requiring fathers, mothers, and children, then we would have to say that people like the Nayar do not have families. We can, however, define the **family** in a less ethnocentric way as a group composed of a woman and her dependent children and at least one adult male joined through marriage or blood relationship.[8] The Nayar family is a **consanguine** one, consisting as it does of women with their brothers and the dependent offspring of the women. In such societies, men and women get married but do not live together as members of a single household. Rather, they spend their lives in the households in which they grew up, with the men "commuting" for sexual activity with their wives. Economic cooperation between men and women takes place between sisters and brothers, rather than husbands and wives.

Conjugal, as opposed to consanguine, families are formed on the basis of marital ties between husband and wife. Minimally, a conjugal family consists of a married couple with their dependent children, otherwise known as the **nuclear family;** other forms of conjugal families are polygynous and polyandrous families, which may be thought of as aggregates of nuclear families with one spouse in common. A polygynous family includes the multiple wives of a single husband, while a polyandrous family includes the multiple husbands of a single wife.

FORMS OF MARRIAGE

Monogamy is the form of marriage with which we are most familiar. It is also the most common, but for economic rather than moral reasons. In many polygynous societies, a man must be fairly wealthy to be able to afford **polygyny,** or marriage to more than one wife. Among the Kapauku of western New Guinea,[9] the ideal is to have as many wives as

---

Family: A residential kin group composed of a woman, her dependent children, and at least one adult male joined through marriage or blood relationship.

Consanguine family: A family consisting of related women, their brothers, and the offspring of the women.

Nuclear family: A family unit consisting of husband, wife, and dependent children.

Polygyny: The marriage custom of a man having several wives at the same time; a form of polygamy.

---

possible, and a woman actually urges her husband to spend money on acquiring additional wives. She even has the legal right to divorce him if she can prove that he has money for bride price and refuses to remarry. As we saw in Chapter 12, wives are desirable because they work in the fields and care for pigs, by which wealth is measured, but not all men are wealthy enough to afford bride price for multiple wives.

Among the Turkana, a pastoral nomadic people of northern Kenya, the number of animals at a family's disposal is directly related to the number of adult women available to care for them. The more wives a man has, the more women there are to look after the livestock, and so the more substantial the family's holdings can be. Thus, it is not uncommon for a man's existing wife to actively search for another woman to marry her husband. Again, however, a substantial bride-price is involved in marriage, and only men of wealth and prominence can afford large numbers of wives.

Although most marriages around the world tend to be monogamous, polygyny is the preferred form in by far a majority of the world's societies. It is particularly common in societies that support themselves by growing crops, and the bulk of the farm work is done by women. Under these conditions, women are valued as workers as well as child bearers. Because wives in polygamous households receive little support from their husbands, at the same time that their labor generates wealth, their bargaining position within the household is a

---

[8]Goodenough, *Description*, p. 19.

[9]Leopold Pospisil, *The Kapauku Papuans of West New Guinea* (New York: Holt, Rinehart and Winston, 1963).

Where polygynous marriages occur, a man's co-wives may occupy separate dwellings in a larger household like the one shown here. Thus, children have a close relationship with their mother, but a distant one with their father.

strong one. Often, they have considerable freedom of movement and some economic independence from the sale of crops. Commonly, each wife within the household lives with her children in her own dwelling, apart from her co-wives and husband who occupy other houses within some sort of larger household compound (note that the terms *house* and *household* need not be synonymous; a household may consist of several houses together, as here). Because of this residential autonomy, fathers are usually remote from their sons, who grow up among women. As noted in Chapter 14, this is the sort of setting conducive to the development of aggressiveness in adult males, who must prove their masculinity. As a consequence, a high value is often placed on military glory, and one reason for going to war is to capture women, who may then become a warrior's co-wives. This wealth-increasing pattern is found in its fullest elaboration in sub-Saharan Africa, though it is known elsewhere as well (the Kapauku are a case in point). More-

over, it is still intact in the world today, as its wealth-generating properties at the household level have made it an economically productive system.[10]

In societies practicing wealth-generating polygyny most men and women enter into polygynous marriage, although some are able to do this earlier in life than others. In societies in which men are more heavily involved in productive work, generally only a small minority of marriages are polygynous. Under these circumstances, women are more dependent on men for support so that they are valued as child bearers more than for the work they do. This makes them especially vulnerable if they prove incapable of bearing children, which is one reason a man may seek another wife. Another reason for a man to take on secondary wives is to demonstrate his high position in soci-

[10]Douglas R. White, "Rethinking Polygyny: Co-wives, Codes and Cultural Systems," *Current Anthropology* 29 (1988): 529–572.

ety. But where most productive work is done by men, they must work exceptionally hard to support more than one wife, and few actually do so. Usually, it is the exceptional hunter, or a shaman ("medicine man") in a food-foraging society, or a particularly wealthy man in an agricultural or pastoral society who is most apt to practice polygamy. When he does, it is usually of the sororal type, in which the women he marries are sisters. Having already lived together before marriage, they continue to do so with their husband, instead of occupying separate dwellings of their own.

Although monogamy and polygyny are the most common forms of marriage in the world today, other forms do occur, however rarely. **Polyandry,** the marriage of one woman to several men at the same time, is known in only a few societies, perhaps in part because a man's life expectancy is shorter than a woman's, and male infant mortality is high, so a surplus of men in a society is unlikely. Another reason is that it limits a man's descendants more than any other pattern. Fewer than a dozen societies are known to have favored polyandry, but they involve people as widely separated from one another as the eastern Inuit (Eskimos), Marquesan Islanders of Polynesia, and Tibetans. In Tibet, where inheritance is in the male line and arable land is limited, the marriage of brothers to a single woman averted the danger of constantly subdividing farmlands among all the sons of any one landholder.

Group marriage, in which several men and women have sexual access to one another, also occurs but rarely. Even in communal groups today, among young people seeking alternatives to modern marriage forms, group marriage seems to be a transitory phenomenon, despite the publicity it may sometimes receive.

THE LEVIRATE AND THE SORORATE

If a husband dies, leaving a wife and children, it is often the custom that the wife marry one of the brothers of the dead man. This custom, called the **levirate,** not only provides social security for the

Polyandry: The marriage custom of a woman having several husbands at one time; a form of polygamy.

Group marriage: Marriage in which several men and women have sexual access to one another.

Levirate: A marriage custom according to which a widow marries a brother of her dead husband.

Sororate: A marriage custom according to which a widower marries his dead wife's sister.

Serial monogamy: A marriage form in which a man or a woman marries or lives with a series of partners in succession.

widow and her children but also is a way for the husband's family to maintain their rights over her sexuality and her future children: it acts to preserve relationships previously established. When a man marries the sister of his dead wife, it is called the **sororate;** in essence, a family of "wife givers" supplies one of "wife takers" with another spouse to take the place of the one who died. In societies that have the levirate and sororate, the relationship between the two families is maintained even after the death of a spouse; and in such societies, an adequate supply of brothers and sisters is generally ensured by the structure of the kinship system (discussed in Chapter 19), in which individuals whom we would call "cousins" are classified as brothers and sisters.

SERIAL MONOGAMY

A form of marriage that is becoming increasingly common in North American society today is **serial monogamy,** in which the man or the woman marries a series of partners in succession. Upon dissolution, the children of each marriage remain with the mother. This pattern is an outgrowth of one first described by sociologists and anthropologists among West Indians and lower-class urban blacks in the United States. Early in life, women begin to bear children by men who are not married to them. In order to support themselves and their children, the women must look for work outside of the household, but to do so, they must seek help from other kin, most commonly the children's mother's mother. As a consequence, households are frequently headed by women (on the average, about 32 percent are so headed in the West Indies). After a number of years, however, an unmarried woman usually does marry a man, who may or may not be the father of some or all of her children. Under conditions of poverty, where this pattern has been most common, women are driven to seek this male support, owing to the difficulties of supporting themselves and their children, while at the same time fulfilling their domestic obligations.

In the United States, with the rise of live-in premarital arrangements between couples, the increasing necessity for women to seek work outside the home, and rising divorce rates, a similar pattern is becoming more common among middle-class whites. Frequently isolated from kin or other assistance, women in single-parent households often find it difficult to cope. One solution is to marry (or in many cases, to remarry), in order to get the assistance of another adult.

CHOICE OF SPOUSE

The Western egalitarian ideal that an individual should be free to marry whomever he or she chooses is an unusual arrangement, certainly not one that is universally embraced. However desirable such an ideal may be in the abstract, it is fraught with difficulties, and certainly contributes to the apparent instability of marital relationships in modern North American society. Part of the problem is the great emphasis that our culture places on the importance of youth and glamour — especially on the part of women — for romantic love. Female youth and beauty are perhaps most glaringly exploited by the women's wear, cosmetics, and beauty parlor industries, but movies, TV, and the recorded music business have generally not lagged far behind; nor do advertisements for cigarettes, hard and soft drinks, beer, automobiles, and a host of other products that make liberal use of young, glamorous women. As anthropologist Jules Henry once observed, "Even men's wear and

The great emphasis our culture continues to place on feminine beauty is illustrated by the use of Vanna White as a prop to turn letters on "Wheel of Fortune."

toiletries could not be marketed as efficiently without an adoring, pretty woman (well under thirty-five years of age) looking at a man wearing a stylish shirt or sniffing at a man wearing a deodorant."[11] By no means are all North Americans taken in by this, but it does tend to nudge people in such a way that marriages may all too easily be based on trivial and transient characteristics. In no other part of the world are such chances taken with something as important as marriage.

In many societies, marriage and the establishment of a family are considered far too important to be left to the whims of young people. The marriage of two individuals who are expected to spend their whole lives together and raise their children together is incidental to the more serious matter of making allies of two families by means of the marriage bond. Marriage involves a transfer of rights between families, including rights to property and

[11]Jules Henry, "The Metaphysic of Youth, Beauty, and Romantic Love," in *The Challenge to Women*, ed. Seymour Farber and Roger Wilson (New York: Basic Books, 1966).

Marriage is a means of creating alliances between groups of people — the relatives of the bride and those of the groom. Since such alliances have important economic and political implications, the decision to marry cannot be left in the hands of the two young and inexperienced people. At the left is shown a Moroccan bride, whose marriage has been arranged between her parents and those of the groom. The picture at the right was taken at the wedding of Princess (now Queen) Elizabeth of England and Prince Philip of Greece.

rights over the children, as well as sexual rights. Thus, marriages tend to be arranged for the economic and political advantage of the family unit.

Arranged marriages, needless to say, are not commonplace in North American society, but they do occur. Among ethnic minorities, they may serve to preserve traditional values that people fear might otherwise be lost. Among families of wealth and power, marriages may be arranged by segre-

gating their children in private schools and carefully steering them toward "proper" marriages. A careful reading of announced engagements in the society pages of the *New York Times* provides clear evidence of such family alliances. The following Original Study illustrates how marriages may be arranged in societies where such practices are commonplace.

ORIGINAL STUDY
Engagement and Marriage in a Moroccan Village[12]

Marriages in Sidi Embarek are all arranged by the parents of the couple involved, although the parties on occasion may make suggestions, or veto those of their parents. The author heard an older woman describe, with obvious glee, how she had foiled her parents' plans for her. The prospective groom's family sent a donkey bearing baskets full of ripe grapes and a large sack of *henna* (a cosmetic made of powdered leaves, used to color hair red in the U.S.) as a gift. To show her disapproval, Fatna dumped all the grapes on the ground, sprinkled the *henna* over them, and set the chickens loose in the mess — and ran away to hide. When her parents found her, they chained her ankles together so she could not run far, and went ahead with the wedding plans. But Fatna was not about to be subdued, and a girl friend helped her remove the chain from one ankle. She put this over her shoulder and ran off to a nearby French farm where she knew some Moroccan workers, and they interceded with the owner. He let her stay, and when her parents came for her persuaded them to delay the marriage. According to Fatna, she was fourteen at the time, and she did not marry (and then it was someone else) for another several years.

Legally, a girl now has the right to refuse the match and is asked if she agrees to it during the engagement ceremony, but the legal prerogative does not always match the reality of the situation. If a girl fears a beating, or lack of further support from her family, she will agree publicly to the marriage, whatever her personal preferences (which are just beginning to be important in village marriages). Traditionally, marriage is an alliance between two families. It was said to often be of the patrilateral parallel cousin type, in which a boy married his father's brother's daughter, which had the effect of keeping jointly owned property in the same patrilineal family. Since the families involved were related and may even have lived together as an extended family, it also meant that it was easier to assess both the types of relationships being entered into and the characters of the actors. Data collected in Sidi Embarek, however, show that in only three of twenty-four cases did persons related by blood (not only parallel cousins) marry, while in the other twenty-one marriages the partners were unrelated. While this was not a random or representatively selected sample, it does indicate that marriage often occurs between unrelated couples.

Since marriage is mainly an alliance between two families, the partners do not have expectations of Western-style "love" (although movies and magazines are beginning to arouse such expectations), but rather work as a partnership with the object of raising a family. In this context arranged marriages are not resented, as many Western observers suspect, but rather accepted as the most sensible way to go about the matter. Even if a girl and boy in the village decide they want to marry, the decision is probably based on only a few meetings, since the sexes do not usually mix and in rural Morocco there is nothing like the custom of dating. Parents have more experience in life and more knowledge of the families which may be involved, so they are the logical agents.

The age at marriage of village girls is considerably higher than was that of their mothers. Many women recall that they had barely reached puberty when they were married ("I hardly had any breasts yet"), were afraid of their husbands, and ran away several times before finally settling down. There is now a Moroccan law setting the minimum age at marriage for girls as sixteen years and boys as eighteen, but this can easily be circumvented (an agreement with the proper official, or a change in the birth certificate) and is thus unlikely to be the cause of the higher age at marriage, now usually seventeen or eighteen for girls and the early or mid-twenties for boys. Unmarried teenage girls are still seen as a threat to the family honor, and in other rural regions of Morocco (e.g., the Southeast, near the Sahara) may still be married when they are eleven or twelve years old. The higher age at marriage in Sidi Embarek is probably due to the general lack of agriculturally based extended families living as a single household unit that could absorb and support the new couple. Marriages now usually do not occur until the male has a job with which he can support his new family, and when the job is not involved with family agriculture (and given the general shortage of jobs available), he is usually in his twenties before he can afford to be married. Thus age at marriage is higher, and most girls approve of this (although some of the boys get impatient). However, girls are still regarded as likely to be old maids if they are not married by the time they are twenty.

It is the male's family which selects the wife for its son and makes the first overtures to her family. The first sign the girl has of her impending marriage (it is improper for a father and daughter to discuss such things) is a visit paid to her home by a few female members of the groom's family, including his mother. While the males of the groom's family are important in selecting with which family they desire further ties, since they are men they can play little part in personally assessing the worthiness of the proposed bride. The women of the family are given this task, both because they can interact with her face-to-face, and because they will be more accurate judges of her housekeeping skills. In fact, household skills and honor are highly correlated; one would not expect to find an honorable girl a sloppy housekeeper, and a messy house suggests also a looseness in a woman's moral character. In this way, even if the women have been overruled initially by the men in the choice of the bride, they still have the opportunity to influence the decision in their favor.

If the groom's family is pleased with the reputation, demeanor (very shy and retiring), and household skills of the potential bride, males of the two families discuss the bride price (*sdaq* in Morocco, *mahr* in classical Arabic and in the Middle East). This sum is included in the marriage contract, and may either be given as a large lump sum to the family of the bride, or given only in part at the marriage with the other portion to be paid only in case of divorce or death of the husband. In either case, the bride price contributes to the stability of the marriage. A man considers seriously before divorcing a woman when it means he will have to pay her family additional money. Even if he has paid the total amount initially, he must still raise the bride price for another wife, for men seldom live as bachelors. Usually his family contributes to the bride price, and their hesitance to invest any further money leads them to put pressure on him to sustain his current marriage.

The inflation of bride prices in recent years is a problem for many bachelors and has also contributed to the rising age at marriage. The family of a country girl in 1972 demanded $100.00 or $200.00, while that of a city girl asked between $700.00 and $1,000.00 (village girls fell in between), in a country where the per capita income was then $80.00 a year. Divorcees and widows are much more easily attainable; their price fell within the $20.00

to $40.00 range (and did not require a large wedding celebration either), but usually only a man who has in some way lost his first wife will marry a woman who is not a virgin.

The Moroccan case also refutes (once again) those who suggest that a bride price involves the "selling" of a daughter. The money is paid to the bride's father, but it is used to buy jewelry for the bride or household furnishings for the new couple, and to finance the elaborate and costly wedding celebration. Guests do bring gifts, but these are usually something personal for the bride (such as a slip or nightgown) or cash, and are not large enough to furnish a house. The bride's father may manage to retain some of the money (for this reason some prospective grooms attempt to provide the furnishings themselves rather than giving cash to the bride's family to do so, confident that in this way they can be more economical), but not a great deal in any case. Rather, he is expected to contribute a similar sum as a dowry, to be used for the celebration, the bride's garments, and household furnishings.

If a bride price is agreed upon by the two families, there are exchanges of gifts and meals between them and a contract is prepared. The legal part of the ceremony of signing the marriage contract in rural Morocco (literally, "they do the paper") is considered as part of the engagement, but is actually also the only legal part of the marriage. If one decides afterwards to break the "engagement," one must obtain a divorce. The marriage is usually not consummated until months or even years later at a marriage ceremony (which is purely secular and consists of several days of celebration and feasting), but it is legally binding from the signing of the contract at the engagement.

The signature of the contract is done at home in the presence of a judge or his assistant and attended by members of each family. The bride is present but is spoken for by her father (or other male relative) except when asked if she agrees to the marriage. Otherwise she maintains a demure silence, her eyes cast down.

[12]Susan S. Davis, *Patience and Power; Women's Lives in a Moroccan Village* (Rochester, Ver.: Schenkman, Books, Inc., 1987), pp. 26–30. Reprinted with permission.

COUSIN MARRIAGE

In the Original Study, mention was made of **patrilateral parallel-cousin marriage,** in which a man marries his father's brother's daughter. Although not obligatory, such marriages have been favored historically among Arabs, the ancient Israelites, and also the people of ancient Greece and traditional China. All of these societies are hierarchical in nature — that is, some people have more

Patrilateral parallel-cousin marriage: Marriage of a man to his father's brother's daughter, or a woman to her father's brother's son.

property than others — and although male dominance and descent are emphasized, property of interest to men is inherited by daughters as well as sons. Thus, when a man marries his father's brother's daughter (or, from the woman's point of view, her father's brother's son), property is retained within the single male line of descent. In these societies, generally speaking, the greater the property, the more this form of parallel-cousin marriage is apt to occur.

Matrilateral cross-cousin marriage — that is, of a man to his mother's brother's daughter, or a woman to her father's sister's son — is a preferred form of marriage in a variety of societies ranging from food foragers (Australian aborigines, for example) to intensive agriculturists (as among various peoples of south India). Among food-foraging peoples, who inherit relatively little in the way of property from adults, such marriages help establish and maintain ties of solidarity between social groups. In agricultural societies, on the other hand, the transmission of property is once again an important determinant. In societies in which descent is traced exclusively in the female line, for instance, property and important rights usually pass from a man to his sister's son; under cross-cousin marriage, the sister's son is at the same time the man's daughter's husband.

MARRIAGE EXCHANGES

In the Trobriand Islands, when a young couple decide to get married, they sit in public on the veranda of the young man's adolescent retreat, where all may see them. Here they remain until the bride's mother brings the couple cooked yams, which they then eat together, making their marriage official. This is followed a day later by the presentation of three long skirts to the bride by the husband's sister, a symbol of the fact that the sexual freedom of adolescence is now over for the newly wed woman. This is followed up by a large presentation of uncooked yams by the bride's father and her mother's brother, who represent both her lineage and that of her father. Meanwhile, the groom's father and mother's brother — representing his father's and his own lineages — collect such valuables as stone axe blades, clay pots, money, and the occasional Kula shell to present to the young wife's maternal kin and father. After the

> **Matrilateral cross-cousin marriage:** Marriage of a woman to her father's sister's son, or a man to his mother's brother's daughter.

first year of the marriage, during which the bride's mother continues to provide the couple's meals of cooked yams, each of the young husband's relatives who provided valuables for his father's and mother's brother to present to the bride's relatives will receive yams from the bride's maternal relatives and father. All of this gift giving back and forth between the lineages to which the husband and wife belong, as well as those of their fathers,

On the day that her marriage is announced, the Trobriand bride must give up the provocative miniskirts she has worn till then in favor of longer skirts, the first of which are provided by the groom's sister. This announces that her days of sexual freedom are gone.

In some societies, when a woman marries, she receives her share of the family inheritance (her dowry), which she brings with her to her new family (unlike bride price, which passes from the groom's to the bride's family). Shown here is a traditional dowry presentation in Czechoslovakia.

serves to bind the four parties together in a way that people respect, honors the marriage, and creates obligations on the part of the woman's kin to take care of her husband in the future.

As among the Trobriand Islanders, marriages in many human societies are formalized by some sort of economic exchange. Among the Trobrianders, this takes the form of a gift exchange, as described above. Far more common is **bride price,** sometimes called bride wealth. This involves payments of money or other valuables to a bride's parents or other close kin. This usually happens in societies where the bride will become a member of the household in which her husband grew up; it is they who will benefit from her labor, as well as the offspring she produces. Thus, her family must be compensated for their loss. Other forms of compensation are an exchange of women between families — my son will marry your daughter if your son will marry my daughter — or **bride service,** a period of time during which the groom works for the bride's family.

Bride price: Compensation paid by the groom or his family to the bride's family upon marriage.

Bride service: A designated period of time after marriage during which the groom works for the bride's family.

Dowry: Payment of a woman's inheritance at the time of her marriage, either to her or to her husband.

In many Eurasian societies in which the economy is based on intensive agriculture, women often bring a **dowry** with them at marriage. In effect, a dowry is a woman's share of parental property which, instead of passing to her upon her parent's death, is distributed to her at the time of her marriage. This is not to say that she retains control of this property after marriage; under traditional European law, for example, a woman's property falls exclusively under the control of her husband. Having benefited by what she has brought to the marriage, however, he is obligated to look out for her future well-being, even after his death. Thus, one of the functions of a dowry is to ensure a woman's support in widowhood (or after divorce), an important consideration in a society where men carry out the bulk of productive work and women are valued for their reproductive potential but not for the work they do. In such societies, women incapable of bearing children are especially vulnerable, but the dowry they bring with them at marriage helps protect them against desertion. Another function of dowry is to reflect the economic status of the woman in societies where differences in economic status are important. Thus, the property that a woman brings with her at marriage demonstrates that the man is marrying a woman whose standing is on a par with his own.

RELATIONSHIPS MODELED ON MARRIAGE

As we have seen, marriage, although defined in terms of a continuing sexual relationship between individuals of opposite sex, always involves various other nonsexual rights and obligations as well. In some societies, however, marriagelike arrangements may occur between individuals of the same sex. Although not marriage in the technical sense of our definition, they are clearly modeled on marriage, and represent legal fictions designed to deal with problems for which ordinary marriage offers no satisfactory solution. Such is the case with woman/woman marriage, a practice sanctioned in many societies of sub-Saharan Africa, although in none does it involve more than a small minority of all women.

Although details differ from one society to another, woman/woman marriages among the Nandi of western Kenya may be taken as reasonably representative of such practices in Africa.[13] The Nandi are a pastoral people who also do considerable farming. Control of most significant property and the primary means of production — livestock and land — is exclusively in the hands of men and may only be transmitted to their male

In Europe, where both men and women inherit, by "marrying" women to the church to become nuns, the wealth that would otherwise pass to a woman's husband and offspring was instead diverted to the church.

heirs, usually their sons. Since polygyny is the preferred form of marriage, a man's property is normally divided equally among his wives for their sons to inherit. Within the household, each wife has her own house in which she lives with her children, but all are under the authority of the woman's husband, who is a remote and aloof figure within the household. In such situations, the position of a woman who bears no sons is difficult; not only does she not help perpetuate her husband's male line — a major concern among the Nandi — but she has no one to inherit the proper share of her husband's property.

To get around these problems, a woman of advanced age to whom no sons have been born may become a female husband by marrying a young

[13]The following is based on Regina Smith Obler, "Is the Female Husband a Man? Woman/Woman Marriage among the Nandi of Kenya," *Ethnology* 19 (1980): 69–88.

woman. The purpose of this arrangement is for the wife to provide the male heirs that her female husband could not. To accomplish this, the young wife enters into a sexual relationship with a man other than her female husband's husband; usually it is one of his male relatives. No other obligations exist between this woman and her male sex partner, and it is her female husband who is recognized as the social and legal father of any children born under these conditions.

In keeping with her role as female husband, this woman is expected to abandon her female gender identity and, ideally, dress and behave as a man. In practice, the ideal is not completely achieved, for the habits of a lifetime are difficult to reverse. Generally it is in the context of domestic activities, which are most highly symbolic of female identity, that female husbands most completely assume a male identity.

For the individuals who are parties to woman/woman marriages, there are several advantages. By assuming a male identity, a barren or son-less woman raises her status considerably, and even achieves near equality with men, who otherwise occupy a far more favored position in Nandi society than do women. A woman who marries a female husband is usually one who is unable to make a good marriage, often because she has lost face as a consequence of premarital pregnancy. By marrying a female husband, she too raises her status, and secures legitimacy for her children. Moreover, a female husband is usually less harsh and demanding, spends more time with her, and allows her a greater say in decision making than does a male husband. The one thing she may not do is engage in sexual activity with her marriage partner; in fact, female husbands are expected to abandon sexual activity altogether, even with their male husbands, to whom they remain married even though the woman now has her own wife.

DIVORCE

Like marriage, divorce in non-Western societies is a matter of great concern to the families of the couple. Since marriage is less often a religious than it is an economic matter, divorce arrangements can be made for a variety of reasons and with varying degrees of difficulty.

Among the Gusii of Kenya, sterility or impotence were grounds for a divorce. Among the Chenchu of Hyderabad and the Caribou Indians of Canada, divorce was discouraged after children were born, and a couple were usually urged by their families to adjust their differences. By contrast, in the southwestern United States, a Hopi woman might divorce her husband at any time merely by placing his belongings outside the door to indicate he was no longer welcome. Divorce was fairly common among the Yahgan, who lived at the southernmost tip of South America, and was seen as justified if the husband was considered cruel or failed as a provider.

Divorce in these societies seems familiar and even sensible, considered in the light of our own entangled arrangements. In one way or another, the children are taken care of. An adult unmarried woman is almost unheard of in most non-Western societies; a divorced woman will soon remarry. In many societies, economic considerations are often the strongest motivation to marry. A man of New Guinea does not marry because he wants to satisfy his sexual needs, which he can readily do out of wedlock, but because he needs a woman to make pots and cook his meals, to fabricate nets and weed his plantings. A man without a wife among the Australian aborigines is in an unsatisfactory position, since he has no one to supply him regularly with food or firewood.

It is of interest to note that divorce rates in Western societies are low when compared with those in some societies, notably matrilineal societies such as that of the Hopi. Yet they are high enough to cause many North Americans to worry about the future of marriage and the family in the contemporary world. Undoubtedly, the causes of divorce in our society are many and varied. Among them are the trivial and transient characteristics that we have already mentioned, on which marriages may all too easily be based. Beyond this, marriage is supposed to involve an enduring, supportive, intimate bond between a man and woman, full of affection and love. In this relationship, we are supposed to find escape from the pressures of the competitive workaday world, as well as from the legal and social constraints that so affect our behavior outside the family. Yet in a society in which people are brought up to seek individual gratification, where this often is seen to come through competition at someone else's expense (see Chapter 14), and in which women have traditionally been expected to be submissive to men, it should not come as a surprise to find that the reality of marriage does not always live up to the ideal. Harsh treatment and neglect of spouses — usually wives by husbands — in our society is neither new nor rare; furthermore, we are more tolerant of violence directed against spouses and children than we are against outsiders. As anthropologists Collier, Rosaldo, and Yanagisako have observed: ". . . a smaller percentage of homicides involving family members are prosecuted than those involving strangers. We are faced with the irony that in our society the place where nurturance and noncontingent [unconditional] affection are supposed to be located is simultaneously the place where violence is most tolerated."[14] What has happened in recent years is that we have become less inclined to moral censure of those — women especially — who seek escape from unsatisfactory marriages. No longer are people as willing to "stick it out at all costs," no matter how intolerable the situation may be. Thus, divorce is increasingly exercised as a sensible reaction to marriages that don't work.

CHAPTER SUMMARY

Among primates, the human female is unique in her ability to engage in sexual behavior whenever she wants to or whenever her culture tells her it is appropriate, irrespective of whether or not she is fertile. While such activity may reinforce social bonds between men and women, it can also be disruptive, so that in every society there are rules that govern sexual access. The near universality of the incest taboo, which forbids sexual relations between parents and their children, and usually between siblings, has long interested anthropologists, but a truly convincing explanation of the taboo has yet to be advanced. Endogamy is marriage within a group of individuals; exogamy is marriage outside the group. If the group is limited to the immediate family, all societies can be said to prohibit endogamy and practice exogamy. At the same time, societies that practice exogamy at one level may practice endogamy at another. Community endogamy, for example, is a relatively common practice. In a few societies, royal families are known to have practiced endogamy rather than exogamy among siblings, in order to preserve intact the purity of the royal line.

Although defined in terms of a continuing sexual relationship between a man and woman, marriage should not be confused with mating. Although mating takes place within marriage, it often takes place outside of it as well. Unlike mating, marriage is backed by social, legal, and economic forces. In some societies, new families are formed through marriage, but this is not true for all societies.

Monogamy, or the taking of a single spouse, is the most common form of marriage, primarily for economic reasons. A man must have a certain amount of wealth to be able to afford polygyny, or marriage to more than one wife at the same time. On the other hand, in societies where most of the productive work is done by women, polygyny may serve as a means of generating wealth for a household. Although few marriages in a given society may be polygynous, it is regarded as an appropriate, and even preferred, form of marriage in the

[14]Jane Collier, Michelle Z. Rosaldo, and Sylvia Yanagisako, "Is There a Family? New Anthropologial Views," in *Rethinking the Family: Some Feminist Problems*, ed. Barrie Thorne and Marilyn Yalom (New York: Longman, 1982), p. 36.

majority of the world's societies. Since few communities have a surplus of men, polyandry, or the custom of a woman having several husbands, is uncommon. Also rare is group marriage, in which several men and several women have sexual access to one another. The levirate ensures the security of a woman by providing that a widow marry her husband's brother; the sororate provides that a widower marry his wife's sister.

Serial monogamy is a form in which a man or woman marries a series of partners. In recent decades, this pattern has become increasingly common among middle-class Americans as individuals divorce and remarry.

In the United States and many of the other industrialized countries of the West, marriages run the risk of being based on an ideal of romantic love, in which youthful beauty is emphasized. In no other parts of the world would marriages based on such trivial and transitory characteristics be expected to work. In non-Western societies, economic considerations are of major concern in arranging marriages. Love follows rather than precedes marriage. The family arranges marriages in societies in which it is the most powerful social institution. Marriage serves to bind two families as allies.

Preferred marriage partners in many societies are cross-cousins (mother's brother's daughter if a man; father's sister's son if a woman), or less commonly, parallel cousins on the paternal side (father's brother's son or daughter). Cross-cousin marriage is a means of establishing and maintaining solidarity between groups. Marriage to a paternal parallel cousin serves to retain property within a single male line of descent.

In many human societies, marriages are formalized by some sort of economic exchange. Sometimes, this takes the form of reciprocal gift exchange between the bride's and groom's relatives. More common is bride price, the payment of money or other valuables from the groom's to the bride's kin; this is characteristic of societies in which the women will work and bear children for the husband's family. An alternative arrangement is for families to exchange daughters. Bride service occurs when the groom is expected to work for a period of time for the bride's family. Dowry is the payment of a woman's inheritance at the time of marriage to her or her husband; its purpose is to ensure support for women in societies where most productive work is done by men and where women are valued for their reproductive potential alone.

In some societies, arrangements exist between individuals that are modeled on marriage. An example is woman/woman marriage, as practiced in many African societies. Such arrangements provide a socially approved way to deal with problems for which conventional marriage offers no satisfactory solution.

Divorce is possible in all societies, though reasons for divorce as well as its frequency vary widely from one society to another. In the United States, factors contributing to the breakup of marriages include the trivial and transitory characteristics on which many marriages are based, and the difficulty of establishing a supportive, intimate bond in a society in which people are brought up to seek individual gratification, often through competition at someone else's expense, and in which women have traditionally been expected to be submissive to men.

SUGGESTED READINGS

Goodenough, Ward H. *Description and Comparison in Cultural Anthropology*. Chicago: Aldine, 1970. The book illustrates the difficulties that anthropologists confront in describing and comparing social organization cross-culturally. The author begins with an examination of marriage and family, clarifying these and related concepts in important ways.

Goody, Jack. *Production and Reproduction: A Comparative Study of the Domestic Domain*. Cambridge: Cambridge University Press, 1976. This book is especially good in its discussion of the interrelationship between marriage, property, and inheritance. Although cross-cultural in its approach, readers will be fascinated by the many insights into the history of marriage in the Western world.

Mair, Lucy. *Marriage*. Baltimore: Penguin, 1971. Dr. Mair traces the evolution of marriage and such alternative relationships as surrogates and protectors. Commenting upon marriage as an institution and drawing her examples from tribal cultures, Dr. Mair deals with the function, rules, symbolic rituals, and economic factors of marriage. She also cites the inferior status of women and discusses the self-determining behavior of "serious free women" as an important factor in social change.

Needham, Rodney, ed. *Rethinking Kinship and Marriage*. London: Tavistock, 1971. This collection of essays is concerned with a definition of kinship and the marriage procedure. It deals cross-culturally with the practices and rituals and the relationship of marriage to the entire social structure. Contributors include Edmund Leach, Francis Korn, and David McKnight.

18

FAMILY AND HOUSEHOLD

A woman of Katmandu with her child. Caring for children is one of the basic functions of the human family.

CHAPTER
P R E V I E W

What Is the Family?

The human family is a group composed of a woman, her dependent children, and at least one adult male joined through marriage or blood relationship. The family may take many forms, ranging all the way from a single married couple with their children, as in our society, to a large group composed of several brothers and sisters with the sisters' children, as in southwest India among the Nayar. The particular form taken by the family is related to particular social, historical, and ecological circumstances.

What Is the Difference between Family and Household?

Households are basic residential units within which economic production, consumption, inheritance, child rearing, and shelter are organized and carried out. In the vast majority of human societies, households consist of families, or else their core members constitute families, even though some members of the household may not be relatives of the family around which it is built. In some societies, although households are present, families are not. Furthermore, in some societies where families are present, they may be less important in peoples' thinking than the households of which they are parts.

What Are Some of the Problems of Family and Household Organization?

Although families and households exist to solve in various ways problems with which all peoples must deal, the different forms that they may take are all accompanied by their own characteristic problems. Where families and households are small and relatively independent, as they are in our society, individuals are isolated from the aid and support of kin and must fend for themselves in many situations. By contrast, families that include several adults within the same large household must find ways of controlling various kinds of tensions that invariably exist between their members.

The family, long regarded by North Americans as a critically necessary, core social institution, today has become a matter of controversy and discussion. Women going outside the home to take jobs rather than staying home with children, young couples living together without the formality of marriage, and soaring divorce rates have raised questions about the functions of the family in North American society and its ability to survive in a period of rapid social change. Evidence of the widespread interest in these questions can be seen in the convening, in 1980, of a White House Conference on Families. Since then, scarcely a political campaign for national office has passed without frequent reference to what candidates like to think are "traditional family values."

Does the family, as presently constituted in North America, offer the best environment for bringing up children? Does it impose an inferior status on the woman, confined and isolated in the

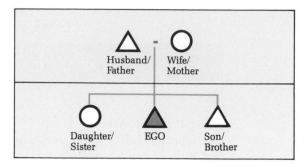

FIGURE 18.1 Anthropologists use diagrams of this sort to illustrate the relationships formed through marriage. The diagram always begins with a hypothetical individual, called Ego, and then demonstrates the kinship and marital ties in Ego's immediate family. The diagram shows the relationships in nuclear families, such as those found in our society. Only two generations are represented, but all possible relationships between the individuals can be determined from the diagram.

home, performing household and child-raising chores? Does the man, locked into an authoritarian role, suffer unduly in his personal development from bearing the primary responsibility for support of the family? Are there adequate substitutes for people who have no family to care for them, such as old people and orphans? If the family as we know it today is found wanting, what are the alternatives?

Historical and cross-cultural studies of the family offer as many different family patterns as the fertile human imagination can invent. The one considered "normal" or "natural" to most North Americans—a discrete and independent living unit consisting of the nuclear family (Figure 18.1)—is in fact no more normal or natural than any other, and cannot be used as the standard against which other forms should be measured. Neither universal nor even common among human societies, the independent nuclear family emerged only recently in human history. Its roots go back to a series of regulations imposed by the Roman Catholic Church in the fourth century A.D. that prohibited close marriages, discouraged adoption, and condemned polygyny, concubinage, divorce, and remarriage (all of which had previously been per-

This picture typifies the North American ideal of the nuclear family.

POSTQVAB CONSVMATI SVNT DIES OCTO VT CIRCVCIDERET PVER VOCATV E NOM ET IHES.LVCE.II.C.

ELONGAVI FVGIENS 7 MANSI INSOLITVDINE . PS. XXXXXV. C

SVRGE ACCIPE PVERVM 7 MATREM ET 7 FVGE INEGIPTVM .MACEI.II.C.

The Holy Family of Christianity. Mary's husband Joseph was her father's brother's son, and was himself the product of a leviratic marriage. Even though both kinds of marriage were considered proper in the early days of Christianity, they were not allowed by the Church after the fourth century.

fectly respectable, as the Old Testament of the Bible, among other sources, makes clear). Not only did this strengthen the conjugal tie between a single man and woman, at the expense of consanguineal, or "blood," ties; it also ensured that large numbers of people would be left with no male heirs. It is a biological fact that 20 percent of all couples will have only daughters, and another 20 percent will have no children at all. By eliminating polygyny, concubinage, divorce, and remarriage and by discouraging adoption, the church removed the means by which people overcame these odds and made sure that they would have male heirs. The result of all this was to facilitate the transfer of property from families to the church, which rapidly became the largest landowner in most European countries, a position it has retained to this day. By insinuating itself into the very fabric of domestic life — heirship and marriage — the church gained tremendous control over the grass roots of society, enriching itself in the process.[1]

With the industrialization of Europe and North America, the nuclear family became further isolated from other kin. One reason for this is that industrial economies require a mobile labor force; people must be prepared to move to where the jobs are, something that is most easily done without excess kin in tow. Another reason is that the family came to be seen as a kind of refuge from a public world that people saw as threatening to their sense of privacy and self-determination.[2] Within the family, relationships were supposed to be enduring and noncontingent, entailing love and affection, based upon cooperation, and governed by feeling and morality. Outside the family, where people sold their work and negotiated contracts, relationships increasingly were seen as competitive, temporary, and contingent upon performance, requiring buttressing by law and legal sanction. Although such views were most widely held in the late nineteenth and early twentieth centuries, they are still widely held today, in spite of the fact that many people find more intimacy and emotional support in relationships outside the family, and that harsh treatment and neglect of children and spouses, especially wives, are all too common within families (in the United States, some 2 million women experience abuse from the men in their families, and at least an equal number of children are also abused).

The family as it has emerged in Europe and North America, then, is the product of particular historical and social circumstances; where these have differed, so have family forms. Thus, how men and women in other societies live together

must be studied, not as bizarre and exotic forms of human behavior, but as logical outcomes of peoples' experience living in particular times, places, and social situations.

FAMILY AND SOCIETY

Although many North Americans continue to think of families as standing in opposition to the rest of society, the truth is that they are affected by, and in turn affect, the values and structure of the society in which they are embedded. For a closer look at this, we may turn to the Kiowa, a people who lived in the nineteenth century on the Great Plains of North America. Like their neighbors, the Comanche and the Cheyenne (discussed in Chapter 15), the Kiowa lived by hunting buffalo from horseback. To get horses, raids were carried out on other groups, and it was through their military exploits that men achieved high status. Kiowa society, however, was less egalitarian than those of their neighbors, being divided into three ranks, with a group of "outcasts" at the bottom who belonged to no rank. Of highest rank were families who had other men to herd and hunt for them, allowing the men in these families the freedom to join raiding parties to capture horses and accumulate war honors for themselves. Of second rank were families whose men were curtailed in their abilities to join raiding parties, since they had no men to do their herding and hunting, even though they themselves did not have to work for others. In third place were families whose ability to accumulate war honors was restricted by obligations to work for their in-laws. Finally, the outcasts consisted of sons who had been disowned by their families for disobedience, orphans, and captives living as "hangers on" with high-ranking families. It was their lifelong dependency that allowed other men to enjoy lifelong freedom from drudgery.

The key to this system of ranking was the way in which families were established, which was through marriage, and the continuing obligations men had to accede to requests made by their wives'

---

[1]Jack Goody, *The Development of the Family and Marriage in Europe* (Cambridge: Cambridge University Press, 1983), pp. 44–46.
[2]Jane Collier, Michelle Z. Rosaldo, and Sylvia Yanagisako, "Is There a Family? New Anthropological Views," in *Rethinking the Family: Some Feminist Problems*, ed. Barrie Thorne and Marilyn Yalom (New York: Longman, 1982), pp. 34–35.

male kin. A Kiowa man could acquire a wife in any of three ways, the most desirable being by exchange of gifts between families, who validated their claims to rank through the amount and quality of the gifts exchanged. This took place between families of equal rank, or between families of unequal rank if that of the groom ranked lower (wife takers were considered to be inferior to wife givers). Another way was for a high-ranking man who was already married to take as secondary wives lower-ranking women; because he had already validated his high rank through the gift exchange for his first (high-ranking) wife, he could now acquire secondary wives through gift exchanges of lesser

value without losing status. What such polygynous marriages did was to confirm the dependence of the bride's low-ranking family on the gifts and patronage her husband could not refuse them; the husband in turn (and his sons by his high-ranking senior wife) was provided with low-status daughters and half-sisters to give to outsiders in return for labor. Only men of highest status could give wives in this way, and only men with no valuables of their own would accept such gifts.

The impact of this system upon relationships within families is described in the following Original Study by Jane Collier.

ORIGINAL STUDY
Marriage and Affinal Relationships among the Kiowa[3]

The marriage system of Kiowa society established what may be seen as a triangular relationship between a woman, her husband, and her male kin whereby cooperation between any two parties jeopardized the interests of the third. This description does not suggest that Kiowa women and men actively colluded with spouses, siblings, or affines to harm one another, although some undoubtedly did; rather, the wider system of inequality organized the meaning and consequences of people's actions in such a way that cooperation between two members of the triad prejudiced the interests of the third whether the two willed it or not.

Cooperation between a husband and wife, for example, prejudiced the interests of her male kin. Ethnographers report that a Kiowa man might refuse a request from his wife's male kin, whose authority was sanctioned by their ability to take back his wife if he balked. A Kiowa informant told Richardson that " a WF [wife's father] always takes W[ife] away when H[usband] refuses a request, even if it is the first time he has refused. But such refusals are rare. In most cases where there is refusal, H thinks he has a strong hold on W and can get away with a refusal without losing her. . . ." As this informant recognized, cooperation between a woman and her husband undermined the ability of her kin to enforce their demands.

Just as cooperation between a woman and her husband allowed him to refuse requests from her kin, so cooperation between a woman and her kin put her husband at a disadvantage. If a woman were willing to return to her kin, then her husband was put in the position of having to comply with his in-law's requests or lose her. Should she leave, it might "cost him and his

Reprinted from *Gender and Kinship: Essays Toward a Unified Analysis*, edited by Jane Fishburne Collier and Sylvia Junko Yanagisako with the permission of the publishers, Stanford University Press. Copyright © 1987 by the Board of Trustees of the Leland Stanford Junior University.

kin considerable property to get her back. . . ." A husband, of course, could decide to forget an estranged wife and look for another, but, as we will see, men varied in their abilities to attract wives.

Finally, cooperation between a woman's husband and her kin put her at a disadvantage. If a woman's kin were unwilling to take her back or if they readily returned her to her husband when he offered valuables, she lost leverage in her marriage. She would be less able to protect herself from an abusive husband and less able to obtain benefits for herself and her children.

The analysis in the previous section suggests that Kiowa women benefited from keeping their children near them. Not only would a woman enjoy having her children and her grandchildren near her as she aged, but married sons who remained in the band would enjoy relative freedom from distant in-law's requests. It thus seems reasonable to assume that most Kiowa women hoped their husbands would provide enough gifts to attract married children, particularly sons, to their band. It seems reasonable, of course, to imagine that Kiowa men also hoped to keep their married children near them; however, men had competing claims on the property to be used as gifts: obligations to their brothers, an interest in taking secondary wives, the need to divide limited resources among multiple wives and children. It thus seems likely that if a woman's kin did not fully back her demands, she could not ensure that her husband's resources would be expended on her and her children, rather than on his brother or on a co-wife's children.

Just as a Kiowa man whose wife cooperated with her brothers could decide to look for another wife, so a woman whose husband had obtained the cooperation of her brothers could decide to look for another man. Evidence indicates that Kiowa women were not pawns in male-initiated marriage exchanges. Mishkin, for example, writes that "the most common form of marriage among the Kiowa was elopement . . . ," and Richardson observes that "trespass upon a husband's exclusive sexual rights to his wife was by far the most frequent source of grievance. . . ." It is thus clear that Kiowa girls did not wait patiently for their male kin to arrange marriages, nor did Kiowa wives faithfully sit home minding their husbands' hearths. Women took active roles in choosing their sexual and marital partners. But even so, the meaning and consequences of their sexual affairs were structured by the wider system of social inequality.

A Kiowa informant told Mishkin that "women seem to love [high-ranking men] more . . . ," and Richardson reports that "no woman would consort with a man of low rank unless he were most attractive. . . ." It would, of course, require a cultural analysis to understand what Kiowa meant by "love" or what women considered "attractive," but it is easy to grasp why Kiowa interpreted a woman's choice of sexual partner as a statement about his rank. In Kiowa society, the woman who took a lover necessarily chose him over another man — either her present husband or the suitor preferred by her kin. As a result, people interpreting a particular affair or elopement had to explain not why a woman chose a certain man, but why she chose him instead of a particular other. They would naturally tend to assume that she preferred the man who could offer her more — unless she were foolishly attracted by a handsome face.

In all societies, men fight men who seduce their wives (just as women fight other women who seduce their husbands), but the prevailing social hierarchy determines the form of such confrontations. Among the Kiowa, women's elopements and adulteries often led to property destructions and gift-giving. Since women's sexual affairs were so easily interpreted as statements about men's rank, such affairs tended to provoke confrontations in which conflicting parties exhibited their ability to give things away.... Only if the conflicting families were unambiguously at opposite ends of the social scale were status confrontations avoided....

Up to this point, I have focused on the effects of this system on the triad of husband, wife, and her male kin, but people's ambitions and possibilities also varied by rank. In theory, every Kiowa man both received requests from his wife's brothers and placed demands on his sisters' husbands who, given the "downhill" relation [wife givers were superior to wife takers] could not be the same people. The man who might never refuse a request from his wife's brothers could, by the same token, make unrefusable requests of his sisters' husbands. In fact, it makes sense to imagine that a man's ability to comply with his wife's brothers' requests rested on his ability to obtain compliance from his sisters' husbands. And, if this were true, then it becomes clear that women's possibilities varied according to the ranking (i.e., the needs) of their brothers.

Richardson reports that "the brother–sister bond was actually the warmest, strongest, yet most respectful, in the culture. It was said, 'A woman can always get another husband, but she has only one brother.'" It is easy to understand why brothers loomed so large in women's lives. A woman whose parents were of high rank and whose brothers exchanged many high-quality gifts with her husband and his kin, could expect to enjoy considerable power with her husband's household. She could expect, for example, that if her husband failed to provide her and her children with the advantages she felt due a woman of her background, then her brothers would support her complaint. Should she wish to leave her husband, her brothers would welcome her. And should her husband try to get her back, her wealthy brothers — who were supported by the labor of youths to whom they had given half sisters and daughters — could afford to demand considerable gifts from him and his kin before deciding whether or not she would return.

A woman whose brothers were of lower rank, and so did not have others to hunt and herd for them, could not enjoy such security if she left her husband. If her brothers had little free time for horse raiding, and so relied on her husband to supply the gifts they needed for their wives' kin, she could expect that her brothers might send her back in return for her husband's gifts or cooperation. Such a woman could run off with another man, but the amount of influence she would have over him would always be affected by her brothers' need for the goods and services he could provide.

At this point I can suggest an answer to the question that Kiowa ethnographers raise but do not answer: Why did some women let their high-ranking kin "give" them to poor youths in exchange for help in hunting and herding? Other evidence confirms that women were not simply pawns in male marriage exchanges; both unmarried and married women eloped with lovers and avoided affairs with low-ranking men unless that were most attractive. . . . Since it is unrealistic to assume that all poor youths who accepted gifts of women were irresistibly attractive, why would the women agree to live with them? The answer to this question provides the key for understanding how inequality was organized in Kiowa society.

In the previous section, I suggested that co-wives and their children were ranked within polygynous families and that high-ranking men gave away not their daughters by high-ranking wives or their full sisters but rather the daughters of their low-ranking wives and of their mothers' co-wives. In this section, I will examine the relationships among these daughters of low-ranking women, their half brothers, and their full brothers in order to suggest why some women let their male kin "give" them to poor youths.

My analysis of Kiowa marriage suggests that, unlike a daughter of parents who differed little in rank, a daughter of a high-ranking man and a low-ranking secondary wife could not count on her brothers—either half or full—to support her in quarrels with her husband. Most brothers, for example, probably had to shelter unhappily married sisters in order to avoid appearing in need of the gifts the abandoned husbands could offer. High-ranking men, however, who engaged in lavish gift exchanges with their full sisters-in-law, were in a position to refuse low-ranking half sisters' requests for aid without having others question their wealth; help could therefore be contingent on the sisters' cooperation.

At the same time, the sons of a low-ranking mother and high-ranking father were probably easily coopted into siding with their higher-ranking half brothers against the interests of their full sisters. Evidence suggests, for example, that high-ranking men regularly provided the horses and valuables their lower-ranking half brothers needed to give their in-laws in order to live virilocally [near their fathers]. In contrast to most men of low rank, therefore, sons of high-ranking fathers and low-ranking mothers did not need to obtain their sisters' cooperation in order to ensure access to horses; such men had more to gain from cooperating with their high-ranking half brothers.

It thus seems reasonable to assume that the Kiowa system of inequality created a group of women whose half brothers could refuse to help them without having their high rank questioned and whose full brothers could refuse to help them without losing access to wealth. Such women were presented (whether they realized it or not) with a choice between two less than ideal options: earning their brothers' support by complying with their brothers' wishes or facing the world without supportive male kinsmen. These, I suggest, were the women high-ranking men "gave" to poor youths. Because such women had to earn their brothers' support, these high-ranking men could tell them when to stay with and when to leave their low-ranking consorts. As a result, the poor youths who accepted such women were also presented with a choice between two less than ideal options: working for their patrons or losing their access to wifely services. In summary, the Kiowa system of inequality ultimately rested on two interrelated processes: (1) the continued reproduction of a group of women for whom the best available option was full cooperation with brothers, and (2) the continued reproduction of a group of men who had to accept such women or remain wifeless.

[3]Jane Fishburne Collier, "Rank and Marriage: Or Why High-Ranking Brides Cost More," in *Gender and Kinship: Essays Toward a Unified Analysis*, Stanford University Press, 1987), pp. 210–214.

FUNCTIONS OF THE FAMILY

Among humans, reliance on group living for survival is a basic characteristic. They have inherited this from their primate ancestors, though they have developed it in their own distinctively human ways. Even among monkeys and apes, group living requires the participation of adults of both sexes. Among those species that, like us, have taken up life on the ground, as well as among those species that are most closely related to us, adult males are normally much larger and stronger than females, and their teeth are usually more efficient for fighting. Thus, they are essential for the group's defense. Moreover, the close and prolonged relationship between infants and their mothers, without which the infants cannot survive, renders the adult primate female less well suited than the males to handle defense.

NURTURANCE OF CHILDREN

Taking care of the young is primarily the job of the adult primate female. Primate babies are born relatively helpless, and remain dependent upon their mothers for a longer time than any other animals (a chimpanzee, for example, cannot survive without its mother until it reaches the age of four or even five) This dependence is not just for food and physical care; as a number of studies have shown, primate infants deprived of normal maternal attention will not grow and develop normally, if they survive at all. The protective presence of adult males shields the mothers from both danger and harassment from other troop members, allowing them to give their infants the attention they require.

Among humans, the sexual division of labor has been developed beyond that of other primates. Until the recent advent of synthetic infant formulas, human females have more often than not been occupied much of their adult lives with child rearing. And human infants need no less active "mothering" than do the young of other primates. For one thing, they are even more helpless at birth, and for another, the period of infant dependency is longer in humans. Besides all this, studies have shown that human infants, no less than other primates, need more than just food and physical care if they are to develop normally. But among humans, unlike other primates, all this "mothering" does not have to be provided by the infant's biological mother. Not only may other women provide children with much of the attention they

A female baboon with her infant and a male friend. Baboon males are protective of their female friends, even though they are not always the fathers of their friends' infants. Thus shielded from danger and harassment from other troop members, females are able to give their infants the attention they require to survive.

need, but so may men. In many societies children may be handled and fondled as much by men as by women, and in some societies men are more nurturant to children than are women.

In all human societies, even though women may be the primary providers of child care, they have other responsibilities as well. While many of the economic activities that they have traditionally engaged in have been compatible with their child-rearing role, and have not placed their offspring at risk, this cannot be said of all of them. As a case in point, the common combination of child care with food preparation, especially if cooking is done over an open fire, creates a potentially hazardous situation for children. With the mother (or other care giver) distracted by some other task, the child may all too easily receive a severe burn, or bad cut, with serious consequences. What can be said is that the economic activities of women have generally complemented those of men, even though in some so-

cieties, individuals may perform tasks normally assigned to the opposite sex, as the occasion dictates. Thus, men and women could share the results of their labors on a regular basis, as was discussed in Chapters 15 and 16.

An effective way both to facilitate economic cooperation between the sexes and at the same time to provide for a close bond between mother and child is through the establishment of residential groups that include adults of both sexes. The differing nature of male and female roles, as these are defined by different cultures, requires a child to have an adult of the same sex available to serve as a proper model for the appropriate adult role. The presence of adult men and women in the same residential group provides for this. As defined in Chapter 17, a family is a residential group composed of a woman, her dependent children, and at least one male joined through marriage or consanguineal ("blood") relationship.

One alternative to the family as a child rearing unit is the Israeli kibbutz. Here, children of a kibbutz are shown on their playground.

Well suited though it may be for the task, we should not suppose that the family is the only unit capable of providing these conditions. In fact, other arrangements are possible, as on the Israeli kibbutz where groups of children are raised by paired teams of male and female specialists. In many food-foraging societies (the !Kung and Mbuti, discussed in Chapters 14 and 15, are good examples), all adult members of a community share in the responsibilities of child care. Thus, when parents go off to hunt or to collect plants and herbs, they may leave their children behind, secure in the knowledge that they will be looked after by whatever adults remain in the camp. Yet another arrangement may be seen among the Mundurucu, a horticultural people of South America's Amazon forest. Their children live in houses with their mothers, apart from all men until the age of 13, whereupon the boys leave their mothers' houses to go live with the men of the village. Because Mundurucu men and women do not live together as

"babysitting" also seen in non-h. primates

> **Household:** The basic residential unit in which economic production, consumption, inheritance, child rearing, and shelter are organized and carried out; may or may not be synonymous with family.

members of discrete residential units, it cannot be said that families are present in their society.

FAMILY AND HOUSEHOLD

Although it is often asserted that some form of family is present in all human societies, the Mundurucu case just cited demonstrates that this is not so. In Mundurucu villages, the men all live together in a single house with all boys over the age of 13; women live with others of their sex as well as younger boys in two or three houses grouped around that of the men. As among the Nayar (discussed in Chapter 17), married men and women are members of separate households, meeting periodically for sexual activity.

Although the family is not universally present in human societies, the **household**, defined as the basic residential unit within which economic production, consumption, inheritance, child rearing, and shelter are organized and carried out, is universally present. Among the Mundurucu, the men's house constitutes one household, and the women's houses constitute others. Although in this case, as in many, each house is in effect a household, there are a number of societies in which households are made up of two or more houses together, as we shall see later in this chapter.

In many human societies, most households in fact constitute families, although other sorts of households may be present as well (single-parent households, for example, in our own society). Often, a household may consist of a family along with some more distant relatives of family members. Or coresidents may be unrelated, as in the case of service personnel in an elaborate royal household, apprentices in the household of craft specialists, or low-status clients of rich and powerful patrons. In such societies, even though people

This photo shows a celebration at the palace in the Yoruba city of Oyo, Nigeria. As is usual in societies in which royal households are found, that of the Yoruba includes many individuals not related to the ruler, as well as the royal family itself.

may think in terms of households, rather than families, it is the latter around which the households are built. Thus, even though the family is not universal, in the vast majority of human societies, the basic core of the household is the family.

FORM OF THE FAMILY

As suggested earlier in this chapter, the family may take any one of a number of forms in response to particular social, historical, and ecological circumstances. At the outset, a distinction must be made between **conjugal families,** which are formed on the basis of marital ties, and consanguine families, which are not. As defined in Chapter 17, consanguine families consist of related women, their brothers, and the women's offspring. Such families are not common; the classic case is the Nayar household group. The Nayar are not unique, however, and consanguine families are found else-

Conjugal Family: A family consisting of one man (or more) married to one woman (or more), and their offspring.

where, for example, among the Tory Islanders, a Roman Catholic, Gaelic-speaking fisher folk living off the coast of Ireland. These people do not marry until they are in their late twenties or early thirties, by which time there is tremendous resistance to breaking up existing household arrangements. The Tory Islanders look at it this way: "Oh well, you get married at that age, it's too late to break up arrangements that you have already known for a long time. . . . You know, I have my sisters and brothers to look after, why should I leave home to go live with a husband? After all, he's got his sisters and his brothers looking after him."[4] Because the community numbers only a

[4]Robin Fox, Interview for Coast Telecourses, Inc., Los Angeles, December 3, 1981.

few hundred people, husbands and wives are within easy commuting distance of one another.

THE NUCLEAR FAMILY

The conjugal family form familiar to most North Americans is the nuclear family, which has come to be regarded as the "standard" in the United States and Canada. In these countries it is not considered desirable for young people to live with their parents beyond a certain age, nor is it considered a moral responsibility for a couple to take their aged parents into their home when the old people are no longer able to care for themselves. For this there are retirement communities and nursing homes, and to take aged parents into one's own home is commonly regarded as not only an economic burden, but a threat to the privacy and independence of the household.

The nuclear family is also apt to be prominent in societies such as the Inuit, which live in harsh environments. In the winter the Inuit husband and wife, with their children, roam the vast arctic wilderness in search of food. The husband hunts and makes shelters. The wife cooks, is responsible for the children, and makes the clothing and keeps it in good repair. One of her chores is to chew her husband's boots to soften the leather for the next day, so that he can resume his search for game. The wife and her children could not survive without the husband, and life for a man is unimaginable without a wife.

Certain parallels can be drawn between the nuclear family in industrial societies and families living under especially harsh environmental conditions. In both cases, the family is an independent unit that must be prepared to fend for itself; this creates a strong dependence of individual members on one another. There is minimal help from outside in the event of emergencies or catastrophes. When their usefulness is at an end, the elderly are cared for only if it is feasible. In the event of death of the mother or father, life becomes precarious for the child. Yet this form of family is well adapted to a life that requires a high degree of geographical mobility. For the Inuit, this mobility

Among the Inuit, nuclear families such as the one shown here are the norm, although they are not as isolated from other kin as are nuclear families in the United States.

permits the hunt for food; for North Americans, it is the hunt for jobs and improved social status that requires a mobile form of family unit.

Not even among the Inuit, however, is the nuclear family as isolated from other kin as it is among most nonnative North Americans. When Inuit families are off by themselves, it is regarded as a matter of temporary expediency; most of the time, they are found in groups of at least a few families together, with members of one having relatives in all of the others.[5] Thus families cooperate with one another on a daily basis, sharing food and other resources, looking out for each others' children, and sometimes even eating together. The sense of shared responsibility for each other's children, and general welfare, in Inuit multi-family groups contrasts with families in the United States, which are basically "on their own." In our society the state has assigned sole responsibility to the family for child care and the welfare of its members, with relatively little assistance from out-

[5]Nelson H. H. Graburn, *Eskimos without Igloos: Social and Economic Development in Sugluk* (Boston: Little, Brown, 1969), pp. 56–58.

Extended families like this one are still found in some parts of rural North America.

side.[6] To be sure, families can and often do help one another out, but they are under no obligation to do so. In fact, once children reach the age of majority, parents have no further legal obligation to them, nor do the children to their parents. When families do have difficulty fulfilling their assigned functions even though it be through no fault of their own, less support is available to them from the community at large than in most of the world's "stateless" societies, including that of the Inuit.

THE EXTENDED FAMILY

In North America, nuclear families have not always had the degree of independence that they do today. In an earlier, more agrarian era, the small nuclear family commonly was part of a larger **extended family.** This kind of family, in part conjugal and in part consanguine, might include grandparents, mother and father, brothers and sisters, perhaps an uncle and aunt, and a stray cousin or two. All these people, some related by blood and some by marriage, lived and worked together. Because members of the younger generation brought their spouses (husbands or wives) to live

[6]Collier, Rosaldo, and Yanagisako, "Is There a Family?" pp. 28–29.

Extended family: A collection of nuclear families, related by ties of blood, that live together in one household.

in the family, extended families, like consanguine families, had continuity through time. As older members died off, new members were born into the family.

Such families, until recently, have survived in some communities, as along the Maine coast.[7] There they developed in response to a unique economy featuring a mix of farming and seafaring, coupled with an ideal of self-sufficiency. Because family farms were incapable of providing self-sufficiency, seafaring was taken up as an economic alternative. Seagoing commerce, however, was periodically afflicted by depression, and so family farming remained important as a cushion against economic hard times. The need for sufficient manpower to tend the farm, while at the same time furnishing officers, crew, or (frequently) both for locally owned vessels, was satisfied by the practice of a couple, when they married, of settling on the farm of either the bride's or the groom's parents. Thus, most people spent their lives cooperating on a day-to-day basis in economic activities with close relatives, all of whom lived together (even if in separate houses) on the same farm.

The Maya of Guatemala and southern Mexico also live in extended family households.[8] In many of their communities, sons bring their wives to live in houses built on the edges of a small open plaza, on one edge of which their father's house already stands. Numerous household activities take place out on this plaza; here women weave, men receive guests, and children play together. The head of the family is the sons' father, who makes most of the important decisions. All members of the family work together for the common good and deal with outsiders as a single unit.

[7]William A. Haviland, "Farming, Seafaring and Bilocal Residence on the Coast of Maine," *Man in the Northeast* 6 (Fall 1973): 31–44.
[8]Evon Z. Vogt, *The Zinacantecos of Mexico, A Modern Maya Way of Life* (New York: Holt, Rinehart and Winston, 1970), pp. 30–34.

Traditionally, Hopi Indians of the southwestern United States lived in large extended family households. Upon marriage, a man would go to live in the household in which his wife grew up. As a consequence, Hopi families consisted of a core of women who were blood relations of one another, along with their husbands, who were "outsiders."

Extended families living together in single households were important social units among the Hopi Indians of Arizona.[9] Ideally, the head of the household was an old woman; her married daugh-

ters, their husbands, and their children lived with her. The women of the household owned land, but it was tilled by the men (usually their husbands). When extra help was needed during the harvest, for example, other male relatives, or friends, or persons designated by local religious organizations, formed work groups and turned the hard

[9]C. Daryll Forde, *Habitat, Economy and Society* (New York: E. P. Dutton, 1950), pp. 225–245.

Members of a modern Maya extended family (*top*). (*bottom*) Family members carry out various activities on the household plaza; here, for example, women weave and interact with outsiders.

Patrilocal residence: A residence pattern in which a married couple lives in the locality associated with the husband's father's relatives.

Matrilocal residence: A residence pattern in which a married couple lives in the locality associated with the wife's mother's relatives.

work into a festive occasion. The women performed household tasks, such as the making of pottery, together.

The 1960s saw a number of attempts on the part of young people in our own society to reinvent a form of extended family living. Their families were groups of unrelated nuclear families that held property in common and lived together. It is further noteworthy that the life-style of these modern families often emphasized the kinds of cooperative ties to be found in the rural North American extended family of old, which provided a labor pool for the many tasks required for economic survival. In some of them the members even reverted to old traditional gender roles; the women took care of the child rearing and household chores, while the men took care of those tasks that took people outside of the household itself.

RESIDENCE PATTERNS

Where some form of conjugal or extended family is the norm, family exogamy requires that either the husband or wife, if not both, must move to a new household upon marriage. There are five common patterns of residence that a newly married couple may adopt:

1. As just described for the Maya, a woman may go to live with her husband in the household in which he grew up; this is known as **patrilocal residence.**
2. As among the Hopi, the man may leave the family in which he grew up to go live with his wife in her parents' household; this is called **matrilocal residence.**
3. As in the case of extended families on the coast of Maine, a married couple may have the option

of choosing whether to live matrilocally or patrilocally, an arrangement that is labeled **ambilocal residence.**

4. As in most of modern North America, a married couple may form a household in an independent location, an arrangement referred to as **neolocal residence.**

5. The final pattern, to which we will return below for an example, is far less common than any of the others; this is **avunculocal residence,** in which a married couple goes to live with the groom's mother's brother.

There are variations of these patterns, but they need not concern us here.

Why do postmarital patterns of residence differ so from one society to another? Briefly, the prime determinants of residence are ecological circumstances, although other factors enter in as well. If these make the role of the man predominant in subsistence, patrilocal residence is a likely result. This is even more likely if in addition men own property that can be accumulated, if polygyny is customary, if warfare is prominent enough to make cooperation among men important, and if there is elaborate political organization in which men wield authority. These conditions are most often found together in societies that rely on animal husbandry and/or intensive agriculture for their subsistence. Where patrilocal residence is customary, it is often the case that the bride must move to a different band or community. In such cases, not only is her parents' family losing the services of a useful family member, but it is losing her potential offspring as well. Hence, some kind of compensation to her family, most commonly bride price, is usual.

Matrilocal residence is a likely result if ecological circumstances make the role of the woman predominant in subsistence. It is found most often in horticultural societies, where political complexity is relatively uncentralized and where cooperation among women is important. Under matrilocal residence, men usually do not move very far from the family in which they were raised, and so they are available to help out there from time to time.

Ambilocal residence: A pattern in which a married couple may choose either matrilocal or patrilocal residence.

Neolocal residence: A pattern in which a married couple may establish their household in a location apart from either the husband's or the wife's relatives.

Avunculocal residence: Residence of a married couple with the husband's mother's brother.

Therefore, marriage usually does not involve compensation to the groom's family.

Ambilocal residence is particularly well suited to situations where economic cooperation of more people than are available in the nuclear family is needed, but where resources are limited in some way. Because one can join either the bride's or the groom's family, family membership is flexible, and one can go where the resources look best or where one's labor is most needed. This was once the situation on the peninsulas and islands along the coast of Maine, where extended family households were based upon ambilocal residence. This pattern of residence is particularly common among food-foraging peoples, as among the Mbuti of Africa's Ituri Forest. Typically, a Mbuti marries someone from another band, so that each individual has in-laws who live elsewhere. Thus, if foraging is bad in one band's part of the forest, there is somewhere else to go where food may be more readily available. Ambilocality greatly enhances the Mbutis' opportunity to find food. It also provides a place to go if a dispute breaks out with someone in the band in which one is currently living. Consequently, Mbuti camps are constantly changing their composition as people split off to go live with their in-laws, while others are joining from other groups. For a people like food foragers, who find their food in nature and who maintain an egalitarian social order, ambilocal residence can be a crucial factor in both survival and conflict resolution.

Neolocal residence occurs where the independence of the nuclear family is emphasized. In industrial societies like our own, where most eco-

This Trobriand chief, shown in front of his house, will be succeeded by his sister's son. Hence, men who will become chiefs live avunculocally.

nomic activity occurs outside rather than inside the family and where it is important for individuals to be able to move where jobs are to be found, neolocal residence is better suited than any of the other patterns.

Avunculocal residence is favored by the same factors that promote patrilocal residence, but only in societies in which descent through women is deemed crucial for the transmission of important rights and property. Such is the case among the people of the Trobriand Islands, where each individual is a member from birth of a group of relatives, all of whom trace their descent back through their mother, their mother's mother, and so on to the one woman from whom all others are descended. Each of these descent groups holds property, consisting of hamlet sites, bush and garden lands, and, in some cases, beachfronts, to which members have rights of access. These properties are controlled each generation by a chief or other leader who inherits these rights and obligations,

but because descent is traced exclusively through women, these cannot be inherited by a man from his father. Thus, succession to positions of leadership passes from a man to his sister's son. For this reason, a man who is in line to take over control of his descent group's assets will take his wife to live with the one he will succeed—his mother's brother. This enables him to observe how the older man takes care of his hamlet's affairs, as well as to learn the oral traditions and magic that he will need to be an effective leader.

Although Trobriand leaders and chiefs live avunculocally, most married couples in this society live patrilocally. This allows sons to fulfill their obligations to their fathers, who helped build up and nurture them when they were small; in return, the sons will inherit personal property such as clay pots and valuable stone ax blades from their fathers. This also gives men access to land controlled by their fathers' descent groups in addition to their own, enabling them to improve their own economic and political position in Trobriand society. In short, here, as in any human society, practical considerations play a central role in determining where people will live following marriage.

PROBLEMS OF FAMILY AND HOUSEHOLD ORGANIZATION

Effective though the family may be at organizing (at the household level) economic production, consumption, inheritance, and child rearing, relationships within the family inevitably involve a certain amount of conflict and tension. This is not to say that they may not also involve a great deal of warmth and affection, for indeed they may. Nevertheless, at least the potential for conflict is always there, and must be dealt with lest families become dysfunctional. Different forms of families are associated with different sorts of tensions, and the means employed to manage these tensions differ accordingly.

Shown here is a North African Bedouin man with his two wives. In polygynous families, ways must be found to prevent tensions between co-wives from erupting in conflict.

POLYGAMOUS FAMILIES

A major source of tension within polygamous families is the potential for conflict that exists between the multiple spouses of the one individual to whom they are married. For example, under polygyny (the most common form of polygamy), the several wives of a man must be able to get along with a minimum of bickering and jealousy. One way to handle this is through sororal polygyny, or marriage to women who are sisters. Presumably, women who have grown up together can get along as co-wives of a man more easily than women who grew up in different households and have never had to live together before. Another mechanism is to provide each wife with a separate apartment or house within a household compound, and perhaps require the husband to adhere to a system of rotation for sleeping purposes. The latter at least prevents the husband from playing obvious favorites

among his wives. Although polygyny can be difficult for the women involved, this is not always the case. In some polygynous societies, women enjoy considerable economic autonomy, and in societies where women's work is hard and boring, polygyny can provide a means of sharing the work load and alleviating boredom through sociability.

EXTENDED FAMILIES

Extended families too, no matter how well they work, have their own potential areas of stress. Decision making in such families usually rests with an older individual, and other family members must defer to the elder's decisions. Among a group of siblings, an older one usually has the authority. Then there is the problem of in-marrying spouses, who must adjust their ways to conform to the expectations of the family in which they now live. To combat these problems, cultures rely on various techniques to enforce harmony, including such things as dependence training and the concept of "face" or "honor." Dependence training, discussed in Chapter 14, is typically associated with extended family organization, and raises people who are more inclined to accept their lot in life than are individuals who have been raised to be independent. One of the many problems faced by young people in our own society who have experimented with extended family living is that they have generally been raised to be independent, making it hard to defer to the wishes of others when they are in disagreement.

The concept of "face" may constitute a particularly potent check on the power of senior members of extended families. Among pastoral nomads of North Africa, for example, young men can escape from ill treatment of a father or older brother by leaving the patrilocal extended family to join the family of his maternal relatives, in-laws, or even an unrelated family willing to take him in.[10] Because men lose face if their sons or brothers flee in this

[10]Lila Abu-Lughod, *Veiled Sentiments: Honor and Poetry in a Bedouin Society* (Berkeley: University of California Press, 1988), pp. 99–103.

Some young North Americans have attempted to re-create the extended family in the formation of communes. These attempts sometimes run into trouble as young people cope with stress associated with extended family organization for which they are unprepared.

way, they are generally at pains to control their behavior in order to prevent this from happening. Women, who are the in-marrying spouses, may also return to their natal families if they are mistreated in their husbands' families. A woman who does this exposes her husband and his family to scolding by her kin, again causing loss of face.

Effective though such techniques may be in societies that stress the importance of the group over the individual, and in which loss of face is to be avoided at almost any cost, not all conflict may be avoided. When all else fails to restore harmony, siblings may be forced to demand their share of family assets in order to set up separate households, and in this way, new families may come into being. Divorce, too, may be possible, although the ease with which this may be accomplished varies considerably from one society to another. In societies that practice matrilocal residence, divorce rates tend to be high, reflecting the ease with which unsatisfactory marriages may be termi-

nated. In some (not all) societies with patrilocal residence, by contrast, divorce may be all but impossible, at least for women (the in-marrying spouses). This was the case in traditional China, for example, where women were raised to be cast out of their families.[11] When they married, they exchanged their dependence on fathers and brothers for absolute dependence on husbands, and later in life, sons. Without divorce as an option, to protect themselves against ill treatment, women went to great lengths to develop the strongest bond possible between themselves and their sons, in order that the latter would rise to their mothers' defense when necessary. So single-minded were many women in developing such relationships with their sons that they often made life miserable for their daughters-in-law, who were seen as competitors for their sons' affections.

[11]Margery Wolf, *Women and the Family in Rural Taiwan* (Stanford, Calif.: Stanford University Press, 1972), pp. 32–35.

NUCLEAR FAMILIES

Just as extended families have built into them certain potentially serious problems, so too do nuclear families, especially in modern industrial societies where the family has lost one of its chief reasons for being: its economic function as a basic unit of production. Instead of staying within the fold, working with and for each other, one or both adults must seek work outside of the family. Furthermore, their work may keep them away for prolonged periods of time. If both spouses are employed (as is increasingly the case, since couples find it more and more difficult to maintain a decent standard of living on a single income), the requirement for workers to go where their jobs take them may pull the husband and wife in different directions. On top of all this, neolocal residence tends to isolate husbands and wives from both sets of kin. Because there are no clearly established patterns of responsibility between husbands and wives, couples must work these out for themselves. Two things make this difficult, one being the traditional dependence of women on men that has for so long been a feature of Western society. In spite of recent changes in the direction of greater equality between men and women, all too often the partners to a marriage do not come to it as equals. The other problem is the great emphasis our society places on the pursuit of individual gratification through competition, often at someone else's expense. The problem is especially acute if the husband and wife grew up in families with widely divergent outlooks on life and ways of doing things. Furthermore, being isolated from their kin, there is no one on hand to help stabilize the new marriage; for that matter, intervention of kin would likely be regarded as interference.

Isolation from kin also means that a young mother-to-be must face pregnancy and childbirth without the aid and support of female kin with whom she already has a relationship, and who have been through pregnancy and childbirth themselves. Instead, she must turn for advice and guidance to physicians (who are more often men than women), books, and friends and neighbors who themselves are likely to be inexperienced. The problem continues through motherhood, in the absence of experienced women within the family, as well as a clear model for child rearing. So reliance on physicians, books, and mostly inexperienced friends for advice and support continues. The problems are exacerbated, for families differ widely in the ways in which they deal with their children. In our competitive society, the children themselves recognize this and often use such differences against their parents to their own ends.

A further problem connected with the raising of children confronts the woman who has devoted herself entirely to this task: what will she do when the children are gone? One answer to this, of course, is to pursue some sort of career, but this, too, may present problems. She may have a husband who thinks "a woman's place is in the home." Or it may be difficult to begin a career in middle age. To begin a career earlier, though, may involve difficult choices: should she have her career at the expense of having children, or should she have both simultaneously? If the latter, there are not likely to be kin available to look after the children, as there would be in an extended family, and so arrangements must be made with people who are nonkin. And, of course, all of these thorny decisions must be made without the aid and support of kin.

The impermanence of the nuclear family itself may constitute a problem, in the form of anxieties over old age. Once the children are gone, who will care for the parents in their old age? In our society, there is no *requirement* for their children to do so. The problem does not arise in an extended family, where one is cared for from womb to tomb.

FEMALE-HEADED HOUSEHOLDS

In North America, as increasing numbers of adults have sought escape from dysfunctional nuclear families through divorces, and as young adults have become more sexually active outside of wedlock, there has been a dramatic rise in the incidence of single-parent households headed by

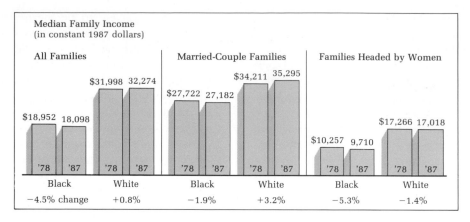

FIGURE 18.2 Median family income: Married-couple families and female-headed families in the United States are compared.

Source: Center on Budget and Policy Priorities, based on Bureau of the Census data.

women. In most cases, any children remain with their mother, who then faces the problem of having to provide for them as well as for herself. In the case of divorces, fathers are usually required to pay child support, but they are not always able or willing to do this; and when they are, the amount paid is often not sufficient to pay for all the food, clothes, and medical care that is needed, let alone the cost of child care so that the woman can seek income-producing work outside the house in order to support herself. As in the case of working women who remain with their husbands, kin may not be available to look after the children, and so outside help must be sought and (usually) paid for, thereupon making it even more difficult for the woman to support herself adequately. To compound the problem, women frequently lack the skills necessary to secure other than menial and low-paying jobs, not having acquired such skills earlier in order to raise children. Even when they do have skills, it is a fact that women are not paid as much as are men who hold the same jobs. Not surprisingly, as the number of female-headed households has increased, so has the number of women (and, of course, their children) who live below the poverty line. Over one-third of all female-headed households in the U.S. now fall into this category, and one-quarter of all children are poor (Figure

18.2). Moreover, these women and children are the ones most severely affected by cutbacks that have been made in social welfare programs since 1980. Even before Reagan was inaugurated president, the purchasing power of women was declining, and since then, the programs that were of most assistance to women and children are the ones that have suffered the deepest cuts.

Female-headed households are neither new, nor restricted to industrialized societies like the United States. They have been known and studied for a long time in the countries of the Caribbean Basin, and are becoming increasingly common in other Third World countries as well, as development projects increasingly restrict the ability of women to earn a living wage (reasons for this are discussed in Chapters 24 and 25). Thus, women constitute the majority of the poor, the underprivileged, and the economically and socially disadvantaged in most of the world's societies, just as is coming to be the case in the United States. In the Third World countries, the situation has been made worse by the recent "reforms" required by the International Monetary Fund in order to renegotiate payment of foreign debts. Cutbacks in government education, health, and social programs for debt service have their most direct (and negative) impact on women and children, at the same

Dealing with Infant Mortality

In 1979 Dr. Margaret Boone, an anthropologist who now works as a social science analyst with the Program Evaluation and Methodology Division of the United States government's General Accounting Office, began a residency on the staff of Washington, D.C.'s only public hospital. Her task was to gain an understanding of the sociocultural basis of poor maternal and infant health among inner-city blacks — something about which little was known at the time — and to communicate that understanding to the relevant public and private agencies, as well as to a wider public. As Dr. Boone put it:

> The problem was death — the highest infant death rate in the United States. In Washington, D.C., babies were dying in their first years of life at the highest rate for any large American city, and nobody could figure out why.*

In Washington, as in the rest of the United States, infant mortality is mainly a black health problem because of the large and increasing number of disadvantaged black women; black infants die at almost twice the rate of white infants. In the hospital in which Boone worked, the population served was overwhelmingly poor and black.

For the next year and a half, Boone worked intensively, reviewing medical, birth, and death records; carrying out statistical analyses; and interviewing women whose infants had died, as well as nurses, physicians, social workers, and administrators. As she herself points out, no matter how important the records review and statistical analyses were (and they were important), her basic understanding of reproduction in the inner-city black community came from the daily experience working in the "community center" for birth and death, which was the hospital — classic anthropological participant observation.

What Boone found out was that infant death and miscarriage are associated with the absence of prenatal care, smoking, the consumption of alcohol, psychological distress during pregnancy and hospitalization, evidence of violence, ineffective contraception, rapid childbearing in the teens (average age at first pregnancy was 18), and the use of several harmful drugs together (contrary to everyone's expectations, heroin abuse was less important a factor than alcohol abuse, and drug abuse in general was no higher among women whose infants died than among those whose infants did not). Cultural factors found to be important include a belief in a birth for every death, a high value placed on children, a value on gestation without necessarily any causal or sequential understanding of the children it will produce, a lack of planning ability, distrust of both men and women, and a separation of men's roles from the process of family formation (indeed, three-quarters of the women in Boone's study were unmarried at the time of delivery). Of course, some of these factors were already known to be related to infant mortality, but many were not.

As a consequence of Boone's work, there have been important changes in policies and programs relating to infant mortality. It is now widely recognized that the problem goes beyond mere medicine, and that medical solutions have gone about as far as they can go. Only by dealing with the social and cultural factors connected to poor black health in the inner city will further progress be made, and new service delivery systems are slowly emerging to reflect this fact.

*Elizabeth S. Boone, "Practicing Sociomedicine: Redefining the Problem of Infant Mortality in Washington, D.C.," in *Anthropological Praxis: Translating Knowledge into Action*, ed. Robert M. Wulff and Shirley J. Fiske (Boulder, Colo.: Westview Press, 1987), p. 56.

time that further development designed to increase foreign exchange (for debt repayment and the financing of further industrialization) also comes at the expense of women and children.

Meanwhile, the prices people must pay for basic necessities of life increase (to cut down on unfavorable balances of trade). If a women is *lucky*, the wage she earns to buy bread for herself and her

In recent years, the United States public has been shocked by reports of abuse of family members by other family members. It has become apparent that domestic violence is far from rare in North American households, where women and children are the usual victims.

children remains constant, even if low, while the price she must pay for that bread continues to rise.

At the start of this chapter we posed a number of questions relating in one way or another to the effectiveness of the family, as we know it today in North America, in meeting human needs. From what we have just discussed, it is obvious that neo-local nuclear families impose considerable anxiety and stress upon the individuals in such families. Deprived of the security and multiplicity of emotional ties to be found in polygamous, extended, or consanguine families, if something goes wrong, it is potentially more devastating to the individuals involved. On the other hand, it is also obvious that alternative forms of family and household organization come complete with their own distinctive stresses and strains. The question that springs to mind is, Which of the alternatives is preferable? And the answer is, It depends on what problems one wishes to overcome, and what price one is willing to pay.

CHAPTER SUMMARY

Dependence on group living for survival is a basic human characteristic. Nurturance of children has traditionally been the job of the adult female, although men may also play a role, and in some societies are even more involved with their children than are women. In addition to at least some child care, women also carry out other economic tasks that complement those of men. The presence of adults of both sexes in a residential group is advantageous, in that it provides the child with an adult model of the same sex, from whom can be learned the gender-appropriate role as defined in that society.

A definition of the family that avoids Western ethnocentrism sees it as a group composed of a woman and her dependent children, with at least one adult male joined through marriage or blood relationship. In most human societies, either families constitute households, or else households are built around them. Although families are not universally present in human societies, households

are. Households are defined as the basic residential units in which economic production, consumption, inheritance, child rearing, and shelter are organized and carried out.

Far from being a stable, unchanging entity, the family may take any one of a number of forms in response to particular social, historical, and ecological circumstances. Conjugal families are those formed on the basis of marital ties. The smallest conjugal unit of mother, father, and their dependent children is called the nuclear family. Contrasting with the conjugal is the consanguine family, consisting of women, their brothers, and the dependent children of the women. The nuclear family, which has become the ideal in North American society, is also found in societies that live in harsh environments, such as the Inuit. In industrial societies as well as societies that exist in particularly harsh environments, the nuclear family has to be able to look after itself. The result is that individual members are strongly dependent on very few people. This form of family is well suited to the mobility required in food-foraging groups and in industrial societies as well, where frequent job changes necessitate family mobility. Among food foragers, however, the nuclear family is not as isolated from other kin as in our own society.

Characteristic of many nonindustrial societies is the large extended, or conjugal–consanguineal, family. Ideally, some of an extended family's members are related by blood, others are related by marriage, and all live and work together as members of a single household. Conjugal or extended families are based upon five basic residence patterns: patrilocal, matrilocal, ambilocal, neolocal, and avunculocal.

Different forms of family organization are accompanied by their own distinctive problems. In polygamous families there is the potential for conflict among the several spouses of the one individual to whom they are married. One way to ameliorate this problem is through sororal polygyny. In extended families, the matter of decision making may be the source of stress, resting as it does with an older individual whose views may not coincide with those of the younger family members. In-marrying spouses in particular may have trouble complying with the demands of the family in which they must now live.

In neolocal, nuclear families, individuals are isolated from the aid and support of kin, and so husbands and wives must work out their own solutions to the problems of living together and having children. The problems are especially difficult owing to the inequality that still persists between men and women, our society's great emphasis on individualism and competition, and an absence of clearly understood patterns of responsibility between husbands and wives, as well as a clear model for child rearing.

In North America, an alternative to the independent nuclear family is the single-parent household, usually headed by a woman. Female-headed households are also common in Third World countries. Because the women in such households are hard-pressed to provide adequately for themselves as well as for their children, more and more women in the United States and abroad find themselves sinking ever more deeply into poverty.

SUGGESTED READINGS

Fox, Robin. *Kinship and Marriage in an Anthropological Perspective.* Baltimore: Penguin, 1968. Fox's book is a good introduction to older, orthodox theories about the family.

Goody, Jack. *The Development of the Family and Marriage in Europe.* Cambridge: Cambridge University Press, 1983. This historical study shows how the nature of the family changed in Europe, in response to regulations introduced by the Catholic church in order to weaken the power of kin groups and gain access to property. This book explains how European patterns of kinship and marriage came to differ from those of the ancient circum-Mediterranean world, and those that succeeded them in the Middle East and North Africa.

Netting, R. M., R. R. Wilk, and E. J. Arnould, eds., *Households: Comparative and Historical Studies of the Domestic Group.* Berkeley: University of California Press, 1984. This collection of essays by 20 anthropologists and historians focuses on how and why households vary within and between societies, and over time within single societies.

Thorne, Barrie, and Marilyn Yalom, eds., *Rethinking the Family: Some Feminist Questions.* New York: Longman, 1982. As anthropologists have paid more attention to how institutions and practices work from a woman's perspective, they have had to reexamine existing assumptions about families in human societies. The 12 original essays in this volume, by scholars in the fields of economics, history, law, literature, philosophy, psychology, and sociology as well as anthropology, examine such topics as the idea of the monolithic family, the sexual division of labor and inequality, motherhood, parenting, mental illness, and relations between family, class, and state. Especially recommended is the essay: "Is There a Family? New Anthropological Views."

19

KINSHIP AND DESCENT

On this altar, King Yax-Pac of the ancient Maya city of Copan portrays himself and his predecessors, thereby tracing his descent back to the founder of the dynasty. In many human societies, such genealogical connections are used to define each individual's rights, privileges, and obligations.

PREVIEW

What Is a Descent Group?

A descent group is a kind of kinship group in which being a lineal descendant of a particular real or mythical ancestor is a criterion of membership. Descent may be reckoned exclusively through men, exclusively through women, or through either at the discretion of the individual. In some cases, two different means of reckoning descent are used at the same time, to assign individuals to different groups for different purposes.

What Functions Do Descent Groups Serve?

Descent groups of various kinds — lineages, clans, phratries, and moieties — are convenient devices for solving a number of problems that commonly confront human societies: how to maintain the integrity of resources that cannot be divided without being destroyed; how to provide work forces for tasks that require a labor pool larger than families can provide; and how to allow members of one sovereign local group to claim support and protection from members of another. Not all societies have descent groups; in many food-foraging and industrial societies, some of these problems are commonly handled by the kindred, a group of people with a living relative in common. The kindred, however, does not exist in perpetuity, as does the descent group, nor is its membership as clearly and explicitly defined. Hence, it is generally a weaker unit than the descent group.

How Do Descent Groups Evolve?

Descent groups arise from extended family organization, so long as there are problems of organization that such groups help to solve. This is most apt to happen in food-producing as opposed to food-gathering societies. First to develop are localized lineages, followed by larger, dispersed groups such as clans and phratries. With the passage of time, kinship terminology itself is affected by and adjusts to the kinds of descent or other kinship groups that are important in a society.

All societies have found some form of family and/ or household organization a convenient way to deal with problems faced by all human groups: how to facilitate economic cooperation between the sexes, how to provide a proper setting within which child rearing may take place, and how to regulate sexual activity. Efficient and flexible though family and household organization may be in rising to challenges connected with such problems, the fact is that many societies confront problems that are beyond the ability of family and household organization to deal with. For one, there is often a need for some means by which members of one sovereign local group can claim support and protection from individuals in another. This can be important for defense against natural or human-made disasters; if people have the right of entry into local groups other than their own, they are able to secure protection or critical resources when their own group cannot provide them. For another, there frequently is a need for a way to share rights in some means of production that cannot be divided without its destruction. This is often the case in horticultural societies, where division of land is impractical beyond a certain point. It can be avoided if ownership of land is vested in a corporate group. Finally, there is often a need for some means of providing cooperative work forces for tasks that require more participants than can be provided by families alone.

There are many ways to deal with these sorts of problems. One is through the development of a formal political system, with personnel to make and enforce laws, keep the peace, allocate resources, and perform other regulatory and societal functions. A more common way in nonindustrial societies — especially horticultural and pastoral societies — is through the development of kinship groups.

DESCENT GROUPS

A common way of organizing a society along kinship lines is by creating what anthropologists call descent groups. A **descent group** is any publicly

> **Descent group:** Any publicly recognized social entity such that being a lineal descendant of a particular real or mythical ancestor is a criterion of membership.
>
> **Unilineal descent:** Descent that establishes group membership exclusively through either the mother's or the father's line.

recognized social entity in which being a lineal descendant of a particular real or mythical ancestor is a criterion of membership. Members of a descent group trace their connections back to a common ancestor through a chain of parent–child links. In this feature, we may have an answer to why descent groups are so common in human societies. They appear to stem from the parent–child bond, which is built upon as the basis for a structured social group. This is a convenient thing to seize upon, and the addition of a few nonburdensome obligations and avoidances acts as a kind of "glue" to help hold the group together.

To operate most efficiently, membership in a descent group ought to be clearly defined. Otherwise, membership overlaps, and it is not always clear where one's primary loyalty belongs. There are a number of means by which membership can be restricted. It can be done on the basis of where you live; for example, if your parents live patrilocally, you might automatically be assigned to your father's descent group. Another way is through choice; each individual might be presented with a number of options, among which he or she may choose. This, though, introduces a possibility of competition and conflict as groups vie for members, and may not be desirable. The most common way to restrict membership is by making sex jurally relevant. Instead of tracing membership back to the common ancestor, sometimes through men and sometimes through women, one does it exclusively through one sex. In this way, each individual is automatically assigned to his or her mother's or father's group, and that group only.

UNILINEAL DESCENT

Unilineal descent (sometimes called *unisexual* or *unilateral descent*) establishes descent-group mem-

Lewis Henry Morgan (1818–1881)

This major theoretician of nineteenth-century North American anthropology has been regarded as the founder of kinship studies. In *Systems of Consanguinity and Affinity of the Human Family* (1871), he classified and compared the kinship systems of peoples around the world in an attempt to prove the Asiatic origin of American Indians. In doing so, he developed the idea that the human family had evolved through a series of evolutionary stages, from primitive promiscuity on the one hand to the monogamous, patriarchal family on the other. Although subsequent work showed Morgan to be wrong about this and a number of other things, his work showed the potential value of studying the distribution of different kinship systems in order to frame hypotheses of a developmental or historical nature and, by noting the connection between terminology and behavior, showed the value of kinship for sociological study. Besides his contributions to kinship and evolutionary studies, he produced an ethnography of the Iroquois, which still stands as a major source of information.

bership exclusively through the male or the female line. In non-Western societies, unilineal descent groups are the most common form. The individual is assigned at birth to membership in a specific descent group, which may be traced either by **matrilineal descent,** through the female line, or by **patrilineal descent,** through the male line. In patrilineal societies the males are far more important than the females, for it is they who are considered to be responsible for the perpetuation of the group. In matrilineal societies, this responsibility falls on the female members of the group.

There seems to be a close relation between the descent system and the economy of a society. Generally, patrilineal descent predominates where the man is the breadwinner, as among pastoralists and intensive agriculturalists, where male labor is a prime factor. Matrilineal descent is important mainly among horticulturists with societies in which women are the breadwinners. Numerous matrilineal societies are found in southern Asia, one of the cradles of food production in the Old World. Matrilineal systems exist in India, Sri Lanka, Indonesia, Sumatra, Tibet, south China, and many Indonesian islands. They were also prominent in parts of aboriginal North America and still are in parts of Africa.

> **Matrilineal descent:** Descent traced exclusively through the female line for purposes of group membership.
>
> **Patrilineal descent:** Descent traced exclusively through the male line for purposes of group membership.

It is now recognized that in all societies, the kin of both mother and father are important components of the social structure. Just because descent may be reckoned patrilineally, for example, does not mean that maternal relatives are necessarily unimportant. It simply means that, for purposes of *group membership,* the mother's relatives are being excluded. Similarly, under matrilineal descent, the father's relatives are being excluded for purposes of group membership.

Patrilineal Descent and Organization

Patrilineal descent (sometimes called *agnatic* or *male descent*) is the more widespread of the two systems of unilineal descent. The male members of a patrilineal descent group trace through other males their descent from a common ancestor (Figure 19.1). Brothers and sisters belong to the descent group of their father's father, their father,

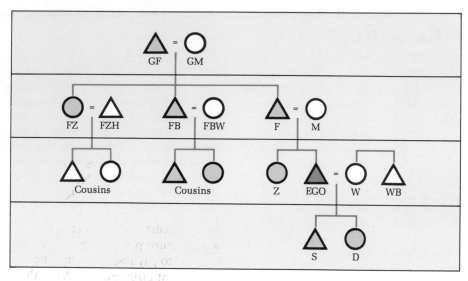

FIGURE 19.1 How patrilineal descent is traced. Only the individuals symbolized by a filled-in circle or triangle are in the same descent group as Ego. The abbreviation *F* stands for father, *B* for brother, *H* for husband, *S* for son, *M* for mother, *Z* for sister, *D* for daughter, and *W* for wife.

their father's siblings, and their father's brother's children. A man's son and daughter also trace their descent back through the male line to their common ancestor. In the typical patrilineal group, the responsibility for training the children rests with the father or his elder brother. A woman belongs to the same descent group as her father and his brothers, but her children cannot trace their descent through them. A person's paternal aunt's children, for example, trace their descent through the patrilineal group of her husband.

Traditional China: A Patrilineal Society   Up until World War II, rural Chinese society was strongly patrilineal. Since then, there have been considerable changes, although vestiges of the old system persist to varying degrees in different regions. Traditionally, the basic unit for economic cooperation was the large extended family, typically including aged parents, their sons, and their sons' wives and sons' children.[1] Residence, therefore,

was patrilocal, as defined in Chapter 18. As in most patrilocal societies, then, children grew up in a household dominated by their father and his male relatives. The father himself was a source of discipline, from whom a child would maintain a respectful social distance. Often, the father's brother and his sons were members of the same household. Thus, one's paternal uncle was rather like a second father and was treated with obedience and respect, while his sons were like one's own brothers. Accordingly, kinship terms applied to one's own father and brothers were extended to father's brother and his sons as well. When families became too large and unwieldy, as frequently happened, one or more sons would move elsewhere to establish their own separate households; when one did so, however, the tie to his natal household remained strong.

Important though family membership was for each individual, it was the *tsu* that was regarded as the primary social unit. Each *tsu* consisted of men who traced their ancestry back through the male line to a common ancestor, usually within about five generations. Although a woman belonged to

---

[1]Most of the following is from Fei Hsiaotung, *Peasant Life in China* (London: Kegan, Paul, Trench and Truber, 1939).

the *tsu* of her father, for all practical purposes she was absorbed by that of her husband, with whom she went to live upon marriage. Nonetheless, members of her natal *tsu* retained some interest in her after her departure. Her mother, for example, would come to assist her in the birth of her children, and her brother or some other male relative would look after her interests, perhaps even intervening if the woman was badly treated by her husband or other members of his family.

The function of the *tsu* was to assist its members economically and to come together for occasions such as weddings, funerals, and ceremonies for honoring the ancestors. Recently deceased ancestors, up to about three generations back, were given offerings of food and paper money on the anniversaries of their births and deaths, while more distant ancestors were collectively worshiped five times a year. Each *tsu* maintained its own place for storage of ancestral tablets, on which the names of all members were recorded. In addition to its economic and ritual functions, the *tsu* also functioned as a legal body, passing judgment on errant members.

Just as families periodically split up into new ones, so would the larger descent groups periodically splinter along the lines of its main family branches. Causes included disputes among brothers over management of landholdings, or suspicion of unfair division of profits. When such separation occurred, a representative of the new *tsu* would return periodically to the ancestral temple in order to pay respect to the ancestors and to record recent births and deaths in the official genealogy. Ultimately, though the tie to the old *tsu* would still be recognized, a copy of the old genealogy would be made and brought home to the younger *tsu*, following which only its births and deaths would be recorded. In this way, over many

In patrilineal and other societies that promote the dominance of men over women, this sometimes goes to the extreme of inflicting physical, as well as social disabilities on women. In the nineteenth century, Chinese women had their feet tightly bound, while in North America, women were often tightly corseted. The result in both cases was actual physical impairment.

centuries, a whole hierarchy of descent groups developed, with all persons having the same surname considering themselves to be members of a great patrilineal clan. With this went surname exogamy, which is still widely practiced today even though clan members no longer carry on ceremonial activities together.

The patrilineal system reached throughout rural Chinese social relations. Children owed obedience and respect to their fathers and older patrilineal relatives in life, and had to marry whomever their parents chose for them. It was the duty of sons to care for their parents when they became old and helpless, and even after death, sons had ceremonial obligations to them. Inheritance passed from fathers to sons, with an extra share going to the eldest, since he ordinarily made the greater contribution to the household and had the greater responsibility to his parents after their deaths. Women, by contrast, had no claims on their families' heritable property. Once married, a woman was in effect cast off by her own patrilineal kin (even though they might continue to take an interest in her) in order to produce children for her husband's family and *tsu*.

As the preceding suggests, a patrilineal society is very much a man's world; no matter how valued they may be, women inevitably find themselves in a difficult position. How they cope with this can be seen by looking more closely at the way women relate to one another in traditional Chinese society.

ORIGINAL STUDY
Coping as a Woman in a Man's World[2]

Women in rural Taiwan do not live their lives in the walled courtyards of their husbands' households. If they did, they might be as powerless as their stereotype. It is in their relations in the outside world (and for women in rural Taiwan that world consists almost entirely of the village) that women develop sufficient backing to maintain some independence under their powerful mothers-in-law. A successful venture into the men's world is no small feat when one recalls that the men of a village were born there and are often related to one another, whereas the women are unlikely to have either the ties of childhood or the ties of kinship to unite them. All the same, shared interests, and common problems of women are reflected in every village in a loosely knit society that can when needed be called on to exercise considerable influence.

Women carry on as many of their activities as possible outside the house. They wash clothes on the riverbank, clean and pare vegetables at a communal pump, mend under a tree that is a known meetingplace, and stop to rest on a bench or group of stones with other women. There is a continual moving back and forth between kitchens, and conversations are carried on from open doorways through the long, hot afternoons of summer. The shy young girl who enters the village as a bride is examined as frankly and suspiciously by the women as an animal that is up for sale. If she is deferential to her elders, does not criticize or compare her new world unfavorably with the one she has left, the older residents will gradually accept her presence on the edge of their conversations and stop changing the topic to general subjects when she brings the family laundry to scrub on the rocks near them. As the young bride meets other girls in her position, she makes allies for the future, but she must also develop relationships with the older women. She learns to use considerable discretion in making and receiving confidences, for a girl who gossips freely about the affairs of her husband's household may find herself always on the outside of the group, or worse yet, accused of snobbery. I described in *The House of Lim* the plight of Lim Chui-ieng, who had little village backing in her troubles with her husband and his family as a result of her arrogance toward the women's community. In Peihotien the young wife of the storekeeper's son suffered a similar lack of support. Warned by her husband's parents not to be too "easy" with the other villagers lest they try to buy things on credit, she obeyed to the point of being considered unfriendly by the women of the village. When she began to have serious troubles with her husband and eventually his family, there was no one in the village she could turn to for solace, advice, and most important, peacemaking.

Once a young bride has established herself as a member of the women's community, she has also established for herself a certain amount of protection. If the members of her husband's family step beyond the limits of propriety in their treatment of her—such as refusing to allow her to return to her natal home for her brother's wedding or beating her without serious justification—she can complain to a woman friend, preferably older, while they are washing vegetables at the communal pump. The story will quickly spread to the other women, and one of them will take it upon herself to check the facts with another member of the girl's household. For a few days the matter will be thoroughly discussed whenever a few women gather. In a young wife's first few years in the community, she can expect to have her mother-in-law's side of any disagreement given fuller weight than her own—her mother-in-law has, after all, been a part of the community a lot longer. However, the discussion itself will serve to curb many offenses. Even if the older woman knows that public opinion is falling to her side, she will be somewhat more judicious about refusing her daughter-in-law's next request. Still, the daughter-in-law who hopes to make use of the village forum to depose her mother-in-law or at least gain herself special privilege will discover just how important the prerogatives of age and length of residence are. Although the women can serve as a powerful protective force for their defenseless younger members, they are also a very conservative force in the village.

Taiwanese women can and do make use of their collective power to lose face for their menfolk in order to influence decisions that are ostensibly not theirs to make. Although young women may have little or no influence over their husbands and would not dare express an unsolicited opinion (and perhaps not even a solicited one) to their fathers-in-law, older women who have raised their sons properly retain considerable influence over their sons' actions, even in activities exclusive to men. Further, older women who have displayed years of good judgement are regularly consulted by their husbands about major as well as minor economic and social projects. But even men who think themselves free to ignore the opinions of their women are never free of their own concept, face. It is much easier to lose face than to have face. We once asked a male friend in Peihotien just what "having face" amounted to. He replied, "When no one is talking about a family, you can say it has face." This is precisely where women wield their power. When a man behaves in a way that they consider wrong, they talk about him—not only among themselves, but to their sons and husbands. No one "tells him how to mind his own business," but it becomes abundantly clear that he is losing face and by continuing in this manner may bring shame to the family of his ancestors and descendants. Few men will risk that.

The rules that a Taiwanese man must learn and obey to be a successful member of his society are well developed, clear, and relatively easy to stay within. A Taiwanese woman must also learn the rules, but if she is to be a successful woman, she must learn not to stay within them, but to appear to stay within them; to manipulate them, but not to appear to be manipulating them; to teach them to her children, but not to depend on her children for her protection. A truly successful Taiwanese woman is a rugged individualist who has learned to depend largely on herself while appearing to lean on her father, her husband, and her son. The contrast between the terrified young bride and the loud, confident, often lewd old woman who has outlived her mother-in-law and her husband reflects the tests met and passed by not strictly following the rules and by making purposeful use of those who must. The Chinese male's conception of women as "narrow-hearted" and socially inept may well be his vague recognition of this facet of women's power and technique.

[2]Reprinted from *Women and the Family in Rural Taiwan* by Margery Wolf with permission of the publisher, Stanford University Press. Copyright © 1972 by the Board of Trustees of the Leland Stanford Junior University.

Matrilineal Descent and Organization

In one respect, matrilineal descent is the opposite of patrilineal: It is reckoned through the female line (Figure 19.2). The matrilineal pattern differs from the patrilineal in that descent does not automatically confer authority. Thus, while patrilineal societies are patriarchal, matrilineal societies are not matriarchal. Although descent passes through the female line, and women may have considerable power, they do not hold exclusive authority in the descent group: they share it with men. These are the brothers, rather than the husbands, of the women through whom descent is reckoned. Apparently, the adaptive purpose of the matrilineal system is to provide continuous female solidarity within the female work group. Matrilineal systems are usually found in farming societies in which women perform much of the productive work.

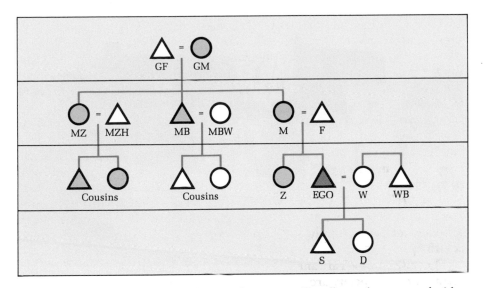

FIGURE 19.2 This diagram, which traces descent matrilineally, can be compared with that in Figure 19.1, showing patrilineal descent. The two patterns are virtually mirror images. Note that a male Ego cannot transmit descent to his own children.

Because women's work is regarded as so important to the society, matrilineal descent prevails.

In the matrilineal system, brothers and sisters belong to the descent group of the mother's mother, the mother, the mother's siblings, and the mother's sister's children. Males belong to the same descent group as their mother and sister, but their children cannot trace their descent through them. For example, the children of a man's maternal uncle are considered members of the uncle's wife's matrilineal descent group. Similarly, a man's own children belong to his wife's, but not his, descent group.

Although not true of all matrilineal systems, a common feature is the weakness of the tie between husband and wife. The wife's brother, and not the husband-father, distributes goods, organizes work, settles disputes, administers inheritance and succession rules, and supervises rituals. The husband has legal authority not in his own household but in that of his sister. Furthermore, his property and status are inherited by his sister's son, rather than his own. Thus, brothers and sisters maintain life-long ties with one another, whereas marital ties are easily severed. In matrilineal societies, unsatisfactory marriages are more easily ended than in patrilineal societies.

The Hopi: A Matrilineal Society In northeastern Arizona are the villages, or pueblos, of the Hopi Indians, a farming people whose ancestors have lived in the region for at least 2,000 years. Their society is divided into a number of named clans, based strictly on matrilineal descent.[3] Each individual is assigned from birth to the clan of his or her mother, and so important is this affiliation that, in a very real sense, a person has no identity apart from it. Two or more clans together constitute larger, supraclan units, or phratries, of which there are nine in Hopi society. Within each of these, member clans are expected to support one another and to observe strict exogamy. Because

[3]Most of the following is from John C. Connelly, "Hopi Social Organization," in *Handbook of North American Indians*, vol. 9, *Southwest*, ed. Alfonso Ortiz (Washington: Smithsonian Institution, 1979), pp. 539–553.

The buildings shown in this 1914 photograph of a traditional Hopi village housed women who were matrilineal relatives of one another — together with their husbands and children.

members of all nine phratries can be found living in any given pueblo, marriage partners can always be found in one's home community. This same dispersal of membership provides individuals with rights of entry into villages other than their own.

Although clans are the major units in Hopi thinking, the functional units consist of subclans, or lineages, of which there are several per village. Each is headed by a senior woman — usually the eldest, although it is her brother or maternal uncle who keeps the sacred "medicine bundle" and plays an active role in running lineage affairs. The woman, however, is not a mere figurehead; she may act as mediator to help resolve disputes between members of the group; nor does she yield any authority to her brother or uncle. Although these men have the right to offer her advice and criticism, they are equally obligated to listen to what she has to say. Most female authority, however, is exerted within the household, and here men clearly take second place. These households consist of the women of the lineage with their husbands and unmarried sons, all of whom used to live in sets of adjacent rooms in single large tenements. Nowadays, nuclear families often live (frequently

with a maternal relative or two) in separate houses, but pickup trucks enable related households to maintain close contacts and to cooperate as before.

Lineages function as landholding corporations, allocating land for the support of member households. These lands are farmed by "outsiders," the husbands of the women whose lineage owns the land, and it is to these women that the harvest belongs. Thus, Hopi men spend their lives laboring for alien lineages (their wives'), in return for which they are given food and shelter (by their wives). Although sons learn from their fathers how to farm, a man has no real authority over his son (the two belong to different lineages). Thus, when parents have difficulty with an unruly child, it is the mother's brother who is called upon to mete out punishment. Male loyalties are therefore divided, between their wives' households on the one hand and their sisters' on the other. If at any time a man is perceived as being an unsatisfactory husband, his wife has merely to place his belongings outside the door, and the marriage is over.

In addition to their economic and legal functions, lineages play a role in Hopi ceremonial activities. Although membership in the associations

APPLICATION
Federal Recognition for Native Americans

In 1981, the Washington (D.C.) Association of Professional Anthropologists bestowed its first annual Praxis Award on James Wherry, for his use of anthropological knowledge to win federal recognition for the Houlton Band of Maliseet Indians in Maine. The Praxis Award is an international competition open to all projects, programs, and activities that illustrate the translation of anthropological knowledge into action. As a consequence of their recognition, the Houlton Band became eligible to receive services and contracts from the Bureau of Indian Affairs and Indian Health Services, and to share in the settlement of the Maine Indian land claim, with which they could purchase land to be held in trust for them. With these arrangements, they were transformed from a poor and powerless minority into a semisovereign people with the means to establish their own land base, as well as a broad range of programs controlled by themselves.

The Houlton Band of Maliseet Indians are one of over 100 Native American communities that were forgotten or overlooked by the federal government, owing to drastic depopulation, forced removals, and other dislocations in the regions in which they lived. Under the U.S. Constitution, Indians are a federal responsibility, but without official recognition, native communities are unable to gain access to government health, education, and other Indian services that derive from treaty obligations of the United States toward Indian "tribes." As a result, unrecognized Indians are poorer, less well educated, and subject to more serious health problems than are those in recognized "tribes." Most unrecognized groups are landless, and some have disintegrated through lack of protection by the federal government.

In 1978, federal regulations were adopted by which unrecognized Indian communities could petition for acknowledgment. In order to do so, they must provide extensive ethnohistorical, genealogical and ethnographic information on their origins, development, and present social and political organization. Genealogical data are especially important, for genealogies of all present "tribal" members are required. Moreover, traditional communities often were structured on the basis of kinship and descent, and recurring marriages between families have been an important means by which community organization has been perpetuated and identity maintained. Since the gathering of such data has long been an anthropological specialty, Native American communities commonly turn to anthropologists like James Wherry to assist in meeting the criteria required for recognition.

that actually perform ceremonies is open to all who have the proper qualifications for membership, they are all owned and managed by clans, and in each village, a leading lineage acts as its clan's representative. Owned by this lineage is a special house in which the clan's religious paraphernalia is stored and cared for by the "clan mother." Together with her brother, the clan's "big uncle," she helps manage ceremonial activity. While most of the associations that do the actual performing are controlled by men, women still have vital roles to play. For example, they provide the cornmeal, symbolic of natural and spiritual life, that is a necessary ingredient in virtually all ceremonies.

Prior to the imposition by the United States government in 1936 of a different system, each Hopi pueblo was politically autonomous, with its own chief and village council. Here again, however, descent group organization made itself felt, for the council was made up of men who inherited their positions through their clans. Moreover, the powers of the chief and his council were limited; the chief's major job was to maintain harmony between his village and the spiritual world, and whatever authority he and his council wielded was directed at coordination of community effort, not enforcement of unilateral decrees. Decisions were made on the basis of consensus, and women's views had to be considered, as well as those of men. Once again, although positions of authority were held by men, women had considerable control over their decisions in a behind-the-scene way. These men, after all, lived in households that were controlled by women, and their position within them depended largely on how well they got along with the senior women. Outside the household, refusal to play their part in the performance of ceremonies gave women the power of the veto. Small wonder, then, that Hopi men readily admit that "women usually get their way."[4]

DOUBLE DESCENT

Double descent, or double unilineal descent, whereby descent is reckoned both patrilineally and matrilineally at the same time, is very rare. In this system, descent is matrilineal for some purposes and patrilineal for others. Generally, where double descent is reckoned, the matrilineal and patrilineal groups take action in different spheres of society.

For example, among the Yakö of eastern Nigeria, property is divided into patrilineal line possessions and matrilineal line possessions.[5] The patrilineage owns perpetual productive resources, such as land, whereas the matrilineage owns consumable property, such as livestock. The legally weaker matrilineal line is somewhat more important in religious matters than the patrilineal line. Through double descent, a Yakö individual might inherit grazing lands from the father's patrilineal group and certain ritual privileges from the mother's matrilineal line.

AMBILINEAL DESCENT

Unilineal descent provides an easy way of restricting descent-group membership so as to avoid problems of divided loyalty and the like. A number

> **Double descent:** A system according to which descent is reckoned matrilineally for some purposes and patrilineally for others.
>
> **Ambilineal descent:** Descent in which the individual may affiliate with either the mother's or the father's descent group.

of societies, many of them in the Pacific and in Southeast Asia, accomplish the same thing in other ways, though perhaps not quite so neatly. The resultant descent groups are known as ambilineal, nonunilineal, or cognatic. **Ambilineal descent** provides a measure of flexibility not normally found under unilineal descent; each individual has the option of affiliating with either the mother's or the father's descent group. In many of these societies an individual is allowed to belong to only one group at any one time, regardless of how many groups he or she may be eligible to join. Thus, the society may be divided into the same sorts of discrete and separate groups of kin as in a patrilineal or matrilineal society. There are other cognatic societies, however, such as the Samoans of the South Pacific or the Bella Coola and the southern branch of the Kwakiutl of the Pacific northwest coast, which allow overlapping membership in a number of descent groups. As anthropologist George Murdock observed, too great a range of individual choice interferes with the orderly functioning of any kin-oriented society: "An individual's plural membership almost inevitably becomes segregated into one primary membership, which is strongly activated by residence, and one or more secondary memberships in which participation is only partial or occasional."[6]

Ambilineal Descent among New York City Jews

For an example of ambilineal organization we might easily turn to a traditional, non-Western society, as we have for patrilineal and matrilineal organization. Instead, we shall turn to contempo-

---

[4]Alice Schlegel, "Male and Female in Hopi Thought and Action," in *Sexual Stratification*, ed. Alice Schlegel (New York: Columbia University Press, 1977), p. 254.

[5]C. Daryll Forde, "Double Descent among the Yakö," in *Kinship and Social Organization*, ed. Paul Bohannan and John Middleton (Garden City, N.Y.: Natural History Press, 1968), pp. 179–191.

[6]George P. Murdock, "Cognatic Forms of Social Organization," in *Social Structure in Southeast Asia*. ed. G. P. Murdock (Chicago: Quadrangle Books, 1960), p. 11.

rary North American society, in order to dispel the common notion that descent groups are necessarily incompatible in structure and function with the demands of modern, industrial society. In fact, large corporate descent groups are to be found in New York City, as well as in every other large city in the United States where a substantial Jewish population of eastern European background is to be found.[7] Furthermore, these descent groups are not survivals of an old eastern European, descent-based organization. Rather, they represent a social innovation designed to restructure and preserve the traditionally close affective family ties of the old eastern European Jewish culture in the face of continuing immigration to the United States, subsequent dispersal from New York City, and the development of significant social and even temperamental differences among their descendants. The earliest of these descent groups did not develop until the end of the first decade of the 1900s, some 40 years after the immigration of eastern European Jews began in earnest. Although some groups have disbanded, they generally have remained alive and vital right down to the present day.

The original Jewish descent groups in New York City are known as *family circles.* The potential members of a family circle consist of all living descendants, with their spouses, of an ancestral pair. In actuality, not all who are eligible join, so there is an element of voluntarism. But eligibility is explicitly determined by descent, using both male and female links, without set order, to establish the connection with the ancestral pair. Thus, individuals are normally eligible for membership in more than one group. To activate one's membership, one simply pays the required dues, attends meetings, and participates in the affairs of the group. Individuals can, and frequently do, belong at the same time to two or three groups for which they are eligible. Each family circle bears a name, usually including the surname of the male ancestor; each has elected officers; and each meets regularly

[7]William E. Mitchell, *Mishpokhe: A Study of New York City Jewish Family Clubs* (The Hague: Mouton, 1978).

This photo shows three generations of a Jewish family. Close family ties have always been important in eastern European Jewish culture. In order to maintain such ties in the United States, the descendants of eastern European Jews developed ambilineal descent groups.

throughout the year rather than just once or twice. At the least, the family circle as a corporation holds funds in common, and some hold title to burial plots for the use of members. Originally, the family circles functioned as mutual-aid societies, as well as for the purpose of maintaining family solidarity. Now, as the mutual-aid functions have been taken over by outside agencies, the promotion of solidarity has become their primary goal. It will be interesting to see if reduced government funding for these agencies leads to a resurgence of the mutual-aid function of family circles.

In the years just prior to World War II, an interesting variant of the ambilineal descent group developed among younger-generation descendants of east European Jewish immigrants. Being more assimilated into North American culture than their elders, some of them sought to separate themselves somewhat from members of older generations, who were perceived as being a bit old-fashioned. Yet they still wished to maintain the traditional Jewish ethic of family solidarity. The result was the *cousins club,* which consists of a group of first cousins, who themselves share a common ancestry; their spouses; and their descendants. Excluded are parents and grandparents of the cousins, with their older views and life-styles. Ambilineal descent remains the primary organizing principle, but it has been modified by a generational principle. Otherwise, cousins clubs are organized and function in many of the same ways as family circles.

FORMS AND FUNCTIONS OF DESCENT GROUPS

Descent groups with restricted membership, regardless of how descent is reckoned, are usually more than just groups of relatives providing warmth and a sense of belonging; in nonindustrial societies they are tightly organized working units providing security and services in the course of what can be a difficult, uncertain life. The tasks performed by descent groups are manifold. Besides acting as economic units providing mutual aid to their members, they may act to support the aged and infirm or help in the case of marriage or death. Often, they play a role in determining whom an individual may or may not marry. The descent group may also act as a repository of religious traditions. Ancestor worship, for example, is a powerful force acting to reinforce group solidarity.

LINEAGE

A **lineage** is a corporate descent group composed of consanguineal kin who claim descent from a common ancestor and who are able to trace descent genealogically through known links. The term is usually employed where some form of unilineal descent is the rule, but there are similar ambilineal groups, such as the Jewish family circles just discussed.

The lineage is ancestor-oriented; membership in the group is recognized only if relationship to a common ancestor can be traced and proved. In many societies an individual has no legal or political status except as a member of a lineage. Since "citizenship" is derived from lineage membership and legal status depends on it, political power and

> **Lineage:** A corporate descent group whose members claim descent from a common ancestor and can trace their genealogical links to that ancestor.
>
> **Fission:** The splitting of a descent group into two or more new descent groups.

religious power are thus derived from it as well. Important religious and magical powers, such as those associated with the cults of gods and ancestors, may also be bound to the lineage.

The lineage, like General Motors or Polaroid, is a corporate group. Because it continues after the death of members as new members are continually being born into it, it has a perpetual existence that enables it to take corporate actions, such as owning property, organizing productive activities, distributing goods and labor power, assigning status, and regulating relations with other groups. The lineage is a strong, effective base of social organization.

A common feature of lineages is that they are exogamous. This means that members of a lineage must find their marriage partners in other lineages. One advantage of lineage exogamy is that potential sexual competition within the group is curbed, promoting the group's solidarity. Lineage exogamy also means that each marriage is more than an arrangement between two individuals; it amounts as well to a new alliance between lineages. This helps to maintain them as components of larger social systems. Finally, lineage exogamy maintains open communication within a society, promoting the diffusion of knowledge from one lineage to another.

CLAN

In the course of time, as generation succeeds generation and new members are born into the lineage, its membership may become too large to be manageable, or too much for the lineage's resources to support. When this happens, **fission** will take place; that is, the lineage will split up into new, smaller lineages. When fission occurs, it is usual for the members of the new lineages to continue to recognize their ultimate relationship to one another. The result of this process is the appearance of a second kind of descent group, the **clan**. The term *clan*, (and its close relative, the term *sib*) has been used differently by different anthropologists, and a certain amount of confusion exists about its meaning. The clan (or sib) will here be defined as a noncorporate descent group in which each member assumes descent from a common ancestor (who may be real or fictive), but is unable to trace the actual genealogical links back to that ancestor. This stems from the great genealogical depth of the clan, whose founding ancestor lived so far in the past that the links must be assumed rather than known in detail. A clan differs from a lineage in another respect: it lacks the residential unity that is generally — though not invariably — characteristic of the core members of a lineage. As with the lineage, descent may be patrilineal, matrilineal, or ambilineal.

Because clan membership is dispersed rather than localized, it usually does not hold tangible property corporately. Instead, it tends to be more a unit for ceremonial matters. Only on special occasions will the membership gather together for specific purposes. Clans, however, may handle important integrative functions. Like lineages, they may regulate marriage through exogamy. Because of their dispersed membership, they give individuals the right of entry into local groups other than their own. One is usually expected to give protection and hospitality to one's fellow clan members. Hence, these can be expected in any local group that includes members of one's own clan.

Clans, lacking the residential unity of lineages, depend on symbols — of animals, plants, natural forces, and objects — to provide members with solidarity and a ready means of identification. These symbols, called *totems*, are often associated with the clan's mythical origin and provide clan members with a means of reinforcing the awareness of their common descent. The word *totem* comes from the Ojibwa American Indian word *ototeman*,

Clan: A noncorporate descent group with each member claiming descent from a common ancestor without actually knowing the genealogical links to that ancestor.

Totemism: The belief that people are descended from animals, plants, or natural objects.

Phratry: A unilineal descent group composed of two or more clans that claim to be of common ancestry. If there are only two such groups, each is a moiety.

meaning "he is a relative of mine." **Totemism** has been defined by A. R. Radcliffe-Brown as a set of "customs and beliefs by which there is set up a special system of relations between the society and the plants, animals, and other natural objects that are important in the social life."[8] Hopi Indian matriclans, for example, bear such totemic names as Bear, Bluebird, Butterfly, Lizard, Spider, and Snake.

Totemism is a changing concept that varies from clan to clan. A kind of "watered-down" totemism may be found even in our own society, where baseball and football teams are given the names of such powerful wild animals as bears, tigers, and wildcats. This extends to the Democratic Party's donkey and the Republican Party's elephant, and to the Elks, the Lions, and other fraternal and social organizations. Our animal emblems, however, do not involve the same notions of descent and strong sense of kinship, nor are they associated with the various ritual observances associated with clan totems.

PHRATRIES AND MOIETIES

Other kinds of descent groups are phratries and moieties (Figure 19.3). A **phratry** is a unilineal descent group composed of two or more clans that are supposedly related, whether or not they really are. Like individuals of the clan, members of the

[8]A. R. Radcliffe-Brown, "Social Organization of Australian Tribes," *Oceania Monographs*, no. 1 (Melbourne: Macmillan, 1931), p. 29.

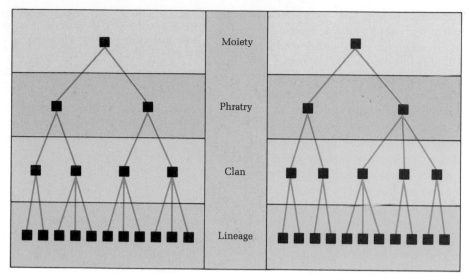

FIGURE 19.3 This diagram shows how lineages, clans, phratries, and moieties form an organization hierarchy. Each moiety is subdivided into phratries, each phratry is subdivided into clans, and each clan is subdivided into lineages.

phratry are unable to trace accurately their descent links to a common ancestor, though they believe such an ancestor existed.

If the entire society is divided into two and only two major descent groups, be they equivalent to clans or phratries, or at an even more all-inclusive level, each group is called a **moiety** (after the French word for "half"). Members of the moiety believe themselves to share a common ancestor, but are unable to prove it through definite genealogical links. As a rule, the feeling of kinship among members of lineages and clans is stronger than that felt among members of phratries and moieties. This may be due to the larger size and more diffuse nature of the latter groups.

BILATERAL DESCENT AND THE KINDRED

Important though descent groups are in many societies, they are not found in all societies, nor are they the only kinds of nonfamilial kinship groups to be found. Bilateral descent, a characteristic of

Moiety: Each group that results from a division of a society into two halves on the basis of descent.

Kindred: A group of people closely related to one living individual through both parents.

Western society, affiliates a person with other close relatives through both sexes; in other words, the individual traces descent through both parents simultaneously and recognizes multiple ancestors. Theoretically, one is associated equally with all relatives on both the mother's and father's sides of the family. Thus, this principle relates an individual lineally to all eight great-grandparents and laterally to all third and fourth cousins. Since such a huge group is too big to be socially practical, the group is usually reduced to a small circle of paternal and maternal relatives, called the **kindred.** The kindred may be defined as a group of people closely related to one living individual through both parents. Unlike descent groups, the kindred is laterally rather than lineally organized. That is, ego, or the focal person from whom the degree of

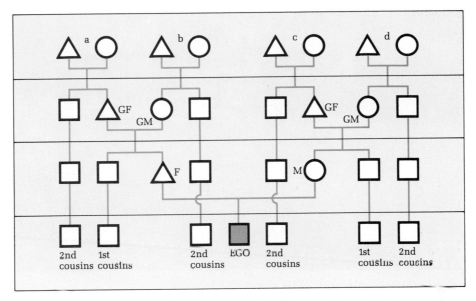

FIGURE 19.4 The kinship pattern of the kindred. These people are related, not to a common ancestor, but rather to a living relative, Ego. The squares represent persons of either sex; sex is not relevant in determining relationship.

each relationship is reckoned, is the center of the group (Figure 19.4). We are all familiar with the kindred; we simply call them relatives. It includes the relatives on both sides of the family whom we see on important occasions, such as family reunions and funerals. Most of us can identify the members of our kindred up to second cousins and grandparents. In our society, the limits of the kindred are variable and indefinite; no one can ever be absolutely certain which relatives to invite to every important function and which to exclude. Inevitably, situations arise that require some debate about whether or not to invite certain, usually distant, relatives. The kindred is thus somewhat vaguely defined, lacking the distinctiveness of the unilineal or ambilineal descent group. (It is also temporary, lasting only as long as the function it has been assembled to attend.)

The kindred possesses one feature that sets it apart from all descent groups: because of its bilateral structure, a kindred is never the same for any two persons except siblings (brothers and sisters).

Thus, no two people (except siblings) belong to the same kindred. Ego's father's kindred, for example, ranges lineally to the father's grandparents and laterally to cousins too distant for ego to know; the same is true of ego's mother, maternal and paternal aunts, and uncles. Thus, the kindred is not composed of people with an ancestor in common, but of people with a living relative in common — ego.

The Ego: Center of the Kindred

Kindreds are referred to as ego-centered or ego-focused groups because ego, or the person viewing the group, is at its center. Even in relation to ego, the membership of the group is constantly changing as ego moves through life. When one is young, it consists of one's parents, siblings, and other close consanguineal relatives, most of whom are older than ego is. As ego grows older and has children, the composition of the kindred changes; it consists of one's descendants and the remaining relatives of one's own generation. Thus, because

Members of this baby's personal kindred shown here are her mother, father, father's mother, mother's father, mother's sister, and mother's sister's husband. Each of us has a unique kindred consisting of relatives on both our mother's and father's sides.

of its vagueness, temporary nature, and changing personnel, the kindred cannot function as a group except in relation to ego. Unlike descent groups, it is not self-perpetuating—it ceases with ego's death. It has no constant leader, nor can it easily hold, administer, or pass on property. In most cases, it cannot organize work, nor can it easily administer justice or assign status. It can, however, be turned to for aid. In non-Western societies, for example, raiding or trading parties may be composed of kindred groups. The group is assembled, does what it was organized to do, shares the spoils, and then disbands. It can also act as a ceremonial group for rites of passage—initiation ceremonies and the like. Thus, kindreds assemble only for specific purposes. Finally, they can also regulate marriage through exogamy.

Kindreds are frequently found in industrial societies such as our own, where mobility weakens contact with relatives. Individuality is emphasized in such societies, and strong kinship organization is usually not as important as it is among non-Western peoples. On the other hand, the bilateral kindred may also be found in societies where kinship ties are important, and in some instances, they even occur alongside descent groups.

EVOLUTION OF THE DESCENT GROUP

Just as different types of families occur in different societies, so do different kinds of descent systems. Descent groups, for example, are not a common feature of hunting and gathering societies, where marriage acts as the social mechanism for integrating individuals within the society. In horticultural, pastoral, or many intensive agricultural societies, however, the descent group usually provides the structural framework upon which the fabric of the society rests.

It is generally agreed that lineages arise from extended family organization, so long as there are problems of organization that such groups help solve. As members of existing extended families find it necessary to split off and establish new families elsewhere, all that is required, really, is that

Iroquoian clans were a legal fiction that allowed people to travel back and forth between villages of the "Five Nations" in what is now New York State. This portrait, done in 1710, shows a member of the Mohawk Nation with (behind him) a bear, which represents his clan.

they not move too far away, that the core members of such related families (men in patrilocal, women in matrilocal, members of both sexes in ambilocal extended families) explicitly acknowledge their descent from a common ancestor, and that they continue to participate in common activities in an organized way. As this proceeds, lineages will develop, and these may with time give rise to clans and ultimately phratries.

Another way that clans may arise is as legal fictions to bring about the integration of otherwise autonomous units. The five Iroquoian Indian tribes of what now is New York State, for example, developed clans by simply behaving as if lineages

of the same name in different villages were related. Thus, their members became fictitious brothers and sisters. By this device, members of, say, a "Turtle" lineage in one village could travel to another and be welcomed in and hosted by members of another "Turtle" lineage. In this way, the Five Nations achieved a wider unity than had previously existed.

As larger, dispersed descent groups develop, the conditions that gave rise to extended families and lineages may change. For example, economic diversity and the availability of alternative occupations among which individuals may choose may conflict with the residential unity of extended families and (usually) lineages. Or lineages may lose their economic bases, if control of resources is taken over by developing political institutions. In such circumstances, lineages would be expected to disappear as important organizational units. Clans, however, might survive, if they continued to provide an important integrative function. In this sense, the Jewish family circles and cousins clubs that we discussed earlier have become essentially clanlike in their function. This helps explain their continued strength and vitality in the United States today: they perform an integrative function among kin who are geographically dispersed as well as socially diverse, but in a way that does not conflict with the mobility that is characteristic of our society.

In societies where the small domestic unit — nuclear families — is of primary importance, bilateral descent and kindred organization are apt to be the result. This can be seen in our own industrial society, as well as in many food-foraging societies throughout the world.

KINSHIP TERMINOLOGY AND KINSHIP GROUPS

Any system of organizing people who are relatives into different kinds of groups, be they descent-based or ego-oriented, is bound to have an important effect upon the ways in which relatives are la-

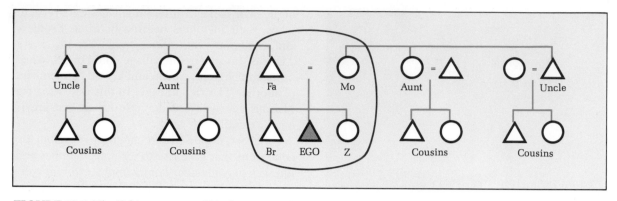

FIGURE 19.5 The Eskimo system of kinship terminology emphasizes the nuclear family (indicated by the red line). Ego's father and mother are distinguished from his aunts and uncles, and his siblings are distinguished from his cousins.

beled in any given society. The fact is, the kinship terminologies of other peoples are far from being the arbitrary and even capricious ways of labeling relatives that Westerners all too often take them to be. Rather, they reflect the positions individuals occupy within their society. In particular, kinship terminology is affected by, and adjusts to, the kinds of kinship groups that exist in a society. There are, however, other factors at work as well in each system of kinship terminology, which help differentiate one kin from another. These factors may be sex, generational differences, or genealogical differences. In the various systems of kinship terminology, any one of these factors may be emphasized at the expense of others, but regardless of the factors emphasized, all kinship terminologies accomplish two important tasks. First, they classify particular kinds of persons into single specific categories; second, they separate different kinds of persons into distinct categories. Generally, two or more kin are merged under the same term when similarity of status exists between the individuals. These similarities are then emphasized by the application of one term to both individuals.

Six different systems of kinship terminology result from the application of the above principles: the Eskimo, Hawaiian, Iroquois, Crow, Omaha, and descriptive systems, each identified according to the way cousins are classified.

Eskimo system: System of kinship terminology, also called lineal system, which emphasizes the nuclear family by specifically identifying mother, father, brother, and sister, while merging together all other relatives.

ESKIMO SYSTEM

Eskimos kinship terminology, comparatively rare among all the systems of the world, is the one used by Anglo-Americans, as well as by a number of food-foraging peoples. The **Eskimo,** or lineal, **system** emphasizes the nuclear family by specifically identifying mother, father, brother, and sister, while merging together all other relatives such as maternal and paternal aunts, uncles, and cousins, without differentiating among them (Figure 19.5). For example, one's father is distinguished from one's father's brother (uncle); but one's father's brother is not distinguished from one's mother's brother (both are called *uncle*). In addition, one uses the term *cousin* to refer to all the sons and daughters of aunts and uncles, without distinguishing the sex of the children or the side of the family to which they belong.

Unlike other terminologies, the Eskimo system provides separate and distinct terms for each member of the nuclear family. This is probably because the Eskimo system is generally found in societies where the dominant kin group is the bi-

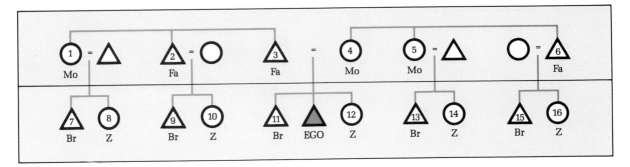

FIGURE 19.6 The Hawaiian kinship system. The men numbered 2 and 6 are called by the same term as father (3) by Ego; the women numbered 1 and 5 are called by the same term as mother (4). All cousins of Ego's own generation (7–16) are considered brothers and sisters.

lateral kindred, in which only the closest members of the family are important in day-to-day affairs. This is especially true of our own society, in which the family is independent, living apart from, and not directly involved with, other kin except on ceremonial occasions. Thus, we distinguish between our closest kin (our parents and siblings), but lump together (as aunts, uncles, cousins) other kin on both sides of the family.

HAWAIIAN SYSTEM

The **Hawaiian system** of kinship terminology, common in Hawaii and other Malayo-Polynesian–speaking areas, but found elsewhere as well, is the least complex system, in that it uses the fewest terms. The Hawaiian system is also called the *generational system*, since all relatives of the same generation and sex are referred to by the same term (Figure 19.6). For example, in one's parents' generation, the term used to refer to one's father is used as well for father's brother and for mother's brother. Similarly, one's mother, her sister, and one's father's sister are all lumped together under a single term. In ego's generation, male and female cousins are distinguished by sex and are equated with brothers and sisters.

The Hawaiian system reflects the absence of strong unilineal descent and is usually associated with ambilineal descent. Because ambilineal rules allow one to trace descent through either side of

Hawaiian system: A mode of kinship reckoning in which all relatives of the same sex and generation are referred to by the same term.

Iroquois system: System of kinship terminology wherein one's father and father's brother are referred to by a single term, as are one's mother and mother's sister, but one's father's sister and one's mother's brother are given separate terms; parallel cousins are classified with brothers and sisters, but not with cross-cousins.

the family, and members on both the father's and the mother's side are looked upon as being more or less equal, a certain degree of similarity is created among the father's and the mother's siblings. Thus, they are all simultaneously recognized as being similar relations and are merged together under a single term. In like manner, the children of the mother's and father's siblings are related to oneself in the same way as one's brother and sister are. Thus, they are ruled out as potential marriage partners.

IROQUOIS SYSTEM

In the **Iroquois system** of kinship terminology, one's father and father's brother are referred to by a single term, as are one's mother and mother's sister; however, one's father's sister and mother's brother are given separate terms (Figure 19.7). In one's own generation, brothers, sisters, and paral-

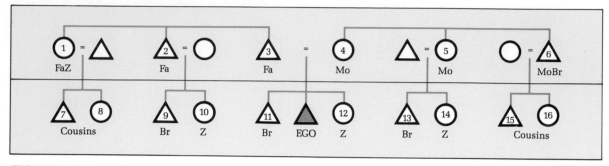

FIGURE 19.7 According to the Iroquois system of kinship terminology, father's brother (2) is called by the same term as father (3); mother's sister (5) is called by the same term as mother (4); but the people 1 and 6 have separate terms for themselves. Those people numbered 9–14 are all considered siblings, but 7, 8, 15, and 16 are cousins.

lel cousins (offspring of parental siblings of the same sex, that is, the children of the mother's sister or the father's brother) of the same sex are referred to by the same terms, which is logical enough considering that they are the offspring of people who are classified in the same category as ego's actual mother and father. Cross-cousins (offspring of parental siblings of opposite sex, that is, the children of the mother's brother or the father's sister) are distinguished by separate terms. In fact, cross-cousins are often preferred as spouses, for marriage to them reaffirms alliances between related lineages.

Iroquois terminology is very widespread and is usually found with unilineal descent groups. It was, for example, the terminology in use until recently in rural Chinese society.

> **Crow system:** A mode of kinship classification usually associated with matrilineal descent, in which father's sister and father's sister's daughter are called by the same term, mother and mother's sister are merged under another, and father and father's brother are merged under a third. Parallel cousins are equated with brothers and sisters.

CROW SYSTEM

In the preceding systems of terminology, some relatives were grouped under common terms, while others of the same generation were separated and given different labels or terms. In the Crow system, another variable enters the picture: the system ignores the distinction that occurs between generations among certain kin.

The **Crow system,** found in many parts of the world, is the one used by the Hopi Indians. Associ-

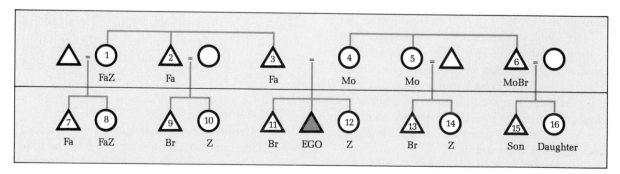

FIGURE 19.8 The Crow system is the obverse of the Omaha system shown in Figure 19.9. Those numbered 4 and 5 are merged under a single term, as are 2, 3, and 7. Ego's parallel cousins (9, 10, 13, 14) are considered siblings, while mother's brother's children (15, 16) are equated with Ego's own children.

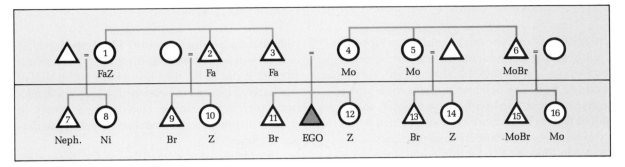

FIGURE 19.9 In the Omaha system, 2 is called by the same term as father (3); 5 is called by the same term as mother (4); but 1 and 6 have separate terms. In Ego's generation, 9–14 are all considered siblings, but 7 and 8 are equated with the generation of Ego's children, while 15 and 16 are equated with the generation of Ego's parents.

ated with strong matrilineal descent organization, it groups differently the relations on the father's side and mother's side (Figure 19.8). Cross-cousins on the father's side are equated with relatives in the parental generation, while those on the mother's side are equated with the generation of ego's children. Otherwise, the system is much like Iroquois terminology.

From our point of view, the Crow system seems terribly complex and illogical. Why does it exist? In societies like that of the Hopi, where individual identity is so dependent on descent group affiliation and where descent is matrilineal, it makes sense to merge father's sister, her daughter, and even her mother together under a single term, regardless of generation. These are women through whom descent is traced in the lineage that sired ego, just as ego's own children, along with those of his mother's brother, were sired by men of ego's own lineage. Thus, it makes sense for ego to equate his maternal cross-cousins with the generation of his own children.

OMAHA SYSTEM

The **Omaha system** is the patrilineal equivalent of the matrilineal Crow system. Thus, one's mother and mother's sister are designated by a single term, one's father and father's brother are merged together under another, while one's parallel cousins are merged with brothers and sisters (Figure 19.9). Cross-cousins on the maternal side

Omaha system: The patrilineal equivalent of the Crow system; the mother's patrilineal kin are equated across generations.

Descriptive system: System of kinship terminology wherein one's father, father's brother, and mother's brother are distinguished from one another as are one's mother, mother's sister, and father's sister; cousins are distinguished from each other as well as from siblings.

are raised a generation, while those on the paternal side are equated with the generation of ego's children. Thus, children born of women from one patrilineage, for the men of another, are lowered by one generation.

DESCRIPTIVE SYSTEM

Although it has replaced Iroquois terminology among the rural Chinese, the **descriptive system** is found among few of the world's societies. In this system, one's mother's brother is distinguished from one's father's brother, who is distinguished from one's father; one's mother's sister is distinguished from one's mother, as well as from one's father's sister. Each cousin is distinguished from all others, as well as from siblings. It is therefore more precise than any of the other systems, including our own, which may be one reason it is so rare. In few societies are all one's aunts, uncles, cousins, and siblings treated differently from one another.

CHAPTER SUMMARY

In nonindustrial societies, kinship groups commonly deal with problems that cannot be handled by families and households alone — problems such as those involving defense, the allocation of property, or the pooling of other resources. As societies become larger and more complex, formal political systems take over many of these matters.

A common form of kinship group is the descent group, which has as its criterion of membership descent from a common ancestor through a series of parent–child links. Unilineal descent establishes kin group membership exclusively through the male or female line. Matrilineal descent is traced through the female line; patrilineal, through the male.

The descent system is closely tied to the economic base of a society. Generally, patrilineal descent predominates where the male is the breadwinner, matrilineal where the female is the breadwinner. Anthropologists now recognize that in all societies the kin of both mother and father are important elements in the social structure, regardless of how descent group membership is defined.

The male members of a patrilineage trace their descent from a common male ancestor. A female belongs to the same descent group as her father and his brother; but her children cannot trace their descent through him. Typically, authority over the children lies with the father or his elder brother. Behavioral rules that require younger men to defer to older men and that require women to defer to men as well as to the women of a household into which they marry are common sources of tension in a patrilineal society.

In one respect, matrilineal descent is the opposite of patrilineal descent, with descent being traced through the female line. Unlike the patrilineal pattern, which confers authority on men, matrilineal descent does not necessarily confer authority on women, although they usually have more of a say in the making of decisions than they do in patrilineal societies. The matrilineal system is common in societies in which women perform much of the productive work. This system may be a source of family tension, since the husband's authority is not in his own household but in that of his sister. This, and the ease with which unsatisfactory marriages may be ended, often results in higher divorce rates in matrilineal than in patrilineal societies.

Double descent is matrilineal for some purposes and patrilineal for others. Ambilineal descent provides a measure of flexibility in that an individual has the option of affiliating with either the mother's or father's descent group.

Descent groups are often highly structured economic units that provide aid and security to their members. They may also be repositories of religious tradition, with group solidarity enhanced by worship of a common ancestor. A lineage is a corporate descent group made up of consanguineal kin who are able to trace their genealogical links to a common ancestor. Since lineages are commonly exogamous, sexual competition within the group is largely avoided. In addition, marriage of a member of the group represents an alliance of two lineages. Lineage exogamy also serves to maintain open communication within a society and fosters the exchange of information among lineages.

Fission is the splitting up of a large lineage group into new, smaller ones, with the original lineage becoming a clan. Clan members claim descent from a common ancestor but without actually knowing the genealogical links to that ancestor. Unlike lineages, clan residence is usually dispersed rather than localized. In the absence of residential unity, clan identification is reinforced by totems, usually symbols from nature, that remind members of their common ancestry. A phratry is a unilineal descent group of two or more clans that are supposedly related.

Bilateral descent, characteristic of Western society, is traced through both parents simultaneously and recognizes several ancestors. An individual is affiliated equally with all relatives on both the mother's and father's sides. Such a large group is socially impractical and is usually reduced to a small circle of paternal and maternal relatives called the kindred. A kindred is never the same for any two persons except siblings.

Different types of descent systems appear in different societies. In industrial societies, as well as among food-foraging peoples where the nuclear family is paramount, bilateral kinship and kindred organization are likely to prevail.

In any society cultural rules dictate the way kinship relationships are defined. Factors such as sex, generational differences, or genealogical differences help distinguish one kin from another. The Hawaiian system is the simplest kinship system. All relatives of the same generation and sex are referred to by the same name. The Eskimo system, used by Anglo-Americans, emphasizes the nuclear family and merges all other relatives without differentiating among them. In the Iroquois system, a single term is used for an individual's father and father's brother, another for one's mother and mother's sister. In the Omaha and Crow systems no distinction is made between generations among certain kinsmen. The relatively rare descriptive system treats all one's aunts, uncles, cousins, and siblings as different from one another.

SUGGESTED READINGS

Fox, Robin. *Kinship and Marriage in an Anthropological Perspective*. Baltimore: Penguin, 1968. An excellent introduction to the concepts of kinship and marriage, outlining some of the methods of analysis used in the anthropological treatment of kinship and marriage. The book updates Radcliffe-Brown's *African Systems of Kinship and Marriage* and features a perspective focused on kinship groups and social organization.

Goodenough, Ward H. *Description and Comparison in Cultural Anthropology*. Chicago: Aldine, 1970. This is an important contribution to the study of social organization, which confronts the problem of describing kinship organization — kindred and clan, sibling and cousin — in such a way that meaningful cross-cultural comparisons can be made.

Keesing, Roger M. *Kin Groups and Social Structure*. New York: Holt, Rinehart and Winston, 1975. This is a high-level introduction to kinship theory suitable for advanced undergraduate students. A strong point of the work is the attention given to nonunilineal, as well as unilineal, systems.

Schusky, Ernest L. *Variation in Kinship*. New York, Holt, Rinehart and Winston, 1975. This book is an introduction to kinship, descent, and residence for the beginner. A reliance on a case-study approach leads the reader from basic data to generalizations, a strategy that helps remove some of the abstraction that students of kinship organization sometimes find confusing.

Schusky, Ernest L. *Manual for Kinship Analysis*, 2d ed. Lanham, Md.: University Press of America, 1983. A useful book that discusses the elements of kinship, diagramming, systems classification, and descent, with specific examples.

20

GROUPING BY SEX, AGE, COMMON INTEREST, AND CLASS

These Brazilian schoolchildren exemplify the phenomenon of age grading, one of a number of means by which people may be organized into groups without recourse to kinship or descent.

PREVIEW

What Principles, besides Kinship and Marriage, Are Used to Organize People within Societies?
Grouping by sex, age, common interest, and position within a ranked hierarchy (class stratification) all may be used to deal with problems not conveniently handled by marriage, the family and/or household, descent group, or kindred. In addition, stratification is a means by which certain groups within society secure preferential treatment for themselves, at the expense of other groups.

What Is Age Grading?
Age grading — the formation of groups on the basis of age — is a means of organizing people that is widely used in human societies, including our own. In industrial societies, or nonindustrial societies in which populations are relatively large, age grades may be broken down into age sets — groups of people of approximately the same age who move as groups through the series of age grades.

What Are Common-Interest Associations?
Common-interest associations are formed to deal with specific problems. They acquire their members through an act of joining on the part of individuals. This act may range all the way from fully voluntary to compulsory. Common-interest associations have been a feature of human societies since the advent of the first farming villages several thousand years ago, but have become especially prominent in modern industrial or industrializing societies.

What Is Social Stratification?
Stratification is the division of society into two or more classes of people that do not share equally in basic resources, influence, or prestige. Such class structure is characteristic of all societies with large and heterogeneous populations and centralized political control. These include the ancient civilizations of the Middle East, Asia, Mexico, and Peru, as well as modern industrial societies, including our own.

Social organization based on kinship and marriage has received an extraordinary amount of attention from anthropologists, and the subject usually is quite prominent in anthropological writing. There are several reasons for this: In one way or another, kinship and marriage operate as organizing principles in all societies; and in the tribal and band societies so often studied by anthropologists, they are usually the most important organizational principles. There is, too, a certain fascination in the almost mathematical way in which kinship systems at least appear to work. To the unwary, all this attention to kinship and marriage may convey the impression that these are the only principles of social organization that really count. Yet it is obvious from the case of our own society that other principles of social organization not only exist but may be quite important. Those that we will examine in this chapter are grouping by sex, age, common interest, and class (stratification).

GROUPING BY SEX

As we have seen in preceding chapters of this book, some division of labor by sex is characteristic of all human societies. Although in some — the !Kung for example (Chapter 15) — many tasks undertaken by men and women may be shared, and people may perform work normally assigned to the opposite sex without loss of face, in some other societies, men and women are rigidly segregated in what they do. For instance, among the Mohawk, Oneida, Onondaga, Cayuga, and Seneca Indians of New York — the famous Five Nations Iroquois — society was divided into two parts, consisting of sedentary women on the one hand and nomadic men on the other. Living in villages were the women, who were blood relatives of one another and whose job it was to grow the corn, beans, and squash on which the Iroquois relied for subsistence. Although the men built houses and the palisades that protected villages and also helped women to clear their fields, their most important work was pursued at some distance from their vil-

lages. This consisted of hunting, fishing, trading, warring, and engaging in diplomacy. As a consequence, men were transients in the villages, being present for only brief periods of time.

Although masculine activities were considered to be more prestigious than those of women, the latter were regarded by all as the sustainers of life. Moreover, women headed the longhouses (dwellings occupied by matrilocal extended families), descent and inheritance passed through women, and ceremonial life centered on the activities of women. Men held all positions of leadership outside of households, on the councils of the villages, tribes, and the League of Five Nations, but it was the women of their lineages who nominated them for these positions and who held the power of the veto over them. Thus, male leadership was balanced by female authority. Overall, the phrase "separate but equal" accurately describes relations between the sexes in Five Nations Iroquoian society, with members of neither sex being dominant nor submissive to the other. Related to this seems to have been a low incidence of rape, at least among the Five Nations. Widely commented upon by outside observers in the nineteenth century was an apparent absence of rape within Iroquoian communities. On the other hand, earlier Jesuit missionaries do record its occurrence in association with the violence directed at peoples outside of the League of Five Nations, over whom the league wished to impose its dominance.

Although Iroquoian men were often absent from the village, when present they ate and slept with women. Among the Mundurucu, discussed briefly in Chapter 18, men not only work apart from women, but eat and sleep separately as well. All men from the age of 13 on live in a large house of their own, while women with their young children occupy two or three houses grouped around that of the men. For all intents and purposes, men associate with men, and women with women. The relation between the sexes, rather than being harmonious, is one of opposition. According to Mundurucu belief, sex roles were once reversed; women ruled over men and controlled the sacred

Among the Iroquoian tribes of New York, society was divided into sedentary women, whose work was carried out in or near the village, and nomadic men, whose work was carried out away from the village.

trumpets that are the symbols of power and represent the generative capacities of women. But because women couldn't hunt, they couldn't supply the meat demanded by the ancient spirits contained within the trumpets, enabling the men to take the trumpets from the women, establishing their dominance in the process. Ever since, the trumpets have been kept carefully guarded and hidden in the men's house, and no woman can see them under penalty of gang rape. Thus, Mundurucu men express fear and envy toward women, whom they seek to control by force. For their part, the women neither like nor accept a submissive status, and even though men occupy all formal positions of political and religious leadership, women are autonomous in the economic realm.

Although there are important differences, there are nonetheless interesting similarities between Mundurucu beliefs and those of traditional European (including Euro-American) culture. The idea of rule by men replacing an earlier state of matriarchy (rule by women), for example, was held by many nineteenth-century intellectuals. Moreover, the idea that men may use force in order to control women is deeply embedded in both Judaic and Christian traditions (and even today, in spite of changing attitudes, one out of three women in the United States is sexually assaulted at some time in her life). A major difference between Mundurucu and traditional European society is that, in the latter, women have not had control of their own economic activities. Although this is now changing, there is still a considerable distance to go before women in North America and other Western countries achieve economic parity with men.

Age grading in modern North American society is exemplified by the educational system, which specifies that at six years of age all children must enter the first grade.

AGE GROUPING

Age grouping is so familiar and so important that it and sex have sometimes been called the only universal factors in the determination of one's position in society. In our own society, our first friends generally are children our own age. Together we are sent off to school, where together we remain until our late teens. At specified ages we are finally allowed to do things reserved for adults, such as driving a car, voting, and drinking alcoholic beverages, and we are required to go off to war if called upon to do so. Ultimately, we retire from our jobs at some specified age and, more and more, live out the final years of our lives in "retirement communities," segregated from the rest of society. We are "teenagers," "middle-aged," "senior citizens," whether we like it or not, and for no other reason than our age.

The pervasiveness of age grouping in our own society is further illustrated by its effects on the Jewish descent groups that we discussed in Chapter 19. Until well into the 1930s, these always took on a more or less conventional ambilineal structure, which united relatives of all generations from the very old to the very young, with no age restrictions. By the late 1930s, however, younger generations of Jews of eastern European background were becoming assimilated into North American culture to such a degree that some of them began to form new descent groups that deliberately excluded any kin of the parental and grandparental generations. In these new cousins clubs, as they are called, descendants of the cousins are eligible for membership, but not until they reach legal majority or are married, whichever comes first. Here again, these newer descent groups contrast with the older family circles, in which membership can be activated at any age, no matter how young.

Age classification also plays a significant role in non-Western societies, where at least a distinction is made among the immature, mature, and older people whose physical powers are waning. Old age often has profound significance, bringing with it the period of greatest respect (for women it may mean the first social equality with men); rarely are the elderly shunted aside or abandoned. Even the Inuit, who are frequently portrayed as a people who quite literally abandon their aged relatives, do so only in truly desperate circumstances, where the physical survival of the group is at stake. In all nonliterate societies, the elders are the repositories of accumulated wisdom; they arc the "living libraries" for their people. To cast them aside would be analogous to closing down all the archives and libraries in our society.

In the United States we rely on the written word, rather than on our elders, for long-term memory. Moreover, we have become so accustomed to rapid change that we tend to assume that the experiences of our grandparents and those of their generation are of little relevance to us in "today's world." Indeed, retirement from earning a living implies that one has nothing further to offer society and that one should stay out of the way of those who are younger. "The symbolism of the traditional gold watch is all too plain: you should have made your money by now, and your time has run out. The watch will merely tick off the hours that remain between the end of adulthood and death."[1] The ultimate irony is that in the United States all of the ingenuity of modern science is used to keep alive the bodies of individuals who, in virtually every other way, have been shunted aside by society.

In the institutionalization of age, cultural rather than biological factors are of prime importance in determining social status. All human societies recognize a number of life stages; precisely how they are defined will vary from one culture to another. Out of this recognition they establish patterns of activity, attitudes, prohibitions, and obligations. In some instances, these are designed to help the transition from one age to another, to teach needed skills, or to lend economic assistance. Often they are taken as the basis for the formation of organized groups.

INSTITUTIONS OF AGE GROUPING

An organized class of people with membership on the basis of age is known as an **age grade.** Theoretically speaking, membership in an age grade ought to be automatic — one reaches the appropriate age, and so one is included, without question, in the particular age grade. Just such situations do exist, among the East African Tiriki, for example, who are the subject of the Original Study later in this chapter. Sometimes, though, one has to buy one's way into the age grade for which one is eligible. By way of illustration, among some of the Indian tribes of the North American plains, boys had to purchase the appropriate costumes, dances, and songs for age-grade membership. In societies where entrance fees are expensive, not all people

[1]Colin M. Turnbull, *The Human Cycle* (New York: Simon & Schuster, 1983), p. 229.

Age grade: A category of people based on age; every individual passes through a series of such categories in the course of a lifetime.

Age sets: Groups of persons who are initiated into age grades at the same time and who move through the series of categories together.

eligible for membership in a particular age grade may actually be able to join.

Entry into and transfer out of age grades may be accomplished individually, either by a biological distinction, such as puberty, or by a socially recognized status, such as marriage or childbirth. Whereas age-grade members may have much in common, engage in similar activities, cooperate with one another, and share the same orientation and aspirations, their membership may not be entirely parallel with physiological age. A specific time is often ritually established for moving from a younger to an older grade. Although members of senior groups commonly expect deference from and acknowledge certain responsibilities to their juniors, this does not necessarily mean that one grade is better or worse or even more important than another. There can be standardized competition (opposition) between age grades, as between first-year students and sophomores on U.S. college campuses. One can, comparably, accept the realities of being a teenager without feeling the need to "prove anything."

In some societies, age grades are subdivided into **age sets.** An age set is a group of persons initiated into an age grade, who will move through the system together. For example, among the Tiriki of East Africa, the age group consisting of those initiated into an age grade over a 15-year period amounts to an age set. Age sets, unlike age grades, do not cease to exist after a specified number of years; the members of an age set usually remain closely associated throughout their lives, or at least through much of their lives.

A certain amount of controversy has arisen over the relative strength, cohesiveness, and stability that go into an age grouping. The age-set notion implies strong feelings of loyalty and mutual sup-

In many societies it is common for children of the same age to play, eat, and learn together, like this group of African boys. Such a group may form the basis of age-set organization.

port. Because such groups may possess property, songs, shield designs, and rituals, and are internally organized for collective decision making and leadership, a distinction is called for between them and simple age grades. We may also distinguish between transitory age grades — which initially concern younger men (sometimes women too), but become less important and disintegrate as the members grow older — and the comprehensive systems that affect people through the whole of their lives.

AGE GROUPING IN AFRICAN SOCIETIES

While age is used as a criterion for group membership in many parts of the world, its most varied and elaborate use is found in Africa, south of the Sahara. An example may be seen among the Tiriki, one of several pastoral nomadic groups who live in Kenya. (In the Original Study, the author uses the term *age group* to refer to what actually is an age set.)

ORIGINAL STUDY
Changing Age-Group Organization among the Tiriki of Kenya[2]

The Tiriki age group organization is directly borrowed from the Nilo–Hamitic Terik who border the Tiriki to the south. There are seven named age groups (Kabalach, Golongolo, Jiminigayi, Nyonje, Mayina, Juma, and Sawe), each embracing approximately a fifteen-year age span. In addition, each age group passes successively through four distinctive age grades. The system is cyclical, each age group being reinstated with new initiates approximately every 105 years.

Perhaps the easiest way to grasp the difference in age groups and age grades is to review the nature of our college class system. Freshmen entering college in the autumn of 1958, for example, immediately become known as the Class of 1962 — the year when they are due to graduate. Thenceforth, for as long as they live, they are known as the Class of 1962. While in college, however, members of the Class of 1962 must pass in successive years through four ranked grades: freshman, sophomore, junior, and senior.

In Tiriki each age group contains those men who were initiated over a fifteen-year age span, not simply during one year. The initiation rites . . . traditionally extend over a six months' period, and are held every four years; thus each age group receives recruits from three or four successive initiations. The four traditional Tiriki age grades are "bandu bi lihe," "balulu" (the warriors), "balulu basaxulu" (the elder warriors), "basaxulu bi bilina," "basaxulu bu luhya" (the judicial elders), and "basaxulu basaalisi" (the ritual elders). Before they were prohibited by the British about 1900, handing-over ceremonies were held at about fifteen-year intervals in conjunction with the closing of an age group to more initiates. At this time the age group just closed to initiates became formally instated in the warriors age grade, the age group that had just been the warriors' moved on to the elder warrior grade, the former elder warriors moved on to the judicial elder grade, and the former judicial elders moved on to the ritual eldership.

The cyclical aspect of Tiriki age groups can also be readily compared with the system of college classes, if one substitutes the Tiriki age group name for "Class of —," and remembers that each Tiriki age group embraces fifteen years. The Class of '62 at Harvard, for example, has been reinstated every 100 years for several centuries with a new group of college men, and thus can be viewed as part of a cyclical process. In Tiriki each cycle lasts 105 years instead of a century, because the seven age groups, "each" embracing fifteen years, cover a total span of 105 years. The Sawe age group, for example, open for initiates from 1948 to 1963, was previously instated and open to initiates from roughly 1843 to 1858.

The "warriors" were formally given the responsibility of guarding the country. They were said "to hold the land." An age group's lasting reputation was principally earned while it was occupying the warrior age grade. Similarly the reputation accompanying a man throughout the remainder of his life and then remembered by his posterity was primarily based on the leadership, courage, and good fortune he exhibited while a warrior.

The duties and prerogatives of the "elder warriors" were neither as glorious nor as well defined as those of the warriors. They had relatively few specialized social tasks, but they gradually assumed an increasing share of administrative type activities in areas that were basically the responsibility of the elder age groups. For example, at public post-funeral gatherings held to settle property claims, usually a man of the elder warrior group was called upon to serve as chairman. His duty was to maintain order, to see that all the claims and counterclaims were heard, to initiate compromises, but always to seek and defer to the judgment of the elders in matters that were equivocal or a departure from tradition. Members of this age grade also served as couriers and envoys when important news needed to be transmitted between elders of different subtribes.

The age group occupying the "judicial elder" age grade fulfilled most of the tasks connected with the arbitration and settlement of local disputes. This included everything from delinquent or contested bridewealth payments to cases of assault or accidental injury. Any major disturbance or legitimate complaint by the head of a household served as sufficient reason for the community judicial elders to gather at the local meeting ground to hear the plaintiff and defendant, question witnesses, and give a judgment.

The "ritual elders" presided over the priestly functions of the homestead ancestral shrine observances, at subclan meetings concerning inheritance and the like, at semiannual community supplications, and at the initiation rites. Also, the ritual elders were accredited with having access to magical powers. They were the group who expelled or killed witches, or at least who were counted on to neutralize their evil powers, and they also were the group who underwrote the death through sorcery of anyone cursed by the community for violating the initiation secrets or for committing some other heinous crime. The advice of the ritual elders was sought in all situations that seemed to hold danger for or entail the general well-being of the community or the tribe. For example, the warriors solicited the auguries of the ritual elders before embarking on a major raid, and postponed the raid if the omens were bad.

Today, over sixty years after the last formal handing-over ceremony, the age group cycle still continues, kept alive by the regular performance of the initiation rites. The four graded statuses are still manifest in informal social behavior and in current social ideology and action, albeit in relatively informal and altered form. Young men, whose age group according to traditional reckoning would now be warriors, are still occasionally called, or referred to as "warriors," but only in a spirit of friendliness and flattery. Today, instead of fighting, young men of this age grade find a modicum of excitement and adventure through extended employment away from the tribe. A fortunate few are pursuing secondary or advanced studies, teaching school, or holding clerical jobs; but in most cases they, too, are employed or are studying off-tribe. Members of the warrior age grade are no longer held in such esteem as formerly, and no one ever speaks of them as "holding the land." Their active participation, however, in the new and rapidly changing world beyond tribal boundaries still lends the warrior age grade a bit of glamour.

In contrast to that of the warriors, the relative status of those occupying the elder warrior age grade has increased dramatically during the last fifty years. Men of this age grade have assumed nearly all the new administrative and executive roles created by the advent and growth of a centralized tribal administrative bureaucracy. With few exceptions they hold all the salaried offices in the tribal administration. It is quite in keeping with traditional age grade expectations that members of this age grade should occupy the executive and administrative positions, but pre-European conditions provided only a minimal number of such roles.

The judicial elders still serve as the local judiciary body, although their authority was somewhat altered and curtailed by the British colonial administration.

The ritual elders have suffered a severe diminution of their functions and powers. During the last twenty years, ancestor worship has declined until today the formal aspects of the cult are virtually extinct. They, like the warriors, have been deprived of a major part of their traditional age grade activity; but unlike the warriors, they have not found any substitute activity. The positions of leadership in the Christian church have been assumed by a small number of men, mostly of the elder warrior age grade. The ritual elders continue, however, to hold the most important positions in the initiation ceremonies, and their power as sorcerers and witchcraft expungers remains almost universally feared and respected.

[2]Walter H. Sangree, "The Bantu Tiriki of Western Kenya," in *Peoples of Africa*, ed. James Gibbs, Jr., pp. 69–72. Copyright © 1965 by Holt, Rinehart and Winston, Inc., Reprinted by permission of the publisher.

COMMON-INTEREST ASSOCIATIONS

The rise of **common-interest associations**, whether out of individual predilection or community need, is a theme intimately associated with world urbanization and its attendant social upheavals; our own society's fondness for joining is incontestably related to its complexity. This phenomenon poses a major threat to the inviolability of age and kinship grouping. Individuals are often separated from their brothers, sisters, or age mates; they obviously cannot obtain their help in learning to cope with life in a new and bewildering environment, in learning a new language or mannerisms necessary for the change from village to city, if they are not present. But such functions must somehow be met. Because common-interest associations are by nature quite flexible, they are increasingly, both in the cities and in tribal villages, filling this gap in the social structure.

Common-interest associations: Associations not based on age, kinship, marriage, or territory that result from an act of joining.

Common-interest associations are not, however, restricted to modernizing societies alone; they are to be found in many traditional societies as well. There is reason to believe that they may have arisen with the emergence of the first horticultural villages.

Common-interest associations have traditionally been referred to in the anthropological literature as voluntary associations, but this term is misleading. The act of joining may range from being fully voluntary to being required by law. For example, in our society, under the draft laws one sometimes became a member of the armed forces without choosing to join. It is not really compulsory to join a labor union, but unless one does, one can't work in a union shop. What is really meant

The diversity of common-interest associations is astounding. Shown here are a spokeswoman for an adoptive parents' group and a street gang.

by the term *voluntary association* are those associations not based on sex, age, kinship, marriage, or territory that result from an act of joining. The act may often be voluntary, but it doesn't have to be.

KINDS OF COMMON-INTEREST ASSOCIATIONS

The diversity of common-interest associations is astonishing. Their goals may include the pursuit of friendship, recreation, and the expression and dis-

tinction of rank, as well as governing function and the pursuit or defense of economic interests. Traditionally, associations have served for the preservation of tribal songs, history, language, and moral beliefs; the Tribal Unions of West Africa, for example, continue to serve this purpose. Similar organizations, often operating clandestinely, have kept traditions alive among North American Indians, who are undergoing a resurgence of ethnic pride despite generations of schooling designed to extinguish tribal identity. Another significant force in the formation of associations may be the supernatural experience common to all members; the Crow Indian Tobacco Society, the secret associations of the Kwakiutl Indians of British Columbia with their cycles of rituals known only to initiates, and the Kachina cults of the Hopi Indians are well-known examples. Among other traditional forms of association are military, occupational, political, and entertainment groups that parallel such familiar groups as the American Legion, labor unions, block associations, and college fraternities and sororities, not to mention "co-ops" of every kind.

Such organizations are frequently exclusive, but a prevailing characteristic is their concern for the general well-being of an entire village or village group. The rain that falls as a result of the work of Hopi rainmakers nourishes the crops of members and nonmembers alike.

Men's and Women's Associations
For many years, women's contributions to common-interest associations were regarded by social scientists as less significant than men's. The reason is that men's associations generally have attracted more notice around the world than women's. Heinrich Schurtz's theory, published in 1902, that underlying the differentiation between kinship and associational groups is a profound difference in the psychology of the sexes, was widely accepted for years. Schurtz regarded women as eminently unsocial beings who preferred to remain in kinship groups based on sexual relations and the reproductive function rather than form

units on the basis of commonly held interests. Men, on the other hand, were said to view sexual relations as isolated episodes, an attitude that fostered the purely social factor that makes "birds of a feather flock together."

In recent years, scholars of both sexes have shown this kind of thinking to be culture-bound. In some societies women have not formed associations to the extent that men have because the demands of raising a family and their daily activities have not permitted it, and because men have not always encouraged them to do so. Given the plethora of women's clubs of all kinds in the United States for several generations, however, one wonders how this belief in women as unsocial beings survived as long as it did. Earlier in our country's history, of course, when women were stuck at home in rural situations, with no near neighbors, they had little chance to participate in common-interest associations. Moreover, some functions of men's associations—like military duties—are often culturally defined as purely for men or repugnant to women. In a number of the world's traditional societies, however, the opportunities for female sociability are so great that there may be little need for women's associations. Among the Indians of northeastern North America (including the Five Nations Iroquois discussed earlier), the men spent extended periods off in the woods hunting, either by themselves or with a single companion. The women, by contrast, spent most of their time in their village, in close, everyday contact with all the other women of the group. Not only were there lots of people to talk to, but there was always someone available to help with whatever tasks required assistance.

Still, as cross-cultural research makes clear, women do play important roles in associations of their own and even in those in which men predominate. Among the Crow Indians, women participated even in the secret Tobacco Society, as well as in their own exclusive groups. Throughout Africa, women's social clubs complement the men's and are concerned with the education of women, with crafts, and with charitable activities. In Sierra Leone, where once-simple dancing societies have developed under urban conditions into complex organizations with a set of new objectives, the dancing *compin* is made up of young women as well as men, who together perform plays based on traditional music and dancing and raise money for various mutual-benefit causes. The Kpelle of Liberia maintain initiation, or "bush," schools for both young men and women; women also alternate with men in ritual supremacy of a chiefdom. The cycle of instruction and rule (four years for males, three for females) that marks these periods derives from the Kpelle's association of the number four with maleness and three with femaleness, rather than from a notion of male superiority.

Women's rights organizations, consciousness-raising groups, and professional organizations for women are examples of some of the associations arising directly or indirectly out of today's social climate. These groups cover the entire range of association, from simple friendship and support groups to political, guildlike, and economic (the publication of magazines, groups designed to influence advertising) associations on a national scale. If an unresolved point does exist in the matter of women's participation, it is in determining why women are excluded from associations in some societies, while in others their participation is essentially equal with that of men.

The importance of common-interest associations in areas of rapid social change is considerable. Increasingly, such organizations assume the roles and functions formerly held by kinship or age groups; in many areas they hold the key both to individual adaptation to new circumstances and to group survival. Where once groups were organized to preserve traditional ways and structure against the intrusion of the modern world, urban associations accept the reality of such intrusions and help their members to cope both socially and economically. Members may turn to associations for support and sympathy while unemployed or sick; the groups may also provide education or socialization. An important need met by many of these associations is economic survival; to achieve

Common-interest associations are not limited to modern industrial societies. This 1832 picture shows a Mandan Indian Bull Dance. The Bulls were one of several common-interest groups that were concerned with both social and military affairs.

such ends they may help raise capital, regulate prices, discourage competition, and organize cooperative activities.

Always the keynote of these groups is adaptation. As Kenneth Little observes, adaptation implies not only the modification of institutions but also the development of new ones to meet the demands of an industrial economy and urban way of life.[3] Modern urbanism involves the rapid diffusion of entirely new ideas, habits, and technical procedures, as well as a considerable reconstruc-

tion of social relationships as a consequence of new technical roles and groups created. Age-old conventions yield to necessity, as women and young people in general gain new status in the urban economy. Women's participation, especially in associations with mixed membership, involves them in new kinds of social relationships with men, including companionship and the chance to choose a spouse by oneself. Young persons on the whole become leaders for their less Westernized counterparts. Even in rural areas, such associations thrive, reflecting the increasing consciousness of the outer world. With an irony implicit in many former colonial situations, the European contact that so frequently shattered permanent age and kinship groups has, partly through the influence of

[3]Kenneth Little, "The Role of Voluntary Associations in West African Urbanization," in *Africa: Social Problems of Change and Conflict*, ed. Pierre Van den Berghe (San Francisco: Chandler, 1964).

education, helped remove restrictions in association membership in both age and sex.

In our own culture, common-interest associations abound, such as women's clubs, street gangs, Kiwanis, Rotary, and PTA. Elements of secret initiatory cults survive, to some extent, in the Masonic lodges and fraternity and sorority initiations. Women's associations recently seem to have proliferated. Although we may think of our own groups as more complex and highly organized than those of traditional non-Western societies, many of the new urban voluntary associations in Africa, for example, are elaborately structured and rival many of our secular and religious organizations. Such traditional groups, with their antecedents reaching far back in history, may have served as models for associations familiar to us; now, in becoming Westernized, they promise to outstrip our own in complexity, an interesting phenomenon to watch as the non-Western countries become "modernized."

SOCIAL STRATIFICATION

The study of social stratification involves the examination of distinctions that strike us as unfair and even outrageous, but social stratification is a common and powerful phenomenon in some of the world's societies. Civilizations, in particular, with their large and heterogeneous populations, are invariably stratified.

Basically, a **stratified society** is one that is divided into two or more groups of people, and these groups are ranked high and low relative to one another. When the people in one such group or stratum are compared with those in another, marked differences in privileges, rewards, restrictions, and obligations become apparent. Members of low-ranked groups will tend to have fewer privileges than those in higher-ranked groups. In addition, they tend not to be rewarded to the same degree and are denied equal access to basic resources. Their restrictions and obligations, too, are usually more onerous, although members of

> **Stratified society:** The division of society into two or more groups of people that do not share equally in the basic resources that support life, influence, and prestige.
>
> **Egalitarian societies:** Social systems in which as many valued positions exist as there are persons capable of filling them.

high-ranked groups will usually have their own distinctive restrictions and obligations to attend to. In short, social stratification amounts to institutionalized inequality. Without ranking—high versus low—there is no stratification; social differences without this do not constitute stratification.

Stratified societies stand in sharp contrast to **egalitarian societies.** As we saw in Chapter 15, societies of food-foraging peoples are characteristically egalitarian, although there are some exceptions. In such societies there are as many valued positions as there are people capable of filling them. Hence, individuals' positions in society depend pretty much on their own abilities alone. A poor hunter may become a good hunter if he has the ability; he is not excluded from such a prestigious position because he comes from a group of poor hunters. Poor hunters do not constitute a social stratum. Furthermore, they have as much right to the resources of their society as any other of its members. No one can deny a poor hunter a fair share of food, the right to be heard when important decisions are to be made, or anything else to which a man is entitled.

GENDER STRATIFICATION

Societies may be stratified in various ways, not just in terms of class and caste (discussed below). For instance, in our earlier discussion of sex as an organizing principle, we saw that in some (but not all) societies, men and women may be regarded as unequal, with the former outranking the latter. This we may speak of as gender stratification. Generally speaking, sexual inequality is characteristic of societies that are stratified in other ways as well; thus women have historically occupied a position of inferiority to men in the class-structured societies of the Western world. In addition, sexual inequality may sometimes be seen in societies that are not otherwise stratified; in such instances, men and women are always physically as well as conceptually separated from one another. On the other hand, as the Iroquoian case cited earlier in this chapter demonstrates, not all societies in which men and women are separated exhibit gender stratification.

CLASS AND CASTE

A **social class** may be defined as a set of families that show equal or nearly equal prestige according to the system of evaluation.[4] The qualification "nearly equal" is important, for there may be a certain amount of inequality even within a given class. If this is so, to an outside observer low-ranking individuals in an upper class may not seem much different from the highest-ranking members of a lower class. Yet there will be marked differences when the classes are compared as wholes with one another. The point here is that class distinctions will not be clear-cut and obvious in societies such as our own, where there is a continuous range of differential privileges, for example, from virtually none to several. Such a continuum can be divided up into classes in a variety of ways. If fine distinctions are made, then many classes may be recognized. If, however, only a few gross distinctions are made, then only a few classes will be recognized. Thus, some speak of our society as divided into three classes: lower, middle, and upper. Others speak of several classes: lower-lower, middle-lower, upper-lower, lower-middle, and so forth.

A **caste** is a particular kind of social class, one in which membership is fairly fixed or impermeable. Castes are strongly endogamous, and offspring are automatically members of their parents' caste. The classic case is the caste system of India. Coupled with strict endogamy and membership by descent

[4]Bernard Barber, *Social Stratification* (New York: Harcourt, 1957), p. 73.

> **Social class:** A set of families that enjoy equal or nearly equal prestige according to the system of evaluation.
>
> **Caste:** A special form of social class in which membership is determined by birth and remains fixed for life.

in Indian castes is an association of particular castes with specific occupations and customs, such as food habits and styles of dress, along with rituals involving notions of purity and impurity. The literally thousands of castes are organized into a hierarchy of four named groups, at the top of which are the priests, or *Brahmins,* the bearers of universal order and values, and of highest ritual purity. Below them are the powerful — though less pure — warriors. Dominant at the local level, besides ful-

One indicator of class standing in stratified societies is how people behave toward one another. Here a village chief in Nigeria has lower standing than the turbaned king, to whom he must pay homage.

filling warrior functions, they control all village lands. Furnishing services to the landowners, and owning the tools of their trade, are two lower-ranking landless caste groups of artisans and laborers. At the bottom of the system, owning neither land nor the tools of their trade, are the outcasts, or "untouchables." These most impure of all people constitute a large pool of labor at the beck and call of those controlling economic and political affairs, the landholding warrior caste.

Although some argue that the term *caste* should be restricted to the Indian situation, others find this much too narrow a usage, since castelike situations are known elsewhere in the world. In South Africa, for example, blacks are relegated to a low-ranking stratum in society, are barred by law from marrying nonblacks, and may not hold property except to a limited degree in specified "black homelands." While blacks perform menial jobs for whites, they are prohibited from living where whites do, or even swimming in the same water, or holding the hand of someone who is white. All of this brings to mind the concepts of ritual purity and pollution so basic to the Indian caste system. In South Africa, whites fear pollution of their purity through improper contact with blacks.

In India and South Africa, untouchables and blacks are categories of landless or near-landless people who constitute a body of mobile laborers always available to those in political control. A similar mobile labor force of landless men at the disposal of the state emerged in China as much as 2,200 years ago (caste, in India, is at least as old). Today, social scientists are increasingly aware of the fact that a similar castelike "underclass" is emerging in our own society, as automation reduces the need for unskilled workers. Its members consist of unemployed, unemployable, or drastically underemployed people who own little if any property and who live "out on the streets" or — at best — in urban or rural slums. Lacking both economic and political power, they have no access to the kinds of educational facilities that would enable them or their children to improve their lot.

India, South Africa, China, and the United States are all very different countries, in different

"Outcast" groups like India's untouchables are a common feature of stratified societies; the United States, for example, has in recent years seen the growth of a castelike underclass.

parts of the world, with different ideologies; and yet a similar phenomenon has emerged, or is emerging, in each. Is there something about the structure of socially stratified states that sooner or later produces some sort of impoverished outcast group? The answer to this is clearly unknown, but the question is deserving of the attention of anthropologists and other social scientists.

The basis of social-class structure is role differentiation. Some role differentiation, of course, exists in any society, at least along the lines of sex and age. Furthermore, any necessary role will always be valued to some degree. In a food-foraging society, the role of "good hunter" will be valued. The fact that one man may already play that role does

Symbolic indicators of class or caste standing include factors of life-style as illustrated here by ways of enjoying oneself on a hot day.

> **Verbal evaluation:** The way people in a stratified society evaluate other members of their own society.
>
> **Symbolic indicators:** In a stratified society, activities and possessions that are indicative of social class.

about others in their own society. For this, anything can be singled out for attention and spoken of favorably or unfavorably: political, military, religious, economic, or professional roles; wealth and property; kinship; personal qualities; community activity; and a host of other things. Different cultures do this differently, and what may be spoken of favorably in one may be spoken of unfavorably in another and ignored in a third. Furthermore, cultural values may change, so that something regarded favorably at one time may not be at another. This is one reason why a researcher may be misled by verbal evaluation, for what people say may not correspond completely with reality.

Social classes are also manifest through patterns of association: not just who interacts with whom, but in what context, and how those who are interacting treat one another. In Western society, informal, friendly relations take place mostly within one's own class. Relations with members of other classes tend to be less informal and occur in the context of specific situations. For example, a corporation executive and a janitor normally are members of different social classes. They may have frequent contact with one another, but it occurs in the setting of the corporation offices and usually requires certain stereotyped behavior patterns.

A third way that social classes are manifest is through **symbolic indicators.** Included here are activities and possessions indicative of class; for example, in our society, occupation (a garbage collector has different class status than a physician), wealth (rich people generally are in a higher social class than poor people), dress (we have all heard the expression "white collar" versus "blue collar"), form of recreation (upper-class people are expected to play golf rather than shoot pool down at the pool hall—but they can do it at home), resi-

not, however, prevent another man from playing it, too, in an egalitarian society. Therefore, role differentiation by itself is not sufficient for stratification. Two more ingredients are necessary: formalized evaluation of roles involving attitudes, such as like-dislike or attraction-revulsion, and restricted access to the more highly valued ones. Obviously, the greater the diversity of roles in a society, the greater the chances for more complex evaluation and restriction. Since great role diversity is most characteristic of civilizations, it is not surprising that stratification is one of its salient features.

Social classes are manifest in several ways. One is through **verbal evaluation**—what people say

Anthropologists and Social Impact Assessment

A kind of policy research frequently done by anthropologists is a social impact assessment, which entails collection of data about a community or neighborhood for use by planners of development projects. Specifically, such an assessment seeks to determine the effect of a project by determining how and upon whom its impact will fall, and whether the impact is likely to be positive or negative. In the United States, any project requiring a federal permit or license, or using federal funds, by law must be preceded by a social impact assessment, as part of the environmental review process. Examples of such projects include highway construction, urban renewal, water diversion schemes, and land reclamation. Often, such projects are sited so that their impact falls most heavily on neighborhoods or communities inhabited by people in low socioeconomic strata, sometimes because they are seen as ways of improving the lives of poor people, and sometimes because the poor people are seen as having less political power to block proposals that others conceive to be (sometimes rightly, sometimes wrongly) in "the public interest."

As an illustration of this kind of work, anthropologist Sue Ellen Jacobs was hired to carry out a social impact assessment of a water diversion project in New Mexico planned by the Bureau of Land Reclamation in cooperation with the Bureau of Indian Affairs. This would have involved construction of a diversion dam and extensive canal system for irrigation on the Rio Grande. Affected by this would be 22 communities inhabited primarily by Spanish Americans, as well as two Indian Pueblos. In the region, unemployment was high (19.1 percent in June 1970), and the project was seen as a way of promoting a perceived trend to urbanism (which theoretically would be associated with industrial development), while bringing new land into production for intensive agriculture. What the planners failed to take into account was the fact that both the Hispanic and Indian populations were heavily committed to farming for household consumption, with some surpluses raised for the market, using a system of established irrigation canals established as many as 300 years ago. This system is maintained by elected supervisors who know the communities as well as the requirements of the land and crops, water laws, and ditch management skills. Such individuals can allocate water equitably in times of scarcity, and can prevent and resolve conflict in the realm of water and land use, as well as community life beyond the ditches. Under the proposed project, this system would be given up in favor of one in which fewer people would control larger tracts of land, and water allocation would be in the hands of a government technocrat. One of the strongest measures of local government would be lost.

Not surprisingly, Jacobs discovered widespread community opposition to this project, and it was her report that helped convince Congress that any positive impact was far outweighed by negative effects.

One of the major objections to the construction of the project is that it would result in the obliteration of the three-hundred-year-old irrigation system structures. Project planners did not seem to recognize the antiquity and cultural significance of the traditional irrigation system. These were referred to as "temporary diversion structures." The fact that the old dams associated with the ditches were attached to local descent groups was simply not recognized by the official documents.*

Other negative effects, besides loss of local control, were problems associated with population growth and relocation, loss of fishing and other river-related resources, and new health hazards, including increased threat of drowning, breeding of insects, and airborne dust. Finally, physical transformation of the communities' life space was seen likely to result in changes in the context of the informal processes of enculturation that go on within the communities.

*John Van Willigen, *Applied Anthropology* (South Hadley, Mass.: Bergain and Garvey, 1986), p. 169.

dential location (upper-class people do not ordinarily live in slums), kind of car, and so on indicate class. The fact is that there are all sorts of status symbols indicative of class position, including such things as how many bathrooms one's house has. At the same time, symbolic indicators may be cruder indicators of class position than verbal indicators or patterns of association. One reason is that access to wealth may not be wholly restricted to upper classes, so that individuals can buy symbols suggestive of upper-class status, whether or not this really is their status. Conversely, a member of an upper class may deliberately choose a simpler life-style than is customary. Instead of driving a Mercedes, he or she may drive a beat-up Volkswagen.

Symbolic indicators involve not only factors of life-style but also differences in life chances. Life is apt to be less hard for members of an upper class as opposed to a lower class. This will show up in a tendency toward lower infant mortality and longer life expectancy for the upper class. One may also see a tendency toward greater physical stature and robustness on the part of upper-class people, the result of better diet and less hardship.

MOBILITY

In all stratified societies there is at least some **mobility,** and this helps to ease the strains that exist in any system of inequality. Even in the Indian caste system, with its guiding ideology that pretends that all arrangements within it are static, there is a surprising amount of flexibility and mobility, not all of it associated with the recent changes that "modernization" has brought to India. As a rather dramatic case in point, in the state of Rajasthan, those who own and control most land and who are wealthy and politically powerful are not of warrior caste, as one would expect, but are of the lowest caste. Their tenants and laborers, by contrast, are Brahmins. Thus, the group that is ritually superior to all others finds itself in the same social position as untouchables, whereas the landowners who are the Brahmins' ritual inferiors are superior in all other ways. Meanwhile, a group of leatherworkers in the untouchable category, who have gained political power in India's new democracy, are trying

Mobility: The ability to change one's class position.

Open-class societies: Stratified societies that permit a great deal of social mobility.

to better their position by claiming that they are Brahmins who were tricked in the past into doing defiling work. Although individuals cannot move up or down the caste hierarchy, whole groups can move up or down depending on claims they are able to make for higher status, and how well they can manipulate others into acknowledging their claims. Interestingly, the people at the bottom of India's caste system have not traditionally questioned the validity of the system itself, so much as their particular position within it.

Societies that permit a great deal in the way of mobility are referred to as **open-class societies.** Even here, however, mobility is apt to be more limited than one might suppose. In the United States, in spite of our "rags to riches" ideology, most mobility involves a move up or down only a notch, although if this continues over several generations, it may add up to a major change. Generally, our culture makes much of those relatively rare examples of great upward mobility that are consistent with our cultural values, and tends not to notice the numerous cases of little or no upward, not to mention downward, mobility.

The degree of mobility in a stratified society is related to the prevailing kind of family organization. Where the extended family is the usual form, mobility is apt to be difficult, the reason being that each individual is strongly tied to the large family group. Hence, for a person to move up to a higher social class, his or her family must move up, too. Mobility is easier for independent nuclear families in which the individual is closely tied to fewer persons. Moreover, under neolocal residence, individuals normally leave the family into which they were born. So it is, then, that through careful marriage, occupational success, and the severing of the tie to a lower-class family in which one was raised, all of which are based on residential mobility, one can more easily "move up" in society.

 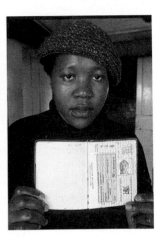

Among the Maya, stratification emerged as certain lineages monopolized important offices. *Left:* A portrayal of a Maya king and his nobles. *Right:* A black with pass book in South Africa, where stratification emerged as conquerors excluded the conquered from positions of importance and access to basic resources.

Because social stratification of any kind tends to make life oppressive for large segments of a population, the lower classes are usually placated by means of religion, which promises them a tolerable existence in the hereafter. If they have this to look forward to, they are more likely to accept the "here and now." In India, for example, belief in reincarnation and the existence of an incorruptible supernatural power that assigns people to a particular caste position as a reward or punishment for the deeds and misdeeds of past lives justifies one's position in this life. If, however, one performs the duties appropriate to one's caste in this lifetime, then one can expect to be reborn into a higher caste in a future existence. Truly exemplary performance of one's duties may even release one from the cycle of rebirth, to be reunited with the divinity from which all existence springs. In the minds of orthodox Hindus, then, one's caste position is something one earns, rather than the accident of birth that it appears to outside observers. Thus, while the caste system explicitly recognizes inequality between people, it is underlain with an implicit assumption of ultimate equality. This contrasts with the situation in the United States, where we explicitly avow the equality of all people while at the same time we treat various groups as unequal.

DEVELOPMENT OF STRATIFICATION

In considering the origin of social stratification, we must reckon with such common tendencies as the desire for prestige, either for oneself or for one's group. Although the impulse need not result inevitably in the ranking of individuals or groups relative to one another, it sometimes may. Among the Iroquois and Hopi Indians and the Sherente and Ugandan peoples, the superiority of some kinship lineages over others is recognized in electing chiefs, performing sacred rituals, and doing other special tasks, whether or not membership entails any economic advantages.

This sort of situation could easily develop into full-fledged stratification. Just such a development may have taken place among the Maya of Central America.[5] There is some indication that these people began as horticulturists with a relatively egalitarian, kinship-based organization. In the last centuries B.C., elaborate rituals developed as a way of

[5]William A. Haviland, "The Ancient Maya and the Evolution of Urban Society," *University of Colorado Museum of Anthropology Miscellaneous Series*, 37, 1975; and William A. Haviland and Hattula Moholy-Nagy, "Distinguishing the High and Mighty from the Hoi Polloi at Tikal, Guatemala," in *Mesoamerican Elites: An Archaeological Assessment*, ed. Arlen F. Chase and Diane Z. Chase (Norman: University of Oklahoma Press, in press).

dealing with the serious problems of agriculture, such as uncertain rains, vulnerability of crops to a variety of pests, and periodic devastation from hurricanes. As this took place, a priesthood arose, along with some craft specialization in the service of religion. Out of the priesthood developed, in the last century B.C., hereditary ruling dynasties. In this developmental process, certain lineages seem to have monopolized the important civic and ceremonial positions, and so came to be ranked above other lineages, forming the basis of an upper class.

Just as lineages may come to be ranked differentially relative to one another, so may ethnic groups. In South Africa, for example, the whites came as conquerors, establishing a social order by which they could maintain their favored position. Even without conquest, though, ethnic differences often lead to diverse classes and even castes, as members of our own society have experienced through the racial stereotyping that leads to social and economic disadvantages.

Classes perform an integrative function in society. They may cut across some or all lines of kinship, residence, occupation, and age group, depending on the particular society, thus counteracting potential tendencies for society to fragment into discrete entities. In India, diverse tribal groups were incorporated into the larger society by certification of their leaders as warriors and by marriage of their women to Brahmins. The problem is that stratification, by its very nature, provides a means by which one group of people may dominate large numbers of others, as in South Africa, where 4.5 million whites dominate 25 million nonwhites. In India a succession of conquerors was allowed to move into the caste hierarchy near its top, as warriors. In any system of stratification, those who dominate are aided by their professed "superior" status. They try to convert this into respect on the part of the lower classes, who (they hope) will then "know their place" and so not contest this domination.

CHAPTER SUMMARY

Grouping by sex separates men and women to varying degrees in different societies; in some, they may be together much of the time, while in others, they may spend much of their time apart, even to the extreme of eating and sleeping separately. Although women are perceived by men to be their inferiors in some sexually segregated societies, in others they are perceived as equals.

Age grouping is another form of association that may augment or replace kinship grouping. An age grade is a category of persons, usually of the same sex, organized on the basis of age. Age grades in some societies are broken up into age sets, which include individuals who are initiated into an age grade at the same time and move together through a series of life stages. A specific time is often ritually established for moving from a younger to an older age grade.

The most varied use of grouping by age is found in African societies south of the Sahara. Among the Tiriki of East Africa, for example, seven named

age sets pass through four successive age grades. Each age set embraces a 15-year age span, and so opens to accept new initiates every 105 years. In principle, the system resembles our college classes, where (say) the "Class of 1990" (an age set) will move through the four age grades: first year, sophomore, junior, senior.

Common-interest associations are linked with rapid social change and urbanization. They are increasingly assuming the roles formerly played by kinship or age groups. In urban areas they help new arrivals cope with the changes demanded by the move from the village to the city. Common-interest associations are also seen in traditional societies, and their roots are probably to be found in the first horticultural villages. Membership may range from voluntary to legally compulsory.

For a long time social scientists mistakenly viewed women's contributions to common-interest associations as less important than men's, largely because of culture-bound assumptions. A question that remains to be resolved is why women are barred from associations in some societies, while in others they participate on an equal basis with men.

A stratified society is one that is divided into two or more categories of people who do not share equally in basic resources, influence, or prestige. This form contrasts with the egalitarian society, in which as many valued positions exist as there are persons capable of filling them. Societies may be stratified in various ways, as by gender, age, social class, or caste. Members of a class enjoy equal or nearly equal access to basic resources and prestige (according to the way the latter is defined). Class differences are not always clear-cut and obvious. Where fine distinctions are made in privileges, the result is a multiplicity of classes. In societies where only gross distinctions are made, only a few social classes may be recognized.

Caste is a special form of social class in which membership is determined by birth and fixed for life. Endogamy is particularly marked within castes, and children automatically belong to their parents' caste. Social-class structure is based on role differentiation, although this by itself is not sufficient for stratification. Also necessary are formalized positive and negative attitudes toward roles, and restricted access to the more valued ones.

Social classes are given expression in several ways. One is through verbal evaluation, or what people say about other people in their society. Another is through patterns of association — who interacts with whom, how, and in what context. Social classes are also manifest through symbolic indicators: activities and possessions indicative of class position.

Mobility is present to a greater or lesser extent in all stratified societies. Open-class societies are those in which mobility is easiest. In most cases, however, the move is limited to one rung up or down the social ladder. The degree of mobility is related to the type of family organization that prevails in a society. Where the extended family is the norm, mobility tends to be severely limited. The independent nuclear family provides a situation in which mobility is easier.

Social stratification can be based on many criteria, such as wealth, legal status, birth, personal qualities, and ideology. A rigidly stratified society in which mobility is limited normally makes life particularly oppressive for large segments of a population.

SUGGESTED READINGS

Bernardi, Bernardo. *Age Class Systems: Social Institutions and Policies Based on Age.* New York: Cambridge University Press, 1985. This book presents a cross-cultural analysis of age as a device for organizing society and seeing to the distribution and rotation of power.

Bradfield, Richard M. *A Natural History of Associations.* New York: International Universities Press, 1973. This two-volume work is the first major anthropological study of common-interest associations since 1902. It attempts to provide a comprehensive theory of the origin of associations and their role in kin-based societies.

Hammond, Dorothy. *Associations.* Reading, Mass.: Addison-Wesley Modular Publications, 14, 1972. This is a brief, first-rate review of anthropological thinking and the literature on common-interest associations and age groups.

Lenski, Gerhard E. *Power and Privilege: A Theory of Social Stratification.* New York: McGraw-Hill, 1966. Who gets what and why is explained by the distributive process and systems of social stratification in industrial nations: the United States, Russia, Sweden, and Britain. Using a broadly comparative approach, the author makes heavy use of anthropological and historical material, as well as the usual sociological materials on modern industrial societies. The basic approach is theoretical and analytical; the book builds on certain postulates about the nature of humans and society, seeking to develop in a systematic manner an explanation of a variety of patterns of stratification. The theory presented is a synthesis of the two dominant theoretical traditions of the past and present, currently represented in both Marxian and functionalist theory.

Sanday, Peggy Reeves. *Female Power and Male Dominance: On the Origins of Sexual Inequality.* Cambridge: Cambridge University Press, 1981. In this cross-cultural study, Professor Sanday reveals the various ways that male–female relations are organized in human societies, and demonstrates that male dominance is not inherent in those relations. Rather, it appears to emerge in situations of stress, as a result of such things as chronic food shortages, migration, and colonial domination.

Art and religion are combined in this Balinese mask used for ritual performances. Art and religion, along with political organization, help ensure the orderly behavior of the individuals in their societies.

THE SEARCH FOR ORDER
Solving the Problem of Disorder

INTRODUCTION

It is an irony of human life that something as fundamental to our existence as cooperation should contain within it the seeds of its own destruction. It is nonetheless true that the groups that people form to take care of important organizational needs do not just facilitate cooperation among the members of those groups; they also create conditions that may lead to the disruption of society. A dramatic illustration of this occurred at the 1985 European Cup soccer playoffs in Belgium, when the fans of a British team went on a rampage, killing 38 fans of the opposing Italian team. The attitude that "my group is better than your group" is not confined to any one of the world's cultures, and it not infrequently takes the form of a sense of rivalry between groups: descent group against descent group, men against women, age grade against age grade, social class against social class, and so forth. This is not to say that such rivalry has to be disruptive; indeed, it may function to ensure that the members of groups perform their jobs well so as not to "lose face" or be subject to ridicule. Rivalry can, however, become a serious problem if it develops into conflict.

The fact is, social living inevitably entails a certain amount of friction — not just between groups, but between individual members of groups as well. Thus, any society can count on some degree of disruptive behavior on the part of some of its members, at some time or other. On the other hand, no one can know precisely when such outbursts will occur or what form they will take. Not only does this uncertainty go against the predictability that social life demands; it also goes against the deep-seated psychological need on the part of each individual for structure and certainty, which we discussed in Chapter 14. Therefore, every society must have means by which conflicts can be resolved and breakdown of the social order prevented. Social control and political systems, which have as their primary function the maintenance of the social order, are the subjects of Chapter 21.

Effective though a culture may be in equipping, organizing, and controlling a society to provide for the needs of its members, there are always certain problems that defy solution through existing technological or organizational means. The response of every culture is to devise a set of rituals, with a set of beliefs to explain them, aimed at solving these problems through the manipulation of supernatural beings and powers. In short, religion and magic exist to transform the uncertainties of life into certainties. At the same time, they may serve as powerful integrative forces through commonly held values, beliefs, and practices. Also important is religion's rationalization of the existing social order, which thereby becomes a moral order as well. Thus, there is a link between religion and magic on the one hand and political organization and social control on the other. Religion and magic are, then, appropriate subjects for discussion in Chapter 22 of this section on the search for order.

Like religion and magic, the arts also contribute to human well-being and help give shape and significance to life. Indeed, the relationship between art and religion goes deeper than this, for much of what we call art has come into being in the service of religion: myths to explain ritual practices, objects to portray important deities, music and dances for ceremonial use, and the like. For that matter, it has sometimes been observed that a religion, like a fine drama, is itself a work of art. Furthermore, art, like religion, expresses the human search for order, in that some essentially formless raw material is given form by the artist. Accordingly, a chapter on the arts follows our chapter on religion and concludes this section.

21

POLITICAL ORGANIZATION AND SOCIAL CONTROL

Social control may be accomplished in a variety of ways in different human societies. Here, a village council meets in Kenya.

PREVIEW

What Is Political Organization?

Political organization refers to the means by which a society maintains order internally and manages its affairs with other societies externally. Such organization may be relatively decentralized and informal, as in bands and tribes, or centralized and formal, as in chiefdoms and states.

How Is Order Maintained Internally?

Social controls may be internalized — "built into" individuals — or externalized, in the form of sanctions. Built-in controls rely on such deterrents as personal shame and fear of supernatural punishment. Sanctions, by contrast, rely on actions taken by other members of society toward behavior that is specifically approved or disapproved. Positive sanctions encourage approved behavior, while negative sanctions discourage behavior that is disapproved. Sanctions that are formalized and enforced by an authorized political body are called laws. Consequently, we may say that laws are sanctions, but not all sanctions are laws. Similarly, societies do not maintain order through law alone.

How Are External Affairs Managed?

Just as the threatened or actual use of force may be employed to maintain order within a society, so may it be used to manage affairs among bands, lineages, clans, or whatever the largest autonomous political units may be. Not all societies, however, rely on force, because there are some that do not practice warfare as we know it. Such societies generally have a view of themselves and their place in the world that has not been characteristic of centrally organized states.

How Do Political Systems Obtain People's Allegiance?

No form of political organization can function without the loyalty and support of those it governs. To a greater or lesser extent, political organizations the world over use religion to legitimize their power. In decentralized systems, loyalty and cooperation are freely given because everyone participates in making decisions. Centralized systems rely more heavily on force, although in the long run these may lessen the effectiveness of the system.

Louis XIV proclaimed, "I am the state." With this sweeping statement, the king declared absolute rule over France; he held himself to be the law, the lawmaker, the courts, the judge, jailer, and executioner — in short, the seat of all political organization in France.

Louis took a great deal of responsibility on his royal shoulders; had he actually performed each of these functions, he would have done the work of thousands of people, the number required to keep the machinery of a large political organization such as a state running at full steam. As a form of political organization, the state of seventeenth-century France was not much different from those that exist in modern times, including our own. All large states require elaborate, centralized structures, involving hierarchies of executives, legislators, and judges, who initiate, pass, and enforce laws for large numbers of people.

Such complex structures, however, have not always been in existence, and even today there are societies that depend on far less formal means of organization. In some societies, flexible and informal kinship systems with leaders who lack real power prevail. Social problems, such as homicide and theft, are perceived as serious "family quarrels," rather than affairs that affect the entire community. Between these two polarities of political organization lies a world of variety, including societies with chiefs, Big Men, or charismatic leaders, and segmented tribal societies with multicentric authority systems. Such disparity prompts the question, What is political organization?

The term *political organization* refers to those aspects of social organization specifically concerned with the management of the affairs of public policy of a society, whether it be organizing a giraffe hunt or raising an army. In other words, political organization is the system of social relationships that provides for the coordination and regulation of behavior, insofar as that behavior is related to the maintenance of public order. Government, on the other hand, consists of an administrative system having specialized personnel that may or may not form a part of the political organization, depending on the complexity of the society.

Band: A small group of related people occupying a single region.

ety. Some form of political organization exists in all societies, but it is not always a government.

KINDS OF POLITICAL SYSTEMS

Political organization is the means through which a society maintains social order and reduces social disorder. It assumes a variety of forms among the peoples of the world, but scholars have simplified this complex subject by identifying four basic kinds of political systems: bands, tribes, chiefdoms, and states. The first two forms are uncentralized systems; the latter two are centralized.

DECENTRALIZED POLITICAL SYSTEMS

Until recently, many non-Western peoples have had neither chiefs with established rights and duties nor any fixed form of government, as we understand the term. Instead, kinship and descent form the principal means of social organization among such peoples. The economies of these societies are of a subsistence type, and populations are typically very small. Leaders do not have real authority to enforce the society's customs or laws, but if individual members do not conform, they may be made the target of scorn and gossip, or even ostracized. Important decisions are usually made in a democratic manner by a consensus of adults, often including women as well as men; dissenting members may decide to act with the majority, or they may choose to adopt some other course of action, if they are willing to risk the social consequences. This form of political organization provides great flexibility, which in many situations confers an adaptive advantage.

Band Organization
The **band** is a small autonomous group, and is the least complicated form of political organization. Bands are usually found among food foragers and

other nomadic societies in which people are organized into politically autonomous groups, numbering anywhere from about 50 to a few hundred. Bands are kin groups, composed of men and/or women who are related (or assumed to be), with their spouses and unmarried children; the closeness of the group is indicated by the usual presence of rules that prohibit marriage between band members. Bands may be characterized as associations of related families who occupy a common territory and who live there together, so long as environmental and subsistence circumstances are favorable. The band is probably the oldest form of political organization, since all humans were once food foragers and remained so until the development of farming and pastoralism over the last 10,000 years.

Since bands are so small in size, there is no real need for formal, centralized political systems. In egalitarian groups, where everyone is related to — and knows on a personal basis — everyone else with whom dealings are required, and where most everyone values "getting along" with the natural order of life, there is reduced potential for conflicts to develop in the first place. Many of those that do arise are settled informally through gossip, ridicule, direct negotiation, or mediation. In the latter instances, the emphasis is on achieving a solution considered "just" by most parties concerned, rather than conforming to some abstract law or rule. Where all else fails, disgruntled individuals have the option of leaving the band to go live in another in which they have relatives. Decisions affecting a band are made with the participation of all its adult members, with an emphasis on achieving consensus, rather than a simple majority. Leaders become such by virtue of their abilities and serve in that capacity only as long as they retain the confidence of the community. Thus, they have neither a guaranteed hold on their position for a specified length of time nor the power to force people to abide by their decisions. People will follow them only as long as they consider it to be in their best interests, and a leader who exceeds what people are willing to accept quickly loses followers.

≠Toma, a !Kung headman known to many college students through the documentary film, *The Hunters*.

An example of the informal nature of leadership in the band is found among the !Kung of the Kalahari Desert, whom we met in Chapter 15. Each !Kung band is composed of a group of families who live together, linked to one another and to the headman, or, less often, headwoman, through kinship. Although each band has rights to the territory it occupies and the resources within it, two or more bands may range over the same territory. The head, called the *kxau*, or "owner," is the focal point for the band's theoretical ownership of the territory. The headman or headwoman does not really own the land or resources, but symbolically personifies the rights of band members to them. If the head leaves a territory to live elsewhere, he or she ceases to be head, as people turn to someone else to lead them.

The head coordinates the band's movements when resources are no longer adequate for subsistence in a particular territory. This leader's chief duty is to plan when and where the group will move; when the move does take place, his or her position is at the head of the line. The leader chooses the site for the new settlement and has the first choice of a spot for his or her own fire. There are no other rewards or duties. For example, a headman does not organize hunting parties, trading expeditions, the making of artifacts, or gift giving; nor does he make marriage arrangements. Instead, individuals instigate their own activities. The headman or headwoman is not a judge and does not punish other band members. Wrongdoers are judged and regulated by public opinion, usually expressed by gossip among band members. A prime technique for resolving disputes, or even avoiding them in the first place, is mobility. Those unable to get along with others of their group simply move to another band to which kinship ties give them rights of entry.

Tribal Organization

The second type of decentralized or multicentric authority system is the **tribe,** in which separate bands or other social units are integrated by pantribal factors, such as clans that unite people in separate bands or communities, or age grades or associations that cross-cut kinship or territorial boundaries. Typically, though not invariably, a tribe has an economy based on some form of farming or herding. Since these methods of production usually yield more food than those of the food-foraging band, tribal membership is usually larger than band membership. Greater population density in tribes than in bands brings a new set of problems to be solved, at the same time permitting new kinds of solutions.

Each tribe consists of one or more small autonomous units, which may then form alliances with one another for various purposes. As in the band, political organization in the tribe is informal and of a temporary nature. Whenever a situation requiring political integration of all or several tribal groups arises, they join to deal with the situation in a cooperative manner. When the problem is satisfactorily solved, each group then returns to its autonomous state.

Leadership among tribes is also informal. Among the Navajo Indians, for example, the individual did not think of government as something

> **Tribe:** A group of bands occupying a specific region, which speak a common language, share a common culture, and are integrated by some unifying factor.
>
> **Segmentary lineage system:** A form of political organization in which a larger group is broken up into clans, which are divided into lineages.

fixed and all-powerful, and leadership was not vested in a central authority. A local leader was a man respected for his age, integrity, and wisdom. His advice was therefore sought frequently, but he had no formal means of control and could not force any decision on those who asked for his help. Group decisions were made on the basis of public consensus, with the most influential man usually somewhat more responsible than others for the final decision. Among the social mechanisms that induced members to abide by group decisions were withdrawal of cooperation, gossip, criticism, and the belief that disease was caused by antisocial actions.[1]

Kinship Organization

In many tribal societies the organizing unit and seat of political authority is the clan, an association of people who consider themselves to be descended from a common ancestor. Within the clan, elders or headmen are responsible for regulating the affairs of members and represent their clan in relations with other clans. As a group, the elders of all the clans may form a council that acts within the tribe or for the tribe in dealings with outsiders. In some societies the strategic and tactical planning for warfare rests in the hands of the clan.

Another form of tribal kinship bond that provides political organization is the **segmentary lineage system.** This system is similar in operation to the clan, but it is less extensive and is a relatively rare form of political organization. The economy of the segmentary tribe is generally just above sub-

[1]Elman Service, *Profiles in Ethnology* (New York: Harper & Row, 1958).

sistence level. Production is small scale, and the tribe probably has a labor pool just large enough to provide necessities. Since each lineage in the tribe produces the same goods, none depends on another for goods or services. Political organization among segmentary lineage societies is usually informal: there are neither political offices nor chiefs, although older tribal members may exercise some personal authority. In his classic study of segmentary lineage organization, Marshall Sahlins describes how this works among the Nuer.[2] According to Sahlins, segmentation is the normal process of tribal growth. It is also the social means of temporary unification of a fragmented tribal society to join in particular action. The segmentary lineage may be viewed as a substitute for the fixed political structure, which a tribe cannot maintain.

Among the Nuer, who number some 200,000 people living in the swampland and savanna of East Africa, there are at least 20 clans. Each is patrilineal and is segmented into maximal lineages; each of these is in turn segmented into major lineages, which are segmented into minor lineages, which in turn are segmented into minimal lineages. The minimal lineage is a group descended from one great-grandfather or a great-great-grandfather.

The lineage segments among the Nuer are all equal, and no real leadership or political organization at all exists above the level of the autonomous minimal or primary segments. The entire superstructure of the lineage is nothing more than an alliance, active only during conflicts between any of the minimal segments. In any serious dispute between members of different minimal lineage segments, members of all other segments take the side of the contestant to whom they are most closely related, and the issue is then joined between the higher-order lineages involved. Such a system of political organization is known as complementary or balanced opposition.

[2]Marshall Sahlins, "The Segmentary Lineage: An Organization of Predatory Expansion," *American Anthropologist* 63 (1961): 322–343.

Disputes among the Nuer are frequent, and under the segmentary lineage system, they can lead to widespread feuds. This possible source of social disruption is minimized by the actions of the "leopard-skin chief," or holder of a ritual office of conciliation. The leopard-skin chief has no political power and is looked on as standing outside the lineage network. All he can do is try to persuade feuding lineages to accept payment in "blood cattle" rather than taking another life. His mediation gives each side the chance to back down gracefully before too many people are killed; but if the participants are for some reason unwilling to compromise, the leopard-skin chief has no authority to enforce a settlement.

Age-Grade Organization

Age-grade systems provide a tribal society with the means of political organization beyond the kin group. Under this system, youths are initiated into an age grade, following which they pass as sets from one age grade to another at appropriate ages. Age grades and sets cut across territorial and kin groupings and so may be important means of political organization. This was the case with the Tiriki of East Africa, whose age grades and sets we examined in Chapter 20. Among them, the warrior age grade guarded the country, while judicial elders resolved disputes. Between these two age grades were elder warriors, who were in a sense understudies to the judicial elders. The oldest age grade, the ritual elders, advised on all matters involving the well-being of all the Tiriki people. Thus, political matters of the tribe were in the hands of the age grades and their officers.

Association Organization

Common-interest associations that function as politically integrative systems within tribes are found in many areas of the world, including Africa, Melanesia, and India. A good example of an association organization is one that functioned during the nineteenth century among the Plains Indians of the United States, such as the Cheyenne, whom we'll talk about again later in this chapter. The

Among the Cheyenne, a council of 44 chiefs, men who embodied all that was valued by the tribe, decided matters of common interest and named one of the military associations to act as police during tribal encampments, hunts, wars, and ceremonies. Shown here are Dull Knife and Little Wolf, two of the most famous nineteenth-century chiefs.

basic territorial and political unit of the Cheyenne was the band, but seven military societies, or warriors' clubs, were common to the entire tribe; the clubs functioned in several areas. A boy might be invited to join one of these societies when he achieved warrior status, whereupon he became familiar with the society's particular insignia, songs, and rituals. In addition to their military functions, the warriors' societies also had ceremonial and social functions.

The Cheyenne warriors' routine daily tasks consisted of overseeing movements in the camp, protecting a moving column, and enforcing rules against individual hunting when the whole tribe was on a buffalo hunt. In addition, each warrior

society had its own repertoire of dances that the members performed on special ceremonial occasions. Since identical military societies bearing identical names existed in each Cheyenne band, the societies thus served to integrate the entire tribe for military and political purposes.[3]

The Melanesian Big Man

Throughout much of Melanesia there appears a type of leader called the Big Man. The Big Man combines a small amount of interest in his tribe's welfare with a great deal of self-interested cunning and calculation for his own personal gain. His authority is personal; he does not come to office, nor is he elected. His status is the result of acts that raise him above most other tribe members and attract to him a band of loyal followers.

Typical of this form of political organization are the Kapauku of west New Guinea. Among them, the Big Man is called the *tonowi,* or "rich one." To achieve this status, one must be male, wealthy, generous, and eloquent; physical bravery and skills in dealing with the supernatural are also frequent characteristics of a *tonowi,* but they are not essential. The *tonowi* functions as the headman of the village unit.

Kapauku culture places a high value on wealth, so it is not surprising that a wealthy individual is considered to be a successful and admirable man. Yet the possession of wealth must be coupled with the trait of generosity, which in this society means not gift giving but willingness to make loans. Wealthy men who refuse to lend money to other villagers may be ostracized, ridiculed, and, in extreme cases, actually executed by a group of warriors. This social pressure ensures that economic wealth is rarely hoarded but is distributed throughout the group.

It is through the loans he makes that the *tonowi* acquires his political power. Other villagers comply with his requests because they are in his debt (often without paying interest), and they do not want to have to repay their loans. Those who have

[3]E. A. Hoebel, *The Cheyennes: Indians of the Great Plains* (New York: Holt, Rinehart and Winston, 1960).

A Kapauku Big Man delivering a political speech. Verbal eloquence is one of the skills necessary for leadership in this society.

not yet borrowed money from the *tonowi* may wish to do so in the future, and so they, too, want to keep his goodwill.

Other sources of support for the *tonowi* are apprentices whom he has taken into his household for training. They are fed, housed, given a chance to learn the *tonowi's* business wisdom, and given a loan to get a wife when they leave; in return, they act as messengers and bodyguards. Even after they leave his household, these men are tied to the *tonowi* by bonds of affection and gratitude. Political support also comes from the *tonowi's* kinsmen, whose relationship brings with it varying obligations.

The *tonowi* functions as a leader in a wide variety of situations. He represents his group in dealing with outsiders and other villages; he acts as

negotiator and/or judge when disputes break out among his followers. Leopold Pospisil, who studied the Kapauku, notes:

> The multiple functions of a *tonowi* are not limited to the political and legal fields only. His word also carries weight in economic and social matters. He is especially influential in determining proper dates for pig feasts and pig markets, in inducing specific individuals to become co-sponsors at feasts, in sponsoring communal dance expeditions to other villages, and in initiating large projects, such as extensive drainage ditches and main fences or bridges, the completion of which requires a joint effort of the whole community.[4]

The *tonowi's* wealth comes from his success at pig breeding (as we discussed in Chapter 12), for pigs are the focus of the entire Kapauku economy. Like all kinds of cultivation and domestication, raising pigs requires a combination of strength, skill, and luck. It is not uncommon for a *tonowi* to lose his fortune rapidly, due to bad management or bad luck with his pigs. Thus the political structure of the Kapauku shifts frequently; as one man loses wealth and consequently power, another gains it and becomes a *tonowi*. These changes confer a degree of flexibility on the political organization, and prevent any one *tonowi* from holding political power for too long a time.

CENTRALIZED POLITICAL SYSTEMS

In bands and tribes, authority is uncentralized, and each group is economically and politically autonomous. Political organization is vested in kinship, age, and common-interest groups. Populations are small and relatively homogeneous, with people engaged for the most part in the same sorts of activities throughout their lives. However, as a society's social life becomes more complex, as population rises and technology becomes more complex, and as specialization of labor and trade networks produces surpluses of goods, the need

[4]Leopold Pospisil, *The Kapauku Papuans of West New Guinea* (New York: Holt, Rinehart and Winston, 1963), pp. 51–52.

for more formally defined, centralized leadership becomes greater. In such societies, political authority and power are concentrated in a single individual—the chief—or in numerous groups of individuals—the state. The state is a form of organization found in societies in which each individual must interact on a regular basis with large numbers of people with diversified interests, who are neither kin nor close acquaintances.

Chiefdoms

A **chiefdom** is a ranked society in which every member has a position in the hierarchy. An individual's status in such a community is determined by membership in a descent group: those in the uppermost levels, closest to the chief, are officially superior and receive deferential treatment from those in lower ranks.

The office of the chief may or may not be hereditary. Unlike the headman of bands and lineages, the chief is generally a true authority figure, and his authority serves to unite his community in all affairs and at all times. For example, a chief can distribute land among his community and recruit members into his military service. In chiefdoms, there is a recognized hierarchy consisting of major and minor authorities who control major and minor subdivisions of the chiefdom. Such an arrangement is, in effect, a chain of command, linking leaders at every level. It serves to bind tribal groups in the heartland to the chief's headquarters, be it a mud-and-dung hut or a marble palace.

On the economic level, a chief controls the economic activities of his people. Chiefdoms are typically redistributive systems; the chief has control over surplus goods and perhaps even the labor force of his community. Thus, he may demand a quota of rice from farmers, which he will redistribute to the entire community. Similarly, he may recruit laborers to build irrigation works, a palace, or a temple.

The chief may also amass a great amount of personal wealth and pass it on to his heirs. Land, cattle, and luxury goods produced by specialists can be collected by the chief and become part of

> **Chiefdom:** A ranked society in which every member has a position in the hierarchy.

his power base. Moreover, high-ranking families of the chiefdom may engage in the same practice and use their possessions as evidence of status.

An example of this form of political organization may be seen among the Kpelle of Liberia, in West Africa.[5] Among them is a class of paramount chiefs, each of whom presides over one of the Kpelle chiefdoms (each of which is now a district of the Liberian nation). The paramount chiefs' traditional tasks are hearing disputes, preserving order, seeing to the upkeep of trails, and maintaining "medicines." In addition, they are now salaried officials of the Liberian government, mediating between it and their own people. Other rewards received by a paramount chief include a commission on taxes collected within his chiefdom, a commission for laborers furnished for the rubber plantations, a portion of court fees collected, a stipulated amount of rice from each household, and gifts brought by people who come to request favors and intercessions. In keeping with his exalted station in life, a paramount chief has at his disposal uniformed messengers, a literate clerk, and the symbols of wealth: many wives, embroidered gowns, and freedom from manual labor.

In a ranked hierarchy, beneath each paramount chief are several lesser chiefs—one for each district within the chiefdom, one for each town within a district, and one for each quarter of all but the smallest towns. Each acts as a kind of lieutenant for his chief of the next higher rank, and serves as well as a liaison between him and those of lower rank. Unlike paramount or district chiefs, who are comparatively remote, town and quarter chiefs are readily accessible to people at the local level.

Stable though the Kpelle political system may be today, traditionally chiefdoms in all parts of the world have been highly unstable. This happens as

[5]James L. Gibbs, Jr., "The Kpelle of Liberia," in *Peoples of Africa*, ed. James L. Gibbs, Jr. (New York: Holt, Rinehart and Winston, 1965), pp. 216–218.

A paramount chief among the Kpelle of Liberia settling a dispute. The defendant's mother pleads for her son in a case heard on the porch of the chief's house.

lesser chiefs try to take power from higher-ranking chiefs, or as paramount chiefs vie with one another for supreme power. In precolonial Hawaii, for example, war was the way to gain territory and maintain power; great chiefs set out to conquer one another in an effort to become paramount chief of all the islands. When one chief conquered another, the loser and all his nobles were dispossessed of all property and were lucky if they escaped alive. The new chief then appointed his own supporters to positions of political power. As a consequence, there was very little continuity of governmental or religious administration.

State Systems

The **state,** the most formal of political organizations, is one of the hallmarks of civilization. In the state, political power is centralized in a govern-

State: In anthropology, a centralized political system with the power to coerce.

ment, which may legitimately use force to regulate the affairs of its citizens, as well as its relations with other states. Although their guiding ideology pretends that they are permanent and stable, the fact is that since their appearance some 5,000 years ago, states have been anything but permanent. Whatever stability they have achieved has been short term at best; over the long term, they show a clear tendency to instability and transience. Nowhere have states even begun to show the staying power exhibited by more decentralized political systems.

An important aspect of the state is its delegation of authority to maintain order within and outside its borders. Police, foreign ministries, war ministries, and other branches of the government function to control and punish disruptive acts of crime, terror, and rebellion. By such agencies, authority in the state is asserted impersonally and (in theory at least) objectively.

The state is found only in societies with numerous diverse groups, social classes, and associations; it brings together under a common rule many kinds of people. In all known states, past and present, society is divided into social classes, and economic functions and wealth are distributed unequally. A market economy is an integral part of most states, as are vast surpluses of goods and services and the intense specialization of labor.

Our own form of government, of course, is a state government, and its organization and workings are undoubtedly familiar to everyone. An example of a not so familiar state is afforded by the Swazi of Swaziland, a Bantu-speaking people who live in southeast Africa.[6] They are primarily farmers, but cattle raising is more highly valued than farming: the ritual, wealth, and power of their au-

[6]Hilda Kuper, "The Swazi of Swaziland," in *Peoples of Africa*, ed. James L. Gibbs, Jr. (New York: Holt, Rinehart and Winston, 1965), pp. 479–512.

Symbolic of the state's authority over its citizens is the power to order executions, whether by electrocution, lethal injection, or gas, as in the United States; by sacrifice, as in Aztec society; or by some other means.

thority system are all intricately linked with cattle. In addition to farming and cattle raising, there is some specialization of labor; certain people become specialists in ritual, smithing, woodcarving, and pottery. Their goods and services are traded, although the Swazi do not have elaborate markets.

The Swazi authority system is characterized by a highly developed dual monarchy, a hereditary aristocracy, and elaborate rituals of kinship, as well as by statewide age sets. The king and his mother are the central figures of all national activity, linking all the people of the Swazi state; they preside over higher courts, summon national gatherings, control age classes, allocate land, disburse national wealth, take precedence in ritual, and help organize important social events.

Advising the king are the senior princes, who are usually his uncles and half-brothers. Between the king and the princes are two specially created *tinsila*, or "blood brothers," who are chosen from certain common clans. These men are his shields, protecting him from evildoers and serving him in intimate personal situations. In addition, the king is guided by two *tindvuna*, or counselors, one civil and one military. The people of the state make their opinions known through two councils: the *liqoqo*, or privy council, composed of senior princes, and the *libanda*, or council of state, composed of chiefs and headmen and open to all adult males of the state. The *liqoqo* may advise the king, make decisions, and execute them. For example, they may rule on such questions as land, education, traditional ritual, court procedure, and transport.

Government extends from the smallest local unit—the homestead—upward to the central administration. The head of a homestead has legal and administrative powers; he is responsible for the crimes of those under him, controls their property, and speaks for them before his superiors. On the district level, political organization is similar to that of the central government. The relationship between a district chief, however, and his subjects is personal and familiar; he knows all the families in his district. The main check on any autocratic tendencies he may exhibit rests in his subjects' ability to transfer their allegiance to a more responsive chief. Swazi officials hold their positions for life and are dismissed only for treason or witchcraft. Incompetence, drunkenness, and stupidity are frowned upon, but they are not considered to be sufficient grounds for dismissal.

POLITICAL LEADERSHIP AND GENDER

Irrespective of cultural configuration or type of political organization, it is a fact that women rarely hold important positions of political leadership. Furthermore, when they do occupy publicly recognized offices, their power and authority rarely exceed those of men. Nevertheless, there have been exceptions, recent ones being Corazon Aquino, Sirimavo Badaranaike, Benazir Bhutto, Indira Ghandi, Golda Meir, and Margaret Thatcher, who have headed governments of the Philippines, Sri Lanka, Pakistan, India, Israel, and Great Britain, respectively. Historically, one might cite the occasional "squaw sachems" (woman chiefs) mentioned in early accounts of New England Indians, or powerful queens such as Elizabeth I of England or Catherine the Great of Russia. When women do hold high office, it is often on account of their relationship to men. Thus, a queen is either the wife of a reigning monarch or else the daughter of a king who died without a male heir to succeed him. Moreover, women in focal positions frequently must adopt many of the characteristics of temperament normally deemed appropriate for men in their societies. In her role as prime minister, Margaret Thatcher, for instance, displays the toughness and assertiveness that, in Western societies, have long been considered to be desirable masculine qualities, rather than the nurturance and compliance that Westerners have traditionally expected of women.

In spite of all this, it is a fact that in a number of societies, women regularly enjoy as much political power as men. In band societies, it is common for them to have as much of a say in public affairs as men, even though the latter more often than not are the nominal heads of their groups. Among the

This Seneca Chief, Cornplanter, participated in three treaties with the United States in the late eighteenth century. Although Iroquoian chiefs were always men, they served strictly at the pleasure of women, whose position in society was equal to that of men.

Iroquoian tribes of New York State (discussed in Chapter 20), all positions of leadership above the household level were, without exception, filled by men. Thus they held all positions on the village and tribal councils, as well as on the great council of the League of Five Nations. However, they were completely beholden to women, for only the latter could appoint men to high office. Moreover, the women actively lobbied the men on the councils and could remove someone from office whenever it suited them to do so.

As the above cases make clear, low visibility of women in politics does not necessarily exclude them from the realm of social control, or mean that men have more power in political affairs. Sometimes, though, women may play more visible roles, as in the dual sex systems of West Africa. Among the Igbo of midwestern Nigeria, in each political unit, separate political institutions for men and women gave each sex their own autonomous spheres of authority, as well as an area of shared responsibility.[7] At the head of each was a male *obi*, considered the head of government though in fact he presided over the male community, and a female *omu*, the acknowledged mother of the whole community but who in practice was concerned with the female section of the community. Unlike a queen (though both she and the *obi* were crowned), the *omu* was neither the wife of the *obi* nor the daughter of the previous one.

Just as the *obi* had a council of dignitaries to advise him and to act as a check against any arbitrary exercise of power, so was the *omu* served by a council of women, in equal number to the *obi's* male councilors. The duties of the *omu* and her councilors involved such things as establishing rules and regulations for the community market (marketing was a woman's activity) and hearing cases involving women brought to her from throughout the town or village. If such cases also involved men, then she and her council would cooperate with the *obi* and his. Widows also went to the *omu* for the final rites required to end their period of mourning for dead husbands. Since the *omu* represented all women, she had to be responsive to her constituency and would seek their approval and cooperation in all major decisions.

In addition to the *omu* and her council, the women's government included a representative body of women chosen from each quarter or section of the village or town on the basis of their ability to think logically and speak well. In addition, at the village or lineage level were political pressure groups of women that acted to stop quarrels and prevent wars. These were of two types,

one being of women born into a community, most of whom lived elsewhere since villages were exogamous and residence was patrilocal. The other consisted of women who had married into the community. Its duties included helping companion wives in times of illness and stress, as well as meting out discipline to lazy or recalcitrant husbands.

In the Igbo system, then, women managed their own affairs, and their interests were represented at all levels of government. Moreover, they had the right to enforce their decisions and rules by recourse to sanctions similar to those employed by men. Included were strikes, boycotts, and "sitting on a man" or woman. Anthropologist Judith Van Allen describes the latter:

> To "sit on" or "make war on" a man involved gathering at his compound, sometimes late at night, dancing, singing scurrilous songs which detailed the women's grievances against him and often called his manhood into question, banging on his hut with the pestles women used for pounding yams, and perhaps demolishing his hut or plastering it with mud and roughing him up a bit. A man might be sanctioned in this way for mistreating his wife, for violating the women's market rules, or for letting his cows eat the women's crops. The women would stay at his hut throughout the day, and late into the night if necessary, until he repented and promised to mend his ways. . . . Although this could hardly have been a pleasant experience for the offending man, it was considered legitimate and no man would consider intervening.[8]

Given the high visibility of women in the Igbo political system, it is surprising to learn that when the British imposed colonial rule upon these people, they failed to recognize the autonomy and power possessed by those women. The reason for this is that the British were blinded by their Victorian values, which then were at their height. To them, a woman's mind was not strong enough for such supposedly masculine subjects as science, business, and politics; her place was clearly in the home. Hence, it was inconceivable that women

---

[7]Kamene Okonjo, "The Dual-Sex Political System in Operation: Igbo Women and Community Politics in Midwestern Nigeria," in *Women in Africa*, ed. Nancy Hafkin and Edna Bay (Stanford, Calif.: Stanford University Press, 1976).

[8]Judith Van Allen, "Sitting on a Man: Colonialism and the Last Political Institutions of Igbo Women," in *Women in Society*, ed. Sharon Tiffany (St. Albans, Vt.: Eden Press, 1979), p. 169.

might play important roles in politics. As a consequence, the British introduced "reforms" that destroyed women's traditional forms of autonomy and power, without providing alternative forms in exchange. Far from enhancing the status of women, as Westerners like to think their influence does, in this case, women lost their equality and became subordinate to men. Nor is the Igbo situation unusual in this regard. Historically, in state-organized societies, women have always been subordinate to men. Hence, when states impose their control on societies in which the sexes are equal to one another, the situation almost invariably changes to one in which women become subordinate to men.

POLITICAL ORGANIZATION AND SOCIAL CONTROL

Whatever form the political organization of a society may take, and whatever else it may do, it is always involved in one way or another with social control. Always it seeks to ensure that people behave in acceptable ways, and it defines the proper action to take when they don't. In the case of chiefdoms and states, some sort of centralized authority has the power to regulate the affairs of society. In bands and tribes, however, people behave generally as they are expected to, without the direct intervention of any centralized political authority. To a large degree, gossip, criticism, fear of supernatural forces, and the like serve as effective deterrents to antisocial behavior.

As an example of how such seemingly informal considerations serve to keep people in line, we may look at the Wape people of Papua New Guinea, who believe that the ghosts of dead ancestors roam lineage lands, protecting them from trespassers and helping their hunting descendants by driving game their way.[9] These ghosts also punish those who have wronged them or their descendants by

[9] William E. Mitchell, "A New Weapon Stirs Up Old Ghosts," *Natural History Magazine*, December 1973, 77–84.

preventing hunters from finding game or causing them to miss their shots, thereby depriving people of much needed meat. Nowadays, the Wape hunt with shotguns, which are purchased by the community for the use of one man, whose job it is to hunt for all the others. The cartridges used in the hunt, however, are supplied always by individual members of the community. Not always is the gunman successful; if he shoots and misses, it is because the owner of the fired shell, or some close relative, has quarreled or wronged another person whose ghost relative is securing revenge by causing the hunter to miss. Or if the gunman fails to find game, it is because vengeful ghosts have chased the animals away. As a proxy hunter for the villagers, the gunman is potentially subject to ghostly sanctions in response to collective wrongs on the part of those for whom he hunts.

For the Wape, then, successful hunting depends upon avoiding quarrels and maintaining tranquility within the community, so as not to antagonize anybody's ghost ancestor. Unfortunately, complete peace and tranquility are impossible to achieve in any human community, and the Wape are no exception. Thus, when hunting is poor, the gunman must discover what quarrels and wrongs have taken place within his village, in order to identify the proper ancestral ghosts to appeal to for renewed success. Usually, this is done in a special meeting, in which confessions of wrongdoing may be forthcoming. If not, questioning accusations are bandied about until resolution occurs, but even if there is no resolution, the meeting must end amicably, in order to create no new antagonisms. Thus, everyone's behavior comes under public scrutiny, reminding all of what is expected of them and encouraging them to avoid acts that will cast them in an unfavorable light.

INTERNALIZED CONTROLS

The Wape concern about ancestral ghosts is a good example of internalized controls — beliefs that are so thoroughly ingrained that each person becomes personally responsible for his or her own

When Papua New Guinea gained its independence in 1975, a major question was: What should be the national legal system of a country whose roughly 3.5 million people speak at least 750 mutually unintelligible languages and maintain something like 1,000 customary legal systems? As an interim measure, the new government adopted the legal system under which people had lived while under Australian colonial rule, even though this often clashed with the customary law of indigenous groups. In order to develop a system more in accord with indigenous customs and traditions, the government established a Law Reform Commission.

The questions faced by the commission were twofold. First, could principles common to all indigenous legal systems be discovered? If so, then could the essence of systems that function smoothly in tribal societies, with their small and relatively homogeneous populations, work in a large, pluralistic nation state? To help find the answers to these questions, the commission established the Customary Law Project, which was to research the nature of customary law and the extent to which it could form the basis for a unique national legal system.

In 1979, the commission hired to head up this project a young anthropologist, Richard Scaglion, whose Ph.D. research a few years earlier had been a study of customary law and legal change among the Abelam. Scaglion's first job was to conduct an extensive bibliographical search and review of the literature. This re-vealed the need for more complete research on specific societies, for which students from the University of Papua New Guinea were employed. Using standard anthropological techniques, usually in their home areas, these students gathered detailed data on all aspects of observed, remembered, and hypothetical cases. By the mid-1980s, roughly 600 case studies had been gathered from all parts of the country and were made available to legal researchers through a computer retrieval system. From these case studies, Scaglion and others have been able to abstract underlying principles, while legal practitioners have made use of them in actual court cases.

The reform of Papua New Guinea's national legal system is an ongoing process. To date, Scaglion and his associates not only have supplied a body of precedent for legal scholars to draw on but have also helped draft legislation. For example, a Family Law Bill recognizes as legal customary marriage arrangements, which under Australian law are not legal. Similarly, legislation was drafted to recognize the principle of customary compensation, by which a variety of conflicts were resolved, while regulating both claims and payments to control inflationary demands. Perhaps the most important accomplishment of the project has been to focus attention on underlying principles and procedures, which can be adapted to changing situations, as opposed to the kinds of inflexible statutory rules with which lawyers are so often preoccupied.

good conduct. Examples of this can also be found in our own society; for instance, people refrain from committing incest not so much from fear of legal punishment as from a sense of deep disgust at the thought of the act and the shame they would feel in performing it (obviously, not all members of our society feel this disgust, or there wouldn't be such a high incidence of incest, especially between fathers and daughters). Built-in or internalized controls rely on such deterrents as the fear of supernatural punishment — ancestral ghosts sabotaging the hunting, for example — and magical retaliation. The individual expects to be punished, even though no one in the community may be aware of the wrongdoing.

EXTERNALIZED CONTROLS

Because internalized controls are not wholly sufficient even in bands and tribes, every society develops institutions designed to encourage conformity

Awards such as Olympic medals are examples of positive sanctions, by which societies promote behavior deemed appropriate.

to social norms. These institutions are referred to as **sanctions;** they are externalized social controls. According to Radcliffe-Brown, "A sanction is a reaction on the part of a society or of a considerable number of its members to a mode of behavior which is thereby approved (positive sanctions) or disapproved (negative sanctions)."[10] Sanctions may also be either formal or informal and may vary significantly within a given society.

Each group and subgroup within a society tends to develop its own distinctive pattern or usages and the

Sanctions: Externalized social controls designed to encourage conformity to social norms.

means of maintaining them without necessary recourse to the municipal law. Sanctions there come to operate within every conceivable set of group relationships: they include not only the organized sanctions of the law but also the gossip of neighbors or the customs regulating norms of production that are spontaneously generated among workers on the factory floor. In small scale communities . . . informal sanctions may become more drastic than the penalties provided for in the legal code.[11]

Sanctions, then, operate within social groups of all sizes. Moreover, they need not be enacted into law in order to play a significant role in social control. If, however, a sanction is to be effective, it cannot be arbitrary. Quite the opposite: sanctions must be consistently applied, and their existence must be generally known by the members of the society.

Negative and Positive Sanctions

Social sanctions may be categorized as either positive or negative. Positive sanctions consist of such incentives to conformity as awards, titles, and recognition by one's neighbors. Negative sanctions consist of such threats as imprisonment, corporal punishment, or ostracism from the community for violation of social norms. One example of a negative sanction discussed earlier is the Igbo practice of "sitting on a man." If some individuals are not convinced of the advantages of social conformity, they are still likely to be more willing to go along with society's rules than to accept the consequences of not doing so.

Formal and Informal Sanctions

Sanctions may also be categorized as either formal or informal, depending on whether or not a legal statute is involved. In our society the man who

[10]A. R. Radcliffe-Brown, *Structure and Function in Primitive Society* (New York: Free Press, 1952), p. 205.

[11]A. L. Epstein, "Sanctions," *International Encyclopedia of Social Sciences,* vol. 14 (New York: Macmillan, 1968), p. 3.

Negative sanctions may involve some form of regulated combat, as seen here as armed dancers near Mt. Hagen in Papua New Guinea demand redress in the case of murder.

wears tennis shorts to a church service may be subject to a variety of informal sanctions, ranging from the glances of the clergyman to the chuckling of other parishioners. If, however, he were to show up without any trousers at all, he would be subject to the formal sanction of arrest for indecent exposure. Only in the second instance would he have been guilty of breaking the **law.**

Formal sanctions, like laws, are always organized, because they attempt to precisely and explicitly regulate people's behavior. Other examples of organized sanctions include, on the positive side, such things as military decorations and monetary rewards. On the negative side are loss of face, exclusion from social life and its privileges, seizure of property, imprisonment, and even bodily mutilation or death.

Informal sanctions are diffuse in nature, involving spontaneous expressions of approval or disapproval by members of the group or community. They are, nonetheless, very effective in enforcing a large number of seemingly unimportant customs. Because most people want to be accepted, they are

> **Law:** A social norm, the neglect or infraction of which is regularly met, in threat or in fact, by the application of physical force on the part of an individual or group possessing the socially recognized privilege of so acting.

willing to acquiesce to the rules that govern dress, eating, and conversation, even in the absence of actual laws.

As an example of how informal sanctions work, we may examine them in the context of power relationships within the society of Bedouins living in the western desert of Egypt. The example is of especial interest, for it shows how sanctions act not only to control peoples' behavior, but to keep them in their place in a hierarchical society.

Another agent of social control in societies, whether or not they possess centralized political systems, may be witchcraft. An individual would naturally hesitate to offend one's neighbor when that neighbor might retaliate by resorting to black magic. Similarly, individuals may not wish to be

ORIGINAL STUDY
Limits on Power in Bedouin Society[12]

Where individuals value their independence and believe in equality, those who exercise authority over others enjoy a precarious status. In Bedouin society, social precedence or power depends not on force but on demonstration of the moral virtues that win respect from others. Persons in positions of power are said to have social standing (*gíma*), which is recognized by the respect paid them. To win the respect of others, in particular dependents, such persons must adhere to the ideals of honor, provide for and protect their dependents, and be fair, taking no undue advantage of their positions. They must assert their authority gingerly lest it so compromise their dependents' autonomy that it provoke rebellion and be exposed as a sham.

Because those in authority are expected to treat their dependents, even children, with some respect, they must draw as little attention as possible to the inequality of their relationships. Euphemisms that obscure the nature

Among the Awlad 'Ali, those who flaunt their authority over others lose face. Accordingly, patrons try to interact with their dependents in a friendly, open manner.

of such relationships abound. For example, Sàádi [free tribes] individuals do not like to call Mrábit [client tribes] associates Mrábtín in their presence. My host corrected me once when I referred to his shepherds by the technical word for shepherd, saying, "We prefer to call them 'people of the sheep' [hal il-ghanam]. It sounds nicer." The use of fictive kin terms serves the same function of masking relations of inequality, as for example in the case of patrons and clients.

Those in authority are also expected to respect their dependents' dignity by minimizing open assertion of their power over them. Because the provider's position requires dependents, he risks losing his power base if he alienates them. When a superior publicly orders, insults, or beats a dependent, he invites the rebellion that would undermine his position. Such moments are fraught with tension, as the dependent might feel the need to respond to a public humiliation to preserve his dignity or honor. Indeed, refusal to comply with an unreasonable order, or an order given in a compromising way, reflects well on the dependent and undercuts the authority of the person who gave it.

Tyranny is never tolerated for long. Most dependents wield sanctions that check the power of their providers. Anyone can appeal to a mediator to intervene on his or her behalf, and more radical solutions are open to all but young children. Clients can simply leave an unreasonable patron and attach themselves to a new one. Young men can always escape the tyranny of a father or paternal uncle by leaving to join maternal relatives or, if they have them, affines, or even to become clients to some other family. For the last twenty years or so, young men could go to Libya to find work.

Younger brothers commonly get out from under difficult elder brothers by splitting off from them, demanding their share of the patrimony and setting up separate households. The dynamic is clear in the case of four brothers who constituted the core of the camp in which I lived. Two had split off and lived in separate households. Another two still shared property, herds, and expenses. While I was there, tensions began to develop. Although the elder brother was more important in the community at large, and the younger brother was slightly irresponsible and less intelligent, for the most part they worked various enterprises jointly and without friction. The younger brother deferred to his older brother and usually executed his decisions.

But one day the tensions surfaced. The elder brother came home at midday in a bad mood only to find that no one had prepared him lunch. He went to one of his wives and scolded her for not having prepared any lunch, asserting that his children had complained that they were hungry. He accused her of trying to starve his children and threatened to beat her. His younger brother tried to intervene, but the elder brother then turned on him, calling him names. Accusing him of being lazy (because he had failed to follow through on a promise involving the care of the sheep that day), he then asked why the younger brother let his wife get away with sitting in her room when there was plenty of work to be done around the household. Then he went off toward his other wife carrying a big stick and yelling.

The younger brother was furious and set off to get their mother. The matriarch, accompanied by another of her sons, arrived and conferred at length with the quarreling men. The younger son wished to split off from his elder brother's household; the other brother scolded him for being so sensitive about a few words, reminding him that this was his elder brother, from whom even a beating should not matter. His mother disapproved of splitting up the households. Eventually everyone calmed down. But it is likely that a few more incidents such as that will eventually lead the younger brother to demand a separate household.

Even a woman can resist a tyrannical husband by leaving for her natal home "angry" (*mughtáża*). This is the approved response to abuse, and it forces the husband or his representatives to face the scolding of the woman's kin and, sometimes, to appease her with gifts. Women have less recourse against tyrannical fathers or guardians, but various informal means to resist the imposition of unwanted decisions do exist. As a last resort there is always suicide, and I heard of a number of both young men and women who committed suicide in desperate resistance to their fathers' decisions, especially regarding marriage. One old woman's tale illustrates the extent to which force can be resisted, even by women. Náfla reminisced:

> My first marriage was to my paternal cousin [*ibn àmm*]. He was from the same camp. One day the men came over to our tent. I saw the tent full of men and wondered why. I heard they were coming to ask for my hand [*yukhultú fiyya*]. I went and stood at the edge of the tent and called out, "If you're planning to do anything, stop. I don't want it." Well, they went ahead anyway, and every day I would cry and say that I did not want to marry him. I was young, perhaps fourteen. When they began drumming and singing, everyone assured me that it was in celebration of another cousin's wedding, so I sang and danced along with them. This went on for days. Then on the day of the wedding my aunt and another relative caught me in the tent and suddenly closed it and took out the washbasin. They wanted to bathe me. I screamed. I screamed and screamed; every time they held a pitcher of water to wash me with, I knocked it out of their hands.
>
> His relatives came with camels and dragged me into the litter and took me to his tent. I screamed and screamed when he came into the tent in the afternoon [for the defloration]. Then at night, I hid among the blankets. Look as they might, they couldn't find me. My father was furious. After a few days he insisted I had to stay in my tent with my husband. As soon as he left, I ran off and hid behind the tent in which the groom's sister stayed. I made her promise not to tell anyone I was there and slept there.
>
> But they made me go back. That night, my father stood guard nearby with his gun. Every time I started to leave the tent, he would take a puff on his cigarette so I could see that he was still there. Finally I rolled myself up in the straw mat. When the groom came, he looked and looked but could not find me.
>
> Finally I went back to my family's household. I pretended to be possessed. I tensed my body, rolled my eyes, and everyone rushed about, brought me incense and prayed for me. They brought the healer [or holyman, *fgih*], who blamed the

unwanted marriage. Then they decided that perhaps I was too young and that I should not be forced to return to my husband. I came out of the seizure, and they were so grateful that they forced my husband's family to grant a divorce. My family returned the bride-price, and I stayed at home.

Náfla could not oppose her father's decision directly, but she was nevertheless able to resist his will through indirect means. Like other options for resistance by dependents unfairly treated, abused, or humiliated publicly, her rebellion served as a check on her father's and, perhaps, more important, her paternal uncle's power.

Supernatural sanctions, which seem to be associated with the weak and with dependents, provide the final check on abuse of authority. Supernatural retribution is believed to follow when the saintly lineages of Mrábtín are mistreated, their curses causing death or the downfall of the offender's lineage. In one Bedouin tale, when a woman denied food to two young girls, she fell ill, and blood appeared on food she cooked—a punishment for mistreating the helpless. Possession, as Náfla's tale illustrates, may also be a form of resistance....

All these sanctions serve to check the abuse of power by eminent persons who have the resources to be autonomous and to control those who are dependent upon them. At the same time, moreover, figures of authority are vulnerable to their dependents because their positions rest on the respect these people are willing to give them.

[12]Lila Abu-Lughod, *Veiled Sentiments: Honor and Poetry in a Bedouin Society* (Berkeley: University of California Press, 1986), pp. 99–103. Copyright © 1986 by the Regents of the University of California. Reprinted by permission.

---

accused of practicing witchcraft themselves, and so they will behave with greater circumspection. Among the Azande of the Sudan, people who think they have been bewitched may consult an oracle, who, after performing the appropriate mystical rites, may then establish or confirm the identity of the offending witch.[13] Confronted with this evidence, the "witch" will usually agree to cooperate in order to avoid any additional trouble. Should the victim die, the relatives of the deceased may choose to make magic against the witch, ultimately accepting the death of some villager as evidence of both guilt and the efficacy of their magic. For the Azande, witchcraft provides not only a sanction

[13]E. E. Evans-Pritchard, *Witchcraft, Oracles and Magic among the Azande* (London: Oxford University Press, 1937).

against antisocial behavior, but also a means of dealing with natural hostilities and death. No one wishes to be thought of as a witch, and surely no one wishes to be victimized by one. By institutionalizing their emotional responses, the Azande successfully maintain social order. (For more on witchcraft, see Chapter 22.)

Another important social control, and one that is likely to be internalized, is the religious sanction. Just as a devout Christian may avoid sinning for fear of hell, so may other worshipers tend to behave in a manner intended not to offend their powerful supernatural beings. The threat of punishment—either in this life or in the next—by gods, ancestral spirits, or ghosts is a strong incentive for proper behavior. In some societies, it is

In Western society, someone who commits an offense against someone else is subject to a series of complex proceedings, in which the emphasis is on assigning and punishing guilt. In non-Western societies, by contrast, the emphasis is often on finding a solution that both parties can live with.

believed that ancestral spirits are very much concerned with the maintenance of good relations among the living members of their lineage. Death or illness in the lineage may be explained by reference to some violation of tradition or custom. Religious sanctions may thus serve not only to regulate behavior but to explain unexplainable phenomena as well.

SOCIAL CONTROL THROUGH LAW

Among the Inuit of northern Canada, all offenses are considered to involve disputes between individuals; thus, they must be settled between the disputants themselves. One way they may do so is through a song duel, in which they heap insults upon one another in songs specially composed for

the occasion. Although "society" does not intervene, its interests are represented by spectators, whose applause determines the outcome. If, however, social harmony cannot be restored — and that, rather than assigning and punishing guilt, is the goal — one or the other disputant may move to another band. Among the Inuit, the alternative to peaceful settlement is to leave the group. Ultimately, there is no binding legal authority.

In Western society, on the other hand, someone who commits an offense against another person is subject to a series of complex legal proceedings. In criminal cases the primary concern is to assign and punish guilt, rather than to help out the victim. The offender will be arrested by the police; tried before a judge and, perhaps, a jury; and, if the crime is serious enough, may be fined, imprisoned, or even executed. Rarely is there restitution or compensation for the victim. Throughout this chain of events, the accused party is dealt with by presumably disinterested police, judges, jurors, and jailers, who may have no personal acquaintance whatsoever with the plaintiff or the defendant. How strange this all seems from the standpoint of traditional Inuit culture! Clearly, the two systems operate under distinctly different assumptions.

Each society establishes institutions to encourage conformity to its rules and to define proper action in the event of breach of those rules. Through its sanctions, a society exercises a degree of control over the behavior of its members. An important part of a society's total system of social controls is that aspect referred to as law.

DEFINITION OF LAW

Once two Inuit settle a dispute by engaging in a song contest, the affair is considered closed; no further action need be expected. Would we choose to describe the outcome of such a contest as a legal decision? If every law is a sanction, but not every sanction is a law, how are we to distinguish between social sanctions in general and those to which we will apply the label *law*?

The definition of law has been a lively point of contention among anthropologists in the twentieth century. In 1926, Malinowski argued that the rules of law are distinguished from the rules of custom in that "they are regarded as the obligation of one person and the rightful claim of another, sanctioned not by mere psychological motive, but by a definite social machinery of binding force based . . . upon mutual dependence."[14] An example of one rule of custom in our own society might be seen in the dictate that guests at a dinner party should repay the person who gave the party with entertainment in the future. A host or hostess who does not receive a return invitation may feel cheated of something thought to be owed, but there is no legal claim against the ungrateful guest for the $22.67 spent on food. If, however, an individual was cheated of the same sum by the grocer when shopping, the law could be invoked. Although Malinowski's definition introduced several important elements of law, his failure to distinguish adequately between legal and nonlegal sanctions left the problem of formulating a workable definition of law in the hands of later anthropologists.

An important pioneer in the anthropological study of law was E. Adamson Hoebel, according to whom "a social norm is legal if its neglect or infraction is regularly met, in threat or in fact, by the application of physical force by an individual or group possessing the socially recognized privilege of so acting."[15] In stressing the legitimate use of physical coercion, Hoebel de-emphasized the traditional association of law with a centralized court system. Although judge and jury are fundamental features of Western jurisprudence, they are not the universal backbone of human law. Some anthropologists have proposed that a precise definition of law is an impossible — and perhaps even undesirable — undertaking. When we speak of "the law," are we not inclined to fall back on our familiar Western conception of rules enacted by an authorized legislative body and enforced by the judicial mechanisms of the state? Can any concept of law be applied to such societies as the Nuer or the Inuit, for whom the notion of a centralized judiciary is virtually meaningless? How shall we categorize duels, song contests, and other socially condoned forms of self-help, which seem to meet some but not all of the criteria of law?

Ultimately, it seems of greatest value to consider each case within its cultural context. That each society exercises a degree of control over its members by means of rules and sanctions, and that some of these sanctions are more formalized than others, is indisputable; yet in distinguishing between legal and nonlegal sanctions, we should be careful not to allow questions of terminology to

---

[14]Bronislaw Malinowski, *Crime and Custom in Savage Society* (London: Routledge, 1951), p. 55.

[15]E. Adamson Hoebel, *The Law of Primitive Man: A Study in Comparative Legal Dynamics* (Cambridge, Mass.: Harvard University Press, 1954), p. 28.

overshadow our efforts to understand individual situations as they arise.

FUNCTIONS OF LAW

In *The Law of Primitive Man* (1954), Hoebel writes of a time when the notion that private property should be generously shared was a fundamental precept of Cheyenne Indian life. Subsequently, however, some men assumed the privilege of borrowing other men's horses without bothering to obtain permission. When Wolf Lies Down complained of such unauthorized borrowing to the members of the Elk Soldier Society, the Elk Soldiers not only had his horse returned to him but also secured an award for damages from the offender. The Elk Soldiers then announced that, to avoid such difficulties in the future, horses were no longer to be borrowed without permission. Furthermore, they declared their intention of retrieving any such property and administering a whipping to anyone who resisted their efforts to return improperly borrowed goods.

The case of Wolf Lies Down and the Elk Soldier Society clearly illustrates three basic functions of law. First, it defines relationships among the members of society, determining proper behavior under specified circumstances. Knowledge of the law permits each person to know his or her rights and duties in respect to every other member of society. Second, law allocates the authority to employ coercion in the enforcement of sanctions. In societies with centralized political systems, such authority is generally vested in the government and its court system. In societies that lack centralized political control, the authority to employ force may be allocated directly to the injured party. Third, law functions to redefine social relations and to ensure social flexibility. As new situations arise, law must determine whether old rules and assumptions retain their validity and to what extent they must be altered. Law, if it is to operate efficiently, must allow room for change.

In actual practice, law is rarely the smooth and well-integrated system described above. In any given society, various legal sanctions may apply at various levels. Because the people in a society are usually members of numerous subgroups, they are subject to the various dictates of these diverse groups. Each individual Kapauku is, simultaneously, a member of a family, a household, a sublineage, and a confederacy, and is subject to all the laws of each. In some cases it may be impossible for an individual to submit to contradictory legal indications:

> In one of the confederacy's lineages, incestuous relations between members of the same clan were punished by execution of the culprits, and in another by severe beating, in the third constituent lineage such a relationship was not punishable and . . . was not regarded as incest at all. In one of the sublineages, it became even a preferred type of marriage.[16]

Furthermore, the power to employ sanctions may vary from level to level within a given society. The head of a Kapauku household may punish a member of his household by means of slapping or beating, but the authority to confiscate property is vested exclusively in the headman of the lineage. An example of a similar dilemma in our own society occurred a few years ago in Oklahoma, a state in which the sale of liquor by the drink is illegal. State officials arrested several passengers and workers on an Amtrak train passing through the state; these people knew their actions were legal under federal law but were unaware that they could be prosecuted under state law. The complexity of legal jurisdiction within each society casts a shadow of doubt over any easy generalization about law.

CRIME

As we have observed, an important function of sanctions, legal or otherwise, is to discourage the breach of social norms. A person contemplating theft is aware of the possibility of being captured and punished. Yet even in the face of severe sanctions, individuals in every society sometimes vio-

---

[16]Leopold Pospisil, *Anthropology of Law: A Comparative Theory* (New York: Harper & Row, 1971), p. 36.

late the norms and subject themselves to the consequences of their behavior. In general, the nature of crime in Western society differs from that in non-Western societies.

In Western society, a clear distinction can be made between offenses against the state and offenses against an individual. Henry Campbell Black said:

> The distinction between a crime and a tort or civil injury is that the former is a breach and violation of the public right and of duties due to the whole community considered as such, and in its social and aggregate capacity; whereas the latter is an infringement or privation of the civil rights of individuals merely.[17]

Thus, a reckless driver who crashes into another car may be guilty of a crime in endangering public safety. The same driver may also be guilty of a tort in causing damages to the other car and can be sued for their cost by the other driver.

In many non-Western societies, however, there is no conception of a central state. Consequently, all offenses are conceived of as offenses against individuals, rendering the distinction between crime and tort of no value. Indeed, a dispute between individuals may seriously disrupt the social order, especially in small groups where the number of disputants, though small in absolute numbers, may be a large percentage of the total population. Although the Inuit have no effective domestic or economic unit beyond the family, a dispute between two people will interfere with the ability of members of separate families to come to one another's aid when necessary, and is consequently a matter of wide social concern. The goal of judicial proceedings in most cases is to restore social harmony, instead of punishing an offender. In distinguishing between offenses of concern to the community as a whole and those of concern only to a few individuals, we may refer to offenses as public or private, rather than distinguishing be-

[17]Henry Campbell Black, *Black's Law Dictionary* (St. Paul, Minn.: West, 1968).

Negotiation: The use of direct argument and compromise by the parties to a dispute to arrive voluntarily at a mutually satisfactory agreement.

Mediation: Settlement of a dispute through negotiation assisted by an unbiased third party.

Adjudication: Mediation, with the ultimate decision made by an unbiased third party.

tween criminal and civil law. In this way we may avoid values and assumptions that are irrelevant to a discussion of non-Western systems of law.

Perhaps the most fruitful path to understanding the nature of law lies in the thorough analysis of individual dispute cases, each within its own unique social context. Basically, a dispute may be settled in either of two ways. On the one hand, disputing parties may, by means of argument and compromise, voluntarily arrive at a mutually satisfactory agreement. This form of settlement is referred to as **negotiation** or, if it involves the assistance of an unbiased third party, **mediation.** In bands and tribes a third-party mediator has no coercive power and so cannot force disputants to abide by his decision, but as a person who commands great personal respect, he may frequently effect a settlement through his judgments.

In chiefdoms and states, an authorized third party may issue a binding decision, which the disputing parties will be obligated to respect. This process is referred to as **adjudication.** The difference between mediation and adjudication is basically a difference in authorization. In a dispute settled by adjudication, the disputing parties present their positions as convincingly as they can, but they do not participate in the ultimate decision making.

Although the adjudication process is not universally characteristic, every society employs some form of negotiation in the settlement of disputes. Often negotiation acts as a prerequisite or an alternative to adjudication. For example, in the resolution of U.S. labor disputes, striking workers may first negotiate with management, often with the

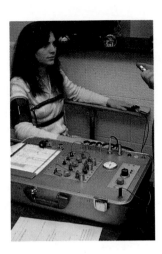

Two means of psychological stress evaluation: a Kpelle trial by ordeal and a Western polygraph ("lie detector").

mediation of a third party. If the state decides that the strike constitutes a threat to the public welfare, the disputing parties may be forced to submit to adjudication. In this case, the responsibility for resolving the dispute is transferred to a presumably impartial judge.

The work of the judge is difficult and complex. Not only must the evidence that is presented be sifted through, but the judge must consider a wide range of norms, values, and earlier rulings in order to arrive at a decision that is intended to be considered just not only by the disputing parties but by the public and other judges as well. In most tribal societies a greater value is placed on reconciling disputing parties and resuming tribal harmony than on administering awards and punishments. Thus, "tribal courts may . . . work in ways more akin to Western marriage conciliators, lawyers, arbitrators, and industrial conciliators than to Western judges in court."[18]

In many societies judgment is thought to be made by incorruptible supernatural, or at least nonhuman, powers, through a trial by ordeal. Among the Kpelle of Liberia, for example, when guilt is in doubt, an ordeal operator licensed by the government may apply a hot knife to the leg of a suspect. If the leg is burned, the suspect is guilty; if not, he is innocent. But the operator does not merely heat the knife and apply it. With his hand, he massages the suspect's legs, and once he has determined that the knife is hot enough, he strokes his own leg with it, without being burned, thus proving that the innocent will escape injury. He then applies the knife to the suspect. What he has done up to this point — consciously or unconsciously — is to read the suspect's nonverbal cues: his gestures, the degree of tension in his legs, how much he perspires, and so forth. From this he is able to judge whether or not the accused is showing so much anxiety as to indicate his probable guilt; in effect, he has carried out a psychological stress evaluation. As he applies the knife, he manipulates it so as to either burn or not burn the suspect, once he has made his judgment. This manipulation is easily done by controlling how long the knife is in the fire, as well as by the pressure and angle at which it is pressed against the leg.[19]

[18]Max Gluckman, *The Judicial Process among the Barotse of Northern Rhodesia* (New York: Free Press, 1975).

[19]James L. Gibbs, Jr., Interview, *Faces of Culture* (Huntington Beach, Calif.: Coast Telecourses, 1983), Program 18.

Similar to this is the use of the lie detector (polygraph) in our own society, although the guiding ideology is scientific rather than supernaturalistic. Still, an incorruptible nonhuman agency is thought to establish who is lying and who is not, whereas in reality the polygraph operator cannot just "read" the needles of the machine. What he or she must do is judge whether or not the subject is registering a high level of anxiety brought on by the testing situation, as opposed to the stress of guilt. Thus, the polygraph operator has much in common with the Kpelle ordeal operator.

POLITICAL ORGANIZATION AND EXTERNAL AFFAIRS

Although the regulation of internal affairs is an important function of any political system, it is by no means the sole function. Another is the management of external affairs — what we would call international relations, but which in the case of bands and tribes amounts to relations among different bands, lineages, clans, or whatever the largest autonomous political unit may be. And just as the threatened or actual use of force may be used to maintain order within a society, so may it be used in the conduct of external affairs.

WAR

One of the responsibilities of the state is the organization and execution of the activities of war. Throughout the last few thousand years of history, people have engaged in a seemingly endless chain of wars and intergroup hostilities. Why do wars occur? Is the need to wage war an instinctive feature of the human personality? What are the alternatives to violence as a means of settling disputes between societies?

War is not a universal phenomenon, for in various parts of the world there are societies in which warfare as we know it is not practiced. Examples include people as diverse as the !Kung of Africa, the Arapesh of New Guinea, and the Hopi of North America. Among those societies where warfare is practiced, levels of violence may differ dramatically. Of warfare in New Guinea, for example, the anthropologist Robert Gordon notes:

> It's slightly more civilized than the violence of warfare which we practice insofar as it's strictly between two groups. And as an outsider, you can go up and interview people and talk to them while they're fighting and the arrows will miss you. It's quite safe and you can take photographs. Now, of course, the problem with modern warfare is precisely that it kills indiscriminately and you can't do much research on it, but at the same time, you can learn a lot talking to these people about the dynamics of how violence escalates into full-blown warfare.[20]

There is ample reason to suppose that war has become a serious problem only in the last 10,000 years, since the invention of food-production techniques, the rise of the city, and the invention of centralized states. It has reached crisis proportions in the last 200 years, with the invention of modern weaponry and increased direction of violence against civilian populations. Thus, war seems not to be so much an age-old problem as a relatively recent one. Among food foragers, with their decentralized political systems, warfare is not unknown, but neither is it common. Because territorial boundaries and membership among food-foraging bands are usually fluid and loosely defined, a man who hunts with one band today may hunt with a neighboring band tomorrow. Warfare is further rendered impractical by the systematic interchange of women among food-foraging groups — it is likely that someone in each band will have a sister, a brother, or a cousin in a neighboring band. Where property ownership is minimal and no state organization exists, the likelihood of warfare is greatly diminished.

Although there are peaceful farmers, despite the traditional view of the farmer as a gentle tiller of the soil, it is among such people, along with pastoralists, that warfare becomes prominent. One

[20]Robert J. Gordon, Interview for Coast Telecourses, Inc., Los Angeles, December 4, 1981.

reason for this may be that food-producing peoples are far more prone to population growth than are food foragers, whose numbers are generally maintained well below carrying capacity. This population growth, if unchecked, can lead to resource depletion, one solution to which may be to seize the resources of some other people. In addition, the commitment to a fixed piece of land inherent in farming makes such societies somewhat less fluid in their membership than among people who are food foragers. In those societies that are rigidly matrilocal or patrilocal, each new generation is bound to the same territory, no matter how small it may be or how large the group trying to live within it.

The availability of virgin land may not serve as a sufficient detriment to the outbreak of war. Among slash-and-burn horticulturists, for example, competition for land cleared of virgin forest frequently leads to hostility and armed conflict. The centralization of political control and the possession of valuable property among farming people provide many more stimuli for warfare. It is among such peoples, especially those organized into states, that the violence of warfare is most apt to result in indiscriminate killing. This development has reached its peak in modern states.

Another difference between food-gathering and food-producing populations lies in their different **world views.** As a general rule, food foragers tend to conceive of themselves as a part of the natural world and in some sort of balance with it. This is reflected in their attitudes toward the animals they kill. Western Abenaki hunters, for example, thought that animals, like humans, were composed of a body and vital self. Although Abenakis hunted and killed animals to sustain their own lives, they clearly recognized that animals were entitled to proper respect. Thus, when beaver, muskrat, or waterfowl were killed, one couldn't just toss their bones into the nearest garbage pit. Proper respect required that their bones be returned to the water, with a request that the species be continued. Such attitudes may be referred to as a naturalistic world view.

World views: The conceptions, explicit and implicit, of a society or an individual of the limits and workings of its world.

The Abenakis' respect for nature contrasts sharply with the kind of world view prevalent among farmers and pastoralists, who do not find their food in nature but actively manipulate it so as to produce food for themselves. The attitude that nature exists only to be used by humans may be referred to as an exploitative world view. With such an outlook, it is a small step from manipulating the rest of nature to manipulating other societies for the benefit of one's own. The exploitative world view, prevalent among food-producing peoples, is an important contributor to intersocietal warfare.

A comparison between the western Abenakis and their Iroquoian neighbors to the west is instructive. Among the Abenakis warfare was essentially a defensive activity. These food foragers, with their naturalistic world view, believed that one could not operate in someone else's territory since one didn't control the necessary supernatural powers. Furthermore, operating far below carrying capacity, they had no need to prey upon the resources of others. The Iroquois, by contrast, were slash-and-burn horticulturists who engaged in predatory warfare. Archaeological evidence indicates that significant environmental degradation took place around their settlements, suggesting overutilization of resources. Although the Iroquois went to war in order to replace men lost in previous battles, the main motive was to achieve dominance by making their victims acknowledge Iroquoian superiority. The relation between victim and victor, however, was one of subjection, rather than outright subordination. The payment of tribute purchased "protection" from the Iroquois, no doubt helping to offset the depletion of resources near the village of the would-be protectors. The price of protection went further than this, though; it included constant and public ceremonial deference to the Iroquois, free passage for

In Ethiopia, as in many former colonial possessions, war has become a common phenomenon as governments controlled by one ethnic group seek to impose their control over other previously autonomous ethnic groups in order to gain access to their resources and labor.

their war parties through the subjugated group's country, and the contribution of young men to Iroquoian war parties.

A comparison between the Iroquois and Europeans is also instructive. Sometime in the sixteenth century, five Iroquoian tribes — the Mohawks, Oneidas, Onondagas, Cayugas, and Senecas — determined to bring to an end warfare among themselves by the simple device of directing their predatory activities against outsiders, rather than each other. In this way the famous League of the Iroquois came into being. Similarly, in the year 1095, Pope Urban II launched the Crusades with a speech in which he urged European barons to bring to an end their ceaseless wars against each other by directing their hostilities outward, against the Turks and Arabs. In that same speech he also alluded to the economic benefits to be realized by seizing the resources of the infidels. Although rationalized as a "holy war," the Crusades clearly were motivated by more than religious ideology.

Although the Europeans never did "liberate" the Holy Land, at least some of them did benefit from the booty obtained in battle, lending credence to the idea that people could live better than they had before by locating and seizing the resources of others. Thus, the state formation that took place in Europe in the centuries after A.D. 1000 was followed by colonial expansion into other parts of the world. Proceeding apace with this growth and outward expansion was the development of the technology and organization of warfare.

The idea that warfare is an acceptable way to bring about economic benefits is still a part of the European cultural tradition, as the following from a letter that appeared in New Hampshire's largest daily newspaper a few years ago illustrates: "If a war is necessary to stabilize the economy, then we shall have a war. It affects the everyday lives of most of us so little that we need hardly acknowledge the fact that it is going on. Surely the sacrifice of a son, husband or father by a hundred or so of our citizens every week is not that overwhelming. They will forget their losses in time."[21] Certainly, we would like to think that this kind of attitude has become relatively rare in our country, and perhaps it has, but we do not know this for a fact. Nor do we really know the extent to which it is or is not held by members of those segments of our society that tend to be influential in the setting of public policy. These are obviously important questions, and we need to find out more about them.

As the above examples illustrate, the causes of warfare are complex; economic, political, and ideological factors are all involved. With the emergence of states (not just in Europe, but in other parts of the world as well) has gone an increase in the scale of warfare. Perhaps this is not surprising, given the state's acceptance of force as a legitimate tool to use in the regulation of human affairs and its ability to organize large numbers of people. In the modern world, we are as far (if not farther) from the elimination of war as humanity ever has been; value systems would seem to be as crucial as any other element in the existence of warfare.

[21]Quoted in Robert MacNeil, *The Right Place at the Right Time* (Boston: Little, Brown, 1982), p. 263.

POLITICAL SYSTEMS AND THE QUESTION OF LEGITIMACY

Whatever form the political system of a society may take, and however it may go about its business, it must always find some way to obtain the people's allegiance. In decentralized systems, in which every adult participates in the making of all decisions, loyalty and cooperation are freely given, since each person is considered to be a part of the political system. As the group grows larger, however, and the organization becomes more formal, the problems of obtaining and keeping public support become greater.

In centralized political systems, increased reliance is placed upon coercion as a means of social control. This, however, tends to lessen the effectiveness of a political system. For example, the staff needed to apply force must often be large and may itself grow to be a political entity. The emphasis on force may also create resentment on the part of those to whom it is applied and so lessens cooperation. Thus, police states are generally short-lived; most societies choose less extreme forms of social coercion.

Also basic to the political process is the concept of legitimacy, or the right of political leaders to rule. Like force, legitimacy is a form of support for a political system; unlike force, legitimacy is based on the values a particular society believes most important. For example, among the Kapauku the legitimacy of the *tonowi's* power comes from his wealth; the kings of Hawaii, and England and France before their revolutions, were thought to have a divine right to rule; the head of the Dahomey state of West Africa acquires legitimacy through his age, as he is always the oldest living male.

Legitimacy grants the right to hold, use, and allocate power. Power based on legitimacy may be distinguished from power based on force: obedience to the former results from the belief that obedience is "right"; compliance to power based on force is the result of fear of the deprivation of liberty, physical well-being, life, and material property. Thus, power based on legitimacy is symbolic and depends not upon any intrinsic value, but upon the positive expectations of those who recognize and accede to it. If the expectations are not met regularly (if the head of state fails to deliver "economic prosperity" or the leader is continuously unsuccessful in preventing horse or camel theft), the legitimacy of the recognized power figure is minimized and may eventually collapse altogether.

RELIGION AND POLITICS

Religion is intricately connected with politics. Religious beliefs may influence laws: acts that people believe to be sinful, such as sodomy and incest, are often illegal as well. Frequently it is religion that legitimizes government.

In both industrial and nonindustrial societies, belief in the supernatural is important and is reflected in the governments of the people. The effect of religion on politics is perhaps best exemplified in medieval Europe. Holy wars were fought over the smallest matter; immense cathedrals were built in honor of the Virgin and other saints; kings and queens pledged allegiance to the pope and asked his blessing in all important ventures, were they marital or martial. In the pre-Columbian Americas the Aztec state was a religious state, or theocracy, which thrived in spite of more or less constant warfare carried out to procure captives for human sacrifices to assuage or please the gods. In Peru the Inca emperor proclaimed absolute authority based on the proposition that he was descended from the sun god. In modern Iran the head of state is the most holy of all Shiite Moslem holy men. In our own country the Declaration of Independence, which is an expression of the social and political beliefs of the United States, stresses a belief in a supreme being. The document states that "all men are created [by God] equal," a tenet that gave rise to our form of democracy, because it implied that all people should participate in governing themselves. The fact that the president of the United States takes the oath of office by swear-

In the United States, in spite of an official separation of church and state, the president is always sworn in over a Christian bible.

ing on the Bible is another instance of the use of religion to legitimize political power, as is the phrase "one nation, under God" in our Pledge of Allegiance. On our coins is the phrase "In God We Trust," and many meetings of government bodies begin with a prayer or invocation. In spite of our official separation of church and state, religious legitimization of government lingers on.

CHAPTER SUMMARY

Through political organization, societies maintain social order, manage public affairs, and reduce social disorder. No group can live together without persuading or coercing its members to conform to agreed-upon rules of conduct. To understand properly the political organization of a society, one needs to view it in the light of its ecological, social, and ideological context.

Four basic types of political systems may be identified. In order of complexity, these range from decentralized bands and tribes to centralized chiefdoms and states. The band, characteristic of food-foraging and some other nomadic societies, is a small autonomous group of associated families or kin occupying a common territory. Political organization in bands is democratic, and informal social control is exerted by public opinion in the form of gossip and ridicule. Band leaders are older men, or occasionally women, whose personal authority lasts only as long as members believe they are leading well and making the right decisions.

The tribe is composed of separate bands or other social units that are brought together by such unifying factors as descent, age grading, or common interest. With an economy usually based on farming or herding, the population of the tribe is larger than that of the band, although family units within the tribe are still relatively autonomous and egalitarian. As in the band, political organization is transitory, and leaders have no formal means of maintaining authority.

Many tribal societies vest political authority in the clan, an association of people who believe themselves to be descended from a common ancestor. A group of elders or headmen regulate the affairs of members and represent their group in relations with other clans. The segmentary lineage system, similar in operation to the clan, is a rare form of tribal organization based on kinship bond. Tribal age-grade systems cut across territorial and kin groupings. Leadership is vested in men in the group who were initiated into the age grade at the same time and passed as a set from one age grade to another until reaching the proper age to become elders.

Common-interest associations wield political authority in some tribes. A boy joins one club or another when he reaches warrior status. These organizations administer the affairs of the tribe. Another variant of authority in tribes in Melanesia is the Big Man, who builds up his wealth and political power until he must be reckoned with as a leader.

As societies become more heterogeneous socially, politically, and economically, leadership becomes more centralized. Chiefdoms are ranked societies in which every member has a position in the hierarchy. Status is determined by the position of an individual's descent group. Power is concentrated in a single chief whose true authority serves to unite his community in all matters. The chief may accumulate great personal wealth, which enhances his power base, and pass it on to his heirs.

The most formal of political organizations is the state. It has a central power that can legitimately use force to administer a rigid code of laws and to maintain order, even beyond its borders. A large bureaucracy functions to uphold the authority of the central power. The state is found only in societies with numerous diverse groups. Typically, it is a stratified society, and economic functions and wealth are distributed unequally. Although thought of as being stable and permanent, it is, in fact, inherently unstable and transitory.

Historically women have rarely held important positions of political leadership, and when they have, it has sometimes been for lack of a qualified man to hold the position. Nonetheless, in a number of societies, women have enjoyed political equality with men, as among the Iroquoian tribes of New York State. Among them, all men held office at the pleasure of women, who not only appointed them but could remove them as well. Among the Igbo of midwestern Nigeria, women held positions in an administrative hierarchy that paralleled and balanced that of the men. Under centralized political systems, women are most apt to be subordinate to men, and when states impose their control on societies marked by sexual egalitarianism, the relationship changes to one in which men dominate women.

There are two kinds of social controls, internalized and externalized. Internalized controls are self-imposed by guilty individuals. These built-in controls, which include morality, rely on such deterrents as personal shame, fear of divine punishment, or magical retaliation. Although bands and tribes rely heavily upon them, internalized controls are generally insufficient by themselves. Every society develops externalized controls, called sanctions. Positive sanctions, in the form of awards or recognition by one's neighbors, reinforce the position that a society, or a number of its members, takes toward behavior that is approved; negative sanctions, such as threat of imprisonment, corporal punishment, or "loss of face," reflect societal reactions to behavior that is disapproved.

Sanctions may also be classified as either formal, involving actual laws, or informal, involving norms but not legal statutes. Formal sanctions are organized and reward or punish behavior through a rigidly regulated social procedure. Informal sanctions are diffuse, involving immediate reactions of approval or disapproval by individual community members to one of their compatriot's behavior. Other important agents of social control are witchcraft beliefs and religious sanctions.

Sanctions serve to formalize conformity to group norms, including actual law, and to maintain each social faction in a community in its "proper" place. Some anthropologists have proposed that to define law is an impossible and perhaps undesirable undertaking. In considering law it appears best to examine each society within its unique cultural context.

Law serves several basic functions. First, it defines relationships among the members of a society and thereby dictates proper behavior under different circumstances. Second, law allocates authority to employ coercion in the enforcement of sanctions. In centralized political systems this authority rests with the government and court system. Decentralized societies may give this authority directly to the injured party. Third, law redefines social relations and aids its own efficient operation by ensuring that there is room for change.

Western societies clearly distinguish offenses against the state, called crimes, from offenses against an individual, called torts. Decentralized societies may view all offenses as against individuals. One way to understand the nature of law is to analyze individual dispute cases against their own cultural background. A dispute may be settled in two ways, negotiation and adjudication. All societies use negotiation to settle individual disputes. In negotiation the parties to the dispute themselves reach an agreement, with or without the help of a third party. In adjudication, not found in some societies, an authorized third party issues a binding decision. The disputing parties present their petitions but play no part in the decision making.

In addition to regulating internal affairs, political systems also attempt to regulate external affairs, or relations among politically autonomous units. In doing so they may resort to the threat or use of force.

War is not a universal phenomenon, since there are societies that do not practice warfare as we know it. Usually these societies are those that have some kind of naturalistic world view, an attitude that until recently had become nearly extinguished in modern industrial societies.

A major problem faced by any form of political organization is obtaining and maintaining people's loyalty and support. Reliance on force and coercion in the long run usually tends to lessen the effectiveness of a political system. A basic instrument of political implementation is legitimacy, or the right of political leaders to exercise authority. Power based on legitimacy stems from the belief of a society's members that obedience is "right," and therefore from the positive expectations of those who obey. It may be distinguished from compliance based on force, which stems from fear, and thus from negative expectations.

Religion is so intricately woven into the life of the people in both industrial and nonindustrial countries that its presence is inevitably felt in the political sphere. To a greater or lesser extent, most governments the world over use religion to legitimize political power.

SUGGESTED READINGS

Bohannan, Paul, ed. *Law and Warfare, Studies in the Anthropology of Conflict.* Garden City, N.Y.: Natural History Press, 1967. Examples of various ways in which conflict is evaluated and handled in different cultures are brought together in this book. It examines institutions and means of conflict resolution, including courts, middlemen, self-help, wager of battle, contest, and ordeal. It also has a selection discussing war — raids, organization for aggression, tactics, and feuds.

Cohen, Ronald, and John Middleton, eds. *Comparative Political Systems.* Garden City, N.Y.: Natural History Press, 1967. The editors have selected some 20 studies in the politics of nonindustrial societies by such well-known scholars as Lévi-Strauss, S. F. Nadel, Marshall Sahlins, and S. N. Eisenstadt.

Fried, Morton. *The Evolution of Political Society: An Essay in Political Anthropology.* New York: Random House, 1967. The author attempts to trace the evolution of political society through a study of simple, egalitarian societies. The character of the state and the means whereby this form of organization takes shape are considered in terms of pristine and secondary states, formed because preexisting states supplied the stimuli or models for organization.

Gordon, Robert J., and Mervyn J. Meggitt. *Law and Order in the New Guinea Highlands.* Hanover, N.H.: University Press of New England, 1985. This ethnographic study of the resurgence of tribal fighting among the Mae-Enga addresses two issues of major importance in today's world: the changing nature of law and order in the Third World and the nature of violence in human societies.

Krader, Lawrence. *Formation of the State.* Englewood Cliffs, N.J.: Prentice-Hall, 1968. This book describes the characteristics of the state type of political organization in the process of trying to account for the way (or ways) in which states develop.

Nader, Laura, ed. *No Access to Law: Alternatives to the American Judicial System.* New York: Academic Press, 1980. This is an eye-opening study of how consumer complaints are resolved in our society. After ten years of study, Nader found repeated and documented offenses by business that cannot be handled by present complaint mechanisms, either in or out of court. The high cost exacted includes a terrible sense of apathy and loss of faith in the system itself.

22

RELIGION AND MAGIC

Ritual is religion in action, and the making of offerings is a common form of ritual. These Maya Indians are sacrificing a chicken at Chichicastenango, Guatemala.

PREVIEW

What Is Religion?

Religion may be regarded as the beliefs and patterns of behavior by which humans try to deal with what they view as important problems that cannot be solved through the application of known technology or techniques of organization. To overcome these limitations, people turn to the manipulation of supernatural beings and powers.

What Are Religion's Identifying Features?

Religion consists of various rituals — prayers, songs, dances, offerings, and sacrifices — through which people try to manipulate supernatural beings and powers to their advantage. These beings and powers may consist of gods and goddesses, ancestral and other spirits, or impersonal powers, either by themselves or in various combinations. In all societies there are certain individuals especially skilled at dealing with these beings and powers, who assist other members of society in their ritual activities. A body of myths rationalizes, or "explains," the system in a manner consistent with people's experience in the world in which they live.

What Functions Does Religion Serve?

Whether or not a particular religion accomplishes what people believe it does, all religions serve a number of important psychological and social functions. They reduce anxiety by explaining the unknown and making it understandable, as well as provide comfort in the belief that supernatural aid is available in times of crisis. They sanction a wide range of human conduct by providing notions of right and wrong, setting precedents for acceptable behavior, and transferring the burden of decision making from individuals to supernatural powers. Through ritual, religion may be used to enhance the learning of oral traditions. Finally, religion plays an important role in maintaining social solidarity.

According to their origin myth, the Tewa Indians of New Mexico emerged from a lake far to the north of where they now live. Once on dry land, they divided into two groups, the Summer People and the Winter People, and migrated south along the Rio Grande. During their travels they made 12 stops before finally being reunited into a single community.

For the Tewa all existence is divided into six categories, three human and three supernatural. Each of the human categories, which are arranged in a hierarchy, is matched by a spiritual category, so that when people die, they immediately pass into their proper spiritual role. Not only are the supernatural categories identified with human categories; they also correspond to divisions in the natural world.

To those of some other religious persuasion, such beliefs may seem, at best, irrational and arbitrary, but in fact they are neither. Alfonso Ortiz, an anthropologist who is also a Tewa, points out that his native religion not only is logical and socially functional, but is the very model of Tewa society.[1] These people have a society that is divided into two independent moieties, each having its own economy, rituals, and authority. The individual is introduced into one of these moieties (which in this case are *not* based on kinship), and his or her membership is regularly reinforced through a series of life-cycle rituals that correspond to the stops on the mythical tribal journey down the Rio Grande. The rites of birth and death are shared by the whole community; other rites differ in the two moieties. The highest status of the human hierarchy belongs to the priests, who also help integrate this divided society; they mediate not only between the human and spiritual world but between the two moieties as well.

Tewa religion enters into virtually every aspect of Tewa life and society. It is the basis of the simultaneously dualistic/unified world view of the individual Tewa. It provides numerous points of mediation through which the two moieties can continue to exist together as a single community. It sanctifies the community by linking its origin with the realm of the supernatural, and it offers divine sanction to those "rites of passage" that soften life's major transitions. In providing an afterworld that is the mirror image of human society, it answers the question of death in a manner that reinforces social structure. In short, Tewa religion, by weaving all elements of Tewa experience into a single pattern, gives a solid foundation to the stability and continuity of their society.

All religions fulfill numerous social and psychological needs. Some of these — the need to confront and explain death, for example — appear to be universal; indeed, we know of no group of people anywhere on the face of the earth who, at any time over the past 100,000 years, have been without religion. Unbound by time, religion gives meaning to individual and group life, drawing power from "the time of the gods in the Beginning" and offering continuity of existence beyond death. It can provide the path by which people transcend their arduous earthly existence and attain, if only momentarily, spiritual selfhood. The social functions of religion are no less important than the psychological functions. A traditional religion reinforces group norms, provides moral sanctions for individual conduct, and furnishes the substratum of common purpose and values upon which the equilibrium of the community depends.

In the nineteenth century the European intellectual tradition gave rise to the idea that science would ultimately destroy religion by showing people the irrationality of their myths and rituals. Indeed, many still believe that as scientific explanations replace those of religion, the latter should wither on the vine. An opposite tendency has occurred, however; not only do traditional, "main line" religions continue to attract new adherents, but there has been a strong resurgence of fundamentalist religions. Examples include the Islamic fundamentalism of the Ayatollah Khomeini in Iran and, in the United States, the Christian fundamentalism of Jerry Falwell and others, with its marked

---

[1]Alfonso Ortiz, *The Tewa World* (Chicago: University of Chicago Press, 1969), p. 43.

Far from causing the death of religion, the growth of scientific knowledge, by producing new anxieties and raising new questions about human existence, may have contributed to the continuing presence of religion in modern life. North Americans continue to participate in traditional religions, such as Judaism (top left), as well as imported sects, such as Hare Krishna (right), and evangelism (bottom left).

antiscience bias.[2] Moreover, interest in astrology and occultism continues to be strong in North America, and there are new religious options, such as sects derived from eastern religions.

Science, far from destroying religion, may have contributed to the creation of a veritable religious boom. It has done this by removing many traditional psychological props, while at the same time creating, in its technological applications, a host of

new problems — threat of nuclear catastrophe, health threats from pollution, fear of loneliness in a society that isolates us from our kin and that places impediments in the way of establishing deep and lasting friendships, to list but a few that people must now deal with. In the face of these new anxieties, religion offers social and psychological support.

The continuing strength of religion in the face of Western rationalism clearly reveals that it is a powerful and dynamic force in society. Although anthropologists are not qualified to pass judgment on the metaphysical truth of any particular religion, they can attempt to show how each religion

[2]Richard J. Norelli and Robert R. Proulx, "Anti-Science as a Component in the Growing Popularity of Scientific Creationism," and Kenneth R. Stunkel, "Understanding Scientific Creationism," in *Confronting the Creationists*, ed. Stephen Pastner and William A. Haviland, *Northeastern Anthropological Association Occasional Proceedings* 1 (1982): 4–11, 51–60.

embodies a number of "truths" about humans and society.

THE ANTHROPOLOGICAL APPROACH TO RELIGION

Anthony F. C. Wallace has defined religion as "a set of rituals, rationalized by myth, which mobilizes supernatural powers for the purpose of achieving or preventing transformations of state in man and nature."[3] What lies behind this definition is a recognition that people, when they cannot deal with serious problems that cause them anxiety through technological or organizational means, try to do so through the manipulation of supernatural beings and powers. This requires ritual, which Wallace sees as the primary phenomenon of religion, or "religion in action." Its major function is to reduce anxiety and keep confidence high, all of which serves to keep people in some sort of shape to cope with reality. It is this that gives religion survival value.

Religion, then, may be regarded as the beliefs and patterns of behavior by which people try to control the area of the universe that is otherwise beyond their control. Since no known culture, our own included, has achieved complete certainty in controlling the universe, religion is a part of all known cultures. There is, however, considerable variability here. At one end of the human spectrum are food-foraging peoples, whose technological ability to manipulate their environment is limited, and who tend to see themselves more as part, rather than masters, of nature. This is what we referred to in Chapter 21 as a naturalistic world view. Among food foragers, religion is apt to be inseparable from the rest of daily life. At the other end of the human spectrum is Western civilization, with its ideological commitment to overcoming problems through technological and organizational skills. Here religion is less a part of daily activities and is restricted to more specific occasions. Even so, there is variation. Religious activity may be less

[3]Anthony F. C. Wallace, *Religion: An Anthropological View* (New York: Random House, 1966), p. 107.

prominent in the lives of social elites, who see themselves as more in control of their own destinies, than it is in the lives of peasants or members of lower classes. Among the latter, religion may afford some compensation for a dependent status in society. On the other hand, religion is still important to elite members of society, in that it rationalizes the system in such a way that people are less likely to question the existing social order. After all, if there is hope for a better existence after death, then one may be more willing to put up with the difficulties of this life. Thus, religious beliefs serve to influence and perpetuate conceptions, if not actual relations, between different classes of people.

THE PRACTICE OF RELIGION

Much of the value of religion comes from the activities called for by its practice. Participation in religious ceremonies may bring a sense of personal transcendence, a wave of reassurance, security, and even ecstasy, or a feeling of closeness to fellow participants. Although the rituals and practices of religions vary considerably, even those rites that seem to us most bizarrely exotic can be shown to serve the same basic social and psychological functions.

SUPERNATURAL BEINGS AND POWERS

One of the hallmarks of religion is a belief in supernatural beings and forces. In attempting to control by religious means what cannot be controlled in other ways, humans turn to prayer, sacrifice, and ritual activity in general. This presupposes a world of supernatural beings that have an interest in human affairs and to whom appeals for aid may be directed. For convenience we may divide these beings into three categories: major deities (gods and goddesses), ancestral spirits, and nonhuman spirit beings. Although the variety of deities and spirits recognized by the world's cultures is tremendous, certain generalizations about them are possible.

The people of Bali believe in the existence of three worlds: an upper one inhabited by gods, a middle one inhabited by people, and a lower one inhabited by demons. Elaborate rituals are the means by which the people keep the inhabitants of all three worlds in balance.

Gods and Goddesses

Gods and goddesses are the great and more remote beings. They are usually seen as controlling the universe, or if several are recognized, each has charge of a particular part of the universe. Such was the case of the gods and goddesses of ancient Greece: Zeus was lord of the sky, Poseidon was ruler of the sea, and Hades was lord of the underworld and ruler of the dead. Besides these three brothers, there were a host of other deities, female as well as male, each similarly concerned with specific aspects of life and the universe. **Pantheons,** or collections of gods and goddesses such as those of the Greeks, are common in non-Western states as well. Since states have frequently grown through conquest, their pantheons often have developed as local deities of conquered peoples were incorporated into the national pantheon. Usually, creators of the present world are included, though this was not the case with the Greeks. Another frequent though not invariable feature of pantheons is the presence of a supreme deity, who may be all but totally ignored by humans. For example, the Aztecs of Mexico recognized a supreme pair, but, logically enough, they did not pay much attention to them. After all, being so remote, they were un-

Pantheon: The several gods and goddesses of a people.

likely to be interested in human affairs. Hence, attention was focused on those deities who were more directly concerned in human matters.

Whether or not a people recognize gods, goddesses, or both has to do with how men and women relate to one another in everyday life. Generally speaking, in societies in which women are subordinate to men, the godhead is defined in exclusively masculine terms. Such societies are generally those with economies based upon the herding of animals or intensive agriculture carried out by men, who, as fathers, are distant and controlling figures to their children. Goddesses, by contrast, are found in societies in which women make a major contribution to the economy and enjoy relative equality with men, and in which men are more involved in their children's lives. Such societies are apt to be those that depend upon farming, much or all of which is done by women. As an illustration, the early Hebrews, like other pastoral nomadic tribes of the Middle East, described their god in masculine, authoritarian terms. By contrast, goddesses played central roles in religious ritual and popular consciousness of the agricultural peoples of the region. Associated with these goddesses were concepts of light, love, fertility, and procreation. Around 1300 B.C., the Hebrew tribes entered the land of Canaan and began to practice agriculture, whereupon they had to establish a new kind of relationship with the soil. As they became dependent upon rainfall and on the rotation of the seasons for crops and became concerned about fertility (as the Canaanites already were), they adopted many of the Canaanite goddess cults. Although diametrically opposed to the original Hebrew cult, belief in the Canaanite goddesses catered to the human desire for security by seeking to control the forces of fertility in the interest of peoples' well-being.

Later on, when the Israelite tribes sought national unity in the face of a military threat by the Philistines, and they strengthened their identity as

The patriarchal nature of Western society is expressed in its theology, in which a masculine God gives life to the first man, as depicted here on the ceiling of the Sistine chapel. Only after this is the first woman created, from the first man.

a "chosen people," the goddess cults lost out to followers of the old, masculine tribal god. This ancient masculine–authoritarian concept of god has been perpetuated down to the present, not just in the Judaic tradition, but also in Christianity and Islam, whose religions stem from the old Hebrew religion. As a consequence, this masculine–authoritarian model has played an important role in perpetuating a relationship between men and women in which the latter traditionally have been

expected to submit to the "rule" of men at every level of Jewish, Christian, and Islamic society.

Ancestral Spirits

A belief in ancestral spirits is consistent with the widespread notion that human beings are made up of two parts, a body and some kind of vital spirit. For example, the Penobscot Indians, whom we met in Chapter 14, maintained that each person had a vital spirit that could even detach itself and travel about apart from the body, while the latter remained inert. Given some such concept, the idea of the spirit being freed by death from the body and having a continued existence seems logical enough.

Where a belief in ancestral spirits exists, these beings are frequently seen as retaining an active interest and even membership in society. In the last chapter, for instance, we saw how ghost ancestors of the Wape acted to provide or withhold meat from their living descendants. Like living persons, ancestral spirits may be benevolent or malevolent, but one is never quite sure what their behavior will be. The same feeling of uncertainty — how will they react to what I have done? — may be displayed toward ancestral spirits that tends to be displayed to those of a senior generation who hold authority over the individual. Beyond this, ancestral spirits closely resemble living humans in appetites, feelings, emotions, and behavior. Thus, they reflect and reinforce social reality.

A belief in ancestral spirits of one sort or another is found in many parts of the world. In several African societies, however, the concept is particularly well developed. Here one frequently finds ancestral spirits behaving just like humans. They are able to feel hot, cold, and pain, and they may be capable of dying a second death by drowning or burning. They may even participate in family and lineage affairs, and seats will be provided for them, even though the spirits are invisible. If they are annoyed, they may send sickness or even death. Eventually, they are reborn as new members of their lineage; and in societies that hold such beliefs, there is a need to observe infants closely in order to determine just who it is that has been reborn.

Deceased ancestors were also important in the patrilineal society of traditional China. For the gift of life, a boy was forever indebted to his parents, owing them obedience, deference, and a comfortable old age. Even after their death, he had to provide for them in the spirit world, offering food, money, and incense to them on the anniversaries of their births and deaths. In addition, collective

> **Animism:** A belief in spirit beings, which are thought to animate nature.

worship of all lineage ancestors was carried out periodically throughout the year. Even the birth of sons was regarded as an obligation to the ancestors, as this ensured that their needs would continue to be attended to even after their sons' own death. To satisfy the needs of ancestors for descendants (and a man's own need to be respectable in a culture that demanded that he satisfy their needs) a man would go so far as to marry a girl who had been adopted into his family as an infant, in order to be raised as a dutiful wife for him, even when this arrangement went against the wishes of both parties. Furthermore, a man would readily force his daughter to marry a man against her will. In fact, a woman was raised to be cast out by her natal family, and yet might not find acceptance in her husband's family for years. Not until after death, when her soul was carried in a tablet and placed in the shrine of her husband's family, was she an official member of it. As a consequence, once a son was born to her, a woman worked long and hard to establish the strongest possible tie between herself and her son to ensure that she would be looked after in life.

Strong beliefs in ancestral spirits are particularly appropriate in a society of descent-based groups with their associated ancestor orientation. More than this, though, they provide a strong sense of continuity in which past, present, and future are all linked.

Animism

One of the most widespread beliefs about supernatural beings is **animism,** which sees nature as animated by all sorts of spirits. In reality, the term masks a wide range of variation. Animals and plants, like humans, may all have their individual spirits, as may springs, mountains, and other natural features. So too may stones, weapons, ornaments, and so on. In addition, the woods may be full of a variety of unattached or free-ranging spir-

Sir Edward B. Tylor (1832–1917)

The concept of animism was first brought to the attention of anthropologists by the British scholar Sir Edward B. Tylor. Though not university-educated himself, Tylor was the first person to hold a chair in anthropology at a British university, with his appointment first as lecturer, then reader, and finally (in 1895) professor at Oxford. His interest in anthropology developed as a consequence of travels that took him as a young man to the United States (where he visited an Indian Pueblo), Cuba, and Mexico, where he was especially impressed by the achievements of the ancient Aztec and the contemporary blend of Indian and Spanish culture.

Tylor's numerous publications ranged over such diverse topics as the possible historical connection between the games of pachisi and patolli (played in India and ancient Mexico), the origin of games of Cat's Cradle, and the structural connections between post-marital residence, descent, and certain other customs such as in-law avoidance and the couvade (the confinement of a child's father following birth). It was also Tylor who formulated the first widely accepted definition of culture (see Chapter 12). The considerable attention paid to religious concepts and practices in his writings stemmed from a lifelong commitment to combat the idea, still widely held in his time, that so-called savage people had degenerated more than civilized people from an original state of grace. To Tylor, "savages" were intellectuals just like anyone else, grappling with their problems, but handicapped (as was Tylor in his intellectual life) by limited information.

---

its. The various spirits involved are a highly diverse lot. Generally speaking, though, they are closer to people than gods and goddesses and are more involved in daily affairs. They may be benevolent, malevolent, or just plain neutral. They may also be awesome, terrifying, lovable, or even mischievous. Since they may be pleased or irritated by human actions, people are obliged to be concerned with them.

Animism is typical of those who see themselves as being a part of nature rather than superior to it. This takes in most food foragers, as well as those food-producing peoples who recognize little difference between a human life and that of any growing thing. Among them, gods and goddesses are relatively unimportant, but the woods are full of all sorts of spirits. (For a good example, see the discussion of the Penobscot behavioral environment in Chapter 14.) Gods and goddesses, if they exist at all, may be seen as having created the world, and perhaps making it fit to live in; but it is

spirits to whom one turns for curing, who help or hinder the shaman, and whom the ordinary hunter may meet in the woods.

Animatism

While supernatural power is often thought of as being vested in supernatural beings, it doesn't have to be. The Melanesians, for example, think of *mana* as a force inherent in all objects. It is not in itself physical, but it can reveal itself physically. A warrior's success in fighting is not attributed to his own strength but to the *mana* contained in an amulet that hangs around his neck. Similarly, a farmer may know a great deal about horticulture, soil conditioning, and the correct time for sowing and harvesting, but nevertheless depend upon *mana* for a successful crop, often building a simple altar to this power at the end of the field. If the crop is good, it is a sign that the farmer has in some way appropriated the necessary *mana*. Far from being a personalized force, *mana* is abstract in the extreme, a power lying always just beyond reach of the senses. As R. H. Codrington described it, "virtue, prestige, authority, good fortune, influence, sanctity, luck are all words which, under certain conditions, give something near the meaning. . . . *Mana* sometimes means a more than natural virtue or power attaching to some person or thing."[4] This concept of impersonal power was also widespread among North American Indians. The Iroquois called it *orenda*; to the Sioux it was *wakonda*; to the Algonquians, *manitu*. Though found on every continent, the concept is not necessarily universal, however. R. R. Marett called this concept of impersonal power **animatism.** The two concepts, animatism (which is inanimate) and animism (a belief in spirit beings), are not mutually exclusive. They are often found in the same culture, as in Melanesia, and also in the Indian societies mentioned above.

People trying to comprehend beliefs in supernatural beings and powers frequently ask how such beliefs are maintained. In part, the answer is through manifestations of power. By this is meant that, given a belief in animatism and/or the powers of supernatural beings, one is predisposed to see what appear to be results of the application of such powers. For example, if a Melanesian warrior is convinced of his power because of his possession of the necessary *mana*, and he is successful, he may very well interpret this success as proof of the power of *mana*. "After all, I would have lost had I not possessed it, wouldn't I?" Beyond this, because of his confidence in his *mana*, he may be less timid in his fighting, and this could indeed mean the difference between success or failure.

Failures, of course, do occur, but they can be explained. Perhaps one's prayer was not answered because a deity or spirit was still angry about some past insult. Or perhaps our Melanesian warrior lost his battle because he was not as successful in bringing *mana* to bear as he thought, or else his opponent had more of it. In any case, humans generally emphasize successes over failures, and long

[4]Quoted by Godfrey Leinhardt in "Religion," in *Man, Culture, and Society,* 2d ed., ed. Harry L. Shapiro (New York: Oxford University Press, 1971), p. 388.

| **Animatism:** A belief that the world is animated by impersonal supernatural powers.

after many of the latter have been forgotten, tales will probably still be told of striking cases of the workings of supernatural powers.

Another feature that tends to perpetuate beliefs in supernatural beings is that they have attributes with which people are familiar. Allowing for the fact that supernatural beings are in a sense larger than life, they are generally conceived of as living the way people do and as being interested in the same sorts of things. For example, the Penobscot Indians believed in a quasi-human being called Gluskabe. Like ordinary mortals, Gluskabe traveled about in a canoe, used snowshoes, lived in a wigwam, and made stone arrowheads. The gods and goddesses of the ancient Greeks had all the familiar human lusts and jealousies. Such features serve to make supernatural beings believable.

The role of mythology in maintaining beliefs should not be overlooked. Myths, which are discussed in some detail in Chapter 23, are explanatory tales that rationalize religious beliefs and practices. To us the word *myth* immediately conjures up the idea of a story about imaginary events, but the people responsible for a particular myth usually don't see it that way. To them myths are true stories, analogous to historical documents in our culture. Myths invariably are full of accounts of the doings of various supernatural beings. Hence, they serve to reinforce beliefs in them.

RELIGIOUS SPECIALISTS

Priests and Priestesses

In all human societies there exist individuals whose job it is to guide and supplement the religious practices of others. Such individuals are highly skilled at contacting and influencing supernatural beings and manipulating supernatural forces. Their qualification for this is that they have undergone special training. In addition, they may display certain distinctive personality traits that particularly suit them for their job. In societies with the

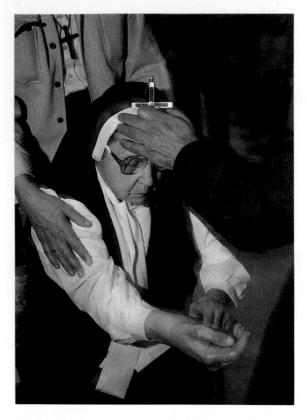

Faith healers, such as the one shown here, conform in every respect to our definition of the shaman. Thus, shamanism is by no means absent in modern, industrial societies.

Priest or priestess: A full-time religious specialist.

Shaman: A person who has special religious power acquired through his or her own initiative and is thought to possess certain special abilities to deal with supernatural beings and powers.

resources to support full-time occupational specialists, the role of guiding religious practices and influencing the supernaturals belongs to the **priest or priestess.** He or she is the socially initiated, ceremonially inducted member of a recognized religious organization, with a rank and function that belong to him or her as the tenant of an office held before by others. The sources of power are the society and the institution in which the priest or priestess functions. The priest, if not the priestess, is a familiar figure in our own society; he is the priest, minister, pastor, rector, rabbi, or whatever the official title may be in some organized religion. With their god defined in masculine, authoritarian terms, it was not surprising that the most impor-

tant religious positions in the Judaic, Christian, and Islamic religions have traditionally been filled by men. Only in societies in which women make a major contribution to the economy, and which recognize goddesses as well as gods, are female religious specialists likely to be found.

Shamans

Even in societies that lack full-time occupational specialization, there have always been individuals who have acquired religious power individually, usually in solitude and isolation, when the Great Spirit, the Power, the Great Mystery, or whatever is revealed to them. Such persons become the recipients of certain special gifts, such as healing or divination; when they return to society, they are frequently given another kind of religious role, that of the **shaman.**

In the United States millions of people have learned something about shamans through their reading of the popular autobiography of Black Elk, a traditional Sioux Indian "medicine man," or Carlos Castaneda's apparently fictional accounts of his experiences with Don Juan, the Yaqui Indian shaman. Few of them may realize, however, that the faith healers and many other evangelists in their own society conform in every respect to our definition of the shaman. Thus, one should not get the idea that shamans are not to be found in modern, industrial societies, for they are. Furthermore, they may become more common, given the current revival of interest in the occult and supernatural that is taking place in the United States.

Typically, one becomes a shaman by passing through stages commonly related by many myths. These stages are often thought to involve torture and violent dismemberment of the body; scraping away of the flesh until the body is reduced to a skeleton; substitution of the viscera and renewal of the blood; a period spent in a nether region, or land of the dead, during which the shaman is taught by the souls of dead shamans and other spirit beings; and an ascent to a sky realm. Among the Crow Indians, for example, any man could become a shaman, since there was no ecclesiastical organization that handed down laws for the guidance of the religious consciousness. The search for shamanistic visions was pursued by most adult Crow males, who would engage in bodily deprivation, even self-torture, to induce such visions. The majority of seekers would not be granted a vision, but failure carried no social stigma. While those who claimed supernatural vision would be expected to manifest some special power in battle or wealth, it was the sincerity of the seeker that carried the essential truth of the experience. Many of the elements of shamanism, such as transvestitism, trance states, and speaking in undecipherable languages, can just as easily be regarded as abnormalities, and it has been frequently pointed out that those regarded as specially gifted in some societies would be outcasts or worse in others. The position

of shaman can provide a socially approved role for what in other circumstances might be unstable personalities.

The shaman is essentially a religious entrepreneur, who acts for some human client. On behalf of the client, the shaman intervenes to influence or impose his or her will on supernatural powers. The shaman can be contrasted with the priest or priestess, whose "clients" are the deities. Priests and priestesses frequently tell people what to do; the shaman tells supernaturals what to do. In return for services rendered, the shaman may collect a fee — fresh meat, yams, a favorite possession. In some cases, the added prestige, authority, and social power attached to the status of shaman are reward enough.

When a shaman acts for a client, he or she may put on something of a show — one in which the basic drama is heightened by a sense of danger. An example of this is afforded by the following discussion of healing among the !Kung of Africa's Kalahari Desert.

ORIGINAL STUDY
Healing among the !Kung[5]

One way the spirits affect humans is by shooting them with invisible arrows carrying disease, death, or misfortune. If the arrows can be warded off, illness will not take hold. If illness has already penetrated, the arrows must be removed to enable the sick person to recover. An ancestral spirit may exercise this power against the living if a person is not being treated well by others. If people argue with her frequently, if her husband shows how little he values her by carrying on blatant affairs, or if people refuse to cooperate or share with her, the spirit may conclude that no one cares whether or not she remains alive and may "take her into the sky."

Interceding with the spirits and drawing out their invisible arrows is the task of !Kung healers, men and women who possess the powerful healing force called n/um. N/um generally remains dormant in a healer until an effort is made to activate it. Although an occasional healer can accomplish this through solo singing or instrumental playing, the usual way of activating n/um is through the medicinal curing ceremony or trance dance. To the

A !Kung healer in a trance.

sound of undulating melodies sung by women, the healers dance around and around the fire, sometimes for hours. The music, the strenuous dancing, the smoke, the heat of the fire, and the healers' intense concentration cause their n/um to heat up. When it comes to a boil, trance is achieved.

At this moment the n/um becomes available as a powerful healing force, to serve the entire community. In trance, a healer lays hands on and ritually cures everyone sitting around the fire. His hands flutter lightly beside each person's head or chest or wherever illness is evident; his body trembles; his breathing becomes deep and coarse; and he becomes coated with a thick sweat—also considered to be imbued with power. Whatever "badness" is discovered in the person is drawn into the healer's own body and met by the n/um coursing up his spinal column. The healer gives a mounting cry that culminates in a soul-wrenching shriek as the illness is catapulted out of his body and into the air.

While in trance, many healers see various gods and spirits sitting just outside the circle of firelight, enjoying the spectacle of the dance. Sometimes the spirits are recognizable—departed relatives and friends—at other times they are "just people." Whoever these beings are, healers in trance usually blame them for whatever misfortune is being experienced by the community. They are barraged by hurled objects, shouted at, and aggressively warned not to take any of the living back with them to the village of the spirits.

To cure a very serious illness, the most experienced healers may be called upon, for only they have enough knowledge to undertake the dangerous spiritual exploration that may be necessary to effect a cure. When they are in a trance, their souls are said to leave their bodies and to travel to the spirit world to discover the cause of the illness or the problem. An ancestral spirit or a god is usually found responsible and asked to reconsider. If the healer is persuasive and the spirit agrees, the sick person recovers. If the spirit is elusive or unsympathetic, a cure is not achieved. The healer may go to the principal god, but even this does not always work. As one healer put it, "Sometimes, when you speak with God, he says, 'I want this person to die and won't help you make him better.' At other times, God helps; the next morning, someone who has been lying on the ground, seriously ill, gets up and walks again."

These journeys are considered dangerous because while the healer's soul is absent his body is in "half-death." Akin to loss of consciousness, this state has been observed and verified by medical and scientific investigators. The power of other healers' n/um is all that is thought to protect the healer in this state from actual death. He receives lavish attention and care—his body is vigorously massaged, his skin is rubbed with sweat, and hands are laid on him. Only when consciousness returns—the signal that his soul has been reunited with his body—do the other healers cease their efforts.

[5]Marjorie Shostak, *Nisa: The Life and Words of !Kung Women* (Cambridge, Mass.: Harvard University Press, 1981), pp. 291–293. Reprinted by permission.

In many human societies trancing is accompanied by sleight-of-hand tricks and ventriloquism. Among Arctic peoples, for example, a shaman may summon spirits in the dark and produce all sorts of flapping noises and strange voices to impress the audiences. To some Western observers, this kind of trickery is regarded as evidence of the fraudulent nature of shamanism; but is this so? The truth is that shamans know perfectly well that they are pulling the wool over people's eyes with their tricks. On the other hand, virtually everyone who has studied them agrees that shamans really believe in their power to deal with supernatural powers and spirits. It is this power that gives them the right as well as the ability to fool people in minor technical matters. In short, the shaman regards his or her ability to perform tricks as proof of superior powers.

The importance of shamanism in a society should not be underestimated. For the individual members of society, it promotes, through the drama of the performance, a feeling of ecstasy and release of tension. It provides psychological assurance through the manipulation of supernatural powers, otherwise beyond human control, of such things as invulnerability from attack, success at love, or the return of health. In fact, a frequent reason for a shamanistic performance is to cure illness, as among the !Kung. The treatment may not be medically effective, but the state of mind induced in the patient may be important to his or her recovery.

APPLICATION
Reconciling Modern Medicine with Traditional Beliefs in Swaziland

Although the biomedical germ theory is generally accepted in Western societies today, this is not the case in many other societies around the world. In southern Africa's Swaziland, for example, all types of illnesses are generally thought to be caused by sorcery, or by loss of ancestral protection. Even where the effectiveness of Western medicine is recognized, the ultimate question remains: Why was the disease sent in the first place? Thus, for the treatment of disease, the Swazi have traditionally relied upon herbalists, diviner mediums through whom ancestor spirits are thought to work, and Christian faith healers. Unfortunately, such individuals have usually been regarded as quacks and charlatans by the medical establishment, even though the herbal medicines used by traditional healers are effective in several ways, and the reassurance provided patient and family alike through stress- and anxiety-reducing rituals plays an important role in the patient's recovery. In a country where there is 1 traditional healer for every 110 people, versus 1 physician for every 10,000, the potential benefit of cooperation between physicians and healers seems self-evident, and yet it was unrecognized until proposed by anthropologist Edward C. Green.

Green, who is now a senior research associate with a private firm, went to Swaziland in 1981 as a researcher for a Rural Water-Borne Disease Control Project, funded by the United States Agency for International Development. Assigned the task of finding out about knowledge, attitudes, and practices related to water and sanitation, and aware of the serious deficiencies of conventional surveys that rely on precoded questionnaires (see Chapter 1), Green used instead the traditional anthropological techniques of open-ended interviews with key informants, along with participant observation. The key informants were traditional healers, patients, and rural health motivators (individuals chosen by their communities to receive eight weeks of training in preventive health care in regional clinics). Without such work, it would have been im-

possible to design and interpret a reliable survey instrument, but the added payoff was that Green learned a great deal about Swazi theories of disease and its treatment. Disposed at the outset to recognize the positive value of many traditional practices, he was able to see as well how cooperation with physicians might be achieved. For example, traditional healers already recognized the utility of Western medicines for the treatment of diseases not indigenous to Africa, and traditional medicines were routinely given to children through inhalation and a kind of vaccination. Thus, nontraditional medicines and vaccinations might be accepted if presented in traditional terms.

Realizing the suspicion that existed on both sides, Green and his Swazi associate Lydia Makhubu (a chemist who had studied the properties of native medicines) recommended to the minister of health a cooperative project focused on a problem of concern to health professionals and native healers alike: infant diarrheal diseases. These had recently become a health problem of high concern to the general public; healers wanted a means of preventing such diseases, and a means of treatment existed—oral rehydration therapy—that was compatible with traditional treatments for diarrhea (herbal preparations taken orally over a period of time). Packets of oral rehydration salts, along with instructions for their use, were provided healers in a pilot project, with positive results. This helped convince health professionals of the benefits of cooperation, while at the same time, the distribution of packets to the healers was seen by them as a gesture of trust and cooperation on the part of the Ministry of Health. Since then, further steps at cooperation have been taken. What all this demonstrates is the importance of finding how to work in ways that are compatible with existing belief systems. To directly challenge traditional beliefs, as all too often happens, does little more than create stress, confusion, and resentment.

What shamanism does for society is to provide a focal point of attention. This is not without danger to the shaman. Someone with so much skill and power has the ability to work evil as well as good, and so is potentially dangerous. Too much nonsuccess on the part of a shaman may result in his or her being driven out of the group or killed. The shaman may also help maintain social control through the ability to detect and punish evildoers.

The benefits of shamanism for the shaman are that it provides prestige and perhaps even wealth. It may also be therapeutic, in that it provides an approved outlet for the outbreaks of an unstable personality. An individual who is psychologically unstable (and not all shamans are) may actually get better by becoming intensely involved with the problems of others. In this respect, shamanism is a bit like self-analysis. Finally, shamanism is a good outlet for the self-expression of those who might be described as being endowed with an "artistic temperament."

RITUALS AND CEREMONIES

Religious ritual is the means through which persons relate to the sacred; it is religion in action. Not only is ritual the means by which the social bonds of a group are reinforced and tensions relieved; it is also one way that many important events are celebrated and crises, such as death, made less socially disruptive and less difficult for the individuals to bear. Anthropologists have classified several different types of ritual, among them **rites of passage,** which pertain to stages in the life cycle of the individual, and **rites of intensification,** which take place during a crisis in the life of the group, serving to bind individuals together.

Rites of Passage

In one of anthropology's classic works, Arnold Van Gennep analyzed the rites of passage that help individuals through the crucial crises of their lives, such as birth, puberty, marriage, parenthood, advancement to a higher class, occupational specialization, and death.[6] He found it useful to divide

Rites of passage: Religious rituals marking important stages in the lives of individuals, such as birth, marriage, and death.

Rites of intensification: Religious rituals that take place during a real or potential crisis for a group.

Separation: In rites of passage, the ritual removal of the individual from society.

Transition: In rites of passage, the isolation of the individual following separation and prior to incorporation.

Incorporation: In rites of passage, reincorporation of the individual into society in his or her new status.

ceremonies for all of these life crises into three stages: **separation, transition,** and **incorporation.** The individual would first be ritually removed from the society as a whole, then isolated for a period, and finally incorporated back into society in his or her new status.

Van Gennep described the male initiation rites of Australian aborigines. When the time for the initiation is decided by the elders, the boys are taken from the village, while the women cry and make a ritual show of resistance. At a place distant from the camp, groups of men from many villages gather. The elders sing and dance, while the initiates act as though they are dead. The climax of this part of the ritual is a bodily operation, such as circumcision or the knocking out of a tooth. Anthropologist A. P. Elkin says:

> This is partly a continuation of the drama of death. The tooth-knocking, circumcision or other symbolical act "killed" the novice; after this he does not return to the general camp and normally may not be seen by any woman. He is dead to the ordinary life of the tribe.[7]

The novice may be shown secret ceremonies and receive some instruction during this period, but the most significant element is his complete removal from society. In the course of these Australian puberty rites, the initiate must learn the

---

[6]Arnold Van Gennep, *The Rites of Passage* (Chicago: University of Chicago Press, 1960).

[7]A. P. Elkin, *The Australian Aborigines* (Garden City, N.Y.: Doubleday, Anchor Books, 1964).

Spears and fly chasers signal the new status of these Benin girls parading in their initiation. Now recognized as adults, they may join the husbands to whom they were married in infancy.

tribal lore; he is given, in effect, a "cram course." The trauma of the occasion is a pedagogical technique that ensures that he will learn and remember everything; in a nonliterate society the perpetuation of cultural traditions requires no less, and so effective teaching methods are necessary.

On his return to society the novice is welcomed with ceremonies, as though he had returned from the dead. This alerts the society at large to the individual's new status — that he can be expected to act in certain ways and in return people must act in the appropriate ways toward him. The individual's new rights and duties are thus clearly defined. He is spared, for example, the problems of "American teenage," a time when an individual is neither adult nor child, but a person whose status is ill defined.

In the Australian case just cited, boys are prepared not just for adulthood, but for *man*hood. In their society, for example, fortitude is considered an important masculine virtue, and the pain of tooth knocking and circumcision helps instill this in initiates. Similarly, female initiation rites help prepare Mende girls in West Africa for womanhood. After they have begun to menstruate, they

are removed from society to spend weeks, or even months, in seclusion. There, they discard the clothes of childhood, smear their bodies with white clay, and dress in brief skirts and many strands of beads. Shortly after their seclusion, they undergo surgery in which their clitoris and part of the labia minora are excised, something that is thought to enhance their procreative potential. Until their return to society, they are trained in the moral and practical responsibilities of potential child bearers by experienced women in the Sande association, an organization to which the initiates will belong once their training has ended. This training is not all harsh, however, for it is accompanied by a good deal of singing, dancing, and storytelling, and the initiates are very well fed. Thus, they acquire both a positive image of womanhood and a strong sense of sisterhood. Once their training is complete, a medicine made by brewing leaves in water is used for a ritual washing, removing the magical protection that has protected them over the period of their confinement.

Mende women emerge from their initiation, then, as women in knowledgeable control of their sexuality, eligible for marriage and childbearing.

The pain and danger of the surgery, which was endured in the context of intense social support from other women, serves as a metaphor for childbirth, which, when it happens, may well take place in the same place of seclusion, again with the support of Sande women. It has also been suggested that, symbolically, excision of the clitoris (a rudiment of the male penis) removed sexual ambiguity.[8] Once done, a woman *knows* she is all woman. Thus, we have symbolic expression of gender as something important in peoples' cultural lives.

Rites of Intensification

Rites of intensification are those rituals that mark occasions of crisis in the life of the group, rather than an individual. Whatever the precise nature of the crisis — a severe lack of rain that threatens crops in the fields, the sudden appearance of an enemy war party, or some other force from outside that disturbs everyone — mass ceremonies are performed to allay the danger to the group. What this does is to unite people in a common effort in such a way that fear and confusion yield to collective action and a degree of optimism. The balance in the relations of all concerned, which has been upset, is restored to normal.

While the death of an individual might be regarded as the ultimate crisis in the life of an individual, it is, as well, a crisis for the entire group, particularly if the group is small. A member of the group has been removed, and so its equilibrium has been upset. The survivors, therefore, must readjust and restore balance. At the same time, they need to reconcile themselves to the loss of someone to whom they were emotionally tied. Funerary ceremonies, then, can be regarded as rites of intensification that permit the living to express in nondisruptive ways their upset over the death, while providing for social readjustment. A frequent feature of such ceremonies is an ambivalence about the dead person. For example, one of the parts of the funerary rites of Melanesians was the eating of the flesh of the dead person. This ritual cannibal-

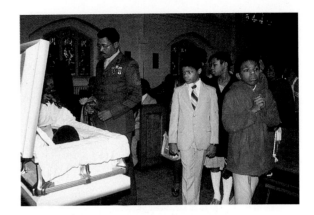

Viewing the body of the deceased is a common part of North American funeral rites. It is one expression of the desire to maintain a tie with the individual even after death. Other expressions of the same desire are common in the funeral rites of other cultures.

ism, witnessed by anthropologist Bronislaw Malinowski, was performed with "extreme repugnance and dread and usually followed by a violent vomiting fit. At the same time it is felt to be a supreme act of reverence, love and devotion."[9] This custom and the emotions accompanying it clearly reveal the ambiguous attitude toward death: on the one hand, there is the desire to maintain the tie to the dead person, and on the other hand, one feels disgust and fear at the transformation wrought by death. According to Malinowski, funeral ceremonies provide an approved collective means by which individuals may express these feelings, while at the same time maintaining social cohesiveness and preventing disruption of society.

The performance of rites of intensification does not have to be limited to times of overt crisis. In regions where the seasons differ enough so that human activities must change accordingly, they will take the form of annual ceremonies. These are particularly common among horticultural and agricultural people, with their planting, first-fruit, and harvest ceremonies. These are critical times in the lives of people in such societies, and the cere-

---

[8]Carol P. MacCormack, "Biological Events and Cultural Control," *Signs* 3(1977): 98.

[9]Bronislaw Malinowski, *Magic, Science and Religion* (Garden City, N.Y.: Doubleday, Anchor Books, 1954), p. 50.

In North America an interest in and the practice of witchcraft have grown dramatically over the past twenty years.

monies express a reverent attitude toward the forces of generation and fertility in nature, on which peoples' very existence depends. If all goes well, as it often does at such times, participation in a happy situation reinforces group involvement. It also serves as a kind of dress rehearsal for serious crisis situations; it promotes a habit of reliance on supernatural forces through ritual activity, which can be easily activated under stressful circumstances when it is important not to give way to fear and despair.

RELIGION, MAGIC, AND WITCHCRAFT

Among the most fascinating of ritual practices is application of the belief that supernatural powers can be compelled to act in certain ways for good or evil purposes by recourse to certain specified formulas. This is a classic anthropological notion of magic. Many societies have magical rituals to ensure good crops, the replenishment of game, the fertility of domestic animals, and the avoidance or cure of illness in humans. Although Western peoples today, in seeking to objectify and demythologize their world, have often tried to suppress the existence of these fantastic notions in their own consciousness, they continue to be fascinated

Sympathetic magic: Magic based on the principle that like produces like.

by them. Not only are books and films about demonic possession and witchcraft avidly devoured and discussed, but by 1967 (after some 40 years of poor sales) sales of ouija boards in the United States passed the 2 million mark. About 100 newspapers carried horoscope columns 30 years ago, but 1,200 of a total of 1,750 daily newspapers regularly carried such columns by 1970. As scientist Stephen Jay Gould points out, occultism is as fashionable in chic intellectual circles as in other segments of society.[10] When he complained to the manager of the Harvard Coop Bookstore that the paperback science section had been moved to a less visible location in order to make room for a large section on astrology and the occult, he was informed that this reflected a "sales reality." Although it is certainly true that non-Western and peasant peoples tend to endow their world quite freely with magical properties, so do many Western peoples.

Sir James George Frazer, author of one of the most widely read anthropological books of all time, *The Golden Bough*, made a strong distinction between religion and magic. Religion he saw as "a propitiation or conciliation of powers superior to man which are believed to direct and control the course of nature and human life."[11] Magic, on the other hand, he saw as an attempt to manipulate certain perceived "laws" of nature. The magician never doubts that the same causes will always produce the same effects. Thus, Frazer saw magic as a sort of pseudoscience, differing from modern science only in its misconception of the nature of the particular laws that govern the succession of events.

Frazer differentiated between two fundamental principles of magic. The first principle, that "like produces like," he called **sympathetic magic.** In

[10]Stephen Jay Gould, *An Urchin in the Storm* (New York: Norton, 1987), p. 241.
[11]James G. Frazer, "Magic and Religion," *The Making of Man: An Outline of Anthropology*, ed. V. F. Calverton (New York: Modern Library, 1931), p. 693.

Burma, for example, a rejected lover might engage a sorcerer to make an image of his scornful love. If this image were tossed into water, to the accompaniment of certain charms, the hapless girl would go mad. Thus, the girl would suffer a fate similar to that of her image.

Frazer's second principle was that of **contagious magic** — the concept that things or persons that have once been in contact can afterward influence one another. The most common example of contagious magic is the permanent relationship between an individual and any part of his or her body, such as hair, fingernails, or teeth. Frazer cites the Basutos of South Africa, who were careful to conceal their extracted teeth, because these might fall into the hands of certain mythical beings who could harm the owner of the tooth by working magic on it. Related to this is the custom, in our own society, of treasuring things that have been touched by special people.

WITCHCRAFT

Two hundred suspected witches were arrested in Salem, Massachusetts, in 1692; of these, 19 were hanged and 1 was hounded to death. Nineteen years later the descendants of some of the victims were awarded damages, but not until 1957 were the last of the Salem witches exonerated by the Massachusetts legislature. One might perhaps suppose that **witchcraft** is something that belongs to a less-enlightened past, but in fact, it is alive and well in the United States today. Indeed, starting in the 1960s, witchcraft began to undergo something of a boom in this country. We are by no means alone in this; for example, as the Ibibio of Nigeria have become increasingly exposed to modern education and scientific training, their reliance on witchcraft as an explanation for misfortune has increased.[12] Furthermore, it is often the younger, more educated members of Ibibio society who accuse others of "bewitching" them. Frequently, the

> **Contagious magic:** Magic based on the principle that things once in contact can influence one another after separation.
>
> **Witchcraft:** An explanation of misfortune based on the belief that certain individuals possess an innate, psychic power capable of causing harm, including sickness and death.

accused are older, more traditional members of society; thus, we have an expression of the intergenerational hostility that often exists in fast-changing traditional societies.

Ibibio Witchcraft

Among the Ibibio, as among most peoples of sub-Saharan Africa, witchcraft beliefs are highly developed and are of long-standing. A rat that eats up a person's crops is not really a rat, but a witch that changed into one; if a young and enterprising man cannot get a job or fails an exam, he has been bewitched; if someone wastes away money, or becomes sick, or is bitten by a snake or struck by lightning, the reason is always the same: it is witchcraft. Indeed, virtually all misfortune, illness, and death are attributed to the malevolent activity of some witch. The Ibibio's modern knowledge of such things as the role played by microorganisms in disease has little impact; after all, it says nothing about why these were sent to the afflicted individual. Although Ibibio religious beliefs provide alternative explanations for misfortune, they carry negative connotations and do not elicit nearly as much sympathy from others. Thus, if evil befalls a person, witchcraft is a far more satisfying explanation than something like "filial disobedience" or violation of some taboo.

Who are these Ibibio witches? They are thought to be those, male or female, who have within them a special substance acquired from some other established witch. This substance is made up of red, white, and black threads, needles, and other ingredients, and one gets it by swallowing it. From it comes a special power that causes harm, up to and including death, irrespective of whether its possessor intends to cause harm or not. The power is purely psychic, and witches do not

[12]Daniel Offiong, "Witchcraft among the Ibibio of Nigeria," in *Magic, Witchcraft and Religion*, ed. Arthur C. Lehmann and James E. Myers (Palo Alto, Calif.: Mayfield, 1985), pp. 152–165.

perform rites, nor make use of "bad medicine." It gives them the ability to change into animals, to travel any distance at incredible speed to get at their victims, whom they may torture, or kill by transferring the victim's soul into an animal, which is then eaten.

To identify a witch, one looks for any person who behaves abnormally. Specifically, some combination of the following may cause one to be labeled a witch: not being fond of greeting people; living alone in a place apart from others; charging too high a price for something; enjoying adultery or committing incest; walking about at night; not showing sufficient grief upon the death of a relative or other member of the community; taking improper care of one's parents, children, or wives; hard-heartedness. Witches are apt to look and act mean, and to be socially disruptive people in the sense that their behavior too far exceeds the range of variance considered acceptable.

Neither the Ibibio in particular nor Africans in general are alone in attributing most malevolent happenings to witchcraft. Similar beliefs can be found in any human society, including — as already noted — our own. As among the Ibibio, the powers (however they may be gained) are generally considered to be innate and uncontrollable; they result in activities that are the antithesis of proper behavior, and persons displaying undesirable characteristics of personality (however these may be defined) are generally the ones accused of being witches. The Ibibio make a distinction between "black witches" — those whose acts are especially diabolical and destructive — and "white witches" — those whose witchcraft is relatively benign, even though their powers are thought to be greater than those of their black counterparts. This exemplifies a common distinction between what Lucy Mair, a British anthropologist, has dubbed "nightmare witches" and "everyday witches."[13] The nightmare witch is the very embodiment of a society's conception of evil, a being that flouts the rules of sexual behavior and disregards every other stan-

dard of decency. Nightmare witches, being almost literally the product of dreams and repressed fantasies, have much in common wherever they appear: the modern Navajo and the ancient Roman, for example, like the Ibibio, conceived of witches that could turn themselves into animals and gather to feast on their victims. Everyday witches are often the nonconformists of a community, who are morose, who eat alone, who are arrogant and unfriendly, but who otherwise cause little trouble. Such witches may be dangerous when offended and retaliate by causing sickness, death, crop failure, cattle disease, or any number of lesser ills; people thought to be witches are usually treated very courteously.

THE FUNCTIONS OF WITCHCRAFT

Why witchcraft? We might better ask, why not? As Mair aptly observed, in a world where there are few proven techniques for dealing with everyday crises, especially sickness, a belief in witches is not foolish; it is indispensable. No one wants to resign oneself to illness, and if the malady is caused by a witch's hex, then magical countermeasures should cure it. Not only does the idea of personalized evil answer the problem of unmerited suffering; it also provides an explanation for many of those happenings for which no cause can be discovered. Witchcraft, then, cannot be refuted. Even if we could convince a person that his or her illness was due to natural causes, the victim would still ask, as the Ibibio do, Why me? Why now? There is no room for pure chance in such a view; everything must be assigned a cause or meaning. Witchcraft provides the explanation, and in so doing, also provides both the basis and the means for taking counteraction.

The positive functions of witchcraft may be seen in many African societies in which sickness and death are regarded as caused by witches. The ensuing search for the perpetrator of the misfortune becomes, in effect, a communal probe into social behavior.

[13]Lucy Mair, *Witchcraft* (New York: McGraw-Hill, 1969), p. 37.

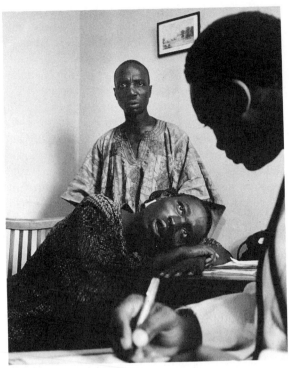

In many societies witchcraft may be an important source of psychological assurance. Here we see a positive application of this possibility. The man at the right is a Nigerian trained as a psychiatrist; helping him treat his patient is the local "witch doctor," who has considerable skill in dealing with severe emotional upsets. He has been incorporated into the staff of the clinic under the title "native therapist."

A witch hunt is, in fact, a systematic investigation, through a public hearing, into all social relationships involving the victim of the sickness or death. Was her husband unfaithful, her son lacking in the performance of his duties; were her friends uncooperative, or was she herself any of these things? Accusations are reciprocal, and before long just about every unsocial or hostile act that has occurred in that society since the last outbreak of witchcraft (sickness or death) is brought into the open.[14]

[14]Colin M. Turnbull, *The Human Cycle* (New York: Simon & Schuster, 1983), p. 181.

Divination: A magical procedure by which the cause of a particular event, such as an illness, may be determined or the future foretold.

Through such periodic public scrutiny of everyone's behavior, people are reminded of what their society regards as both strengths and weaknesses of character. This encourages individuals to suppress as best they can those traits of personality that are looked upon with disapproval, for if they do not, they may at some time be accused of being a witch. A belief in witchcraft thus serves a function of social control.

Psychological Functions of Witchcraft among the Navajo

Widely known among American Indians are the Navajo, who possess a detailed concept of witchcraft. Several types of witchcraft are distinguished. Witchery encompasses the practices of witches, who are said to meet at night to practice cannibalism and kill people at a distance. Sorcery is distinguished from witchery only by the methods used by the sorcerer, who casts spells on individuals, using the victim's fingernails, hair, or discarded clothing. Wizardry is not distinguished so much by its effects as by its manner of working; wizards kill by injecting a cursed substance, such as a tooth from a corpse, into the victim's body.

Whether or not a particular illness results from witchcraft is determined by **divination,** a magical procedure by which the identity of the witch is also learned. Once a person is charged with witchcraft, he or she is publicly interrogated, possibly even tortured, until there is a confession. It is believed that the witch's own curse will turn against the witch once this happens, so it is expected that the witch will die within a year. Some confessed witches have been allowed to live in exile.

According to Clyde Kluckhohn, Navajo witchcraft served to channel anxieties, tensions, and frustrations that were caused by the pressures from the white man.[15] The rigid rules of decorum

[15]Clyde Kluckhohn, "Navajo Witchcraft," *Papers of the Peabody Museum of American Archaeology and Ethnology* 22, no. 2 (1944).

among the Navajo allow little means of expression of hostility, except through accusations of witchcraft. Such accusations funnel pent-up negative emotions against individuals, without upsetting the wider society. Another function of accusations of witchcraft is that they permit the direct expression of hostile feelings against people to whom one would ordinarily be unable to express anger or enmity.

THE FUNCTIONS OF RELIGION

Just as a belief in witchcraft may serve a variety of psychological and social functions, so too do religious beliefs and practices in general. Here we may summarize these functions in a somewhat more systematic way. One psychological function is to provide an orderly model of the universe, the importance of which for orderly human behavior is discussed in Chapter 14. Beyond this, by explaining the unknown and making it understandable, the fears and anxieties of individuals are reduced. As we have seen, the explanations usually assume the existence of various sorts of supernatural beings and powers, which may potentially be appealed to or manipulated by people. This being so, a means is provided for dealing with crises: divine aid is, theoretically, available when all else fails.

A social function of religion is to sanction a wide range of conduct. In this context, religion plays a role in social control, which, as we saw in Chapter 21, does not rely on law alone. This is done through notions of right and wrong. If one does the right thing, one earns the approval of whatever supernatural powers are recognized by a particular culture. If, on the other hand, one does the wrong thing, one may suffer retribution through supernatural agencies. Religion does more than this, though; it sets precedents for acceptable behavior. We have already noted the connection between myths and religion. Usually, myths are full of tales of various supernatural beings, which in various ways illustrate the society's ethical code in action. So it is that Gluskabe, the

Penobscot culture hero, is portrayed in the Penobscot myths as tricking and punishing those who mock others, lie, are greedy, or go in for extremes of behavior. Moreover, the specific situations serve as precedents for human behavior in similar circumstances. The Old and New Testaments of the Bible are rich in the same sort of material. Related to this, by the models it presents and the morals it espouses, religion serves to justify and perpetuate a particular social order. Thus, in the Jewish, Christian, and Islamic traditions, a masculine, authoritarian godhead along with a creation story in which a woman is seen responsible for a fall from grace serves to justify a social order in which men have had control over women.

There is a psychological function tied up in all this. The moral code of a society, since it is held to be divinely fixed, lifts the burden of responsibility for one's conduct from the shoulders of the individual members of society, at least in important situations. It can be a tremendous relief to individuals to know that the responsibility for the way things are rests with the gods, rather than with themselves.

Another social function of religion is its role in the maintenance of social solidarity. In our discussion of the shaman we saw how such individuals provide focal points of interest, thus supplying one ingredient of assistance in maintaining the unity of the group. In addition, common participation in rituals, coupled with a basic uniformity of beliefs, helps to bind people together and reinforce their identification with their group. Particularly effective may be their participation together in rituals, when the atmosphere is charged with emotion. The exalted feelings people may experience in such circumstances serve as a positive reinforcement in that they "feel good" as a result. Here, once again, we find religion providing psychological assurance, while providing for the needs of society.

One other area in which religion serves a social function is education. In our discussion of rites of passage, we noted that Australian puberty rites served as a kind of cram course in tribal lore. By providing a memorable occasion, initiation rites can serve to enhance learning and so help ensure the perpetuation of a nonliterate culture. And as we saw in the case of female initiation rites among the Mende, they can serve to ensure that individuals have the knowledge that they will need to fulfill their adult roles in society. Education may also be served by rites of intensification. Frequently such rites involve dramas that portray matters of cultural importance. For example, among a food-foraging people dances may imitate the movement of game and techniques of hunting. Among farmers a fixed round of ceremonies may emphasize the steps necessary for good crops. What this does is to help preserve knowledge that is of importance to a people's material well-being.

RELIGION AND CULTURE CHANGE

Although the subject of culture change is taken up in a later chapter, no anthropological consideration of religion is complete without some mention of revitalization movements. In 1931, at Buka in the Solomon Islands, a native religious cult suddenly emerged, its prophets predicting that a deluge would soon engulf all whites. This would be followed by the arrival of a ship laden with European goods. The believers were to construct a storehouse for the goods and to prepare themselves to repulse the colonial police. Because the ship would arrive only after the natives had used up all their own supplies, they ceased working in the fields. Although the leaders of the cult were arrested, the movement continued for some years.

This was not an isolated instance. Such "cargo cults" — and many other movements that have promised the resurrection of the dead, the destruction or enslavement of Europeans, and the coming of utopian riches — have sporadically appeared throughout Melanesia ever since the beginning of this century. Since these cults are widely separated in space and time, their similarities are apparently the result of similarities in social conditions. In these areas the traditional cultures of the indigenous peoples have been

Young Melanesian men parade with mock rifles made of bamboo in a cargo cult ritual. Many of the believers are also Christians, converted by missionaries; the people see nothing contradictory in the two faiths.

uprooted. Europeans, or European-influenced natives, hold all political and economic power. Natives are employed in unloading and distributing Western-made goods, but have no practical knowledge of how to attain these goods. When cold reality offers no hope from the daily frustrations of cultural deterioration and economic deprivation, religion offers the solution.

REVITALIZATION MOVEMENTS

From the 1890 Ghost Dance of the North American Indians to the Mau Mau of Africa to the "cargo cults" of Melanesia, extreme and sometimes vio-

Revitalization movements are not restricted to non-Western cultures. In Western countries, they are frequently seen among segments of the population where there is dissatisfaction with life as it is. This picture was taken at Fiesta Island, Mission Bay, San Diego, California.

lent religious reactions to European colonial domination are so common that anthropologists have sought to formulate their underlying causes and general characteristics. Yet **revitalization movements,** as they are now called, are by no means restricted to the colonial world, and in the United States alone hundreds of such movements have sprung up. Among the more widely known are Mormonism, which began in the nineteenth century, the more recent Unification Church of the Reverend Sun Myung Moon, and the People's Temple of the Reverend Jim Jones. As these three examples suggest, revitalization movements show a great deal of diversity, and some have been much more successful than others.

A revitalization movement is a deliberate effort by members of a society to construct a more satisfying culture. The emphasis in this definition is on the reformation not just of the religious sphere of

Revitalization movements: Social movements, often of a religious nature, with the purpose of totally reforming a society.

activity, but of the entire cultural system. Such a drastic solution is attempted when a group's anxiety and frustration have become so intense that the only way to reduce the stress is to overturn the entire social system and replace it with a new one.

Anthropologist Anthony Wallace has outlined a sequence common to all expressions of the revitalization process.[16] First is the normal state of society, in which stress is not too great and there exist sufficient cultural means of satisfying needs. Under certain conditions, such as domination by a more powerful group or severe economic depres-

[16]Anthony F. C. Wallace, *Culture and Personality*, 2d ed. (New York: Random House, 1970), pp. 191–196.

sion, stress and frustration will be steadily amplified; this ushers in the second phase, or the period of increased individual stress. If there are no significant adaptive changes, a period of cultural distortion follows, in which stress becomes so chronic that socially approved methods of releasing tension begin to break down. This steady deterioration of the culture may be checked by a period of revitalization, during which a dynamic cult or religious movement grips a sizable proportion of the population. Often the movement will be so out of touch with reality that it is doomed to failure from the beginning. This was the case with the Ghost Dance, which was supposed to make the participants impervious to the bullets of the white men's guns. This was the case also with the cult of the Reverend Jim Jones, where the murder of a U.S. congressman was followed by the mass suicide of Jones and many of his followers. More rarely, a movement may tap long-dormant adaptive forces underlying a culture, and a long-lasting religion may result. Such was the case with Mormonism. Indeed, it appears that revitalization movements lie at the root of all known religions, Judaism, Christianity, and Islam included. We shall return to revitalization movements in Chapter 24.

CHAPTER SUMMARY

Religion is a part of all cultures. It consists of beliefs and behavior patterns by which people try to control the area of the universe that is otherwise beyond their control. Among food-foraging peoples, religion is a basic ingredient of everyday life. As societies become more complex, religion is less a part of daily activities and tends to be restricted to particular occasions.

Religion is characterized by a belief in supernatural beings and forces. Through prayer, sacrifice, and general ritual activity, people appeal to the supernatural world for aid. Supernatural beings may be grouped into three categories: major deities (gods and goddesses), nonhuman spirit beings, and ancestral spirits. Gods and goddesses are the great but remote beings. They are usually thought of as controlling the universe or a specific part of it. Whether or not people recognize gods, goddesses, or both has to do with how men and women relate to one another in everyday life. Animism is a belief in spiritual beings other than ancestors who are believed to animate all of nature. These spirit beings are closer to humans than gods and goddesses and are intimately concerned with human activities. Animism is typical of peoples who see themselves as a part of nature rather than as superior to it. A belief in ancestral spirits is based on the idea that human beings are made up of a body and soul. At death the spirit is freed from the body and continues to participate in human affairs. Belief in ancestral spirits is particularly characteristic of descent-based groups with their associated ancestor orientation. Animatism, as described by R. H. Codrington, may be found with animism in the same culture. Animatism is a force or power directed to a successful outcome, which may make itself manifest in any object.

Beliefs in supernatural beings and powers are maintained, first, through what are interpreted as manifestations of power. Second, they are perpetuated because supernatural beings possess attributes with which people are familiar. Finally, myths serve to rationalize religious beliefs and practices.

All human societies have specialists — priests and priestesses and/or shamans — to guide religious practices and to intervene with the supernatural world. Shamanism, with its often dramatic ritual, promotes a release of tension among individuals in a society. The shaman provides a focal point of attention for society and can help to maintain social control. The benefits of shamanism for the shaman are prestige, sometimes wealth, and an outlet for artistic self-expression.

Ritual is religion in action. Through ritual acts, social bonds are reinforced. Times of life crises are occasions for ritual. Arnold Van Gennep divided such rites of passage into rites of separation, transition, and incorporation. Rites of intensification are rituals to mark occasions of crisis in the life of the group rather than the individual. They serve to unite people, allay fear of the crisis, and prompt collective action. Funerary ceremonies are rites of intensification that provide for social readjustment after the loss of the deceased. Rites of intensification may also involve annual ceremonies to seek favorable conditions surrounding such critical activities as planting and harvesting.

Ritual practices of peasant and non-Western peoples are often an expression of the belief that supernatural powers can be made to act in certain ways through the use of certain prescribed formulas. This is the classic anthropological notion of magic. Sir James Frazer saw magic as a pseudoscience and found two principles of magic — "like produces like," or sympathetic magic, and the law of contagion.

Witchcraft functions as an effective way for people to explain away personal misfortune without having to shoulder any of the blame themselves. In spite of its negative effects in a society, witchcraft may function positively in the realm of social control. It may also provide an outlet for feelings of hostility and frustration without disturbing the norms of the larger group.

Religion serves several important social functions. First, it sanctions a wide range of conduct by providing notions of right and wrong. Second, it sets precedents for acceptable behavior and helps perpetuate an existing social order. Third, religion serves to lift the burden of decision making from individuals and places responsibility with the gods. Fourth, religion plays a large role in maintaining social solidarity. Finally, religion serves education. Ritual ceremonies enhance learning of tribal lore and so help to ensure the perpetuation of a nonliterate culture.

Domination by Western society has been the cause of certain religious manifestations in non-Western societies. In the islands of Melanesia, cargo cults have appeared spontaneously at different times since the beginning of the century. Anthony Wallace has interpreted religious reformations as revitalization movements in which an attempt is made, sometimes successfully, to change the society. He argues that all religions stem from revitalization movements.

SUGGESTED READINGS

Kalwet, Holger. *Dreamtime and Inner Space: The World of the Shaman*. New York: Random House, 1988. Written by an ethnopsychologist, this book surveys the practices and paranormal experiences of healers and shamans from Africa, the Americas, Asia, and Australia.

Lehmann, Arthur C., and James E. Myers, eds. *Magic, Witchcraft and Religion: An Anthropological Study of the Supernatural*, 2d ed. Palo Alto, Calif.: Mayfield, 1988. This anthology of readings is cross-cultural in scope and covers traditional as well as nontraditional themes. Well represented are both "tribal" and "modern" religions. The book provides a good way to discover the relevance and vitality of anthropological approaches to the supernatural.

Malinowski, Bronislaw. *Magic, Science and Religion, and Other Essays*. Garden City, N.Y.: Doubleday, Anchor Books, 1954. The articles collected here provide a discussion of the Trobri-

and Islanders as illustrative of conceptual and theoretical knowledge of humankind. The author covers such diversified topics as religion, life, death, character of "primitive" cults, magic, faith, and myth.

Norbeck, Edward. *Religion in Human Life: Anthropological Views*. New York: Holt, Rinehart and Winston, 1974. The author presents a comprehensive view of religion based on twin themes: the description of religious events, rituals, and states of mind and the nature of anthropological aims, views, procedures, and interpretations.

Wallace, Anthony F. C. *Religion: An Anthropological View*. New York: Random House, 1966. This is a standard textbook treatment of religion by an anthropologist who has specialized in the study of revitalization movements.

23

THE ARTS

No human culture is known to be without some form of art, even though that art may be applied to a purely utilitarian object. In Colombia, this bus serves as a means of transportation, not as an object of art. Yet, it is certainly artistic.

CHAPTER

PREVIEW

What Is Art?
Art is the creative use of the human imagination to interpret, understand, and enjoy life. Although the idea of art serving nonuseful, nonpractical purposes seems firmly entrenched in the thinking of modern Western peoples, in other cultures art often serves what are regarded as important, practical purposes.

Why Do Anthropologists Study Art?
Anthropologists have found that art reflects the cultural values and concerns of a people. This is especially true of the verbal arts — myths, legends, and tales. From these the anthropologist may learn how a people order their universe, and may discover much about a people's history as well. Also, music and the visual arts, such as sculpture, may provide insights into a people's world view and, through distributional studies, may suggest things about a people's history.

What Are the Functions of the Arts?
Aside from adding enjoyment to everyday life, the various arts serve a number of functions. Myths, for example, set standards for orderly behavior, and the verbal arts generally transmit and preserve a culture's customs and values. Songs, too, may do this, within the restrictions imposed by musical form. And any form of art, to the degree that it is characteristic of a particular society, may contribute to the cohesiveness or solidarity of that society.

Art is the product of a specialized kind of human behavior: the creative use of our imagination to help us interpret, understand, and enjoy life. Whether one is talking about a Chinese love song, a Hopi pot, a Balinese dance, or an African woodcarving, it is clear that everyone involved in the activity we call art—the creator, the performer, the participant, the spectator—is making use of a uniquely human ability to use and comprehend symbols and to shape and interpret the physical world for something beyond a purely utilitarian purpose. After all, if a Hopi Indian wanted a useful container, a simple, undecorated pot would do just as well as a carefully shaped, smoothed, and elaborately painted one, and could be more quickly and easily made. Yet Hopi potters typically devote much time and technical skill to the production of pottery vessels that are aesthetically pleasing not just to other Hopi but to many non-Hopi peoples as well.

The idea of art serving nonuseful, nonpractical purposes seems firmly entrenched in the thinking of modern Western peoples. Today, for example, the objects from the tomb of the young Egyptian king Tutankhamen are on display in a museum, where they may be seen and admired as the exquisite works of art that they are. They were made, however, to be hidden away from human eyes, where they were to guarantee the eternal life of the king and to protect him from evil forces that might enter his body and gain control over it. Or we may listen to the singing of a sea chantey purely for aesthetic pleasure, as a form of entertainment. In fact, in the days of sail, sea chanteys served very useful and practical purposes. They set the appropriate rhythm for the performance of specific shipboard tasks, and the same qualities that make them pleasurable to listen to today served to relieve the boredom of those tasks. Such links between art and other aspects of culture are common in human societies around the world.

To us, the making of exquisite objects of gold and precious stones to place in a tomb might seem like throwing them away. Yet something of the same sort happens when a Navajo Indian creates an intricate sand painting as part of a ritual act, only to destroy it once the ritual is over. Johann Sebastian Bach was also doing the same thing when, almost 300 years ago, he composed his cantatas to be used in church services. These were "throwaway" music, to be discarded after the services for which they were written. That many of them are still performed today is something of an accident, for Bach was not composing them for posterity. In many human societies the "doing" of art is often of greater importance than the final product itself.

Whether a particular work of art is intended to be appreciated purely as such or to serve some practical purpose, as in the examples shown here, it will in every case require the same special combination of the symbolic representation of form and the expression of feeling that constitutes the creative imagination. Insofar as the creative use of the human ability to symbolize is universal and either expresses or is shaped by cultural values and concerns, it is properly and eminently an area of investigation for anthropology.

There appears to be no culture in the world without at least some kind of storytelling, singing, dancing, or other activity that gives aesthetic pleasure. Reasoning backward from effect to cause, some writers in recent times have proposed that humans may have an actual need or drive—either innate or acquired—to use their faculties of imagination. Just as we need food and shelter to survive, we may also need to nourish and exercise our active minds, which are not satisfied, except in times of crisis, with the mere business of solving the immediate problems of daily existence. Without the free play of the imagination there is boredom, and boredom may lead to a lack of productivity, perhaps even in extreme cases to death. It is art that provides the means and the materials for our imaginative play and thus helps to sustain life. According to this way of thinking, art is therefore not a luxury to be afforded or appreciated by a minority of aesthetes or escapists, but a necessary kind of social behavior in which every normal and active human being participates.

Much of the world's art is created for practical, rather than aesthetic purposes. Shown here are examples of art used for curing (a Navajo sand painting), to express cultural identity (the Mardi Gras costume of one of New Orleans' "Black Indians"), and as political expression (wall painting in Northern Ireland).

As an activity or kind of behavior that contributes to well-being and helps give shape and significance to life, art must be at the same time related to, yet differentiated from, religion. The dividing line between the two is not distinct: it is not easy to say, for example, precisely where art stops and religion begins in an elaborate ceremony involving ornamentation, masks, costumes, songs, dances, and effigies. Does religion inspire art, or is religion perhaps a kind of art in which the supernatural happens to be the central element?

This problem in semantics is not easy to solve, but it is often convenient to distinguish between secular and religious art, if not between art and religion. In what we call purely secular art, whether it is light or serious, it is clear that our imaginations are free to roam without any ulterior motives — creating and re-creating patterns, plots, rhythms, and feelings at leisure and without any thought of consequence or aftermath. In religious art, on the other hand, the imagination is working still, but the whole activity is somehow aimed at assuring our well-being through propitiation, celebration, and acknowledgment of forces beyond ourselves. At any rate, whether categorized as secular or religious, art of all varieties can be expected to reflect the values and concerns of the people who create and enjoy it; the nature of the things reflected and expressed in art is the concern of the anthropologist.

The world's earliest known pictorial art is from Australia, and is not unlike this example from a cave in Arnhem Land.

THE ANTHROPOLOGICAL STUDY OF ART

In approaching art as a cultural phenomenon, the anthropologist has the pleasant task of cataloging, photographing, recording, and describing all possible forms of imaginative activity in any particular culture. There is an enormous variety of forms and modes of artistic expression in the world. Because people everywhere continue to create and develop in new directions, there is no foreseeable point of diminishing returns in the interesting process of collecting and describing the world's ornaments, body decorations, variations in clothing, blanket and rug designs, pottery and basket styles, architectural embellishments, monuments, ceremonial masks, legends, work songs, social dances, and other art forms. The process of collecting, however, must eventually lead to some kind of analysis, and then (it is hoped) to some illuminating generalizations about relationships between art and culture.

Folklore: A nineteenth-century term first used to refer to the traditional oral stories and sayings of the European peasant, and later extended to those traditions preserved orally in all societies.

Probably the best way to begin a study of this problem of the relationships between art and culture is to examine critically some of the generalizations that have already been made about specific arts. Rather than trying to cover all forms of art, we shall concentrate on just a few: verbal arts, music, and sculpture. We shall start with the verbal arts, for we have already touched upon them in our earlier discussions of religion (Chapter 22) and world view (Chapter 14).

VERBAL ARTS

The term **folklore** was coined in the nineteenth century to denote the unwritten stories, beliefs, and customs of the European peasant, as opposed

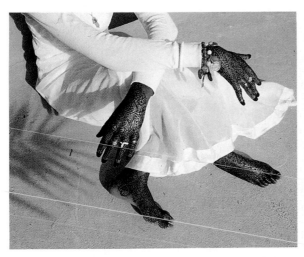

Perhaps the oldest means of artistic expression is body decorating. Shown here is a Moroccan woman whose hands and feet are dyed with henna (to celebrate a royal wedding), and a man from New England with a tattooed chest.

to the traditions of the literate elite. The subsequent study of folklore, concentrating on folktales, has become a discipline allied to but somewhat independent of anthropology, working on cross-cultural comparisons of themes, motifs, and structures, often more from a literary than an ethnological point of view. In general, both linguists and anthropologists prefer to speak of the oral traditions and verbal arts of a culture rather than its folklore and folktales, recognizing that creative verbal expression takes many forms and that the implied distinction between folk and "sophisticated" art is a projection of our own culture's attitude onto others.

The verbal arts include narrative, drama, poetry, incantations, proverbs, riddles, word games, and even naming procedures, compliments, and insults, when these take elaborate and special forms. The narrative seems to be one of the easiest kinds of verbal arts to record or collect. Perhaps because it is also the most publishable, with popular appeal in our own culture, it has received the most study and attention. Generally, narratives have been divided into three basic and recurring categories: myth, legend, and tale.

Myth: A traditional narrative in which people explain the nature of the world and their place in it; a myth deals with the ultimate questions of human existence.

MYTH

The word *myth*, in popular usage, refers to something that is widely believed to be true, but probably isn't. Actually, a true **myth** is basically religious, in that it provides a rationale for religious beliefs and practices. Its subject matter is the ultimates of human existence: where we and the things in our world came from, why we are here, and where we are going. As was noted in Chapter 22, the myth has an explanatory function; it depicts and describes an orderly universe, which sets the stage for orderly behavior. Below is a typical origin myth traditional with the Western Abenaki of northwestern New England and southern Quebec.

In the beginning, *Tabaldak*, "The Owner," created all living things but one — the spirit being who was to accomplish the final transformation of the earth. Man and woman *Tabaldak* made out of a piece of

stone, but he didn't like the result, and so he broke
them up. He tried again, this time using living wood,
and from them came all later Abenakis. The one living thing not created by *Tabaldak* was *Odziózo*, "He
Makes Himself from Something." This being seems
to have created himself out of dust, but since he was
more transformer than creator, he wasn't able to accomplish it all at once. At first, he managed only his
head, body, and arms; the legs came later, growing
slowly as legs do on a tadpole. Not waiting until his
legs were grown, he set out to change the shape of
the earth. He dragged his body about with his hands,
gouging channels that became the rivers. To make
the mountains, he piled dirt up with his hands. Once
his legs grew, *Odziózo's* task was made easier; by
merely extending his legs, he made the tributaries of
the main streams.

Anthropologist Gordon Day has described *Odziózo's* last act of landscape transformation as
follows:

> It was Odziózo who laid out the river channels and
> lake basins and shaped the hills and mountains. Just
> how long he took is a subject which Abenakis, only
> recently deceased, used to discuss over their camp-
> fires. At last he was finished, and like Jehovah in
> Genesis, he surveyed his handiwork and found it was
> good. The last work he made was Lake Champlain
> and this he found especially good. It was his master-
> piece. He liked it so much that he climbed onto a
> rock in Burlington Bay and changed himself into
> stone so that he could better sit there and enjoy the
> spectacle through the ages. He still likes it, because
> he is still there and used to be given offerings of to-
> bacco as long as Abenakis went this way by canoe, a
> practice which continued until about 1940. The rock
> is also called Odziózo, since it is the Transformer
> himself.[1]

Such a myth, insofar as it is believed, accepted,
and perpetuated in a culture, may be said to express a part of the world view of a people: the un-
expressed but implicit conceptions of their place in
nature and of the limits and workings of their

Odziózo's last work was Lake Champlain. So pleased
was he with this masterpiece that he climbed onto a
rock and changed himself into stone so that he could sit
there and enjoy it through the ages.

world. This concept we discussed in Chapters 14
and 21. The concepts of world view and science
are intimately related, and it may be said that myth
is the science of cultures that do not employ scientific methods. Extrapolating from the details of the
Abenaki myth, for example, we might arrive at the
conclusion that these people recognize a kinship
among all living things; after all, they were all part
of the same creation, and humans were even made
from living wood. Moreover, an attempt to make
them of nonliving stone was not satisfactory. This
idea of a closeness between all living things led the
Abenaki to show special respect to the animals that
they hunted in order to sustain their own lives. For
example, when one killed a beaver, muskrat, or
waterfowl, one couldn't unceremoniously toss
their bones into the nearest garbage pit. Proper
respect demanded that their bones be returned to
the water, with a request that their kind be continued. Similarly, before eating meat, an offering of
grease was placed on the fire to thank *Tabaldak*.
More generally, waste was to be avoided, so as not
to offend the animals. Failure to respect their
rights would result in their no longer being willing
to sacrifice their lives, that people might live.

[1]Gordon M. Day, quoted in William A. Haviland and Marjory
W. Power, *The Original Vermonters: Native Inhabitants, Past and
Present* (Hanover, N.H.: University Press of New England,
1981), p. 189.

In transforming himself into stone, in order to enjoy his work for all eternity, *Odziózo* may be seen as setting an example for people; they should see the beauty in things as they are, and not seek to alter what is already so good. To question the goodness of existing reality would be to call into question the judgment of an important deity. It is characteristic of an explanatory myth, such as this one, that the unknown will be simplified and explained in terms of the known. This myth accounts in terms of human experience for the existence of rivers, mountains, lakes, and other features of the landscape, as well as for the existence of humans and all other living things. It also serves to sanction particular attitudes and behaviors. It is a product of creative imagination, and it is a work of art, as well as a potentially religious statement.

One aspect of mythology that has attracted a good deal of interest over the years is the similarity of certain themes in the stories of peoples living in separate parts of the world. One of these themes is the myth of matriarchy, or one-time rule by women. In a number of societies, stories tell about a time when women ruled over men. Eventually, so these stories go, men were forced to rise up and assert their dominance over women, in order to combat their tyranny or incompetence (or both). In the nineteenth century, a number of eminent scholars interpreted such myths as evidence for an early stage of matriarchy in the evolution of human culture, an idea that has recently been revived by some feminists. Although a number of societies are known in which the two sexes relate to one another as equals (Western Abenaki society was one), never have anthropologists found one in which women rule over or dominate men. The interesting thing about myths of matriarchy is that they are generally found in societies in which men dominate women, while at the same time the latter have considerable autonomy.[2] Under such conditions, male dominance is insecure, and a rationale is needed to justify it. Thus, myths of men over-

[2]Peggy Reeves Sanday, *Female Power and Male Dominance: On the Origins of Sexual Inequality* (Cambridge: Cambridge University Press, 1981), p. 181.

> **Legends:** Semihistorical narratives coming down from the past that recount the deeds of heroes, the movements of peoples, and the establishment of local customs.

throwing women and taking control mirror an existing paradoxical relationship between the two sexes.

The analysis and interpretation of myths have been carried to great lengths, becoming a field of study almost unto itself. It is certain that myth making is an extremely important kind of human creativity, and the study of the myth-making process and its results can give some valuable clues to the way people perceive and think about their world. The dangers and problems of interpretation, however, are great. Several questions arise. Are myths literally believed or perhaps accepted symbolically or emotionally as a different kind of truth? To what extent do myths actually determine or reflect human behavior? Can an outsider read into a myth the same meaning that it has in its own culture? How do we account for contradictory myths in the same culture? New myths arise and old ones die. Is it then the content or the structure of the myth that is important? All of these questions deserve, and are currently receiving, serious consideration.

LEGEND

Less problematical, but perhaps more complex than myth, is the legend. **Legends** are semihistorical narratives that account for the deeds of heroes, the movements of peoples, and the establishment of local customs, typically with a mixture of realism and the supernatural or extraordinary. As stories, they are not necessarily believed or disbelieved, but they usually serve to entertain as well as to instruct and to inspire or bolster pride in family, tribe, or nation.

To a degree, in literate states such as our own, the function of legends has been taken over by history. Yet much of what passes for history, as one

The telling of legends and tales is no less important in the education of children in the United States than it is on the Ivory Coast.

historian has put it, consists of "the myths we develop to make ourselves feel better about who we are."[3] (The word *myth* is used here in its popular sense.) The trouble is that history does not always tell people what they want to hear about themselves, or, conversely, it tells them things that they would prefer not to hear. By projecting their culture's hopes and expectations onto the record of the past, they seize upon and even exaggerate some past events, while ignoring or giving scant attention to others. Although this often takes place unconsciously, so strong is the motivation to trans-

Epics: Long oral narratives, sometimes in poetry or rhythmic prose, recounting the glorious events in the life of a real or legendary person.

form history into legend that states have often gone so far as to deliberately rewrite it, as when the Aztecs in the reign of their fifteenth-century king Itzcoatl rewrote their history in a way befitting their position of dominance in ancient Mexico. An example from our own past may be seen in the deliberate "slanting" (and in some cases destruction) of written documents by the Puritan authorities of colonial New England, so that their policies toward Indians might be seen in the most favorable light.[4] Similar practices have been noted in modern times in the Soviet Union. Historians, in their attempts to separate fact from fiction, frequently incur the wrath of people who will not willingly abandon what they wish to believe is true, whether or not it really is.

Long legends, sometimes in poetry or in rhythmic prose, are known as **epics.** In parts of West and Central Africa there are remarkably elaborate and formalized recitations of extremely long legends, lasting several hours, and even days. These long narratives have been described as veritable encyclopedias of the most diverse aspects of a culture, with direct and indirect statements about history, institutions, relationships, values, and ideas. Epics are typically found in nonliterate societies with a form of state political organization; they serve to transmit and preserve a culture's legal and political precedents and practices. The Mwindo epic of the Nyanga people, the Lianja epic of the Mongo, and the Kambili epic of the Mande, for example, have been the subject of extensive and rewarding study by French, British, and American anthropologists in the last several years.

Legends may incorporate mythological details, especially when they make appeal to the supernatural, and are therefore not always clearly distinct from myth. The legend about Mwindo follows

[3]Mark Stoler, "To Tell the Truth," *Vermont Visions* 82, no. 3 (1982): 3.

[4]Francis Jennings, *The Invasion of America* (New York: Norton, 1976), p. 182.

him through the earth, the atmosphere, the underworld, and the remote sky, and gives a complete picture of the Nyanga people's view of the organization and limits of the world. Legends may also incorporate proverbs and incidental tales, and thus be related to other forms of verbal art as well. A recitation of the legend of Kambili, for example, has been said to include as many as 150 proverbs.

Below is an example of a short legend that instructs, traditional with the Western Abenakis of northwestern New England and southern Quebec.

> This is a story of a lonesome little boy who used to wander down to the riverbank at Odanak or downhill toward the two swamps. He used to hear someone call his name but when he got to the swamp pond, there was no one to be seen or heard. But when he went back, he heard his name called again. As he was sitting by the marshy bank waiting, an old man came and asked him why he was waiting. When the boy told him, the old man said that the same thing happened long ago. What he heard was the Swamp Creature and pointed out the big tussocks of grass where it hid; having called out it would sink down behind them. The old man said: "It just wants to drown you. If you go out there you will sink in the mud. You better go home!"[5]

The moral of this story is quite simple: Swamps are dangerous places; stay away from them. When told well, the story is a lot more effective in keeping children away from swamps than just telling them, "Don't go near swamps."

For the anthropologist the major significance of the secular and apparently realistic portions of legends, whether long or short, is probably in the clues they provide to what constitutes approved or model ethical behavior in a culture. The subject matter of legends is essentially problem solving, and the content is likely to include combat, warfare, confrontations, and physical and psychological trials of many kinds. Certain questions may be

[5]Gordon M. Day, quoted in the film *Prehistoric Life in the Champlain Valley*, by Thomas C. Vogelman and others (Burlington: Department of Anthropology, University of Vermont, 1972).

Tale: A creative narrative recognized as fiction for entertainment.

answered explicitly or implicitly. Does the culture justify homicide? What kinds of behavior are considered to be brave or cowardly? What is the etiquette of combat or warfare? Is there a concept of altruism or self-sacrifice? Here again, however, there are pitfalls in the process of interpreting art in relation to life. It is always possible that certain kinds of behavior are acceptable or even admirable with the distance or objectivity afforded by art, but are not at all so approved in daily life. In our own culture, murderers, charlatans, and rakes have sometimes become popular "heroes" and the subjects of legends; we would object, however, to the inference of an outsider that we necessarily approved or wanted to emulate the morality of Billy the Kid or Jesse James.

TALE

The term **tale** is a nonspecific label for a third category of creative narratives, those that are purely secular and nonhistorical and are recognized as fiction for entertainment, though they may draw a moral or teach a practical lesson as well. Consider this brief summary of a tale from Ghana, known as "Father, Son, and Donkey":

> A father and his son farmed their corn, sold it, and spent part of the profit on a donkey. When the hot season came, they harvested their yams and prepared to take them to storage, using their donkey. The father mounted the donkey and they all three proceeded on their way until they met some people. "What? You lazy man!" the people said to the father. "You let your young son walk barefoot on this hot ground while you ride on a donkey? For shame!" The father yielded his place to the son, and they proceeded until they came to an old woman. "What? You useless boy!" said the old woman. "You ride on the donkey and let your poor father walk barefoot on this hot ground? For shame!" The son dismounted, and both father and son walked on the road, leading the donkey behind them until they came to an old

man. "What? You foolish people!" said the old man. "You have a donkey and you walk barefoot on the hot ground instead of riding?" And so it goes. Listen: When you are doing something and other people come along, just keep on doing what you like.

This is precisely the kind of tale that is of special interest in traditional folklore studies. It is an internationally popular "numbskull" tale; versions of it have been recorded in India, the Middle East, the Balkans, Italy, Spain, England, and the United States, as well as in West Africa. It is classified or cataloged as exhibiting a basic **motif,** or story situation — father and son trying to please everyone — one of the many thousands that have been found to recur in world folktales. In spite of variations in detail, every version will be found to have about the same basic structure in the sequence of events, sometimes called the *syntax* of the tale; a peasant father and son work together, a beast of burden is purchased, the three set out on a short excursion, the father rides and is criticized, the son rides and is criticized, both walk and are criticized, and a conclusion is drawn.

Tales of this sort with an international distribution sometimes raise more problems than they solve: Which one is the original? What is the path of its diffusion? Could it be sheer coincidence that different cultures have come up with the same motif and syntax, or could it be a case of independent invention with similar tales developing in similar situations in response to like causes? A surprisingly large number of motifs in European and African tales are traceable to ancient sources in India. Is this good evidence of a spread of culture from a "cradle" of civilization, or is it an example of diffusion of tales in contiguous areas? There are, of course, purely local tales, as well as tales with a wide distribution. Within any particular culture it will probably be found possible to categorize local types of tales: animal, human experience, trickster, dilemma, ghost, moral, scatological, nonsense, and so on. In West Africa there is a remarkable prevalence of animal stories, for example, with such creatures as the spider, the rabbit, and the hyena as the protagonists. Many were car-

■ **Motif:** A story situation in a folktale.

ried to the slave-holding areas of the Americas; the Uncle Remus stories about Brer Rabbit, Brer Fox, and other animals may be a survival of this tradition.

The significance of tales for the anthropologist rests partly in this matter of their distribution. They provide evidence for either cultural contacts or cultural isolation, and for limits of influence and cultural cohesion. It has been debated for decades now, for example, to what extent the culture of West Africa was transmitted to the southeast United States. So far as folktales are concerned, one school of folklorists has always found and insisted on European origins; another school, somewhat more recently, points to African prototypes. The anthropologist can be interested, however, in more than these questions of distribution. Like legends, tales very often illustrate local solutions to universal human ethical problems, and in some sense they state a moral philosophy. The anthropologist sees that whether the tale of the father, the son, and the donkey originated in West Africa or arrived there from Europe or the Middle East, the very fact that it has been accepted in West Africa suggests that it states something valid for that culture. The tale's lesson of a necessary degree of self-confidence in the face of arbitrary social criticism is therefore something that can be read into the culture's values and beliefs.

OTHER VERBAL ARTS

Myths, legends, and tales, prominent as they are in anthropological studies, turn out to be no more important than the other verbal arts in many cultures. In the culture of the Awlad 'Ali Bedouins of Egypt's western desert, for example, poetry is a lively and active verbal art, especially as a vehicle for personal expression and private communication. Among these people, there are two forms of poetry, one being the elaborately structured and heroic poems chanted or recited by men on cere-

The "little songs" of the Awlad 'Ali Bedouins punctuate conversations carried out while performing every day chores, like making bread, as these girls are doing.

monial occasions and in specific public contexts. The other is the *ghinnáwa*, or "little songs," which punctuate everyday conversations. Simple in structure, these deal with personal matters and feelings more appropriate to informal social situations, and are regarded by older men as the unimportant productions of women and youths. In spite of this official devaluation in the male-dominated society of the Bedouins, however, they play a vital part in peoples' daily lives.

ORIGINAL STUDY
The "Little Songs" of the Awlad 'Ali[6]

It is clear that individuals are shielded from the consequences of making statements and expressing sentiments that contravene the moral system if they do so in poetry. By sharing these "immoral" sentiments only with intimates and veiling them in impersonal traditional formulas, they even demonstrate that they have a certain control, which actually enhances their moral standing. But if we turn from how individuals use poems to the poetry itself as a cultural discourse, as a set of rule-bound statements that represent a vision of reality, an even more intriguing set of questions presents itself. If the disjunction between the messages carried by the two discourses occurs not just on the individual level but on the cultural level as well, and if ordinary discourse is that generated in accordance with the values that support the dominant social and political system, then is poetry the discourse of antistructure? If poetry is associated with opposition to the system, why is it not condemned or repressed? Why is it glorified?

The *ghinnáwa's* antistructural character is evident not just in the type of sentiments regularly carried by it, but in its association as well. Its closest association is with the traditional Bedouin romance. Poems are always included in love tales that celebrate the often tragic course of romance, a force usually condemned as threatening to the social system. Thwarted love, especially between a man and a woman from different tribes, is the theme of the most poignant Bedouin love stories, which are recounted as true tales of the distant past. In a few, cousins fall in love but are prevented from marrying by the girl's wealthy father who does not wish to let her marry his poor brother's son; from what I could gather, those stories usually ended happily with the young nephew triumphing. More commonly, the sweethearts are unrelated, and their love is thwarted by the girl's cousin, as in the following archetypal love story:

Once upon a time there was a boy and a girl who were in love with each other. The girl's father's brother's son heard about this and was furious. He swore she would never marry the boy and claimed her . . . for himself.

Now, the girl and the boy used to meet secretly to talk at the tent of an old lady, a neighbor of theirs. One day, the boy announced that he was leaving on a journey. He was going to the oasis of Siwa to get dates. He promised that after he returned, he would marry the girl. He said to her:

> Happiness in my absence is a failing
> and grief between us the sign of love . . .

With that he set off with a caravan of camels. He was away for a long time. On his way back, only two days from home, he fell ill and died. He had instructed his companion earlier, "If I die on the way, please carry my body home so my family can bury me." So his companion loaded his corpse on a camel and journeyed the rest of the way home.

When his family heard what had happened, they wailed and cried. Meanwhile, the girl had seen the camels returning to his camp but wondered, "Why don't I hear trilling and the firing of rifles [signs of celebration]?" She ran to find out, and when she did, she wailed and cried with his kinswomen.

Her cousin discovered that she had gone to her lover's camp and followed her. He ran in and grabbed her from among the mourners and started beating her. She tried to run away, but he chased her, beating her until she fell dead, right on the fresh grave of her sweetheart.

Her cousin was enraged. He swore at her, "Even in death you're a slut!" He demanded that they not bury her near the boy, so they carried her about a kilometer away and buried her.

After a while, a palm tree sprang from the head of the boy's grave and a tree sprang from the head of the girl's. The trees grew and grew until their fronds crossed high in the sky. The cousin grew angry when he saw this, thinking, "She still can't keep away from him, even in death?" So he went to find a woodcutter to cut down the trees.

As the woodcutter was trying to chop down the tree that grew over her grave, the axe flew out of his hand and into his eye, blinding him. He went home and fell ill. In his sleep a vision of the boy came to him and said:

> May God cut you down, oh woodcutter
> you cut the rope as they were filling [at the well] . . .

Then he parted with the words:

> Love must bring forth fruits
> which join each other in their sky . . .

This story has several remarkable features. It celebrates the desires of individuals against the demands of the system, as codified in the first cousin's right to his father's brother's daughter—the cousin seeks to enforce the system as the girl and her lover refuse to accept it. The heroine is both defiant and a "slut," hence lacking in modesty; her tragic end may hold a lesson for Awlad 'Ali about the ultimate power of the system. At the same time, however, she and her sweetheart are heroic, and their defiance ends in a victory of sorts. People who listen to such tales admire the behavior of lovers and do not condemn it as immoral, and they appreciate the poetry that expresses the lover's feelings.

Poetry is associated with antistructure in ways other than this explicit link to romance and sexuality. People perceive poetry as un-Islamic and poetic recitation as impious, just as "crying" at funerals is wrong from a religious point of view (and so is not done by women who have been on the pilgrimage to Mecca). The fact that the very word "to sing" . . . cannot be said in mixed-sex company suggests its antistructural quality. Another indication is that people say they *tahashsham* or are embarrassed/ashamed/modest about singing in front of nonintimates, especially elders. Elders, too, avoid settings such as weddings and sheep shearings where, at least in the past, *ghinnáwas* were publicly sung. Even the rhetoric of poetry gives it an antistructural flavor, as if poetry were the language of the unsocialized child as opposed to the ordinary discourse of adult conformity. The final and most persuasive link is in who sings or recites *ghinnáwas*. Although older men occasionally recite them, *ghinnáwas* are most closely associated with youths and women, the disadvantaged dependents who least embody the ideals of Bedouin society and have least to gain in the system as structured. Poetry is, in so many ways, the discourse of opposition to the system and of defiance of those who represent it: it is antistructure just as it is antimorality.

The existence of dissident or subversive discourses is probably not unusual. What may be peculiar to Awlad 'Ali is that their discourse of rebellion is both culturally elaborated and sanctioned. Although poetry refers to personal life, it is not individual, spontaneous, idiosyncratic, or unofficial but public, conventional, and formulaic—a highly developed art. More important, this poetic discourse of defiance is not condemned, or even just tolerated, as well it might be given all the constraints of time and place and form that bind it. Poetry is a privileged discourse in Awlad 'Ali society. Like other Arabs, and perhaps like many oral cultures, the Bedouins cherish poetry and other verbal arts. Everyone listens attentively whenever poems are recited or sung. People memorize poems, repeat them, and are moved by them. For Awlad 'Ali, poetry represents what is best in their culture, what they consider distinctively Bedouin. Poetry is associated with the glorious past, when Awlad 'Ali lived without Egyptian government interference, migrating freely, herding sheep, riding horses, and being brave and tough.

People are thrilled by poetry. They are drawn to *ghinnáwas*, and at the same time they consider them risqué, against religion, and slightly improper — as befits something antistructural. This ambivalence about poetry is significant, and it makes sense only in terms of the cultural meaning of opposition. Because ordinary discourse is informed by the values of honor and modesty, the moral correlates of the ideology that upholds the Awlad 'Ali social and political system, we would expect the antistructural poetic discourse with its contradictory messages, to be informed by an opposing set of values. This is not the case. Poetry as a discourse of defiance of the system symbolizes freedom — the ultimate value of the system and the essential entailment of the honor code.

[6]Lila Abu-Lughod, *Veiled Sentiments: Honor and Poetry in a Bedouin Society* (Berkeley, Calif.: University of California Press, 1986), pp. 248–252. Copyright © 1986 by The Regents of the University of California.

In all cultures the words of songs constitute a kind of poetry. Poetry and stories recited with gesture, movement, and props become drama. Drama combined with dance, music, and spectacle becomes a public celebration. The more we look at the individual arts, the clearer it becomes that they are often interrelated and interdependent. The verbal arts are, in fact, simply differing manifestations of the same creative imagination that produces music and the plastic arts.

THE ART OF MUSIC

The study of music in specific cultural settings, beginning in the nineteenth century with the collection of folksongs, has developed into a specialized field, called **ethnomusicology.** Like the study of folktales for their own sake, ethnomusicology is at the same time related to and somewhat independent of anthropology. Nevertheless, it is

Ethnomusicology: The study of a society's music in terms of its cultural setting.

possible to sort out from the various concerns of the field several concepts that are of interest in general anthropology.

In order to talk intelligently about the verbal arts of a culture, it is, of course, desirable to know as much as possible about the language itself. In order to talk about the music of a culture, it is equally desirable to know the language of music — that is, its conventions. The way to approach a totally unfamiliar kind of musical expression is to learn first how it functions in respect to melody, rhythm, and form.

In general, human music is said to differ from natural music — the songs of birds, wolves, and whales, for example — in being almost everywhere perceived in terms of a repertory of tones at fixed or regular intervals from each other: in other words, a scale. We have made closed systems out of a formless range of possible sounds by dividing the distance between a tone and its first overtone or sympathetic vibration (which always has exactly twice as many vibrations as the basic tone) into a series of measured steps. In the Western or European system, the distance between the basic tone and the first overtone is called the octave; it consists of seven steps — five "whole" tones and two "semitones" — which are named with the letters A through G. The whole tones are further divided into semitones, for a total working scale of 12 tones. Westerners learn at an early age to recognize and imitate this arbitrary system and its conventions, and it comes to sound natural. Yet the overtone series, on which it is partially based, is the only part of it that can be considered a wholly natural phenomenon.

One of the most common alternatives to the semitonal system is the pentatonic system, which divides the octave into five nearly equidistant tones. In Japan there is a series of different pentatonic scales, in which some semitones are employed. In Java there are scales of both five and seven equal steps, which have no relation to the intervals we hear as "natural" in our system. In Arabic and Persian music there are smaller units of a third of a tone (some of which we may accidentally produce on an "out-of-tune" piano), with scales of 17 and 24 steps in the octave. There are even quarter-tone scales in India and subtleties of interval shading that are nearly indistinguishable to a Western ear. Small wonder, then, that even when we can hear what sounds like melody and rhythm in these systems, the total result may sound to us peculiar or out of tune. The anthropologist needs a very practiced ear to learn to appreciate — perhaps even to tolerate — some of the music heard, and only some of the most skilled folksong collectors have attempted to notate and analyze the music of nonsemitonal systems.

Scale systems and their modifications constitute what is known as **tonality** in music. Tonality determines the possibilities and limits of both melody and harmony. Not much less complex than

Tonality: In music, scale systems and their modifications.

tonality is the matter of rhythm. Rhythm, whether regular or irregular, is an organizing factor in music, sometimes more important than the melodic line. Traditional European music is rather neatly measured into recurrent patterns of two, three, and four beats, with combinations of weak and strong beats to mark the division and form patterns. Non-European music is likely to move also in patterns of five, seven, or eleven, with complex arrangements of internal beats and sometimes polyrhythms: one instrument or singer going in a pattern of three beats, for example, while another is in a pattern of five or seven. Polyrhythms are frequent in the drum music of West Africa, which shows remarkable precision in the overlapping of rhythmic lines. In addition to polyrhythms, non-European music may also contain shifting rhythms: a pattern of three, for example, followed by a pattern of two, or five, with little or no regular recurrence or repetition of any one pattern, though the patterns themselves are fixed and identifiable as units.

Although it is not necessarily the concern of anthropologists to untangle all these complicated technical matters, they will want to know enough to be aware of the degree of skill or artistry involved in a performance and to have some measure of the extent to which people in a culture have learned to practice and respond to this often important creative activity. Moreover, as with myths, legends, and tales, the distribution of musical forms and instruments can reveal much about cultural contact or isolation.

FUNCTIONS OF MUSIC

Even without concern for technical matters, the anthropologist can profitably investigate the function of music in a society. First, rarely has a culture been reported to be without any kind of music. Bone flutes and whistles as much as 30,000 years old have been found by archaeologists. Nor have historically known food-foraging peoples been

While songs and dances are often performed in Western society for enjoyment, in non-Western societies they are often more important as adjuncts to ritual. At the top, people who live on the Sepik River in Papua New Guinea dance to mourn for a dead child.

without their music. In the Kalahari Desert, for example, a !Kung hunter off by himself would play a tune for himself on his bow simply to help while away the time (long before anyone thought of beating swords into plowshares some genius discovered — when and where we do not know — that bows could be used not just to kill, but to make music as well). In northern New England, Abenaki shamans used cedar flutes to call game, lure enemies, and attract women. In addition, a drum over which two rawhide strings were stretched to produce a buzzing sound, thought to represent singing, gave the shaman the power to communicate with the spirit world. But however played, and for

whatever reason, music (like all art) is an individual creative skill that one can cultivate and be proud of, whether from a sense of accomplishment or the sheer pleasure of performing; and it is a form of social behavior through which there is a communication or sharing of feelings and life experience with other humans.

The social function of music is perhaps most obvious in song. Songs very often express as much as tales the values and concerns of the group, but they do so with the increased formalism that results from the restrictions of closed systems of tonality, rhythm, and musical form. Early investigators of non-European song were struck by the apparent simplicity of pentatonic scales and a seemingly endless repetition of phrases. They often did not give sufficient credit to the formal function of repetition in such music, confusing repetition with repetitiveness or lack of invention. A great deal of non-European music was dismissed as "primitive" and formless, and typically treated as trivial.

Repetition is, nevertheless, a fact of music, including European music, and a basic formal principle. Consider this little song from Nigeria:

Ijangbon l'o ra,
Ijangbon l'o ra,
Eni r'asho Oshomalo,
Ijangbon l'o ra.

(He buys trouble,
He buys trouble,
He who buys Oshomalo cloth,
He buys trouble.)

Several decades ago, the Oshomalo were cloth sellers in Egba villages who sold on credit and then harassed, intimidated, and even beat their customers to make them pay before the appointed day. The message of the song is simple, and both words and music are the same for three lines out of four; the whole song may be repeated many times at will. What is it that produces this kind of artistic expression and makes it more than primitive trivia? A single Egba undoubtedly improvised the song first, reacting to a personal experience or observation, lingering on one of its elements by repeating it. The repetition gives the observation not emphasis but symbolic form, and therefore a kind of concreteness or permanence. In this concrete form, made memorable and attractive with melody and rhythm, the song was taken up by other Egba, perhaps with some musical refinements or embellishments from more creative members of the group, including clapping or drumming to mark the rhythm. Thus a bit of social commentary was crystallized and preserved even after the situation had passed into history.

Whether the content of songs is didactic, satirical, inspirational, religious, political, or purely emotional, the important thing is that the formless has been given form, and feelings are communicated in a symbolic and memorable way that can be repeated and shared. The group is consequently united and probably has the sense that the experience, whatever it may be, has shape and meaning.

THE ART OF SCULPTURE

In the broadest sense, sculpture is art in the round. Any three-dimensional product of the creative imagination may be called a piece of sculpture: a ceremonial knife, a decorative pot, a hand-crafted lute, an ornamental gate, a funerary monument, or a public building display the same essential artistic process as a statue, a mask, or a figurine. All of these human creations represent an imaginative organization of materials in space. The artist has given tangible shape to his or her feelings and perceptions, creating or re-creating symbolically meaningful form out of formlessness. In a narrower sense, sculpture means only those artifacts that serve no immediate utilitarian purpose and are fashioned from hard or semipermanent materials. It is, however, difficult to state unequivocally what may or may not qualify as a piece of sculpture, even with this limitation. Are the beautiful and highly imaginative tiny brass figurines of the Ashanti, for example, which were formerly used as weights for measuring out quantities of gold, not to be considered sculpture, even though the somewhat larger brass figurines of comparable design in Dahomey, which have never had a practical use,

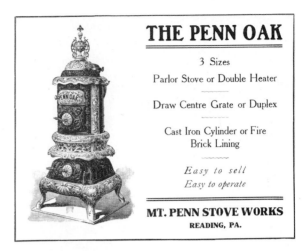

THE PENN OAK

3 Sizes
Parlor Stove or Double Heater

Draw Centre Grate or Duplex

Cast Iron Cylinder or Fire
Brick Lining

Easy to sell
Easy to operate

MT. PENN STOVE WORKS
READING, PA.

Though once mass produced as a utilitarian item, a stove like this one today, if in good condition, will fetch a price of several hundred dollars as an object of "art in the round." Although not created as a piece of sculpture, that is what it has, in effect, become.

are obviously to be so considered? Or should we perhaps now call the Ashanti figurines sculpture, as we now do, because they are no longer put to use?

ART AND CRAFT

Our use of the word *sculpture* in English seems to impose a distinction between types of creative activity where none may in fact exist. One solution is to substitute the modern term *plastic art*, but the phenomenon remains the same. Objects that are obviously skillfully made but still do not quite qualify as sculpture by virtue of being somewhat trivial, low in symbolic content, or impermanent — by the standards of the culture — are generally known and considered as the products of craft (or, in modern times, industry). An automobile, for example, however beautifully it may be designed, however lovingly it may be displayed in front of the house as an object for admiration, and however cleverly we may interpret its parts and its functions as symbolic in our culture, is for us above all a mass-produced consumable, and to treat it as sculpture would be misrepresenting its *usual* value in our society. Furthermore, we must also consider

Michelangelo's "David."

ture and abstracts patterns of ideal beauty, ugliness, or typical expressions of emotion. Michelangelo's *David* is representational sculpture, clearly depicting a human being; it is also abstract insofar as it generalizes an ideal of masculine beauty, quiet strength, and emotional calm, therefore functioning symbolically. Henry Moore's gigantic women with holes through their midsections are abstractions, using nature but exaggerating and deliberately transforming some of its shapes for the purpose of expressing a particular feeling toward them.

WEST AFRICAN SCULPTURE

West African sculpture, only comparatively recently studied and described in adequate detail, is an especially rich non-Western tradition that may help illustrate some of the anthropological aspects of representational and abstract sculpture, its subjects, materials, and meanings.

Ancestor worship and reverence of royalty have found expression in a realistic or portrait-style sculpture throughout the region of the Niger and Congo River basins. Probably the most dramatically realistic are the so-called Benin bronzes: hundreds of finely detailed heads of royal ancestors, produced first at the sacred Yoruba city of Ife (in present-day Nigeria) in the fifteenth century and later in the Benin capital itself. Upon the death of a ruler of Benin, a memorial head was cast in bronze to be placed on the shrine of the departed ruler. Most of these heads were carried off to England at the end of the nineteenth century, and they have served as a forcible reminder to Westerners that the Mediterranean region is not the only source of fine realistic sculpture.

In addition to the Benin bronzes, the royal statues of the Bakuba kings in the Congo River region, the ancestor figures of the Guro on the Ivory Coast, the secular and satirical representations of Europeans by the Yoruba in Nigeria, and the small brasses depicting the royalty and animals of the Fon in Dahomey are also naturalistic in detail, and are obviously often intended to represent real persons or animals in characteristic moods or poses.

the intention of the creator. What we call sculpture or plastic art is not ordinarily artistic by accident or through after-the-fact interpretation, but by design. Detroit does not intentionally produce sculpture.

As a type of symbolic expression, sculpture may be representational, imitating closely the forms of nature, or it may be abstract, drawing from natural forms but representing only their basic patterns or arrangements. Representational sculpture is partly abstract to the extent that it generalizes from na-

Head of one of the Kings of Benin cast in bronze at the time of his death.

A wooden figure made by the Yoruba of Nigeria, probably in the 1920s as a cult item. It was used as a container for kola nuts used in divination ceremonies.

Features and proportions may be somewhat stylized according to regional conventions of what is appropriate or possible in sculpture: heads may be disproportionately large, necks elongated, and sexual parts either exaggerated or minimized. It is of note that most of these sculptures come from cultures in which subsistence techniques were efficient enough to produce a surplus, which was used to support a variety of occupational specialists. The artist was one such specialist, much of whose work was commissioned by other specialists, such as priests and government officials.

The majority of West African sculpture is abstract or expressionistic — giving form to human feelings and attitudes toward gods, spirits, other humans, and animals. Generalizations about the nonrepresentational styles and purposes for the region are, however, almost impossible. Every West African culture that produces or has produced sculpture has its own identifiable styles, and this artistic cohesion undoubtedly reinforces the social unity of the group. A Fon recognizes a Yoruba mask, and is disassociated from whatever symbolic significance it has for the Yoruba. Materials as well as styles differ in neighboring cultures. The most common material is wood, but there is also regional use of brass, iron, terra-cotta, mud, and raffia. Sculpture may be rubbed with ash, smoked in banana leaves, oiled, waxed, painted, and adorned with cowrie shells, teeth, iron or brass nails, strips of metal, or cloth.

Symbolic Content

In all these varieties of sculpture, whatever their style and material, anthropologists are interested in exactly what is abstracted from nature and why. They are also interested in the extent to which traditions are perpetuated, and what meanings may be developing or changing. It appears that any single piece of sculpture in West Africa may be interpreted in terms of its symbolic significance for the group, which is well known by the people who make and look at the sculpture. Consequently the anthropologist has only to ask.

A small wooden figure of a person, with a head, rudimentary limbs, and a large trunk purposely riddled with holes, may be found among the Balega of the northeast Congo region. The figure is known as a *katanda*, meaning the scattering of red ants when attacked; it is interpreted as symbolizing the bad effect of internal fighting on the unity of local descent groups. The *kanaga* mask of the Dogon in Upper Volta is an elongated head with triangular eyes, long pointed ears and nose, and a cap surmounted with an enormous crest, four or five times the size of the head, in the form of a double-armed cross. For young initiates the cross symbolizes a bird with outstretched wings, the beginning of active flight into life, and for older initiates of high rank its structure symbolizes a synthesis of contradictory or competing life forces. The *akua'ba* dolls of the Ashanti in Ghana, flat disk-headed figures on a long, narrow, legless body with a simple crosspiece for arms, are said to symbolize an Ashanti ideal of beauty in the high, wide forehead; the dolls are tucked into the waistcloths of young girls, who carry them like real babies, perhaps as talismans to assure their own physical development or that of their children.

Ritual Masks

The widest variety of expression in African sculpture is certainly to be found in the ritual mask. Styles range from the relatively realistic and serene

Mask made by the Baluba of Zaire.

faces made by the Baule on the Ivory Coast to the frightening, violent, and extroverted faces with protruding eyes produced by the neighboring Ngere of Liberia. Theories about the symbolism of the masks have arisen beside the explanations of local informants, particularly in cases where certain masks are no longer produced or known. One of the more interesting is the notion that the unnatural features of some of the masks representing spirits of the dead are made systematically unnatural in order to suggest that the other world, or the spirit world, is somehow an opposite of this one: noses are long instead of short, ears are large rather than small, eye cavities are hollow rather than filled, and so on. The mask, as well as other sculpture, therefore becomes, as much as the myth, an expression of world view. The sculptor again gives shape and meaning to that which is unknown.

As in musical expression, sculpture also crystallizes feeling in a form that can be shared and perpetuated. Much, though not all, African sculpture is impermanent because of the impermanent na-

APPLICATION
Reviving Lost Heritages

In these last years of the twentieth century, the time is long past when the anthropologist could go out and describe small tribal groups in out-of-the-way places that had not been "contaminated" by contact with Westerners. Not only are there few such groups in the world today, but those that do remain face strong pressures to abandon their traditional ways in the name of "progress." All too often, tribal peoples are made to forfeit their indigenous identity and are pressed into a mold that allows them neither the opportunity nor the motivation to rise above the lowest rung of the social ladder. From an autonomous people able to provide for their own needs, with pride and a strong sense of their own identity as a people, they are transformed into a deprived underclass with neither pride nor a sense of their own identity, often despised by more fortunate members of some national society.

The basic right of groups of people to be themselves and not to be deprived of their own distinctive cultural identities is and should be our paramount consideration, and will be dealt with in the final two chapters of this book. There are, however, additional reasons to be concerned about the disappearance of the societies with which anthropologists have been so often concerned. For one thing, the need for information about them has become steadily more apparent. If we are ever to have a realistic understanding of that elusive thing called human nature, we need reliable data on all humans. There is more to it than this, though; once a tribal society is gone, it is lost to humanity, unless an adequate record of it exists. When

this happens, humanity is the poorer for the loss. Hence, anthropologists have in a sense rescued many such societies from oblivion. This not only helps to preserve human heritage; it may also be important to an ethnic group that, having become Westernized, wishes to rediscover and reassert its past cultural identity. As an example, native arts on the northwest coast of North America had all but disappeared as a consequence of the Canadian government's decision that native practices such as potlatching (discussed in Chapter 16) had to stop.

With the dropping of the ban on potlatching in 1951, there was a resurgence of ethnic pride and, in consequence, a revival of native arts, in which Bill Holm, an anthropologist at the University of Washington, played a key role. Through analysis of 400 of the finest old pieces of northwest coast art in museums, he was able to rediscover the aesthetic rules that had governed the works of traditional wood sculptors. Reawareness of the rules has breathed new life into the work of native artists, who are again creating splendid works of art that are vital to traditional northwest coast social and ceremonial life.

In this instance, Bill Holm was not working as an applied anthropologist in the strict sense — that is, he was not putting his anthropological talents to work for a specific client; he was just "doing research." Yet the practical outcome of his work was as if he had. The fact is that the distinction that is often made between "basic" and "applied" research is not nearly as clear as is often made out.

ture of its materials (50 years has been suggested as an average lifetime for a wooden figure exposed to weather), but it is generally considered a great shame when a mask or piece of sculpture disintegrates. An important piece of sculpture may be replaced by imitation, copied, and perpetuated so that the traditions and beliefs may be preserved. There is often a ritual in mask making, with great care taken to preserve and copy exactly the tradi-

tional specifications. Similarly, there is still in some places a special reverence in the process of sculpting in general, and the soul of the wood must be respected with attendant rituals and beliefs. Traditional West African sculpture is currently in decline, but it is not by any means everywhere dead. An excursion beyond the major urban centers reveals continuing activity in this important kind of symbolic creativity.

CHAPTER SUMMARY

Art is the creative use of the human imagination to interpret, understand, and enjoy life. It stems from the uniquely human ability to use symbols to give shape and significance to the physical world for more than just a utilitarian purpose. Anthropologists are concerned with art as a reflection of the cultural values and concerns of people.

Oral traditions denote the unwritten stories, beliefs, and customs of a culture. Verbal arts include narrative, drama, poetry, incantations, proverbs, riddles, and word games. Narratives, which have received the most study, have been divided into three categories: myths, legends, and tales.

Myths are basically religious, with their subject matter the large questions of human existence. In describing an orderly universe, myths function to set standards for orderly behavior. Legends are semihistorical narratives that recount the exploits of heroes, the movements of people, and the establishment of local customs. Epics, which are long legends in poetry or prose, are typically found in nonliterate societies with a form of state political organization. They serve to transmit and preserve a culture's legal and political practices. In literate states, these functions have been taken over to one degree or another by history. Anthropologists are interested in legends because they provide clues to what constitutes model ethical behavior in a culture. Tales are fictional, secular, nonhistorical narratives that sometimes teach moral or practical lessons. Anthropological interest in tales centers on the fact that their distribution provides evidence of cultural contacts or cultural isolation.

The study of music in specific cultural settings has developed into the specialized field of ethnomusicology. Almost everywhere human music is perceived in terms of a scale. Scale systems and their modifications constitute tonality in music. Tonality determines the possibilities and limits of melody and harmony. Rhythm is an organizing factor in music. Traditional European music is measured into recurrent patterns of two, three, and four beats.

The social function of music is most obvious in song. Like tales, songs may express the concerns of the group, but with greater formalism because of the restrictions imposed by closed systems of tonality, rhythm, and musical form.

Sculpture is any three-dimensional product of the creative imagination fashioned from hard or semipermanent materials. Sculpted objects, such as a statue, a ceremonial knife, or a public building, represent an imaginative organization of materials in space. A more modern term for sculpture is plastic art. Certain objects, although skillfully made, do not qualify as sculpture. This may be because by the standards of the culture they are trivial, low in symbolic content, or impermanent. Such objects are generally considered as the products of crafts — or in modern times, industry. Sculpture may be representational, imitating the forms of nature, or it may be abstract, representing only basic patterns of natural forms. West African sculpture illustrates some of the anthropological aspects of representational and abstract sculpture in its subject matter, materials, and meanings.

SUGGESTED READINGS

Boas, Franz. *Primitive Art*. Gloucester, Mass.: Peter Smith, 1962. This is a reprint of an old "classic," which gives an analytical description of the basic traits of "primitive" art. Its treatment is based on two principles: the fundamental sameness of mental processes in all races and cultural forms of the present day, and the consideration of every cultural phenomenon in a historical context. It covers formal elements in art, symbolism, and style and has sections on "primitive" literature, music, and dance.

Dundes, Alan. *Interpreting Folk Lore*. Bloomington: Indiana University Press, 1980. This collection of articles assesses the materials that folklorists have amassed and classified; the articles seek to broaden and refine traditional assumptions about the proper subject matter and methods of folklore.

Fraser, Douglas. *Primitive Art*. Garden City, N.Y.: Doubleday, 1962. The book presents a systematic survey of non-Western art, aiming to place each style studied in relation both to its local setting and to other styles near and far away. The author covers the three main geographical areas of Africa, Asia-Oceania, and America. The color illustrations are especially good.

Hatcher, Evelyn Payne. *Art as Culture: An Introduction to the Anthropology of Art*. New York: University Press of America, 1985. This handy, clearly written book does a nice job of relating the visual arts to other aspects of culture. Topics include "The Technological Means," "The Psychological Perspective," "Social Contexts and Social Functions," "Art as Communication," and "The Time Dimension." Numerous line drawings help the reader to understand the varied forms of art in non-Western societies.

Merriam, Alan P. *The Anthropology of Music*. Chicago: Northwestern University Press, 1964. This book focuses upon music as a complex of behavior, which resonates throughout all of culture: social organization, aesthetic activity, economics, and religion.

Otten, Charlotte M., ed. *Anthropology and Art: Readings in Cross-cultural Aesthetics*. Garden City, N.Y.: Natural History Press, 1971. This is a collection of articles by anthropologists and art historians, with an emphasis on the functional relationships between art and culture.

This space helmet is symbolic of the changes sweeping the world today. Unfortunately, our success at putting humans into space has not been matched by similar success in alleviating hunger, poverty, and pollution, or in controlling violence.

PART VII

CHANGE
AND THE
FUTURE

Solving the Problem of Adjusting to Changed Conditions

INTRODUCTION

Without the ability to conceive new ideas and change existing behavior patterns, no human society could survive. Human culture is remarkably stable, but it is also resilient and therefore able to adapt to altered circumstances.

Understanding the processes of change, the subject of Chapter 24, is one of the most important and fundamental of anthropological goals. Unfortunately, the task is made difficult by our cultural biases, which predispose us to see change as a progressive process leading in a predictable and determined way to where we are now, and even on beyond into a future to which we are leading the way. So pervasive is our notion of progress that it motivates our thinking in a great many ways of which we are hardly aware. Among other things, it leads us to view cultures not like our own as "backward" and "underdeveloped"; as two well-known economists put it, "we . . . have the feeling that we are encountering in the present the anachronistic counterparts of the static societies of antiquity."[1] Of course, they are no such thing; as we saw in Chapter 15, no culture is static, and cultures may be very highly developed in quite different ways. A simple analogy with the world of nature may be helpful here. In the course of evolution, single-celled organisms appeared long before vertebrate animals, and land vertebrates like mammals are relative latecomers indeed. Yet single-celled organisms abound in the world today, not as relics of the past, but as creatures highly adapted to situations for which mammals are totally unsuited. Just because mammals got here late does not mean that a dog is "better" or "more progressive" than an amoeba.

Belief in "progress" and its inevitability has important implications for ourselves as well as others. For us, it means that change has become necessary for its own sake, for whatever we have today is, by definition, not as good as what we will have tomorrow. Put another way, whatever is old is, by virtue of that fact alone, not very good, and should be gotten rid of, no matter how well it seems to be working. This virtually guarantees the continuing existence of significant dissatisfaction within our own society. For others, the logic runs like this: If the old must inevitably give way to the new, then societies that we perceive as being "old" or "out of the past" must also give way to the new. Since our way of life is a recent development in human history, we must represent the new. "Old" societies must therefore become like us, or else it is their fate to disappear altogether. What this amounts to is a charter for massive intervention into the lives of others, whether they want this or not; the outcome, more often than not, is the destabilization and even destruction of other societies in the world at large.

A conscious attempt to identify and eliminate the biases of our culture allows us to see change in a very different way. It allows us to recognize that, although people can respond deliberately to problems in such a way as to change their culture, much change

[1]Robert L. Heilbroner and Lester C. Thurow, *The Economic Problem*, 6th ed. (Englewood Cliffs, N.J.: Prentice-Hall, 1981), p. 607.

occurs accidentally. This should not surprise us, though, when we consider that in biological evolution, accidents (called mutations) are the ultimate source of all change. The fact is that the historical record, too, is quirky, and full of random events. And while it is true that without change, cultures could never adapt to changed conditions, we must recognize that too much in the way of large-scale, continuing change may also place a culture in jeopardy. This is because it conflicts with the social need for predictability, discussed in Chapter 12; the need of individuals for regularity and structure, discussed in Chapter 14; and the need of populations for an adaptive "fit" with their environment, discussed in Chapter 15. In short, just as a runaway rate of mutation is a threat to the survival of a biological species, so is a runaway rate of change to a human society.

The more anthropologists study change and learn about the various ways people go about solving their problems of existence, the more aware they become of a great paradox of culture. While the basic business of culture is to solve problems, in doing so, inevitably, new problems are created, which themselves demand solution. Throughout this book we have seen examples of this — the problem of forming groups in order to cooperate in solving the problems of staying alive, the problem of finding ways to overcome the stresses and strains on individuals as a consequence of their membership in groups, as well as the structural problems that are inherent in the division of society into a number of smaller groups, to mention but a few. It is apparent that every solution to a problem has its price, but so long as culture is able to keep at least a step ahead of the problems, all is reasonably well. This seems to have been the case generally over the past 2 million years.

When we see all of the problems that face the human species today (Chapter 25), most of them the result of cultural practices, we may wonder if we haven't passed some critical threshold where culture has begun to fall a step behind the problems. This is not to say that the future necessarily has to be bleak for the generations that come after us, but it would certainly be irresponsible to project some sort of rosy, science-fiction type of future as inevitable, at least on the basis of present evidence. To prevent the future from being bleak, humans will have to rise to the challenge of changing their behavior and ideas in order to conquer the large problems that threaten to annihilate them: overpopulation and unequal access to basic resources with their concomitant starvation, poverty, and squalor; environmental pollution and poisoning; and the culture of discontent and bitterness that rises out of the widening economic gap separating industrialized and nonindustrialized countries as well as the "haves" from the "have-nots" within countries.

24

CULTURAL CHANGE

The capacity to change has always been important to human cultures. Perhaps at no time has the pace of culture change equalled that of today, as symbolized by these Maori children using a calculator. In the space of a single generation, many traditional peoples are attempting to undergo the kind of culture change that took Western industrialized societies generations to accomplish.

Why Do Cultures Change?

All cultures change at one time or another, for a variety of reasons. Although people may deliberately change their ways in response to some perceived problem, much change is accidental, including the unforeseen outcome of existing events. Or, contact with other peoples may lead to the introduction of "foreign" ideas, bringing about changes in existing values and behavior. This may even involve the massive imposition of foreign ways through conquest of one group by another. Through change, cultures are able to adapt to altered conditions; on the other hand, not all change is adaptive.

How Do Cultures Change?

The mechanisms of change are innovation, diffusion, cultural loss, and acculturation. Innovation occurs when someone within a society discovers something new that is then accepted by other members of the society. Diffusion is the borrowing of something from another group, and cultural loss is the abandonment of an existing practice or trait, with or without replacement. Acculturation is the massive change that occurs with the sort of intensive, firsthand contact that has occurred under colonialism.

What Is Modernization?

Modernization is an ethnocentric term used to refer to a global process of change by which traditional, nonindustrial societies seek to acquire characteristics of industrially "advanced" societies. Although modernization has generally been assumed to be a good thing, and there have been some successes, it has frequently led to the development of a new "culture of discontent," a level of aspirations far exceeding the bounds of an individual's local opportunities. Sometimes it leads to the destruction of cherished customs and values people had no desire to abandon.

Culture is the medium through which the human species solves the problems of existence as perceived by members of the species. Various cultural institutions, such as kinship and marriage, political and economic organization, and religion, mesh together to form an integrated cultural system. Because systems generally work to maintain stability, cultures are often fairly stable and remain so unless either the conditions to which they are adapted, or human perceptions of those conditions, change. Archeological studies have revealed how elements of a culture may persist for long periods of time. In Chapter 15, for example, we saw how the culture of the native inhabitants of northwestern New England and southern Quebec remained relatively stable over thousands of years.

Although stability may be a striking feature of many cultures, none is ever changeless, as the cultures of food foragers, subsistence farmers, or pastoralists are all too often assumed to be. In a stable society, change may occur gently and gradually, without altering in any fundamental way the underlying logic of the culture. Sometimes, though, the pace of change may increase dramatically, causing a radical cultural alteration in a relatively short period of time. The modern world is full of examples as diverse as what happened in Iran with the overthrow of the Shah, or what is happening to the native peoples of the Amazon forest as Brazil presses ahead to "develop" this vast region.

The causes of change are many and include the unexpected outcome of existing activities. To cite an example from our own history, the settlement of what we now call New England by English-speaking people had nothing to do with their culture being "better" or "more progressive" than those of the region's native inhabitants (it was neither, but merely different). Rather, it was the outcome of a series of unrelated events that happened to coincide at a critical moment in time. In England, economic and political developments that drove large numbers of farmers off the land, occurring at a time of growing populations, together favored an outward migration of people; that this happened shortly after the European discovery of the Americas was purely a matter of chance. Even

at that, attempts to establish British colonies in New England ended in failure, until an epidemic of unprecedented scope resulted in the sudden death of about 90 percent of the native inhabitants of coastal New England. This epidemic did not happen because without it, the British would be unable to settle, but rather because the Indians had contracted the disease during regular contact with European fishermen and fur traders, whose activities were independent of British attempts at colonization. For centuries up to this time, Europeans had been living under conditions that were ideal for the incubation and spread of all sorts of infectious diseases, but the Indians had not. Consequently, the Europeans had developed over time a degree of resistance to them, which Indians lacked altogether. To be sure, the consequences were inevitable once direct contact between these people occurred; nonetheless, differential immunity did not occur in order to clear the coast of New England for English settlement. And even once those settlements were established, it is unlikely that the colonists would have been able to alienate the remaining natives from their land had they not come equipped with the techniques previously used to impose control upon other peoples, for example the Scots, Irish, and Welsh. In sum, had not a number of otherwise unrelated phenomena come together by chance at just the right moment in time, English might very well not be the language spoken by most North Americans today.

Not just the unexpected outcome of existing activities, but other sorts of accidents, too, may bring about changes, if people perceive them to be useful. Of course, people may also respond deliberately to altered conditions, thereby correcting the perceived problem that made the cultural modification seem necessary. Change may also be forced upon one group by another, as happened in colonial New England and as is happening in many parts of the world today, in the course of especially intense contact between two societies. Progress and adaptation, on the other hand, are *not* causes of change; the latter is a consequence of it that happens to work well for a population, and the former is a judgment of those consequences in terms of the group's cultural values. Progress is whatever it is defined as.

MECHANISMS OF CHANGE

INNOVATION

The ultimate source of all change is through innovation: any new practice, tool, or principle that gains widespread acceptance within a group. Those that involve the chance discovery of some new principle we refer to as **primary innovations;** those that result from the deliberate applications of known principles are **secondary innovations.** It is the latter that correspond most closely with our culture's model of change as predictable and determined, while the former involves accidents of one sort or another.

An example of a primary innovation is the discovery that the firing of clay makes it permanently hard. Presumably, accidental firing of clay took place frequently in ancient cooking fires. An accidental occurrence is of no account, however, unless some application of it is perceived. This actually happened about 25,000 years ago, for figurines were made then of fired clay. Pottery vessels were not made, however, and the practice of making things of fired clay did not reach the Middle East at this time; at least if it did, it failed to take root. Not until some time between 7000 and 6500 B.C. did people living in the Middle East recognize a significant application of fired clay, at which time they began using it to make cheap, durable, easy-to-produce containers and cooking vessels.

As nearly as we can reconstruct, the development of the earliest known pottery vessels came about in the following way.[1] By 7000 B.C., cooking areas in the Middle East included clay-lined basins built into the floor, clay ovens, and hearths, making the accidental firing of clay inevitable. More-

[1]Ruth Amiran, "The Beginnings of Pottery-Making in the Near East," in *Ceramics and Man*, ed. Frederick R. Matson (Viking Fund Publications in Anthropology, 1965), no. 41, pp. 240–247.

Clay-lined basins in the floor of an ancient cooking area at Jericho, in the Middle East. The proximity of clay and fire must have accidentally fired clay on numerous occasions; under the circumstances, the invention of pottery containers was bound to happen.

Primary innovation: The chance discovery of some new principle.

Secondary innovation: Something new that results from the deliberate application of known principles.

over, people were already familiar with the working of clay, which they used to build houses, line storage pits, and model figurines. For containers, however, they still relied upon baskets, and leather bags.

Once the significance of fired clay — **primary innovation** — was perceived, then the application of known techniques to it — **secondary innovation** — became possible. Clay could be modeled in the familiar way into the known shapes of baskets, leather bags, and stone bowls and then fired, either in an open fire or in the same ovens used for cooking food. In fact, the earliest known Middle East pottery is imitative of leather and stone containers, and the decoration consists of motifs transferred from basketry, even though they were ill suited to the new medium. Eventually, shapes and decorative techniques more suited to the new technology were developed.

Since men are never the potters in traditional societies unless the craft has become something of a commercial operation, the first pottery was probably made by women. The vessels that they produced were initially handmade, and the earliest kilns were the same ovens that were used for cooking. As people became more adept at making pottery, there were further technological refinements. As an aid in production, the clay could be modeled on a mat or other surface, which the woman could move as work progressed. Hence, she could sit in one place while she worked, without having to get up to move around the clay. A further refinement was to mount the movable surface on a vertical rotating shaft — an application of a known principle used for drills — which produced the potter's wheel and permitted mass production. Kilns, too,

were improved for better circulation of heat by separating the firing chamber from the fire itself. By chance, it happened that these improved kilns produced enough heat to smelt some ores such as copper, tin, gold, silver, and lead. Presumably, this discovery was made by accident — another primary innovation — and the stage was set for the eventual development of the forced-draft furnace out of the earlier pottery kiln.

The accidents responsible for primary innovations are not generated by environmental change or some other "need," nor are they preferentially oriented in an adaptive direction (Figure 24.1). They are, however, given structure by the cultural context in which they occur. Thus, the outcome of the discovery of fired clay by mobile food foragers 25,000 years ago was very different from what it was when discovered later on by more sedentary farmers in the Middle East, where it set off a veritable chain reaction as one invention led to another. Indeed, given certain sets of cultural goals, values, and knowledge, particular innovations are

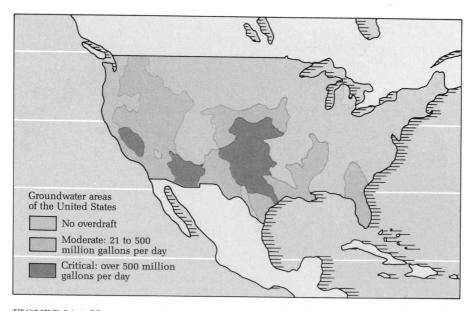

Groundwater areas
of the United States

☐ No overdraft

☐ Moderate: 21 to 500
million gallons per day

■ Critical: over 500 million
gallons per day

FIGURE 24.1 Human practices may or may not be adaptive. In the United States, for example, it is not adaptive over the long run to deplete ground water in regions of fast growing populations, yet this is being done.

almost bound to be made, as illustrated by the case of penicillin. This antibiotic was discovered in 1928 when a mold blew in through the window of Sir Alexander Fleming's lab and landed on a microbial colony of staphylococcus, which it then dissolved. Fleming recognized the importance of this accident, because he had become aware of the need for more than antiseptics and immunization, the mainstays of medicine at the time, to fight infection. Of course, he was not alone in his awareness, nor was the accident involved at all unusual. Any physician who studied medicine in the early part of this century has stories about having to scrub down laboratories when their studies in bacteriology were brought to a halt by molds that persisted in contaminating cultures and killing off the bacteria. To them, it was an annoyance; to Fleming, it was a "magic bullet" to fight infection. Under the circumstances, however, had he not made the discovery, someone else would have before long.

Although a culture's internal dynamics may encourage certain innovative tendencies, they may discourage others, or even remain neutral with respect to yet others. Copernicus's discovery of the rotation of the planets around the sun and Mendel's discovery of the basic laws of heredity are instances of genuine creative insights out of step with the established needs, values, and goals of their times and places. In fact, Mendel's work remained obscure until 16 years after his death, when three scientists working independently rediscovered, all in the same year (1900), the same laws of heredity. Thus, in the context of turn-of-the-century Western culture, Mendel's laws were bound to be discovered, even had Mendel himself not hit upon them earlier.

While an innovation must be reasonably consistent with a society's needs, values, and goals, if it is to be accepted, this is not sufficient to assure its acceptance. Force of habit tends to be an obstacle to acceptance; people will generally tend to stick with what they are used to, rather than adopt something new that will require some adjustment on their part. An example of this can be seen in the continued British practice of driving on the left-

While a culture may be "open" to change in some areas, it may be resistant to change in others. British drivers continue to drive on the left, even though other Europeans do not. So ingrained do bodily reflexes associated with driving become that changing is physically difficult.

Diffusion: The spread of customs or practices from one culture to another.

hand side of the road, rather than on the right. Driving on the left is no more natural than driving on the right, but to someone from Britain it seems so, because of the body reflexes that have developed in the course of driving on the left. In this case, the individual's very body has become adjusted to certain patterns of behavior that bypass any presumed "openness" to change. An innovation's chance of acceptance tends to be greater if it is obviously better than the thing or idea it replaces. Beyond this, much may depend on the prestige of the innovator and imitating groups. If the innovator's prestige is high, this will help gain acceptance for the innovation. If it is low, acceptance is less likely, unless the innovator can attract a sponsor who has high prestige.

DIFFUSION

When the Pilgrims established their colony of New Plymouth in North America, they very likely would have starved to death, had the Indian Squanto not showed them how to grow the native American crops — corn, beans, and squash. The borrowing of cultural elements from one society by members of another is known as **diffusion,** and the donor society is, for all intents and purposes, the "inventor" of that element. So common is borrowing that the late Ralph Linton, a North American anthropologist, suggested that borrowing accounts for as much as 90 percent of any culture's content. People are creative about their borrowing, however, picking and choosing from multiple possibilities and sources. Usually their selections are limited to those compatible with the existing culture. In modern-day Guatemala, for example, Maya Indians, who make up over half of that country's population, will adopt Western ways if the value of what they adopt is self-evident and does not conflict with traditional ways and values. The use of metal hoes, shovels, and machetes has long since become standard, for they are superior to stone tools, and yet they are compatible with the cultivation of corn in the traditional way by men using hand tools. Yet certain other "modern" practices, which might appear advantageous to the Maya, tend to be resisted if they are perceived as running counter to Indian tradition. Thus, a young man in one community who tried his hand at truck gardening, using chemical fertilizers and pesticides to grow cash crops with market value only in the city — vegetables never eaten by the Maya — could not secure a "good" woman for a wife (a "good" woman is one who has never had sex with another man, who is skilled at domestic chores, not lazy, and willing to attend to her husband's needs). Upon abandonment of his unorthodox ways, however, he became accepted by his community as a "real man," no longer different from the rest of them and conspicuous. (A "real man" is one who will work steadily to provide the members of his household with what they need to live by farming and making charcoal in the traditional ways.) Before long, he was well married.[2]

[2]Ruben E. Reina, *The Law of the Saints.* (Indianapolis: Bobbs-Merrill, 1966), pp. 65–68.

While the tendency toward borrowing is so great as to lead Robert Lowie to comment, "Culture is a thing of shreds and patches," the borrowed traits usually undergo sufficient modifications to make this wry comment more colorful than critical. Moreover, existing cultural traits may be modified to accommodate the borrowed one. An awareness of the extent of borrowing can be eye opening. Take, for example, the numerous things we have borrowed from American Indians. Domestic plants that were developed ("invented") by the Indians — "Irish" potatoes, corn, beans, squash, and sweet potatoes — furnish nearly half the world's food supply. Among drugs and stimulants, tobacco (Figure 24.2) is the best known, but others include coca in cocaine, ephedra in ephedrine, datura in pain relievers, and cascara in laxatives. All but a handful of drugs known today made from plants native to America were used by Indians, and over 200 plants and herbs that they used for medicinal purposes have at one time or another been included in the *Pharmacopeia of the United States* or in the *National Formulary.* Varieties of cotton developed by Indians supply much of the world's clothing needs, while the woolen poncho, the parka, and moccasins are universally familiar items. Not only has Anglo-American literature been permanently shaped by such works as Longfellow's *Hiawatha* and James Fenimore Cooper's *Leatherstocking Tales*, but American Indian music has contributed to world music such ultramodern devices as unusual intervals, arbitrary scales, conflicting rhythms, and hypnotic monotony. These borrowings are so well integrated into our culture that few people are aware of their source.

Despite the obvious importance of diffusion, there are probably more obstacles to accepting an innovation from another culture than there are to accepting one that is "homegrown." In addition to the same obstacles that stand in the way of "homegrown" inventions is the fact that a borrowed one is, somehow, "foreign." In the United States, for example, this is one reason why people have been so reluctant to abandon completely the awkward and cumbersome old English system of weights and measures for the far more logical metric sys-

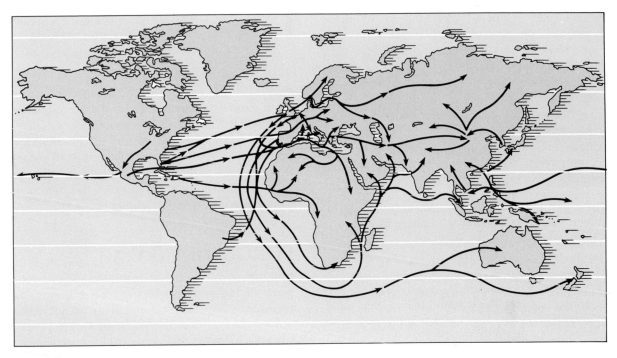

FIGURE 24.2 The diffusion of tobacco from its starting points in the Americas to Europe and its rapid spread throughout the world.

tem, which has been adopted by just about everyone else on the face of the earth. (The only holdouts besides the United States are Brunei and Burma.) Hence, the ethnocentrism of the potential borrowing culture may act as a barrier to acceptance.

CULTURAL LOSS

Most often we tend to think of change as an accumulation of innovations, new things being added to those already there. We do so because this seems so much a part of the way we live. A little reflection, however, leads to the realization that frequently the acceptance of a new innovation leads to the loss of an older one. This sort of replacement is not just a feature of Western civilization. For example, back in biblical times, chariots and carts were in widespread use in the Middle East, but by the sixth century A.D., wheeled vehi-

cles had virtually disappeared from Morocco to Afghanistan. They were replaced by camels, not because of some reversion to the past on the part of the region's inhabitants, but because camels, used as pack animals, worked better. By the sixth century, Roman roads had deteriorated, but camels, so long as they were not used as draft animals, were not bound to them. Not only that, their longevity, endurance, and ability to ford rivers and traverse rough ground without having to build roads in the first place made pack camels admirably suited for the region. Finally, there was a saving in labor: A wagon required a man for every two draft animals, whereas a single person can manage from three to six pack camels. Stephen Jay Gould comments:

We are initially surprised . . . because wheels have come to symbolize in our culture the sine qua non of intelligent exploitation and technological progress. Once invented, their superiority cannot be gainsaid

In our culture, the wheel is the symbol of technological progress, but wheeled transport is not always superior to other forms.

or superseded. Indeed, "reinventing the wheel" has become our standard metaphor for deriding the repetition of such obvious truths. In an earlier era of triumphant social Darwinism, wheels stood as an ineluctable stage of human progress. The "inferior" cultures of Africa slid to defeat; their conquerors rolled to victory. The "advanced" cultures of Mexico and Peru might have repulsed Cortés and Pizarro if only a clever artisan had thought of turning a calendar stone into a cartwheel. The notion that carts could ever be replaced by pack animals strikes us not only as backward but almost sacrilegious.

The success of camels reemphasizes a fundamental theme. . . . Adaptation, be it biological or cultural, represents a better fit to specific, local environments, not an inevitable stage in a ladder of progress. Wheels were a formidable invention, and their uses are manifold (potters and millers did not abandon them, even when cartwrights were eclipsed). But camels may work better in some circumstances. Wheels, like wings, fins, and brains, are exquisite devices for certain purposes, not signs of intrinsic superiority.[3]

Often overlooked is another facet of the loss of apparently useful traits: loss without replacement. An example of this is the absence of boats among the inhabitants of the Canary Islands, an archipelago isolated in the stormy seas off the coast of

[3]Stephen Jay Gould, *Hen's Teeth and Horses' Toes* (New York: Norton, 1983), p. 159.

| **Acculturation:** Major culture changes that occur as a result of prolonged contact between societies.

West Africa. The ancestors of these people must have had boats, for without them they could never have transported themselves and their domestic livestock to the islands in the first place. Later, without boats, they had no way to communicate between islands. The cause of this loss of something useful was that the islands contain no stone suitable for making polished stone axes, which in turn limited the islanders' carpentry.[4]

FORCIBLE CHANGE

Innovation, diffusion, and cultural loss all may take place among peoples who are free to decide for themselves what they will or will not accept in the way of change. Not always, however, are people left free to make their own choices; frequently, changes that they would not willingly make themselves have been forced on them by some other group, usually in the course of colonialism and conquest. A direct outcome in many cases is a phenomenon that anthropologists call acculturation.

ACCULTURATION

Acculturation occurs when groups having different cultures come into intensive firsthand contact, with subsequent massive changes in the original culture patterns of one or both groups. It always involves an element of force, either directly, as in the case of conquest, or indirectly, as in the implicit or explicit threat that force will be used if people refuse to make the changes that those in the other group expect them to make. Other variables include degree of cultural difference; circumstances, intensity, frequency, and hostility of contact; relative status of the agents of contact; who is dominant and who is submissive; and whether the nature of the flow is reciprocal or nonreciprocal. It

[4]Carleton S. Coon, *The Story of Man* (New York: Knopf, 1954), p. 174.

should be emphasized that acculturation and diffusion are not equivalent terms; one culture can borrow from another without being in the least acculturated.

In the course of acculturation, any one of a number of things may happen. Merger or fusion occurs when two cultures lose their separate identities and form a single culture, as expressed by the "melting pot" ideology of Anglo-American culture in the United States. Sometimes, though, one of the cultures loses its autonomy but retains its identity as a subculture, such as a caste, class, or ethnic group; this is typical of conquest or slavery situations, and there are examples in the United States despite its melting-pot ideology. One need look no farther afield than the nearest Indian reservation. Today, in nearly all parts of the world, people are faced with the indignity of forced removal from their traditional homelands, as entire communities are uprooted to make way for hydroelectric projects, grazing lands for cattle, mining operations, or the construction of highways. In Brazil's rush to develop the Amazon Basin, for instance, whole villages are frequently relocated to "national parks," where resources are inadequate for so many people and where former enemies are often forced to live in close proximity.

Extinction is the phenomenon in which so many carriers of a culture die that those who survive become refugees, living among peoples of other cultures. Examples of this may be seen in many parts of the world today; the closest examples are to be found in many parts of South America, again as in Brazil's Amazon basin. One particularly well-documented case occurred in the 1960s, when hired killers tried to wipe out the Cinta-Larga Indians. Using arsenic, dynamite, and machine guns from light planes, these killers chose a time when an important native ceremony was taking place to attack a Cinta-Larga village, seen as an obstacle to development. Violence continues to be used in Brazil as a means of dealing with native people; in 1983, for instance, 17 Indian defenders of their group's land rights were assassinated, but as of mid-1984, not a single assassin had

> **Genocide:** The extermination of one people by another, often in the name of "progress," either as a deliberate act or as the accidental outcome of activities carried out by one people with little regard for their impact on others.

been arrested or brought to trial.[5] In 1988, two Kayapo Indians and an anthropologist were charged with violating the Brazilian Foreign Sedition Act for traveling to the United States where they spoke with members of several congressional committees, as well as officials of the Department of State, the Treasury, and the World Bank about the destruction of their land and way of life caused by internationally financed development projects.

GENOCIDE

The case of the Cinta-Largas just cited raises the issue of **genocide** — the extermination of one group of people by another, often deliberately and in the name of "progress." Genocide is not new in the world, as we need look no farther than our own history to see. In 1637, for example, the Pequot Indians were effectively destroyed by setting afire their village at Mystic, Connecticut, and then shooting down all those — women and children included — who sought to escape being burned alive. Several other massacres of Indian peoples occurred thereafter, up until the last one at Wounded Knee, South Dakota, in 1890. Of course, such acts were by no means restricted to North America; one of the most famous nineteenth-century acts of genocide was the extermination of the aboriginal inhabitants of Tasmania, a large island just south of Australia. In this case, the use of military force failed to achieve the complete elimination of the Tasmanians, but what the military could not achieve, a missionary could. George Augustus Robinson was able to round up the surviving natives, and at his mission station, the deadly combination of psychological depression

[5]Robin Wright, "Towards a New Indian Policy in Brazil," *Cultural Survival Quarterly* 8, no. 1 (Spring 1984): 76–78.

Genocide is not new in the world; this 1638 illustration shows English colonists with their Narragansett allies (the outer ring of bowmen) shooting down Pequot Indian women, children, and unarmed men attempting to flee their homes, which have been set afire.

and European diseases brought about the demise of the last full-blooded Tasmanians in time for Robinson to retire to England a moderately wealthy man.

The most widely known act of genocide in recent history was the attempt of the Nazi Germans to wipe out European Jews and gypsies in the name of racial superiority. Unfortunately, the common practice of referring to this as "*the* holocaust" — as if it were something unique — tends to blind us to the fact that it is simply one more example of an all too common phenomenon. Moreover, genocide continues to occur in the world today in places like Iraq, where, in 1988, poison gas began to be used against Kurdish villagers, and (as we will see in Chapter 25) Guatemala, to mention but two

cases. If such practices are ever to be ended, we must gain a better understanding of them than currently exists. Anthropologists are actively engaged in this, carrying out cross-cultural as well as individual case studies. One finding to emerge is the regularity with which religious, economic, and political interests are allied in cases of genocide. In Tasmania, for example, wool growers wanted Aborigines off the land so that they could have it for their sheep. The government advanced their interests through its military campaigns against the natives, but it was Robinson's missionary work that finally secured Tasmania for the wool interests. Today, the !Kung living in Namibia find themselves in a situation remarkably similar to that experienced earlier by the Tasmanians; a combina-

Genocide in the twentieth century: Germany against Jews and Gypsies in the 1930s and 1940s, and Iraq against the Kurds in the 1980s. These are but two cases out of the many that not only have occurred, but continue to occur.

tion of religious (Dutch Reformed church), political (South African government), and economic (agricultural, pastoral, and touristic) interests have brought about the people's confinement to a place where disease and apathy are causing death rates to outstrip birth rates. Other such cases might be cited; for example, a cooperative relationship among Oblate missions, the Royal Canadian Mounted Police, and the Hudson Bay Company was instrumental in bringing about the demise, in the 1950s, of the Ihalmiut who lived in Canada's "Barren Grounds" west of Hudson Bay.[6] The latter case is important, for it clearly illustrates that genocide is not always a deliberate act. It also occurs as the unforseen outcome of activities carried out with little regard for their impact on other peoples. For the people whose lives are ended, however, it makes no difference whether the geno-

[6]Farley Mowat, *The Desperate People* (Boston: Little, Brown, 1959).

Franz Boas (1858–1942)

Born in Germany, where he studied physics and geography, Franz Boas came to the United States to live in 1888. His interest in anthropology began a few years earlier with a trip to Baffinland, where he met his first so-called "primitive" people. Thereafter, he and his students came to dominate anthropology in North America through the first three decades of the 1900s. Through meticulous and detailed fieldwork, which set new standards for excellence, Boas and his students were able to expose the shortcomings of the grandiose schemes of cultural evolution which had been proposed by earlier social theorists. His thesis that a culture must be judged according to its own standards and values, rather than those of the investigator, represented a tremendously liberating philosophy in his time. (The photo shows Boas posing as a Kwakiutl hanatsa dancer for a National Museum diorama, 1895).

Growing Trees In Haiti

When foreigners go to Haiti, one of the things that impresses them is the massive deforestation that has taken place. Since colonial times, this country's population has swelled from fewer than half a million to more than six million — too many people for too little arable land. In their quest for fields, peasants have cut down all but a few stands of trees in remote areas. The resultant erosion, coupled with over-utilization of crop land has led to catastrophic declines in yields, sending many peasants into the capitol, Port au Prince, in search of other work. This in turn has created a growing demand for construction wood and charcoal in that city, which the rural poor are all to happy to satisfy by going after the country's few remaining trees. Responding to this crisis, international development organizations poured millions of dollars into studies of the problem, as well as into reforestation schemes, all to no avail. Not only were very few seedlings planted, but those that were quickly became forage for the goats of peasants, who were reluctant to devote any of their scarce land holdings to the growing of state-owned trees.

Faced with failure, the United States Agency for International Development (AID) in Haiti invited anthropologist Gerald F. Murray to develop an alternative approach to reforestation, and subsequently hired him as Project Director. Already familiar with peasant land usage in Haiti, Murray knew that typical reforestation projects, such as the planting of fruit trees by agents of the government for purposes of soil conservation, would not work. To peasants, fruit trees were of little commercial or nutritional value, especially if they were perceived as being state owned. What they needed was a cash crop which was their's to do with as they wished. Accordingly, what Murray did was to make available, through nongovernmental organiza-

tions rather than state agencies, seedlings of leucaena, ocassia, and eucalyptus, fast-growing wood trees good for charcoal and basic construction material, for which there was a ready market. Moreover, the trees could be cut in some instances as early as four years after planting, and could be grown along borders of fields, or even intercropped among other plants, rather than in large unbroken uncropped stands. Thus, their growth was compatible with continued subsistence farming. Moreover, any potential loss from decreased food production was far offset by income the trees would generate.

The idea that trees were meant to be cut, while heretical to the international development "establishment," was extremely popular with the peasants. As Murray observes, "though it had taken AID two years to decide about the project; it took about twenty minutes with any group of skeptical but economically rational peasants to generate a list of enthusiastic potential tree planters . . . Cash-flow dialogues and ownership . . . were a far cry from the finger-wagging ecological sermons to which many peasant groups had been subjected on the topic of trees."[*] When first conceived, the planting of three million trees, on the land of six thousand peasants, was set as the project's four-year goal. In fact, by the end of the fourth year, twenty million trees had been planted by 75,000 peasants. Unlike bureaucratically conceived projects, this anthropologically conceived and carried-out agroforestry project has turned out to be a resounding success.

[*]Gerald F. Murray, "The Domestication of Wood in Haiti: A Case Study in Applied Evolution," in *Applying Anthropology, An Introductory Reader*, ed. Aaron Podolefsky and Peter J. Brown (Mountain View, Calif.: Mayfield, 1989), pp. 151–152.

cide is deliberate or not; for them, the outcome is the same.

DIRECTED CHANGE

The most extreme cases of acculturation usually occur as a result of military conquest and displacement of traditional political authority by conquerors who know or care nothing about the culture they control. The indigenous people, unable to resist imposed changes and prevented from carrying out many of their traditional social, religious, and economic activities, may be forced into new activities that tend to isolate individuals and tear apart the integration of their societies. Such a people are the !Kung of Namibia, who have been rounded up and confined to a region where they cannot possibly provide for their own needs. In this situation, they are provided by the government with rations that are insufficient to meet their nutritional needs. In poor health and prevented from developing meaningful alternatives to traditional activities, the people have become argumentative and depressed, and as already noted, their death rate now exceeds that of birth.

One by-product of colonial dealings with indigenous peoples has been the growth of **applied anthropology** and the use of anthropological techniques and knowledge for certain "practical" ends. For example, British anthropology has often been considered the "handmaiden" of that country's colonial policy, for it typically provided the kind of information of particular use in maintaining effective colonial rule. In the United States, the Bureau of American Ethnology was founded toward the end of the nineteenth century, to gather reliable data on which the government might base its Indian policies. At the time, North American anthropologists were convinced of the usefulness of their discipline, and many who carried out ethnographic work among Indians devoted a great deal of time, energy, and even money to assisting their informants, whose interests were frequently threatened from outside. In the present century the scope of applied anthropology has broadened. Early on, the applied work of Franz Boas, who almost single-handedly trained a generation of

Applied anthropology: The use of anthropological knowledge and techniques for the purpose of solving "practical" problems, often for a specific "client."

anthropologists in the United States, was instrumental in reforming the country's immigration policies. In the 1930s, anthropologists carried out a number of studies in industrial and other institutional settings, with avowedly applied goals. With World War II came the first efforts at colonial administration beyond our own borders, especially in the Pacific, made by officers trained in anthropology. The rapid recovery of Japan was due in no small measure to the influence of anthropologists in structuring the U.S. occupation. Anthropologists continue to play an active role today in administering the U.S. trust territories in the Pacific.

Today, applied anthropologists are in some demand in the field of international development, on account of their specialized knowledge of social structure, value systems, and the functional interrelatedness of Third World cultures targeted for development. The role of the applied anthropologists, however, is far from easy; as anthropologists, they respect the dignity of other peoples and the integrity of their cultures, yet they are being asked for advice on how to change certain aspects of those cultures. If the request comes from the people themselves, that is one thing, but more often than not, the request comes from some outside "expert." Supposedly, the proposed change is for the good of the targeted populations, yet they don't always see it that way. Just how far applied anthropologists should go in advising how people — especially ones without the power to resist — can be made to embrace changes that have been proposed for them is a serious ethical question.

Despite such difficulties, applied anthropology is flourishing today as never before. As the several "Application" boxes spaced throughout this book illustrate, anthropologists now practice their profession in many different nonacademic settings, in a wide variety of ways.

In the past few decades, Western countries have sent technological "missionaries" to teach people in other countries new ways of doing old tasks. Unless they have had anthropological training, however, such "missionaries" are apt to be unaware of the side effects their new ways will have.

REACTIONS TO FORCIBLE CHANGE

The reactions of indigenous peoples to the changes that have been thrust upon them by outsiders have varied considerably. Some have responded by removing themselves to the nearest available forest, desert, or other inhospitable place, in hopes of being left alone. In Brazil, a number of communities once located near the coast took this option a few hundred years ago, and were successful until the great push to develop the Amazon forest began in the 1960s. Others, like the Ik of Uganda (discussed in Chapter 12) have lapsed into apathy. These former hunters and gatherers were rounded up, loaded into trucks, and transported out of their homeland virtually overnight; they are now, quite literally, dying out. Sometimes, though, people have managed to keep faith

Syncretism: In acculturation, the blending of indigenous and foreign traits to form a new system.

with their own traditions by inventing creative and ingenious ways of expressing them in the face of powerful foreign domination. This blending of indigenous and foreign elements into a new system is known as **syncretism,** and a fine illustration of it is the game of cricket as played by the Trobriand Islanders, some of whose practices we looked at in Chapters 16, 17, and 18.

Under British rule, the Trobrianders were introduced by missionaries to the rather staid British game of cricket to replace the erotic dancing and open sexuality that normally followed the harvest of yams. Traditionally, this was the time when chiefs sought to spread their fame by hosting nights of dancing, in the course of which they provided food for the hundreds of young married people who participated. For two months or so, there would be night after night of provocative dancing, accompanied by chanting and shouting full of sexual innuendo, each night ending as couples disappeared off into the bush together. Since no chief wished to be outdone by any other (to be outdone reflected on the strength of one's magic), there was a strong competitive element to all of this dancing, and fighting sometimes erupted. To the missionaries, cricket seemed a good way to end all of this in a way that would encourage conformity to "civilized" comportment in dress, religion, and "sportsmanship." The Trobrianders, however, were determined to "rubbish" (throw out) the British game, and they eventually turned it into the same kind of distinctly Trobriand event that their dance competitions had once been.[7]

The Trobrianders made cricket their own by adding battle dress and battle magic, and by incorporating erotic dancing into the festivities. Instead of inviting dancers each night, chiefs now arrange games of cricket. Pitching has been modified from the British style to one closer to their old way of throwing a spear. After the game, they hold massive feasts, where wealth is displayed to enhance their prestige. Cricket, in its altered form, has been made to serve traditional systems of prestige and exchange. Neither "primitive" nor benignly accepted in its original form, Trobriand cricket was thoughtfully and creatively adapted into a sophisticated activity reflecting the importance of basic indigenous cultural premises. Exuberance and pride are displayed by everyone associated with the game, and the players are as much concerned with conveying the full meaning of who they are as with scoring well. From the sensual dressing in preparation for the game to the team chanting of songs full of sexual metaphors and to erotic chorus-line dancing between the innings, there is little doubt that each player is playing for his own importance, for the fame of his team, and for the hundreds of

[7]Annette B. Weiner, review of "Trobriand Cricket: An Ingenious Response to Colonialism," *American Anthropologist*, 79 (1977): 506.

attractive young women who usually watch the game.

REVITALIZATION MOVEMENTS

Another common reaction to forcible change is revitalization, a process already touched on in Chapter 22. Revitalization may be defined as a deliberate attempt by some members of a society to construct a more satisfactory culture by the rapid acceptance of a pattern of multiple innovations. Once primary ties of culture, social relationships, and activities are broken, and meaningless activity is imposed by force, individuals and groups char-

Revitalization movements that are revivalistic in nature are not restricted to Third World countries like Iran; in the United States Jerry Falwell is the leader of one such movement.

In Iran, the Ayatollah Khomeini led a revitalization movement that was in part revivalistic and in part revolutionary.

acteristically react with fantasy, withdrawal, and escape.

Examples of revitalization movements have been common in the history of the United States whenever significant segments of the population have found their conditions in life to be at odds with the values of "the American Dream." For example, in the nineteenth century, periodic depression and the disillusionment of the decades after the Civil War produced a host of revitalization movements, of which the most successful was that of the Mormons. In the twentieth century, movements have repeatedly sprung up in the slums of major cities, as well as in depressed rural areas such as in the Appalachian mountain area. By the 1960s, a number of movements were becoming less inward-looking and more "activist," a good example being the rise of the Black Muslim movement. The 1960s also saw the rise of revitalization movements among the young of middle-class and even upper-class families. In their case, the pro-

fessed values of peace, equality, and individual freedom were seen to be at odds with the reality of persistent war, poverty, and constraints on individual action imposed by a variety of impersonal institutions. Their reaction to these things was expressed by their use of drugs, in their outlandish or "freaky" clothes, hair styles, music, speech, and in their behavior toward authority and authority figures.

By the 1980s, revitalization movements were becoming prominent even among older, more affluent segments of society, as in the rise of the Moral Majority. In these cases, the reaction is not so much against a perceived failure of the American dream as it is against perceived threats to that dream by dissenters and activists within their society, by foreign governments, by new ideas that challenge other ideas that they would like to believe, and by the sheer complexity of modern life.

Clearly, when value systems get out of step with existing realities, for whatever reason, a condition of cultural crisis is likely to build up that may breed some form of reactive movement. Not all suppressed, conquered, or colonized people eventually rebel against established authority, although why they do not is still a debated issue. When they do, however, resistance may take one of several forms, all of which are varieties of revitalization movements. A culture may seek to speed up the acculturation process in order to share more fully in the supposed benefits of the dominant cultures. Melanesian cargo cults of the post-World War II era have generally been of this sort, although earlier ones stressed a revival of traditional ways. Movements that try to reconstitute a destroyed but not forgotten way of life are known as **nativistic** or **revivalistic movements.** A movement that attempts to resurrect a suppressed pariah group, which has long suffered in an inferior social standing and which has its own special subcultural ideology, is referred to as **millenarism;** the most familiar examples of this to us are prophetic Judaism and early Christianity. If the aim of the movement is directed primarily to the ideological system and the attendant social structure of a cultural system from within, it is then called **revolutionary.**

REBELLION AND REVOLUTION

When the scale of discontent within a society reaches a certain level, the possibilities for rebellion and revolution — such as the Iranian Revolution or the Sandinista Revolution in Nicaragua — are high.

The question of why revolutions come into being, as well as why they frequently fail to live up to the expectations of the people initiating them, is a problem. It is clear, however, that the colonial policies of countries such as England, France, Spain, Portugal, and the United States during the nineteenth and early twentieth centuries have created a worldwide situation in which revolution has become nearly inevitable. Despite the political independence most colonies have gained since World War II, many of them continue to be exploited by more powerful countries for their natural resources and cheap labor, causing a deep re-

> **Nativistic or revivalistic movement:** A revitalization movement that tries to reconstitute a destroyed but not forgotten way of life.
>
> **Millenarism:** A revitalization movement that attempts to resurrect a suppressed pariah group that has long suffered in an inferior social position and that has its own special subcultural ideology.
>
> **Revolutionary:** A revitalization movement from within, directed primarily at the ideological system and the attendant social structure of a culture.

sentment of rulers beholden to foreign powers. Further discontent has been caused by the attempts of newly independent states to assert their control over peoples living within their boundaries who, by virtue of a common ancestry, possession of distinct cultures, persistent occupation of their own territories, and traditions of self-determination identify themselves as distinct nations and refuse to recognize the sovereignty of what they regard as a foreign government. Thus, in many a former colony, large numbers of people have taken up arms to resist annexation and absorption by imposed state regimes that would strip them of their lands, resources, and sense of identity as a people. One of the most important facts of our time is that the vast majority of the distinct peoples of the world have never consented to rule by the governments of states within which they find themselves living.[8] In many a newly emerged country, such peoples feel they have no other option.

On the basis of an examination of four revolutions of the past — English, American, French, and Bolshevik — the following conditions have been offered as precipitators of rebellion and revolution:

1. Loss of prestige of established authority, often as a result of the failure of foreign policy, financial difficulties, dismissals of popular ministers, or alteration of popular policies.

[8]Bernard Nietschmann, "The Third World War," *Cultural Survival Quarterly* 11, no. 3 (1987): 3.

2. Threat to recent economic improvement. In France and Russia, those sections of the population (professional classes and urban workers) whose economic fortunes had previously taken an upward swing were "radicalized" by unexpected setbacks, such as steeply rising food prices and unemployment.

3. Indecisiveness of government, as exemplified by lack of consistent policy; such governments appear to be controlled by, rather than in control of, events.

4. Loss of support of the intellectual class. Such a loss deprived the prerevolutionary governments of France and Russia of philosophical support, thus leading to their lack of popularity with the literate public.

5. A leader or group of leaders with enough charisma to mobilize a substantial part of the population against the establishment.

Apart from resistance to internal authority, such as in the English, French, and Russian revolutions, many revolutions in modern times have been struggles against an authority imposed on them by outsiders. Such resistance usually takes the form of independence movements that wage campaigns of armed defiance against colonial powers. The Algerian struggle for independence from France and the American Revolution are typical examples. Of the 120 or so armed conflicts in the world today, 98 percent are in the economically poor countries of the "Third World," almost all of which were at one time under European colonial domination. Of these wars, 75 percent are between the state and one or more peoples within the state's borders who are seeking to maintain or regain control of their persons, communities, lands, and resources in the face of what, to them, is subjugation by a foreign power.[9]

Not all revolts are truly revolutionary in their consequences. According to Max Gluckman, rebellions:

"throw the rascals out" and substitute another set, but there is no attempt to alter either the cultural ideology or the form of the social structure. In political revolution, attempts are made to seize the offices of power in order to change social structure, belief systems, and their symbolic representations. Political revolutions are usually turbulent, violent, and not long-lasting. A successful revolution soon moves to re-establish a stable, though changed, social structure; yet it has far-reaching political, social and sometimes economic and cultural consequences.[10]

Not always are revolutions successful about accomplishing what they set out to do. One of the stated goals of the Chinese revolution, for example, was to liberate women from the oppression of a strongly patriarchal society in which a woman owed life-long obedience to some man or other—first her father, later her husband and, after his death, her sons. Although some progress was made, the effort overall has been frustrated by the cultural lens through which the revolutionaries have viewed their work. A tradition of extreme patriarchy extending back at least 22 centuries is not easily overcome, and has unconsciously influenced many of the decisions made by China's leaders since 1949. In rural China today, as in the past, a woman's life is still usually determined by her relationship to some man, be it her father, husband, or son, rather than her own efforts—successes or failures. What's more, women are being told more and more that their primary role is as wives and mothers. When they do work outside the house, it is generally at jobs with low pay, low status, and no benefits. Thus, despite whatever autonomy they may achieve for a while, they become totally dependent in their old age on their sons. What we see here is that subversion of revolutionary goals, if it occurs, is not necessarily brought about by political opponents. Rather, it may be a consequence of the revolutionaries' own cultural background. In rural China, so long as women marry out of the family, and land is held by

[9]Bernard Nietschmann, p. 7.

[10]E. Adamson Hoebel, *Anthropology: The Study of Man*, 4th ed. (New York: McGraw-Hill, 1972), p. 667.

families, daughters will always be seen as something of a liability.

It should be pointed out that revolution is a relatively recent phenomenon, occurring only during the last 5,000 years or so. The reason for this is that it requires a centralized political authority (or state) to rebel against, and the state has been in existence for only 5,000 years. In those societies typified by tribes and bands, and in other nonindustrial societies lacking central authority, there could not have been rebellion or political revolution.

MODERNIZATION

One of the most frequently used terms to describe social and cultural change as these are occurring today is **modernization.** This is most clearly defined as an all-encompassing and global process of cultural and socioeconomic change, whereby developing societies seek to acquire some of the characteristics common to industrially advanced societies. If one looks very closely at this definition, one sees that "becoming modern" really means "becoming like us," with the very clear implication that not being like us is to be antiquated and obsolete. Not only is this ethnocentric, it also fosters the notion that these other societies must be changed to be more like us, irrespective of other considerations. It is unfortunate that the term "modernization" continues to be so widely used. Since we seem to be stuck with it, the best we can do at the moment is to recognize its inappropriateness, even though we continue to use it.

The process of modernization may be best understood as consisting of four subprocesses, of which one is technological development. In the course of modernization, traditional knowledge and techniques give way to the application of scientific knowledge and techniques borrowed mainly from the West. Another subprocess is agricultural development, represented by a shift in emphasis from subsistence farming to commercial

Modernization: The process of cultural and socioeconomic change, whereby developing societies acquire some of the characteristics of Western industrialized societies.

Structural differentiation: The division of single traditional roles, which embrace two or more functions (for example, political, economic, and religious) into two or more roles, each with a single specialized function.

Integrative mechanisms: Cultural mechanisms, such as nationalistic ideologies, formal governmental structures, political parties, legal codes, labor and trade unions, and common-interest associations, that oppose forces for differentiation in a society.

Tradition: In a modernizing society, old cultural practices, which may oppose new forces of differentiation and integration.

farming. Instead of raising crops and livestock for their own use, people turn more and more to the production of cash crops, with greater reliance on a cash economy and markets for the sale of farm products and purchase of goods. A third subprocess is industrialization, with a greater emphasis placed on inanimate forms of energy—especially fossil fuels—to power machines. Human and animal power become less important, as do handicrafts in general. The fourth subprocess is urbanization, marked particularly by population movements from rural settlements into cities. Although all four subprocesses are interrelated, there is no fixed order of appearance.

As modernization takes place, other changes are likely to follow. In the political realm, political parties and some sort of electoral machinery frequently appear, along with the development of a bureaucracy. In education, there is an expansion of learning opportunities, literacy increases, and an indigenous educated elite develops. Religion becomes less important in many areas of thought and behavior, as traditional beliefs and practices are undermined. The traditional rights and duties connected with kinship are altered, if not elimi-

Structural differentiation. Whereas most items for daily use were once made at home, as in this quilting party (*top*), almost everything we use today is the product of specialized production, as are the quilts shown in this linens boutique (*below*).

nated, especially where distant kin are concerned. Finally, where stratification is a factor, mobility increases as ascribed status becomes less important and achievement counts for more.

Two other features of modernization go hand in hand with those already noted. One, **structural differentiation,** is the division of single traditional roles, which embrace two or more functions, into two or more roles, each with a single specialized function. This represents a kind of fragmentation of society, which must be counteracted by new **integrative mechanisms,** if the society is not to disintegrate into a number of discrete units. These new mechanisms take such forms as new nationalistic ideologies, formal governmental structures, political parties, legal codes, labor and trade unions, and common-interest associations. All of these cross-cut other societal divisions and so serve to oppose differentiating forces. These two forces, however, are not the only ones in opposition in a situation of modernization; to them must be added a third, the force of **tradition.** This opposes the new forces of both differentiation and integration. On the other hand, the conflict does not have to be total. Traditional ways may on occasion facilitate modernization. For example, rural people may be assisted by traditional kinship ties as they move into cities, if they have relatives already there to whom they may turn for aid. One's relatives, too, may provide the financing that is necessary for business success.

One aspect of modernization, the technological explosion, has made it possible to transport human beings and ideas from one place to another with astounding speed and in great numbers. Formerly independent cultural systems have been brought into contact with others. The cultural differences between New York and Pukapuka are declining, while the differences between fishing people and physicists are increasing. No one knows whether this implies a net gain or net loss in cultural diversity, but the worldwide spread of anything, whether it is DDT or a new idea, should be viewed with at least caution. That human beings and human cultural systems are different is the most exciting thing about them, yet the destruction of diversity is implicit in the worldwide spread of rock-and-roll, communism, capitalism, or anything else. When a song is forgotten or a ceremony ceases to be performed, a part of the human heritage is destroyed forever.

An examination of two traditional cultures that have felt the impact of modernization or other cultural changes will help to pinpoint some of the problems these cultures have met. The cultures are the Skolt Lapps of Finland and the Shuar Indians of the Amazon Forest.

SKOLT LAPPS AND THE SNOWMOBILE REVOLUTION

The Skolt Lapps, whose homeland straddles the Arctic Circle in Finland, traditionally supported themselves by fishing and the herding of reindeer.[11] Although they depended on the outside world for certain material goods, the resources crucial for their system were to be had locally and were for all practical purposes available to all. No one was denied access to critical resources, and there was little social and economic differentiation among people. Theirs was basically an egalitarian society.

Of particular importance to the Skolt Lapps was reindeer herding. Indeed, herd management is central to their definition of themselves as a people. These animals were a source of meat for home consumption or for sale in order to procure outside goods. They were also a source of hides for shoes and clothing, sinews for sewing, and antler and bone for making various things. Finally, reindeer were used to pull sleds in the winter and as pack animals when there was no snow on the ground. Understandably, the animals were the objects of much attention. The herds were not large, but without a great deal of attention, productivity suffered. Hence, most winter activities centered on reindeer. Men, operating on skis, were closely associated with their herds, intensively, from November to January and, periodically, from January to April.

In the early 1960s, these reindeer herders speedily adopted snowmobiles on the premise that the new machines would make herding physically easier and economically more advantageous. The first machine arrived in Finland in 1962; by 1971, there were 70 operating machines owned by the Skolt Lapps and non-Lapps in the same area. Although men on skis still carry out some herding activity, their importance and prestige are now diminished. As early as 1967, only four people were still using reindeer sleds for winter travel; most had gotten rid of draft animals. Those who had not converted to snowmobiles felt themselves disadvantaged compared with the rest.

The consequences of this mechanization were extraordinary and far reaching. The need for snowmobiles, parts and equipment to maintain them, and a steady supply of gasoline created a dependency on the outside world unlike anything that had previously existed. As traditional skills were replaced by snowmobile technology, the ability of the Lapps to determine their own survival without dependence on outsiders, should this be necessary, was lost. Snowmobiles are also expensive, costing on the order of $1000 (1973 dollars) in the Arctic. Maintenance and gasoline expenses must be added to this initial cost. Accordingly, there has been a sharp rise in the need for cash. To get this, men must go outside the Lapp community for wage work more than just occasionally, as had once been the case, or else rely on such sources as government pensions or welfare.

The argument may be made that dependency (the need for cash) is a price worth paying for an improved system of reindeer herding; but has it improved? In truth, snowmobiles have contributed in a significant way to a disastrous decline in reindeer herding. By 1971, the average size of the family herd was down from 50 to 12. Not only is this too small a number to be economically viable, it is too small to maintain at all. The reason is that the animals in such small herds will take the first opportunity to run off to join another larger one. What happened was that the old close, prolonged, and largely peaceful relationship between herdsman and beast changed to a noisy, traumatic relationship. Now, when men appear, it is to come speeding out of the woods on snarling, smelly machines that invariably chase animals, often for long distances. Instead of helping the animals in their winter food quest, helping females with their calves, and protecting them from predators, the appearance of men now means either slaughter or castration. Naturally enough, the reindeer have become suspicious. The result has been actual

---

[11]Pertti J. Pelto, *The Snowmobile Revolution: Technology and Social Change in the Arctic* (Menlo Park, Calif.: Cummings, 1973).

dedomestication, with reindeer scattering and running off to more inaccessible areas, given the slightest chance. Moreover, there are indications that snowmobile harassment has adversely affected the number of viable calves added to the herds. What we have here is a classic illustration of the fact that change is not always adaptive.

The cost of mechanized herding — and the decline of the herds — has led many Lapps to abandon it altogether. Now, the majority of males are no longer herders at all. This constitutes a serious economic problem, since few economic alternatives are available. The problem is compounded by the fact that participation in a cash–credit economy means that most people, employed or not, have payments to make. Furthermore, this is more than just an economic problem, for in the traditional culture of this people, being a herder of reindeer is the very essence of manhood. Hence, the new nonherders are not only poor in a way that they could not be in previous times, but they are in a sense inadequate as "men" quite apart from this.

This economic differentiation with its evaluation of roles is leading to the development of a stratified society out of the older egalitarian one. Differences are developing in terms of wealth, and with this, in life-styles. It is difficult to break into reindeer herding now, for one needs a substantial cash outlay. And herding now requires skills and knowledge that were not a part of traditional culture. Not everyone has these, and those without them are dependent on others if they are to participate. Hence, there is now restricted access to critical resources, where once there had been none.

Although the Skolt Lapps have not escaped many negative aspects of modernization, the choice to modernize or not was essentially theirs. The Shuar Indians, by contrast, deliberately avoided modernization, until they felt that they had no other option, if they were to fend off the same outside forces that elsewhere in the Amazon Basin have resulted in the destruction of whole societies.

ORIGINAL STUDY
The Shuar Solution[12]

The Shuar are a Jivaroan-speaking, forest-dwelling group in Ecuador, who by their own estimate numbered over 26,000 people in 1975. Traditionally they were self-sufficient cultivators and hunters, living in dispersed extended families. They are widely famous as "head-hunters" and for their successful resistance to foreign domination since the arrival of the Spanish in 1540. The Shuar still retained control over much of their traditional territory, and their basic culture remained viable well into the present century. However, by 1959 they were outnumbered by colonists and were rapidly losing their most valuable subsistence lands. Their entire way of life was threatened with disintegration.

At this point the Shuar in the most heavily invaded areas set about developing what they called an "original self-solution" to the crisis. They concluded that their situation had been irrevocably altered by circumstances, but felt that they could still make a satisfying adjustment. The basic objective was to retain control over their own futures — they sought self-determination. They realized that the key to self-determination lay in retaining an adequate community land base, which would require effective participation in the government colonization program. If the Shuar sought individual land titles, only a few would succeed, given the pro-colonist bias in the entitlement process. In the end the Shuar community would be destroyed. The solution was the creation in 1964 of a fully independent, but officially recognized, corporate body—a federation, based on regional associations of many local Shuar communities. The Federation became a legal entity, the *Federación de Centros Shuar*, that as of 1978 contained some 20,000 members organized into 160 local centers and 13 regional associations. . . . According to the Federation's official statutes, the basic objectives of the organization are to promote the social, economic, and moral advancement of its members, and to coordinate development efforts with official government agencies. There are elected officials with carefully specified duties, and five specialized commissions to deal with such matters as health, education, and land.

The Federation quickly opted for a system of community land titles through the appropriate government body IERAC (*Instituto Ecuatoriano de Reforma Agraria y Colonización*), and promoted cooperative cattle ranching as the new economic base. Cattle ranching was especially important because land was titled on the basis of actual use and the legitimate requirement for pastureland was greater than for other forms of land use. The Federation obtained financial and technical assistance from various national and international agencies; by 1975, 95,704 hectares were securely in community titles. By 1978, the cattle herd had grown to more than 15,000 head and had become the primary source of outside income.

With the approval and support of the Ecuadorian ministry of education, and with the cooperation of the Salesian mission, the Federation has developed an education system suited to local needs and supportive of the traditional culture. Much of the instruction utilizes the Shuar language and Shuar teachers. In order to minimize the family disruption caused by boarding schools, and to spread educational opportunities as widely as possible, the Federation established its own system of radio-broadcast bilingual education beginning in 1972. The program has successfully reduced the elementary school role of the mission-operated boarding schools, and these have now been converted into technical schools for advanced training. The Federation has operated its own radio station since 1968, broadcasting in both Shuar and Spanish. In addition, since 1972 it has published a bilingual newspaper, *Chicham*, the official organ of the Shuar Federation.

The Federation solution is in many ways unique in Amazonia. The Shuar are the only native group to have retained such effective control over its own future. The initiative for the major adaptive changes that have occurred in the Shuar system as well as the administration of the entire program has been carried out by the Shuar themselves. Of course, the Federation itself was a response to uninvited outside pressures, and its early formation was facilitated by the Salesian missionaries who had been in the area since 1893, but there is no doubt that the Shuar have created a distinctly *Shuar* solution to the problem. The Federation has not yet become fully self-sufficient, but it has drawn on a very broad base of financial support so that no single outside interest has been able to assert undesired influence. Technical volunteers from many countries have been recruited on a temporary basis, but they have not dominated any programs.

The Shuar are very proud of the Federation and of the clear gains they have made. They recognize that they have had to make enormous changes in their culture, but they feel that they are still Shuar. Certainly, many traditional patterns have been abandoned with few regrets, and many material elements are disappearing or have been converted to the tourist trade. But the Federation has succeeded in strengthening the Shuar language and cultural identity, and in securing a viable resource base. The Shuar are actively promoting selected qualities which they feel represent the essence of their culture and which clearly distinguish them from their non-Indian neighbors. These qualities include: communal land tenure, cooperative production and distribution, a basically egalitarian economy, kin-based local communities with maximum autonomy, and a variety of distinctive cultural markers.

The Federation has not existed without problems. Understandably, the colonists have resented its successes. In 1969, the Federation's central office was burned down, presumably by colonists, and Federation leaders have been jailed and tortured for crimes for which they were never convicted. . . . While the government officially recognizes and cooperates with the Federation, actual support for their programs has been sporadic, and outside interests have consistently been favored by government agencies over the needs of the Shuar. The government has also forcefully attempted to prevent the Shuar from promoting the political organization of other Ecuadorian Indians and generally seems opposed to the idea of Ecuador becoming a multiethnic nation. . . . The Federation has also been criticized by leftist organizations for accepting aid from capitalists, while at the same time some missionaries have accused Federation leaders of being communists. In the long run, the Federation faces other problems as well. Economic differentiation related to cattle ranching and the gradual emergence of an educated and salaried elite may be difficult to contain within the traditional egalitarian ideal to which the Federation still aspires. Furthermore, the present land base, which is broken up into discontinuous islands, may prove in a short time to be inadequate for the needs of a growing population.

[12]John H. Bodley, *Victims of Progress*, 3rd ed. (Palo Alto, Calif.: Mayfield, 1982), pp. 172–174. Copyright 1982 by Mayfield Publishing Company. Reprinted by permission.

MODERNIZATION AND THE THIRD WORLD

In the two examples that we have just examined, we have seen how modernization has affected tribal peoples in otherwise "modern" nations. Elsewhere in the so-called Third World, whole nations are in the throes of modernization. Throughout Africa, Asia, and South and Central America, we are witnessing the widespread removal of economic activities from the family–community setting; the altered structure of the family in the face of the changing labor market; the increased reliance of young children on parents alone for affection, instead of on the extended family; the decline of general parental authority; schools replacing the family as the primary educational unit; the discovery of a generation gap; and many others. The difficulty is that change happens so fast that traditional societies are unable to adapt themselves gradually. Changes that took generations to accomplish in Europe and North America are attempted within the span of a single generation in developing countries. In the process, they are frequently faced with the erosion of a number of dearly held values they had no intention of giving up.

Commonly the burden of modernization falls most heavily on women. For example, the commercialization of agriculture often involves land reforms which overlook or ignore traditional land rights of women. At the same time that this reduces their control of and access to resources, mechanization of food production and processing drastically reduces their opportunities for employment. As a consequence, they are confined more and more to traditional domestic tasks which, as commercial production becomes peoples' dominant concern, are increasingly downgraded in value. To top it all off, the domestic work load tends to increase as men become less available to

Although many third world countries have improved the educational levels of their populations remarkably, they are frequently unable to provide the kinds of employment opportunities for which people are educated. A consequence is widespread discontent, as people are unable to realize their aspirations.

help out, and tasks such as fuel gathering and water collection become more difficult as common land and resources come under private ownership and woodlands are reserved for commercial exploitation. In short, with modernization, women frequently find themselves in an increasingly marginal position. At the same time that their work load increases, the value assigned the work they do declines, as does their relative and absolute health, nutritional, and educational status.

MODERNIZATION: MUST IT ALWAYS BE PAINFUL?

Although most anthropologists see the change that is affecting traditional, non-Western peoples caught up in the modern technological world as an ordeal, some scholars, like sociologist Alex Inkeles, see emerging from the process of modernization a new kind of person. This person is a kind of prototype, who — whether from an African tribe, a South American village, or a North American city — will be open to accept and benefit from the changes in the modern world. The first element in Inkeles's definition of the "modern person" is a readiness for new experience and an openness to innovation and change. Here, he is talking of a "state of mind, a psychological disposition, an inner readiness" rather than of specific techniques and skills an individual or group may possess because of an attained level of technology. In this sense, therefore, someone working with a wooden plow may be more modern in spirit than someone in another part of the world who drives a tractor.

Second, an individual is more "modern" if he or she "has a disposition to form or hold opinions over a large number of the problems and issues that arise not only in [the] immediate environment but also outside of it."[13] Such people show awareness of the diversity of attitude and opinion around them rather than closing themselves off in the be-

In Guatemala, where these bananas are grown, agricultural development has caused increased levels of malnutrition. As in many developing countries, modernization of agriculture has meant the conversion of land from subsistence farming to the raising of crops for export, making it increasingly difficult for people to satisfy their basic nutritional needs.

lief that everyone thinks alike and, indeed, is just like themselves. They are able to acknowledge differences of opinion without needing to deny differences out of fear that these will upset their own view of the world; they are also less likely to approach opinion in a strictly autocratic or hierarchical way.

Inkeles's view of modernization, unfortunately, is based more on the hopes and expectations of our own culture than it is on reality. There is no doubt that we would like to see the non-Western world attain the high levels of development seen in Europe and North America, as the Japanese in fact have done. Overlooked is the stark fact that the standard of living in the Western world is based on a rate of consumption of nonrenewable resources, where far less than 50 percent of the world's population uses a good deal more than 50 percent of these resources. By the early 1970s, for example, the people of the United States — a mere 6 percent (approximately) of the world's population — were

---

[13]Alex Inkeles, "The Modernization of Man" in *Modernization: The Dynamics of Growth*, ed. Myron Weiner (New York: Basic Books, 1966), pp. 141–144.

consuming about 66 percent of the world's annual output of copper, coal, and oil. This and other figures like it suggest that it is not realistic to expect most peoples of the world to achieve a standard of living comparable to that of the Western world in the near future, if at all. At the very least, the countries of the Western world would have to cut drastically their consumption of nonrenewable resources. So far, they have shown no inclination to do this, and if they did, their living standards would have to change. Yet more and more non-Western people, quite understandably, aspire to a standard of living such as Western countries now enjoy, even though the gap between the rich and poor people of the world is widening rather than narrowing. This has led to the development of what anthropologist Paul Magnarella (see "Suggested Readings") has called a new "culture of discontent," a level of aspirations that far exceeds the bounds of an individual's local opportunities. No longer satisfied with traditional values, people all over the world are fleeing to the cities to find a "better life," all too often to live out their days in poor, congested, and diseased slums in an attempt to achieve what is usually beyond their reach. So far it appears that this, and not Inkeles's prototype, is the person of the future.

CHAPTER SUMMARY

Although cultures may be remarkably stable, culture change is characteristic to a greater or lesser degree of all cultures. Change is often caused by accidents, including the unexpected outcome of existing events. Another cause is the deliberate attempt of people to solve some perceived problem. Finally, change may be forced on one group in the course of especially intense contact between two societies. Adaptation and progress are consequences rather than causes of change, although not all changes are necessarily adaptive. Progress is whatever a culture defines it as.

The mechanisms involved in cultural change are innovation, diffusion, cultural loss, and acculturation. The ultimate source of change is through innovation; some new practice, tool, or principle. Other individuals adopt the innovation, and it becomes socially shared. Primary innovations are chance discoveries of new principles, for example, the discovery that the firing of clay makes the material permanently hard. Secondary innovations are improvements made by applying known principles, for example, modeling the clay that is to be fired by known techniques into familiar objects. Primary innovations may prompt rapid culture change and stimulate other inventions. An innovation's chance of being accepted depends on its perceived superiority to the method or object it replaces. Its acceptance is also connected with the prestige of the innovator and imitating groups. Diffusion is the borrowing by one society of a cultural element from another. Cultural loss involves the abandonment of some trait or practice with or without replacement. Anthropologists have given considerable attention to acculturation. It stems from intensive firsthand contact of groups with different cultures and produces major changes in the cultural patterns of one or both groups. The actual or threatened use of force is always a factor in acculturation.

Applied anthropology arose as anthropologists sought to provide colonial administrators with a better understanding of native cultures, so as to avoid serious disruption of them, or as anthropologists tried to help indigenous people cope with outside threats to their interests. A serious ethical issue for applied anthropologists is how far they should go in trying to change the ways of other peoples.

Reactions of indigenous peoples to changes that are forced on them vary considerably. Some have retreated to inaccessible places in hopes of being

25

THE FUTURE OF HUMANITY

A Quiché Maya soldier on patrol in Guatemala. Throughout the world, ethnic groups are trying to retain and reassert their distinctive identities and traditions. A common response of the governments of the artificially created states in which such peoples live is to institute repressive measures in order to maintain control over people who never consented to that control in the first place.

CHAPTER

PREVIEW

What Can Anthropologists Tell Us of the Future?
Anthropologists cannot any more accurately predict future forms of culture than biologists can predict future forms of life or geologists future landforms. They can, though, identify certain trends of which we might otherwise be unaware, and anticipate some of the consequences these might have if they continue. They can also shed light on problems already identified by non-anthropologists, by showing how these relate to each other as well as to cultural practices and attitudes of which "experts" in other fields are often unaware. This ability to place problems in their wider context is an anthropological specialty, and it is essential if these problems are ever to be solved.

What Present-Day Trends Are Taking Place in the Evolution of Culture?
One major trend in present-day cultural evolution is toward the worldwide adoption of the products, technology, and practices of the industrialized world. This apparent gravitation toward a homogenized, one-world culture is, however, opposed by another very strong trend for ethnic groups all over the world to reassert their own distinctive identities. A third trend, of which we are just becoming aware, is that the problems created by cultural practices seem to be outstripping the capacity of culture to find solutions to problems.

What Problems Will Have to Be Solved if Humanity Is to Have a Future?
If humanity is to have a future, human cultures will have to find solutions to problems of population growth, food and other resource shortages, pollution, and a growing culture of discontent. One difficulty is that, up to now, there has been a tendency to see these as if they were discrete and unrelated. Thus, attempts to deal with one problem, such as short food supplies, are often at cross-purposes with others, such as an inequitable global system for the distribution of basic resources. Unless humanity has a more realistic understanding of the "global society" than presently exists, it will not be able to solve the problems that are crucial for its future.

Anthropology is often described by those who know little about it as a backward-looking discipline. The most popular stereotype is that anthropologists devote all of their attention to the interpretation of the past and the description of present-day tribal remnants. Yet as we saw in Chapter 1, as well as in the Applications boxes for Chapters 3 and 15, not even archaeologists, the most backward-looking anthropologists, limit their interests to the past, nor are ethnologists uninterested in their own cultures. Thus, throughout this book we have constantly made comparisons between "us" and "others." Moreover, anthropologists have a special concern with the future and the changes it may bring. Like many members of Western industrialized societies, they wonder what the "postindustrial" society now being predicted will hold. They also wonder what changes the coming years will bring to non-Western cultures. As we saw in the preceding chapter, when non-Western peoples are thrown into contact with Western industrialized peoples, their culture rapidly changes, often for the worse, becoming both less supportive and less adaptive. Since Westerners show no inclination to leave non-Westerners alone, we may ask, How can these threatened cultures adapt to the future?

THE CULTURAL FUTURE OF HUMANITY

Whatever the biological future of the human species, culture remains the mechanism by which people solve their problems of existence. Yet some anthropologists have noted with concern — and interpret as a trend — that the problems of human existence seem to be outstripping culture's ability to find solutions. The main problem seems to be that in solving existing problems, culture inevitably poses new ones. To paraphrase anthropologist Jules Henry, although culture is "for" people, it is also "against" them.[1] As we shall see, this is now posing serious new problems for human beings.

[1]Jules Henry, *Culture against Man* (New York: Vintage Books, 1965), p. 12

What can anthropologists tell us about the culture of the future?

Anthropologists — like geologists and evolutionary biologists — are historical scientists; as such, they can identify and understand the processes that have shaped the past and will shape the future. They cannot, however, tell us precisely what these processes will produce in the way of future cultures, any more than biologists can predict future forms of life, or geologists future landforms. The cultural future of humanity, though, will certainly be affected in important ways by decisions that we humans will be making in the future. This being so, if those decisions are to be made intelligently, it behooves us to have a clear understanding of the way things are in the world today. It is here that anthropologists have something vital to offer.

To comprehend anthropology's role in understanding and solving the problems of the future, we must look at certain flaws frequently seen in the enormous body of future-oriented literature that has appeared over the past few decades, not to mention the efforts to plan for the future that have become commonplace on regional, national, and international levels. For one, rarely do futurist writers or planners look more than about 50 years into the future, and the trends they project into it, more often than not, are those of recent history. This predisposes people to think that a trend that seems fine today will always be so, and that it may be projected indefinitely into the future. The danger inherent in this is neatly captured in anthropologist George Cowgill's comment: "It is worth recalling the story of the person who leaped from a very tall building and on being asked how things were going as he passed the 20th floor replied 'Fine, so far.'"[2]

Another flaw is a tendency to treat subjects in isolation, without reference to pertinent trends outside an expert's field of competence. For example, agricultural planning is often predicated upon the assumption that a certain amount of water is available for irrigation, whether or not urban plan-

[2]George L. Cowgill, Letter, *Science* 210 (1980): 1305.

ners or others have designs upon that same water. Thus—as in the southwestern United States, where more of the Colorado River's water has been allocated than actually exists—people may be counting on resources in the future that will not, in fact, be available. One would suppose that this would be a cause for concern, but as two well-known futurists put it, "if you find inconsistencies the model is better off without them."[3] These same two authorities, in editing a volume aimed at refuting the somewhat pessimistic projections of *Global 2000* (the first attempt at a coordinated analysis of global resources on the part of the U.S. government), deliberately avoided going into population growth and its implications, because they knew that to do so would lead their contributing authors to disagree with one another.[4] This brings us to yet another common flaw: a tendency to project the hopes and expectations of our own culture into the future interferes with the scientific objectivity that we ought to bring to the problem.

Against this background, anthropology's contribution to our view of the future is clear. With our holistic perspective, we are specialists at seeing how parts fit together into a larger whole; with our evolutionary perspective, we are able to see short-term trends in longer-term perspective; with over 100 years of cross-cultural research behind us, we are able to recognize culture-bound assertions when we encounter them; and we are familiar with alternative ways of dealing with a wide variety of problems.

ONE-WORLD CULTURE

A popular belief in recent years has been that the future world will see the development of a single, homogeneous world culture. The idea that such a "one-world culture" is emerging is based largely on the observation that developments in communication, transportation, and trade so link the peoples of the world that they are increasingly wearing the same kinds of clothes, eating the same kinds of

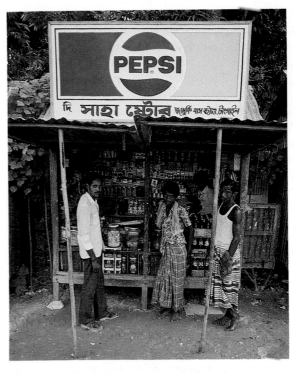

The worldwide spread of such products as Pepsi Cola is taken by some as a sign that a single homogeneous world culture is developing.

food, reading the same kinds of newspapers, watching the same kinds of television programs, and so on. The continuation of such trends, so this thinking goes, should lead North Americans, traveling in the year 2100 to Tierra del Fuego, China, or New Guinea, to find the inhabitants of these areas living in a manner identical or similar to theirs.

Certainly it is striking, the extent to which such things as Western-style clothing, transistor radios, Coca-Cola, and McDonald's hamburgers have spread to virtually all parts of the world; and many countries—Japan, for example—have gone a long way toward becoming "Westernized." Moreover, if one looks back over the past 5,000 years of human history, one will see that there has been a clear-cut trend for political units to become larger and more all-encompassing, while becoming at the same time fewer in number. A logical outcome of

---

[3]Constance Holden, "Simon and Kahn versus *Global 2000*," *Science* 221 (1983): 342.
[4]Ibid., p. 343.

the continuation of this trend into the future would be the reduction of autonomous political units to a single one, encompassing the entire world. In fact, by extrapolation from this past trend into the future, some anthropologists have gone so far as to predict that the world will become politically integrated, perhaps by the twenty-third century, but no later than the year 4850.[5]

One problem with such a prediction is that it ignores the one thing that all large states, past and present, irrespective of other differences between them, share in common: a tendency to come apart. Not only have the great empires of the past, without exception, broken up into numbers of smaller independent states, but countries in virtually all parts of the world today are showing a tendency to fragment. We can see this, for example, in separatist movements such as that of French-speaking peoples in Canada; Basque and Catalonian nationalist movements in Europe; Scottish, Irish, and Welsh nationalist movements in Britain; Armenian and Georgian nationalism in the Soviet Union; Kurdish nationalism in Turkey, Iran, and Iraq; Bangladesh separatism in Pakistan; Sikh separatism in India; Tamil separatism in Sri Lanka; Igbo separatism in Nigeria; Eritrean and Tigrean secession movements in Ethiopia; Namibian nationalism; and so on — this list is far from exhaustive. Nor is the United States immune, as can be seen from Puerto Rican nationalist movements and native American attempts to secure greater political self-determination and autonomy. These examples all involve peoples who consider themselves to be members of distinct nations by virtue of birth and cultural and territorial heritage, over whom peoples of some other ethnic background have tried to assert control. There are some 3,000 to 5,000 such national groups in the world today, as opposed to a mere 168 recognized states.[6] Although some of these groups are quite small in population and area — 100 or so people living on a few acres — some are quite large. The Karen peo-

ple of Burma, for example, number some 4.5 to 5 million, making them larger than 48 percent of United Nations member states. Reactions of these peoples to attempts at annexation and absorption by imposed state regimes controlled by other peoples range all the way from the successful fight for independence from Pakistan on the part of Bangladesh (or the Igbos' unsuccessful fight for independence from Nigeria) to the nonviolence of Scottish and Welsh nationalism. Many struggles for independence have been going on for years, as in the case of Karen resistance to the Burmese invasion of their territory in 1948, or the takeover of Kurdistan by Iraq, Iran, and Turkey in 1925. Even in cases of relative nonviolence, the stresses and strains are obviously there. Similar stresses and strains may even develop in the absence of ethnic differences, as regional interests within a large country come into increasing competition. Again, hints of this may be seen in the United States — for example, in arguments over access to Colorado River water, in attempts by oil- and gas-producing states to get the most out of their resources at the expense of other states ("Let the Bastards Freeze in the Dark" proclaimed bumper stickers in oil- and gas-producing states during the Arab oil embargo of the 1970s) or in the refusal in some states to curb smokestack emissions that cause acid rain, which is destroying resources and endangering the health of people in other states.

Expansionist attempts on the part of existing states to annex all or parts of other states also seem to be running into difficulty, as in the case of Soviet attempts to take over Afghanistan, Iraqi attempts to annex parts of Iran, or Libyan attempts to take over all or part of Chad. At the same time, voluntary efforts for the strengthening of international law seem to have hit a snag, as exemplified by the U.S. refusal to ratify the "Law of the Sea" treaty and, more recently, its refusal to accept the jurisdiction of the World Court in its quarrel with Nicaragua. It is just possible that we are reaching a point at which the old tendency for political units to increase in size, while decreasing in number, is being canceled out by the tendency to fragment into a greater number of smaller units.

[5]Carol R. Ember and Melvin Ember, *Cultural Anthropology*, 4th ed. (Englewood Cliffs, N.J.: Prentice-Hall, 1985), p. 230.
[6]Bernard Nietschmann, "The Third World War," *Cultural Survival Quarterly* 11, no. 3 (1987): 1–3.

THE RISE OF THE MULTINATIONALS

The resistance of the world to political integration seems to be offset, at least partially, by the rise of multinational corporations. Because these cut across the boundaries between states, they are a force for global unity in spite of the political differences that divide people. Situations like this are well known to anthropologists, as illustrated by this description of Zuni Indian integrative mechanisms:

> Four or five different planes of systemization cross-cut each other and thus preserve for the whole society an integrity that would speedily be lost if the planes merged and thereby inclined to encourage segregation and fission. The clans, the fraternities, the priesthoods, the kivas, in a measure the gaming parties, are all dividing agencies. If they coincided, the rifts in the social structure would be deep; by countering each other they cause segmentations which produce an almost marvelous complexity, but can never break apart the national entity.[7]

Multinational corporations are not new in the world (the Dutch East India Company is a good example from the seventeenth century), but they were comparatively rare until the 1950s. Since then they have become a major force in the world. These modern-day giants are actually clusters of corporations of diverse nationality, joined together by ties of common ownership and responsive to a common management strategy. More and more tightly controlled by a head office in one particular country, these multinationals are able to organize and integrate production across international boundaries for interests formulated in corporate board rooms, irrespective of whether or not these are consistent with the interests of the countries within which they operate. In a sense they are products of the technological revolution, for without sophisticated data-processing equipment, the multinationals could not keep adequate track of their worldwide operations.

[7]Alfred L. Kroeber, quoted in Edward Dozier, *The Pueblo Indians of North America* (New York: Holt, Rinehart and Winston, 1970), p. 19.

Multinational corporations are run from corporate boardrooms where decisions are made in the corporate interests whether or not these are consistent with those of the countries in which they operate.

So great is the power of multinationals that they are increasingly able to thwart the wishes of governments. Because the information processed by these corporations is kept from flowing in a meaningful way to the population at large, or even to lower levels within the organization, it becomes difficult for governments to get the information they need for informed policy decisions. For example, the U.S. Congress repeatedly expressed its frustration in trying to get from corporations the information that it needed in order to consider what federal energy policies should be. Beyond this, though, the multinationals have shown themselves able to overrule foreign-policy decisions, as when they got around the U.S. embargo on pipeline equipment for the Soviet Union. While some might see this as a hopeful augury for the transcendence of national vices and rivalries, it raises the unsettling issue of whether or not the global order should be determined by corporations interested only in their own profits.

If the ability of multinational corporations to ignore the wishes of sovereign governments is cause for concern, so is their ability to act in concert with such governments. Here, in fact, is where their worst excesses have taken place. In Brazil, for example, where the situation is hardly unique but is especially well documented, a partnership emerged, after the military coup of 1964, between a government anxious to proceed as rapidly as possible with the "development" of the Amazon Basin, a number of multinational corporations such as ALCOA, Borden, Union Carbide, Swift-Armour, and Volkswagen, to mention only a very few, and several international lending institutions, such as the Export–Import Bank, the Inter-American Development Bank, and the World Bank.[8] In order to realize their goals, these allies have introduced inappropriate technology and ecologically unsound practices into the region, which have already converted vast areas into semidesert. Far more shocking, however, has been the practice of uprooting whole human societies because they are seen as obstacles to economic growth. Literally overnight, people are deprived of the means to provide for their own needs and forcibly removed to places where they do not choose to live. Little distinction is made here between Indians and Brazilian smallholders who were brought into the region in the first place by a government anxious to alleviate acute land shortages in the northeast. Bad as this is for these Brazilian smallholders, the amount of disease, death, and human suffering unleashed upon the Indians can only be described as massive; in the process, whole peoples have been (and are still being) destroyed with a thoroughness not achieved even by the Nazis in World War II. Were it not so well documented, it would be beyond belief. This is "culture against people" with a vengeance.

The power of multinational corporations creates problems on the domestic as well as on the international scene. Anthropologist Jules Henry, in his classic study of life in the United States, observed that working for any large corporation — multinational or not — tends to generate "hostility, instability, and fear of being obsolete and unprotected. For most people their job was what they had to do rather than what they wanted to

do, . . . taking a job, therefore, meant giving up part of their selves."[9]

Consumers, too, have their problems with big business. After a ten-year intensive study of relations between producers and consumers of products and services, the anthropologist Laura Nader found repeated and documented offenses by business that cannot be handled by present complaint mechanisms, either in or out of court. Viable alternatives to a failed judicial system do not seem to be emerging. Face-to-faceless relations between producers and consumers, among whom there is a grossly unequal distribution of power, exact a high cost: a terrible sense of apathy, even a loss of faith in the system itself.

These problems are exacerbated, and new ones arise, in the "sprawling, anonymous, networks" that are the multinational corporations.[10] Not only are corporate decisions made in board rooms far removed from where other corporate operations take place, but given their dependence on ever more sophisticated data-processing systems to keep their operations running smoothly, many decisions can be and are being made by computers programmed for given contingencies and strategies. As anthropologist Alvin Wolfe has observed, "a social actor has been created which is much less under the control of men than we expected it to be, much less so than many even think it to be."[11] In the face of such seemingly mindless systems for making decisions in the corporate interest, employees become ever more fearful that if they ask too much of the corporation, it may simply shift its operations to some other part of the globe where it can find cheaper, more submissive personnel, as has happened with some frequency with respect to labor forces. Indeed, whole communities become fearful that if they do not acquiesce to corporate interests, local operations may be closed down.

---

[8]Shelton H. Davis, *Victims of the Miracle* (Cambridge: Cambridge University Press, 1982).

[9]Henry, *Culture*, p. 127.

[10]David Pitt, "Comment," *Current Anthropology* 18 (1977): 628.

[11]Alvin W. Wolfe, "The Supranational Organization of Production: An Evolutionary Perspective," *Current Anthropology* 18 (1977): 619.

In Third World countries, women have become a source of cheap labor for large corporations, as subsistence farming has given way to mechanized agriculture. Unable to contribute to their families' well-being in any other way, they have no choice but to take on menial jobs for low wages.

In their never-ending search for cheap labor, multinational corporations more and more have come to favor women for low-skilled assembly jobs. In Third World countries, as subsistence farming gives way to mechanical agriculture for production of crops for export, women are less able to contribute to their families' survival. Together with devaluation of the worth of domestic work, this places pressure on women to seek jobs outside the household in order to contribute to its support. Since most women do not have the time or resources to get an education or to develop special job skills, only low-paying jobs are open to them. Corporate officials, for their part, assume that female workers are strictly temporary, and high turnover means that wages can be kept low. Unmarried women are especially favored for employment, for it is assumed that they are free from family responsibilities until they marry, whereupon they will leave the labor force. Thus, the increasing importance of the multinationals in developing countries is contributing to the emergence of a division of labor in which gender segregation is prominent. On top of their housework, women hold low-paying jobs that require little skill; altogether, they may work as many as 15 hours a day. Higher-paying jobs, or at least those that require special skills, are generally held by men, whose workday may be shorter since they do not have additional domestic tasks to perform. Those men who lack special skills — and there are many — are often doomed to lives of unemployment.

In sum, multinational corporations have become a major force in the world today, drawing people more firmly than ever before into a system of relationships that is truly global in scope. While this brings with it potential benefits, it is also clear that it poses whole new sets of problems, which now must be solved.

ONE WORLD CULTURE: A GOOD IDEA OR NOT?

In the abstract, the idea of a single culture for all the world's people is one that has had a degree of popular appeal, in that it might offer fewer chances for the kinds of misunderstandings to develop that, so often in the past few hundred years, have led to wars. Some anthropologists question this, though, in the face of evidence that traditional ways of thinking of oneself and the rest of the world may persist, even in the face of massive changes in other aspects of culture. Indeed, one might argue that the chances for misunderstandings actually increase; an example of this is the Penobscot Indian land-claims case mentioned in Chapter 14. Many non-Indian residents of the state of Maine simply cannot comprehend how a people who look and act so much like themselves cannot see things as they do.

Some have argued that perhaps a generalized world culture would be desirable in the future, because certain cultures of today may be too specialized to survive in a changed environment. Examples of this situation are sometimes said to abound in modern anthropology. When a tradi-

Advocacy for the Rights of Indigenous Peoples

Anthropologists are increasingly concerned about the rapid disappearance of the world"'s remaining tribal peoples for a number of reasons, foremost among them a basic issue of human rights. In the world today there is a rush to develop those parts of the planet earth that have so far escaped industrialization, or the extraction of resources regarded as vital to the well-being of developed economies. These efforts at national and international development are planned, financed, and carried out by both governments and businesses (generally the huge multinational corporations) and international lending institutions. Unfortunately, the rights of native peoples generally have not been incorporated into the programs and concerns of these organizations, even where laws exist that are supposed to protect the rights of such peoples.

For example, the typical pattern for development of Brazil's Amazon Basin has been for the government to build roads, along which poor people from other parts of the country are settled. This brings them into conflict with Indians already living there, and who begin to die off in large numbers from diseases contracted from the settlers. Before long, the settlers learn that the soils are not suited for their kind of farming; at the same time, outside logging, mining, and agribusiness interests exert pressure to get them off the land. Ultimately, the poor people wind up living in disease-ridden slums, while the Indians end up decimated by the diseases and violence unleashed upon them by the outsiders. Those who survive are usually relocated to places where resources are inadequate to support them.

In an attempt to do what they can to help indigenous peoples gain title to their land and avoid exploitation by outsiders, anthropologists in various countries have formed advocacy groups. The major one in the United States is Cultural Survival, Inc., based in Cambridge, Massachusetts. The interest of this organization is not in preserving indigenous cultures in some sort of romantic, pristine condition, so that they will be there to study or to serve as "living museum exhibits," as it were. Rather, it is to provide the information and support to help endangered groups to comprehend their situation, maintain or even strengthen their sense of self, and adapt to the changing circumstances. It does not regard "mainstreaming" these groups into national societies as necessarily desirable; rather, the groups should be allowed the freedom to make their own decisions about how they wish to live. Instead of designing projects and then imposing them on endangered societies, Cultural Survival prefers to respond to the requests and desires of groups that see a problem and the need to address it. Cultural Survival can suggest ways to help and can activate extensive networks of anthropologists, other indigenous peoples who have already dealt with similar problems, and those government officials whose support can be critical to success.

Most projects funded or assisted by Cultural Survival have been focused on securing the land rights of indigenous peoples and organizing native federations. It has also identified and funded a number of locally designed experiments in sustainable development. Of major importance, Cultural Survival was instrumental in getting the World Bank, in 1982, to require as a matter of policy that the rights and autonomy of tribal peoples and minorities be *guaranteed* in any project in which the bank is involved. In spite of such successes, however, much remains to be done to secure the survival of indigenous peoples in all parts of the world.

tional culture that is highly adapted to a specific environment — such as that of the Indians of Brazil, who are well adapted to life in a tropical rain forest — meets European-derived culture and the social environment changes suddenly and drastically, the traditional culture often collapses. The reason for this, it is argued, is that its traditions and its political and social organizations are not at all adapted to "modern" ways. Here we have, once again, the ethnocentric notion (discussed in Chapter 24) that "old" cultures are destined to give way to the new. Since this is regarded as inevitable, actions are taken that by their very nature virtually guarantee that the traditional cultures will not survive; it is a classic case of the self-fulfilling prophecy.

A problem with this argument is that, far from being unable to adapt, traditional societies in places like Brazil's Amazon Forest are usually given no chance to work out their own adaptations. That Amazonian Indians can adapt themselves to the modern world if left alone to do so, without losing their own distinctive ethnic and cultural identity, is demonstrated by the Shuar case, noted in the preceding chapter. In Brazil, however, the pressures to develop the Amazon are so great that whole groups of people are swept aside, as multinational corporations and agribusiness pursue their own particular interests. People do not have much chance to work out their own adaptations to the modern world if they are transported en masse from their homelands and deprived literally overnight of their means of survival so that more acreage can be devoted to the raising of beef cattle. Few Brazilians get to eat any of this meat, for the bulk of it is shipped to Europe; nor do many of the profits stay in Brazil, since the major ranches are owned and operated by corporations based elsewhere. The process continues apace, nonetheless.

There is an important issue at stake in such situations, for what has happened is that some of the world's people have defined others — indeed, whole societies — as obsolete. This is surely a dangerous precedent, which, if allowed to stand, means that any of the world's people may at some time in the future be declared obsolete by someone else.

ETHNIC RESURGENCE

In spite of the worldwide adoption of such things as Coca-Cola and the Big Mac, and in spite of pressure for traditional cultures to disappear, it is clear that cultural differences are still very much with us in the world today. In fact, there is a strengthening tendency for peoples all around the world to resist modernization, and in many cases

retreat from it. Manifestations of this to which we have already alluded are the separatist movements around the world, and the success so far of the Shuar in retaining their own ethnic and cultural identity.

During the 1970s indigenous peoples around the world began to organize self-determination movements, culminating in the formation of the World Council of Indigenous Peoples in 1975. This now has official status as a nongovernmental organization of the United Nations which allows it to present the case of indigenous people before the world community. Leaders of this movement see their own societies as community-based, egalitarian, and close to nature, and are intent upon maintaining them that way.

North Americans often have difficulty adjusting to the fact that not everyone wants to be just like us. As children we are taught to believe that "the American way of life" is one to which all other peoples aspire, but it isn't only people like the Shuar who resist becoming "just like us." There are in the world today whole countries that, having striven to emulate Western ways, have suddenly backed off. The most striking recent case of such a retreat from modernity is Iran. With the overthrow of the Shah, a policy of deliberate modernization was abandoned in favor of a radical attempt to return to an Islamic republic out of a past "golden age" (mythical though the latter is). A somewhat similar, though far less radical, retreat from modernity seemed to be under way in the United States, which in 1984 reelected a government dedicated to a return to certain "traditional values" out of its past. To note just two other parallels between the two situations, in the United States, the analogue to the control of the Iranian government by a fundamentalist religious leader is the strong sympathy shown by members of the Reagan administration, as well as some members of Congress, to fundamentalist religious views;[12] the analogue to Iran's outlawing of Western-style

[12]Joan Marsella, "Pulling It Together: Discussion and Comments," in *Confronting the Creationists*, ed. Stephen Pastner and William A. Haviland, Northeastern Anthropological Association, Occasional Proceedings, no. 1, 1982, pp. 79–80.

These Australian Aborigines are calling relatives to ceremonies over a short-wave radio powered by solar batteries. Indigenous peoples can manage to adapt themselves to the modern world without losing their own distinctive identity, providing they are allowed to do so.

dress for women, who were ordered to return to traditional-style clothing, was the directive to women on the White House staff that pants were no longer acceptable dress and that skirts must be worn.

CULTURAL PLURALISM

If a single homogeneous world culture is not necessarily the wave of the future, what is? Some see **cultural pluralism,** in which more than one culture exists in a given society, as the future condition of humanity. Cultural pluralism is the social and political interaction within the same society of people with different ways of living and thinking. Ideally, it implies the rejection of bigotry, bias, and racism in favor of respect for the cultural traditions of other peoples. In reality, it has rarely worked out that way.

> **Cultural pluralism:** Social and political interaction within the same society of people with different ways of living and thinking.

Elements of pluralism are to be found in the United States, in spite of its melting-pot ideology. For example, in New York City there are neighborhoods where Puerto Ricans, with their own distinctive cultural traditions and values, exist side by side with other New Yorkers. Besides living in their own *barrio,* the Puerto Ricans have their own language, music, religion, and food. This particular pluralism, however, may be of a temporary nature, a stage in the process of integration into what is sometimes referred to as "standard American culture." Thus, the Puerto Ricans, in four or five generations, like many Italians, Irish, and east European Jews before them, may also become

All large North American cities contain pockets of immigrant cultures; shown here is a Chinese produce market in New York's Chinatown.

North Americanized to the point where their lifestyle will be indistinguishable from others around them. On the other hand, some Puerto Ricans, blacks, American Indians, Chicanos, and others have strongly resisted abandoning their distinctive cultural identities. Whether this marks the beginning of a trend away from the melting-pot philosophy and toward real pluralism, however, remains to be seen.

Some familiar examples of cultural pluralism may be seen in Switzerland, where Italian, German, and French cultures exist side by side; in Belgium, where the French Walloons and the Flemish have somewhat different cultural heritages; and in Canada, where French- and English-speaking Canadians live in a pluralistic society. In none of these cases, though, are the cultural differences of the magnitude seen in many a non-Western pluralistic society. As an example of one such society —

and its attendant problems — we may look at the Central American country of Guatemala.

Guatemalan Cultural Pluralism

Guatemala, like many another pluralistic country, came into being through conquest. In Guatemala's case the conquest was about as violent and brutal as it could be, given the technology of the time, as a rough gang of Spanish adventurers defeated a people whose civilization was far older than Spain's. The aim of the conquerors was quite simply to extract as much wealth as they could, primarily for themselves but also for Spain, by seizing the riches of those they conquered and by putting the native population to work extracting the gold and silver they hoped to find. Although the treasures to be had did not live up to the expectations of the conquerors (no rich deposits of ore were found), their main interest in their new possession continued to be in whatever they could extract from it that could be turned into wealth for themselves. Over the nearly 500 years since, their "Ladino" descendants have continued to be motivated by the same interests, even after independence from Spain.

Following its conquest, there was never substantial immigration from Spain, or anywhere else in Europe, into Guatemala. The conquerors and their descendants, for their part, wished to restrict the spoils of victory as much as possible to themselves, even though those spoils did not live up to advance expectations. There was, in fact, little to attract outsiders to the country. Thus, Indians have always outnumbered non-Indians in Guatemala, and continue to do so today. Nonetheless, Indians have never been allowed to hold any important political power at all; the apparatus of state, with its instruments of force (the police and army), remained firmly in the hands of the Ladino minority. This enabled them to continue exacting tribute and forced labor from Indian communities.

In the nineteenth century Guatemala's Ladino population saw the export of coffee and cotton as a new source of wealth for themselves. For this, they took over huge amounts of Indian lands to create their plantations, at the same time placing Indians in a situation where they had no option but to work for the plantation owners at wages cheap beyond belief. Any reluctance on the part of these native laborers was dealt with by brute force.

In the 1940s democratic reforms took place in Guatemala. Although Indians played no role in bringing them about, they benefited from them; for the first time in over 400 years native peoples could hold municipal offices in their own communities. In the 1950s the Roman Catholic church began to promote agricultural, consumer, and credit cooperatives in rural areas (which, in Guatemala, are predominantly Indian).

With the military coup of 1954 (carried out with U.S. aid) this brief interlude, in which the government recognized that Indians had social, economic, and cultural rights, came to an end. As before, the Indians stayed out of politics except within their own villages. And for the most part, they remained aloof from the guerrilla activities that arose in reaction to a succession of military regimes. But because the guerrillas operated in the countryside, these regimes came to regard all rural people, most of whom are Indian, with deep suspicion. Inevitably, the latter were drawn into the conflict, for reasons that are made clear in the following Original Study by an anthropologist with long experience in rural Guatemala.

ORIGINAL STUDY
The Indians Become Guerrillas: A Quiché Case[13]

Santa Cruz del Quiché produced no authentic guerrillas before 1980. This does not mean that there were no sympathizers, peasant organizations, or even some contacts with guerrillas.

In September of 1980 a terrorist act occurred in Santa Cruz that revolutionized the Indians of Santa Cruz. On the 23rd of September, 1980, Santa Cruz' first Indian *alcalde* [mayor] after centuries of Ladino rule was assassinated while riding home on his bicycle. His name was Abelino Zapeta y Zapeta. He was an acculturated Indian who lived in a hamlet a few kilometers from town, practiced carpentry, and was deeply committed to the Catholic Action movement of the community.

I interviewed Alcalde Zapeta the morning of his assassination. He related an incident of great interest to me, telling of some Indians in one of his hamlets, La Estancia, who had become guerrillas. According to him, men from that hamlet had been harassed by the Army. Some were even killed. They consequently took up arms to defend themselves. Though Catholics, he said, they became guerrillas and would fire on the Army as it passed alongside the hamlet on maneuvers. This was the first reliable testimony I had received that there were guerrillas in Santa Cruz.

By 1980 La Estancia was a large community, numbering about 4,000 persons, all Indians. It was heavily agricultural, approximately 63% of the families subsisting primarily from the cultivation of traditional highland crops. Weaving was an important secondary means of subsistence; some 25% of the families lived from the sale of weavings. Another 10% of the families made a living as travelling merchants, and another few (perhaps 2% of the families) owned trucks and pickups and made money through transportation.

Few of the La Estancia Indians worked on Pacific Coastal plantations. Such work was unnecessary because, through the use of fertilizers, cooperatives (La Estancia had five), and other progressive means the Indians of La Estancia were relatively wealthy. Most of the families earned from $1,000 to $3,000 per year. Thus, while the hamlet was overwhelmingly peasant, the vast majority owned lands and lived comfortably through income earned from agriculture and/or crafts.

The peasant Indians of La Estancia were overwhelmingly involved in the Catholic Action movement. At least 80% of the families were active — almost all agriculturalists and weavers. The merchants were comparatively secular in their beliefs. There were only a handful of traditionalists in the community and only a single family of Adventists.

As might be expected, the Christian Democratic party received a wide majority of votes from the Indians of La Estancia, especially in national elections; the two conservative parties polled only about 25% of the votes. The religious and political unity of most La Estancia Indians gave the community a strong collective spirit.

The collective spirit of the community is seen even more clearly in the strength of the Peasant Organization, CUC (Committee for Peasant Unity). CUC came to La Estancia in 1974. In 1980 almost everyone except the merchants had joined. CUC appears to have gradually replaced the Catholic Action organization as the collective secular structure of La Estancia; all its leaders came directly out of the Church leadership. Though originally set up under the direction of outside peasant leaders, it later became locally autonomous. While not directly militarized, it functioned to provide vigilance against outside interference, to gather intelligence information, to coordinate activities with peasants from other Santa Cruz hamlets and the region, and to promote political education — especially to awaken the Indians to their subordinate position as peasants in Guatemalan society. In La Estancia CUC was not seen as Marxist or revolutionary, but as a local organization necessary to protect the vast majority of inhabitants against an increasingly hostile government.

Incredible as it may seem, given the conditions outlined above, before the end of 1980 the entire community of La Estancia, some 4,000 individuals, except for a few families in an isolated mountainous zone, had disappeared. A band of about 40 young men and women had joined the EGP (Guerrilla Army of the Poor) guerrillas. The rest of the people had become refugees, scattered throughout Guatemala and neighboring countries; all had become guerrilla sympathizers. The situation was actually much more radical than Alcalde Zapeta had understood. How did this incredible transformation take place?

One big step, as noted before, was the assassination of Indian leaders like Alcalde Zapeta. Zapeta's family had seen the Ladino assassins, who were picked up by a speeding Army jeep shortly after the assassination. A few months before, one of the cooperative leaders from La Estancia had also been assassinated. The murder was highly symbolic, for the young man was killed in front of the Utatlan ruins, where the ancient Quiché capital had been. On that occasion too, the assassins were seen by Indian witnesses; they were once again Ladinos affiliated with the Army. The killing of Alcalde Zapeta and the cooperative leader, neither of whom were revolutionaries, greatly alarmed and angered the Indians of La Estancia. Little did they know that the terror directed against them by their own government was just beginning.

Three days after the assassination of Alcalde Zapeta some thirty to fifty armed men arrived in jeeps at La Estancia early in the morning. In a house to house search, using lists, they tracked down the Catholic Action, CUC, and cooperative leaders of the hamlet. By the time they completed their assignment, fifteen people, including several adolescents, had been massacred. One CUC–Catholic Action leader was crucified between two trees, his side pierced with a knife. According to witnesses from La Estancia these paramilitary assassins were Ladinos from the Oriente.

The terrified La Estancia Indians redoubled their vigilant guard. The men guarded by night, the children by day. At that time, many of the men began to sleep together, occupying a different house each night. They still had no modern weapons, and armed themselves with slings, machetes, and stones.

In November, Guatemalan soldiers arrived in force, this time by a different road (though they sent a jeep as a decoy along the same route the paramilitary assassins had come). Starting from the southern end of the hamlet, the soldiers systematically began searching homes for arms. According to witnesses, one of the Lieutenants was black, and many of the soldiers were Indians. Entire families, unarmed, were killed in cold blood, riddled with machine gun bullets as they cowered or slept in their beds. In all, fifty people were killed, including many women and children; they even killed a seventy-year-old man.

> **The dazed La Estancia Indians buried their dead in large holes dug in the ground — to have brought coffins from the town center for proper burial would have been seen as subversive. It was not even possible to officially report the killings.**
>
> **The women of the hamlet collectively beat to death a suspected informer in the marketplace of a nearby town, and a band of 30–40 youth left for the north to join the guerrillas. Then, as the rain poured down, the remaining inhabitants of La Estancia broke into families and silently left their homes. A community that had existed for a thousand years disappeared!**

[13]Robert M. Carmack, "Indians and the Guatemalan Revolution," *Cultural Survival Quarterly* 12, no. 7 (Summer 1983): 52–54.

What Carmack's case study describes has become commonplace in rural Guatemala. Whole communities have been wiped out, and an estimated 2 million people have been displaced. One would like to think that Guatemala represents the exception rather than the rule so far as pluralistic societies go, but unfortunately cases like it abound, in South and Central America and other parts of the world. A few random examples from elsewhere will make the point. In Ethiopia several ethnic groups are in revolt against a repressive regime controlled by a minority ethnic group, the Amharas. In South Africa a white minority government regularly makes use of force to maintain its grip over a black majority. In Southeast Asia Indonesians maintain their control over the people of East Timor and western New Guinea by force of arms. In the 1980s, on average, states borrow more money for the purpose of fighting peoples within their boundaries than for all other programs combined.[14]

Switzerland may be about the only country where pluralism has really worked out to the satisfaction of all parties to the arrangement, perhaps because in spite of linguistic differences, they are all heirs to a common European cultural tradition.

[14]Jason W. Clay, "Genocide in the Age of Enlightenment," *Cultural Survival Quarterly* 12, no. 3 (1988): 1.

In Northern Ireland, on the other hand, being heirs to a common tradition has not prevented violence and bloodshed. The more divergent cultural traditions are, the more difficult it appears to be to make pluralism work.

In Guatemala, so-called "model villages" like this one are inhabited by refugees from communities that have been destroyed by the army. Thrown together with people from different regions, who often speak different languages, they have been deprived of the ability to sustain themselves, and have become utterly dependent upon a government that neither trusts nor respects them.

ETHNOCENTRISM

The major problem associated with cultural pluralism has to do with ethnocentrism, a concept introduced in Chapter 12. In order to function effectively, a culture must instill the idea that its ways are "best," or at least preferable to those of all other cultures. It provides individuals with a sense of pride in and loyalty to their traditions, from which they derive psychological support, and which binds them firmly to their group. In societies in which one's self-identification derives from the group, ethnocentrism is essential to a sense of personal worth. The problem with ethnocentrism is that it can all too easily be taken as a charter for manipulating other cultures for the benefit of one's own, even though — as we saw in Chapter 21 — it does not have to be taken as such. When it is, however, unrest, hostility, and violence commonly result.

A typical expression of ethnocentrism is provided by President James Monroe's view, expressed in 1817, of Native American rights:

> The hunter state can exist only in the vast uncultivated deserts. It yields to the . . . greater force of civilized population; and of right, it ought to yield, for the earth was given to mankind to support the greater number of which it is capable; and no tribe or people have a right to withhold from the wants of others, more than is necessary for their support and comfort.[15]

This attitude is, of course, alive and well in the world today, and the idea that no group has the right to stand in the way of "the greater good for the greater number" is frequently used by governments to justify the development of resources in regions occupied by subsistence farmers, pastoral nomads, or food foragers — irrespective of the wishes of those peoples. But is it the greater good for the greater number? A look at the world as it exists today as a kind of global society, in which all the world's peoples are bound by interdependency, raises serious questions.

[15]Quoted in Jack D. Forbes, *The Indian in America's Past* (Englewood Cliffs, N.J.: Prentice-Hall, 1964), p. 103.

GLOBAL APARTHEID

Apartheid, which is the official policy of the government of South Africa, consists of programs or measures that aim to maintain racial segregation.[16] Structurally, it serves to perpetuate the dominance of a white minority over a nonwhite majority through the social, economic, political, military, and cultural constitution of society. Nonwhites are denied effective participation in political affairs, are restricted as to where they can live and what they can do, and are denied the right to travel freely. Whites, by contrast, control the government, including, of course, the military and police. Although there are 4.7 nonwhites for every white, being white and belonging to the upper stratum of society tend to go together. The richest 20 percent of South Africa take 58 percent of the country's income and enjoy a high standard of living, while the poorest 40 percent of the population receive but 6.2 percent of the national product.

What has South Africa to do with a global society? Structurally, the latter is very similar — almost a mirror image of South Africa's society, even though there is no stated policy of global apartheid. In the world society about two-thirds of the population is nonwhite and one-third white. In the world as a whole, being white and belonging to the upper stratum tend to go together. Although this upper stratum is not a homogeneous group, including as it does Communist and non-Communist peoples, neither is the upper stratum of South African society, where there is friction between the English, who control business and industry, and the Afrikaners, who control the government and military. In the world, the poorest 40 percent of the population receive about 5.2 percent of the world product, while the richest 20 percent take about 71.3 percent of world income (Figure 25.1). Life expectancy, as in South Africa, is poorest among nonwhites. Most of the world's weapons of mass destruction are owned by whites: the United States, U.S.S.R., France, and Britain. As in South

[16]Material on global apartheid is drawn from Gernot Kohler, "Global Apartheid," *World Order Models Project Working Paper 7* (New York: Institute for World Order, 1978).

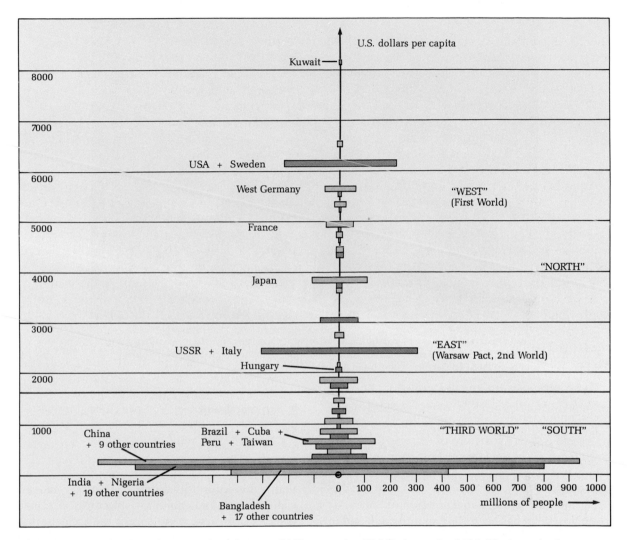

FIGURE 25.1 World income tree. Vertical axis = GNP per capita (U.S.$), intervals of 100. Horizontal axis = number of persons living at each income level.

Africa, death and suffering from war and violence are distributed unequally; in the world, the poorest 70 percent of the population suffer over 90 percent of violent death in all categories.

One could go on, but enough has been said to make the point: the parallels between the current world situation and that in South Africa are striking. We may sum up global apartheid as a de facto structure of world society which combines socio-economic and racial antagonisms and in which (1) a minority of whites occupies the pole of affluence, while a majority composed of other races occupies the pole of poverty; (2) social integration of the two groups is made extremely difficult by barriers of complexion, economic position, political boundaries, and other factors; (3) economic development of the two groups is interdependent; and (4) the affluent white minority possesses a dis-

Under apartheid, blacks have had to live in separate reserves, like the one shown here. Because these "Bantustans" cannot be self-supporting, whites have had available a pool of cheap labor to perform their menial work.

proportionately large share of the world society's political, economic, and military power. Global apartheid is thus a structure of extreme inequality in cultural, racial, social, political, economic, military, and legal terms, as in South African apartheid.[17]

Around the world, condemnation of South African apartheid has been close to universal, and in the United States the Congress in 1985 passed antiapartheid legislation. Since global apartheid is, if anything, even more severe, we ought to be much more concerned about it than we have been up to now.

PROBLEMS OF STRUCTURAL VIOLENCE

One of the consequences of a system of apartheid, be it official or unofficial, national or global, is a great deal of **structural violence,** that is, violence

[17]Ibid., p. 4.

> **Structural violence:** Violence exerted by situations, institutions, and social, political, and economic structures.

that is exerted by situations, institutions, and social, political, and economic structures. A classic instance of structural violence is the accident that occurred in December of 1984, when gas released from Union Carbide's plant in Bhopal, India, killed 2,000 people and seriously injured at least 200,000 more. As far as the victims of this accident are concerned, the effect was violent, even though the cause was not the hostile act of a specific individual. The source of the violence was an anonymous structure, and this is what structural violence is all about. In what remains of this chapter, there is not sufficient space to go into all aspects of structural violence, but we can look at some aspects of it that have been of particular concern to anthropologists. They are of concern to other specialists, too, and anthropologists draw on the work of these specialists as well as their own, thereby fulfilling their traditional role as synthesizers (discussed in Chapter 1). Moreover, anthropologists are less apt than other specialists to see these aspects of structural violence as discrete and unrelated. Thus, they have a key contribution to make to our understanding of such modern-day problems as overpopulation, food shortages, pollution, and widespread discontent in the world.

WORLD HUNGER

As recently dramatized by events in Ethiopia and other parts of Africa, a major source of structural violence in the world today is our failure to provide food for all of the people. Not only is Africa losing the capacity to feed itself; by 1980, 52 countries were producing less food per capita than they were ten years previously, and in 42 countries, available supplies of food were not adequate to supply the caloric requirements of their populations.[18] One factor that has contributed to this food crisis is a dramatic growth in the world's population.

Population growth is more than a simple addition of people. If it were just that, the addition of 20 people a year to a population of 1,000 would result in that population's being doubled in 50 years; but because the added people produce more people, the doubling time is actually much less than 50 years. Hence, it took the whole of human history and prehistory for the world's population to reach 1 billion people, which it had done by 1850 (Figure 25.2). By 1950, world population had reached almost 2.5 billion, representing an annual growth rate of about 0.8 percent. Between 1950 and 1960, the rate of growth had climbed to 1.8 percent (doubling time, 39 years), and in the 1960s fluctuated between 1.8 percent and 2 percent (doubling time, 35 years at 2 percent). There are now almost 5 billion people in the world, with growth rates ranging from less than 1 percent (Europe and North America), to 2.4–2.6 percent (southern Asia, Central and South America), to close to 3 percent (Africa).

[18]John H. Bodley, *Anthropology and Contemporary Human Problems*, 2d ed. (Mountain View, Calif.: Mayfield, 1985), p. 114.

In 1986 an "accident" at the Soviet Union's Chernobyl nuclear plant released massive amounts of radioactivity into the atmosphere. Fallout from this devastated the reindeer herding economy of Scandinavian Lapps: a classic example of structural violence.

The obvious question arising from the burgeoning world population is, Can we produce enough food to feed all of those people? The majority opinion among those in the field of agriculture is that we can do so, although we probably won't be able to in the future if populations continue to grow as they have. In the 1960s a major effort was launched to expand food production in the poor countries of the world by introducing new high-yield strains of grains. Yet in spite of some dramatic gains from this "green revolution" — India, for example, was able to double its wheat crop in six years and was on the verge of grain self-sufficiency by 1970 — and in spite of the impressive output of North American agriculture, millions of people on the face of the globe continue to face malnutrition and starvation. In the United States, meanwhile, about $85 million worth of *edible* food is thrown out every day (far more food than is sent out for famine relief), and farms are going out of business in record numbers.

The immediate cause of world hunger has less to do with food production than with food distribution. For example, millions of acres in Africa, Asia, and Latin America, which once were devoted

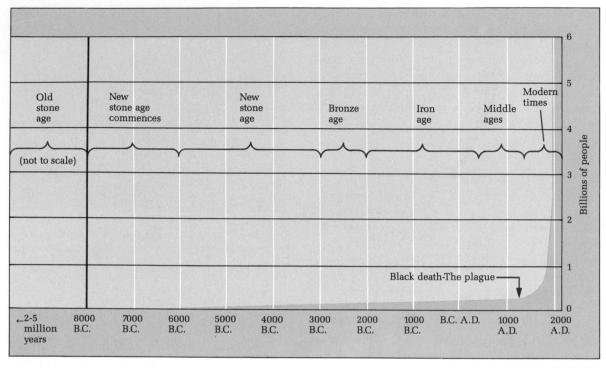

FIGURE 25.2 World population growth through history.

to subsistence farming, have been given over to the raising of cash crops for export, to satisfy appetites in the "developed" countries of the world for such things as coffee, tea, chocolate, bananas, and beef. Those who used to farm the land for their own food needs are relocated, either to urban areas, where all too often there is no employment for them, or to other areas that are ecologically unsuited for farming. In Africa such lands are often occupied by pastoral nomads; as these are encroached upon by farmers, insufficient pasturage is left for livestock. The resultant overgrazing, coupled with the clearing of the land for farming, leads to increased loss of both soil and water, with disastrous consequences to nomad and farmer alike. In Brazil, which is highly dependent on outside sources of fossil fuels for its energy needs, millions of acres in the northeast part of the country were taken over for sugar production, which could be used to make alcohol to fuel the vehicles in Rio.

The people who were displaced by this were given small holdings in the Amazon, where they are now being uprooted to make way for huge ranches on which beef is raised for export.

One strategy urged upon Third World nations, especially by government officials and development advisors from the United States, is to adopt the practices that have made North American agriculture so incredibly productive. On the face of it, this seems like a good idea; what it overlooks is the fact that it requires investment in expensive seeds and chemicals that neither small farmers nor poor countries can afford. Intensive agriculture on the U.S. model requires enormous inputs of chemical fertilizers, pesticides, and herbicides, not to mention the fossil fuels needed to run all the mechanized equipment. Even where high production lowers costs, the price is likely to be beyond the reach of poor farmers. And there are other problems: farming U.S.-style is energy inefficient.

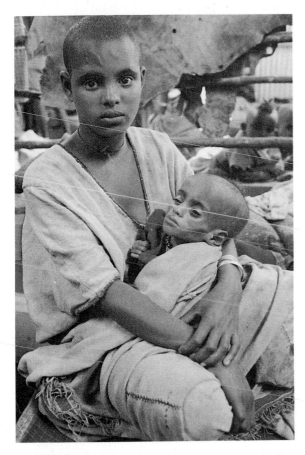

Hunger stalks much of the world as a result of a world food system geared to satisfy the appetites of an affluent minority living in the "developed" nations of the world.

For every calorie that is produced, at least 8 — some say as many as 20 — calories go into its production and distribution.[19] By contrast, an Asian wet rice farmer using traditional methods produces 300 calories for each one expended. North American agriculture is wasteful of other resources as well: about 30 pounds of fertile topsoil are ruined for every pound of food produced.[20] Meanwhile, toxic substances from chemical nutrients and pesticides pile up in unexpected places, poisoning ground and surface waters, killing fish, birds, and other useful forms of life, upsetting natural ecological cycles, and causing major public health problems. In spite of its spectacular short-term success, there are serious questions about whether such a profligate system of food production can be sustained over the long run, even in North America.

POLLUTION

It is ironic that a life-sustaining activity such as food production should constitute a health hazard, but that is precisely what it becomes, as agricultural chemicals poison soils and waters, and food additives (over 2,500 are or have been used) expose people to substances that all too often turn out to be harmful. This, though, is but a part of a larger problem of environmental pollution. Industrial activities are producing highly toxic waste at unprecedented rates, and emissions from factories are poisoning the air. For example, smokestack gases are clearly implicated in acid rain, which is causing damage to lakes and forests all over northeastern North America. Air containing water vapor with a high acid content is, of course, harmful to the lungs, but the health hazard is greater than this. As surface and ground waters become more acidic, the solubility of lead, cadmium, mercury, and aluminum increases sharply. The increase of dissolved aluminum, in particular, is becoming truly massive, and aluminum has been found to be associated with senile dementia and Alzheimer's and Parkinson's diseases. These, in turn, are ranked as major health problems in the United States.

As with world hunger, the structural violence that results from pollution tends to be greatest in the poorer countries of the world, where chemicals banned for use in nations like the United States are still widely used. And as manufacturing shifts from the developed to the less developed countries of the world, a trend encouraged in part by fewer safety and environmental regulations to comply with, lethal accidents such as the one already mentioned at Bhopal, India, may be expected to in-

[19]Ibid., p. 128.
[20]Barbara H. Chasin and Richard W. Franke, "U.S. Farming: A World Model?" *Global Reporter* 1, no. 2 (1983): 10.

"Progress" comes to the Amazon: Debris from oil exploration.

crease. Indeed, development itself seems to be a health hazard; it is well known that indigenous peoples in Africa, the Pacific Islands, South America, and elsewhere are relatively free from diabetes, obesity, hypertension, and a variety of circulatory diseases, until they adopt the ways of the developed countries. With this, rates of these "diseases of development" escalate dramatically.

Modern humanity knows the causes of pollution, and realizes it is a danger to future survival. Why, then, can humanity not control this evil by which it fouls its own nest? At least part of the answer lies in philosophical and theological traditions. As we saw in Chapter 21, Western industrialized societies accept the biblical assertion that they have dominion over the earth with all that

grows and lives on it, which it is their duty to subdue.

This exploitative world view, characteristic of all civilizations, extends to all natural resources. Only when problems have reached crisis proportions have Western peoples protected or replaced what greed and acquisitiveness have prompted them to take from the environment. In recent years, recognizing the seriousness of the environmental crisis that people were creating for themselves, authorities have passed laws against such activities as hunting whales out of existence, dumping toxic wastes into streams and rivers, and poisoning the air with harmful fumes. That these laws have been at best only partially successful is illustrated by attempts to deal with the destruction of the earth's protective ozone layer that is being caused by the chlorofluorocarbons used in aerosol sprays, refrigerators, air conditioners, and the manufacture of Styrofoam. First, a ban was imposed on the use of these chemicals in sprays, in spite of which deterioration of the ozone layer preceded about twice as fast as scientists predicted it would, even in the absence of the ban. More recently, an international treaty restricting the use of chlorofluorocarbons has been ratified, but even this will merely slow down, rather than halt, further deterioration. Obviously, many more people will have to suffer from skin cancers than presently do before more meaningful steps will be taken, by which time it could be too late.

A large part of the problem in this and similar situations is a reluctance to perceive as disadvantageous those practices that previously seemed to work well. What frequently happens is that practices that were carried out on one particular scale, or that were suited to one particular context, become unsuitable when carried out on another scale or in another context. Because they are trained to look at customs in their broader context, anthropologists would seem to have an important role to play in convincing people that solutions to many problems require changed behavior.

Indigenous peoples, in particular, are apt to stand in awe of natural forces, bestowing on them a special place in their religious system. For example, many people believe that rushing rapids, storms, the mountains, and the jungles possess awesome powers. This is also true of fire, which warms and destroys. For farmers, the sun, rain, and thunder are important to their existence and are often considered divine. Such world views may not be foolproof checks to the kind of environmental manipulation that causes severe pollution, but they certainly act as powerful restraining influences.

POPULATION CONTROL

Although the problems we have discussed so far may not be caused by population growth, they are certainly made worse by it. For one thing, it increases the scale of the problems; thus, the waste generated by a small population is far easier to deal with than that generated by a large one. For another, it often nullifies efforts made to solve the problems, as when increased food production is offset by increased numbers of people to be fed. While solving the problem of population growth will not make the other problems go away, it is unlikely that those other problems can be solved unless population growth is arrested.

As our earlier look at population demonstrated, the world's population has grown enormously since the beginning of the industrial age. With the exception of European and North American populations, there was no sign of a significant decline in birthrates before 1976. Since then there have been some encouraging signs, as in China, where there has been a steep decline in fertility. In southern Asia, Africa, and much of Central and South America, however (again, the poorer countries of the world), the impact on fertility of programs to reduce birthrates is yet to be felt. In these countries, growing populations make it difficult even to maintain their present per capita share of food and other resources. Even if, through some miracle, those countries having policies aimed at population control were able to bring about an immediate balance between birthrates and death rates (**replacement reproduction**), their populations would continue to grow for the next 60 years or so.

Replacement reproduction: When birthrates and death rates are in equilibrium; people produce no more offspring than necessary to replace themselves when they die.

The case of India — a country that has been working for some time to curb population growth — illustrates the problem. This country's population currently is about one-ninth of the world total, and is growing by 13 million people per year. If by 25 years from now India achieved replacement reproduction, its population would continue to grow for another 60 years, making it 2.5 times its present size.

The severity of the problem becomes clear when it is realized that the present world population of nearly 5 billion people can be sustained only by using up what are really nonrenewable resources, which is like living off income-producing capital. It works for a time, but once the capital is gone, so is the possibility of even having an income to live on. In recognition of the importance of bringing population growth under control, some 59 developing countries have programs for the dissemination of birth-control information. By contrast, agencies of the United States government have been actively working against such programs since 1980.

Evident though the problem is, efforts to bring about reduced birthrates face enormous cultural and structural obstacles. Some of these, as well as the kinds of new problems that may arise, are well illustrated by China's much publicized policy to promote one-child families. While this has slowed the rate of growth of China's population, it has given rise to some serious new problems. The difficulty stems from a basic contradiction with another policy, to raise agricultural productivity by granting more economic autonomy to rural households, and the continued existence of families that, as in old China, are strongly patriarchal. Within such families, men are responsible for farm work, perpetuation of the male line of descent is considered essential to everyone's well-being, and

An ad for China's "one child" family policy. Necessary though population control policies may be, existing cultural practices may make them difficult to carry out.

postmarital residence is strictly patrilocal. Under these circumstances, the birth of male children is considered essential; without them, the household will not have the manpower it needs and will suffer economically. Furthermore, the parents will have no one to support them once they are too old for physical labor. Daughters are of little use to them since they will marry out of the household and can offer little aid to their parents. Since married couples are supposed to have only one child, the birth of a daughter is greeted with dismay, for if the couple tries again for a boy, tremendous pressures will be brought to bear by local officials of the state for the woman to have an abortion, and for her or her husband to undergo sterilization.

Not surprisingly, in the face of all this, female infanticide is on the rise in China, and women who bear daughters are often physically and mentally abused by their husbands and mothers-in-law, sometimes to the point of committing suicide (although the state teaches that men determine the sex of a baby, most rural Chinese believe that the woman is still responsible for the outcome of birth, perhaps through her diet and behavior). Women pay in other ways with their bodies; when a second pregnancy occurs, it is the woman who must have the abortion, and it is usually she who is sterilized (surgical intervention in men in their prime is discouraged, owing to the importance of their labor in agriculture). Under such circumstances, a man may divorce his daughter-bearing wife in order to try again for a son with a new wife. As a consequence, his old wife is left on her own, with no son to care for her in her old age. In a married woman, one means by which unauthorized pregnancy is prevented is through placement of an intrauterine device (IUD) in her womb. This cannot be removed without official permission, which is hard to get even in the face of compelling medical reasons to do so, since removal is contrary to official policy. Nor is an attached cord for removal provided, all of which has led to proliferation of back-alley practitioners who remove IUDs with improvised hooks, often leading to infection and death.

THE CULTURE OF DISCONTENT

In spite of the difficulties, stabilization of the world's population appears to be a necessary step if the problems of the future are ever to be solved. Without this, whatever else is done, an inability to provide enough food seems inevitable. Up until about 1950, growth in the world's food supply came almost entirely from expanding the amount of land under cultivation. Since then, it has come increasingly from high energy inputs in the form of chemical fertilizers (upon which new high-yield varieties of crops depend), pesticides, and herbicides, as well as fuel to run tractors and other mechanical equipment, including irrigation pumps. The source of almost all this energy is oil; yet while the demand for food is projected to rise until at least the middle of the next century, oil supplies are diminishing and will surely decline over this same period. Insufficient supplies of food are bound to result in increased structural violence in the form of higher death rates in the "underdeveloped" countries of the world. This will surely have an impact on the "developed" countries, with their relatively stable populations and high standards of living. It is hard to see how such countries could exist peacefully side by side with others experiencing high death rates and abysmally low living standards.

Necessary though it may be in solving problems of the future, there is no reason to suppose that birth control will be sufficient by itself. The result would be only to stabilize things as they are. The problem is twofold. Over the past several years, the poor countries of the world have been sold on the idea that they should enjoy a standard of living comparable to that of the rich countries, while at the same time the resources necessary to maintain such a standard of living are running out. As we saw in Chapter 24, this situation has led to the creation of a culture of discontent, whereby people's aspirations far exceed their opportunities. The problem involves not just a case of population

The need for ever more resources on the part of the richer countries condemns many people in poorer countries to lives of misery. In Bolivia, tin is the number one export. It is mined by Quechua Indians, who sacrifice their health for the equivalent of one U.S. dollar a day. Rarely do they live more than seven years after entering the mines.

growth outstripping food supplies; it is also one of unequal access to decent jobs, housing, sanitation, health care, and adequate police and fire protection. And it is one of steady deterioration of the natural environment as a result of increasing industrialization.

What are required are some dramatic changes in cultural values and motivations, as well as in social institutions. The emphasis on individual self-interest, materialism, and conspicuous production, acquisition, and consumption, which is characteristic of the richer countries of the world, needs to be abandoned in favor of a more human self-image and social ethic, which can be created from values still to be found in many of the world's cultures. These include a world view that sees humanity as a part of nature rather than superior to it. Included, too, is a sense of social responsibility that recognizes that no individual, people, or state has the right to monopolize important resources. Finally, there is needed an awareness of the importance of the supportive ties among individuals, such as are seen in kinship or other associations in the traditional societies of the world.

CHAPTER SUMMARY

Since future forms of culture will be shaped by decisions humans have yet to make, they cannot be predicted with any accuracy. Thus, instead of trying to foretell the future, a number of anthropologists are trying for a better understanding of the existing world situation, so that those decisions may be made intelligently. Anthropologists are especially well suited to do this, owing to their experience at seeing things in context, their long-term evolutionary perspective, their ability to recognize culture-bound biases, and their familiarity with cultural alternatives.

However humanity changes biologically, culture remains the chief means by which humans try to solve their problems of existence. Some anthropologists are concerned that there is a trend for the problems to outstrip culture's ability to find solutions. Rapid developments in communication, transportation, and world trade, some believe, will link people together to the point that a single world culture will result. Their thinking is that such a homogenized superculture would offer fewer chances for conflict between peoples than in the past. A number of anthropologists are skeptical of such an argument, in view of the recent tendency for ethnic groups to reassert their own distinctive identities, and in view of the persistence of traditional ways of thinking about oneself and others, even in the face of massive changes in other aspects of culture. Anthropologists are also concerned about the tendency for many of the world's traditional societies to be treated as obsolete when they appear to stand in the way of "development."

Another alternative is for humanity to move in the direction of cultural pluralism, in which more than one culture exists in a society. To work, cultural pluralism must reject bigotry, bias, and racism. Some anthropologists maintain that pluralistic arrangements are the only feasible means for achieving global equilibrium and peace. A problem associated with cultural pluralism is ethnocentrism. All too often, it has led one group to impose its control on others, often leading to prolonged, violent, and bloody political upheavals, including genocide.

Adopting a global perspective, a picture emerges that is strikingly similar to South Africa's system of apartheid. It serves to maintain the dominance of a white minority over a nonwhite majority, through the social, economic, political, military, and cultural constitution of the "global society."

One consequence of any system of apartheid is a great deal of structural violence exerted by situations, institutions, and social, political, and economic structures. Such violence involves things like overpopulation and food shortages, which anthropologists are actively working to understand and help alleviate. One challenge the world over is to provide food resources to keep pace with the burgeoning population. The immediate problem, though, is not so much one of overpopulation as it is a food-distribution system that is geared to the satisfaction of appetites in the "rich" countries of the world, at the expense of those living in poorer nations.

Pollution has become a direct threat to humanity. Western peoples have protected their environments only when some crisis forced them to do so; they have felt no long-term responsibilities toward the earth or its resources. Western societies could learn much from those non-Western peoples who see themselves as integral parts of the earth.

Meeting the problems of structural violence that beset the human species today probably can be done only if we are able to reduce the birthrate. Effective birth-control methods are now available. Whether or not these methods are used on a vast enough scale depends on their availability and acceptance. Many of the world's developing countries have policies aimed at controlling population growth, but these sometimes conflict with other policies and give rise to new kinds of problems. Even if replacement reproduction were immediately achieved, their populations would continue to grow. At the moment, some elements in the United States actively oppose such policies.

Solving the problems of the global society depends also on lessening the gap between the living standards of poor and developed countries. This will call for dramatic changes in the values of Western societies with their materialistic, consumer orientation. All people need to see themselves as a part of nature, rather than as superior to it. Also needed are a social responsibility that recognizes that no nation has a right to monopolize important resources and an awareness of the importance of supportive ties between individuals.

SUGGESTED READINGS

Bodley, John H. *Victims of Progress*, 2d. ed. Mountain View, Calif.: Mayfield, 1982. Anthropologist Bodley explores the impact of industrial civilization on the indigenous peoples of the world and reports how the latter are organizing to protect themselves.

Bodley, John H. *Anthropology and Contemporary Human Problems*, 2d ed. Mountain View, Calif.: Mayfield, 1985. In this book, Bodley examines some of the most serious problems in the world today: overconsumption, resource depletion, hunger and starvation, overpopulation, violence, and war.

Davis, Shelton H. *Victims of the Miracle*. Cambridge: Cambridge University Press, 1982. An anthropologist looks at Brazil's efforts to develop the Amazon region, the motivations behind those efforts, and their impact on indigenous peoples. Davis pays special attention to what role multinational corporations play, how they relate to the Brazilian government, and who benefits from it all.

Maybury-Lewis, David, ed. *The Prospects for Plural Societies*. 1982 Proceedings of the American Ethnological Society, 1984. In 1982, a group of anthropologists met to discuss one of the most crucial issues of our time, the prospects for multiethnic societies. What emerged as the "villain" of the conference was the state; not just particular countries but states as a kind of political structure and the hold that they have over modern thought and political action. Maybury-Lewis confronts this issue in the concluding essay, which by itself makes this volume worth getting hold of.

Wolf, Eric R. *Europe and the People without History*. Berkeley: University of California Press, 1982. As far back as the Crusades, Europeans learned that seizure of external resources allowed them to live better than they had before, and they have been living beyond their means ever since. In this book, Eric Wolf looks at the role of Europeans as part of a global community, and how this has made the world what it is today.

BIBLIOGRAPHY

Aberle, David F., 1961. "Culture and Socialization," in F. Hsu, ed., *Psychological Anthropology: Approaches to Culture and Personality*. Homewood, Ill.: Dorsey Press, pp. 381–399.

Aberle, David F., Urie Bronfenbrenner, Eckhard H. Hess, Daniel R. Miller, David H. Schneider, and James N. Spuhler, 1963. "The Incest Taboo and the Mating Patterns of Animals," *American Anthropologist*, 65: 253–265.

Abu-Lughold, Lila, 1988. *Veiled Sentiments: Honor and Poetry in A Bedouin Society*, Berkeley, Calif.: University of California Press.

Adams, Richard E. W., 1977. *Prehistoric Mesoamerica*. Boston: Little, Brown.

Adams, Robert McC., 1965. *Land Behind Baghdad*. Chicago: University of Chicago Press.

Adams, Robert McC., 1966. *The Evolution of Urban Society*. Chicago: Aldine.

Al-Issa, Ihsan, and Wayne Dennis, eds., 1970. *Cross-cultural Studies of Behavior*. New York: Holt, Rinehart and Winston.

Alland, Alexander, Jr., 1971. *Human Diversity*. New York: Columbia University Press.

Alland, Alexander, Jr., 1970. *Adaptation in Cultural Evolution: An Approach to Medical Anthropology*. New York: Columbia University Press.

Allen, Susan L., 1984. "Media Anthropology: Building a Public Perspective," *Anthropology Newsletter*, 25: 6.

Amiran, Ruth, 1965. "The Beginnings of Pottery-Making in the Near East," in Frederick R. Matson, ed., *Ceramics and Man*. Viking Fund Publications in Anthropology, No. 41.

Anderson, Connie M. "Neanderthal Pelves and Gestational Length," *American Anthropologist*, 1989, 91: 327–340.

Arensberg, Conrad M., 1961. "The Community as Object and Sample," *American Anthropologist*, 63: 241–264.

Arensberg, Conrad M., and Arthur H. Niehoff, 1964. *Introducing Social Change:*

A Manual for Americans Overseas. Chicago: Aldine.

Ashmore, Wendy, ed., 1981. *Lowland Maya Settlement Patterns*. Albuquerque: University of New Mexico Press.

Balandier, Georges, 1971. *Political Anthropology*. New York: Pantheon.

Banton, Michael, 1968. "Voluntary Association: Anthropological Aspects," *International Encyclopedia of the Social Sciences*, 16: 357–362.

Bar-Yosef, O., 1986. "The Walls of Jericho: An Alternative Interpretation," *Current Anthropology*, 27: 157–162.

Barber, Bernard, 1957. *Social Stratification*. New York: Harcourt.

Barfield, Thomas J., 1984. "Introduction," *Cultural Survival Quarterly*, 8: 2.

Barnett, H. G., 1953. *Innovation: The Basis of Cultural Change*. New York: McGraw-Hill.

Barnouw, Victor, 1963. *Culture and Personality*. Homewood, Ill.: Dorsey Press.

Barth, Frederick, 1961. *Nomads of South Persia: The Basseri Tribe of the Khamseh Confederacy*. Boston: Little, Brown (Series in Anthropology).

Barton, R. F., 1919. *Ifugao Law*. Berkeley: *University of California Publications in American Archaeology and Ethnology*, Vol. XV.

Bascom, William, 1969. *The Yoruba of Southwestern Nigeria*. New York: Holt, Rinehart and Winston.

Bateson, Gregory, 1958. *Naven*. Stanford, Calif.: Stanford University Press.

Beals, Alan R., 1972. *Gopalpur: A South Indian Village*. New York: Holt, Rinehart and Winston.

Beattie, John, 1964. *Other Cultures: Aims, Methods and Achievements*. New York: Free Press.

Beidelman, T. O., ed., 1971. *The Transition of Culture: Essays to E. E. Evans-Pritchard*. London: Tavistock.

Belshaw, Cyril S., 1958. "The Significance of Modern Cults in Melanesian

Development," in William Lessa and Evon Z. Vogt, eds., *Reader in Comparative Religion: An Anthropological Approach*. New York: Harper & Row.

Benedict, Ruth, 1959. *Patterns of Culture*. New York: New American Library.

Bennett, John W., 1964. "Myth, Theory and Value in Cultural Anthropology," in E. W. Caint and G. T. Bowles, eds., *Fact and Theory in Social Science*. Syracuse, N.Y.: Syracuse University Press.

Berdan, Frances F., 1982. *The Aztecs of Central Mexico*. New York: Holt, Rinehart and Winston.

Bernal, I., 1969. *The Olmec World*. Berkeley: University of California Press.

Bernard, H. Russell, and Willis E. Sibley, 1975. *Anthropology and Jobs*. Washington, D.C.: American Anthropological Association.

Bernardi, Bernardo, 1985. *Age Class Systems: Social Institutions and Policies Based on Age*. New York: Cambridge University Press.

Bernstein, Basin, 1961. "Social Structure, Language and Learning," *Educational Research*, 3: 163–176.

Berreman, Gerald D., 1962. *Behind Many Masks: Ethnography and Impression Management in a Himalayan Village*. Ithaca, N.Y.: Society for Applied Anthropology (Monograph No. 4).

Berreman, Gerald D. 1968. "Caste: The Concept of Caste," *International Encyclopedia of the Social Sciences*, 2: 333–338.

Bicchieri, M. G., ed., 1972. *Hunters and Gatherers Today: A Socioeconomic Study of Eleven Such Cultures in the Twentieth Century*. New York: Holt, Rinehart and Winston.

Bidney, David, 1953. *Theoretical Anthropology*. New York: Columbia University Press.

Binford, L. R., 1972. *An Archaeological Perspective*. New York: Seminar Press.

Birdwhistell, Ray 1970. *Kinesics and Context*. Philadelphia: University of Pennsylvania Press.

Boas, Franz, 1962. *PrimitiveArt.* Gloucester, Mass.: Peter Smith.

Boas, Franz, 1966. *Race, Language and Culture.* New York: Free Press.

Bodley, John H., 1982. *Victims of Progress,* 2d ed. Palo Alto, Calif.: Mayfield.

Bodley, John H., 1985. *Anthropology and Contemporary Human Problems,* 2d ed. Palo Alto, Calif.: Mayfield.

Bohannan, Paul, 1966. *Social Anthropology,* New York: Holt, Rinehart and Winston.

Bohannan, Paul, ed., 1967. *Law and Warfare: Studies in the Anthropology of Conflict.* Garden City, N.Y.: Natural History Press.

Bohannan, Paul, and George Dalton, eds., 1962. *Markets in Africa.* Evanston, Ill.: Northwestern University Press.

Bohannan, Paul, and John Middleton, eds., 1968. *Kinship and Social Organization.* Garden City, N.Y.: Natural History Press (American Museum Source Books in Anthropology).

Bohannan, Paul, and John Middleton, eds., 1968. *Marriage, Family, and Residence.* Garden City, N.Y.: Natural History Press (American Museum Source Books in Anthropology).

Bolinger, Dwight, 1968. *Aspects of Language.* New York: Harcourt.

Bordes, Franrois, 1972. *A Tale of Two Caves.* New York: Harper & Row.

Bornstein, Marc H., 1975. "The Influence of Visual Perception on Culture," *American Anthropologist,* 77 (4): 774–798.

Brace, C. Loring, 1981. "Tales of the Phylogenetic Woods: The Evolution and Significance of Phylogenetic Trees," *American Journal of Physical Anthropology,* 56: 411–429.

Brace, C. Loring, and M. F. Ashley Montagu, 1977. *Human Evolution: An Introduction to Biological Anthropology,* 2d ed., New York: Macmillan.

Brace, C. Loring, Harry Nelson, and Noel Korn, 1979. *Atlas of human Evolution,* 2d ed., New York: Holt, Rinehart and Winston.

Brace, C. Loring, Alan S. Ryan, and B. Holly Smith, 1981. "Comment," *Current Anthropology,* 22 (4): 426–430.

Bradfield, Richard 1973. *A Natural History of Associations.* New York: International Universities Press.

Braidwood, Robert J., 1960. "The Agricultural Revolution," *Scientific American,* 203: 130–141.

Braidwood, Robert J., 1975. *Prehistoric Men,* 8th ed. Glenview, Ill.: Scott, Foresman.

Braidwood, Robert J., and Gordon R. Willey, 1962. *Courses Toward Urban Life: Archeological Consideration of Some Cultural Alternatives.* Chicago: Aldine (Publications in Anthropology Series, No. 32).

Brain, C. K., 1968. "Who Killed the Swartkrnas Ape-Men?" *South African Museums Association Bulletin,* 9: 127–139.

Brain, C. K., 1969. The Contribution of Namib Desert Hottentots to an Understanding of Australopithecine Bone Accumulations. *Scientific Papers of the Namib Desert Research Station* 13.

Brew, John O., 1968. *One Hundred Years of Anthropology.* Cambridge, Mass.: Harvard University Press.

Brinton, Crane, 1953. *The Shaping of the Modern Mind.* New York: Mentor.

Brothwell, D. R., and E. Higgs, eds., 1969. *Science in Archaeology,* rev. ed. London: Thames and Hudson.

Brues, Alice M., 1977. *People and Races.* New York: Macmillan.

Bruner, Edward M., 1970. "Medan: The Role of Kinship in an Indonesian City," in William Mangin, ed., *Peasants in Cities: Readings in the Anthropology of Urbanization.* Boston: Houghton Mifflin.

Burling, Robbins, 1969. "Linguistics and Ethnographic Description," *American Anthropologist,* 71: 817–827.

Burling, Robbins, 1970. *Man's Many Voices: Language in Its Cultural Context.* New York: Holt, Rinehart and Winston.

Butzer, K. 1971. *Environment and Anthropology: An Ecological Approach to Prehistory,* 2d ed. Chicago: Aldine.

Byers, D. S., ed., 1967. *The Prehistory of the Tehuacan Valley: Vol. 1. Environment and Subsistence.* Austin: University of Texas Press.

Carmack, Robert 1983. "Indians and The Guatemalan Revolution," *Cultural Survival Quarterly,* 7 (3): 52–54.

Carneiro, Robert L., 1961. "Slash and Burn Cultivation among the Kuikuru and Its Implications for Cultural Development in the Amazon Basin," in J. Wilbert, ed., *The Evolution of Horticultural Systems in Native South America: Causes and Consequences.* Caracas: Sociedad de Ciencias Naturales La Salle, pp. 47–68.

Carneiro, Robert L., 1970. "A Theory of the Origin of the State," *Science,* 169: 733–738.

Carpenter, Edmund, 1973. *Eskimo Realities.* New York: Holt, Rinehart and Winston.

Carroll, John B., ed., 1956. *Language, Thought and Reality: Selected Writings of Benjamin Lee Whorf.* New York: Wiley.

Carroll, John B., ed., 1956. *Language, Thought and Reality: Selected Writings of Benjamin Lee Whorf.* New York: Wiley.

Cavalli-Sforza, L. L., 1977. *Elements of Human Genetics.* Menlo Park, Calif.: W. A. Benjamin.

Chagnon, Napoleon A., 1988. *Yanomamo(diar): The Fierce People.* 3rd ed., New York: Holt, Rinehart and Winston.

Chagnon, N. A., and William Irons, eds., 1979. *Evolutionary Biology and Human Social Behavior.* North Scituate, Mass.: Duxbury Press.

Chambers, Robert, 1983. *Rural Development: Putting The Last First.* New York: Longman.

Chang, K. C., ed., 1968. *Settlement Archaeology.* Palo Alto, Calif.: National Press.

Chapple, Eliot D., 1970. *Cultural and Biological Man: Explorations in Behavioral Anthropology.* New York: Holt, Rinehart and Winston.

Childe, V. Gordon, 1951, orig. 1936. *Man Makes Himself.* New York: New American Library.

Childe, V. Gordon, 1954. *What Happened in History.* Baltimore: Penguin.

Ciochon, Russell L., and John G. Fleagle, eds. 1987. *Primate Evolution and Human Origins.* Hawthorne, N.Y.: Aldine de Gruyter.

Clark, Ella E., 1966. *Indian Legends of the Pacific Northwest.* Berkeley: University of California Press.

Clark, Grahame, 1967. *The Stone Age Hunters.* New York: McGraw-Hill.

Clark, Grahame, 1972. *Starr Carr: A Case Study in Bioarchaeology.* Reading, Mass.: Addison-Wesley.

Clark, J. G. D., 1962. *Prehistoric Europe: The Economic Basis.* Stanford, Calif.: Stanford University Press.

Clark, W. E. LeGros, 1960. *The Antecedents of Man.* Chicago: Quadrangle Books.

Clark, W. E. LeGros, 1966. *History of the Primates,* 5th ed. Chicago: University of Chicago Press.

Clark, W. E. LeGros, 1967. *Man-Apes or Ape-Men? The Story of Discoveries in Africa.* New York: Holt, Rinehart and Winston.

Clay, Jason W., "Genocide in the Age of Enlightenment," *Cultural Survival Quarterly* 12, No. 3.

Clough, S. B., and C. W. Cole, 1952. *Economic History of Europe,* 3d ed. Lexington, Mass.: Heath.

Codere, Helen, 1950. *Fighting with Property*. Seattle: University of Washington Press (American Ethnological Society, Monograph 18).

Coe, William R., 1967. *Tikal: A Handbook of the Ancient Maya Ruins*. Philadelphia: University of Pennsylvania Museum.

Cohen, Mark N., 1977. *The Food Crisis in Prehistory*. New Haven, Conn.: Yale University Press.

Cohen, Mark, and George Armelegos, eds. 1984. *Paleopathology and the Origins of Agriculture*. Orlando, Fla.: Academic Press.

Cohen, Myron L., 1967. "Variations in Complexity among Chinese Family Groups: The Impact of Modernization," *Transactions of the New York Academy of Sciences*, 295: 638–647.

Cohen, Myron L., 1968. "A Case Study of Chinese Family Economy and Development," *Journal of Asian and African Studies*, 3: 161–180.

Cohen, Ronald, and John Middleton, eds., 1967. *Comparative Political Systems*. Garden City, N.Y.: Natural History Press.

Cohen, Yehudi, 1968. *Man in Adaptation: The Cultural Present*. Chicago: Aldine.

Cole, Sonia, 1975. *Leakey's Luck: The Life of Louis Seymour Bazett Leakey, 1903–1972*. New York: Harcourt Brace Jovanovich.

Collier, Jane Fishburne and Sylvia Junko Yanagisako, eds., 1987. *Gender and Kinship: Essays Toward a Unified Analysis*. (Stanford, Calif.: Stanford University Press).

Constable, George, and the Editors of Time-Life, 1973. *The Neanderthals*. New York: Time-Life.

Cook, S. F., 1972. *Prehistoric Demography*. Reading, Mass.: Addison-Wesley.

Coon, Carleton S., 1948. *A Reader in General Anthropology*. New York: Holt, Rinehart and Winston.

Coon, Carleton S., 1954. *The Story of Man*. New York: Knopf.

Coon, Carleton S., 1954. "Climate and Race." Smithsonian Report for 1953, pp. 277–298.

Coon, Carleton S., 1957. *The Seven Caves*. New York: Knopf.

Coon, Carleton S., 1958. *Caravan: The Story of the Middle East*, 2d ed. New York: Holt, Rinehart and Winston.

Coon, Carleton S., 1971. *The Hunting Peoples*. Boston: Little, Brown.

Coon, Carleton S., Stanley N. Garn, and Joseph Birdsell, 1950. *Races: A Study of the Problems of Race Formation in Man*.

Springfield, Ill.: Charles C Thomas.

Coppens, Yves, F. Clark Howell, Glyn L. Isaac, and Richard E. F. Leakey, eds., 1976. *Earliest Man and Environments in the Lake Rudolf Basin: Stratigraphy, Paleoecology, and Evolution*. Chicago: University of Chicago Press.

Cornish, Andrew, 1987. "Participant Observation on a Motorcycle," *Anthropology Today* 3 (6) (December 1987).

Cottrell, Fred, 1965. *Energy and Society: The Relation between Energy, Social Changes and Economic Development*. New York: McGraw-Hill.

Cottrell, Leonard, 1963. *The Lost Pharaohs*. New York: Grosset & Dunlap.

Courlander, Harold, 1971. *The Fourth World of the Hopis*. New York: Crown.

Cox, Oliver Cromwell, 1959. *Caste, Class and Race: A Study in Dynamics*. New York: Monthly Review Press.

Crane, L. Ben, Edward Yeager, and Randal L. Whitman, 1981. *An Introduction to Linguistics*. Boston: Little, Brown.

Culbert, T. P., ed., 1973. *The Classic Maya Collapse*. Albuquerque: University of New Mexico Press.

Cultural Survival Quarterly, 1983. "Death and Disorder in Guatemala." *Cultural Survival Quarterly*, 7 (1).

Dalton, George, 1971. *Traditional Tribal and Peasant Economics: An Introductory Survey of Economic Anthropology*. Reading, Mass.: Addison-Wesley.

Dalton, George, ed., 1967. *Economic Anthropology and Development: Essays on Tribal and Peasant Economics*. New York: Basic Books.

Dalton, George, ed., 1967. *Tribal and Peasant Economics: Readings in Economic Anthropology*. Garden City, N.Y.: Natural History Press.

Daniel, Glyn, 1970. *The First Civilizations: The Archaeology of Their Origins*. New York: Apollo Editions.

Daniel, Glyn, 1970. *The Origins and Growth of Archaeology*. Baltimore, Md.: Penguin.

Daniel, Glyn, 1975. *A Hundred and Fifty Years of Archaeology*, 2d ed. London: Duckworth.

Darwin, Charles, 1936; orig. 1871. *The Descent of Man and Selection in Relation to Sex*. New York: Random House (Modern Library).

Darwin, Charles, 1967; orig. 1859. *On the Origin of Species*. New York: Atheneum.

Davenport, 1959. "Linear Descent and Descent Groups." *American Anthropologist*, 61: 557–573.

Davis, Shelton 1982. *Victims of the*

Miracle. Cambridge, Eng.: Cambridge University Press.

Davis, Susan S., n.d. *Patience, and Power, Women's Lives in a Moroccan Village*. Cambridge, Mass.: Schenkman.

de Laguna, Frederica, 1977. *Voyage to Greenland: A Personal Initiation into Anthropology*. New York: Norton.

de Laguna, Grace A., 1966. *On Existence and the Human World*. New Haven, Conn.: Yale University Press.

de Pelliam, Alison, and Francis D. Burton, 1976. "More on Predatory Behavior in Nonhuman Primates," *Current Anthropology*, 17 (3).

DeBeer, Sir Gavin R., 1964. *Atlas of Evolution*. London: Nelson.

Deetz, James, 1967. *Invitation to Archaeology*. New York: Doubleday.

Deevy, Edward S., Jr., 1960. "The Human Population," *Scientific American*, 203: 194–204.

del Castillo, Bernal Diaz. *The Discovery and Conquest of Mexico*. Alfred P. Maudsley, translator and ed. New York: Grove Press, 1956.

Despres, Leo A., 1968. "Cultural Pluralism and the Study of Complex Societies," *Current Anthropology*, 9: 3–26.

Devereux, George, 1963. "Institutionalized Homosexuality of the Mohave Indians," in Hendrik M. Ruitenbeck, ed., *The Problem of Homosexuality in Modern Society*. New York: Dutton.

DeVore, Irven, ed., 1965. *Primate Behavior: Field Studies of Monkeys and Apes*. New York: Holt, Rinehart and Winston.

Dixon, J. E., J. R. Cann, and C. Renfrew, 1968. "Obsidian and the origins of Trade," *Scientific American*, 218: 38–46.

Dobyns, Henry F., Paul L. Doughty, and Harold D. Lasswell, eds., 1971. *Peasants, Power, and Applied Social Change*. London: Sage.

Dobzhansky, Theodosius, 1962. *Mankind Evolving*. New Haven, Conn.: Yale University Press.

Douglas, Mary, 1958. "Raffia Cloth Distribution in the Lele Economy," *Africa*, 28: 109–122.

Dozier, Edward 1970. *The Pueblo Indians of North America*. New York: Holt, Rinehart and Winston.

Driver, Harold, 1964. *Indians of North America*. Chicago: University of Chicago Press.

Dubois, Cora, 1944. *The People of Alor*. Minneapolis: University of Minnesota Press.

Dubos, René, 1968. *So Human an Animal*. New York: Scribner.

Dumond, Don E., 1977. "Science in Archaeology: The Saints Go Marching In," *American Antiquity*, 42 (3): 330–349.

Dundes, Alan, 1980. *Interpreting Folk Lore*. Bloomington: Indiana University Press.

Durkheim, Emile, 1964. *The Division of Labor in Society*. New York: Free Press.

Durkheim, Emile, 1965. *The Elementary Forms of the Religious Life*. New York: Free Press.

Edey, Maitland, and the Editors of Time-Life, 1972. *The Missing Link*. New York: Time-Life.

Edey, Maitland A., and Donald Johanson. *Blueprints: Solving the Mystery of Evolution*. Boston: Little, Brown, 1989.

Edmonson, Munro S., 1971. *Lore: An Introduction to the Science of Folklore*. New York: Holt, Rinehart and Winston.

Edwards, Stephen W., 1978. "Nonutilitarian Activities on the Lower Paleolithic: A Look at the Two Kinds of Evidence," *Current Anthropology*, 19 (1): 135–137.

Eggan, Fred, 1954. "Social Anthropology and the Method of Controlled Comparison," *American Anthropologist*, 56: 743–763.

Ehrlich, Paul R., and Anne H. Ehrlich, 1970. *Population, Resources, Environment*. San Francisco: Freeman.

Eiseley, Loren, 1958. *Darwin's Century: Evolution and the Men Who Discovered It*. New York: Doubleday.

Eisenstadt, S. N., 1956. *From Generation to Generation: Age Groups and Social Structure*. New York: Free Press.

Elkin, A. P., 1964. *The Australian Aborigines*. Garden City, N.Y.: Doubleday, Anchor Books.

Ember, Melvin, and Carol R. Ember, 1971. "The Conditions Favoring Matrilocal vs. Patrilocal Residence," *American Anthropologist*, 73: 571–594.

Epstein, A. 1968. "Sanctions," *International Encyclopedia of the Social Sciences*, Vol. 14.

Erasmus, C. J., 1950. "Patolli, Pachisi, and the Limitation of Possibilities," *Southwestern Journal of Anthropology*, 6: 369–381.

Erasmus, C. J., and W. Smith, 1967. "Cultural Anthropology in the United States since 1900," *Southwestern Journal of Anthropology*, 23: 11–40.

Ervin-Tripp, Susan 1973. *Language Acquisition and Communicative Choice*. Stanford, Calif.: Stanford University Press.

Evans, William 1968. *Communication in the Animal World*. New York: Crowell.

Evans-Pritchard, E. E., 1937. *Witchcraft, Oracles, and Magic among the Azande*. London: Oxford University Press.

Evans-Pritchard, E. E., 1968. *The Nuer: A Description of the Modes of Livelihood and Political Institutions of a Nilotic People*. London: Oxford University Press.

Fagen, Brian M., 1977. *People of the Earth–An Introduction to World Prehistory*, 2d ed. Boston: Little, Brown.

Falk, Dean, 1975. "Comparative Anatomy of the Larynx in Man and the Chimpanzee: Implications for Language in Neanderthal," *American Journal of Physical Anthropology*, 43 (1): 123–132.

Farsoun, Samih K., 1970. "Family Structures and Society in Modern Lebanon," in Louise E. Sweet, ed., *Peoples and Cultures of the Middle East*, Vol. 2. Garden City, N.Y.: Natural History Press.

Fedigan, Linda Marie, 1986. "The Changing Role of Women in Models of Human Evolution," *Annual Review of Anthropology*, 15: 25–56.

Firth, Raymond, 1952. *Elements of Social Organization*. London: Watts.

Firth, Raymond, 1957. *Man and Culture: An Evaluation of Bronislaw Malinowski*. London: Routledge.

Firth, Raymond, 1963. *We the Tikopia*. Boston: Beacon Press.

Firth, Raymond, ed., 1967. *Themes in Economic Anthropology*. London: Tavistock.

Flannery, Kent V., 1973. "The Origins of Agriculture," Bernard J. Siegel, Alan R. Beals, and Stephen A. Tyler, eds., *Annual Review of Anthropology*, Palo Alto, Calif.: Annual Reviews, Inc., 1973, pp. 271–310. vol. 2.

Flannery, Kent V., ed., 1976. *The Mesoamerican Village*. New York: Seminar Press.

Flannery, Kent V., and Joyce Marcus, 1976. "Formative Oaxaca and the Zapotec Cosmos," *American Scientist*, 64.

Forde, C. Daryll, 1955. "The Nupe," in Daryll Forde, ed., *Peoples of the Niger–Benue Confluence*. London: International African Institute (Ethnographic Survey of Africa. Western Africa, part 10), pp. 17–52.

Forde, C. Daryll, 1963. *Habitat, Economy and Society*. New York: Dutton.

Forde, C. Daryll, 1968. "Double Descent among the Yako," in Paul Bohannan and J. Middleton, eds., *Marriage, Family and Residence*. Garden City, N.Y.: Natural History Press, pp. 179–192.

Fortes, Meyer, 1950. "Kinship and Marriage among the Ashanti," in A. R. Radcliffe-Brown and C. Daryll Forde, eds., *African Systems of Kinship and Marriage*. London: Oxford University Press.

Fortes, Meyer, 1969. *Kinship and the Social Order: The Legacy of Lewis Henry Morgan*. Chicago: Aldine.

Fortes, Meyer, and E. E. Evans-Pritchard, eds., 1962; orig. 1940. *African Political Systems*. London: Oxford University Press.

Fossey, Dian, 1983. *Gorillas in The Mist*. Burlington, Mass.: Houghton Mifflin.

Foster, G. M., 1955. "Peasant Society and the Image of the Limited Good," *American Anthropologist*, 67: 293–315.

Fox, Robin, 1968. *Encounter with Anthropology*. New York: Dell.

Fox, Robin, 1968. *Kinship and Marriage in an Anthropological Perspective*. Baltimore, Md.: Penguin.

Frankfort, Henri, 1968. *The Birth of Civilization in the Near East*. New York: Barnes & Noble.

Fraser, Douglas, 1962. *Primitive Art*. New York: Doubleday.

Fraser, Douglas, ed., 1966. *The Many Faces of Primitive Art: A Critical Anthology*. Englewood Cliffs, N.J.: Prentice-Hall.

Frayer, David W., 1981. "Body Size, Weapon Use, and Natural Selection in the European Upper Paleolithic and Mesolithic," *American Anthropologist*, 83: 57–73.

Frazer, Sir James George, 1931. "Magic and Religion," in V. F. Claverton, ed., *The Making of Man: An Outline of Anthropology*. Westport, Conn.: Greenwood, pp. 693–713.

Frazer, Sir James George, 1961 reissue. *The New Golden Bough*. New York: Doubleday, Anchor Books.

Freeman, J. D., 1960. "The Iban of Western Borneo," in G. P. Murdock, ed., *Social Structure in Southeast Asia*. Chicago: Quadrangle Books.

Fried, Morton, 1960. "On the Evolution of Social Stratification and the State," in S. Diamond, ed., *Culture in History: Essays in Honor of Paul Radin*. New York: Columbia University Press, pp. 713–731.

Fried, Morton, 1967. *The Evolution of Political Society: An Essay in Political Anthropology*. New York: Random House.

Fried, Morton, 1972. *The Study of Anthropology*. New York: Crowell.

Fried, Morton, Marvin Harris, and Robert Murphy, 1968. *War: The Anthropology of Armed Conflict and Aggression*. Garden City, N.Y.: Natural History Press.

Friedl, Ernestine, 1975. *Women and Men: An Anthropologist's View.* New York: Holt, Rinehart and Winston.

Frye, Marilyn, 1983. "Sexism," in *The Politics of Reality* New York: The Crossing Press.

Gamst, Frederick C., and Edward Norbeck, 1976. *Ideas of Culture: Sources and Uses.* New York: Holt, Rinehart and Winston.

Garn, Stanley M., 1970. *Human Races,* 3d ed. Springfield, Ill.: Charles C Thomas.

Geertz, Clifford, 1963. *Agricultural Involution: The Process of Ecological Change in Indonesia.* Berkeley: University of California Press.

Geertz, Clifford, 1965. "The Impact of the Concept of Culture on the Concept of Man," in John R. Platt, ed., *New Views of Man.* Chicago: University of Chicago Press.

Geertz, Clifford, 1968. "Religion: Anthropological Study," *International Encyclopedia of the Social Sciences,* Vol. 13. New York: Macmillan.

Geertz, Clifford, 1984. "Distinguished Lecture: Anti Anti-Relativism," *American Anthropologist,* 86: 263–278.

Gelb, Ignace J., 1952. *A Study of Writing.* London: Routledge.

Gellner, Ernest, 1969. *Saints of the Atlas.* Chicago: University of Chicago Press (The Nature of Human Society Series).

Gibbs, James L., Jr., 1965. "The Kpelle of Liberia," in James L. Gibbs, ed., *Peoples of Africa.* New York: Holt, Rinehart and Winston.

Gleason, H. A., Jr., 1966. *An Introduction to Descriptive Linguistics,* rev. ed. New York: Holt, Rinehart and Winston.

Glob, P., 1969. *The Bog People.* London: Faber & Faber.

Gluckman, Max, 1955. *The Judicial Process among the Barotse of Northern Rhodesia.* New York: Free Press.

Godlier, Maurice, 1971. "Salt Currency and the Circulation of Commodities among the Baruya of New Guinea," in George Dalton, ed., *Studies in Economic Anthropology.* Washington, D.C.: American Anthropological Association (Anthropological Studies No. 7).

Golden, M., B. Birns, W. Bridger, and A. Moss, 1971. "Social-Class Differentiation in Cognitive Development among Black Preschool Children," *Child Development,* 42: 37–45.

Goodall-Van Lawick, Jane, 1972. *In the Shadow of Man.* New York: Dell.

Goodall Jane, 1986. *The Chimpanzees of Gombe: Patterns of Behavior.* Cambridge, Mass.: Belknap Press.

Goode, William 1963. *World Revolution and Family Patterns.* New York: Free Press.

Goodenough, Ward, 1956. "Residence Rules," *Southwestern Journal of Anthropology,* 12: 22–37.

Goodenough, Ward, 1961. "Comment on Cultural Evolution," *Daedalus,* 90: 521–528.

Goodenough, Ward, ed., 1964. *Explorations in Cultural Anthropology: Essays in Honor of George Murdock.* New York: McGraw-Hill.

Goodenough, Ward, 1965. "Rethinking Status," and "Role: Toward a General Model of the Cultural Organization of Social Relationships," in Michael Benton, ed., *The Relevance of Models for Social Anthropology, ASA Monographs 1.* New York: Praeger.

Goodenough, Ward, 1970. *Description and Comparison in Cultural Anthropology.* Chicago: Aldine (Lewis H. Morgan Lecture Series).

Goodman, Mary Ellen, 1967. *The Individual and Culture.* Homewood, Ill.: Dorsey Press.

Goody, John, 1969. *Comparative Studies in Kinship.* Stanford, Calif.: Stanford University Press.

Goody, Jack, ed., 1972. *Developmental Cycle in Domestic Groups.* New York: Cambridge University Press (papers in Social Anthropology, No. 1).

Goody, Jack, 1976. *Production and Reproduction: A Comparative Study of the Domestic Domain.* Cambridge: Cambridge University Press.

Goody, Jack, 1983. *The Development of the Family and Marriage in Europe.* Cambridge, Eng.: Cambridge University Press.

Gordon, Robert J., and Mervyn J. Meggitt, 1985. *Law and Order in the New Guinea Highlands.* Hanover, N.H.: University Press of New England.

Gornick, Vivian and Barbara K. Moran, eds. 1971. *Woman in Sexist Society.* New York: Basic Books.

Gould, Stephen J., 1981. *The Mismeasure of Man.* New York: W.W. Norton, pp. 155–157.

Gould, Stephen J., 1985. *The Flamingo's Smile: Reflections in Natural History.* New York: Norton, pp. 408–410.

Gould, Stephen J., 1986. "Of Kiwi Eggs and the Liberty Bell," *Natural History,* 95: 20–29.

Graburn, Nelson H. H., 1969. *Eskimos Without Igloos: Social and Economic Develonment in Sugluk.* Boston: Little Brown.

Graburn, Nelson H., 1971. *Readings in Kinship and Social Structure.* New York: Harper & Row.

Graham, Susan Brandt, 1979. "Biology and Human Social Behavior: A Response to van den Berghe and Barash," *American Anthropologist,* 81 (2): 357–360.

Greenberg, Joseph H., 1968. *Anthropological Linguistics: An Introduction.* New York: Random House.

Greene, John C., 1959. *The Death of Adam.* Ames: Iowa State University Press.

Greenfield, Leonard Owen, 1979. "On the Adaptive Pattern of Ramapithecus" *American Journal of Physical Anthropology,* 50: 527–547.

Greenfield, Leonard Owen, 1980. "A Late Divergence Hypothesis," *American Journal of Physical Anthropology,* 52: 351–366.

Gulliver, P., 1968. "Age Differentiation," *International Encyclopedia of the Social Sciences,* 1: 157–162.

Hafkin, Nancy, and Edna Bay, eds. 1976. *Women in Africa.* Stanford, Calif.: Stanford University Press.

Hall, Edward T., and Mildred Reed Hall, "The Sounds of Silence," in *Anthropology 86/87,* Elvio Angeloni, ed. Guilford, Conn.: Dushkin, 1986.

Hall, K. R. L., and Irven DeVore, 1965. "Baboon Social Behavior," in Irven DeVore, ed., *Primate Behavior.* New York: Holt, Rinehart and Winston.

Hallowell, A. Irving, 1955. *Culture and Experience.* Philadelphia: University of Pennsylvania Press.

Halverson, John. "Review of *Altimira Revisited and Other Essays on Early Art,*" *American Antiquity,* 1989, 54: 883.

Hamblin, Dora Jane, and the Editors of Time-Life, 1973. *The First Cities.* New York: Time-Life.

Hamburg, David A., and Elizabeth R. McGown, eds., 1979. *The Great Apes.* Menlo Park, Calif.: Cummings.

Hammond, Dorothy, 1972. *Associations.* Reading, Mass.: Addison-Wesley (Modular Publications, 14).

Harlow, Harry F., 1962. "Social Deprivation in Monkeys," *Scientific American,* 206: 1–lO.

Harris, Marvin, 1965. "The Cultural Ecology of India's Sacred Cattle," *Current Anthropology,* 7: 51–66.

Harris, Marvin, 1968. *The Rise of Anthropological Theory: A History of Theories of Culture*. New York: Crowell.

Harrison, Gail G., 1975. "Primary Adult Lactase Deficiency: A Problem in Anthropological Genetics," *American Anthropologist*, 77: 812–835.

Harrison, G. A., et al., 1964. *Human Biology: An Introduction to Human Evolution, Variation and Growth*. New York: Oxford.

Hart, Charles W., Arnold R. Pilling, and Jane Goodale, 1988. *Tiwi of North Australia*, 3d ed. New York: Holt, Rinehart and Winston.

Hatcher, Evelyn Payne, 1985. *Art As Culture: An Introduction to the Anthropology of Art*. New York: University Press of America.

Haviland, W. 1970. "Tikal, Guatemala and Mesoamerican Urbanism," *World Archaeology*, 2: 186–198.

Haviland, W. A., 1972. "A New Look at Classic Maya Social Organization at Tikal," *Ceramica de Cultura Maya*, 8: 1–16.

Haviland, W. A., 1974. "Farming, Seafaring and Bilocal Residence on the Coast of Maine," *Man in the Northeast*, 6: 31–44.

Haviland, W. A., 1975. "The Ancient Maya and the Evolution of Urban Society," *University of Northern Colorado Museum of Anthropology, Miscellaneous Series*, No. 37.

Haviland, W. A., 1983. *Human Evolution and Prehistory*, 2d ed. New York: Holt, Rinehart and Winston.

Haviland, William A., and Hattula Moholy-Nagy, in press. "Distinguishing the High and Mighty from the Hoi Polloi at Tikal, Guatemala," in *Mesoamerican Elites: an Archaeological Assessment*, ed. Arlen F and Diane Z. Chase. Norman, Okla.: University of Oklahoma Press.

Haviland, W., and M. W. Power, 1981. *The Original Vermonters: Native Inhabitants, Past and Present*. Hanover, N.H.: University Press of New England.

Hawkins, Gerald S., 1965. *Stonehenge Decoded*. New York: Doubleday.

Hays, H. R., 1965. *From Ape to Angel: An Informal History of Social Anthropology*. New York: Knopf.

Heichel, G. 1976. "Agricultural Production and Energy Resources," *American Scientist*, Vol. 64.

Heilbroner, Robert L., 1972. *The Making of Economic Society*, 4th ed. Englewood Cliffs, N.J.: Prentice-Hall.

Helm, June, 1962. "The Ecological Approach in Anthropology," *American Journal of Sociology*, 67: 630–649.

Henry, Jules, 1965. *Culture against Man*. New York: Vintage Books.

Henry, Jules, 1974. "A Theory for an Anthropological Analysis of American Culture," in Joseph G. Jorgensen and Marcello Truzzi, eds., *Anthropology and American Life*. Englewood Cliffs, N.J.: Prentice-Hall.

Herskovits, Melville J., 1952. *Economic Anthropology: A Study in Comparative Economics*, 2d ed. New York: Knopf.

Herskovits, Melville J., 1964. *Cultural Dynamics*. New York: Knopf.

Hewes, Gordon W., 1973. "Primate Communication and the Gestural Origin of Language," *Current Anthropology*, 14: 5–24.

Hickerson, Nancy Parrot, 1980. *Linguistic Anthropology*. New York: Holt, Rinehart and Winston.

Hjelmsiev, Louis, 1970. *Language: An Introduction*, Francis J. Whitfield, trans. Madison: University of Wisconsin Press.

Hodgen, Margaret, 1964. *Early Anthropology in the Sixteenth and Seventeenth Centuries*. Philadelphia: University of Pennsylvania Press.

Hoebel, E. A., 1954. *The Law of Primitive Man: A Study in Comparative Legal Dynamics*. Cambridge, Mass.: Harvard University Press; Atheneum, 1968.

Hoebel, E. A., 1960. *The Cheyennes: Indians of the Great Plains*. New York: Holt, Rinehart and Winston.

Hoebel, E. A., 1972. *Anthropology: The Study of Man*, 4th ed. New York: McGraw-Hill.

Hogbin, Ian, 1964. *A Guadalcanal Society*. New York: Holt, Rinehart and Winston.

Hole, Frank, 1966. "Investigating the Origins of Mesopotamian Civilization," *Science*, 153: 605–611.

Hole, Frank, and Robert F. Heizer, 1977. *An Introduction to Prehistoric Archeology, A Brief Introduction*. New York: Holt, Rinehart and Winston.

Holloway, Ralph L., 1980. "The O. H. 7 (Olduvai Gorge, Tanzania) Hominid Partial Brain Endocast Revisited," *American Journal of Physical Anthropology*, 53: 267–274.

Holloway, Ralph L., 1981."Volumetric and Asymmetry Determinations on Recent Hominid Endocasts: Spy I and II, Djebel Jhroud 1, and the Salb *Homo erectus* specimens, with some Notes on Neanderthal Brain Size," *American Journal of Physical Anthropology*, 55: 385–393.

Holloway, Ralph L., 1981. "The Indonesian Homo erectus Brain Endocast Revisited," *American Journal of Physical Anthropology*, 55: 503–521.

Hostetler, John, and Gertrude Huntington, 1971. *Children in Amish Society*. New York: Holt, Rinehart and Winston.

Howell, F. Clark, 1970, *Early Man*. New York: Time-Life.

Hsu, Francis L. 1961. *Psychological Anthropology: Approaches to Culture and Personality*. Homewood, Ill.: Dorsey Press.

Hsu, Francis L. K., 1977. "Role, Affect, and Anthropology," *American Anthropologist*, 79: 805–808.

Hsu, Francis L. K., 1979. "The Cultural Problems of the Cultural Anthropologist," *American Anthropologist*, 81: 517–532.

Hubert, Henri, and Marcel Mauss, 1964. *Sacrifice*. Chicago: University of Chicago Press.

Hunt, Robert C., ed., 1967. *Personalities and Cultures: Readings in Psychological Anthropology*. Garden City, N.Y.: Natural History Press.

Hymes, Dell, 1964. *Language in Culture and Society: A Reader in Linguistics and Anthropology*. New York: Harper & Row.

Hymes, Dell, ed., 1972. *Reinventing Anthropology*. New York: Pantheon.

Inkeles, Alex, 1966. "The Modernization of Man," in Myron Weiner, ed., *Modernization: The Dynamics of Growth*. New York: Basic Books.

Inkeles, Alex, Eugenia Hanfmann, and Helen Beier, 1961. "Modal Personality and Adjustment to the Soviet Sociopolitical System," in Bert Kaplan, ed., *Studying Personality Cross-culturally*. New York: Harper & Row.

Inkeles, Alex, and D. J. Levinson, 1954. "National Character: The Study of Modal Personality and Socio-cultural Systems," in G. Lindzey, ed., *Handbook of Social Psychology*. Reading, Mass.: Addison-Wesley, pp. 977–1020.

Jennings, Francis, 1976. *The Invasion of America*. New York: Norton.

Jennings, Jesse D., 1974. *Prehistory of North America*, 2d ed., New York: McGraw-Hill.

Johanson, Donald C., and Maitland Edey, 1981. *Lucy, The Beginnings of Humankind*. New York: Simon & Schuster.

Johanson, D. C., and T. D. White, 1979. "A Systematic Assessment of Early African Hominids," *Science*, 203: 321–330.

John, V., 1971. "Whose Is the Failure?" in C. L. Brace, G. R. Gamble, and J. T. Bond, ods., *Race and Intelligence*. Washington, D.C.: American Anthropological Association (Anthropological Studies No. 8).

Jolly, Allison, 1972. *The Evolution of Primate Behavior*. New York: Macmillan.

Jolly, Alison, 1985. "The Evolution of Primate Behavior," *American Scientist* 73 (3): 230–239.

Jolly, C. J., 1970. "The Seed Eaters: A New Model of Hominid Differentiation Based on a Baboon Analogy," *Man*, 5: 5–26.

Jolly, Clifford J., and Fred Plog, 1986. *Physical Anthropology and Archaeology*, 4th ed. New York: Knopf, p. 216.

Jopling, Carol F., 1971. *Art and Aesthetics in Primitive Societies: A Critical Anthology*. New York: Dutton.

Jorgensen, Joseph, 1972. *The Sun Dance Religion*. Chicago: University of Chicago Press.

Joukowsky, Martha A., 1980. *A Complete Field Manual of Archeology: Tools and Techniques of Field Work for Archaeologists*. Englewood Cliffs, N.J.: Prentice-Hall.

Kahn, Herman, and Anthony J. Wiener, 1967. *The Year 2000*. New York: Macmillan.

Kaplan, David, 1968. "The Superorganic: Science or Metaphysics," in Robert Manners and David Kaplan, eds., *Theory in Anthropology: A Sourcebook*. Chicago: Aldine.

Kaplan, David, 1972. *Culture Theory*. Englewood Cliffs, N.J.: Prentice-Hall (Foundations of Modern Anthropology).

Kardiner, Abram, 1939. *The Individual and His Society. The Psycho-dynamics of Primitive Social Organization*. New York: Columbia University Press.

Kardiner, Abram, and Edward Preble, 1961. *They Studied Men*. New York: Mentor.

Kay, Richard F., 1981. "The Nut-Crackers — A New Theory of the Adaptations of the Ramapithecinae," *American Journal of Physical Anthropology*, 55: 141–151.

Kay, R. F., J. F. Fleagle, and E. L. Simons, 1981. "A Revision of the Oligocene Apes of the Fayum Province, Egypt," *American Journal of Physical Anthropology*, 55: 293–322.

Keesing, Roger M., 1975. *Kin Groups and Social Structure*. New York: Holt, Rinehart and Winston.

Keesing, Roger M., 1976. *Cultural Anthropology: A Contemporary Perspective*.

New York: Holt, Rinehart and Winston.

Kenyon, Kathleen, 1957. *Digging Up Jericho*. London: Ben.

Kerri, James N., 1976. "Studying Voluntary Associations as Adaptive Mechanisms: A Review of Anthropological Perspectives," *Current Anthropology*, 17(1).

Kessler, Evelyn, 1975. *Women*. New York: Holt, Rinehart and Winston.

Kleinman, Arthur, 1982. "The Failure of Western Medicine," in David Hunter and Phillip Whitten, *Anthropology: Contemporary Perspectives*. Boston: Little, Brown.

Kluckhohn, Clyde, 1944. "Navajo Witchcraft." Cambridge, Mass.: Harvard University Press. (Papers of the Peabody Museum of American Archaeology and Ethnology 22, 2).

Kluckhohn, Clyde, 1970. *Mirror for Man*. Greenwich, Conn.: Fawcett.

Kohler, Gernot, 1978. "Global Apartheid," in *World Order Models Project*, *Paper 7*. New York: Institute for World Order.

Kolata, Gina Bari, 1974. "!Kung Hunter-Gatherers: Feminism, Diet, and Birth Control," *Science*, 185: 932–934.

Krader, Lawrence, 1968. *Formation of the State*. Englewood Cliffs, N.J.: Prentice-Hall (Foundation of Modern Anthropology).

Kroeber, A. L., 1939. "Cultural and Natural Areas of Native North America," *American Archaeology and Ethnology*, Vol. 38. Berkeley, Calif.: University of California Press.

Kroeber, A. 1958. "Totem and Taboo: An Ethnologic Psychoanalysis," in William Lessa and Evon Z. Vogt, eds., *Reader in Comparative Religion: An Anthropological Approach*. New York: Harper & Row.

Kroeber, A. L., 1963. *Anthropology: Cultural Processes and Patterns*. New York: Harcourt.

Kroeber, A. L., and Clyde Kluckhohn, 1952. *Culture: A Critical Review of Concepts and Definitions*. Cambridge, Mass.: Harvard University Press (Papers of the Peabody Museum of American Archaeology and Ethnology, 47).

Kuhn, Thomas 1968. *The Structure of Scientific Revolutions*. Chicago: University of Chicago Press [International Encyclopedia of Unified Science, 2 (27)].

Kummer, Hans, 1971. *Primate Societies: Group Techniques of Ecological Adaptation*. Chicago: Aldine.

Kuper, Hilda, 1965. "The Swazi of Swaziland," in James L. Gibbs, ed., *peoples of Africa*. New York: Holt, Rinehart and Winston, pp. 497–511.

Kurath, Gertrude Probosch, 1960. "Panorama of Dance Ethnology," *Current Anthropology*, 1: 233–254.

Kushner, Gilbert, 1969. *Anthropology of Complex Societies*. Stanford, Cal.: Stanford University Press.

LaBarre, Weston, 1945. "Some Observations of Character Structure in the Orient: The Japanese," *Psychiatry*, 8: 319–342.

Lancaster, Jane B., 1975. *Primate Behavior and the Emergence of Human Culture*. New York: Holt, Rinehart and Winston.

Lanning, Edward P., 1967. *Peru before the Incas*. Englewood Cliffs, N.J.: Prentice-Hall.

Lanternari, Vittorio, 1963. *The Religions of the Oppressed*. New York: Mentor.

Lasker, Gabriel W., and Robert Tyzzer, 1982. *Physical Anthropology*, 3d ed. New York: Holt, Rinehart and Winston.

Laughlin, W. S., and R. H. Osborne, eds., 1967. *Human Variation and Origins*. San Francisco: Freeman.

Leach, Edmund, 1961. *Rethinking Anthropology*. London: Athione Press.

Leach, Edmund, 1962. "On Certain Unconsidered Aspects of Double Descent Systems," *Man*, 214: 13(nd34.

Leach, Edmund, 1962. "The Determinants of Differential Cross-cousin Marriage," *Man*, 62: 238.

Leach, Edmund, 1965. *Political Systems of Highland Burma*. Boston: Beacon Press.

Leach, Edmund, 1982. *Social Anthropology*. Glasgow: Fontana Paperbacks.

Leacock, Eleanor, 1981. *Myths of Male Dominance: Collected Articles on Women Cross Culturally*. New York: Monthly Review Press.

Leakey, L. S. B., 1965. *Olduvai Gorge, 1951–1961*, Vol. 1. London: Cambridge University Press.

Leakey, L. S. B., 1967. "Development of Aggression as a Factor in Early Man and Prehuman Evolution," in C. Clements and D. Lundsley, eds., *Aggression and Defense*. Los Angeles: University of California Press.

Leakey, M. D., 1971. *Olduvai Gorge: Excavations in Beds I and II, 1960–1963*. London and New York: Cambridge University Press.

LeClair, Edward, and Harold K. Schneider, eds., 1968. *Economic Anthropology: Readings in Theory and Analysis*. New York: Holt, Rinehart and Winston.

Lee, Richard B., 1969. "!Kung Bushman Subsistence: An Input–Output Analysis," in Andrew P. Vayda, ed., *Environment and Cultural Behavior*. Garden City, N.Y.: Natural History Press, pp. 47–49.

Lee, Richard B., 1984. *The Dobe !Kung: Foragers in a Changing World*. New York: Holt, Rinehart and Winston.

Lee, Richard B., and Irven DeVore, eds., 1968. *Man the Hunter*. Chicago: Aldine.

Leeds, Anthony, and Andrew P. Vayda, eds., 1965. *Man, Culture and Animals: The Role of Animals in Human Ecological Adjustments*. Washington, D.C.: American Association for the Advancement of Science.

Lees, Robert, 1953. "The Basis of Glottochronology," *Language*, 29: 113–127.

Lehmann, Arthur C., and James E. Myers, eds., 1988. *Magic, Witchcraft and Religion*, 2d ed. Palo Alto, Calif.: Mayfield.

Lehmann, Winifred 1973. *Historical Linguistics, An Introduction*, 2d ed. New York: Holt, Rinehart and Winston.

Leinhardt, Godfrey, 1964. *Social Anthropology*. London: Oxford University Press.

Leinhardt, Godfrey, 1971. "Religion," in Harry Shapiro, ed., *Man, Culture and Society*, 2d ed. London: Oxford University Press, pp. 382–401.

LeMay, Marjorie, 1975. "The Language Capability of Neanderthal Man," *American Journal of Physical Anthropology*, 43 (1): 9–14.

Lenski, Gerhard, 1966. *Power and Privilege: A Theory of Social Stratification*. New York: McGraw-Hill.

Leonard, William R., and Michelle Hegman, 1987. "Evolution of P₃ Morphology in *Australopithecus afarensis*," *American Journal of Physical Anthropology*, 73: 41–63.

Leroi-Gourhan, A., 1968. "The Evolution of Paleolithic Art," *Scientific American*, 218: 58ff.

Levanthes, Louise E., 1987. "The Mysteries of the Bog," *National Geographic*, 171: 397–420.

Lévi-Strauss, Claude, 1963. *Totemism*. Boston: Beacon Press.

Lévi-Strauss, Claude, 1963. *Structural Anthropology*. New York: Basic Books.

Lévi-Strauss, Claude, 1966. *The Savage Mind*. Chicago: University of Chicago Press.

Lévi-Strauss, Claude, 1969. *The Elementary Structures of Kinship*. Boston: Beacon Press.

Lévi-Strauss, Claude, 1971. "The Family," in Harry L. Shapiro, ed., *Man, Culture and Society*. London: Oxford

University Press, pp. 333–357.

Levine, Robert Paul, 1968. *Genetics*. New York: Holt, Rinehart and Winston.

LeVine, Robert 1973. *Culture, Behavior and Personality*. Chicago: Aldine.

Lewin, Roger, 1983. "Is the Orangutan a Living Fossil?" *Science*, 222: 1223.

Lewin, Roger, 1985. "Tooth Enamel Tells a Complex Story," *Science*, 228: 707.

Lewin, Roger, 1986. "Myths and Methods in Ice Age Art," *Science*, 234: 938.

Lewin, Roger, 1986. "New Fossil Upsets Human Family," *Science*, 1986, 233: 720–721.

Lewin, Roger, 1987 "Four Legs Bad, Two Legs Good," *Science*, 235: 969–971.

Lewin, Roger, 1987. "Debate over Emergence of Human Tooth Pattern," *Science*, 235: 749.

Lewin, Roger, 1987. "The Earliest Humans Were More Like Apes," *Science*, 236: 106–163.

Lewin, Roger, 1987. "Why Is Ape Tool Use So Confusing?" *Science*, 236: 776–777.

Lewin, Roger, 1988. "Molecular Clocks Turn a Quarter Century," *Science*, 235: 969–971.

Lewis, I. M. 1965. "Problems in the Comparative Study of Unilineal Descent," in Michael Banton, ed., *The Relevance of Models for Social Organization* (A.S.A. Monograph No. 1). London: Tavistock.

Lewis, I. M., 1976. *Social Anthropology in Perspective*. Harmondsworth, Eng.: Penguin.

Linton, Ralph, 1936. *The Study of Man: An Introduction*. New York: Appleton.

Little, Kenneth, 1964. "The Role of Voluntary Associations in West African Urbanization," in Pierre van den Berghe, ed., *Africa: Social Problems of Change and Conflict*. San Francisco: Chandler.

Livingstone, Frank B., 1973. "The Distribution of Abnormal Hemoglobin Genes and Their Significance for Human Evolution," in C. Loring Brace and James Metress, eds., *Man in Evolutionary Perspective*. New York: Wiley.

Lounsbury, F., 1964. "The Structural Analysis of Kinship Semantics," in Horace G. Lunt, ed., *Proceedings of the Ninth International Congress of Linguists*. The Hague: Mouton, pp. 1073–1093.

Lovejoy, C. Owen, 1981. "Origin of Man," *Science*, 211 (4480): 341–350.

Lowie, Robert H., 1948. *Social Organi-*

zation. New York: Holt, Rinehart and Winston.

Lowie, Robert H., 1956. *Crow Indians*. New York: Holt, Rinehart and Winston.

Lowie, Robert H., 1966. *Culture and Ethnology*. New York: Basic Books.

Lustig-Arecco, Vero, 1975. *Technology: Strategies for Survival*. New York: Holt, Rinehart and Winston.

MacCormack, Carol P. 1977. "Biological Events and Cultural Control," *Signs*, 3 (1977).

MacNeish, Richard S., 1964. "Ancient Mesoamerican Civilization," *Science*, 143: 531–537.

Magnarella, Paul J., 1974. *Tradition and Change in a Turkish Town*. New York: Wiley.

Mair, Lucy, 1969. *Witchcraft*. New York: McGraw-Hill.

Mair, Lucy, 1971. *Marriage*. Baltimore, Md.: Penguin.

Malefijt, Annemarie de Waal, 1969. *Religion and Culture: An Introduction to Anthropology of Religion*. London: Macmillan.

Malefijt, Annemarie de Waal, 1974. *Images of Man*. New York: Knopf.

Malinowski, Bronislaw, 1922. *Argonauts of the Western Pacific*. New York: Dutton.

Malinowski, Bronislaw, 1945. *The Dynamics of Culture Change*. New Haven, Conn.: Yale University Press.

Malinowski, Bronislaw, 1951. *Crime and Custom in Savage Society*. London: Routledge.

Malinowski, Bronislaw, 1954. *Magic, Science and Religion*. Garden City, N.Y.: Doubleday, Anchor Books.

Marano, Lou, 1982. "Windigo Psychosis: The Anatomy of an Emic–Etic Confusion," *Current Anthropology*, 23: 385–412.

Marshack, Alexander, 1972. *The Roots of Civilization: A Study in Prehistoric Cognition; The Origins of Art, Symbol and Notation*. New York: McGraw-Hill.

Marshack, Alexander, 1976. "Some Implications of the Paleolithic Symbolic Evidence for the Origin of Language," *Current Anthropology*, 17 (2): 274–282.

Marshall, Lorna, 1961. "Sharing, Talking and Giving: Relief of Social Tensions among !Kung Bushmen," *Africa*, 31: 231–249.

Mason, J. Alden, 1957. *The Ancient Civilizations of Peru*. Baltimore, Md.: Penguin.

Matson, Frederick R., ed., 1965. *Ceramics and Man*. New York: Viking Fund Publications in Anthropology No. 41.

Maybury-Lewis, David, 1960. "Parallel Descent and the Apinaye Anomaly," *Southwestern Journal of Anthropology*, 16: 191–216.

Maybury-Lewis, David, 1984. *The Prospects for Plural Societies*. 1982 Proceedings of the American Ethnological Society.

McFee, Malcolm, 1972. *Modern Blackfeet: Montanans on a Reservation*. New York: Holt, Rinehart and Winston.

McGimsey, Charles R., 1972. *Public Archaeology*. New York: Seminar Press.

McHale, John, 1969. *The Future of the Future*. New York: Braziller.

McHenry, Henry, 1975. "Fossils and the Mosaic Nature of Human Evolution," *Science*, October, 190: 524–431.

Mead, Margaret, 1928. *Coming of Age in Samoa*. New York: Morrow.

Mead, Margaret, 1963. *Sex and Temperament in Three Primitive Societies*, 3d ed. New York: Morrow.

Mead, Margaret, 1970. *Culture and Commitment*. Garden City, N.Y.: Natural History Press.

Meadows, Donella H., Dennis L. Meadows, Jorgen Randers, and William W. Behrens III, 1974. *The Limits to Growth*. New York: Universe Books.

Melaart, James, 1967. *Catal Hüyük: A Neolithic Town in Anatolia*. London: Thames and Hudson.

Merrell, David J., 1962. *Evolution and Genetics: The Modem Theory of Genetics*. New York: Holt, Rinehart and Winston.

Merriam, Alan, 1964. *The Anthropology of Music*. Chicago: Northwestern University Press.

Mesghinua, Haile Michael, 1966. "Salt Mining in Enderta," *Journal of Ethiopian Studies*, 4 (2).

Michaels, Joseph W., 1973. *Dating Methods in Archaeology*. New York: Seminar Press.

Middleton, John, ed., 1970. *From Child to Adult: Studies in the Anthropology of Education*. Garden City, N.Y.: Natural History Press (American Museum Source Books in Anthropology).

Millon, René, 1973. *Urbanization of Teotihuacán, Mexico, Vol. 1, Part 1: The Teotihuacán Map*. Austin: University of Texas Press.

Mitchell, William E., 1973. "A New Weapon Stirs Up Old Ghosts," *Natural History Magazine*, December, pp. 77–84.

Mitchell, William E., 1978. *Mishpokhe: A Study of New York City Jewish Family Clubs*. The Hague: Mouton.

Montagu, Ashley, 1963. *Human Heredity*, 2d ed. New York: Signet Books.

Montagu, Ashley, 1964. *The Concept of Race*. London: Macmillan.

Montagu, Ashley, 1964. *Man's Most Dangerous Myth: The Fallacy of Race*, 4th ed. New York: World Publishing.

Montagu, Ashley, 1969. *Man: His First Two Million Years*. New York: Columbia University Press.

Montagu, Ashley, 1975. *Race and IQ*. New York: Oxford University Press.

Morgan, Lewis H., 1877. *Ancient Society*. New York: World Publishing.

Moscati, Sabatino, 1962. *The Face of the Ancient Orient*. New York: Doubleday.

Mowat, Farley, 1981. *People of the Deer*. Toronto: Bantam Books.

Murdock, George 1960. "Cognatic Forms of Social Organization," in G. P. Murdock, ed., *Social Structure in Southeast Asia*. Chicago: Quadrangle Books.

Murdock, George P., 1965. *Social Structure*. New York: Free Press.

Murdock, George P., 1971. "How Culture Changes," in Harry L. Shapiro, ed., *Man, Culture and Society*, 2d ed. New York: Oxford University Press, pp. 319–332.

Murphy, Robert, 1971. *The Dialectics of Social Life: Alarms and Excursions in Anthropological Theory*. New York: Basic Books.

Murphy, Robert, and Leonard Kasdan, 1959. "The Structure of Parallel Cousin Marriage," *American Anthropologist*, 61: 17–29.

Myrdal, Gunnar, 1974. "Challenge to Affluence: The Emergence of an "Under-class," in Joseph G. Jorgensen and Marcello Truzzi, eds., *Anthropology and American Life*. Englewood Cliffs, N.J.: Prentice-Hall.

Nader, Laura, ed., 1965. "The Ethnography of Law," *American Anthropologist*, Part II, 67 (6).

Nader, Laura, ed., 1969. *Law in Culture and Society*. Chicago: Aldine.

Nader, Laura, ed., 1980. *No Access To Law: Alternatives to the American Judicial System*. New York: Academic Press.

Naroll, Raoul, 1973. "Holocultural Theory Tests," in Raoul Naroll and Frada Naroll, eds., *Main Currents in Cultural Anthropology*. New York: Appleton.

Nash, Manning, 1966. *Primitive and Peasant Economic Systems*. San Francisco: Chandler.

Needham, Rodney, ed., 1971. *Rethinking Kinship and Marriage*. London: Tavistock.

Needham, Rodney, 1972. *Belief, Language and Experience*. Chicago: University of Chicago Press.

Neer, Robert M., 1975. "The Evolutionary Significance of Vitamin D, Skin Pigment and Ultraviolet Light," *American Journal of Physical Anthropology*, 43: 409–416.

Nesbitt, L. M., 1935. *Hell-Hole of Creation*. New York: Knopf.

Nettl, Bruno, 1956. *Music in Primitive Culture*. Cambridge, Mass.: Harvard University Press.

Newman, Philip L., 1965. *Knowing the Gururumba*. New York: Holt, Rinehart and Winston.

Nietschmann, Bernard, 1978. "The Third World War," *Cultural Survival Ouarterly* 11, (3): pp. 1–16.

Norbeck, Edward, 1974. *Religion in Human Life: Anthropological Views*. New York: Holt, Rinehart and Winston.

Norbeck, Edward, Douglas Price-Williams, and William McCord, eds., 1968. *The Study of Personality: An Interdisciplinary Appraisal*. New York: Holt, Rinehart and Winston.

Nye, E. Ivan, and Felix M. Berardo, 1975. *The Family: Its Structure and Interaction*. New York: Macmillan.

O'Mahoney, Kevin, 1970. "The Salt Trade," *Journal of Ethiopian Studies*, 8(2).

Oakley, Kenneth P., 1964. *Man the Tool-Maker*. Chicago: University of Chicago Press.

Obler, Regina Smith, 1980. "Is the Female Husband a Man? Woman/Woman Marriage Among the Nandi of Kenya," *Ethnology* 19.

Oliver, Douglas Z., 1964. *Invitation to Anthropology*. Garden City, N.Y.: Natural History Press.

Ortiz, Alfonso, 1969. *The Tewa World*. Chicago: University of Chicago Press.

Oswalt, Wendell H., 1970. *Understanding Our Culture*. New York: Holt, Rinehart and Winston.

Oswalt, Wendell H., 1972. *Habitat and Technology*. New York: Holt, Rinehart and Winston.

Oswalt, Wendell H., 1972. *Other Peoples Other Customs: World Ethnography and Its History*. New York: Holt, Rinehart and Winston.

Otten, Charlotte N., 1971. *Anthropology and Art: Readings in Cross-cultural Aesthetics*. Garden City, N.Y.: Natural History Press (American Museum Sourcebooks in Anthropology).

Ottenberg, Phoebe, 1965. "The Afikpo Ibo of Eastern Nigeria," in James L. Gibbs, ed., *Peoples of Africa*. New York: Holt, Rinehart and Winston.

Otterbein, Keith F., 1971. *The Evolution of War*. New Haven, Conn.: HRAF Press.

Parker, Seymour, and Hilda Parker, 1979. "The Myth of Male Superiority: Rise and Demise," *American Anthropologist*, 81 (2): 289–309.

Partridge, William ed., 1984. *Training Manual in Development Anthropology*. Washington, D.C.: American Anthropological Association.

Pastner, Stephen, and William A. Haviland, eds., 1982. "Confronting the Creationists," *Northeastern Anthropological Association Occasional Proceedings*, I.

Patterson, Francine, and Eugene Linden, 1981. *The Education of Koko*. New York: Holt, Rinehart and Winston.

Patterson, Thomas C., 1981. *Archeology: The Evolution of Ancient Societies*. Englewood Cliffs, N.J.: Prentice-Hall.

Pelliam, Alison de, and Francis D. Burton, 1976. "More on Predatory Behavior in Nonhuman Primates," *Current Anthropology*, 17 (3): 512–513.

Pelto, Pertti J., 1966. *The Nature of Anthropology*. Columbus, O.: Merrill (Social Science Perspectives).

Pelto, Pertti J., 1973. *The Snowmobile Revolution: Technology and Social Change in the Arctic*. Menlo Park, Calif.: Cummings.

Penniman, T. K., 1965. *A Hundred Years of Anthropology*. London: Duckworth.

Peters, Charles R., 1979. "Toward an Ecological Model of African Plio-Pleistocene Hominid Adaptations," *American Anthropologist*, 81 (2): 261–278.

Peterson, Frederick L., 1962. *Ancient Mexico, An Introduction to the Pre-Hispanic Cultures*. New York: Capricorn Books.

Pfeiffer, John E., 1977. *The Emergence of Society*. New York: McGraw-Hill.

Pfeiffer, John E., 1978. *The Emergence of Man*. New York: Harper & Row.

Piddocke, Stuart, 1965. "The Potlatch System of the Southern Kwakiutl: A New Perspective," *Southwestern Journal of Anthropology*, 21: 244–264.

Piggott, Stuart, 1965. Ancient Europe. Chicago: Aldine.

Pilbeam David, 1986. *Human Origins*. David Skamp Distinguished Lecture in Anthropology, Indiana University.

Pilbeam, David, 1987. "Rethinking Human Origins," in *Primate Evolution and Human Origins*. Hawthorne, N.Y.: Aldine de Gruytar, p. 217.

Pilbeam, David, and Stephen Jay Gould, 1974. "Size and Scaling in Human Evolution," *Science*, 186: 892–901.

Pimentel, David, L. E. Hurd, A. C. Bellotti, M. J. Forster, 1. N. Oka, O. D. Sholes, and R. J. Whitman, 1973. "Food Production and the Energy Crisis," *Science*, Vol. 182.

Podplefsky, Aaron and Peter J. Brown, eds., 1989. *Applying Anthropology, An Introductopry Reader*. Mountain View, Colo.: Mayfield.

Polanyi, Karl, 1968. "The Economy as Instituted Process," In E. E. LeClair, Jr., and H. K. Schneider, eds., *Economic Anthropolgy: Readings in Theory and Analysis*. New York: Holt, Rinehart and Winston.

Pope, Geoffrey G., 1989. "Bamboo and Human Evolution," *Natural History*, 10/89, pp. 48–57.

Pospisil, Leopold, 1963. *The Kapauku Papuans of West New Guinea*. New York: Holt, Rinehart and Winston.

Pospisil, Leopold, 1971. *Anthropology of Law: A Comparative Theory*. New York: Harper & Row.

Powdermaker, Hortense, 1966. *Stranger and Friend: The Way of an Anthropologist*. New York: Norton.

Premack, Ann James, and David Premack, 1972. "Teaching Language to an Ape," *Scientific American*, 277 (4): 92–99.

Price-Williams, D. R., ed., 1970. *Cross-cultural Studies: Selected Readings*. Baltimore, Md.: Penguin (Penguin Modern Psychology Readings).

Prideaux, Tom, and the Editors of Time-Life, 1973. *Cro-Magnon Man*. New York: Time-Life.

Prins, A. H. 1953. *East African Class Systems*. Gronigen, The Netherlands: J. B. Walters.

Radcliffe-Brown, A. R., 1931. "Social Organization of Australian Tribes," *Oceania Monographs*, No. 1. Melbourne: Macmillan, 1931.

Radcliffe-Brown, A. 1952. *Structure and Function in Primitive Society*. New York: Free Press.

Radcliffe-Brown, A. R., and C. D. Forde, eds., 1950. *African Systems of Kinship and Marriage*. London: Oxford University Press.

Rappaport, Roy, 1968. *Pigs for the Ancestors*. New Haven, Conn.: Yale University Press.

Rappaport, Roy A., 1969. "Ritual Regulation of Environmental Relations among a New Guinea People," in Andrew P. Vayda, ed., *Environment and Cultural Behavior*. Garden City, N.Y.: Natural History Press, pp. 181–201.

Rappaport, Roy, 1984. *Pigs for the Ances-*

tors, new enlarged ed. New Haven, Conn.: Yale University Press.

Rathje, William L., 1974, "The Garbage Project: A New Way of Looking at the Problems of Archaeology," *Archaeology*, 27: 236–241.

Read, Catherine E., 1973. "The, Role of Faunal Analysis in Reconstructing Human Behavior: A Mousterian Example," paper presented at the meetings of the California Academy of Sciences, Long Beach.

Read-Martin, Catherine E., and Dwight W. Read, 1975. "Australopithecine Scavenging and Human Evolution: An Approach from Faunal Analysis," *Current Anthropology*, 16 (3): 359–368.

Redfield, Robert, Ralph Linton, and Melville J. Herskovits, 1936. "Memorandum of the Study of Acculturation," *American Anthropologist*, 38: 149–152.

Redman, Charles L., 1978. *The Rise of Civilization: From Early Farmers to Urban Society in the Ancient Near East*. San Francisco: Freeman.

Reid, J. J., M. B. Schiffer, and W. L. Rathje, 1975. "Behavioral Archaeology: Four Strategies," *American Anthropologist*, 77: 864–869.

Reina, Ruben, 1966. *The Law of the Saints*. Indianapolis: Bobbs-Merrill.

Reiter, Rayna, ed.,1975 *Toward an Anthropology of Women* New York: Monthly Review Press.

Renfrew, Cohn, 1973. *Before Civilization: The Radiocarbon Revolution and Prehistoric Europe*. London: Jonathan Cape.

Rice, Don S. and Prudence M. Rice, 1984. "Lessons from the Maya," *Latin American Research Review*, 19 (3).

Rindos, David, 1984. *The Origins of Agriculture: An Evolutionary Perspective*. Orlando, Fla.: Academic Press.

Rodman, Hyman, 1968. "Class Culture," *International Encyclopedia of the Social Sciences*, Vol. 15. New York: Macmillan, pp. 332–337.

Rowe, Timothy, 1988. "New Issues for Phylogenetics," *Science*, 239: 1183–1184.

Sabloff, Jeremy, and C. C. Lambert-Karlovsky, 1973. *Ancient Civilization and Trade*. Albuquerque: University of New Mexico Press.

Sabloff, J. A., and C. C. Lamberg-Karlovsky, eds., 1974. *The Rise and Fall of Civilizations, Modern Archaeological Approaches to Ancient Cultures*. Menlo Park, Calif.: Cummings.

Sahlins, Marshall, 1961. "The Segmentary Lineage: An Organization of Predatory Expansion," *American Anthropologist*, 63: 322–343.

Sahlins, Marshall, 1968. *Tribesmen.* Englewood Cliffs, N.J.: Prentice-Hall (Foundations of Modern Anthropology).

Sahlins, Marshall, 1972. *Stone Age Economics.* Chicago: Aldine.

Salthe, Stanley N., 1972. *Evolutionary Biology.* New York: Holt, Rinehart and Winston.

Salzman, Philip C., 1967. "Political Organization among Nomadic Peoples," *proceedings of the American Philosophical Society,* 3: 115–131.

Sanday, Peggy R., 1975. "On the Causes of IQ Differences Between Groups and Implications for Social Policy," in Ashley Montagu, ed., *Race and IQ.* London: Oxford.

Sanday, Peggy Reeves, 1981. *Female Power and Male Dominance: On the Origins of Sexual Inequality.* Cambridge: Cambridge University Press.

Sangree, Walter H., 1965. "The Bantu Tiriki of Western Kenya," in James L. Gibbs, ed., *Peoples of Africa.* New York: Holt, Rinehart and Winston.

Sapir, E., 1916. *Time Perspective in Aboriginal American Culture: A Study in Method.* Ottawa: Geological Society of Canada (Memoir 90, Anthropological Series, No. 13).

Sapir, E., 1917. "Do We Need a Superorganic?" *American Anthropologist,* 19: 441–447.

Sapir, E., 1921. *Language.* New York: Harcourt.

Sapir, E., 1924. "Culture, Genuine or Spurious?" *American Journal of Sociology,* 29: 401–429.

Savage, Jay M., 1969. *Evolution,* 3d ed. New York: Holt, Rinehart and Winston.

Scarr-Salapatek, S., 1971. "Unknowns in the I.Q. Equation," *Science,* 174: 1223–1228.

Schaller, George B., 1963. *The Mountain Gorilla.* Chicago: Chicago University Press.

Schaller, George B., 1971. *The Year of the Gorilla.* New York: Ballantine.

Scheflen, Albert E., 1972. *Body Language and the Social Order.* Englewood Cliffs, N.J.: Prentice-Hall.

Scheper-Hughes, Nancy, 1979. *Saints, Scholars and Schizophrenics.* Berkeley: University of California Press.

Schrire, Carmel, ed., 1984. *Past and Present in Hunter-Gatherer Studies.* Orlando, Fla.: Academic Press.

Schurtz, Heinrich, 1902. *Alterklassen und Männerbünde.* Berlin: Reimer.

Schusky, Ernest L., 1975. *Variation in Kinship.* New York: Holt, Rinehart and Winston.

Schwartz, Jeffrey H., 1984. "Hominoid Evolution: A Review and a Reassessment." *Current Anthropology* 25 (5): 655–672.

Semenov, S. A., 1964. *Prehistoric Technology.* New York: Barnes & Noble.

Sen, Gita, and Caren Grown, 1987. *Development, Crisis, and Alternative Visions: Third World Women's Perspectives.* New York: Monthly Review Press.

Service, Elman R., 1958. *Profiles in Ethnology.* New York: Harper & Row.

Service, Elman R., 1971. *Primitive Social Organization: An Evolutionary Perspective,* 2d ed. New York: Random House.

Shapiro, Harry, ed., 1971. *Man, Culture and Society.* 2d. ed. New York: Oxford University Press.

Sharer, Robert J., and Wendy Ashmore, 1987. *Archaeology: Discovering Our Past.* Palo Alto, Calif.: Mayfield.

Sharp, Lauriston, 1952. "Steel Axes for Stone Age Australians," in Edward H. Spicer, ed., *Human Problems in Technological Change.* New York: Russell Sage.

Shaw, Dennis G., 1984. "A Light at the End of the Tunnel: Anthropological Contributions Toward Global Competence," *Anthropology Newsletter,* 25: 16.

Sheets Payson, 1987. "Dawn of a New Stone Age in Eye Surgery" in *Archaeology: Discovering Our Past,* by Robert J. Sharer and Wendy Ashmore. Palo Alto, Calif.: Mayfield.

Shimkin, Dimitri B., Sol Tax, and John W. Morrison, eds., 1978. *Anthropology for the Future.* Urbana, Ill.: Department of Anthropology, University of Illinois, Research Report No. 4.

Shinnie, Margaret, 1970. *Ancient African Kingdoms.* New York: New American Library.

Shostak, Marjorie, 1981. *Nisa: The Life and Words of a !Kung Woman.* Cambridge, Mass.: Harvard University Press.

Shuey, A. M., 1966. *The Testing of Negro Intelligence.* New York: Social Science Press.

Simons, Elwyn L., 1972. *Primate Evolution.* New York: Macmillan.

Simons, Elwyn, L. "Human Origins," *Science,* 1989, 245: 1343–1350.

Simons, E. L., D. T. Rasmussen, and D. L. Gebo, 1987. "A New Species of Propliopithecus from the Fayum Egypt," *American Journal of Physical Anthropology,* 73: 139–147.

Simpson, George G., 1949. *The Meaning of Evolution.* New Haven, Conn.: Yale University Press.

Sjoberg, Gideon, 1960. *The Preindustrial City.* New York: Free Press.

Skelton, Randall R., Henry M. McHenry, and Gerrell M. Drawhorn, 1986. "Phylogenetic Analysis of Early Hominids," Current Anthropology, 27: 21–43.

Slobin, Dan I., 1971. *Psycholinguistics.* Glenview, Ill.: Scott, Foresman.

Smith, Allan H., and John L. Fisher, 1970. *Anthropology.* Englewood Cliffs, N.J.: Prentice-Hall.

Smith, Bruce D., 1977. "Archaeological Inference and Inductive Confirmation," *American Anthropologist,* 79 (3): 598–617.

Smith, Fred H., and Gail C. Raynard, 1980. "Evolution of the Supraorbital Region in Upper Pleistocene Fossil Hominids from South-Central Europe," *American Journal of Physical Anthropology,* 53: 589–610.

Smith, Philip E. L., 1976. *Food Production and Its Consequences,* 2d ed. Menlo Park, Calif.: Cummings.

Smith, Raymond, 1970. "Social Stratification in the Caribbean," in Leonard Plotnicov and Arthur Tudin, eds., *Essays in Comparative Social Stratification.* Pittsburgh: University of Pittsburgh Press.

Smuts, Barbara, 1987. "What Are Friends For?" *Natural History.* 96 (2): 41.

Speck, Frank G., 1920. "Penobscot Shamanism," *Memoirs of the American Anthropological Association,* 6: 239–288.

Speck, Frank G., 1935. "Penobscot Tales and Religious Beliefs," *Journal of American Folk-Lore,* 48 (187): 1–107.

Speck, Frank G., 1940. *Penobscot Man.* Philadelphia: University of Pennsylvania Press.

Spencer, Frank, and Fred H. Smith, 1981. "The Significance of Ales Hrdlicka's 'Neanderthal Phase of Man': A Historical and Current Assessment," *American Journal of Physical Anthropology,* 56: 435–459.

Spencer, Herbert, 1896. *Principles of Sociology.* New York: Appleton.

Spiro, Melford E., 1966. "Religion: Problems of Definition and Explanation," in Michael Banton, ed., *Anthropological Approaches to the Study of Religion* (A.S.A. Monographs). London: Tavistock.

Spitz, René A., 1949. "Hospitalism," *The Psychoanalytic Study of the Child, Vol. 1.* New York: International Universities Press.

Spradley, James P., 1979. *The Ethnographic Interview.* New York: Holt, Rinehart and Winston.

Spradley, James P., 1980. *Participant Observation.* New York: Holt, Rinehart and Winston.

Stahl, Ann Brower, 1984. "Hominid Dietary Selection Before Fire," *Current Anthropology,* 25: 151–168.

Stanley, Stephen M., 1979. *Macroevolution*, San Francisco: Freeman.

Stanner, W. E. 1968. "Radcliffe-Brown, A. R.," *International Encyclopedia of the Social Sciences*, Vol. 13. New York: Macmillan.

Steward, Julian H., 1972. *Theory of Culture Change: The Methodology of Multilinear Evolution*. Urbana: University of Illinois Press.

Stiles, Daniel, 1979. "Early Acheulian and Developed Oldowan," *Current Anthropology*, 20 (1): 126129.

Stirton, Ruben Arthur, 1967. *Time, Life, and Man*. New York: Wiley.

Stocker, Terry, 1987. "A Technological Mystery Resolved," *Invention and Technology*, Spring: 64.

Stocking, George W., Jr., 1968. *Race, Culture and Evolution: Essays in the History of Anthropology*. New York: Free Press.

Straus, W. L., and A. J. E. Cave, 1957. "Pathology and the Posture of Neanderthal Man," *Quarterly Review of Biology*, 32.

Swadesh, Morris, 1959. "Linguistics as an Instrument of Prehistory," *Southwestern Journal of Anthropology*, 15: 20–35.

Swartz, Marc J., Victor W. Turner, and Arthur Tuden, 1966. *Political Anthropology*. Chicago: Aldine.

Tattersall, Ian, 1975. *The Evolutionary Significance of Ramapithecus*. Minneapolis: Burgess.

Tax, Sol, 1953. *Penny Capitalism: A Guatemalan Indian Economy*, Smithsonian Institution, Institute of Social Anthropology, Pub. No. 16. Washington, D.C.: Government Printing Office.

Tax, Sol, ed., 1962. *Anthropology Today: Selections*. Chicago: University of Chicago Press.

Tax, Sol, Sam Stanley, and others, 1975. "In Honor of Sol Tax," *Current Anthropology*. 16: 507–540.

Thomas, David H., 1974. *Predicting the Past*. New York: Holt, Rinehart and Winston.

Thomas, David H., 1989. *Archaeology*, 2d. ed. New York: Holt, Rinehart and Winston.

Thomas, W. L., ed., 1956. *Man's Role in Changing the Face of the Earth*. Chicago: University of Chicago Press.

Thompson, Stith, 1960. *The Folktale*. New York: Holt, Rinehart and Winston.

Thompson, J. E. S., 1960. *Maya Hieroglyphic Writing: Introduction*. Norman: University of Oklahoma Press.

Thompson, Stith, 1960. *The Folktale*.

New York: Holt, Rinehart and Winston.

Thorne, Alan G., and Melford H. Wolpoff, 1981. "Regional Continuity in Australasian Pleistocene Hominid Evolution," *American Journal of Physical Anthropology*, 55: 337–349.

Thorne, Barrie, and Marilyn Yalom, eds., 1982. *Rethinking the Family: Some Feminist Problems*. New York: Longman.

Tiffany, Sharon, ed., 1979. *Women in Africa*. St. Albans, Vt.: Eden Press.

Tobias, Philip V., 1980. "The Natural History of the Heliocoidal Occlusal Plane and Its Evolution in Early Homo," *American Journal of Physical Anthropology*, 53: 173–187.

Tobias, Philip V., and G. H. R. von Koenigswald, 1964. "A Comparison Between the Olduvai Hominines and Those of Java and Some Implications for Hominid Phylogeny," *Nature*, 204: 515–518.

Trager, George L., 1964. "Paralanguage: A First Approximation," in Dell Hymes, ed., *Language in Culture and Society*. New York: Harper & Row.

Trinkaus, Erik, 1986. "The Neanderthals and Modern Human Origins," *Annual Review of Anthropology*, 15: 197.

Tuden, Arthur, 1970. "Slavery and Stratification among the Ila of Central Africa," in Arthur Tuden and Leonard Plotnicov, eds., *Social Stratification in Africa*. New York: Free Press.

Tumin, Melvin M., 1967. *Social Stratification: The Forms and Functions of Inequality*. Englewood Cliffs, N.J.: Prentice-Hall (Foundations of Modern Sociology).

Turnbull, Colin M., 1961. *The Forest People*. New York: Simon & Schuster.

Turnbull, Colin M., 1972. *The Mountain People*. New York: Simon & Schuster.

Turnbull, Colin M., 1983. *The Human Cycle*. New York: Simon & Schuster.

Turnbull, Colin 1983. *Mbuti Pygmies: Change and Adaptation*. New York: Holt, Rinehart and Winston.

Turner, V. W., 1957. *Schism and Continuity in an African Society*. Manchester, Eng.: The University Press.

Turner, V. W., 1969. *The Ritual Process*. Chicago: Aldine.

Tylor, Edward Burnett, 1871. *Primitive Culture: Researches into the Development of Mythology, Philosophy, Religion, Language, Art and Customs*. London: Murray.

Tylor, Sir Edward B., 1931. "Animism," in V. F. Calverton, ed., *The Making of Man: An Outline of Anthropology*. New York: Modern Library.

Ucko, Peter J., and Andrée Rosenfeld,

1967. *Paleolithic Cave Art*. New York: McGraw-Hill.

Ucko, P. J., R. Tringham, and G. W. Dimbleby, eds., 1972. *Man, Settlement and Urbanism*. London: Duckworth.

Valentine, Charles A., 1968. *Culture and Poverty*. Chicago: University of Chicago Press.

Van Gennep, Arnold, 1960. *The Rites of Passage*. Chicago: University of Chicago Press.

Vansina, Jan, 1965. *Oral Tradition: A Study in Historical Methodology*, H. M. Wright, trans. Chicago: Aldine.

Van Willigen, John, 1986. *Applied Anthropology, An Introduction*. South Hadley, Mass.: Bergin and Garvey.

Vayda, Andrew P., 1961. "A Re-examination of Northwest Coast Economic Systems," *Transactions of the New York Academy of Sciences*, 2d series, 23: 618–624.

Vayda, Andrew P., 1961. "Expansion and Warfare among Swidden Agriculturalists," *American Anthropologist*, 63: 346–358.

Vayda, Andrew ed., 1969. *Environment and Cultural Behavior: Ecological Studies in Cultural Anthropology*, Garden City, N.Y.: Natural History Press.

Vincent, John, 1979. "On the Special Division of Labor, Population, and the Origins of Agriculture," *Current Anthropology*, 20 (2): 422–425.

Vogelman, Thomas C., and others, 1972. Film: *Prehistoric Life in the Champlain Valley*. Burlington, Vt.: Department of Anthropology, University of Vermont.

Voget, F. W., 1960. "Man and Culture: An Essay in Changing Anthropological Interpretation," *American Anthropologist*, 62: 943–965.

Voget, F. W., 1975. *A History of Ethnology*. New York: Holt, Rinehart and Winston.

Wagner, Philip L., 1960. *A History of Ethnology*. New York: Holt, Rinehart and Winston.

Wagner, Philip L., 1960. *The Human Use of the Earth*. New York: Free Press.

Wallace, Anthony F.C. 1956. "Revitalization Movements," *American Anthropologist*, 58: 264–281.

Wallace, Anthony F. C., 1965, "The Problem of the Psychological Validity of Componential Analysis," *American Anthropologist, Special Publication*, Part 2, 67 (5): 229–248.

Wallace, Anthony F. C., 1966. *Religion: An Anthropological View*. New York: Random House.

Wallace, Anthony F. C., 1970. *Culture and Personality*, 2d ed. New York: Random House.

Wallace, Ernest, and E. Adamson Hoebel, 1952. *The Comanches*. Norman: University of Oklahoma Press.

Wardhaugh, Ronald, 1972. *Introduction to Linguistics*. New York: McGraw-Hill.

Washburn, S. L., and Ruth Moore, 1980. *Ape into Human: A Study of Human Evolution*, 2d ed. Boston: Little, Brown.

Weaver, Muriel P., 1972. *The Aztecs, Maya and Their Predecessors*. New York: Seminar Press.

Weiner, Annette, 1988. *The Trobrianders of Papua New Guinea*. New York: Holt, Rinehart and Winston.

Weiner, J. S., 1955. *The Piltdown Forgery*. Oxford: Oxford University Press.

Weiner, Myron, 1966. *Modernization: The Dynamics of Growth*. New York: Basic Books.

Weiss, Mark L., and Alan E. Mann, 1990. *Human Biology and Behavior*, 5th ed. Boston: Little, Brown.

Wells, Calvin, 1964. Bones, *Bodies and Disease*. London: Thames and Hudson.

Wernick, Robert, and the Editors of Time-Life, 1973. *The Monument Builders*. New York: Time-Life.

Westermarck, Edward A., 1926. *A Short History of Marriage*. New York: Macmillan.

Whelehan, Patricia, 1985. "Review of Incest, a Biosocial View," *American Anthropologist* 87: 678.

White, Douglas R., 1988. "Rethinking Polygyny: Co-Wives, Codes and Cultural Systems," *Current Anthropology* 29.

White, Edmond, Dale Brown, and the Editors of Time-Life, 1973. *The First Men*. New York: Time-Life.

White, Leslie, 1940. "The Symbol: The Origin and Basis of Human Behavior," *Philosophy of Science*, 7: 451–463.

White, Leslie, 1949. *The Science of Culture: A Study of Man and Civilization*. New York: Farrar, Strauss.

White, Leslie, 1959. *The Evolution of Culture: The Development of Civilization to the Fall of Rome*. New York: McGraw-Hill.

White, Peter, 1976. *The Past Is Human*, 2d ed. New York: Maplinger.

White, Tim D., 1979. "Evolutionary Implications of Pliocene Hominid Footprints," *Science*, 208: 175–176.

Whiting, Beatrice B., ed., 1963. *Six Cultures: Sudies of Child Rearing*. New York: Wiley.

Whiting, John W. M., and J. Child, 1953..*Child Training and Personality: A Cross-cultural Study*. New Haven, Conn.: Yale University Press.

Whiting, John W. M., John A. Sodergern, and Stephen M. Stigler, 1982. "Winter Temperature as a Constraint to the Migration of Preindustrial Peoples," *American Anthropologist*, 84: 289.

Willey, Gordon R., 1966. *An Introduction to American Archaeology, Vol. 1: North America*. Englewood Cliffs, N.J.: Prentice-Hall.

Willey, Gordon R., 1971. *An Introduction to American Archaeology, Vol. 2: South America*. Englewood Cliffs, N.J.: Prentice-Hall.

Wilson, A. K., and V. M. Sarich, 1969. "A Molecular Time Scale for Human Evolution," *Proceedings of the National Academy of Science* 63: 1089–1093.

Wingert, Paul, 1962. *Primitive Art: Its Tradition and Styles*. London: Oxford University Press; New York: World, 1965.

Wirsing, Rolf L., 1985. "The Health of Traditional Societies and the Effects of Acculturation," *Current Anthropology* 26 (3): 303–322.

Wittfogel, Karl A., 1957. *Oriental Despotism, A Comparative Study of Total Power*. New Haven, Conn.: Yale University Press.

Wolf, Eric, 1959. *Sons of the Shaking Earth*. Chicago: University of Chicago Press.

Wolf, Eric, 1966. *Peasants*. Englewood Cliffs, N.J.: Prentice-Hall (Foundations of Modern Anthropology).

Wolf, Eric, 1982. *Europe and the People without History*. Berkeley: University of California Press.

Wolf, Margery, 1972. *Women and the Family in Rural Taiwan*. Stanford, Calif.: Stanford University Press.

Wolf, Margery, 1985. *Revolution Postponed — Women in Contemporary China*. Stanford, Calif.: Stanford University Press.

Wolfe, Alvin W., 1977. "The Supranational Organization of Production: An Evolutionary Perspective." *Current Anthropology*, 18: 615–635.

Wolpoff, M. H., 1971. "Interstitial Wear," *American Journal of Physical Anthropology*, 34: 205–227.

Wolpoff, M. H., 1977. "Review of Earliest Man in the Lake Rudolf Basin," *American Anthropologist*, 79: 708–711.

Wolpoff, Milford H., 1982. *"Ramapithecus* and Hominid Origins," *Current Anthropology*, 23: 501–522.

Woolfson, Peter, 1972. "Language, Thought, and Culture," in Virginia P. Clark, Paul A. Escholz, and Alfred F. Rosa, eds., *Language*. New York: St. Martins.

World Bank, 1982. *Tribal Peoples and Economic Development*. Washington, D.C.: World Bank.

Wright, Robin, 1984. "Towards a New Indian Policy in Brazil," *Cultural Survival Quarterly* 8, (1).

Wulff, Robert M. and Shirley J. Fiske, 1987. *Anthropological Praxis: Translating Knowledge into Action*. Boulder, Colo.: Westview.

CREDITS

This listing is continued from page iv. The author is indebted to the following for photographs and permission to reproduce them. Copyright for each photograph belongs to the photographer or agency credited, unless specified otherwise.

cover and title page: Peruvian man at Inti Raymi, Inca Sun Festival, at Sacsayhuaman in Cuzco, Peru. Odyssey Productions.

David L. Brill. *37*, William Haviland. *40*, David L. Brill, Copyright © The National Geographic Society. *44*, The Tikal Project, The University Museum, University of Pennsylvania. *45*, MASCA, The University Museum, University of Pennsylvania. **Chapter 3:** Chapter Opener, *50*, Ed Degginger/Color-Pic, Inc. *54*, Photo Researchers, Inc. *57 (left and right)*, Dr. Jean Lusher, The Children's Hospital of Michigan. *60 (upper left)*, Obremski/Image Bank; *(upper right)*, Steve Elmore; *(bottom left)*, Lawrence Manning/Woodfin Camp and Associates. *61*, Department of Library Services, American Museum of Natural History. *62 (left)*, E.R. Degginger; *(right)*, Geoloski-Paleontologi Musej/David L. Brill. *64 (left and right)*, Leonard Lee Rue III/Taurus Photos. *66*, Otorohanga Zoological Society. *68*, Leonard Lee Rue III/Animals Animals. **Chapter 4:** Chapter Opener, *74*, Taurus Photos. *83*, Anthro-Photo. *86 (upper)*, N. R. Christensen/Taurus Photos; *(center)*, S.C. Bisserot/Nature Photographers Ltd., *(bottom)*, Mark Pidgeon/Nature Photo Researchers. *87*, Arthur Ambler/Photo Researchers, Inc. *89, (upper)*, D. Chivers/Anthro-Photo; *(bottom)*, Peter Drowne/E.R. Degginger, *90 (left)*, M. Austerman/Animals Animals; *(right)*, Watts/Anthro-Photo. *92*, Tom McHugh/Photo Researchers, Inc. *93*, I. DeVore/Anthro-Photo. *94*, Jim Moore/Anthro-Photo.

Part II: Part Opener, *103*, Tony Marks/Southern Methodist University. **Chapter 5:** Chapter Opener, *106*, David Brill/Elwyn Simms. *122*, Anthro-Photo. *115 (upper and lower)*, National Museums of Kenya/David L. Brill © National Geographic Society. *117*, Margo Crabtree/*Science*. *118*, Tom McHugh/Photo Researchers, Inc. *122 (upper)*, I. DeVore/Anthro-Photo; *(lower)*, Townsend P. Dickinson/Photo Researchers, Inc. **Chapter 6:** Chapter Opener, *126*, K. Cannon-Benventre/Anthro-Photo. *130*, David Brill, The National Museum of Kenya. *133*, Henry Bunn, University of Wisconsin-Madison/David L. Brill, Copyright © The National Geographic Society. *136 (left)*, National Museum of Tanzania/David L. Brill, Copyright © The National Geographic Society; *(right)*, The National Museums of

Kenya/David L. Brill, Copyright © The National Geographic Society. *138*, Institute of Human Origins. *140*, Des Bartlett/Photo Researchers, Inc. *141 (upper)*, National Museum of Ethiopia/David L. Brill with assistant John Nienhuis, Copyright © The National Geographic Society; *(middle)*, National Museum of Tanzania/David L. Brill with assistant John Nienhuis, Copyright © The National Geographic Society; *(lower)*, National Museums of Kenya/David L. Brill with assistant John Nienhuis, Copyright © The National Geographic Society. *144 (all)*, David L. Brill, Copyright © The National Geographic Society. *149*, Philip V. Tobias, University of Witwatersrand, Republic of South Africa, courtesy of Professor G.H.R. Koenigswald. **Chapter 7:** Chapter Opener, *152*, I. DeVore/Anthro-Photo. *154*, Department of Library Services, American Museum of Natural History. *156 (left)*, National Museums of Kenya/David L. Brill, Copyright © National Geographic Society; *(right)*, University of Thessaloniki/David L. Brill, Copyright © The National Geographic Society. *158 (left and right)*, Lee Bolton. **Chapter 8:** Chapter Opener, *170*, Rapho Agency/Photo Researchers. *172*, Dr. Jon E. Kalb/University of Texas at Austin. *175 (left)*, Ed Degginger/Color-Pic, Inc.; *(right)*, Bernard Vandermeersch/University of Bordeaux. *177 (left and right)*, Lee Boltin. *181 (left and right)*, Alexander Marshack, New York University. *185 (left)*, Museum National d'Histoire/David Brill; *(right)*, Chris Stringer. *192 (all)*, J. Oster/Musée des Antiquités Nationales, Copyright © American Museum of Natural History. *193*, Department of Library Services, American Museum of Natural History. *194 (upper)*, Joe Ben Wheat, University of Colorado Museum; *(lower)*, Anthro-Photo.

Part III: Part Opener, *202*, The National Geographic Society. **Chapter 9:** Chapter Opener, *206*, Adam Woolfitt/Woodfin Camp. *210 (upper)*, Dr. W. van Zeist, Biologisch-Archaeologisch Institut, Rijksuniveriteit Gronigen. *214* Pierre Boulat/Woodfin Camp and Associates. *219*, Ankara Archaeological Museum/Ara Guler, Instanbul. *218 (left and right)*, British School of

Archaeology in Jerusalem. *222*, Department of Library Services, American Museum of Natural History. *224 (upper and lower)*, Allan H. Goodman, Hampshire College. **Chapter 10:** Chapter Opener, *230*, David Brill. *236*, Anita de L. Haviland. *237*, Anita de L. Haviland. *239*, The University Museum, University of Pennsylvania/Paulus Leeser. *240 (upper left)*, Lee Boltin; *(upper right)*, The Metropolitan Museum of Art, New York; *(lower left)*, Department of Library Services, American Museum of Natural History. *241*, William Haviland. *242*, Anita de L. Haviland. *250*, Cultural Relics Bureau, Beijing, and The Metropolitan Museum of Art, New York. **Chapter 11:** Chapter Opener, *254*, Myrleen Ferguson/Photo Edit. *257 (upper left)*, Cyril Toker/Photo Researchers, Inc.; *(right)*, E.R. Degginger; *(lower left)*, George Holton/Photo Researchers, Inc. *258*, Pam Hasegawa/Taurus Photos. *262*, Steve Elmore. *263 (upper)*, Beryl Goldberg; *(bottom left)*, Farrell Graham/Photo Researchers, Inc.; *(bottom center)*, Richard Wood/Taurus Photos; *(bottom right)*, E.R. Degginger. *270*, Paula Agosti, M. Courtney-Clarke/Photo Researchers, Inc. *271*, E.R. Degginger. *272*, NASA.

Part IV: Part Opener, *275*, Dallas Museum of Art. **Chapter 12:** Chapter Opener, *278*, Lila Abu-Lughod/Anthro-Photo. *281 (left)*, Susan Leavines/Photo Researchers; *(right)*, Spencer Grant/Photo Researchers, Inc. *283*, Eric Kroll/Taurus Photos. *284*, E.R. Degginger. *286 (left and right)*, Ronald Cohn from *The Education of Koko* by Patterson and Linder, Copyright © 1982 by Holt, Rinehart and Winston, Inc. *287*, UPI/Bettmann Newsphotos. *288*, UPI/Bettmann Newsphotos. *290*, Annette B. Weiner, Department of Anthropology, New York University. *291*, UPI/Bettmann Newsphotos. *293*, Annette Weiner, Department of Anthropology, New York University. *296*, Alec Duncan/Taurus Photos. *298 (upper)*, Culver Pictures; *(lower)*, UPI/Bettmann Newsphotos. *299*, Alexandra Avakian/Woodfin Camp & Associates. *300*, Colin Turnbull. **Chapter 13:** Chapter Opener, *304*, Bruno Maso/Photo Edit. *308*, Megan Biesele/Anthro-Photo. *312*, Innervisions. *313*, John Chellman/Animals Animals. *102 (left)*, Julien Bryan/Photo Researchers, Inc., *(middle)*, Pamela Johnson Meyer/Photo Researchers, Inc., *(right)*, John Moss/Photo Researchers, Inc. *320*, Dr. J.F.E. Bloss/Anthro-Photo. *326*, Will and Demi McIntre/Photo Researchers, Inc. *328 (left)*, Charles H. Southwick; *(right)*, Wide World. **Chapter 14:** Chapter Opener, *332*, David A. Harvey/Woodfin Camp, Inc. *334*, Martin Bell. *336 (all)*, Colin Turnbull. *340*, Ken

Heyman. *341*, S. Washburn/Anthro-Photo. *343*, Bettmann Archive. *344*, E.R. Derringer. *345*, Colin Turnbull. *350*, Napoleon Chagnon, Department of Anthropology, University of California at Santa Barbara. *351*, The Granger Collection. *352 (left)*, G. Aschendorf/Photo Researchers, Inc.; *(right)*, UPI/Bettmann Newsphotos. *354 (left)*, Lowell Georgia, Photo Researchers, Inc.; *(right)*, Dan Cabe/Photo Researchers, Inc. *355*, Museum of the American Indian, Heye Foundation. *359*, Beryl Goldberg. **Chapter 15:** Chapter Opener, *362*, Ulrike Welsch. *365*, Rappaport. *367 (left)*, William W. Bacon III/Photo Researchers, Inc.; *(right)*, Smithsonian Institution. *372*, Copyright © 1984 Twentieth Century Fox Film Corporation/Museum of Modern Art, Film Stills Archive. *373 (left)*, James Barker; *(right)*, Anita de L. Haviland. *376 (all)*, Richard B. Lee, Department of Anthropology, University of Toronto. *383*, Richard Quataert/Taurus Photos. *384*, from *Knowing the Gururumba* by Phillip L. Newman, Copyright 1965 by Holt, Rinehart and Winston, Inc. *385*, Tony Howarth/Woodfin Camp & Associates. *388*, American Museum of Natural History. *389*, Spencer Grant/Taurus Photos. **Chapter 16:** Chapter Opener, *392*, Stuart Cohen/Comnstock. *396*, Annette Weiner, Department of Anthropology, New York University, *398 (upper)*, Victor Englebert; *(bottom)*, Loren McIntyre/Woodfin Camp & Associates. *399*, Eric Kroll/Taurus Photos. *400 (upper)*, David Allen Harvey/Woodfin Camp & Associates; *(bottom)*, Byron Augustin/D. Donne Bryant. *401*, Charles Harbutt/Actuality, Inc. *403*, Frank Cancian, Department of Anthropology, University of California at Irvine. *408 (all)*, Annette Weiner, Department of Anthropology, New York University. *409*, Alan Carey/The Image Works. *411*, from *The Kwakiutl: The Indians of British Columbia* by Ronald P. Rohner and Evelyn C. Rohner. *413*, Jan Halaska/Photo Researchers, Inc. *414*, Elsa Peterson. *415 (left)*, Beryl Goldberg; *(right)* Colin Turnbull. *417*, Robert Caputo/Stock Boston.

Part V: Part Opener, *421*, University of Pennsylvania Museum. **Chapter 17:** Chapter Opener, *424*, Annette Weiner, Department of Anthropology, New York University. *426 (all)*, Annette Weiner, Department of Anthropology, New York University. *428*, Michael K. Nichols as Published by Aperture Press/Magnum. *431*, Giraudon/Art Resource. *432*, French Cultural Services. *434*, Photo Researchers. *436*, Museum of The American Indian. *438*, E.J. Camp/Onyx. *439 (left)*, Stephanie Dinkins/Photo Researchers; *(left)*, UPI/Bettmann

INDEX

Terms in **boldface** type are defined in the running glossaries on the text page indicated by boldface numbers. *n* indicates reference to a footnote.

Papua (New Guinea), legal system of, 542
Paralanguage, 310, 310–311
Parallel evolution, 366, 366
Parapithecus, 114–115
Participant observation, 13–16
Pastoralism, 227, 227
 Bakhtari, 384–386
 Mesolithic roots of, 208
 See also Agriculture; Domestication; Farming; Food production
Pastoralist, 384
Patrilateral parallel-cousin marriage, 442, 442
Patrilineal descent, 479, 479
 and organization, 475–484
Patrilocal residence, 466, 466–467
Patterns of affect, 338, 338
Pei, W.C., 154
Pelto, P.J., 637*n*
Penobscot Indians (North America)
 and group personality, 351
 vital self of, 337–338, 568–569
Pentadactyly, 83, 83
Percussion method, 143, 143
Permian period, 108–110
Personality, 339, 338–349
 abnormal, 354–358
 development of, 339–349
 group, 349–353
 modal, 349–351
Phenotype, 56, 56
Phonemes, 307, 307
Phonetics, 307, 307
Phonology, 307, 307–308
Phratry, 491, 491–492
Physical anthropology, **8,** 9
Physiological stress, 223–225
Pig-keeping
 Gururumba, 383
 Kapauku, 288–289
Piggott, S., 41*n*
Pilbeam, D., 116, 122*n*, 140
Pitt, D., 654*n*
Plains Indians (North America), 354–355, 368
Platyrrhinii, 78, 78
Play, among primates, 93
Plesiadapiformes, 112, 112
Plog, F., 123*n*
Pluralistic societies, 282, 282
Poetry, 600–604
Pokotyle, D., 201
Political organization
 centralized, 535–539
 decentralized, 530–535
 defined, 530
 and external affairs, 554–556
 and legitimacy, 557
 and religion, 557–558
 types of, 530–535

Polyandry, 437, 437
Polanyi, K., 404
Pollution, 669–671
Polygamous families, problems of, 469
Polygenes, 57, 57
Polygyny, 288–289, **435,** 435–437
Polymorphic, 256, 256
Polytypic, 257, 257
Pope, G.G., 159–163, 164*n*
Population
 breeding, separation of, 67–68
 control of, 671–673
 defined, **57**
 evolution of, 66–67
 genetics of, 57–69
 stability of, 58
Positive sanctions, 543
Pospisil, L., 288, 535, 551
Potassium-argon analysis, 45, 45–46
Potlatch, 410–412
Potts, 146
Power, M.W., 248*n*, 596*n*
Preadaptations, 366, 366
Prehensile, 83, 83
Preindustrial cities, 388, 388–389
Pressure flaking, **185,** 185–186
Priests and priestesses, 571–572, **572**
Primary innovation, 621, 621
Primate order, 52, 77–79
Primates, 52
 behavior, 98
 brain of, 80
 characteristics of, 79–85
 communication, 93, 326–327
 dentition, 80–81
 of Eocene Epoch, 112–114
 evolutionary relationships among, 84–85
 fossil remains, 108
 home range, 93–94
 hunting, 97–98
 interaction among, 91–92
 of Miocene Epoch, 115–116
 modern, 85–89
 of Oligocene Epoch, 114–115
 origins, and mammalian evolution, 108–110
 of Paleocene Epoch, 112
 play, 93
 reproduction and care of young, 84
 rise of, 110–123
 sense organs, 79
 sexual activity, 92–93
 skeleton, 81–83
 social behavior, 90–98
 tool use by, 95–96
Proconsul, 115
Progress
 concept of, 226–227
Psychoses, 357–358

Psychological anthropology, 334–358
 current trends in, 358–359

Race, 67, 67, **258**
 and behavior, 265
 as biological concept, 259–260
 concept of, 260–261
 and intelligence, 266–268
 skin color, 258, 262–265
 social significance of, 265–269
Racism, 265, 265–269
Radcliffe-Brown, A.R., 288, 491
Radiocarbon analysis, 44, 44–45
Ramaphithecines, 116, 116–117
 adaptations of, 118–123
 and human origins, 117–118
Rappaport, R.A., 364*n*
Rasmussen, D.T., 114*n*
Rebellion, 634–635. *See also* Revolution
Reciprocity, 404, 404–406
Redistribution, 409, of wealth, 408–409
Reindeer herding, 637–638
Reischauer, E., 25
Relative dating, 42, 42–44
Religion
 anthropological approach to, 566
 and civilization, 248–249
 and culture change, 585–587
 functions of, 584–585
 magic, and witchcraft, 580–584
 and politics, 557–558
 practice of, 566–579
 rituals and ceremonies, 577–580
 specialists in, 571–577
 supernatural in, 566–571
Replacement reproduction, 671, 671
Residence patterns, 466–468
Resources
 labor, 396–401
 land, 401–403
 leveling mechanisms, 403–404
 technology, 402–403
Revitalization movement, 585–587, **586,** 632–634, **633**
Revolution
 rebellion and, 634–635
 snowmobile, 637–641
Revolutionary, 634, 634
Rice, D.S., 252*n*
Rice, P.M., 252*n*
Ricisak, J., 33
Rindos, D., 208*n*
Rites of intensification, 577, 579–580
Rites of passage, 577, 577
Ritual, 577–580
 among Mbuti, 346–348
Ritual masks, 610–611
Robinson, G.A., 627
Robinson, J., 139
Robust *Australopithecus,* 139–141